revolve

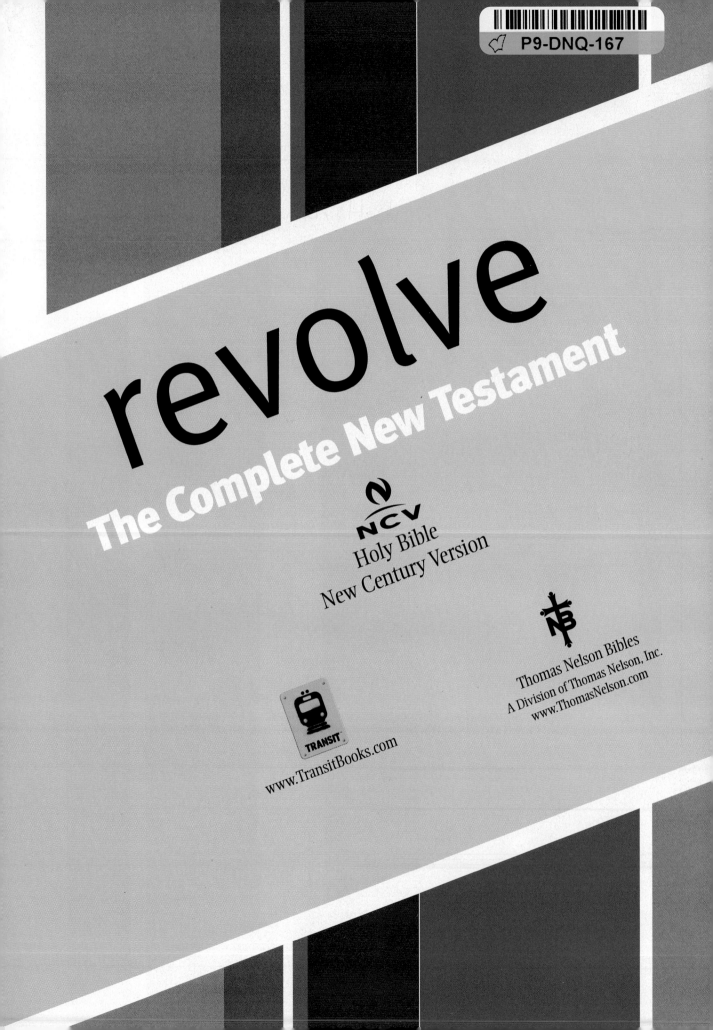

The Complete New Testament

NCV
Holy Bible
New Century Version

Revolve: The Complete New Testament

The Holy Bible, New Century Version.

The preliminary research and development of the *New Century Version* was done by the World Bible Translation Center, Inc., Fort Worth, TX 76182.

Creative Design: Four 5 One Design, Dublin, Ireland (special thanks to Robin Lenowitz and Jon Averill)

Cover Design: Four 5 One Design, Dublin, Ireland

Creative Team: Kate Etue (Managing Editor), Jenny Eaton, Corinne Hyde, Jamie Menzie, Beth Ann Patton, Joy Spooner.

Calendar teen illustrations by Margaret Pesek, www.designmonkee.com

Composition and design: Koechel Peterson & Associates, Minneapolis, MN.

Printed in the United States of America

1 2 3 4 5 6 7 8 9 10 — 11 10 09 08 07 06 05 04 03

TABLE OF CONTENTS

INTRODUCTION

This Bible is about radical devotion and revolutionary people. It is a book that God breathed into the hearts and minds of people who were grappling with life and rising to the challenge of faith in the extreme.

The stories were written by and about dreamers and risk-takers—people who bet their lives on what they could only see through faith. They were people who took a chance on God and dared to believe that this world we live in is a virtual world compared to the reality of who God is and how he wants to connect with us.

They didn't pretty-up their lives. They told the truth even when it was raw. They admitted their mistakes. God inspired a book that reveals life with all its problems and all of humankind's frailties. He gave us a picture of the out-on-a-limb-life that is the life of faith.

This whole Bible is really about God connecting with us through Jesus Christ. It is about Jesus' life and the universal shock waves from his death and resurrection.

Jesus was all-the-way man and all-the-way God. He was the truest revolutionary of all time. He wasn't afraid to blast the hypocritical religious leaders or to cry when his friend died. He lived through a life just like ours, with its frustrations and hard times, to do something no one else has done: die as a sacrifice for our sins. The truth he spoke and the fact that he beat death turned the world upside down.

THIS BIBLE IS A SURVIVAL GUIDE.

The Bible is a lot of books strapped together. They are all inspired by God, but written by different kinds of people in all kinds of circumstances and for different reasons. These people weren't setting out to write a book of the Bible. They were facing life and surviving as best they could. Their stories teach us to survive as well by God's power. Because God inspired them, they're one hundred percent accurate and reliable.

Some of these books are stories, listings of events. Some are letters, and some are sermons. When you read the Bible, any part of it, understand the big picture. Understand why that book was written, what that writer was trying to accomplish. What were the people involved struggling with? What were they trying to make sense of? Each book has an **Introduction** written specifically to help answer these kinds of questions.

There are other special features to help you get as deep inside the Bible as you can.

Blabs are questions and answers with experts on a variety of topics important to you every day. **Promises** point out the commitments that God makes to us. **Radical Faith** notes push us to trust God in the extreme. **Learn It and Live It** give real-life application of tons of Bible verses. **Bible Bios** tell the stories of real-life girls who lived during the Bible times. **Beauty Secrets** show ways that you can beautify your inner-self. There are notes on **Relationships** and **Issues** that you deal with daily. **Guys Speak Out!** give you the opinion of real-life teen guys on questions you wonder about. There's just a ton of info for you to learn from.

It's all here—truth, inspiration, bottom-line *actual reality*. Are you up for the challenge?

FROM THE EDITORS OF *REVOLVE:*

A note about the *New Century Version*

God never intended the Bible to be too difficult for his people. To make sure God's message was clear, the authors of the Bible recorded God's word in familiar everyday language. These books brought a message that the original readers could understand. These first readers knew that God spoke through these books. Down through the centuries, many people wanted a Bible so badly that they copied different Bible books by hand!

Today, now that the Bible is readily available, many Christians do not regularly read it. Many feel that the Bible is too hard to understand or irrelevant to life.

The *New Century Version* captures the clear and simple message that the very first readers understood. This version presents the Bible as God intended it: clear and dynamic.

A team of scholars from the World Bible Translation Center worked together with twenty-one other experienced Bible scholars from all over the world to translate the text directly from the best available Greek and Hebrew texts. You can trust that this Bible accurately presents God's Word as it came to us in the original languages.

Translators kept sentences short and simple. They avoided difficult words and worked to make the text easier to read. They used modern terms for places and measurements. And they put figures of speech and idiomatic expressions ("he was gathered to his people") in language that even children understand ("he died").

Following the tradition of other English versions, the *New Century Version* indicates the divine name, *Yahweh*, by putting LORD, and sometimes GOD, in capital letters. This distinguishes it from *Adonai*, another Hebrew word that is translated Lord.

We acknowledge the infallibility of God's Word and yet our own frailty. We pray that God will use this Bible to help you understand his rich truth for yourself. To God be the glory.

Kate and Laurie

The New Testament

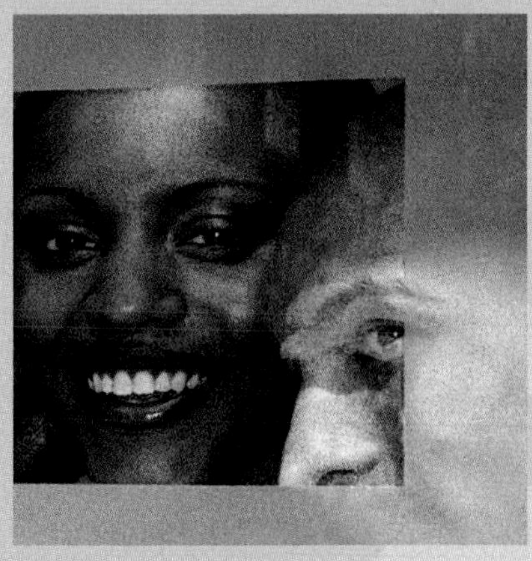

Imagine this: You've just reclined on a soft clump of grass on a Galilean hillside. The air is crisp and warm. Your schedule is clear . . . nothing to do but listen. You're there with thousands of others who have arrived to hear Jesus teach. Your mind is ready to drink in all that Jesus has to say. Your heart is eager for a divine touch. As Jesus begins to teach, suddenly it's just you and him. No more thousands of people. Just you.

That's the spirit of Matthew. The book was intended for hundreds of thousands of millions of people. But it reads like it's for one person. You.

Matthew is the first of four New Testament books about Jesus. Like any collection of stories about one person, each version is different.

Matthew TELLS THE JEWISH PEOPLE ABOUT JESUS

And there's something unique enough about Matthew's story to have inspired Christian leaders long ago to put this ahead of all others in the New Testament. So, what's so unique?

In Matthew, you won't find as much dramatic action as you'll discover in Mark, or as many spotlights on compassion as in Luke, or even as much proof of the deity of Jesus as you'll uncover in John. But in Matthew, you'll find the most complete record of what Jesus taught. And you'll learn how his teachings grow out of Old Testament Scriptures. Matthew's book is like an encyclopedia of Jesus. This is the total good news.

Totally complete. Totally true.

THE FAMILY HISTORY OF JESUS

1 This is the family history of Jesus Christ. He came from the family of David, and David came from the family of Abraham.

2 Abraham was the father[n] of Isaac.
Isaac was the father of Jacob.
Jacob was the father of Judah and his brothers.
3 Judah was the father of Perez and Zerah.
(Their mother was Tamar.)
Perez was the father of Hezron.
Hezron was the father of Ram.
4 Ram was the father of Amminadab.
Amminadab was the father of Nahshon.
Nahshon was the father of Salmon.
5 Salmon was the father of Boaz.
(Boaz's mother was Rahab.)
Boaz was the father of Obed.
(Obed's mother was Ruth.)
Obed was the father of Jesse.
6 Jesse was the father of King David.
David was the father of Solomon.
(Solomon's mother had been Uriah's wife.)
7 Solomon was the father of Rehoboam.
Rehoboam was the father of Abijah.
Abijah was the father of Asa.

DIDYA KNOW

72% OF 15-TO 25-YEAR-OLDS HAVE DONATED TO A COMMUNITY ORGANIZATION.

8 Asa was the father of Jehoshaphat.
Jehoshaphat was the father of Jehoram.
Jehoram was the ancestor of Uzziah.
9 Uzziah was the father of Jotham.
Jotham was the father of Ahaz.
Ahaz was the father of Hezekiah.
10 Hezekiah was the father of Manasseh.
Manasseh was the father of Amon.
Amon was the father of Josiah.
11 Josiah was the grandfather of Jehoiachin and his brothers.
(This was at the time that the people were taken to Babylon.)
12 After they were taken to Babylon:
Jehoiachin was the father of Shealtiel.
Shealtiel was the grandfather of Zerubbabel.
13 Zerubbabel was the father of Abiud.
Abiud was the father of Eliakim.
Eliakim was the father of Azor.
14 Azor was the father of Zadok.
Zadok was the father of Akim.
Akim was the father of Eliud.
15 Eliud was the father of Eleazar.
Eleazar was the father of Matthan.
Matthan was the father of Jacob.
16 Jacob was the father of Joseph.
Joseph was the husband of Mary,
and Mary was the mother of Jesus.
Jesus is called the Christ.

17 So there were fourteen generations from
Abraham to David. And there were fourteen
generations from David until the people were
taken to Babylon. And there were fourteen generations from the time when the people were
taken to Babylon until Christ was born.

THE BIRTH OF JESUS CHRIST

18 This is how the birth of Jesus Christ came
about. His mother Mary was engaged[n] to marry
Joseph, but before they married, she learned
she was pregnant by the power of the Holy
Spirit. 19 Because Mary's husband, Joseph, was a
good man, he did not want to disgrace her in
public, so he planned to divorce her secretly.

20 While Joseph thought about these things, an
angel of the Lord came to him in a dream. The
angel said, "Joseph, descendant of David, don't
be afraid to take Mary as your wife, because the
baby in her is from the Holy Spirit. 21 She will
give birth to a son, and you will name him Jesus,[n]
because he will save his people from their sins."

22 All this happened to bring about what the
Lord had said through the prophet: 23 "The virgin
will be pregnant. She will have a son, and they
will name him Immanuel,"[n] which means "God
is with us."

bible basics

The Bible is a collection of sixty-six books written by different men through history, but all divinely inspired by God. This means that God controlled what they wrote. He wrote it *through* them. Christians believe that the Bible is "living and active." This means that it still applies to us today, that God uses it to speak to us. They believe that everything in the Bible is absolutely true and will never change. The Word of God will last forever.

notes

1:2 father "Father" in Jewish lists of ancestors can sometimes mean grandfather or more distant relative. **1:18 engaged** For the Jewish people an engagement was a lasting agreement, which could only be broken by a divorce. If a bride-to-be was unfaithful, it was considered adultery, and she could be put to death. **1:21 Jesus** The name "Jesus" means "salvation." **1:23 "The virgin . . . Immanuel"** Quotation from Isaiah 7:14.

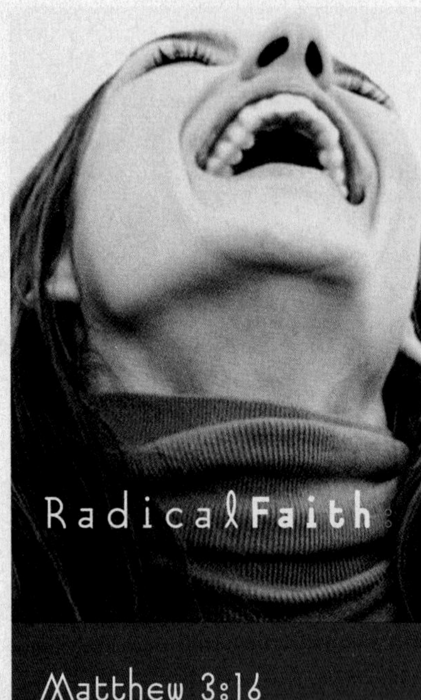

Matthew 3:16

There are two ceremonies Jesus gave for every believer to observe—communion and baptism. Why should we get baptized? Because Jesus did, and he did it publicly. Getting baptized tells the world about your faith in Jesus as your Savior. This lets people know that you mean business with God, and that you're going to live for him, with courage and excitement! Not only does God want you to profess him by being baptized in water, but he also wants you to be a witness for him by being filled daily with his Holy Spirit. Why be baptized in the Holy Spirit? Because we need the power we receive from it. Acts 1:8 says, "But when the Holy Spirit comes to you, you will receive power." We don't need to depend on our own strength and ability. God makes unlimited strength and power available to us through his Holy Spirit. As a teenager, you need that power to make a difference for him. Everyone does. Jesus is the baptizer. Let him baptize you with his power today!

24When Joseph woke up, he did what the
Lord's angel had told him to do. Joseph took
Mary as his wife, 25but he did not have sexual
relations with her until she gave birth to the
son. And Joseph named him Jesus.

WISE MEN COME TO VISIT JESUS

2 Jesus was born in the town of Bethlehem
in Judea during the time when Herod was
king. When Jesus was born, some wise men
from the east came to Jerusalem. 2They asked,
"Where is the baby who was born to be the king
of the Jews? We saw his star in the east and
have come to worship him."

3When King Herod heard this, he was troubled, as well as all the people in Jerusalem.
4Herod called a meeting of all the leading
priests and teachers of the law and asked
them where the Christ would be
born. 5They answered, "In the
town of Bethlehem in Judea.
The prophet wrote about this
in the Scriptures:

6'But you, Bethlehem, in
the land of Judah,
are important among the tribes
of Judah.
A ruler will come from you
who will be like a shepherd for my people
Israel.' " *Micah 5:2*

7Then Herod had a secret meeting with the
wise men and learned from them the exact time
they first saw the star. 8He sent the wise men
to Bethlehem, saying, "Look carefully for
the child. When you find him, come tell me
so I can worship him too."

9After the wise men heard the king, they left.
The star that they had seen in the east went
before them until it stopped above the place
where the child was. 10When the wise men saw
the star, they were filled with joy. 11They came
to the house where the child was and saw him
with his mother, Mary, and they bowed down
and worshiped him. They opened their gifts
and gave him treasures of gold, frankincense,
and myrrh. 12But God warned the wise men in a
dream not to go back to Herod, so they returned
to their own country by a different way.

Psalm 23:6
Surely your goodness and love will be with me all my life, and I will live in the house of the LORD forever.

JESUS' PARENTS TAKE HIM TO EGYPT

13After they left, an angel of the Lord came
to Joseph in a dream and said, "Get up! Take the
child and his mother and escape to Egypt,
because Herod is starting to look for the child
so he can kill him. Stay in Egypt until I tell you
to return."

14So Joseph got up and left for Egypt during
the night with the child and his mother. 15And
Joseph stayed in Egypt until Herod died. This
happened to bring about what the Lord had
said through the prophet: "I called my son out
of Egypt."[n]

HEROD KILLS THE BABY BOYS

16When Herod saw that the wise
men had tricked him, he was
furious. So he gave an order to
kill all the baby boys in
Bethlehem and in the surrounding area who were
two years old or younger. This
was in keeping with the time he learned
from the wise men. 17So what God had said
through the prophet Jeremiah came true:

18"A voice was heard in Ramah
of painful crying and deep sadness:
Rachel crying for her children.
She refused to be comforted,
because her children are dead." *Jeremiah 31:15*

JOSEPH AND MARY RETURN

19After Herod died, an angel of the Lord
spoke to Joseph in a dream while he was in
Egypt. 20The angel said, "Get up! Take the child
and his mother and go to the land of Israel,
because the people who were trying to kill the
child are now dead."

21So Joseph took the child and his mother
and went to Israel. 22But he heard that
Archelaus was now king in Judea since his
father Herod had died. So Joseph was afraid to

notes

2:15 "I called . . . Egypt." Quotation from Hosea 11:1.

go there. After being warned in a dream, he went to the area of Galilee, 23to a town called Nazareth, and lived there. And so what God had said through the prophets came true: "He will be called a Nazarene."[n]

THE WORK OF JOHN THE BAPTIST

3 About that time John the Baptist began preaching in the desert area of Judea. 2John said, "Change your hearts and lives because the kingdom of heaven is near." 3John the Baptist is the one Isaiah the prophet was talking about when he said:

"This is a voice of one
 who calls out in the desert:
'Prepare the way for the Lord.
 Make the road straight for him.' " *Isaiah 40:3*

4John's clothes were made from camel's hair, and he wore a leather belt around his waist. For food, he ate locusts and wild honey. 5Many people came from Jerusalem and Judea and all the area around the Jordan River to hear John. 6They confessed their sins, and he baptized them in the Jordan River.

7Many of the Pharisees and Sadducees came to the place where John was baptizing people. When John saw them, he said, "You are all snakes! Who warned you to run away from God's coming punishment? 8Do the things that show you really have changed your hearts and lives. 9And don't think you can say to yourselves, 'Abraham is our father.' I tell you that God could make children for Abraham from these rocks. 10The ax is now ready to cut down the trees, and every tree that does not produce good fruit will be cut down and thrown into the fire.[n]

11"I baptize you with water to show that your hearts and lives have changed. But there is one coming after me who is greater than I am, whose sandals I am not good enough to carry. He will baptize you with the Holy Spirit and fire. 12He will come ready to clean the grain, separating the good grain from the chaff. He will put the good part of the grain into his barn, but he will burn the chaff with a fire that cannot be put out."[n]

JESUS IS BAPTIZED BY JOHN

13At that time Jesus came from Galilee to the Jordan River and wanted John to baptize him. 14But John tried to stop him, saying, "Why do you come to me to be baptized? I need to be baptized by you!"

15Jesus answered, "Let it be this way for now. We should do all things that are God's will." So John agreed to baptize Jesus.

16As soon as Jesus was baptized, he came up out of the water. Then heaven opened, and he saw God's Spirit coming down on him like a dove. 17And a voice from heaven said, "This is my Son, whom I love, and I am very pleased with him."

THE TEMPTATION OF JESUS

4 Then the Spirit led Jesus into the desert to be tempted by the devil. 2Jesus ate

"AND SO WHAT GOD HAD SAID THROUGH THE PROPHETS CAME TRUE."

BEAUTY SECRET

TIME WITH GOD

As you apply your sunscreen, use that time to talk to God. Tell him how grateful you are for how he made you. Soon, you'll be so used to talking to him, it might become as regular and familiar as shrinking your pores.

TOPten

RANDOM WAYS TO HAVE FUN WITH YOUR FRIENDS

01	Go to a Christian Concert.
02	Make flower arrangements and leave them at strangers' doors.
03	Have a themed sleepover.
04	Volunteer at an animal shelter together.
05	Have a formal dinner party.
06	Get creative and make a wedding cake together!
07	Give each other makeovers.
08	Host a chick-flick night for your friends and their moms.
09	Go shopping and see who can get the coolest item for $10 or less.
10	Keep a prayer journal together.

notes

2:23 Nazarene A person from the city of Nazareth, a name probably meaning "branch" (see Isaiah 11:1). **3:10 The ax . . . fire.** This means that God is ready to punish his people who do not obey him. **3:12 He will . . . out.** This means that Jesus will come to separate good people from bad people, saving the good and punishing the bad.

Blab

Q. The Bible says I'm supposed to be loving my enemies. Does this mean I'm supposed to love Satan?

A. The answer is *no*, we are not to love Satan. Satan is the enemy of God. He is more than a foe to us; he is evil itself and as children of light we cannot love darkness or have any part in it.

Q. I found my grandmother's Catholic Bible and it has added books. What are they?

A. Catholics believe that these "added" books are also the inspired Word of God. They call them the "deuterocanon." These books can help to give us a better understanding of what happened in the 400 years between the Old and New Testaments. However, Protestants believe that they are only writings from the same time period, not the Word of God.

Q. I'm nearly fourteen and I have never even had a boyfriend. Am I the only one? All the people in my class must think I'm pathetic!

A. Don't let what the world thinks is important become important to you. You live by a different set of rules than other people. You live by God's Word. God wants you to seek him first and he'll give you all the rest in good time.

BIBLE BIOS: ABIGAIL

On the run from Saul, David and his men needed food and supplies. So, David sent some men to request these things from Nabal. Nabal rudely refused this request, which made David very angry.

However, Nabal's wife, Abigail, heard of David and all he had done, and she took him some food, wine, and gifts to repent and make reconciliation for her husband's hasty decision. Days later, Nabal died, and David quickly took Abigail as his wife.

From Abigail, we can learn to be both wise and generous.

[1 SAMUEL 25]

nothing for forty days and nights. After this, he
was very hungry. 3The devil came to Jesus to
tempt him, saying, "If you are the Son of God,
tell these rocks to become bread."

4Jesus answered, "It is written in the
Scriptures, 'A person does not live by eating
only bread, but by everything God says.' "*n*

5Then the devil led Jesus to the holy city of
Jerusalem and put him on a high place of the
Temple. 6The devil said, "If you are the Son of
God, jump down, because it is written in the
Scriptures:

'He has put his angels in charge of you.
They will catch you in their hands
so that you will not hit your foot
on a rock.' " *Psalm 91:11-12*

7Jesus answered him, "It also says in the
Scriptures, 'Do not test the Lord your God.' "*n*

8Then the devil led Jesus to the top of a very
high mountain and showed him all the kingdoms
of the world and all their splendor. 9The devil said,
"If you will bow down and worship me, I will give
you all these things."

10Jesus said to the devil, "Go away from me,
Satan! It is written in the Scriptures, 'You must
worship the Lord your God and serve only him.' "*n*

11So the devil left Jesus, and angels came
and took care of him.

JESUS BEGINS WORK IN GALILEE

12When Jesus heard that John had been put
in prison, he went back to Galilee. 13He left
Nazareth and went to live in Capernaum, a
town near Lake Galilee, in the area near
Zebulun and Naphtali. 14Jesus did this to bring
about what the prophet Isaiah had said:

15"Land of Zebulun and land of Naphtali
along the sea,
beyond the Jordan River.
This is Galilee where the non-Jewish
people live.
16These people who live in darkness
will see a great light.
They live in a place covered with
the shadows of death,
but a light will shine on them." *Isaiah 9:1-2*

JESUS CHOOSES SOME FOLLOWERS

17From that time Jesus began to preach, saying, "Change your hearts and lives, because the
kingdom of heaven is near."

18As Jesus was walking by Lake Galilee, he
saw two brothers, Simon (called Peter) and his
brother Andrew. They were throwing a net into

notes

4:4 'A person . . . says.' Quotation from Deuteronomy 8:3. **4:7 'Do . . . God.'** Quotation from Deuteronomy 6:16. **4:10 'You . . . him.'** Quotation from Deuteronomy 6:13.

January 04

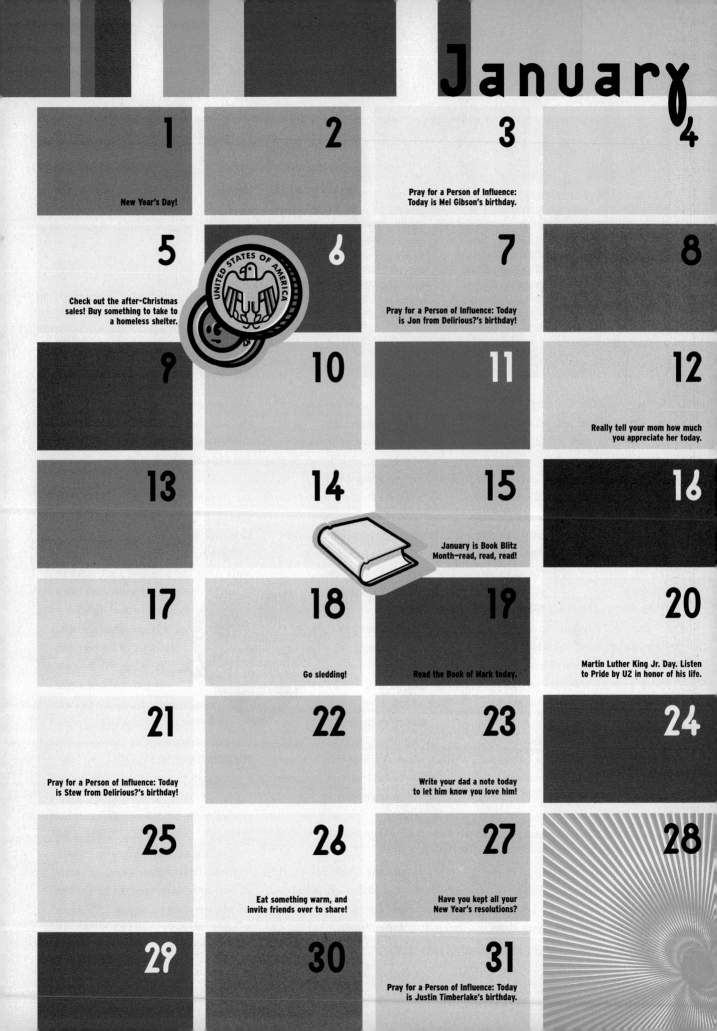

1 New Year's Day!	2	3 Pray for a Person of Influence: Today is Mel Gibson's birthday.	4
5 Check out the after-Christmas sales! Buy something to take to a homeless shelter.	6	7 Pray for a Person of Influence: Today is Jon from Delirious?'s birthday!	8
9	10	11	12 Really tell your mom how much you appreciate her today.
13	14	15 January is Book Blitz Month—read, read, read!	16
17	18 Go sledding!	19 Read the Book of Mark today.	20 Martin Luther King Jr. Day. Listen to Pride by U2 in honor of his life.
21 Pray for a Person of Influence: Today is Stew from Delirious?'s birthday!	22	23 Write your dad a note today to let him know you love him!	24
25	26 Eat something warm, and invite friends over to share!	27 Have you kept all your New Year's resolutions?	28
29	30	31 Pray for a Person of Influence: Today is Justin Timberlake's birthday.	

ISSUES: Rape

Rape is a serious crime of violence. If you or a friend has been raped by a stranger, a family member, or on a date, you need to tell someone. You have several options. You can either call the national rape crisis line at 1-800-656-HOPE for immediate help, or you can talk with a trusted parent, teacher, or counselor. Silence is not a defense against this horrible act of aggression. Please take courage to talk with someone (parents, counselor, teachers, youth pastors) about how you have been abused. In doing so, you will begin the process of healing. Rape is a severe act of brutality against women physically, psychologically, emotionally, and spiritually. There are numerous support groups available where you will find other women who understand your pain. Let others pray for you, comfort you, and talk with you so that you might receive healing for your emotional scars.

the lake because they were fishermen. 19Jesus said, "Come follow me, and I will make you fish for people." 20So Simon and Andrew immediately left their nets and followed him.

21As Jesus continued walking by Lake Galilee, he saw two other brothers, James and John, the sons of Zebedee. They were in a boat with their father Zebedee, mending their nets. Jesus told them to come with him. 22Immediately they left the boat and their father, and they followed Jesus.

JESUS TEACHES AND HEALS PEOPLE

23Jesus went everywhere in Galilee, teaching in the synagogues, preaching the Good News about the kingdom of heaven, and healing all the people's diseases and sicknesses. 24The news about Jesus spread all over Syria, and people brought all the sick to him. They were suffering from different kinds of diseases. Some were in great pain, some had demons, some were epileptics,[n] and some were paralyzed. Jesus healed all of them. 25Many people from Galilee, the Ten Towns,[n] Jerusalem, Judea, and the land across the Jordan River followed him.

JESUS TEACHES THE PEOPLE

5 When Jesus saw the crowds, he went up on a hill and sat down. His followers came to him, 2and he began to teach them, saying:

3"Those people who know they have great
spiritual needs are happy,
because the kingdom of heaven belongs
to them.
4Those who are sad now are happy,
because God will comfort them.
5Those who are humble are happy,
because the earth will belong to them.
6Those who want to do right more than
anything else are happy,
because God will fully
satisfy them.
7Those who show mercy to
others are happy,
because God will show
mercy to them.
8Those who are pure in their
thinking are happy,
because they will be with God.
9Those who work to bring peace are happy,
because God will call them his children.
10Those who are treated badly for doing good
are happy,
because the kingdom of heaven belongs
to them.

11"People will insult you and hurt you. They will lie and say all kinds of evil things about you because you follow me. But when they do, you will be happy. 12Rejoice and be glad, because you have a great reward waiting for you in heaven. People did the same evil things to the prophets who lived before you.

YOU ARE LIKE SALT AND LIGHT

13"You are the salt of the earth. But if the salt loses its salty taste, it cannot be made salty again. It is good for nothing, except to be thrown out and walked on.

14"You are the light that gives light to the world. A city that is built on a hill cannot be hidden. 15And people don't hide a light under a bowl. They put it on a lampstand so the light shines for all the people in the house. 16In the same way, you should be a light for other people. Live so that they will see the good things you do and will praise your Father in heaven.

Psalm 33:18
But the LORD looks after those who fear him, those who put their hope in his love.

THE IMPORTANCE OF THE LAW

17"Don't think that I have come to destroy the law of Moses or the teaching of the prophets. I have not come to destroy them but to bring about what they said. 18I tell you the truth, nothing will disappear from the law until heaven and earth are gone. Not even the smallest letter or the smallest part of a letter will be lost until everything has happened. 19Whoever refuses to obey any command and teaches

notes

4:24 epileptics People with a disease that causes them sometimes to lose control of their bodies and maybe faint, shake strongly, or not be able to move. **4:25 Ten Towns** In Greek, called "Decapolis." It was an area east of Lake Galilee that once had ten main towns.

other people not to obey that command will be
the least important in the kingdom of heaven.
But whoever obeys the commands and teaches
other people to obey them will be great in the
kingdom of heaven. [20]I tell you that if you are
no more obedient than the teachers of the law
and the Pharisees, you will never enter the
kingdom of heaven.

JESUS TEACHES ABOUT ANGER

[21]"You have heard that it was said to
our people long ago, 'You must not murder
anyone.'[n] Anyone who murders another
will be judged.' [22]But I tell you, if you are
angry with a brother or sister,[n] you will be
judged. If you say bad things to a brother
or sister, you will be judged by the council.
And if you call someone a fool, you will be
in danger of the fire of hell.

[23]"So when you offer your gift to God at
the altar, and you remember that your
brother or sister has something against
you, [24]leave your gift there at the altar. Go
and make peace with that person, and then
come and offer your gift.

[25]"If your enemy is taking you to court,
become friends quickly, before you go to court.
Otherwise, your enemy might turn you over to
the judge, and the judge might give you to a
guard to put you in jail. [26]I tell you the truth,
you will not leave there until you have paid
everything you owe.

JESUS TEACHES ABOUT SEXUAL SIN

[27]"You have heard that it was said, 'You
must not be guilty of adultery.'[n] [28]But I tell you
that if anyone looks at a woman and wants to
sin sexually with her, in his mind he has
already done that sin with the woman. [29]If your
right eye causes you to sin, take it out and
throw it away. It is better to lose one part of
your body than to have your whole body
thrown into hell. [30]If your right hand causes
you to sin, cut it off and throw it away. It is better to lose one part of your body than for your
whole body to go into hell.

JESUS TEACHES ABOUT DIVORCE

[31]"It was also said, 'Anyone who divorces his
wife must give her a written divorce paper.'[n]
[32]But I tell you that anyone who divorces his
wife forces her to be guilty of adultery. The only
reason for a man to divorce his wife is if she has
sexual relations with another man. And anyone
who marries that divorced woman is guilty of
adultery.

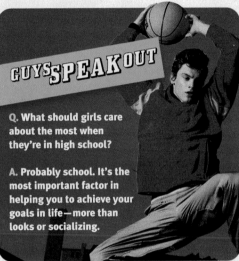

GUYS SPEAK OUT

Q. What should girls care about the most when they're in high school?

A. Probably school. It's the most important factor in helping you to achieve your goals in life—more than looks or socializing.

MAKE PROMISES CAREFULLY

[33]"You have heard that it was said to our
people long ago, 'Don't break your promises,
but keep the promises you make to the Lord.'[n]
[34]But I tell you, never swear an oath. Don't
swear an oath using the name of heaven,
because heaven is God's throne. [35]Don't swear
an oath using the name of the earth, because
the earth belongs to God. Don't swear an oath
using the name of Jerusalem, because that is
the city of the great King. [36]Don't even swear
by your own head, because you cannot make
one hair on your head become white or black.
[37]Say only yes if you mean yes, and no if you
mean no. If you say more than yes or no, it is
from the Evil One.

DON'T FIGHT BACK

[38]"You have heard that it was said, 'An eye
for an eye, and a tooth for a tooth.'[n] [39]But I tell
you, don't stand up against an evil person. If
someone slaps you on the right cheek, turn
to him the other cheek also. [40]If someone
wants to sue you in court and take your
shirt, let him have your coat also. [41]If
someone forces you to go with him one
mile, go with him two miles. [42]If a person
asks you for something, give
it to him. Don't refuse to give to someone
who wants to borrow from you.

LOVE ALL PEOPLE

[43]"You have heard that it was said,
'Love your neighbor[n] and hate your enemies.' [44]But I say to you, love your enemies. Pray for those who hurt you. [45]If
you do this, you will be true children of
your Father in heaven. He causes the sun to
rise on good people and on evil people, and
he sends rain to those who do right and to
those who do wrong. [46]If you love only the
people who love you, you will get no reward.
Even the tax collectors do that. [47]And if you
are nice only to your friends, you are no better than other people. Even those who don't
know God are nice to their friends. [48]So you
must be perfect, just as your Father in heaven
is perfect.

JESUS TEACHES ABOUT GIVING

6 "Be careful! When you do good things,
don't do them in front of people to be
seen by them. If you do that, you will have no
reward from your Father in heaven.

[2]"When you give to the poor, don't be like

42% OF YOUNG ADULTS HAVE A "QUIET TIME" DURING THE WEEK.

5:21 You . . . anyone. Quotation from Exodus 20:13; Deuteronomy 5:17. **5:22 brother . . . sister** Although the Greek text reads "brother" here and throughout this book, Jesus' words were meant for the entire church, including men and women. **5:27 'You . . . adultery.'** Quotation from Exodus 20:14; Deuteronomy 5:18. **5:31 'Anyone . . . divorce paper.'** Quotation from Deuteronomy 24:1. **5:33 'Don't . . . Lord.'** This refers to Leviticus 19:12; Numbers 30:2; Deuteronomy 23:21. **5:38 'An eye . . . tooth.'** Quotation from Exodus 21:24; Leviticus 24:20; Deuteronomy 19:21. **5:43 'Love your neighbor'** Quotation from Leviticus 19:18.

ARE YOU INTROVERTED OR EXTROVERTED?

WHEN I'M UPSET ABOUT SOMETHING, I USUALLY:
A. TALK TO SOMEONE ABOUT IT.
B. DON'T SAY ANYTHING.

IN THE MIDDLE OF A BIG CROWD I FEEL:
A. COMFORTABLE.
B. SCARED.

WHEN I CREATE SOMETHING THAT I AM PROUD OF (LIKE ART, WRITING OR MUSIC) I:
A. SHOW IT TO PEOPLE.
B. KEEP IT TO MYSELF.

I SING IN THE SHOWER:
A. ALL THE TIME.
B. RARELY.

WOULD I CONSIDER RUNNING FOR A SCHOOL OFFICE?
A. SURE, THAT SOUNDS LIKE FUN.
B. NO, I WOULDN'T BE VERY GOOD AT THAT.

MY FRIENDS COME TO ME FOR ADVICE:
A. MOST OF THE TIME.
B. RARELY.

I'M BETTER AT:
A . ENGLISH.
B. MATH.

MY ROLE IN A GROUP OF PEOPLE IS:
A. THE ENTERTAINER.
B. THE LISTENER.

AT A PARTY I AM MOST LIKELY:
A. TELLING ALL THE JOKES.
B. HELPING WITH THE FOOD, MUSIC, ETC.

DO I LIKE TO INITIATE IDEAS?
A. ALL THE TIME!
B. NOT REALLY; I LET OTHERS DO THAT.

IF YOU PICKED MOSTLY A'S, YOU ARE AN EXTROVERT.
For you, life is all about hanging out with friends—you like to share your feelings and experiences. And you probably love adding new people to your group. You don't usually enjoy time alone, because it's not as much fun as having others around. That's great, but remember that everyone needs some quiet time every once in a while. Learn to enjoy being with just yourself and God!

IF YOU PICKED MOSTLY B'S, YOU ARE AN INTROVERT.
As an introvert, you prefer to keep personal things like feelings and thoughts to yourself. You are probably pretty quiet in groups, and you don't prefer to draw attention to yourself. It's great to spend some time looking inward, and it's fine to be your own best friend. But, try to reach out to others and learn to welcome them into your life. We all need friends to love and support us as we walk through life!

LEARN IT & LIVE IT

Matthew 1:1-17:
Learn It: Family is important.
Live It: Today find out something about your family that you never knew before.

Matthew 3:1-2:
Learn It: Your heart is sinful and needs to be changed.
Live It: Figure out one thing about the way you're thinking that's wrong. Ask God to help you really focus on changing it for two weeks.

Matthew 5:23-24:
Learn It: You shouldn't take Communion if you are in a fight with a friend or family member.
Live It: Next time the plate passes, if you're in a bad place with one of your friends, don't take it. Go straight to them and tell them you want to work things out.

the hypocrites. They blow trumpets in the synagogues and on the streets so that people will
see them and honor them. I tell you the truth,
those hypocrites already have their full reward.
3So when you give to the poor, don't let anyone
know what you are doing. 4Your giving should
be done in secret. Your Father can see what is
done in secret, and he will reward you.

JESUS TEACHES ABOUT PRAYER

5"When you pray, don't be like the hypocrites.
They love to stand in the synagogues and on the
street corners and pray so people will see them.
I tell you the truth, they already have their full
reward. 6When you pray, you should go into
your room and close the door and pray to your
Father who cannot be seen. Your Father can see
what is done in secret, and he will reward you.

7"And when you pray, don't be like those
people who don't know God. They continue
saying things that mean nothing, thinking that
God will hear them because of their many
words. 8Don't be like them, because your
Father knows the things you need before you
ask him. 9So when you pray, you should pray
like this:

'Our Father in heaven,
may your name always be kept holy.
10May your kingdom come
and what you want be done,
here on earth as it is in heaven.
11Give us the food we need for each day.
12Forgive us for our sins,
just as we have forgiven those who
sinned against us.
13And do not cause us to be tempted,
but save us from the Evil One.'

14Yes, if you forgive others for their sins, your
Father in heaven will also forgive you for your
sins. 15But if you don't forgive others, your
Father in heaven will not forgive your sins.

JESUS TEACHES ABOUT WORSHIP

16"When you give up eating,[n] don't put on a
sad face like the hypocrites. They make their
faces look sad to show people they are giving
up eating. I tell you the truth, those hypocrites
already have their full reward. 17So when you
give up eating, comb your hair and wash your
face. 18Then people will not know that you are
giving up eating, but your Father, whom you
cannot see, will see you. Your Father sees what
is done in secret, and he will reward you.

GOD IS MORE IMPORTANT THAN MONEY

19"Don't store treasures for yourselves here
on earth where moths and rust will destroy
them and thieves can break in and steal them.
20But store your treasures in heaven where
they cannot be destroyed by moths or rust and
where thieves cannot break in and steal them.
21Your heart will be where your treasure is.

22"The eye is a light for the body. If your eyes
are good, your whole body will be full of light.
23But if your eyes are evil, your whole body
will be full of darkness. And if the only light
you have is really darkness, then you have the
worst darkness.

24"No one can serve two masters. The person will hate one master and love the other, or
will follow one master and refuse to follow the
other. You cannot serve both God and worldly
riches.

DON'T WORRY

25"So I tell you, don't worry about the food
or drink you need to live, or about the clothes
you need for your body. Life is more than food,
and the body is more than clothes. 26Look at
the birds in the air. They don't plant or harvest
or store food in barns, but your heavenly Father
feeds them. And you know that you are worth
much more than the birds. 27You cannot add
any time to your life by worrying about it.

28"And why do you worry about clothes?
Look at how the lilies in the field grow. They
don't work or make clothes for themselves.
29But I tell you that even Solomon with his
riches was not dressed as beautifully as one of
these flowers. 30God clothes the grass in the
field, which is alive today but tomorrow is
thrown into the fire. So you can be even more
sure that God will clothe you. Don't have so little faith! 31Don't worry and say, 'What will we

notes

6:16 give up eating This is called "fasting." The people would give up eating for a special time of prayer and worship to God. It was also done to show sadness and disappointment.

Matthew 5:13-14

Jesus teaches in Matthew 5:13-14 that part of being a Christian is being salt and light to this world. Being salt means that a follower of Jesus creates a thirst for greater information. When you meet someone who is different and has qualities superior to your own, you want to know why that person is different. Have you ever met someone who was really cool, had a great attitude even when life was hard, did nice things for no obvious reason, and later found out that she was a Christian? That explained it! That person was being salt. She made people want to know what made her different.

How about light? A light shines and gives direction. It points people toward the right path. Do you know Christians who radiate Jesus? Others are drawn to them. Their lives are examples that many want to follow. People see their goodness and know it is Jesus who lives in them. Jesus says don't hide who you are. Don't put your light under a basket where others can't see it. Go boldly into the world and give 'em Jesus. You are bound to change the place where you are when others see Jesus in you.

eat?' or 'What will we drink?' or 'What will we
wear?' 32The people who don't know God keep
trying to get these things, and your Father in
heaven knows you need them. 33The thing you
should want most is God's kingdom and doing
what God wants. Then all these other things
you need will be given to you. 34So don't worry
about tomorrow, because tomorrow will have
its own worries. Each day has enough trouble
of its own.

BE CAREFUL ABOUT JUDGING OTHERS

7 "Don't judge other people, or you will be
judged. 2You will be judged in the same
way that you judge others, and the amount you
give to others will be given to you.

3"Why do you notice the little piece of dust
in your friend's eye, but you don't notice the
big piece of wood in your own eye? 4How can
you say to your friend, 'Let me take that little
piece of dust out of your eye'? Look at yourself!
You still have that big piece of wood in your
own eye. 5You hypocrite! First, take the wood
out of your own eye. Then you will see clearly
to take the dust out of your friend's eye.

6"Don't give holy things to dogs, and don't
throw your pearls before pigs. Pigs will only trample on them, and dogs will turn to attack you.

ASK GOD FOR WHAT YOU NEED

7"Ask, and God will give to you. Search, and
you will find. Knock, and the door will open
for you. 8Yes, everyone who asks will receive.
Everyone who searches will find. And everyone
who knocks will have the door opened.

9"If your children ask for bread, which of
you would give them a stone? 10Or if your
children ask for a fish, would you give them a
snake? 11Even though you are bad, you know
how to give good gifts to your children. How
much more your heavenly Father will give
good things to those who ask him!

THE MOST IMPORTANT RULE

12"Do to others what you want them to do to
you. This is the meaning of the law of Moses
and the teaching of the prophets.

THE WAY TO HEAVEN IS HARD

13"Enter through the narrow gate. The gate is
wide and the road is wide that leads to hell, and
many people enter through that gate. 14But the
gate is small and the road is narrow that leads to
true life. Only a few people find that road.

PEOPLE KNOW YOU BY YOUR ACTIONS

15"Be careful of false prophets. They come

"THE THING YOU SHOULD WANT MOST IS GOD'S KINGDOM AND DOING WHAT GOD WANTS."

to you looking gentle like sheep, but they are
really dangerous like wolves. 16You will know
these people by what they do. Grapes don't
come from thornbushes, and figs don't come
from thorny weeds. 17In the same way, every
good tree produces good fruit, but a bad tree
produces bad fruit. 18A good tree cannot produce bad fruit, and a bad tree cannot produce
good fruit. 19Every tree that does not produce
good fruit is cut down and thrown into the fire.
20In the same way, you will know these false
prophets by what they do.

21"Not all those who say that I am their Lord
will enter the kingdom of heaven. The only people who will enter the kingdom of heaven are
those who do what my Father in heaven wants.
22On the last day many people will say to me,
'Lord, Lord, we spoke for you, and through you
we forced out demons and did many miracles.'
23Then I will tell them clearly, 'Get away from
me, you who do evil. I never knew you.'

TWO KINDS OF PEOPLE

24"Everyone who hears my words and obeys
them is like a wise man who built his house on
rock. 25It rained hard, the floods came, and the
winds blew and hit that house. But it did not
fall, because it was built on rock. 26Everyone
who hears my words and does not obey them is
like a foolish man who built his house on sand.

27It rained hard, the floods came, and the winds blew and hit that house, and it fell with a big crash."

28When Jesus finished saying these things, the people were amazed at his teaching, 29because he did not teach like their teachers of the law. He taught like a person who had authority.

JESUS HEALS A SICK MAN

8 When Jesus came down from the hill, great crowds followed him. 2Then a man with a skin disease came to Jesus. The man bowed down before him and said, "Lord, you can heal me if you will."

3Jesus reached out his hand and touched the man and said, "I will. Be healed!" And immediately the man was healed from his disease. 4Then Jesus said to him, "Don't tell anyone about this. But go and show yourself to the priest[n] and offer the gift Moses commanded[n] for people who are made well. This will show the people what I have done."

JESUS HEALS A SOLDIER'S SERVANT

5When Jesus entered the city of Capernaum, an army officer came to him, begging for help. 6The officer said, "Lord, my servant is at home in bed. He can't move his body and is in much pain."

7Jesus said to the officer, "I will go and heal him."

8The officer answered, "Lord, I am not worthy for you to come into my house. You only need to command it, and my servant will be healed. 9I, too, am a man under the authority of others, and I have soldiers under my command. I tell one soldier, 'Go,' and he goes. I tell another soldier, 'Come,' and he comes. I say to my servant, 'Do this,' and my servant does it.

10When Jesus heard this, he was amazed. He said to those who were following him, "I tell you the truth, this is the greatest faith I have found, even in Israel. 11Many people will come from the east and from the west and will sit and eat with Abraham, Isaac, and Jacob in the kingdom of heaven. 12But those people who should be in the kingdom will be thrown outside into the darkness, where people will cry and grind their teeth with pain."

13Then Jesus said to the officer, "Go home. Your servant will be healed just as you believed he would." And his servant was healed that same hour.

JESUS HEALS MANY PEOPLE

14When Jesus went to Peter's house, he saw that Peter's mother-in-law was sick in bed with a fever. 15Jesus touched her hand, and the fever left her. Then she stood up and began to serve Jesus.

16That evening people brought to Jesus many who had demons. Jesus spoke and the demons left them, and he healed all the sick. 17He did these things to bring about what Isaiah the prophet had said:

"He took our suffering on him
and carried our diseases." *Isaiah 53:4*

"EVERYONE WHO HEARS MY WORDS AND OBEYS THEM IS LIKE A WISE MAN WHO BUILT HIS HOUSE ON ROCK."

PEOPLE WANT TO FOLLOW JESUS

18When Jesus saw the crowd around him, he told his followers to go to the other side of the lake. 19Then a teacher of the law came to Jesus and said, "Teacher, I will follow you any place you go."

20Jesus said to him, "The foxes have holes to live in, and the birds have nests, but the Son of Man has no place to rest his head."

21Another man, one of Jesus' followers, said to him, "Lord, first let me go and bury my father."

22But Jesus told him, "Follow me, and let

Blab

Q. I don't feel like telling anyone I'm a Christian or I'll get teased and mocked around. What should I do?

A. Jesus said, "But all who stand before others and say they do not believe in me, I will say before my Father in heaven that they do not belong to me" (Matthew 10:33). What should you do? Don't deny him if you love him.

Q. Hey, my question is how do you tell a friend that's your crush that you're into him without ruining your friendship?

A. Telling a guy friend that he is your crush is risky. You could end a great friendship. If you really dig him, just enjoy being with him. If he feels the same about you, and it is meant to be, it will happen in time. Crushes come and go; friendships can last a lifetime.

Q. When I'm at school I do stuff Christ wouldn't like. How can I quit doing bad stuff?

A. First, confess your sins to God. Then think about what your life will be like if you keep doing this bad stuff. Be imaginative and honest. Check out God's Word to see what he says about people who continually sin. This should inspire you to stop dead in your tracks.

notes

8:4 show . . . priest The Law of Moses said a priest must say when a Jewish person with a skin disease was well. **8:4 Moses commanded** Read about this in Leviticus 14:1–32.

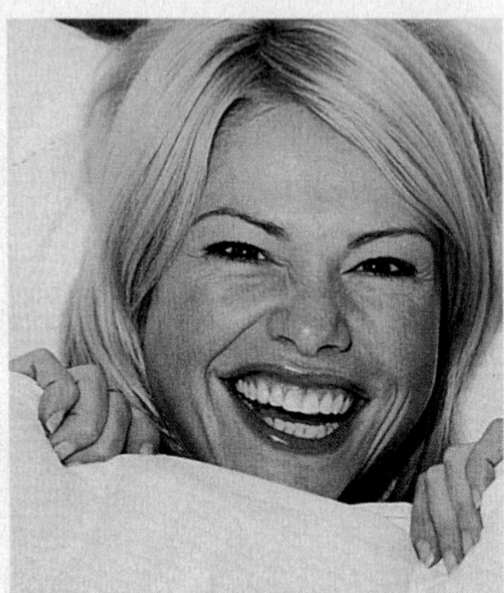

Radical**Faith**:

Matthew 7:12

This verse has been called the "Golden Rule." It's as valuable as gold and it'll work every time you use it. It's been quoted and misquoted for years. It isn't just about being nice; it's a lot more than that. Look at what Jesus says leading up to this. Love people who are against you; pray for the person who's mean to you; if someone wants to borrow something, give him more than what he asks for and don't ask him to give it back. You wouldn't dare *ask* anyone to treat you that well—you'd feel like you were using her—but you'd like it if she did, right?

Jesus isn't telling you to be a doormat. He's showing you how to follow his example. His whole life was about two things: pleasing God and helping other people. He wants you to be more concerned about others than you are about yourself. Look out for others and trust God to look out for you. Always think about how you'd want someone to treat you. That's the heart of the Golden Rule.

the people who are dead bury their own dead."

JESUS CALMS A STORM

23 Jesus got into a boat, and his followers went with him. 24 A great storm arose on the lake so that waves covered the boat, but Jesus was sleeping. 25 His followers went to him and woke him, saying, "Lord, save us! We will drown!"

26 Jesus answered, "Why are you afraid? You don't have enough faith." Then Jesus got up and gave a command to the wind and the waves, and it became completely calm.

27 The men were amazed and said, "What kind of man is this? Even the wind and the waves obey him!"

JESUS HEALS TWO MEN WITH DEMONS

28 When Jesus arrived at the other side of the lake in the area of the Gadarene[n] people, two men who had demons in them met him. These men lived in the burial caves and were so dangerous that people could not use the road by those caves. 29 They shouted, "What do you want with us, Son of God? Did you come here to torture us before the right time?"

30 Near that place there was a large herd of pigs feeding. 31 The demons begged Jesus, "If you make us leave these men, please send us into that herd of pigs."

32 Jesus said to them, "Go!" So the demons left the men and went into the pigs. Then the whole herd rushed down the hill into the lake and were drowned. 33 The herdsmen ran away and went into town, where they told about all of this and what had happened to the men who had demons. 34 Then the whole town went out to see Jesus. When they saw him, they begged him to leave their area.

JESUS HEALS A PARALYZED MAN

9 Jesus got into a boat and went back across the lake to his own town. 2 Some people brought to Jesus a man who was paralyzed and lying on a mat. When Jesus saw the faith of these people, he said to the paralyzed man, "Be encouraged, young man. Your sins are forgiven."

3 Some of the teachers of the law said to themselves, "This man speaks as if he were God. That is blasphemy!"[n]

4 Knowing their thoughts, Jesus said, "Why are you thinking evil thoughts? 5 Which is easier: to say, 'Your sins are forgiven,' or to tell him, 'Stand up and walk'? 6 But I will prove to you that the Son of Man has authority on earth to forgive sins." Then Jesus said to the paralyzed man, "Stand up, take your mat, and go home." 7 And the man stood up and went home. 8 When the people saw this, they were amazed and praised God for giving power like this to human beings.

Psalm 136:1
Give thanks to the LORD because he is good. His love continues forever.

JESUS CHOOSES MATTHEW

9 When Jesus was leaving, he saw a man named Matthew sitting in the tax collector's booth. Jesus said to him, "Follow me," and he stood up and followed Jesus.

10 As Jesus was having dinner at Matthew's house, many tax collectors and "sinners" came and ate with Jesus and his followers. 11 When the Pharisees saw this, they asked Jesus' followers, "Why does your teacher eat with tax collectors and sinners?"

12 When Jesus heard them, he said, "It is not the healthy people who need a doctor, but the sick. 13 Go and learn what this means: 'I want kindness more than I want animal sacrifices.'[n] I did not come to invite good people but to invite sinners."

JESUS' FOLLOWERS ARE CRITICIZED

14 Then the followers of John[n] came to Jesus and said, "Why do we and the Pharisees often give up eating for a certain time,[n] but your followers don't?"

15 Jesus answered, "The friends of the

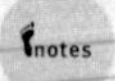

8:28 Gadarene From Gadara, an area southeast of Lake Galilee. **9:3 blasphemy** Saying things against God or not showing respect for God. **9:13 'I want . . . sacrifices.'** Quotation from Hosea 6:6. **9:14 John** John the Baptist, who preached to people about Christ's coming (Matthew 3, Luke 3). **9:14 give up . . . time** This is called "fasting." The people would give up eating for a special time of prayer and worship to God. It was also done to show sadness and disappointment.

bridegroom are not sad while he is with them. But the time will come when the bridegroom will be taken from them, and then they will give up eating.

16“No one sews a patch of unshrunk cloth over a hole in an old coat. If he does, the patch will shrink and pull away from the coat, making the hole worse. 17Also, people never pour new wine into old leather bags. Otherwise, the bags will break, the wine will spill, and the wine bags will be ruined. But people always pour new wine into new wine bags. Then both will continue to be good.”

JESUS GIVES LIFE TO A DEAD GIRL AND HEALS A SICK WOMAN

18While Jesus was saying these things, a leader of the synagogue came to him. He bowed down before Jesus and said, “My daughter has just died. But if you come and lay your hand on her, she will live again.” 19So Jesus and his followers stood up and went with the leader.

20Then a woman who had been bleeding for twelve years came behind Jesus and touched the edge of his coat. 21She was thinking, “If I can just touch his clothes, I will be healed.”

28% OF YOUNG ADULTS ATTEND CHURCH ON A GIVEN SUNDAY.

22Jesus turned and saw the woman and said, “Be encouraged, dear woman. You are made well because you believed.” And the woman was healed from that moment on.

23Jesus continued along with the leader and went into his house. There he saw the funeral musicians and many people crying. 24Jesus said, “Go away. The girl is not dead, only asleep.” But the people laughed at him. 25After the crowd had been thrown out of the house, Jesus went into the girl's room and took hold of her hand, and she stood up. 26The news about this spread all around the area.

JESUS HEALS MORE PEOPLE

27When Jesus was leaving there, two blind men followed him. They cried out, “Have mercy on us, Son of David!”

28After Jesus went inside, the blind men went with him. He asked the men, “Do you believe that I can make you see again?”

They answered, “Yes, Lord.”

29Then Jesus touched their eyes and said, “Because you believe I can make you see again, it will happen.” 30Then the men were able to see. But Jesus warned them strongly, saying, “Don't tell anyone about this.” 31But the blind men left and spread the news about Jesus all around that area.

32When the two men were leaving, some people brought another man to Jesus. This man could not talk because he had a demon in him. 33After Jesus forced the demon to leave the man, he was able to speak. The crowd was amazed and said, “We have never seen anything like this in Israel.”

34But the Pharisees said, “The prince of demons is the one that gives him power to force demons out.”

35Jesus traveled through all the towns and villages, teaching in their synagogues, preaching the Good News about the kingdom, and healing all kinds of diseases and sicknesses. 36When he saw the crowds, he felt sorry for them because they were hurting and helpless, like sheep without a shepherd. 37Jesus said to his followers, “There are many people to harvest but only a few workers to help harvest them. 38Pray to the Lord, who owns the harvest, that he will send more workers to gather his harvest.”[n]

JESUS SENDS OUT HIS APOSTLES

10 Jesus called his twelve followers together and gave them authority to drive out evil spirits and to heal every kind of disease and sickness. 2These are the names of the twelve apostles: Simon (also called Peter) and his brother Andrew; James son of Zebedee, and his brother John; 3Philip and Bartholomew; Thomas and Matthew, the tax collector; James son of Alphaeus, and Thaddaeus; 4Simon the Zealot and Judas Iscariot, who turned against Jesus.

5Jesus sent out these twelve men with the following order: “Don't go to the non-Jewish people or to any town where the Samaritans live. 6But go to the people of Israel, who are like lost sheep. 7When you go, preach this: ‘The kingdom of heaven is near.’ 8Heal the sick, raise the dead to life again, heal those who have skin diseases, and force demons out of people. I give you these powers freely, so help other people freely. 9Don't carry any money with you—gold or silver or copper. 10Don't carry a bag or extra clothes or sandals or a walking stick. Workers should be given what they need.

“WHEN JESUS WAS LEAVING THERE, TWO BLIND MEN FOLLOWED HIM. THEY CRIED OUT, ‘HAVE MERCY ON US, SON OF DAVID!’”

11“When you enter a city or town, find some worthy person there and stay in that home until you leave. 12When you enter that home, say, ‘Peace be with you.’ 13If the people there welcome you, let your peace stay there. But if they don't welcome you, take back the peace you wished for them. 14And if a home or town refuses to welcome you or listen to you, leave that place and shake its dust off your feet.[n] 15I tell you the truth, on the Judgment Day it will be better for the towns of Sodom and Gomorrah[n] than for the people of that town.

JESUS WARNS HIS APOSTLES

16“Listen, I am sending you out like sheep among wolves. So be as smart as snakes and as

notes
9:37-38 “There are . . . harvest.” As a farmer sends workers to harvest the grain, Jesus sends his followers to bring people to God. **10:14 shake . . . feet.** A warning. It showed that they had rejected these people.
10:15 Sodom and Gomorrah Two cities that God destroyed because the people were so evil.

Matthew 7:29

This passage of Scripture tells us that the crowds were surprised because Jesus taught with authority. We're not talking about your basic authority; we're talking about power! There is power in the words of Jesus. Look at what Hebrews 4:12 says: "God's word is alive and working and is sharper than a double-edged sword. It cuts all the way into us, where the soul and the spirit are joined, to the center of our joints and bones. And it judges the thoughts and feelings in our hearts." Start putting the Word of God in your mind and heart today, so that when troubles come against you, you can use it like a sword.

When the devil tempted Jesus in the wilderness, what did Jesus do? He spoke the Word of God. He said, "It is written . . ." (see Matthew 4:4, 6, 10). And you know what? The devil split. We need to do the same. John 1:1 tells us, "In the beginning there was the Word. The Word was with God, and the Word was God." Jesus is the Word, and he wants to teach you today. As you begin to study the Scriptures, you will begin to gain understanding of what the verses mean. This will help you live every day of the week and cause you to walk in victory! Remember, the Bible isn't meant to be difficult. You'll never know until you dive in. Let Jesus be *your* teacher!

innocent as doves. 17Be careful of people, because they will arrest you and take you to court and whip you in their synagogues. 18Because of me you will be taken to stand before governors and kings, and you will tell them and the non-Jewish people about me. 19When you are arrested, don't worry about what to say or how to say it. At that time you will be given the things to say. 20It will not really be you speaking but the Spirit of your Father speaking through you.

21"Brothers will give their own brothers to be killed, and fathers will give their own children to be killed. Children will fight against their own parents and have them put to death. 22All people will hate you because you follow me, but those people who keep their faith until the end will be saved. 23When you are treated badly in one city, run to another city. I tell you the truth, you will not finish going through all the cities of Israel before the Son of Man comes.

"THOSE WHO TRY TO HOLD ON TO THEIR LIVES WILL GIVE UP TRUE LIFE."

24"A student is not better than his teacher, and a servant is not better than his master. 25A student should be satisfied to become like his teacher; a servant should be satisfied to become like his master. If the head of the family is called Beelzebul, then the other members of the family will be called worse names!

FEAR GOD, NOT PEOPLE

26"So don't be afraid of those people, because everything that is hidden will be shown. Everything that is secret will be made known. 27I tell you these things in the dark, but I want you to tell them in the light. What you hear whispered in your ear you should shout from the housetops. 28Don't be afraid of people, who can kill the body but cannot kill the soul. The only one you should fear is the one who can destroy the soul and the body in hell. 29Two sparrows cost only a penny, but not even one of them can die without your Father's knowing it. 30God even knows how many hairs are on your head. 31So don't be afraid. You are worth much more than many sparrows.

TELL PEOPLE ABOUT YOUR FAITH

32"All those who stand before others and say they believe in me, I will say before my Father in heaven that they belong to me. 33But all who stand before others and say they do not believe in me, I will say before my Father in heaven that they do not belong to me.

34"Don't think that I came to bring peace to the earth. I did not come to bring peace, but a sword. 35I have come so that

'a son will be against his father,
a daughter will be against her mother,
a daughter-in-law will be against her
mother-in-law.
36 A person's enemies will be members
of his own family.' *Micah 7:6*

37"Those who love their father or mother more than they love me are not worthy to be my followers. Those who love their son or daughter more than they love me are not worthy to be my followers. 38Whoever is not willing to carry the cross and follow me is not worthy of me. 39Those who try to hold on to their lives will give up true life. Those who give up their lives for me will hold on to true life. 40Whoever accepts you also accepts me, and whoever accepts me also accepts the One who sent me. 41Whoever meets a prophet and accepts him will receive the reward of a prophet. And whoever accepts a good person because that person is good will receive the reward of a good person. 42Those who give one of these little ones a cup of cold water because they are my followers will truly get their reward."

LEARN IT & LIVE IT

Matthew 5:42:
Learn It: We need to be generous.
Live It: When your sister asks to borrow your favorite shirt, let her.

Matthew 8:10:
Learn It: We are saved by faith.
Live It: Ask God to help you do something today that you believe is impossible without his help—make it really hard!

Matthew 9:37:
Learn It: We need more people sharing the good news of God!
Live It: Tell one friend or acquaintance about Christ today—someone who doesn't know him.

CHECK IT OUT

WORLD VISION INTERNATIONAL

World Vision International is a Christian relief and development organization working for the well being of all people, especially children. Through emergency relief, education, health care, economic development and promotion of justice, World Vision helps communities help themselves.

Established in 1950 to care for orphans in Asia, World Vision has grown to embrace the larger issues of community development and advocacy for the poor in its mission to help children and their families build sustainable futures. Working on six continents, World Vision is one of the largest Christian relief and development organizations in the world.

The heart of World Vision's work is in helping communities build stronger and healthier relationships. The absence of such relationships impoverishes communities. World Vision focuses on children because they are the best indicator of a community's social health. When children are fed, sheltered, schooled, protected, valued, and loved, a community thrives.

*Get involved by visiting **www.worldvision.org**.*

JESUS AND JOHN THE BAPTIST

11 After Jesus finished telling these
things to his twelve followers, he left
there and went to the towns in Galilee to teach
and preach.
2John the Baptist was in prison, but he heard
about what Christ was doing. So John sent
some of his followers to Jesus. 3They asked
him, "Are you the One who is to come, or
should we wait for someone else?"
4Jesus answered them, "Go tell John what
you hear and see: 5The blind can see, the crippled can walk, and people with skin diseases
are healed. The deaf can hear, the dead are
raised to life, and the Good News is preached to
the poor. 6Those who do not stumble in their
faith because of me are blessed."
7As John's followers were leaving, Jesus
began talking to the people about John. Jesus
said, "What did you go out into the desert to
see? A reed[n] blown by the wind? 8What did you
go out to see? A man dressed in fine clothes?
No, those who wear fine clothes live in kings'
palaces. 9So why did you go out? To see a
prophet? Yes, and I tell you, John is more than
a prophet. 10This was written about him:

'I will send my messenger ahead of you,
who will prepare the way for you.'

Malachi 3:1

11I tell you the truth, John the Baptist is greater

notes

11:7 reed It means that John was not ordinary or weak like grass blown by the wind.

than any other person ever born, but even the least important person in the kingdom of heaven is greater than John. 12Since the time John the Baptist came until now, the kingdom of heaven has been going forward in strength, and people have been trying to take it by force. 13All the prophets and the law of Moses told about what would happen until the time John came. 14And if you will believe what they said, you will believe that John is Elijah, whom they said would come. 15You people who can hear me, listen!

16"What can I say about the people of this time? What are they like? They are like children sitting in the marketplace, who call out to each other,

17'We played music for you, but you
did not dance;
we sang a sad song, but you
did not cry.'

18John came and did not eat or drink like other people. So people say, 'He has a demon.' 19The Son of Man came, eating and drinking, and people say, 'Look at him! He eats too much and drinks too much wine, and he is a friend of tax collectors and sinners.' But wisdom is proved to be right by what it does."

JESUS WARNS UNBELIEVERS

20Then Jesus criticized the cities where he did most of his miracles, because the people did not change their lives and stop sinning. 21He said, "How terrible for you, Korazin! How terrible for you, Bethsaida! If the same miracles I did in you had happened in Tyre and Sidon,[n] those people would have changed their lives a long time ago. They would have worn rough cloth and put ashes on themselves to show they had changed. 22But I tell you, on the Judgment Day it will be better for Tyre and Sidon than for you. 23And you, Capernaum,[n] will you be lifted up to heaven? No, you will be thrown down to the depths. If the miracles I did in you had happened in Sodom,[n] its people would have stopped sinning, and it would still be a city today. 24But I tell you, on the Judgment Day it will be better for Sodom than for you."

JESUS OFFERS REST TO PEOPLE

25At that time Jesus said, "I praise you, Father, Lord of heaven and earth, because you have hidden these things from the people who are wise and smart. But you have shown them to those who are like little children. 26Yes, Father, this is what you really wanted.

27"My Father has given me all things. No one knows the Son, except the Father. And no one knows the Father, except the Son and those whom the Son chooses to tell.

28"Come to me, all of you who are tired and have heavy loads, and I will give you rest. 29Accept my teachings and learn from me, because I am gentle and humble in spirit, and you will find rest for your lives. 30The teaching that I ask you to accept is easy; the load I give you to carry is light."

JESUS IS LORD OF THE SABBATH

12 At that time Jesus was walking through some fields of grain on a Sabbath day. His followers were hungry, so they began to pick the grain and eat it. 2When the Pharisees saw this, they said to Jesus, "Look! Your followers are doing what is unlawful to do on the Sabbath day."

3Jesus answered, "Have you not read what David did when he and the people with him were hungry? 4He went into God's house, and he and those with him ate the holy bread, which was lawful only for priests to eat. 5And have you not read in the law of Moses that on every Sabbath day the priests in the Temple break this law about the Sabbath day? But the priests are not wrong for doing that. 6I tell you that there is something here that is greater than the Temple. 7The Scripture says, 'I want kindness more than I want animal sacrifices.'[n] You don't really know what those words mean. If you understood them, you would not judge those who have done nothing wrong.

8"So the Son of Man is Lord of the Sabbath day."

JESUS HEALS A MAN'S HAND

9Jesus left there and went into their synagogue, 10where there was a man with a crippled hand. They were looking for a reason to accuse Jesus, so they asked him, "Is it right to heal on the Sabbath day?"[n]

11Jesus answered, "If any of you has a sheep, and it falls into a ditch on the Sabbath day, you will help it out of the ditch. 12Surely a human being is more important than a sheep. So it is lawful to do good things on the Sabbath day."

13Then Jesus said to the man with the crippled hand, "Hold out your hand." The man held out his hand, and it became well again, like the other hand. 14But the Pharisees left and made plans to kill Jesus.

JESUS IS GOD'S CHOSEN SERVANT

15Jesus knew what the Pharisees were doing, so he left that place. Many people followed him, and he healed all who were sick. 16But Jesus warned the people not to tell who he was. 17He did these things to bring about what Isaiah the prophet had said:

18"Here is my servant whom I have chosen.
I love him, and I am pleased with him.
I will put my Spirit upon him,

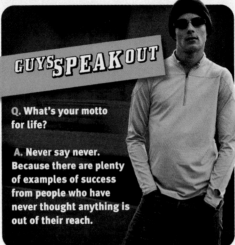

GUYS SPEAK OUT

Q. What's your motto for life?

A. Never say never. Because there are plenty of examples of success from people who have never thought anything is out of their reach.

notes

11:21 Tyre and Sidon Towns where wicked people lived. **11:21, 23 Korazin . . . Bethsaida . . . Capernaum** Towns by Lake Galilee where Jesus preached to the people. **11:23 Sodom** A city that God destroyed because the people were so evil. **12:7 'I . . . sacrifices.'** Quotation from Hosea 6:6. **12:10 "Is it right . . . day?"** It was against Jewish Law to work on the Sabbath day.

and he will tell of my justice to all
people.
19 He will not argue or cry out;
no one will hear his voice in the streets.
20 He will not break a crushed blade of grass
or put out even a weak flame
until he makes justice win the victory.
21 In him will the non-Jewish people
find hope." *Isaiah 42:1-4*

JESUS' POWER IS FROM GOD

22 Then some people brought to Jesus a man who was blind and could not talk, because he had a demon. Jesus healed the man so that he could talk and see. 23 All the people were amazed and said, "Perhaps this man is the Son of David!"

24 When the Pharisees heard this, they said, "Jesus uses the power of Beelzebul, the ruler of demons, to force demons out of people."

25 Jesus knew what the Pharisees were think-

against God. But whoever speaks against the Holy Spirit will not be forgiven. 32 Anyone who speaks against the Son of Man can be forgiven, but anyone who speaks against the Holy Spirit will not be forgiven, now or in the future.

PEOPLE KNOW YOU BY YOUR WORDS

33 "If you want good fruit, you must make the tree good. If your tree is not good, it will have bad fruit. A tree is known by the kind of fruit it produces. 34 You snakes! You are evil people, so how can you say anything good? The mouth speaks the things that are in the heart. 35 Good people have good things in their hearts, and so they say good things. But evil people have evil in their hearts, so they say evil things. 36 And I tell you that on the Judgment Day people will be responsible for every careless thing they have said. 37 The words you have said will be used to judge you. Some of your words will

DIDYA KNOW  **IN A TYPICAL WEEK, 32% OF YOUNG ADULTS READ THE BIBLE.**

ing, so he said to them, "Every kingdom that is divided against itself will be destroyed. And any city or family that is divided against itself will not continue. 26 And if Satan forces out himself, then Satan is divided against himself, and his kingdom will not continue. 27 You say that I use the power of Beelzebul to force out demons. If that is true, then what power do your people use to force out demons? So they will be your judges. 28 But if I use the power of God's Spirit to force out demons, then the kingdom of God has come to you.

29 "If anyone wants to enter a strong person's house and steal his things, he must first tie up the strong person. Then he can steal the things from the house.

30 "Whoever is not with me is against me. Whoever does not work with me is working against me. 31 So I tell you, people can be forgiven for every sin and everything they say

prove you right, but some of your words will prove you guilty."

THE PEOPLE ASK FOR A MIRACLE

38 Then some of the Pharisees and teachers

"WHOEVER DOES NOT WORK WITH ME IS WORKING AGAINST ME."

of the law answered Jesus, saying, "Teacher, we want to see you work a miracle as a sign."

39 Jesus answered, "Evil and sinful people are the ones who want to see a miracle for a sign. But no sign will be given to them, except the sign of the prophet Jonah. 40 Jonah was in the stomach of the big fish for three days and three nights. In the same way, the Son of Man will be in the grave three days and three nights. 41 On the Judgment Day the people from

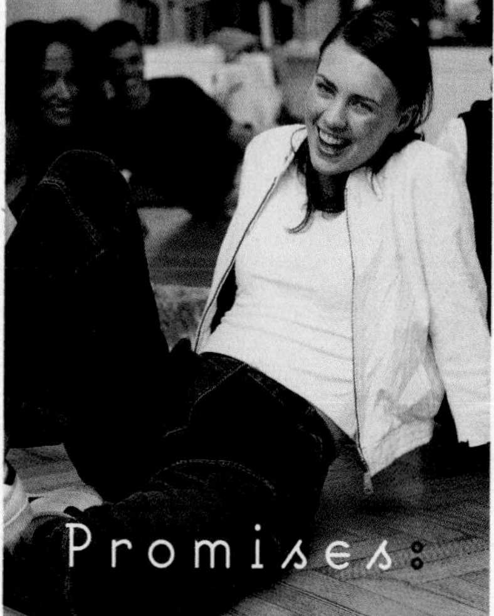

Matthew 10:20

Have you ever been in a situation where you just didn't know what to say? Maybe you were "smack-dab" in the middle of witnessing to someone, and suddenly you didn't know what to do? This has happened to everybody. In this verse, Jesus was telling his followers that he was sending them out to be witnesses, and he assured them they should not be worried about what to say or how to say it. Why? Because the Holy Spirit was going to give them the words to say.

One of the cool parts of being a Christian is that you don't have to live on your own. Jesus is right there with you. He's never going to leave you or stand you up. He's always ready to speak to you and through you. So the next time you're sharing Jesus with a friend, or someone at school is drilling you about Christianity, remember *he* is the One who speaks. The Holy Spirit will give you the words to say. Just calm down, and let him do it. He always will, because his Word never fails!

"THE HOLY SPIRIT WAS GOING TO GIVE THEM THE WORDS TO SAY."

Matthew 11:28

Have you ever been hiking in the mountains with a huge backpack strapped to your back all day long? What's the first thing you did when you finally reached your destination—the top? You unstrapped that pack, stretched out on the ground, and rested, right? Oh, what a feeling! At that very moment, there was nothing better than removing that weight, lying down, and resting.

A lot of people carry around heavy backpacks every day of their lives. Now they don't carry a literal pack, but a backpack of sin, a suitcase full of guilt, or a huge load of worry. Jesus wants to give us rest. He wants to help us. It's not worth carrying around a bunch of heavy junk when all we have to do is come to Jesus and let him take the weight off our shoulders. He paid the price to carry it so we don't have to!

When he says that he will give you rest, he means it. If you can learn to rest in Jesus as a teenager, you'll be a step ahead of a lot of adults. The key is to really learn what Jesus has done for you—what burdens he bears for you—and then to let him have them. When you do what you're supposed to do and let him do what he's supposed to do, then you can rest in him.

"LEARN WHAT JESUS HAS DONE FOR YOU."

Nineveh[n] will stand up with you people who
live now, and they will show that you are
guilty. When Jonah preached to them, they
were sorry and changed their lives. And I tell
you that someone greater than Jonah is here.
42On the Judgment Day, the Queen of the
South[n] will stand up with you people who live
today. She will show that you are guilty,
because she came from far away to listen to
Solomon's wise teaching. And I tell you that
someone greater than Solomon is here.

PEOPLE TODAY ARE FULL OF EVIL

43"When an evil spirit comes out of a person, it travels through dry places, looking for
a place to rest, but it doesn't find it. 44So the
spirit says, 'I will go back to the house I left.'
When the spirit comes back, it finds the house
still empty, swept clean, and made neat.
45Then the evil spirit goes out and
brings seven other spirits even
more evil than it is, and they
go in and live there. So the
person has even more trouble than before. It is the
same way with the evil people who
live today."

Isaiah 54:10

"The mountains may disappear, and the hills may come to an end, but my love will never disappear; my promise of peace will not come to an end," says the LORD who shows mercy to you.

JESUS' TRUE FAMILY

46While Jesus was talking to the people, his
mother and brothers stood outside, trying to
find a way to talk to him. 47Someone told
Jesus, "Your mother and brothers are standing
outside, and they want to talk to you."

48He answered, "Who is my mother? Who
are my brothers?" 49Then he pointed to his
followers and said, "Here are my mother and
my brothers. 50My true brother and sister and
mother are those who do what my Father in
heaven wants."

A STORY ABOUT PLANTING SEED

13 That same day Jesus went out of the
house and sat by the lake. 2Large
crowds gathered around him, so he got into a
boat and sat down, while the people stood on
the shore. 3Then Jesus used stories to teach
them many things. He said: "A farmer went out
to plant his seed. 4While he was planting, some
seed fell by the road, and the birds came and ate
it all up. 5Some seed fell on rocky ground,
where there wasn't much dirt. That seed grew
very fast, because the ground was not deep.
6But when the sun rose, the plants dried up,
because they did not have deep roots. 7Some
other seed fell among thorny weeds, which
grew and choked the good plants. 8Some other
seed fell on good ground where it grew and produced a crop. Some plants made a hundred
times more, some made sixty times more, and
some made thirty times more. 9You people
who can hear me, listen."

WHY JESUS USED STORIES TO TEACH

10The followers came to Jesus and asked,
"Why do you use stories to teach the people?"
11Jesus answered, "You have
been chosen to know the
secrets about the kingdom of
heaven, but others cannot
know these secrets.
12Those who have
understanding will be given more,
and they will have all they need. But
those who do not have understanding, even
what they have will be taken away from them.
13This is why I use stories to teach the people:
They see, but they don't really see. They hear,
but they don't really hear or understand. 14So
they show that the things Isaiah said about
them are true:

'You will listen and listen, but you will not
understand.
You will look and look, but you will not
learn.
15For the minds of these people have become
stubborn.
They do not hear with their ears,
and they have closed their eyes.
Otherwise they might really understand
what they see with their eyes
and hear with their ears.

notes

12:41 Nineveh The city where Jonah preached to warn the people. Read Jonah 3. **12:42 Queen of the South** The Queen of Sheba. She traveled a thousand miles to learn God's wisdom from Solomon. Read 1 Kings 10:1–13.

They might really understand in their minds
and come back to me and be healed.'

Isaiah 6:9-10

16But you are blessed, because you see with your eyes and hear with your ears. 17I tell you the truth, many prophets and good people wanted to see the things that you now see, but they did not see them. And they wanted to hear the things that you now hear, but they did not hear them.

JESUS EXPLAINS THE SEED STORY

18"So listen to the meaning of that story about the farmer. 19What is the seed that fell by the road? That seed is like the person who hears the message about the kingdom but does not understand it. The Evil One comes and takes away what was planted in that person's heart. 20And what is the seed that fell on rocky ground? That seed is like the person who hears the teaching and quickly accepts it with joy. 21But he does not let the teaching go deep into his life, so he keeps it only a short time. When trouble or persecution comes because of the teaching he accepted, he quickly gives up. 22And what is the seed that fell among the thorny weeds? That seed is like the person who hears the teaching but lets worries about this life and the temptation of wealth stop that teaching from growing. So the teaching does not produce fruit[n] in that person's life. 23But what is the seed that fell on the good ground? That seed is like the person who hears the teaching and understands it. That person grows and produces fruit, sometimes a hundred times more, sometimes sixty times more, and sometimes thirty times more."

"THAT PERSON GROWS AND PRODUCES FRUIT, SOMETIMES A HUNDRED TIMES MORE."

A STORY ABOUT WHEAT AND WEEDS

24Then Jesus told them another story: "The kingdom of heaven is like a man who planted good seed in his field. 25That night, when everyone was asleep, his enemy came and planted weeds among the wheat and then left. 26Later, the wheat sprouted and the heads of

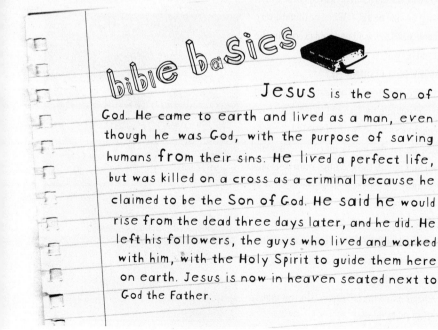

Jesus is the Son of God. He came to earth and lived as a man, even though he was God, with the purpose of saving humans from their sins. He lived a perfect life, but was killed on a cross as a criminal because he claimed to be the Son of God. He said he would rise from the dead three days later, and he did. He left his followers, the guys who lived and worked with him, with the Holy Spirit to guide them here on earth. Jesus is now in heaven seated next to God the Father.

Blab

Q. My pastor tells me that he senses a strong evangelistic spirit within me. What exactly does this mean?

A. The gift of evangelism is that of sharing the truth of God with other people. It means that you are meant to spread the word about him!

Q. Am I a bad person? I have been going out with this one guy for a while, but he is not a Christian.

A. Dating a nonbeliever is like playing with fire. God wants Christians to marry other Christians, and since dating often leads to marriage, it's best not to get involved in a love relationship with someone who doesn't care about God. It's time for you to make a choice between God and this guy.

Q. Is fantasizing wrong? I sometimes imagine things about guys, not nasty things, but just wishing things would happen. Is that wrong?

A. It is no less a sin to think or fantasize about it than it is to actually do it. As soon as a bad thought comes into your mind you have to stop it. Temptation is not a sin, but yielding to that temptation—turning it into a fantasy that you think about over and over—is a sin.

notes

13:22 produce fruit To produce fruit means to have in your life the good things God wants.

grain grew, but the weeds also grew. 27Then the man's servants came to him and said, 'You planted good seed in your field. Where did the weeds come from?' 28The man answered, 'An enemy planted weeds.' The servants asked, 'Do you want us to pull up the weeds?' 29The man answered, 'No, because when you pull up the weeds, you might also pull up the wheat. 30Let the weeds and the wheat grow together until the harvest time. At harvest time I will tell the workers, "First gather the weeds and tie them together to be burned. Then gather the wheat and bring it to my barn." ' "

IN A GIVEN WEEK, 75% OF YOUNG ADULTS REPORT PRAYING.

STORIES OF MUSTARD SEED AND YEAST

31Then Jesus told another story: "The kingdom of heaven is like a mustard seed that a man planted in his field. 32That seed is the smallest of all seeds, but when it grows, it is one of the largest garden plants. It becomes big enough for the wild birds to come and build nests in its branches."

33Then Jesus told another story: "The kingdom of heaven is like yeast that a woman took and hid in a large tub of flour until it made all the dough rise."

34Jesus used stories to tell all these things to the people; he always used stories to teach them. 35This is as the prophet said:

"I will speak using stories;
I will tell things that have been secret
since the world was made." *Psalm 78:2*

JESUS EXPLAINS ABOUT THE WEEDS

36Then Jesus left the crowd and went into the house. His followers came to him and said, "Explain to us the meaning of the story about the weeds in the field."

37Jesus answered, "The man who planted the good seed in the field is the Son of Man. 38The field is the world, and the good seed are all of God's children who belong to the kingdom. The weeds are those people who belong to the Evil One. 39And the enemy who planted the bad seed is the devil. The harvest time is the end of the world, and the workers who gather are God's angels.

40"Just as the weeds are pulled up and burned in the fire, so it will be at the end of the world. 41The Son of Man will send out his angels, and they will gather out of his kingdom all who cause sin and all who do evil. 42The angels will throw them into the blazing furnace, where the people will cry and grind their teeth with pain. 43Then the good people will shine like the sun in the kingdom of their Father. You people who can hear me, listen.

STORIES OF A TREASURE AND A PEARL

44"The kingdom of heaven is like a treasure hidden in a field. One day a man found the treasure, and then he hid it in the field again. He was so happy that he went and sold everything he owned to buy that field.

45"Also, the kingdom of heaven is like a man looking for fine pearls. 46When he found a very valuable pearl, he went and sold everything he had and bought it.

A STORY OF A FISHING NET

47"Also, the kingdom of heaven is like a net that was put into the lake and caught many different kinds of fish. 48When it was full, the fishermen pulled the net to the shore. They sat down and put all the good fish in baskets and threw away the bad fish. 49It will be this way at the end of the world. The angels will come and separate the evil people from the good people. 50The angels will throw the evil people into the blazing furnace, where people will cry and grind their teeth with pain."

51Jesus asked his followers, "Do you understand all these things?"

They answered, "Yes, we understand."

52Then Jesus said to them, "So every teacher of the law who has been taught about the kingdom of heaven is like the owner of a house. He brings out both new things and old things he has saved."

JESUS GOES TO HIS HOMETOWN

53When Jesus finished teaching with these stories, he left there. 54He went to his hometown and taught the people in the synagogue, and they were amazed. They said, "Where did this man get this wisdom and this power to do miracles? 55He is just the son of a carpenter. His mother is Mary, and his brothers are James, Joseph, Simon, and Judas. 56And all his sisters are here with us. Where then does this man get all these things?" 57So the people were upset with Jesus.

But Jesus said to them, "A prophet is honored everywhere except in his hometown and in his own home."

58So he did not do many miracles there because they had no faith.

HOW JOHN THE BAPTIST WAS KILLED

14 At that time Herod, the ruler of Galilee, heard the reports about Jesus. 2So he said to his servants, "Jesus is John

notes

Anna, who was a prophetess, had awaited the day of the Lord's birth her whole life, and it finally came. By the time Jesus was born, she was old and widowed. She practically lived at the Temple, spending time praying and fasting there. When she finally laid her eyes upon the baby Jesus, she began praising God and proclaiming the redemption of Jerusalem. Wait upon the Lord, and trust that he will come.

[LUKE 2]

the Baptist, who has risen from the dead. That
is why he can work these miracles."
[3]Sometime before this, Herod had arrested
John, tied him up, and put him into prison.
Herod did this because of Herodias, who had
been the wife of Philip, Herod's brother. [4]John
had been telling Herod, "It is not lawful for you
to be married to Herodias." [5]Herod wanted to
kill John, but he was afraid of the people,
because they believed John was a prophet.
[6]On Herod's birthday, the daughter of Herodias danced for Herod and his
guests, and she pleased him.
[7]So he promised with an oath
to give her anything she
wanted. [8]Herodias told her
daughter what to ask for, so
she said to Herod, "Give me the head
of John the Baptist here on a platter."
[9]Although King Herod was very sad, he had
made a promise, and his dinner guests had
heard him. So Herod ordered that what she
asked for be done. [10]He sent soldiers to the
prison to cut off John's head. [11]And they
brought it on a platter and gave it to the girl,
and she took it to her mother. [12]John's followers came and got his body and buried it. Then
they went and told Jesus.

MORE THAN FIVE THOUSAND FED

[13]When Jesus heard what had happened to
John, he left in a boat and went to a lonely
place by himself. But the crowds heard about it
and followed him on foot from the towns.
[14]When he arrived, he saw a great crowd waiting. He felt sorry for them and healed those
who were sick.
[15]When it was evening, his followers came to him and said,
"No one lives in this place,
and it is already late. Send
the people away so they
can go to the towns and
buy food for themselves."
[16]But Jesus answered, "They don't
need to go away. You give them something to
eat."
[17]They said to him, "But we have only five
loaves of bread and two fish."
[18]Jesus said, "Bring the bread and the fish to
me." [19]Then he told the people to sit down on
the grass. He took the five loaves and the two
fish and, looking to heaven, he thanked God for
the food. Jesus divided the bread and gave it to
his followers, who gave it to the people. [20]All
the people ate and were satisfied. Then the followers filled twelve baskets with the leftover pieces of food. [21]There were about five
thousand men there who ate, not counting
women and children.

JESUS WALKS ON THE WATER

[22]Immediately Jesus told his followers to get
into the boat and go ahead of him across the
lake. He stayed there to send the people home.
[23]After he had sent them away, he went by himself up into the hills to pray. It was late, and
Jesus was there alone. [24]By this time, the boat
was already far away from land. It was being hit
by waves, because the wind was blowing
against it.
[25]Between three and six o'clock in the morning, Jesus came to them, walking on the water.
[26]When his followers saw him walking on the
water, they were afraid. They said, "It's a
ghost!" and cried out in fear.
[27]But Jesus quickly spoke to them, "Have
courage! It is I. Do not be afraid."
[28]Peter said, "Lord, if it is really you, then
command me to come to you on the water."
[29]Jesus said, "Come."
And Peter left the boat and walked on the
water to Jesus. [30]But when Peter saw the wind
and the waves, he became afraid and began to
sink. He shouted, "Lord, save me!"
[31]Immediately Jesus reached out his hand
and caught Peter. Jesus said, "Your faith is
small. Why did you doubt?"
[32]After they got into the boat, the wind
became calm. [33]Then those who were in the
boat worshiped Jesus and said, "Truly you are
the Son of God!"
[34]When they had crossed the lake, they
came to shore at Gennesaret. [35]When the people there recognized Jesus, they told people all
around there that Jesus had come, and they

Ezekiel 16:8
Later when I passed by you and looked at you, I saw that you were old enough for love. So I spread my robe over you and covered your nakedness. I also made a promise to you and entered into an agreement with you so that you became mine, says the Lord God.

LEARN IT & LIVE IT

Matthew 10:16:
Learn It: We need wisdom.
Live It: Be very careful in all your decisions today, but don't offend—be very gracious to your friends.

Matthew 10:42:
Learn It: We will be rewarded for helping others.
Live It: Buy someone a Coke today—and tell them that you're doing it in the name of Christ.

Matthew 12:34:
Learn It: You talk about what's important to you.
Live It: Be courageous enough to ask a friend to tell you what you obsess over when you talk. It might be very revealing.

brought all their sick to him. 36They begged
Jesus to let them touch just the edge of his coat,
and all who touched it were healed.

OBEY GOD'S LAW

15 Then some Pharisees and teachers
of the law came to Jesus from
Jerusalem. They asked him, 2"Why don't your
followers obey the unwritten laws which have
been handed down to us? They don't wash
their hands before they eat."

3Jesus answered, "And why do you refuse to
obey God's command so that you can follow
your own teachings? 4God said, 'Honor your
father and your mother,'[n] and 'Anyone who
says cruel things to his father or mother must
be put to death.'[n] 5But you say a person can tell
his father or mother, 'I have something I could
use to help you, but I have given it to God
already.' 6You teach that person not to honor
his father or his mother. You rejected what God
said for the sake of your own rules. 7You are
hypocrites! Isaiah was right when he said
about you:

8'These people show honor to me with
words,
but their hearts are far from me.
9Their worship of me is worthless.
The things they teach are nothing but
human rules.' " *Isaiah 29:13*

10After Jesus called the crowd to him, he
said, "Listen and understand what I am saying.
11It is not what people put into their mouths
that makes them unclean. It is what comes out
of their mouths that makes them unclean."

12Then his followers came to him and
asked, "Do you know that the Pharisees are
angry because of what you said?"

> **"BUT WHAT PEOPLE SAY WITH THEIR MOUTHS COMES FROM THE WAY THEY THINK."**

13Jesus answered, "Every plant that my
Father in heaven has not planted himself will
be pulled up by the roots. 14Stay away from
the Pharisees; they are blind leaders. And if a
blind person leads a blind person, both will fall
into a ditch."

15Peter said, "Explain the example to us."

16Jesus said, "Do you still not understand?
17Surely you know that all the food that enters
the mouth goes into the stomach and then goes
out of the body. 18But what people say with
their mouths comes from the way they think;
these are the things that make people unclean.
19Out of the mind come evil thoughts, murder,
adultery, sexual sins, stealing, lying, and
speaking evil of others. 20These things make
people unclean; eating with unwashed hands
does not make them unclean."

JESUS HELPS A NON-JEWISH WOMAN

21Jesus left that place and went to the area of
Tyre and Sidon. 22A Canaanite woman from
that area came to Jesus and cried out, "Lord,
Son of David, have mercy on me! My daughter
has a demon, and she is suffering very much."

23But Jesus did not answer the woman. So
his followers came to Jesus and begged him,

RELATIONSHIPS

"Christ loved the church and gave himself for it" (Ephesians 5:25). How is your guy in this department? Does he do things for you just so he can have you around and get stuff from you? If so, he is using you. Don't become some guy's play toy. Make sure that he is treating you the way Christ treated the church. With respect. With dignity. Selflessly. For their own good, not his own.

15:4 'Honor . . . mother.' Quotation from Exodus 20:12; Deuteronomy 5:16. **15:4 'Anyone . . . death.'** Quotation from Exodus 21:17.

Notes

"Tell the woman to go away. She is following us
and shouting."
24 Jesus answered, "God sent me only to the
lost sheep, the people of Israel."
25 Then the woman came to Jesus again and
bowed before him and said, "Lord, help me!"
26 Jesus answered, "It is not right to take the
children's bread and give it to the dogs."
27 The woman said, "Yes, Lord, but even the
dogs eat the crumbs that fall from their masters' table."
28 Then Jesus answered, "Woman, you have
great faith! I will do what you asked." And
at that moment the woman's daughter was
healed.

JESUS HEALS MANY PEOPLE

29 After leaving there, Jesus went along
the shore of Lake Galilee. He went up on a
hill and sat there.
30 Great crowds came to Jesus, bringing
with them the lame, the blind, the crippled,
those who could not speak, and many others. They put them at Jesus' feet, and he
healed them. 31 The crowd was amazed
when they saw that people who could not
speak before were now able to speak. The
crippled were made strong. The lame could
walk, and the blind could see. And they praised
the God of Israel for this.

MORE THAN FOUR THOUSAND FED

32 Jesus called his followers to him and said,
"I feel sorry for these people, because they have
already been with me three days, and they have
nothing to eat. I don't want to send them away
hungry. They might faint while going home."
33 His followers asked him, "How can we get
enough bread to feed all these people? We are
far away from any town."
34 Jesus asked, "How many loaves of bread do
you have?"
They answered, "Seven, and a few small fish."
35 Jesus told the people to sit on the ground.
36 He took the seven loaves of bread and the fish
and gave thanks to God. Then he divided the
food and gave it to his followers, and they gave
it to the people. 37 All the people ate and were
satisfied. Then his followers filled seven baskets
with the leftover pieces of food. 38 There were
about four thousand men there who ate,
besides women and children. 39 After sending
the people home, Jesus got into the boat and
went to the area of Magadan.

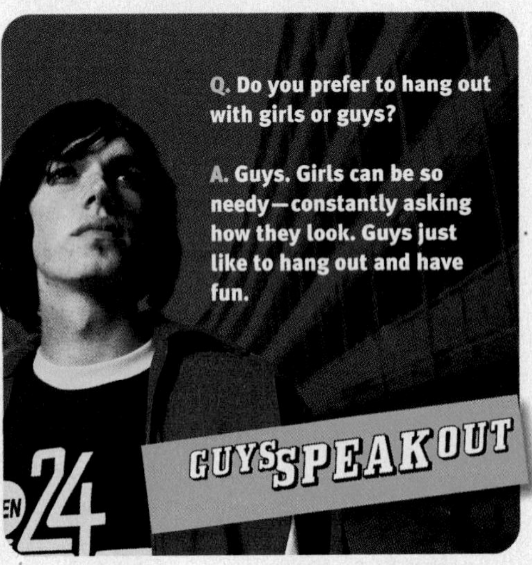

Q. Do you prefer to hang out with girls or guys?
A. Guys. Girls can be so needy—constantly asking how they look. Guys just like to hang out and have fun.
GUYS SPEAK OUT
24

56% OF YOUNG ADULTS SAY THEIR FAITH IS VERY IMPORTANT IN THEIR LIFE.

THE LEADERS ASK FOR A MIRACLE

16 The Pharisees and Sadducees came
to Jesus, wanting to trick him. So
they asked him to show them a miracle
from God.
2 Jesus answered, "At sunset you say we will
have good weather, because the sky is red. 3 And
in the morning you say that it will be a rainy
day, because the sky is dark and red. You see
these signs in the sky and know what they
mean. In the same way, you see the things that
I am doing now, but you don't know their
meaning. 4 Evil and sinful people ask for a miracle as a sign, but they will not be given any
sign, except the sign of Jonah."[n] Then Jesus left
them and went away.

GUARD AGAINST WRONG TEACHINGS

5 Jesus' followers went across the lake, but
they had forgotten to bring bread. 6 Jesus said
to them, "Be careful! Beware of the yeast of
the Pharisees and the Sadducees."
7 His followers discussed the meaning of
this, saying, "He said this because we forgot to
bring bread."
8 Knowing what they were talking about,
Jesus asked them, "Why are you talking
about not having bread? Your faith is small.
9 Do you still not understand? Remember
the five loaves of bread that fed the five
thousand? And remember that you filled
many baskets with the leftovers? 10 Or the
seven loaves of bread that fed the four
thousand and the many baskets you filled
then also? 11 I was not talking to you about
bread. Why don't you understand that? I
am telling you to beware of the yeast of the
Pharisees and the Sadducees." 12 Then the
followers understood that Jesus was not
telling them to beware of the yeast used
in bread but to beware of the teaching of the
Pharisees and the Sadducees.

PETER SAYS JESUS IS THE CHRIST

13 When Jesus came to the area of Caesarea
Philippi, he asked his followers, "Who do people say the Son of Man is?"
14 They answered, "Some say you are John
the Baptist. Others say you are Elijah, and still
others say you are Jeremiah or one of the
prophets."
15 Then Jesus asked them, "And who do you
say I am?"
16 Simon Peter answered, "You are the
Christ, the Son of the living God."
17 Jesus answered, "You are blessed, Simon
son of Jonah, because no person taught you
that. My Father in heaven showed you who I
am. 18 So I tell you, you are Peter."[n] On this rock

notes

16:4 sign of Jonah Jonah's three days in the fish are like Jesus' three days in the tomb. The story about Jonah is in the Book of Jonah. **16:18 Peter** The Greek name "Peter," like the Aramaic name "Cephas," means "rock."

I will build my church, and the power of death
will not be able to defeat it. 19I will give you the
keys of the kingdom of heaven; the things you
don't allow on earth will be the things that God
does not allow, and the things you allow on
earth will be the things that God allows."
20Then Jesus warned his followers not to tell
anyone he was the Christ.

JESUS SAYS THAT HE MUST DIE

21From that time on Jesus began telling his
followers that he must go to Jerusalem, where
the older Jewish leaders, the leading priests,
and the teachers of the law would make him
suffer many things. He told them he must be
killed and then be raised from the dead on the
third day.

"HE TOOK THE SEVEN LOAVES OF BREAD AND THE FISH AND GAVE THANKS TO GOD."

22Peter took Jesus aside and told him not to
talk like that. He said, "God save you from
those things, Lord! Those things will never happen to you!"

23Then Jesus said to Peter, "Go away from
me, Satan![n] You are not helping me! You don't
care about the things of God, but only about
the things people think are important."

24Then Jesus said to his followers, "If people
want to follow me, they must give up the things
they want. They must be willing even to give
up their lives to follow me. 25Those who want
to save their lives will give up true life, and
those who give up their lives for me will have
true life. 26It is worth nothing for them to have
the whole world if they lose their souls. They
could never pay enough to buy back their
souls. 27The Son of Man will come again with
his Father's glory and with his angels. At that
time, he will reward them for what they have
done. 28I tell you the truth, some people standing here will see the Son of Man coming with
his kingdom before they die."

JESUS TALKS WITH MOSES AND ELIJAH

17 Six days later, Jesus took Peter,
James, and John, the brother of
James, up on a high mountain by themselves.
2While they watched, Jesus' appearance was
changed; his face became bright like the sun,
and his clothes became white as light. 3Then
Moses and Elijah[n] appeared to them, talking
with Jesus.

4Peter said to Jesus, "Lord, it is good that we
are here. If you want, I will put up three tents
here—one for you, one for Moses, and one for
Elijah."

5While Peter was talking, a bright cloud covered them. A voice came from the cloud and
said, "This is my Son, whom I love, and I am
very pleased with him. Listen to him!"

6When his followers heard the voice, they
were so frightened they fell to the ground. 7But
Jesus went to them and touched them and said,
"Stand up. Don't be afraid." 8When they looked
up, they saw Jesus was now alone.

9As they were coming down the mountain,
Jesus commanded them not to tell anyone
about what they had seen until the Son of Man
had risen from the dead.

10Then his followers asked him, "Why do
the teachers of the law say that Elijah must
come first?"

11Jesus answered, "They are right to say that
Elijah is coming and that he will make everything the way it should be. 12But I tell you that
Elijah has already come, and they did not recognize him. They did to him whatever they
wanted to do. It will be the same with the Son
of Man; those same people will make the Son of
Man suffer." 13Then the followers understood
that Jesus was talking about John the Baptist.

JESUS HEALS A SICK BOY

14When Jesus and his followers came back
to the crowd, a man came to Jesus and bowed

Q. I know you aren't supposed to have "it" before you're married, but is it okay to think about "it"? I talk about "it" with my friends; is that wrong?

A. Sex is a beautiful gift that God has given to married people. To wonder is okay, to learn about it from a purely educational standpoint is okay too. But to fantasize about it, to think about doing it with someone, is sinful.

Q. What does the Bible teach about women wearing pants and makeup and cutting their hair?

A. What you have to know about Scripture is that some passages are what we call "prescriptive" (they tell us what to do today) and some are "descriptive" (they talk about Bible times). Today it is generally not a scandal for women to wear pants, wear makeup, or cut their hair.

Q. There is a guy on my street and God wants me to witness to him. Every time I try to talk about God, I can't get it out. What should I do?

A. If God wants you to witness to this guy, ask how he wants you to do that. Is it by being his friend and telling him about your relationship with Christ? Or is it by giving him a book or some other method? Share from your heart and trust God to be the one to draw him to himself. God doesn't ask you to convert him, just to tell him.

notes

16:23 Satan Name for the devil, meaning "the enemy." Jesus means that Peter was talking like Satan. **17:3 Moses and Elijah** Two of the most important Jewish leaders in the past. God had given Moses the Law, and Elijah was an important prophet.

LEARN IT & LIVE IT

Matthew 13:44:
Learn It: God's kingdom is priceless.
Live It: Give away something you hold as valuable for the sake of the kingdom. Tell the person you give it to that you're doing it for Christ.

Matthew 17:20:
Learn It: Faith the size of a mustard seed can move mountains.
Live It: Set a super-high goal for yourself. Stretch yourself to reach that goal. Believe in yourself and in Christ's strength to attain it.

Matthew 18:20:
Learn It: Jesus is with you whenever two or three are gathered in his name.
Live It: Ask a few friends over for a time of prayer. Know that Jesus is with you.

before him. 15The man said, "Lord, have mercy on my son. He has epilepsy[n] and is suffering very much, because he often falls into the fire or into the water. 16I brought him to your followers, but they could not cure him."

17Jesus answered, "You people have no faith, and your lives are all wrong. How long must I put up with you? How long must I continue to be patient with you? Bring the boy here." 18Jesus commanded the demon inside the boy. Then the demon came out, and the boy was healed from that time on.

"YOU MUST CHANGE AND BECOME LIKE LITTLE CHILDREN. OTHERWISE, YOU WILL NEVER ENTER THE KINGDOM OF HEAVEN."

19The followers came to Jesus when he was alone and asked, "Why couldn't we force the demon out?"

20Jesus answered, "Because your faith is too small. I tell you the truth, if your faith is as big as a mustard seed, you can say to this mountain, 'Move from here to there,' and it will move. All things will be possible for you." 21[n]

JESUS TALKS ABOUT HIS DEATH

22While Jesus' followers were gathering in Galilee, he said to them, "The Son of Man will be handed over to people, 23and they will kill him. But on the third day he will be raised from the dead." And the followers were filled with sadness.

JESUS TALKS ABOUT PAYING TAXES

24When Jesus and his followers came to Capernaum, the men who collected the Temple tax came to Peter. They asked, "Does your teacher pay the Temple tax?"

25Peter answered, "Yes, Jesus pays the tax."

Peter went into the house, but before he could speak, Jesus said to him, "What do you think? The kings of the earth collect different kinds of taxes. But who pays the taxes—the king's children or others?"

26Peter answered, "Other people pay the taxes."

Jesus said to Peter, "Then the children of the king don't have to pay taxes. 27But we don't want to upset these tax collectors. So go to the lake and fish. After you catch the first fish, open its mouth and you will find a coin. Take that coin and give it to the tax collectors for you and me."

WHO IS THE GREATEST?

18 At that time the followers came to Jesus and asked, "Who is greatest in the kingdom of heaven?"

2Jesus called a little child to him and stood the child before his followers. 3Then he said, "I tell you the truth, you must change and become like little children. Otherwise, you will never enter the kingdom of heaven. 4The greatest person in the kingdom of heaven is the one who makes himself humble like this child.

5"Whoever accepts a child in my name accepts me. 6If one of these little children believes in me, and someone causes that child to sin, it would be better for that person to have a large stone tied around the neck and be drowned in the sea. 7How terrible for the people of the world because of the things that cause them to sin. Such things will happen, but how terrible for the one who causes them to happen! 8If your hand or your foot causes you to sin, cut it off and throw it away. It is better for you to lose part of your body and live forever than to have two hands and two feet and be thrown into the fire that burns forever. 9If your eye causes you to sin, take it out and throw it away. It is better for you to have only one eye and live forever

John 3:16
God loved the world so much that he gave his one and only Son so that whoever believes in him may not be lost, but have eternal life.

notes

17:15 epilepsy A disease that causes a person sometimes to lose control of his body and maybe faint, shake strongly, or not be able to move. **17:21 Verse 21** Some Greek copies add verse 21: "That kind of spirit comes out only if you use prayer and give up eating."

than to have two eyes and be thrown into the fire of hell.

A LOST SHEEP

[10]"Be careful. Don't think these little children are worth nothing. I tell you that they have angels in heaven who are always with my Father in heaven. [11][n]

[12]"If a man has a hundred sheep but one of the sheep gets lost, he will leave the other ninety-nine on the hill and go to look for the lost sheep. [13]I tell you the truth, he is happier about that one sheep than about the ninety-nine that were never lost. [14]In the same way, your Father in heaven does not want any of these little children to be lost.

WHEN A PERSON SINS AGAINST YOU

[15]"If your fellow believer sins against you, go and tell him in private what he did wrong. If he listens to you, you have helped that person to be your brother or sister again. [16]But if he refuses to listen, go to him again and take one or two other people with you. 'Every case may be proved by two or three witnesses.'[n] [17]If he refuses to listen to them, tell the church. If he refuses to listen to the church, then treat him like a person who does not believe in God or like a tax collector.

[18]"I tell you the truth, the things you don't allow on earth will be the things God does not allow. And the things you allow on earth will be the things that God allows.

[19]"Also, I tell you that if two of you on earth agree about something and pray for it, it will be done for you by my Father in heaven. [20]This is true because if two or three people come together in my name, I am there with them."

AN UNFORGIVING SERVANT

[21]Then Peter came to Jesus and asked, "Lord, when my fellow believer sins against me, how many times must I forgive him? Should I forgive him as many as seven times?"

[22]Jesus answered, "I tell you, you must forgive him more than seven times. You must forgive him even if he wrongs you seventy times seven.

[23]"The kingdom of heaven is like a king who decided to collect the money his servants owed him. [24]When the king began to collect his money, a servant who owed him several million dollars was brought to him. [25]But the servant did not have enough money to pay his master, the king. So the master ordered that everything the servant owned should be sold, even the servant's wife and children. Then the money would be used to pay the king what the servant owed.

"HOW MANY TIMES MUST I FORGIVE HIM? SHOULD I FORGIVE HIM AS MANY AS SEVEN TIMES?"

[26]"But the servant fell on his knees and begged, 'Be patient with me, and I will pay you everything I owe.' [27]The master felt sorry for his servant and told him he did not have to pay it back. Then he let the servant go free.

[28]"Later, that same servant found another servant who owed him a few dollars. The servant grabbed him around the neck and said, 'Pay me the money you owe me!'

[29]"The other servant fell on his knees and begged him, 'Be patient with me, and I will pay you everything I owe.'

[30]"But the first servant refused to be patient. He threw the other servant into prison until he could pay everything he owed. [31]When the other servants saw what had happened, they were very sorry. So they went and told their master all that had happened.

[32]"Then the master called his servant in and said, 'You evil servant! Because you begged me to forget what you owed, I told you that you did not have to pay anything. [33]You should have showed mercy to that other servant, just as I

TOPten

RANDOM WAYS TO SHOW YOUR MOM YOU LOVE HER

01	**Make her breakfast in bed.**
02	**Follow her advice.**
03	**Offer to baby-sit the sibs so your parents can go on a date.**
04	**Cook dinner one night a week.**
05	**Send her flowers at work or home.**
06	**Write her a letter or poem.**
07	**Take her out for dinner and a girl movie.**
08	**Tell her you pray for her.**
09	**Knit her a scarf.**
10	**Make her a scrapbook filled with fun memories!**

notes

18:11 Verse 11 Some Greek copies add verse 11: "The Son of Man came to save lost people." **18:16 'Every . . . witnesses.'** Quotation from Deuteronomy 19:15.

Matthew 22:36-37

Well, this is it. This is *the* most important commandment. If you've decided to get serious about God, then this commandment is the place to start. Every element of being Christlike is built on this principle. Learning to love the Lord with your heart, soul, and mind will be a continual process that lasts your whole life. But you've got to start.

So what does it look like to love the Lord with every part of you? It means that you begin to love the way God loves, think the way God thinks, act the way God acts, and hate the things God hates. If you have begun to get serious about God, don't hold back. His love for you has no limits or hesitations. You have absolutely nothing to lose and everything to gain by going for it.

Don't be disappointed if you're not an overnight sensation. Remember, this is a process—learning to spend time with him; giving and receiving grace; working on areas that don't look anything like God; forgiving and being forgiven; trusting; slowly, ever so wonderfully, looking more and more like the One you love. Imitation is the highest form of adoration. Be an imitator of God.

showed mercy to you.' 34The master was very angry and put the servant in prison to be punished until he could pay everything he owed.

35"This king did what my heavenly Father will do to you if you do not forgive your brother or sister from your heart."

JESUS TEACHES ABOUT DIVORCE

19 After Jesus said all these things, he left Galilee and went into the area of Judea on the other side of the Jordan River. 2Large crowds followed him, and he healed them there.

3Some Pharisees came to Jesus and tried to trick him. They asked, "Is it right for a man to divorce his wife for any reason he chooses?"

4Jesus answered, "Surely you have read in the Scriptures: When God made the world, 'he made them male and female.'[n] 5And God said, 'So a man will leave his father and mother and be united with his wife, and the two will become one body.'[n] 6So there are not two, but one. God has joined the two together, so no one should separate them."

7The Pharisees asked, "Why then did Moses give a command for a man to divorce his wife by giving her divorce papers?"

8Jesus answered, "Moses allowed you to divorce your wives because you refused to accept God's teaching, but divorce was not allowed in the beginning. 9I tell you that anyone who divorces his wife and marries another woman is guilty of adultery. The only reason for a man to divorce his wife is if his wife has sexual relations with another man."

John 13:1
Jesus knew that it was time for him to leave this world and go back to the Father. He had always loved those who were his own in the world, and he loved them all the way to the end.

10The followers said to him, "If that is the only reason a man can divorce his wife, it is better not to marry."

11Jesus answered, "Not everyone can accept this teaching, but God has made some able to accept it. 12There are different reasons why some men cannot marry. Some men were born without the ability to become fathers. Others were made that way later in life by other people. And some men have given up marriage because of the kingdom of heaven. But the person who can marry should accept this teaching about marriage."[n]

JESUS WELCOMES CHILDREN

13Then the people brought their little children to Jesus so he could put his hands on them[n] and pray for them. His followers told them to stop, 14but Jesus said, "Let the little children come to me. Don't stop them, because the kingdom of heaven belongs to people who are like these children." 15After Jesus put his hands on the children, he left there.

A RICH YOUNG MAN'S QUESTION

16A man came to Jesus and asked, "Teacher, what good thing must I do to have life forever?"

17Jesus answered, "Why do you ask me about what is good? Only God is good. But if you want to have life forever, obey the commands."

18The man asked, "Which commands?"

Jesus answered, " 'You must not murder anyone; you must not be guilty of adultery; you must not steal; you must not tell lies about your neighbor; 19honor your father and mother;[n] and love your neighbor as you love yourself.' "[n]

20The young man said, "I have obeyed all these things. What else do I need to do?"

21Jesus answered, "If you want to be perfect, then go and sell your possessions and give the money to the poor. If you do this, you will have treasure in heaven. Then come and follow me."

22But when the young man heard this, he left sorrowfully, because he was rich.

23Then Jesus said to his followers, "I tell you the truth, it will be hard for a rich person to enter the kingdom of heaven. 24Yes, I tell you that it is easier for a camel to go through the eye

19:4 'he made . . . female.' Quotation from Genesis 1:27 or 5:2. **19:5 'So . . . body.'** Quotation from Genesis 2:24. **19:12 But . . . marriage.** This may also mean, "The person who can accept this teaching about not marrying should accept it." **19:13 put his hands on them** Showing that Jesus gave special blessings to these children. **19:18-19 'You . . . mother.'** Quotation from Exodus 20:12-16; Deuteronomy 5:16-20. **19:19 'love . . . yourself.'** Quotation from Leviticus 19:18.

of a needle than for a rich person to enter the kingdom of God."

25When Jesus' followers heard this, they were very surprised and asked, "Then who can be saved?"

26Jesus looked at them and said, "This is something people cannot do, but God can do all things."

27Peter said to Jesus, "Look, we have left everything and followed you. So what will we have?"

28Jesus said to them, "I tell you the truth, when the age to come has arrived, the Son of Man will sit on his great throne. All of you who followed me will also sit on twelve thrones, judging the twelve tribes of Israel. 29And all those who have left houses, brothers, sisters, father, mother, children, or farms to follow me will get much more than they left, and they will have life forever. 30Many who have the highest place now will have the lowest place in the future. And many who have the lowest place now will have the highest place in the future.

A STORY ABOUT WORKERS

20 "The kingdom of heaven is like a person who owned some land. One morning, he went out very early to hire some people to work in his vineyard. 2The man agreed to pay the workers one coin[n] for working that day. Then he sent them into the vineyard to work. 3About nine o'clock the man went to the marketplace and saw some other people standing there, doing nothing. 4So he said to them, 'If you go and work in my vineyard, I will pay you what your work is worth.' 5So they went to work in the vineyard. The man went out again about twelve o'clock and three o'clock and did the same thing. 6About five o'clock the man went to the marketplace again and saw others standing there. He asked them, 'Why did you stand here all day doing nothing?' 7They answered, 'No one gave us a job.' The man said to them, 'Then you can go and work in my vineyard.'

8"At the end of the day, the owner of the vineyard said to the boss of all the workers, 'Call the workers and pay them. Start with the last people I hired and end with those I hired first.'

9"When the workers who were hired at five o'clock came to get their pay, each received one coin. 10When the workers who were hired first came to get their pay, they thought they would be paid more than the others. But each one of them also received one coin. 11When they got their coin, they complained to the man who owned the land. 12They said, 'Those people were hired last and worked only one hour. But you paid them the same as you paid us who worked hard all day in the hot sun.' 13But the man who owned the vineyard said to one of those workers, 'Friend, I am being fair to you. You agreed to work for one coin. 14So take your pay and go. I want to give the man who was hired last the same pay that I gave you. 15I can do what I want with my own money. Are you jealous because I am good to those people?'

16"So those who have the last place now will have the first place in the future, and those who have the first place now will have the last place in the future."

JESUS TALKS ABOUT HIS OWN DEATH

17While Jesus was going to Jerusalem, he took his twelve followers aside privately and said to them, 18"Look, we are going to Jerusalem. The Son of Man will be turned over to the leading priests and the teachers of the law, and they will say that he must die. 19They will give the Son of Man to the non-Jewish people to laugh at him and beat him with whips and crucify him. But on the third day, he will be raised to life again."

63% OF YOUNG ADULTS BELIEVE THAT GOD IS THE ALL-POWERFUL, ALL-KNOWING, PERFECT CREATOR WHO RULES THE WORLD TODAY.

A MOTHER ASKS JESUS A FAVOR

20Then the wife of Zebedee came to Jesus with her sons. She bowed before him and asked him to do something for her.

21Jesus asked, "What do you want?"

She said, "Promise that one of my sons will sit at your right side and the other will sit at your left side in your kingdom."

22But Jesus said, "You don't understand what you are asking. Can you drink the cup that I am about to drink?"[n]

"THIS IS SOMETHING PEOPLE CANNOT DO, BUT GOD CAN DO ALL THINGS."

The sons answered, "Yes, we can."

23Jesus said to them, "You will drink from my cup. But I cannot choose who will sit at my right or my left; those places belong to those for whom my Father has prepared them."

24When the other ten followers heard this, they were angry with the two brothers.

25Jesus called all the followers together and said, "You know that the rulers of the non-Jewish people love to show their power over the people. And their important leaders love to use all their authority. 26But it should not be that way among you. Whoever wants to become great among you must serve the rest of you like a servant. 27Whoever wants to become first among you must serve the rest of you like a slave. 28In the same way, the Son of Man did not come to be served. He came to serve others and to give his life as a ransom for many people."

JESUS HEALS TWO BLIND MEN

29When Jesus and his followers were leaving Jericho, a great many people followed him. 30Two blind men sitting by the road heard that

notes

20:2 coin A Roman denarius. One coin was the average pay for one day's work. **20:22 drink . . . drink** Jesus used the idea of drinking from a cup to ask if they could accept the same terrible things that would happen to him.

Jesus was going by, so they shouted, "Lord, Son of David, have mercy on us!"

31 The people warned the blind men to be quiet, but they shouted even more, "Lord, Son of David, have mercy on us!"

32 Jesus stopped and said to the blind men, "What do you want me to do for you?"

33 They answered, "Lord, we want to see."

34 Jesus felt sorry for the blind men and touched their eyes, and at once they could see. Then they followed Jesus.

JESUS ENTERS JERUSALEM AS A KING

21 As Jesus and his followers were coming closer to Jerusalem, they stopped at Bethphage at the hill called the Mount of Olives. From there Jesus sent two of his followers 2 and said to them, "Go to the town you can see there. When you enter it, you will quickly find a donkey tied there with its colt. Untie them and bring them to me. 3 If anyone asks you why you are taking the donkeys, say that the Master needs them, and he will send them at once."

4 This was to bring about what the prophet had said:

5 "Tell the people of Jerusalem,
'Your king is coming to you.
He is gentle and riding on a donkey,
on the colt of a donkey.' " *Isaiah 62:11; Zechariah 9:9*

6 The followers went and did what Jesus told them to do. 7 They brought the donkey and the colt to Jesus and laid their coats on them, and Jesus sat on them. 8 Many people spread their coats on the road. Others cut branches from the trees and spread them on the road. 9 The people were walking ahead of Jesus and behind him, shouting,

"Praise[n] to the Son of David!
God bless the One who comes in the name of the Lord! *Psalm 118:26*
Praise to God in heaven!"

10 When Jesus entered Jerusalem, all the city was filled with excitement. The people asked, "Who is this man?"

11 The crowd said, "This man is Jesus, the prophet from the town of Nazareth in Galilee."

JESUS GOES TO THE TEMPLE

12 Jesus went into the Temple and threw out all the people who were buying and selling there. He turned over the tables of those who were exchanging different kinds of money, and he upset the benches of those who were selling doves. 13 Jesus said to all the people there, "It is written in the Scriptures, 'My Temple will be called a house for prayer.'[n] But you are changing it into a 'hideout for robbers.' "[n]

14 The blind and crippled people came to Jesus in the Temple, and he healed them. 15 The leading priests and the teachers of the law saw that Jesus was doing wonderful things and that the children were praising him in the Temple, saying, "Praise[n] to the Son of David." All these things made the priests and the teachers of the law very angry.

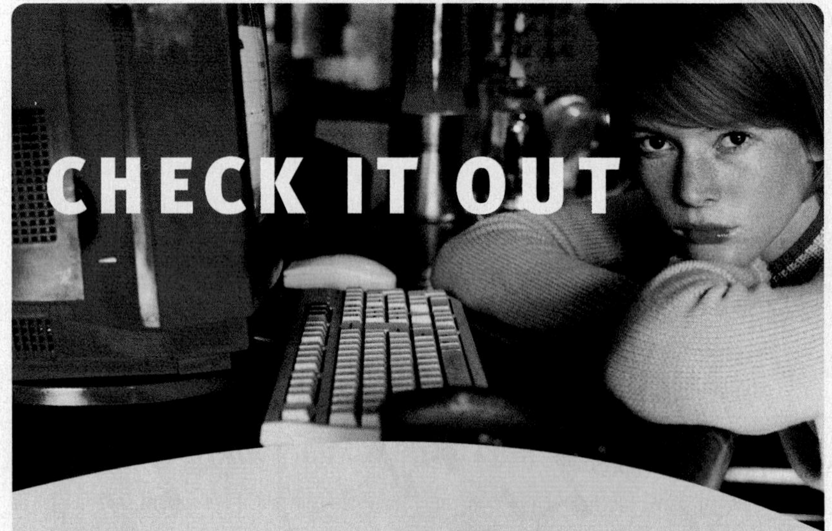

DATA

DATA aims to raise awareness about the crisis swamping Africa: unpayable DEBTS, uncontrolled spread of AIDS, and unfair TRADE rules, which keep AFRICANS poor. We are asking that the governments of the world's wealthy nations—the United States, Europe, Canada and Japan—respond quickly and generously to this emergency.

We also ask Africa's leaders to practice DEMOCRACY, ACCOUNTABILITY and TRANSPARENCY—to make sure that help for African people goes where it's intended and makes a real difference.

DATA is working to bring people and organizations from all around the United States and the world together to stop the spread of AIDS and extreme poverty in Africa. We have offices in Washington, DC, and London, where we work to get the word out about the crisis in Africa—and work to tell our leaders and politicians that people like you want to see action.

Again and again, politicians tell us they want to do more for Africa. Then they don't. Why? Because they don't hear from you—taxpayers, voters and consumers—that you care and want to see something done. We're here to help you get the word to your leaders—and we want your help in finding the very best ways to do that.

Get involved by visiting ***www.datadata.org.***

notes

21:9, 15 Praise Literally, "Hosanna," a Hebrew word used at first in praying to God for help. At this time it was probably a shout of joy used in praising God or his Messiah. **21:13 'My Temple . . . prayer.'** Quotation from Isaiah 56:7. **21:13 'hideout for robbers.'** Quotation from Jeremiah 7:11.

DO YOU HAVE A HEALTHY BODY IMAGE?

I ENJOY SHOPPING FOR CLOTHES.
A. NEVER B. SOMETIMES
C. OFTEN D. ALWAYS

I FEEL SELF-CONSCIOUS WHEN I'M AROUND SOMEONE I THINK IS BEAUTIFUL.
A. ALWAYS B. OFTEN
C. SOMETIMES D. NEVER

I LOVE HAVING MY PICTURE TAKEN.
A. NEVER B. SOMETIMES
C. OFTEN D. ALWAYS

I TRY ON A FEW DIFFERENT OUTFITS BEFORE I FINALLY DECIDE WHAT TO WEAR.
A. ALWAYS B. OFTEN
C. SOMETIMES D. NEVER

I FEEL COMFORTABLE IN A SWIMSUIT.
A. NEVER B. SOMETIMES
C. OFTEN D. ALWAYS

WHEN I LOOK AT MYSELF IN THE MIRROR, I CRINGE.
A. ALWAYS B. OFTEN
C. SOMETIMES D. NEVER

THERE ARE PARTS OF MY BODY THAT I'M REALLY PROUD OF.
A. NEVER B. SOMETIMES
C. OFTEN D. ALWAYS

I AM CRITICAL OF OTHER WOMEN'S BODIES, NO MATTER HOW BEAUTIFUL.
A. ALWAYS B. OFTEN
C. SOMETIMES D. NEVER

I EAT WHAT I WANT WITHOUT REALLY THINKING ABOUT THE FAT OR CALORIES.
A. NEVER B. SOMETIMES
C. OFTEN D. ALWAYS

I WEIGH MYSELF MORE THAN ONCE A DAY.
A. ALWAYS B. OFTEN
C. SOMETIMES D. NEVER

IF YOU PICKED MOSTLY A's AND B's, YOU HAVE A POOR BODY IMAGE.

Come on, girl! Don't you know that God created you, and he calls your body a "temple for the Holy Spirit" (1 Corinthians 6:19-20)? It's time to start being thankful for the body that God gave you and glorifying him with it! Here are some ideas to get you going:
(1) Start a balanced fitness routine, and make sure you are eating well.
(2) Make it a goal to run in a charity race in a few months—it will give you something to work towards, and you will also be helping others.
(3) Ask some close friends to support you in your efforts.

IF YOU PICKED MOSTLY B's AND C's, YOU HAVE AN AVERAGE BODY IMAGE.

You're not crazy about your body, but at the same time, you don't hate it either. Good for you; you're off to a good start! Remember that no one is perfect and God created you exactly the way that is the very best for you. Try some new things—a new haircut, eating healthier foods—and then rest in God's plan and his love for you.

IF YOU PICKED MOSTLY C's AND D's, YOU HAVE A SUPER BODY IMAGE!

Congratulations! You love your body! It is great to have such a positive attitude about your body—and it's rare among women these days. Thank God for your healthy attitude and ask him to help you always remember that, no matter how you feel, your body is a temple for the Holy Spirit. But also remember that your body is not the most important part of you. The Bible says, "People look at the outside of a person, but the LORD looks at the heart" (1 Samuel 16:7).

Matthew 23:8-9

As you learn about Jesus' life on earth, one thing you notice is that he seemed to enjoy hanging around notorious sinners more than he did the Jewish religious leaders. To thieves and prostitutes he said, "Your sins are forgiven" (see Luke 7:48), but he warned the Pharisees and teachers, "How terrible for you!" (Matthew 23:16).

The Pharisees were snobs. These religious leaders actually thought they were better than the rest of the Jewish people. Because they knew a lot about Scripture and religious customs, they figured that God liked them more than he liked everybody else. Jesus could see their conceited attitude and hated it.

Jesus told his followers that God's kingdom is not made up of special people and regular people. The people who follow Jesus are all equal, and he loves each one exactly the same. If you've struggled with feelings of inferiority or insecurity, know that God never sees you as inferior to anyone. If you've gotten an attitude about how cool you are, God isn't impressed. God can peer into a high school classroom and see the most popular student in school sitting beside the biggest outcast; yet he loves them both the same. No matter how you feel, God thinks you're awesome—just as awesome as the next person. Everybody's equal with him. No one has a better chance than you do!

16They asked Jesus, "Do you hear the things
these children are saying?"
Jesus answered, "Yes. Haven't you read in the Scriptures, 'You have taught children and babies to sing praises'?"[n]
17Then Jesus left and went out of the city to
Bethany, where he spent the night.

THE POWER OF FAITH

18Early the next morning, as Jesus was going
back to the city, he became hungry. 19Seeing a
fig tree beside the road, Jesus went to it, but there were no figs on the tree, only leaves. So Jesus said to the tree, "You will never again have fruit." The tree immediately dried up.
20When his followers saw this, they were
amazed. They asked, "How did the fig tree dry up so quickly?"
21Jesus answered, "I tell you
the truth, if you have faith and do not doubt, you will be able to do what I did to this tree and even more. You will be able to say to this mountain, 'Go, fall into the sea.' And if you have faith, it will happen.
22If you believe, you will get anything you ask for
in prayer."

Ephesians 1:5
Because of his love, God had already decided to make us his own children through Jesus Christ.

LEADERS DOUBT JESUS' AUTHORITY

23Jesus went to the Temple, and while he
was teaching there, the leading priests and the older leaders of the people came to him. They said, "What authority do you have to do these things? Who gave you this authority?"
24Jesus answered, "I also will ask you a ques-
tion. If you answer me, then I will tell you what
authority I have to do these things. 25Tell me:
When John baptized people, did that come from God or just from other people?"
They argued about Jesus' question, saying, "If we answer, 'John's baptism was from God,' Jesus will say, 'Then why didn't you believe
him?' 26But if we say, 'It was from people,' we
are afraid of what the crowd will do because they all believe that John was a prophet."
27So they answered Jesus, "We don't know."
Jesus said to them, "Then I won't tell you what authority I have to do these things.

A STORY ABOUT TWO SONS

28"Tell me what you think about this: A man
had two sons. He went to the first son and said,
'Son, go and work today in my vineyard.' 29The
son answered, 'I will not go.' But later the son
changed his mind and went. 30Then the father
went to the other son and said, 'Son, go and work today in my vineyard.' The son answered, 'Yes, sir, I will go and work,' but he did not go.
31Which of the two sons obeyed his father?"
The priests and leaders answered, "The first son."
Jesus said to them, "I tell you the truth, the tax collectors and the prostitutes will enter the kingdom of God before you do.
32John came to show you the
right way to live. You did not believe him, but the tax collectors and prostitutes believed him. Even after seeing this, you still refused to change your ways and believe him.

A STORY ABOUT GOD'S SON

33"Listen to this story: There was a man who
owned a vineyard. He put a wall around it and dug a hole for a winepress and built a tower. Then he leased the land to some farmers and
left for a trip. 34When it was time for the grapes
to be picked, he sent his servants to the farmers
to get his share of the grapes. 35But the farmers
grabbed the servants, beat one, killed another,
and then killed a third servant with stones. 36So
the man sent some other servants to the farmers, even more than he sent the first time. But the farmers did the same thing to the servants
that they had done before. 37So the man decid-
ed to send his son to the farmers. He said, 'They
will respect my son.' 38But when the farmers
saw the son, they said to each other, 'This son will inherit the vineyard. If we kill him, it will
be ours!' 39Then the farmers grabbed the son,
threw him out of the vineyard, and killed him.

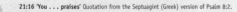

21:16 'You . . . praises' Quotation from the Septuagint (Greek) version of Psalm 8:2.

[40]So what will the owner of the vineyard do to these farmers when he comes?"

[41]The priests and leaders said, "He will surely kill those evil men. Then he will lease the vineyard to some other farmers who will give him his share of the crop at harvest time."

[42]Jesus said to them, "Surely you have read this in the Scriptures:

'The stone that the builders rejected
became the cornerstone.
The Lord did this,
and it is wonderful to us.'

Psalm 118:22-23

[43]"So I tell you that the kingdom of God will be taken away from you and given to people who do the things God wants in his kingdom. [44]The person who falls on this stone will be broken, and on whomever that stone falls, that person will be crushed."[n]

[45]When the leading priests and the Pharisees heard these stories, they knew Jesus was talking about them. [46]They wanted to arrest him, but they were afraid of the people, because the people believed that Jesus was a prophet.

A STORY ABOUT A WEDDING FEAST

22 Jesus again used stories to teach the people. He said, [2]"The kingdom of heaven is like a king who prepared a wedding feast for his son. [3]The king invited some people to the feast. When the feast was ready, the king sent his servants to tell the people, but they refused to come.

[4]"Then the king sent other servants, saying, 'Tell those who have been invited that my feast is ready. I have killed my best bulls and calves for the dinner, and everything is ready. Come to the wedding feast.'

[5]"But the people refused to listen to the servants and left to do other things. One went to work in his field, and another went to his business. [6]Some of the other people grabbed the servants, beat them, and killed them. [7]The king was furious and sent his army to kill the murderers and burn their city.

[8]"After that, the king said to his servants, 'The wedding feast is ready. I invited those people, but they were not worthy to come. [9]So go to the street corners and invite everyone you find to come to my feast.' [10]So the servants went into the streets and gathered all the people they could find, both good and bad. And the wedding hall was filled with guests.

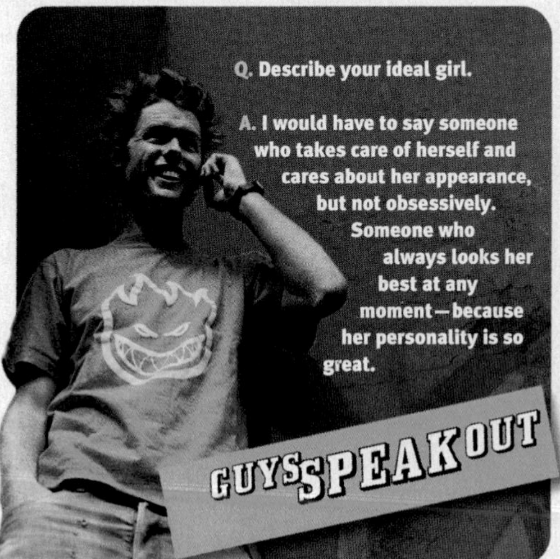

Q. Describe your ideal girl.
A. I would have to say someone who takes care of herself and cares about her appearance, but not obsessively. Someone who always looks her best at any moment—because her personality is so great.
GUYS SPEAK OUT

DIDYA KNOW

AMONG BORN-AGAIN CHRISTIANS, YOUNG ADULTS AND BOOMERS ARE THE GENERATION MORE LIKELY THAN ANY OTHERS TO EVANGELIZE.

[11]"When the king came in to see the guests, he saw a man who was not dressed for a wedding. [12]The king said, 'Friend, how were you allowed to come in here? You are not dressed for a wedding.' But the man said nothing. [13]So the king told some servants, 'Tie this man's hands and feet. Throw him out into the darkness, where people will cry and grind their teeth with pain.'

[14]"Yes, many people are invited, but only a few are chosen."

IS IT RIGHT TO PAY TAXES OR NOT?

[15]Then the Pharisees left that place and made plans to trap Jesus in saying something wrong. [16]They sent some of their own followers and some people from the group called Herodians.[n] They said, "Teacher, we know that you are an honest man and that you teach the truth about God's way. You are not afraid of what other people think about you, because you pay no attention to who they are. [17]So tell us what you think. Is it right to pay taxes to Caesar or not?"

"THE PERSON WHO FALLS ON THIS STONE WILL BE BROKEN, AND ON WHOMEVER THAT STONE FALLS, THAT PERSON WILL BE CRUSHED."

[18]But knowing that these leaders were trying to trick him, Jesus said, "You hypocrites! Why are you trying to trap me? [19]Show me a coin used for paying the tax." So the men showed him a coin.[n] [20]Then Jesus asked, "Whose image and name are on the coin?"

[21]The men answered, "Caesar's."

Then Jesus said to them, "Give to Caesar the things that are Caesar's, and give to God the things that are God's."

[22]When the men heard what Jesus said, they were amazed and left him and went away.

SOME SADDUCEES TRY TO TRICK JESUS

[23]That same day some Sadducees came to Jesus and asked him a question. (Sadducees believed that people would not rise from the dead.) [24]They said, "Teacher, Moses said if a

notes **21:44 Verse 44** Some copies do not have verse 44. **22:16 Herodians** A political group that followed Herod and his family. **22:19 coin** A Roman denarius. One coin was the average pay for one day's work.

Q. Sometimes I feel as if I'm living a double life. At school, I cuss a little, wear makeup and more expensive clothes; at church I'm all "love everybody" and pretty much a model Christian-youth group prez and ultra-volunteer. Please help!

A. Which you is the real you? The church-girl or the school-girl? Start with prayer. Tell God you know you've messed up and that you want to change. Expect him to help you, but know that you have to work at it too. It's up to you what you choose who you want to be, but you have to believe in it and want to live it. Then find someone to hold you accountable. Give them your list. Tell them they can call you on it anytime you are not living what you believe.

Q. I am really worried about my friend. She has been so depressed lately, but she won't tell me what's wrong! How should I deal with this?

A. It definitely sounds like something is wrong with your friend, but if she won't tell you what it is, there isn't much you can do. The first thing you should do is talk to a teacher or counselor. Remember that you do have the most powerful being in the world to go to in Jesus. Show her by your daily actions and words that you don't judge people, but that you love them no matter what, just like Jesus.

married man dies without having children, his
brother must marry the widow and have children
for him. 25Once there were seven brothers among
us. The first one married and died. Since he had
no children, his brother married the widow.
26Then the second brother also died. The same
thing happened to the third brother and all the
other brothers. 27Finally, the woman died.
28Since all seven men had married her, when people rise from the dead, whose wife will she be?"
29Jesus answered, "You don't understand,
because you don't know what the Scriptures say,
and you don't know about the power of God.

"LOVE THE LORD YOUR GOD WITH ALL YOUR HEART, ALL YOUR SOUL, AND ALL YOUR MIND."

30When people rise from the dead, they will not
marry, nor will they be given to someone to
marry. They will be like the angels in heaven.
31Surely you have read what God said to you
about rising from the dead. 32God said, 'I am the
God of Abraham, the God of Isaac, and the God of
Jacob.'[n] God is the God of the living, not the dead."
33When the people heard this, they were amazed
at Jesus' teaching.

THE MOST IMPORTANT COMMAND

34When the Pharisees learned that the
Sadducees could not argue with Jesus' answers to
them, the Pharisees met together. 35One Pharisee,
who was an expert on the law of Moses, asked
Jesus this question to test him: 36"Teacher, which
command in the law is the most important?"
37Jesus answered, " 'Love the Lord your God
with all your heart, all your soul, and all your
mind.'[n] 38This is the first and most important
command. 39And the second command is like
the first: 'Love your neighbor as you love yourself.'[n] 40All the law and the writings of the
prophets depend on these two commands."

JESUS QUESTIONS THE PHARISEES

41While the Pharisees were together, Jesus
asked them, 42"What do you think about the
Christ? Whose son is he?"

They answered, "The Christ is the Son of David."

43Then Jesus said to them, "Then why did
David call him 'Lord'? David, speaking by the
power of the Holy Spirit, said,
44'The Lord said to my Lord:

Sit by me at my right side,
until I put your enemies under your
control.' *Psalm 110:1*

45David calls the Christ 'Lord,' so how can the
Christ be his son?"
46None of the Pharisees could answer Jesus'
question, and after that day no one was brave
enough to ask him any more questions.

JESUS ACCUSES SOME LEADERS

23 Then Jesus said to the crowds and
to his followers, 2"The teachers of
the law and the Pharisees have the authority to
tell you what the law of Moses says. 3So you
should obey and follow whatever they tell you,
but their lives are not good examples for you to
follow. They tell you to do things, but they
themselves don't do them. 4They make strict
rules and try to force people to obey them, but
they are unwilling to help those who struggle
under the weight of their rules.
5"They do good things so that other people
will see them. They make the boxes[n] of Scriptures that they wear bigger, and they make
their special prayer clothes very long. 6Those
Pharisees and teachers of the law love to have
the most important seats at feasts and in the
synagogues. 7They love people to greet them
with respect in the marketplaces, and they love
to have people call them 'Teacher.'
8"But you must not be called 'Teacher,' because you have only one Teacher, and you are
all brothers and sisters together. 9And don't call
any person on earth 'Father,' because you have
one Father, who is in heaven. 10And you should

notes

22:32 'I am . . . Jacob.' Quotation from Exodus 3:6. **22:37 'Love . . . mind.'** Quotation from Deuteronomy 6:5. **22:39 'Love . . . yourself.'** Quotation from Leviticus 19:18. **23:5 boxes** Small leather boxes containing four important Scriptures. Some Jews tied these to their foreheads and left arms, probably to show they were very religious.

not be called 'Master,' because you have only one Master, the Christ. [11]Whoever is your servant is the greatest among you. [12]Whoever makes himself great will be made humble. Whoever makes himself humble will be made great.

[13]"How terrible for you, teachers of the law and Pharisees! You are hypocrites! You close the door for people to enter the kingdom of heaven. You yourselves don't enter, and you stop others who are trying to enter. [14][n]

[15]"How terrible for you, teachers of the law and Pharisees! You are hypocrites! You travel across land and sea to find one person who will change to your ways. When you find that person, you make him more fit for hell than you are.

[16]"How terrible for you! You guide the people, but you are blind. You say, 'If people swear by the Temple when they make a promise, that means nothing. But if they swear by the gold that is in the Temple, they must keep that promise.' [17]You are blind fools! Which is greater: the gold or the Temple that makes that gold holy? [18]And you say, 'If people swear by the altar when they make a promise, that means nothing. But if they swear by the gift on the altar, they must keep that promise.' [19]You are blind! Which is greater: the gift or the altar that makes the gift holy? [20]The person who swears by the altar is really using the altar and also everything on the altar. [21]And the person who swears by the Temple is really using the Temple and also everything in the Temple. [22]The person who swears by heaven is also using God's throne and the One who sits on that throne.

[23]"How terrible for you, teachers of the law and Pharisees! You are hypocrites! You give to God one-tenth of everything you earn—even your mint, dill, and cumin.[n] But you don't obey the really important teachings of the law—justice, mercy, and being loyal. These are the things you should do, as well as those other things. [24]You guide the people, but you are blind! You are like a person who picks a fly out of a drink and then swallows a camel![n]

[25]"How terrible for you, teachers of the law and Pharisees! You are hypocrites! You wash the outside of your cups and dishes, but inside they are full of things you got by cheating others and by pleasing only yourselves. [26]Pharisees, you are blind! First make the inside of the cup clean, and then the outside of the cup can be truly clean.

[27]"How terrible for you, teachers of the law and Pharisees! You are hypocrites! You are like tombs that are painted white. Outside, those tombs look fine, but inside, they are full of the bones of dead people and all kinds of unclean things. [28]It is the same with you. People look at you and think you are good, but on the inside you are full of hypocrisy and evil.

[29]"How terrible for you, teachers of the law and Pharisees! You are hypocrites! You build tombs for the prophets, and you show honor to the graves of those who lived good lives. [30]You say, 'If we had lived during the time of our ancestors, we would not have helped them kill the prophets.' [31]But you give proof that you are children of those who murdered the prophets. [32]And you will complete the sin that your ancestors started.

[33]"You are snakes! A family of poisonous snakes! How are you going to escape God's judgment? [34]So I tell you this: I am sending to you prophets and wise men and teachers. Some of them you will kill and crucify. Some of them

"THE PERSON WHO SWEARS BY HEAVEN IS ALSO USING GOD'S THRONE AND THE ONE WHO SITS ON THAT THRONE."

bible basics

The Old Testament is a collection of the thirty-nine books that were written before Jesus lived on the earth. They tell the story of the creation of the world and mankind, the beginnings of the nation of Israel, and they predict the coming of the Messiah. They're divided into the History, Prophecy, and Poetry and Wisdom books.

notes

23:14 Verse 14 Some Greek copies add verse 14: "How terrible for you, teachers of the law and Pharisees. You are hypocrites. You take away widows' houses, and you say long prayers so that people will notice you. So you will have a worse punishment." **23:23 mint, dill, and cumin** Small plants grown in gardens and used for spices. Only very religious people would be careful enough to give a tenth of these plants. **23:24 You . . . camel!** Meaning, "You worry about the smallest mistakes but commit the biggest sin."

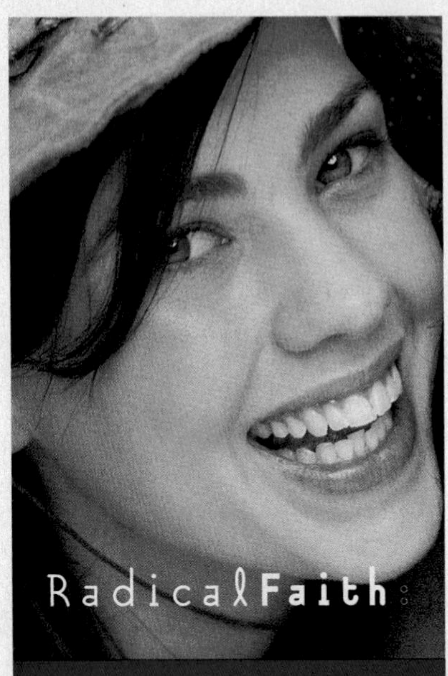

Matthew 24:4

This is a great chapter in the Bible. Jesus is foretelling some of the things that are going to happen before he comes back to the earth—wars, stories of wars, famines, earthquakes, etc. He goes on to tell us not to worry or be afraid because these things must happen before he comes back. But before he goes into all of this, he says that there will be many people who claim to be Jesus and then warns us not to be fooled by them. You've seen this already.

Remember the suicide by the cult group called "Heaven's Gate"? All of the people in that compound died because they allowed themselves to be fooled. Adam and Eve were cast out of the garden because they allowed themselves to be fooled. Esau lost his inheritance because he allowed himself to be fooled. Samson lost his strength because he allowed himself to be fooled.

You don't have to allow yourself to be fooled by some false prophet who claims to be Jesus or from God. If something doesn't line up with the Word of God, then don't believe it. There are more fruitcakes around today than ever before. This is what we call *a sign of the times.*

Jesus is coming back. No one knows exactly when, so stay tight with God and don't be fooled!

you will beat in your synagogues and chase
from town to town. 35So you will be guilty for
the death of all the good people who have been
killed on earth—from the murder of that good
man Abel to the murder of Zechariah[n] son of
Berakiah, whom you murdered between the
Temple and the altar. 36I tell you the truth, all of
these things will happen to you people who are
living now.

JESUS FEELS SORRY FOR JERUSALEM

37"Jerusalem, Jerusalem! You kill the prophets
and stone to death those who are sent to you.
Many times I wanted to gather your people as a
hen gathers her chicks under her wings, but
you did not let me. 38Now your house will be
left completely empty. 39I tell you, you will not
see me again until that time when you will say,
'God bless the One who comes in the name of
the Lord.' "[n]

THE TEMPLE WILL BE DESTROYED

24 As Jesus left the Temple and was
walking away, his followers came
up to show him the Temple's buildings. 2Jesus
asked, "Do you see all these buildings? I tell
you the truth, not one stone will be left on
another. Every stone will be thrown down to
the ground."

3Later, as Jesus was sitting on the Mount of
Olives, his followers came to be alone with
him. They said, "Tell us, when will these
things happen? And what will be the sign that
it is time for you to come again and for this
age to end?"

4Jesus answered, "Be careful that no one
fools you. 5Many will come in my name, saying, 'I am the Christ,' and they will fool many
people. 6You will hear about wars and stories of
wars that are coming, but don't be afraid. These
things must happen before the end comes.
7Nations will fight against other nations; kingdoms will fight against other kingdoms. There
will be times when there is no food for people
to eat, and there will be earthquakes in different
places. 8These things are like the first pains
when something new is about to be born.

9"Then people will arrest you, hand you over
to be hurt, and kill you. They will hate you
because you believe in me. 10At that time,
many will lose their faith, and they will turn
against each other and hate each other. 11Many
false prophets will come and cause many people to believe lies. 12There will be more and
more evil in the world, so most people will stop
showing their love for each other. 13But those
people who keep their faith until the end will
be saved. 14The Good News about God's kingdom will be preached in all the world, to every
nation. Then the end will come.

"THERE WILL BE MORE AND MORE EVIL IN THE WORLD, SO MOST PEOPLE WILL STOP SHOWING THEIR LOVE FOR EACH OTHER. BUT THOSE PEOPLE WHO KEEP THEIR FAITH UNTIL THE END WILL BE SAVED."

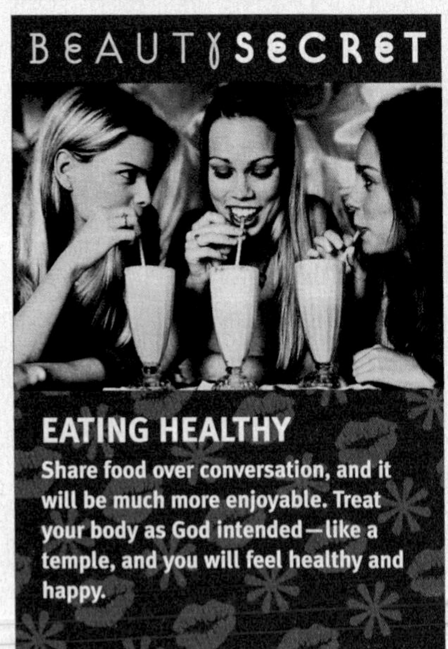

BEAUTYSECRET
EATING HEALTHY
Share food over conversation, and it will be much more enjoyable. Treat your body as God intended—like a temple, and you will feel healthy and happy.

23:35 Abel . . . Zechariah In the order of the books of the Hebrew Old Testament, the first and last men to be murdered. **23:39 'God . . . Lord.'** Quotation from Psalm 118:26.

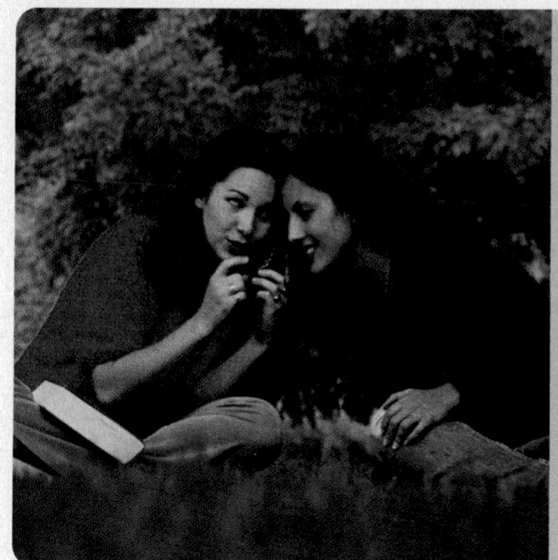

LEARN IT & LIVE IT

Matthew 19:30:
Learn It: The first will be last and the last, first.
Live It: Next time you are in line somewhere, let others behind you go before you.

Matthew 21:22:
Learn It: Ask and you will receive.
Live It: Make a prayer list. Spend some time talking with God in faith; then await his answer.

Matthew 22:37-38:
Learn It: The first and greatest commandment is to love God; the second is to love your neighbor.
Live It: Do something kind for your next-door neighbors. Offer to wash the car, baby-sit the kids, or walk the dog. Show them the love of God.

61% OF YOUNG ADULTS AND 60% OF BOOMERS SHARED THEIR FAITH WITH SOMEONE DURING A GIVEN 12-MONTH PERIOD IN HOPE THAT THE PERSON WOULD ACCEPT JESUS CHRIST AS THEIR SAVIOR.

15“Daniel the prophet spoke about ‘the destroying terror.’[n] You will see this standing in the holy place.” (You who read this should understand what it means.) 16“At that time, the people in Judea should run away to the mountains. 17If people are on the roofs[n] of their houses, they must not go down to get anything out of their houses. 18If people are in the fields, they must not go back to get their coats. 19At that time, how terrible it will be for women who are pregnant or have nursing babies! 20Pray that it will not be winter or a Sabbath day when these things happen and you have to run away, 21because at that time there will be much trouble. There will be more trouble than there has ever been since the beginning of the world until now, and nothing as bad will ever happen again. 22God has decided to make that terrible time short. Otherwise, no one would go on living. But God will make that time short to help the people he has chosen. 23At that time, someone might say to you, ‘Look, there is the Christ!’ Or another person might say, ‘There he is!’ But don’t believe them. 24False Christs and false prophets will come and perform great wonders and miracles. They will try to fool even the people God has chosen, if that is possible. 25Now I have warned you about this before it happens.

26“If people tell you, ‘The Christ is in the desert,’ don’t go there. If they say, ‘The Christ is in the inner room,’ don’t believe it. 27When the Son of Man comes, he will be seen by everyone, like lightning flashing from the east to the west. 28Wherever the dead body is, there the vultures will gather.

29“Soon after the trouble of those days,
‘the sun will grow dark,
and the moon will not give its light.
The stars will fall from the sky.
And the powers of the heavens
will be shaken.’ *Isaiah 13:10; 34:4*

30“At that time, the sign of the Son of Man will appear in the sky. Then all the peoples of the world will cry. They will see the Son of Man coming on clouds in the sky with great power and glory. 31He will use a loud trumpet to send his angels all around the earth, and they will gather his chosen people from every part of the world.

32“Learn a lesson from the fig tree: When its branches become green and soft and new leaves appear, you know summer is near. 33In the same way, when you see all these things happening, you will know that the time is near, ready to come. 34I tell you the truth, all these things will happen while the people of this time are still living. 35Earth and sky will be destroyed, but the words I have said will never be destroyed.

WHEN WILL JESUS COME AGAIN?

36“No one knows when that day or time will be, not the angels in heaven, not even the Son. Only the Father knows. 37When the Son of Man comes, it will be like what happened during Noah’s time. 38In those days before the flood, people were eating and drinking, marrying and giving their children to be married, until the day Noah entered the boat. 39They knew nothing about what was happening until the flood came and destroyed them. It will be the same when the Son of Man comes. 40Two men will be in the field. One will be taken, and the other will be left. 41Two women will be grinding grain with a mill.[n] One will be taken, and the other will be left.

notes **24:15 ‘the destroying terror’** Mentioned in Daniel 9:27; 12:11 (see also Daniel 11:31). **24:17 roofs** In Bible times houses were built with flat roofs. The roof was used for drying things such as flax and fruit. And it was used as an extra room, as a place for worship, and as a cool place to sleep in the summer. **24:41 mill** Two large, round, flat rocks used for grinding grain to make flour.

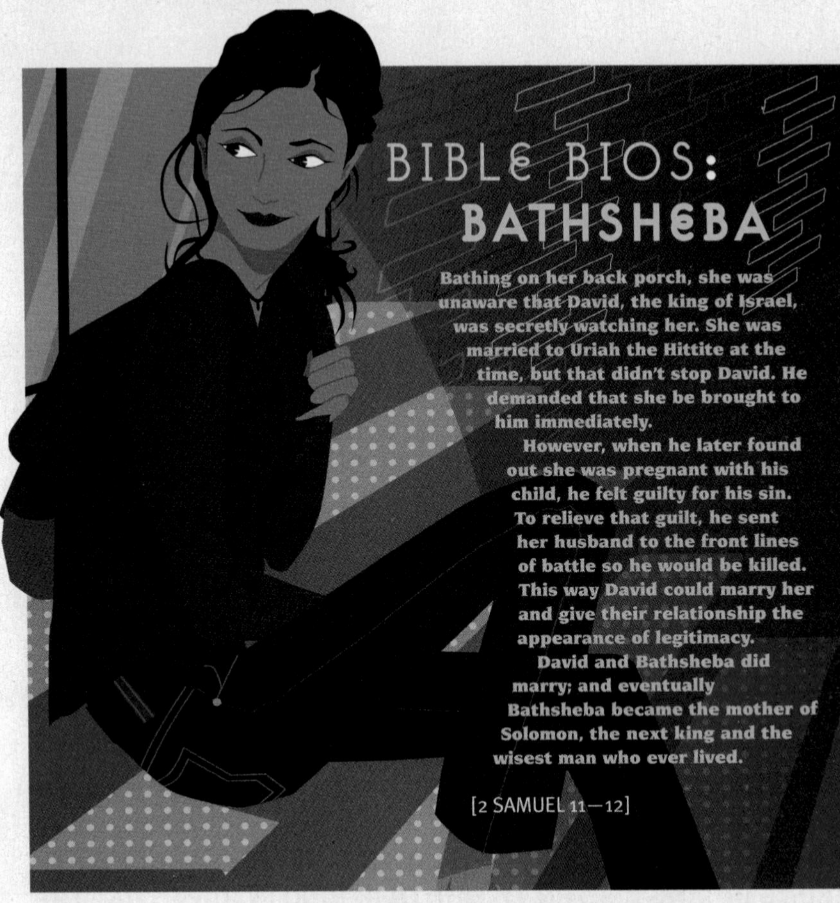

BIBLE BIOS:
BATHSHEBA
Bathing on her back porch, she was unaware that David, the king of Israel, was secretly watching her. She was married to Uriah the Hittite at the time, but that didn't stop David. He demanded that she be brought to him immediately.
However, when he later found out she was pregnant with his child, he felt guilty for his sin. To relieve that guilt, he sent her husband to the front lines of battle so he would be killed. This way David could marry her and give their relationship the appearance of legitimacy.
David and Bathsheba did marry; and eventually Bathsheba became the mother of Solomon, the next king and the wisest man who ever lived.
[2 SAMUEL 11—12]

42“So always be ready, because you don't
know the day your Lord will come. 43Remember
this: If the owner of the house knew what time of
night a thief was coming, the owner would watch
and not let the thief break in. 44So you also must
be ready, because the Son of Man will come at a
time you don't expect him.

45“Who is the wise and loyal servant that the
master trusts to give the other servants their
food at the right time? 46When the master comes
and finds the servant doing his work, the servant will be blessed. 47I tell you the truth, the
master will choose that servant to take care of
everything he owns. 48But suppose that evil
servant thinks to himself, 'My master will not
come back soon,' 49and he begins to beat the
other servants and eat and get drunk with others like him? 50The master will come when that
servant is not ready and is not expecting him.
51Then the master will cut him in pieces and
send him away to be with the hypocrites,
where people will cry and grind their teeth
with pain.

A STORY ABOUT TEN BRIDESMAIDS

25 “At that time the kingdom of heav-
en will be like ten bridesmaids who
took their lamps and went to wait
for the bridegroom. 2Five of
them were foolish and five
were wise. 3The five foolish
bridesmaids took their
lamps, but they did not take
more oil for the lamps to burn. 4The
wise bridesmaids took their lamps and
more oil in jars. 5Because the bridegroom was
late, they became sleepy and went to sleep.

6“At midnight someone cried out, 'The
bridegroom is coming! Come and meet him!'
7Then all the bridesmaids woke up and got
their lamps ready. 8But the foolish ones said to
the wise, 'Give us some of your oil, because our
lamps are going out.' 9The wise bridesmaids
answered, 'No, the oil we have might not be
enough for all of us. Go to the people who sell
oil and buy some for yourselves.'

10“So while the five foolish bridesmaids
went to buy oil, the bridegroom came. The
bridesmaids who were ready went in with the
bridegroom to the wedding feast. Then the door
was closed and locked.

11“Later the others came back and said, 'Sir,

“WHEN THE SON OF MAN COMES, IT WILL BE LIKE WHAT HAPPENED DURING NOAH'S TIME.”

sir, open the door to let us in.' 12But the bridegroom answered, 'I tell you the truth, I don't
want to know you.'

13“So always be ready, because you don't
know the day or the hour the Son of Man will
come.

A STORY ABOUT THREE SERVANTS

14“The kingdom of heaven is like a man who
was going to another place for a visit. Before he
left, he called for his servants and told them to
take care of his things while he was gone. 15He
gave one servant five bags of gold, another servant two bags of gold, and a third
servant one bag of gold, to
each one as much as he could
handle. Then he left. 16The
servant who got five
bags went quickly to
invest the money and earned five
more bags. 17In the same way, the servant
who had two bags invested them and earned
two more. 18But the servant who got one bag
went out and dug a hole in the ground and hid
the master's money.

19“After a long time the master came home
and asked the servants what they did with his
money. 20The servant who was given five bags
of gold brought five more bags to the master

1 John 3:1
The Father has loved us so much that we are called children of God. And we really are his children. The reason the people in the world do not know us is that they have not known him.

February
1
2
3
4
5
Bake a loaf of bread with your mom. Celebrate your family by enjoying it for dinner!
6
7
How's the semester going so far? Do you need to step back and recheck your priorities?
8
Get some exercise, take a vitamin. February is the month that most people suffer depression.
9
10
11
Take pillows and blankets to a homeless shelter tonight.
12
13
Read 1 Corinthians 13 in preparation for the big day tomorrow!
14
Valentine's Day. How are you going to show people you love them?
15
16
17
Pray for a Person of Influence: Today is Michael Jordan's birthday.
18
20
21
Pray for a Person of Influence: Jennifer Love Hewett turns another year older today.
22
25
Spring is almost here!
26
27
28
Meditate on God's grace today.
29

and said, 'Master, you trusted me to care for five bags of gold, so I used your five bags to earn five more.' 21The master answered, 'You did well. You are a good and loyal servant. Because you were loyal with small things, I will let you care for much greater things. Come and share my joy with me.'

22"Then the servant who had been given two bags of gold came to the master and said, 'Master, you gave me two bags of gold to care for, so I used your two bags to earn two more.' 23The master answered, 'You did well. You are a good and loyal servant. Because you were loyal with small things, I will let you care for much greater things. Come and share my joy with me.'

24"Then the servant who had been given one bag of gold came to the master and said, 'Master, I knew that you were a hard man. You harvest things you did not plant. You gather crops where you did not sow any seed. 25So I was afraid and went and hid your money in the ground. Here is your bag of gold.' 26The master answered, 'You are a wicked and lazy servant! You say you knew that I harvest things I did not plant and that I gather crops where I did not sow any seed. 27So you should have put my gold in the bank. Then, when I came home, I would have received my gold back with interest.'

28"So the master told his other servants, 'Take the bag of gold from that servant and give it to the servant who has ten bags of gold. 29Those who have much will get more, and they will have much more than they need. But those who do not have much will have everything taken away from them.' 30Then the master said, 'Throw that useless servant outside, into the darkness where people will cry and grind their teeth with pain.'

Isaiah 62:3
You will be like a beautiful crown in the Lord's hand, like a king's crown in your God's hand.

THE KING WILL JUDGE ALL PEOPLE

31"The Son of Man will come again in his great glory, with all his angels. He will be King and sit on his great throne. 32All the nations of the world will be gathered before him, and he will separate them into two groups as a shepherd separates the sheep from the goats. 33The Son of Man will put the sheep on his right and the goats on his left.

34"Then the King will say to the people on his right, 'Come, my Father has given you his blessing. Receive the kingdom God has prepared for you since the world was made. 35I was hungry, and you gave me food. I was thirsty, and you gave me something to drink. I was alone and away from home, and you invited me into your house. 36I was without clothes, and you gave me something to wear. I was sick, and you cared for me. I was in prison, and you visited me.'

37"Then the good people will answer, 'Lord, when did we see you hungry and give you food, or thirsty and give you something to drink? 38When did we see you alone and away from home and invite you into our house? When did we see you without clothes and give you something to wear? 39When did we see you sick or in prison and care for you?'

"I WAS ALONE AND AWAY FROM HOME, AND YOU INVITED ME INTO YOUR HOUSE."

40"Then the King will answer, 'I tell you the truth, anything you did for even the least of my people here, you also did for me.'

41"Then the King will say to those on his left, 'Go away from me. You will be punished. Go into the fire that burns forever that was prepared for the devil and his angels. 42I was hungry, and you gave me nothing to eat. I was thirsty, and you gave me nothing to drink. 43I was alone and away from home, and you did not invite me into your house. I was without clothes, and you gave me nothing to wear. I was sick and in prison, and you did not care for me.'

44"Then those people will answer, 'Lord, when did we see you hungry or thirsty or alone and away from home or without clothes or sick or in prison? When did we see these things and not help you?'

45"Then the King will answer, 'I tell you the truth, anything you refused to do for even the least of my people here, you refused to do for me.'

46"These people will go off to be punished forever, but the good people will go to live forever."

THE PLAN TO KILL JESUS

26 After Jesus finished saying all these things, he told his followers, 2"You know that the day after tomorrow is the day of the Passover Feast. On that day the Son of Man

RELATIONSHIPS

"She should be holy and without blemish" (Ephesians 5:27 NKJV). Sorry, you don't get to blame your newest pimple on your boyfriend. However, if he is pressuring you to do anything you know is wrong, he's not treating you right. This can be trying to get you to sleep with him, getting you to sneak out on your parents, or even getting you to give him the latest gossip. Now, while your latest crush isn't supposed to fill the role of a husband to you, if he's asking you to do things that aren't in line with God's commands he's gotta go. If you're dating, make sure he's someone who takes the Scriptures seriously.

will be given to his enemies to be crucified."

3Then the leading priests and the older leaders had a meeting at the palace of the high priest, named Caiaphas. 4At the meeting, they planned to set a trap to arrest Jesus and kill him. 5But they said, "We must not do it during the feast, because the people might cause a riot."

PERFUME FOR JESUS' BURIAL

6Jesus was in Bethany at the house of Simon, who had a skin disease. 7While Jesus was there, a woman approached him with an alabaster jar filled with expensive perfume. She poured this perfume on Jesus' head while he was eating.

8His followers were upset when they saw the woman do this. They asked, "Why waste that perfume? 9It could have been sold for a great deal of money and the money given to the poor."

10Knowing what had happened, Jesus said, "Why are you troubling this woman? She did an excellent thing for me. 11You will always have the poor with you, but you will not always have me. 12This woman poured perfume on my body to prepare me for burial. 13I tell you the truth, wherever the Good News is preached in all the world, what this woman has done will be told, and people will remember her."

JUDAS BECOMES AN ENEMY OF JESUS

14Then one of the twelve apostles, Judas Iscariot, went to talk to the leading priests. 15He said, "What will you pay me for giving Jesus to you?" And they gave him thirty silver coins. 16After that, Judas watched for the best time to turn Jesus in.

JESUS EATS THE PASSOVER MEAL

17On the first day of the Feast of Unleavened Bread, the followers came to Jesus. They said, "Where do you want us to prepare for you to eat the Passover meal?"

18Jesus answered, "Go into the city to a certain man and tell him, 'The Teacher says: The chosen time is near. I will have the Passover with my followers at your house.' " 19The followers did what Jesus told them to do, and they prepared the Passover meal.

20In the evening Jesus was sitting at the table with his twelve followers. 21As they were eating, Jesus said, "I tell you the truth, one of you will turn against me."

22This made the followers very sad. Each one began to say to Jesus, "Surely, Lord, I am not the one who will turn against you, am I?"

23Jesus answered, "The man who has dipped his hand with me into the bowl is the one who will turn against me. 24The Son of Man will die, just as the Scriptures say. But how terrible it will be for the person who hands the Son of Man over to be killed. It would be better for him if he had never been born."

25Then Judas, who would give Jesus to his enemies, said to Jesus, "Teacher, surely I am not the one, am I?"

Jesus answered, "Yes, it is you."

THE LORD'S SUPPER

26While they were eating, Jesus took some bread and thanked God for it and broke it. Then he gave it to his followers and said, "Take this bread and eat it; this is my body."

27Then Jesus took a cup and thanked God for it and gave it to the followers. He said, "Every one of you drink this. 28This is my blood which is the new agreement that God makes with his people. This blood is poured out for many to forgive their sins. 29I tell you this: I will not drink of this fruit of the vine[n] again until that day when I drink it new with you in my Father's kingdom."

DIDYA KNOW

56% OF YOUNG ADULTS ARE SEARCHING FOR MEANING IN LIFE.

Blab

Q. My cousin who sexually abused me when I was younger is going to be moving into my house. I tried talking to Mom and Dad, but they will not listen. I am scared and not sure what to do about it.

A. Speak up, that's the first step in confronting evil like this. Keep telling your parents and other people in authority—counselor, teacher, police, principal, parents of friends—whomever you can find. Don't ever be alone with this person. Stay with friends if necessary 'til he is gone. Take heart, God hears your prayers. [If you live in the United States, call Child Help at 1-800-422-4453. They can give you more help.]

Q. In school, I have three friends I always hang out with. I am really close with one, and the others I am not so close to. It's really hard on me because the two friends I am not so close to sometimes pull my really close friend and me apart on purpose. What should I do?

A. Talk to the girls individually and make sure you are all on the same page. Tell them that you really like their company and want to be good friends with them. If they don't soften up to you then, visit a pastor or parent to talk about it.

Q. This girl from church told me that she was in love, yes, in love with one of her female teachers. This girl is fourteen years old. I just need some advice on what I should say to her if I get to speak to her again.

A. For a woman to fall in love with another woman is considered a sin according to the Bible. You've got to remember one thing though: It's the Holy Spirit's job to convict her and teach her. In the Bible it says that God remains faithful even when we are faithless. Your job is to show this girl the love of God. How? Stay her friend. Prayer changes things. It can move mountains. It can radically alter lives. Just make sure you remember who God is and that you're not him.

notes **26:29 fruit of the vine** Product of the grapevine; this may also be translated "wine."

Matthew 27:4

When Judas found out that the Jewish leaders intended to have Jesus executed, it was like a lightbulb came on in his head. He suddenly realized what he had done—the simple kiss that had earned him thirty silver coins was going to cost Jesus his life. Judas knew that Jesus was innocent of all the charges the Jews brought against him, and they were going to kill him anyway.

But Jesus wasn't just innocent under the man-made law of the land; he was also innocent in God's eyes. He *literally* never did anything wrong. And his innocence wasn't just a natural thing because he was God's Son. He still had to make choices. Meanwhile Satan did all he could to convince Jesus not to choose God's way. Hebrews 4:15 says, "For our high priest is able to understand our weaknesses. When he lived on earth, he was tempted in every way that we are, but he did not sin."

Because Jesus is innocent, his blood is an acceptable sacrifice to God for your sins. And because he didn't give in to temptation, he paved the way for you to stand up to Satan's tricks, because his Spirit lives in you. When you do sin, confess, repent, and ask his forgiveness and Jesus will declare you innocent too.

[30]After singing a hymn, they went out to the Mount of Olives.

JESUS' FOLLOWERS WILL LEAVE HIM

[31]Jesus told his followers, "Tonight you will all stumble in your faith on account of me, because it is written in the Scriptures:

'I will kill the shepherd,
and the sheep will scatter.' *Zechariah 13:7*

[32]But after I rise from the dead, I will go ahead of you into Galilee."

[33]Peter said, "Everyone else may stumble in their faith because of you, but I will not."

[34]Jesus said, "I tell you the truth, tonight before the rooster crows you will say three times that you don't know me."

[35]But Peter said, "I will never say that I don't know you! I will even die with you!" And all the other followers said the same thing.

JESUS PRAYS ALONE

[36]Then Jesus went with his followers to a place called Gethsemane. He said to them, "Sit here while I go over there and pray." [37]He took Peter and the two sons of Zebedee with him, and he began to be very sad and troubled. [38]He said to them, "My heart is full of sorrow, to the point of death. Stay here and watch with me."

[39]After walking a little farther away from them, Jesus fell to the ground and prayed, "My Father, if it is possible, do not give me this cup[n] of suffering. But do what you want, not what I want." [40]Then Jesus went back to his followers and found them asleep. He said to Peter, "You men could not stay awake with me for one hour? [41]Stay awake and pray for strength against temptation. The spirit wants to do what is right, but the body is weak."

[42]Then Jesus went away a second time and prayed, "My Father, if it is not possible for this painful thing to be taken from me, and if I must do it, I pray that what you want will be done."

[43]Then he went back to his followers, and again he found them asleep, because their eyes were heavy. [44]So Jesus left them and went away and prayed a third time, saying the same thing.

[45]Then Jesus went back to his followers and said, "Are you still sleeping and resting? The time has come for the Son of Man to be handed over to sinful people. [46]Get up, we must go. Look, here comes the man who has turned against me."

JESUS IS ARRESTED

[47]While Jesus was still speaking, Judas, one of the twelve apostles, came up. With him were many people carrying swords and clubs who had been sent from the leading priests and the older Jewish leaders of the people. [48]Judas had planned to give them a signal, saying, "The man I kiss is Jesus. Arrest him." [49]At once Judas went to Jesus and said, "Greetings, Teacher!" and kissed him.

"EVERYONE ELSE MAY STUMBLE IN THEIR FAITH BECAUSE OF YOU, BUT I WILL NOT."

[50]Jesus answered, "Friend, do what you came to do."

Then the people came and grabbed Jesus and arrested him. [51]When that happened, one of Jesus' followers reached for his sword and pulled it out. He struck the servant of the high priest and cut off his ear.

[52]Jesus said to the man, "Put your sword back in its place. All who use swords will be killed with swords. [53]Surely you know I could ask my Father, and he would give me more than twelve armies of angels. [54]But it must happen this way to bring about what the Scriptures say."

[55]Then Jesus said to the crowd, "You came to get me with swords and clubs as if I were a criminal. Every day I sat in the Temple teaching, and you did not arrest me there. [56]But all these things have happened so that it will come about as the prophets wrote." Then all of Jesus' followers left him and ran away.

notes

26:39 cup Jesus is talking about the terrible things that will happen to him. Accepting these things will be very hard, like drinking a cup of something bitter.

ISSUES: Pregnancy

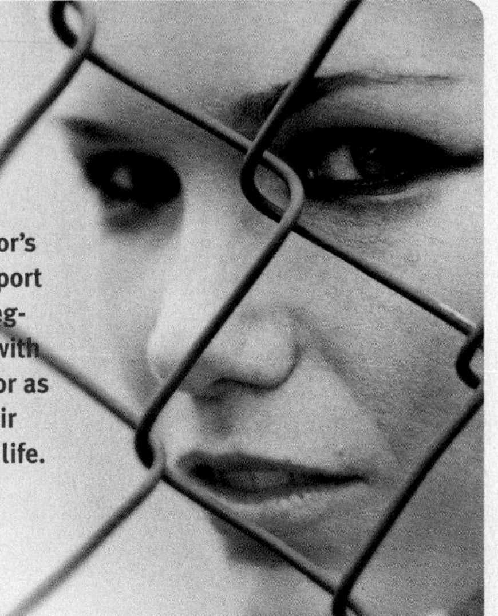

First and foremost, abstinence until marriage is commanded by God and is a liberating lifestyle choice for women. Are you pregnant? Or do you think you might be pregnant? If you have skipped your period, you need to take a pregnancy test either at home (from an over-the-counter test), at your doctor's office, or at a Crisis Pregnancy Support Center or Hope Clinic. If you are pregnant, we highly advise you to talk with a trusted parent, counselor or pastor as soon as possible. You will need their counsel on how to handle this new life.

JESUS BEFORE THE LEADERS

57 Those people who arrested Jesus led him
to the house of Caiaphas, the high priest, where
the teachers of the law and the older leaders
were gathered. 58 Peter followed far behind to
the courtyard of the high priest's house, and he
sat down with the guards to see what
would happen to Jesus.
59 The leading priests and the whole
Jewish council tried to find something
false against Jesus so they could kill him.
60 Many people came and told lies about
him, but the council could find no real
reason to kill him. Then two people came
and said, 61 "This man said, 'I can destroy
the Temple of God and build it again in
three days.' "
62 Then the high priest stood up and
said to Jesus, "Aren't you going to
answer? Don't you have something to
say about their charges against you?"
63 But Jesus said nothing.
Again the high priest said to Jesus, "I command you by the power of the living God: Tell
us if you are the Christ, the Son of God."
64 Jesus answered, "Those are your words.
But I tell you, in the future you will see the Son
of Man sitting at the right hand of God, the
Powerful One, and coming on clouds in the sky."
65 When the high priest heard this, he tore
his clothes and said, "This man has said things
that are against God! We don't need any more
witnesses; you all heard him say these things
against God. 66 What do you think?"

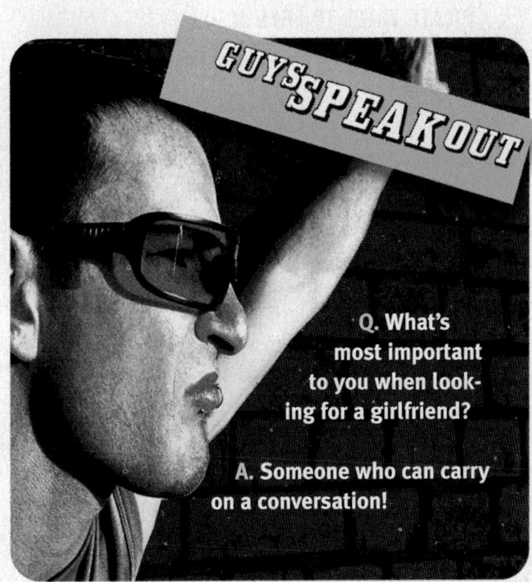

GUYS SPEAK OUT
Q. What's most important to you when looking for a girlfriend?
A. Someone who can carry on a conversation!

The people answered, "He should die."
67 Then the people there spat in Jesus' face
and beat him with their fists. Others slapped
him. 68 They said, "Prove to us that you are a
prophet, you Christ! Tell us who hit you!"

PETER SAYS HE DOESN'T KNOW JESUS

69 At that time, as Peter was sitting in the
courtyard, a servant girl came to him and said,
"You also were with Jesus of Galilee."
70 But Peter said to all the people there that
he was never with Jesus. He said, "I don't know
what you are talking about."
71 When he left the courtyard and was at the
gate, another girl saw him. She said to the
people there, "This man was with Jesus of
Nazareth."
72 Again, Peter said he was never with him,
saying, "I swear I don't know this man Jesus!"
73 A short time later, some people
standing there went to Peter and said,
"Surely you are one of those who followed
Jesus. The way you talk shows it."
74 Then Peter began to place a curse on
himself and swear, "I don't know the
man." At once, a rooster crowed. 75 And
Peter remembered what Jesus had told
him: "Before the rooster crows, you will
say three times that you don't know me."
Then Peter went outside and cried painfully.

JESUS IS TAKEN TO PILATE

27 Early the next morning, all the
leading priests and older leaders of
the people decided that Jesus should die. 2 They
tied him, led him away, and turned him over to
Pilate, the governor.

LEARN IT & LIVE IT

Matthew 25:40:
Learn It: When we do things for those suffering, we are doing them for Jesus.
Live It: Volunteer one afternoon a month to visit a center for juvenile delinquents, a homeless shelter, or a nursing home.

Mark 10:45:
Learn It: The greatest person is the greatest servant.
Live It: Offer to help clean up the kitchen after dinner at home, or clean up after your friends after lunch at school.

Mark 16:16:
Learn It: The one who believes and is baptized will be saved.
Live It: Share your faith with someone who may not know Jesus.

JUDAS KILLS HIMSELF

[3]Judas, the one who had given Jesus to his enemies, saw that they had decided to kill Jesus. Then he was very sorry for what he had done. So he took the thirty silver coins back to the priests and the leaders, [4]saying, "I sinned; I handed over to you an innocent man."

The leaders answered, "What is that to us? That's your problem, not ours."

[5]So Judas threw the money into the Temple. Then he went off and hanged himself.

DIDYA KNOW

50% OF YOUNG ADULTS DESCRIBE THEMSELVES AS DEEPLY SPIRITUAL.

[6]The leading priests picked up the silver coins in the Temple and said, "Our law does not allow us to keep this money with the Temple money, because it has paid for a man's death." [7]So they decided to use the coins to buy Potter's Field as a place to bury strangers who died in Jerusalem. [8]That is why that field is still called the Field of Blood. [9]So what Jeremiah the prophet had said came true: "They took thirty silver coins. That is how little the Israelites thought he was worth. [10]They used those thirty silver coins to buy the potter's field, as the Lord commanded me."[n]

PILATE QUESTIONS JESUS

[11]Jesus stood before Pilate the governor, and Pilate asked him, "Are you the king of the Jews?"

Jesus answered, "Those are your words."

[12]When the leading priests and the older leaders accused Jesus, he said nothing.

[13]So Pilate said to Jesus, "Don't you hear them accusing you of all these things?"

[14]But Jesus said nothing in answer to Pilate, and Pilate was very surprised at this.

PILATE TRIES TO FREE JESUS

[15]Every year at the time of Passover the governor would free one prisoner whom the people chose. [16]At that time there was a man in prison, named Barabbas, who was known to be very bad. [17]When the people gathered at Pilate's house, Pilate said, "Whom do you want me to set free: Barabbas or Jesus who is called the Christ?" [18]Pilate knew that the people turned Jesus in to him because they were jealous.

[19]While Pilate was sitting there on the judge's seat, his wife sent this message to him: "Don't do anything to that man, because he is innocent. Today I had a dream about him, and it troubled me very much."

[20]But the leading priests and older leaders convinced the crowd to ask for Barabbas to be freed and for Jesus to be killed.

[21]Pilate said, "I have Barabbas and Jesus. Which do you want me to set free for you?"

The people answered, "Barabbas."

[22]Pilate asked, "So what should I do with Jesus, the one called the Christ?"

They all answered, "Crucify him!"

[23]Pilate asked, "Why? What wrong has he done?"

But they shouted louder, "Crucify him!"

[24]When Pilate saw that he could do nothing about this and that a riot was starting, he took some water and washed his hands[n] in front of the crowd. Then he said, "I am not guilty of this man's death. You are the ones who are causing it!"

[25]All the people answered, "We and our children will be responsible for his death."

[26]Then he set Barabbas free. But Jesus was beaten with whips and handed over to the soldiers to be crucified.

[27]The governor's soldiers took Jesus into the governor's palace, and they all gathered around him. [28]They took off his clothes and put a red robe on him. [29]Using thorny branches, they made a crown, put it on his head, and put a stick in his right hand. Then the soldiers bowed before Jesus and made fun of him, saying, "Hail, King of the Jews!" [30]They spat on Jesus. Then they took his stick and began to beat him on the head. [31]After they finished, the soldiers took off

notes **27:9-10 "They . . . commanded me."** See Zechariah 11:12-13 and Jeremiah 32:6-9. **27:24 washed his hands** He did this as a sign to show that he wanted no part in what the people did.

the robe and put his own clothes on him again. Then they led him away to be crucified.

JESUS IS CRUCIFIED

[32]As the soldiers were going out of the city with Jesus, they forced a man from Cyrene, named Simon, to carry the cross for Jesus. [33]They all came to the place called Golgotha, which means the Place of the Skull. [34]The soldiers gave Jesus wine mixed with gall[n] to drink. He tasted the wine but refused to drink it. [35]When the soldiers had crucified him, they threw lots to decide who would get his clothes. [36]The soldiers sat there and continued watching him. [37]They put a sign above Jesus' head with a charge against him. It said: THIS IS JESUS, THE KING OF THE JEWS. [38]Two robbers were crucified beside Jesus, one on the right and the other on the left.

[39]People walked by and insulted Jesus and shook their heads, [40]saying, "You said you could destroy the Temple and build it again in three days. So save yourself! Come down from that cross if you are really the Son of God!"

[41]The leading priests, the teachers of the law, and the older Jewish leaders were also making fun of Jesus. [42]They said, "He saved others, but he can't save himself! He says he is the king of Israel! If he is the king, let him come down now from the cross. Then we will believe in him. [43]He trusts in God, so let God save him now, if God really wants him. He himself said, 'I am the Son of God.' " [44]And in the same way, the robbers who were being crucified beside Jesus also insulted him.

JESUS DIES

[45]At noon the whole country became dark, and the darkness lasted for three hours. [46]About three o'clock Jesus cried out in a loud voice, "Eli, Eli, lama sabachthani?" This means, "My God, my God, why have you rejected me?"

[47]Some of the people standing there who heard this said, "He is calling Elijah."

[48]Quickly one of them ran and got a sponge and filled it with vinegar and tied it to a stick and gave it to Jesus to drink. [49]But the others said, "Don't bother him. We want to see if Elijah will come to save him."

[50]But Jesus cried out again in a loud voice and died.

[51]Then the curtain in the Temple[n] was torn into two pieces, from the top to the bottom. Also, the earth shook and rocks broke apart. [52]The graves opened, and many of God's people who had died were raised from the dead. [53]They came out of the graves after Jesus was raised from the dead and went into the holy city, where they appeared to many people.

[54]When the army officer and the soldiers guarding Jesus saw this earthquake and everything else that happened, they were very frightened and said, "He really was the Son of God!"

2 Corinthians 11:2

I am jealous over you with a jealousy that comes from God. I promised to give you to Christ, as your only husband. I want to give you as his pure bride.

[55]Many women who had followed Jesus from Galilee to help him were standing at a distance from the cross, watching. [56]Mary Magdalene, and Mary the mother of James and Joseph, and the mother of James and John were there.

JESUS IS BURIED

[57]That evening a rich man named Joseph, a follower of Jesus from the town of Arimathea, came to Jerusalem. [58]Joseph went to Pilate and asked to have Jesus' body. So Pilate gave orders for the soldiers to give it to Joseph. [59]Then Joseph took the body and wrapped it in a clean linen cloth. [60]He put Jesus' body in a new tomb that he had cut out of a wall of rock, and he rolled a very large stone to block the entrance of the tomb. Then Joseph went away. [61]Mary Magdalene and the other woman named Mary were sitting near the tomb.

THE TOMB OF JESUS IS GUARDED

[62]The next day, the day after Preparation

Matthew 28:19

Notice what this verse is saying. It instructs us to go and make followers—not just converts, but followers in the same way of Jesus' first twelve. We want to do more than just see people give their hearts to the Lord. We want to help them mature and grow in him. Aren't you glad that someone helped you? When you gave your heart to Jesus, God just didn't throw you out and say, "Okay, you're on your own now."

If people are going to be developed, they have to be mentored in the growth of their faith. That's where *we* come in, *showing* them as well as *telling* them how to follow Christ. That's our job—to assist in spreading the Good News, to be totally devoted to God, and to stick to him like glue. We want to see people get saved and stick with it. Let's help our friends develop and grow so they can help others!

notes

27:34 gall Probably a drink of wine mixed with drugs to help a person feel less pain. **27:51 curtain in the Temple** A curtain divided the Most Holy Place from the other part of the Temple. That was the special building in Jerusalem where God commanded the Jewish people to worship him.

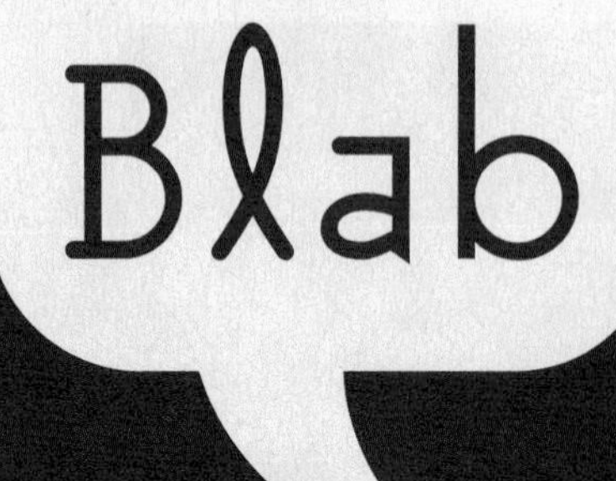

Q. I have this anxiety inside that won't go away. I just want peace and I pray for it, but once I feel like I'm at peace the worry starts up again. Do you have any idea what this may be? I love Jesus, but I feel like I try to be perfect and it makes me worry about the littlest things.

A. Anxiety can be a super hard thing. If you have one particular thing that makes you anxious, visualize it, and then see Jesus there with you. Invite him into the place and let him give you peace. Sometimes anxiety can be caused by a physical condition like hormones or nonactivity. Talk to a nurse or doctor and counselor about your condition too.

Q. I have a friend who says that she is a witch. I'm really worried about her and know she is going against God. Please help. What can I say to her?

A. Your job is to introduce her to Jesus. Invite her to your church so she can hear the truth. God'll take it from there. What she is looking for is the mystery of God that we haven't been able to show her. It is appealing to her craving for spiritual depth and mystery. Pray for her daily, for her salvation, her healing, and her future. God will change her heart.

Q. How modestly do you think people should dress? How do you determine what is modest or not?

A. The big thing to remember is that what you show by how you dress is what guys think of you and about you. The style right now might be "skimpy is best," but you have another code to live by if you are a Christian. Don't tempt guys where they don't need to be tempted. You can still dress totally cute, just cut down on the skin exposure and super-tight clothes.

Day, the leading priests and the Pharisees
went to Pilate. 63They said, "Sir, we remember
that while that liar was still alive he said, 'After
three days I will rise from the dead.' 64So give
the order for the tomb to be guarded closely till
the third day. Otherwise, his followers might
come and steal the body and tell people that he
has risen from the dead. That lie would be even
worse than the first one."
65Pilate said, "Take some soldiers and go
guard the tomb the best way you know." 66So
they all went to the tomb and made it safe from
thieves by sealing the stone in the entrance and
putting soldiers there to guard it.

JESUS RISES FROM THE DEAD

28 The day after the Sabbath day was
the first day of the week. At dawn
on the first day, Mary Magdalene and another
woman named Mary went to look at the tomb.
2At that time there was a strong earthquake.

CHERNOBYL CHILDREN'S PROJECT

The Chernobyl Children's Project is Ireland's leading charity specializing in alleviating the suffering of the victims caused by the world's worst nuclear accident at Chernobyl. Our charity was born as a result of receiving a heartrending message from Belarussian and Ukrainian doctors, which said: SOS Appeal: 'For God's sake, help us to get the children out.' The CCP exists to provide humanitarian support to the victims still living in the stricken regions of Belarus, Western Russia and Northern Ukraine.

The Project saw that the human impact of the Chernobyl disaster had to be dealt with. The Project was anxious not only to apply a healing bandage and has, at a very practical level, devised and implemented fourteen aid programs, each of which is designed to tackle a different consequence of the disaster.

The child victims of Chernobyl offer living proof of the impact of such a technological disaster on human society. Their lives are a testament to its ravages, but they offer hope and inspiration that such a tragedy will not happen anywhere else on this fragile planet.

Get involved by visiting ***www.adiccp.org***.

An angel of the Lord came down from heaven,
went to the tomb, and rolled the stone away
from the entrance. Then he sat on the stone.
[3]He was shining as bright as lightning, and his
clothes were white as snow. [4]The soldiers
guarding the tomb shook with fear because of
the angel, and they became like dead men.
[5]The angel said to the women, "Don't be
afraid. I know that you are looking for Jesus,
who has been crucified. [6]He is not here. He has
risen from the dead as he said he would. Come
and see the place where his body was. [7]And go
quickly and tell his followers, 'Jesus has risen
from the dead. He is going into Galilee ahead
of you, and you will see him there.' " Then
the angel said, "Now I have told you."
[8]The women left the tomb quickly. They
were afraid, but they were also very happy.
They ran to tell Jesus' followers what had
happened. [9]Suddenly, Jesus met them and
said, "Greetings." The women came up to
him, took hold of his feet, and worshiped
him. [10]Then Jesus said to them, "Don't be
afraid. Go and tell my followers to go on to
Galilee, and they will see me there."

"JESUS HAS RISEN FROM THE DEAD. HE IS GOING INTO GALILEE AHEAD OF YOU, AND YOU WILL SEE HIM THERE."

THE SOLDIERS REPORT TO THE LEADERS

[11]While the women went to tell Jesus' followers, some of the soldiers who had been
guarding the tomb went into the city to tell
the leading priests everything that had happened. [12]Then the priests met with the older
leaders and made a plan. They paid the soldiers a large amount of money [13]and said to
them, "Tell the people that Jesus' followers
came during the night and stole the body
while you were asleep. [14]If the governor hears
about this, we will satisfy him and save you
from trouble." [15]So the soldiers kept the money
and did as they were told. And that story is
still spread among the people even today.

JESUS TALKS TO HIS FOLLOWERS

[16]The eleven followers went to Galilee to
the mountain where Jesus had told them to
go. [17]On the mountain they saw Jesus and
worshiped him, but some of them did not
believe it was really Jesus. [18]Then Jesus came
to them and said, "All power in heaven and on
earth is given to me. [19]So go and make followers of all people in the world. Baptize them in
the name of the Father and the Son and the
Holy Spirit. [20]Teach them to obey everything
that I have taught you, and I will be with you
always, even until the end of this age."

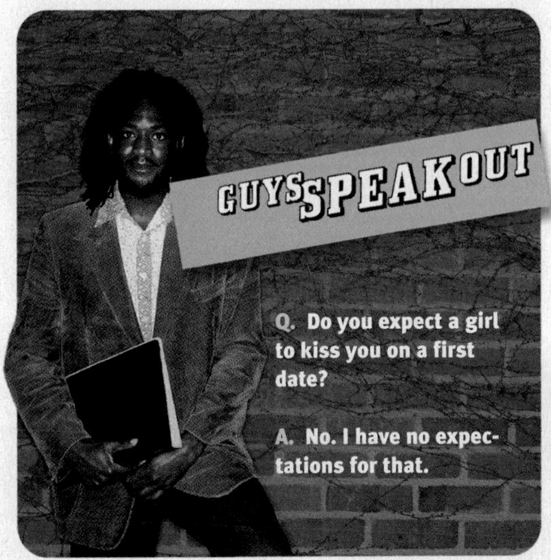

GUYS SPEAK OUT
Q. Do you expect a girl to kiss you on a first date?
A. No. I have no expectations for that.

bible basics

The New Testament is the twenty-seven books that were written after Jesus' life on earth. It talks about how he was born, shows what Jesus taught, describes the beginnings of the early church, and ends with the Book of Revelation, which tells about Christ's future, final triumph over evil.

Mark describes Jesus' service and sacrifice

If you're looking for a great action-packed story about Jesus, you've come to the right place. Here you'll find Jesus moving from place to place . . . healing to healing . . . miracle to miracle. Mark follows along and doesn't miss a beat.

Mark's Gospel is the shortest in the New Testament, but it includes so much information in such a small number of chapters, it feels a lot bigger than it is. And guess what! Mark's Gospel was highly influential in the development of Matthew and Luke. When Matthew and Luke sat down to write their Gospels, they had probably already read Mark. Their books show signs of borrowing from the Book of Mark.

This story makes one thing crystal-clear—Jesus suffered on our behalf. Almost 40 percent of this short book lays out details of the final, traumatic week of Jesus' life. And the earlier part of the book throws the spotlight on the pain Jesus endured from the very beginning of his ministry: confrontation with hostile spiritual forces and human beings intent on humiliating and then killing him. It even describes the suffering and rejection he endured from his family and lifelong friends. Words alone can't accurately convey all that Jesus went through to help us understand how much God loves us. But this action story about his life is an excellent place to begin.

JOHN PREPARES FOR JESUS

1 This is the beginning of the Good News
about Jesus Christ, the Son of God,[n] 2as
the prophet Isaiah wrote:

"I will send my messenger ahead of you,
who will prepare your way." *Malachi 3:1*
3"This is a voice of one
who calls out in the desert:
'Prepare the way for the Lord.
Make the road straight
for him.' " *Isaiah 40:3*

4John was baptizing people in the desert and
preaching a baptism of changed hearts and lives
for the forgiveness of sins. 5All the people from
Judea and Jerusalem were going out to him.
They confessed their sins and were baptized by
him in the Jordan River. 6John wore clothes made
from camel's hair, had a leather belt around his
waist, and ate locusts and wild honey. 7This is
what John preached to the people: "There is one
coming after me who is greater than I; I am not
good enough even to kneel down and untie his
sandals. 8I baptize you with water, but he will
baptize you with the Holy Spirit."

JESUS IS BAPTIZED

9At that time Jesus came from the town of
Nazareth in Galilee and was baptized by John
in the Jordan River. 10Immediately, as Jesus was
coming up out of the water, he saw heaven open.
The Holy Spirit came down on him like a dove,
11and a voice came from heaven: "You are my Son,
whom I love, and I am very pleased with you."

12Then the Spirit sent Jesus into the desert.
13He was in the desert forty days and was
tempted by Satan. He was with the wild animals,
and the angels came and took care of him.

JESUS CHOOSES SOME FOLLOWERS

14After John was put in prison, Jesus went
into Galilee, preaching the Good News from
God. 15He said, "The right time has come. The
kingdom of God is near. Change your hearts
and lives and believe the Good News!"

16When Jesus was walking by Lake Galilee,
he saw Simon[n] and his brother Andrew throwing a net into the lake because they were fishermen. 17Jesus said to them, "Come follow
me, and I will make you fish for people." 18So
Simon and Andrew immediately left their nets
and followed him.

19Going a little farther, Jesus saw two more
brothers, James and John, the sons of Zebedee.
They were in a boat, mending their nets.
20Jesus immediately called them, and they left
their father in the boat with the hired workers
and followed Jesus.

JESUS FORCES OUT AN EVIL SPIRIT

21Jesus and his followers went to Capernaum.
On the Sabbath day He went to the synagogue
and began to teach. 22The people were amazed
at his teaching, because he taught like a person
who had authority, not like their teachers of
the law. 23Just then, a man was there in the

"THE EVIL SPIRIT SHOOK THE MAN VIOLENTLY, GAVE A LOUD CRY, AND THEN CAME OUT OF HIM."

synagogue who had an evil spirit in him. He
shouted, 24"Jesus of Nazareth! What do you
want with us? Did you come to destroy us? I
know who you are—God's Holy One!"

25Jesus commanded the evil spirit, "Be quiet!
Come out of the man!" 26The evil spirit shook
the man violently, gave a loud cry, and then
came out of him.

27The people were so amazed they asked
each other, "What is happening here? This

DIDYA KNOW  **23% OF YOUNG ADULTS DESCRIBE THEMSELVES AS EVANGELICAL CHRISTIAN.**

Mark 1:10-11

Where are you from? In what part of the world were you raised? One of the first things we ask a stranger is, "Where are you from?" Knowing where someone is from tells us a lot about her—why she has an accent, what kind of climate she's used to, which sports teams she might like the most. We can ask questions about favorite foods and whether she knows the one person we know from her city.

The Son of God is from heaven, and there is so much we can know about him because we know where he's from. He comes from the place reserved for the King of kings. He has been there with God the Father and God the Holy Spirit from the very beginning. Heaven is God's home and the place he created for those who know him. To live in heaven is an honor—a gift to those who accept Jesus here on earth.

In heaven, the Lord is continually being praised by angels. There is no sickness or sadness there. We know that Jesus is royal, perfect, and worthy of our praise because he has come from the perfect place of heaven. He has walked among us, but he is not from around here. His righteousness and holiness give him away. He is from heaven.

notes **1:1 the Son of God** Some Greek copies omit these words. **1:16 Simon** Simon's other name was Peter.

Notes

man is teaching something new, and with authority. He even gives commands to evil spirits, and they obey him." [28]And the news about Jesus spread quickly everywhere in the area of Galilee.

JESUS HEALS MANY PEOPLE

[29]As soon as Jesus and his followers left the synagogue, they went with James and John to the home of Simon[n] and Andrew. [30]Simon's mother-in-law was sick in bed with a fever, and the people told Jesus about her. [31]So Jesus went to her bed, took her hand, and helped her up. The fever left her, and she began serving them.

[32]That evening, after the sun went down, the people brought to Jesus all who were sick and had demons in them. [33]The whole town gathered at the door. [34]Jesus healed many who had different kinds of sicknesses, and he forced many demons to leave people. But he would not allow the demons to speak, because they knew who he was.

[35]Early the next morning, while it was still dark, Jesus woke and left the house. He went to a lonely place, where he prayed. [36]Simon and his friends went to look for Jesus. [37]When they found him, they said, "Everyone is looking for you!"

[38]Jesus answered, "We should go to other towns around here so I can preach there too. That is the reason I came." [39]So he went everywhere in Galilee, preaching in the synagogues and forcing out demons.

JESUS HEALS A SICK MAN

[40]A man with a skin disease came to Jesus. He fell to his knees and begged Jesus, "You can heal me if you will."

[41]Jesus felt sorry for the man, so he reached out his hand and touched him and said, "I will. Be healed!" [42]Immediately the disease left the man, and he was healed.

[43]Jesus told the man to go away at once, but he warned him strongly, [44]"Don't tell anyone about this. But go and show yourself to the priest. And offer the gift Moses commanded for people who are made well.[n] This will show the people what I have done." [45]The man left there, but he began to tell everyone that Jesus had healed him, and so he spread the news about Jesus. As a result, Jesus could not enter a town if people saw him. He stayed in places where nobody lived, but people came to him from everywhere.

JESUS HEALS A PARALYZED MAN

2 A few days later, when Jesus came back to Capernaum, the news spread that he was at home. [2]Many people gathered together so that there was no room in the house, not even outside the door. And Jesus was teaching them God's message. [3]Four people came, carrying a paralyzed man. [4]Since they could not get to Jesus because of the crowd, they dug a hole in the roof right above where he was speaking. When they got through, they lowered the mat with the paralyzed man on it. [5]When Jesus saw the faith of these people, he said to the paralyzed man, "Young man, your sins are forgiven."

[6]Some of the teachers of the law were sitting there, thinking to themselves, [7]"Why does this man say things like that? He is speaking as if he were God. Only God can forgive sins."

[8]Jesus knew immediately what these teachers of the law were thinking. So he said to them, "Why are you thinking these things? [9]Which is easier: to tell this paralyzed man, 'Your sins are forgiven,' or to tell him, 'Stand up. Take your mat and walk'? [10]But I will prove to you that the Son of Man has authority on earth to forgive sins." So Jesus said to the paralyzed man, [11]"I tell you, stand up, take your mat, and go home." [12]Immediately the paralyzed man stood up, took his mat, and walked out while everyone was watching him.

The people were amazed and praised God. They said, "We have never seen anything like this!"

[13]Jesus went to the lake again. The whole crowd followed him there, and he taught them.

Mark 1:38

Not too long after Jesus started traveling around telling people about God's kingdom, he visited his hometown. On the Sabbath, he went to the local synagogue, where someone asked him to read from the Scriptures. He read from the Book of Isaiah: "The Lord has put his Spirit in me, because he appointed me to tell the Good News to the poor. He has sent me to tell the captives they are free and to tell the blind that they can see again. God sent me to free those who have been treated unfairly and to announce the time when the Lord will show his kindness." When Jesus finished reading, he said, "While you heard these words just now, they were coming true!" (Luke 4:16-21).

Jesus wanted the people to know that what seemed impossible was possible with God. When matters seemed hopeless, God was able to turn things around.

Jesus knew why he was on earth and put his whole heart into fulfilling the purpose God had given him. What he came to earth to do then in the flesh, his Word and his Spirit continue to do today. Be serious about reading his Word.

WHEN MATTERS SEEMED HOPELESS, GOD WAS ABLE TO TURN THINGS AROUND.

notes

1:29 Simon Simon's other name was Peter. **1:44 Moses . . . well** Read about this in Leviticus 14:1–32.

[14]While he was walking along, he saw a man named Levi son of Alphaeus, sitting in the tax collector's booth. Jesus said to him, "Follow me," and he stood up and followed Jesus.

[15]Later, as Jesus was having dinner at Levi's house, many tax collectors and "sinners" were eating there with Jesus and his followers. Many people like this followed Jesus. [16]When the teachers of the law who were Pharisees saw Jesus eating with the tax collectors and "sinners," they asked his followers, "Why does he eat with tax collectors and sinners?"

"THE MAN HELD OUT HIS HAND AND IT WAS HEALED."

[17]Jesus heard this and said to them, "It is not the healthy people who need a doctor, but the sick. I did not come to invite good people but to invite sinners."

JESUS' FOLLOWERS ARE CRITICIZED

[18]Now the followers of John[n] and the Pharisees often gave up eating for a certain time.[n] Some people came to Jesus and said, "Why do John's followers and the followers of the Pharisees often give up eating, but your followers don't?"

[19]Jesus answered, "The friends of the bridegroom do not give up eating while the bridegroom is still with them. As long as the bridegroom is with them, they cannot give up eating. [20]But the time will come when the bridegroom will be taken from them, and then they will give up eating.

[21]"No one sews a patch of unshrunk cloth over a hole in an old coat. Otherwise, the patch will shrink and pull away—the new patch will pull away from the old coat. Then the hole will be worse. [22]Also, no one ever pours new wine into old leather bags. Otherwise, the new wine will break the bags, and the wine will be ruined along with the bags. But new wine should be put into new leather bags."

JESUS IS LORD OF THE SABBATH

[23]One Sabbath day, as Jesus was walking through some fields of grain, his followers began to pick some grain to eat. [24]The Pharisees said to Jesus, "Why are your followers doing what is not lawful on the Sabbath day?"

[25]Jesus answered, "Have you never read what David did when he and those with him were hungry and needed food? [26]During the time of Abiathar the high priest, David went into God's house and ate the holy bread, which is lawful only for priests to eat. And David also gave some of the bread to those who were with him."

[27]Then Jesus said to the Pharisees, "The Sabbath day was made to help people; they were not made to be ruled by the Sabbath day. [28]So then, the Son of Man is Lord even of the Sabbath day."

JESUS HEALS A MAN'S HAND

3 Another time when Jesus went into a synagogue, a man with a crippled hand was there. [2]Some people watched Jesus closely to see if he would heal the man on the Sabbath day so they could accuse him.

[3]Jesus said to the man with the crippled hand, "Stand up here in the middle of everyone."

[4]Then Jesus asked the people, "Which is lawful on the Sabbath day: to do good or to do evil, to save a life or to kill?" But they said nothing to answer him.

[5]Jesus was angry as he looked at the people, and he felt very sad because they were stubborn. Then he said to the man, "Hold out your hand." The man held out his hand and it was healed. [6]Then the Pharisees left and began making plans with the Herodians[n] about a way to kill Jesus.

MANY PEOPLE FOLLOW JESUS

[7]Jesus left with his followers for the lake, and a large crowd from Galilee followed him. [8]Also many people came from Judea, from Jerusalem, from Idumea, from the lands across the Jordan River, and from the area of Tyre and Sidon. When they heard what Jesus was doing, many people came to him. [9]When Jesus saw the crowds, he told his followers to get a boat ready for him to keep people from crowding against him. [10]He had healed many people, so all the sick were pushing toward him to touch him. [11]When evil spirits saw Jesus, they fell down before him and shouted, "You are the

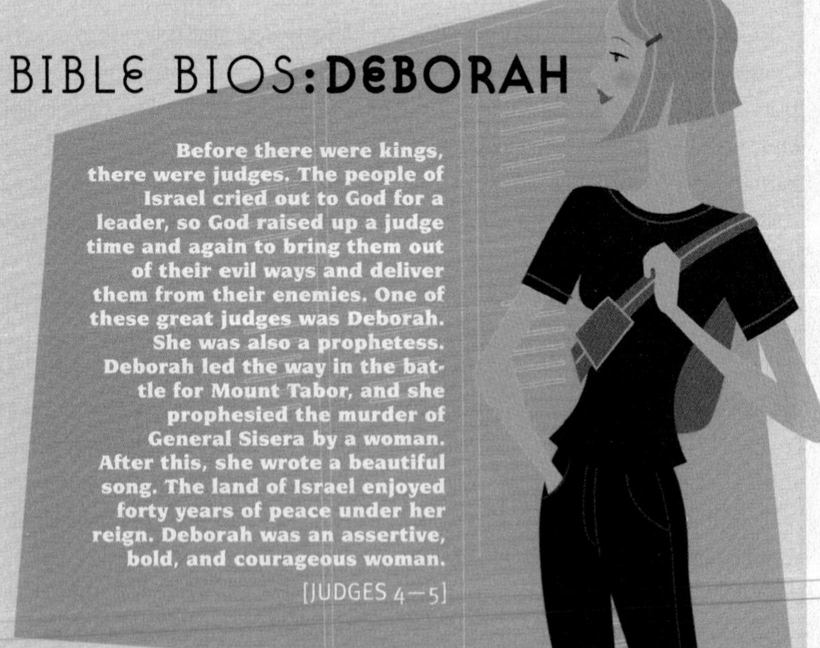
BIBLE BIOS: DEBORAH
Before there were kings, there were judges. The people of Israel cried out to God for a leader, so God raised up a judge time and again to bring them out of their evil ways and deliver them from their enemies. One of these great judges was Deborah. She was also a prophetess. Deborah led the way in the battle for Mount Tabor, and she prophesied the murder of General Sisera by a woman. After this, she wrote a beautiful song. The land of Israel enjoyed forty years of peace under her reign. Deborah was an assertive, bold, and courageous woman.
[JUDGES 4—5]

notes

2:18 John John the Baptist, who preached to the Jewish people about Christ's coming (Mark 1:4–8). **2:18 gave . . . time** This is called "fasting." The people would give up eating for a special time of prayer and worship to God. It was also done to show sadness and disappointment. **3:6 Herodians** A political group that followed Herod and his family.

Son of God!" 12But Jesus strongly warned them not to tell who he was.

JESUS CHOOSES HIS TWELVE APOSTLES

13Then Jesus went up on a mountain and called to him the men he wanted, and they came to him. 14Jesus chose twelve men and called them apostles. He wanted them to be with him, and he wanted to send them out to preach 15and to have the authority to force demons out of people. 16These are the twelve men he chose: Simon (Jesus named him Peter), 17James and John, the sons of Zebedee (Jesus named them Boanerges, which means "Sons of Thunder"), 18Andrew, Philip, Bartholomew, Matthew, Thomas, James the son of Alphaeus, Thaddaeus, Simon the Zealot, 19and Judas Iscariot, who later turned against Jesus.

SOME PEOPLE SAY JESUS HAS A DEVIL

20Then Jesus went home, but again a crowd gathered. There were so many people that Jesus and his followers could not eat. 21When his family heard this, they went to get him because they thought he was out of his mind. 22But the teachers of the law from Jerusalem were saying, "Beelzebul is living inside him! He uses power from the ruler of demons to force demons out of people."

23So Jesus called the people together and taught them with stories. He said, "Satan will not force himself out of people. 24A kingdom that is divided cannot continue, 25and a family that is divided cannot continue. 26And if Satan is against himself and fights against his own people, he cannot continue; that is the end of Satan. 27No one can enter a strong person's house and steal his things unless he first ties up the strong person. Then he can steal things from the house. 28I tell you the truth, all sins that people do and all the things people say against God can be forgiven. 29But anyone who speaks against the Holy Spirit will never be forgiven; he is guilty of a sin that continues forever."

30Jesus said this because the teachers of the law said that he had an evil spirit inside him.

JESUS' TRUE FAMILY

31Then Jesus' mother and brothers arrived. Standing outside, they sent someone in to tell him to come out. 32Many people were sitting around Jesus, and they said to him, "Your mother and brothers are waiting for you outside."

33Jesus asked, "Who are my mother and my brothers?" 34Then he looked at those sitting around him and said, "Here are my mother and my brothers! 35My true brother and sister and mother are those who do what God wants."

A STORY ABOUT PLANTING SEED

4 Again Jesus began teaching by the lake. A great crowd gathered around him, so he sat down in a boat near the shore. All the people stayed on the shore close to the water. 2Jesus taught them many things, using stories. He said, 3"Listen! A farmer went out to plant his seed. 4While he was planting, some seed fell by the road, and the birds came and ate it up. 5Some seed fell on rocky ground where there wasn't much dirt. That seed grew very fast, because the ground was not deep. 6But when the sun rose, the plants dried up because they did not have deep roots. 7Some other seed fell among thorny weeds, which grew and choked the good plants. So those plants did not produce a crop. 8Some other seed fell on good ground and began to grow. It got taller and produced a crop. Some plants made thirty times more, some made sixty times more, and some made a hundred times more."

9Then Jesus said, "You people who can hear me, listen!"

JESUS TELLS WHY HE USED STORIES

10Later, when Jesus was alone, the twelve apostles and others around him asked him about the stories.

11Jesus said, "You can know the secret about the kingdom of God. But to other people I tell everything by using stories 12so that:

'They will look and look,
but they will not learn.

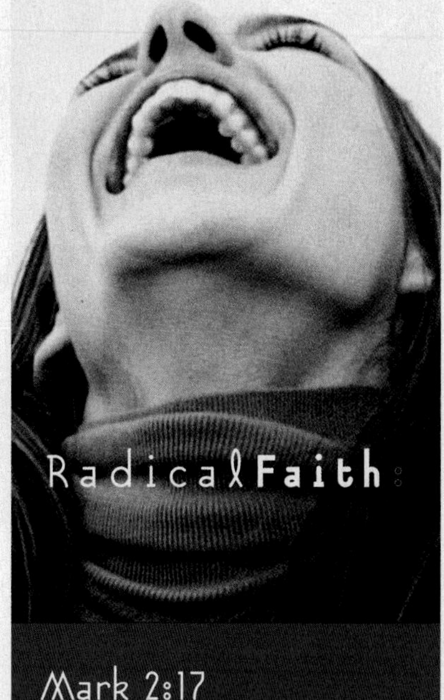

Mark 2:17

The Pharisees didn't understand what Jesus was all about. For one thing, he hung out with people they would have crossed the street to avoid. The Pharisees thought they were way too holy to rub elbows with those people.

What Jesus said to them is like music to your ears if you think you've done such horrible things that God could never love you. He lets you know right off the bat that he's more interested in changing sinners than in recruiting good, religious people to his cause.

But does that mean that Jesus isn't interested in you if you haven't gotten messed up in sex or drugs or haven't broken the law? Not at all. When he said he wasn't inviting "the righteous," he was talking about the attitude in people's hearts. People who consider themselves "righteous" (good), like the Pharisees, don't think they need Jesus. People who know they are sinners—whether their sins are obvious to everyone or the invisible sins of the heart—know they need Jesus. He welcomes them with open arms.

LEARN IT & LIVE IT

Luke 6:44:
Learn It: Every tree is known by its fruit.
Live It: Bear good fruits, the fruits of the Spirit. Take time to be gentle and kind today. Show self-control, joy, and peace to those around you.

Luke 6:49:
Learn It: A good foundation for a house makes the house stand firm.
Live It: Take time to build a foundation of faith. Spend time in prayer and meditation on God's Word today.

Luke 12:2:
Learn It: All secrets will be disclosed at some time or another.
Live It: Have a heart-to-heart with a good friend. Share your deep secrets and find comfort in a trusted friend.

They will listen and listen,
but they will not understand.
If they did learn and understand,
they would come back to me
and be forgiven.' " *Isaiah 6:9-10*

JESUS EXPLAINS THE SEED STORY

13Then Jesus said to his followers, "Don't
you understand this story? If you don't, how
will you understand any story? 14The farmer
is like a person who plants God's message in
people. 15Sometimes the teaching falls on the
road. This is like the people who hear the
teaching of God, but Satan quickly comes and
takes away the teaching that was
planted in them. 16Others are
like the seed planted on rocky
ground. They hear the teaching and quickly accept it
with joy. 17But since they don't
allow the teaching to go deep into
their lives, they keep it only a short time.
When trouble or persecution comes because
of the teaching they accepted, they quickly
give up. 18Others are like the seed planted
among the thorny weeds. They hear the teaching, 19but the worries of this life, the temptation of wealth, and many other evil desires
keep the teaching from growing and producing
fruit[n] in their lives. 20Others are like the seed
planted in the good ground. They hear the
teaching and accept it. Then they grow and produce fruit—sometimes thirty times more,
sometimes sixty times more, and sometimes a
hundred times more."

Song of Solomon 4:9
My sister, my bride,
you have thrilled my heart;
you have thrilled my heart
with a glance of your eyes,
with one sparkle
from your necklace.

USE WHAT YOU HAVE

21Then Jesus said to them, "Do you hide a
lamp under a bowl or under a bed? No! You put
the lamp on a lampstand. 22Everything that is
hidden will be made clear and every secret
thing will be made known. 23You people who
can hear me, listen!

24"Think carefully about what you hear. The
way you give to others is the way God will give
to you, but God will give you even
more. 25Those who have
understanding will be given
more. But those who do not
have understanding,
even what they have will be
taken away from them."

JESUS USES A STORY ABOUT SEED

26Then Jesus said, "The kingdom of God is
like someone who plants seed in the ground.
27Night and day, whether the person is asleep or
awake, the seed still grows, but the person does
not know how it grows. 28By itself the earth produces grain. First the plant grows, then the
head, and then all the grain in the head. 29When
the grain is ready, the farmer cuts it, because
this is the harvest time."

A STORY ABOUT MUSTARD SEED

30Then Jesus said, "How can I show you
what the kingdom of God is like? What story
can I use to explain it? 31The kingdom of God
is like a mustard seed, the smallest seed you
plant in the ground. 32But when planted, this
seed grows and becomes the largest of all garden plants. It produces large branches, and the
wild birds can make nests in its shade."

33Jesus used many stories like these to teach
the crowd God's message—as much as they
could understand. 34He always used stories to
teach them. But when he and his followers
were alone, Jesus explained everything to them.

JESUS CALMS A STORM

35That evening, Jesus said to his followers,
"Let's go across the lake." 36Leaving the crowd
behind, they took him in the boat just as he
was. There were also other boats with them.
37A very strong wind came up on the lake. The
waves came over the sides and into the boat so
that it was already full of water. 38Jesus was at
the back of the boat, sleeping with his head on
a cushion. His followers woke him and said,
"Teacher, don't you care that we are drowning!"

39Jesus stood up and commanded the wind
and said to the waves, "Quiet! Be still!" Then the
wind stopped, and it became completely calm.

40Jesus said to his followers, "Why are you
afraid? Do you still have no faith?"

4:19 producing fruit To produce fruit means to have in your life the good things God wants.

41The followers were very afraid and asked each other, "Who is this? Even the wind and the waves obey him!"

A MAN WITH DEMONS INSIDE HIM

5 Jesus and his followers went to the other side of the lake to the area of the Gerasene people. 2When Jesus got out of the boat, instantly a man with an evil spirit came to him from the burial caves. 3This man lived in the caves, and no one could tie him up, not even with a chain. 4Many times people had used chains to tie the man's hands and feet, but he always broke them off. No one was strong enough to control him. 5Day and night he would wander around the burial caves and on the hills, screaming and cutting himself with stones. 6While Jesus was still far away, the man saw him, ran to him, and fell down before him.

7The man shouted in a loud voice, "What do you want with me, Jesus, Son of the Most High God? I command you in God's name not to torture me!" 8He said this because Jesus was saying to him, "You evil spirit, come out of the man."

9Then Jesus asked him, "What is your name?"

He answered, "My name is Legion,[n] because we are many spirits." 10He begged Jesus again and again not to send them out of that area.

11A large herd of pigs was feeding on a hill near there. 12The demons begged Jesus, "Send us into the pigs; let us go into them." 13So Jesus allowed them to do this. The evil spirits left the man and went into the pigs. Then the herd of pigs—about two thousand of them—rushed down the hill into the lake and were drowned.

14The herdsmen ran away and went to the town and to the countryside, telling everyone about this. So people went out to see what had happened. 15They came to Jesus and saw the man who used to have the many evil spirits, sitting, clothed, and in his right mind. And they were frightened. 16The people who saw this told the others what had happened to the man who had the demons living in him, and they told about the pigs. 17Then the people began to beg Jesus to leave their area.

18As Jesus was getting back into the boat, the man who was freed from the demons begged to go with him.

19But Jesus would not let him. He said, "Go home to your family and tell them how much the Lord has done for you and how he has had mercy on you." 20So the man left and began to tell the people in the Ten Towns[n] about what Jesus had done for him. And everyone was amazed.

JESUS GIVES LIFE TO A DEAD GIRL AND HEALS A SICK WOMAN

21When Jesus went in the boat back to the other side of the lake, a large crowd gathered around him there. 22A leader of the synagogue, named Jairus, came there, saw Jesus, and fell at his feet. 23He begged Jesus, saying again and again, "My daughter is dying. Please come and put your hands on her so she will be healed and will live." 24So Jesus went with him.

A large crowd followed Jesus and pushed very close around him. 25Among them was a woman who had been bleeding for twelve years. 26She had suffered very much from many doctors and had spent all the money she had, but instead of improving, she was getting worse. 27When the woman heard about Jesus, she came up behind him in the crowd and touched his coat. 28She thought, "If I can just touch his clothes, I will be healed." 29Instantly her bleeding stopped, and she felt in her body that she was healed from her disease.

30At once Jesus felt power go out from him. So he turned around in the crowd and asked, "Who touched my clothes?"

31His followers said, "Look at how many people are pushing against you! And you ask, 'Who touched me?' "

32But Jesus continued looking around to see who had touched him. 33The woman, knowing that she was healed, came and fell at Jesus' feet. Shaking with fear, she told him the whole truth. 34Jesus said to her, "Dear woman, you

Mark 3:28

Be encouraged! It doesn't matter what you've done in the past, where you've done it, or who you've done it with. God loves you and wants to forgive you. You may *feel* like you've blown it, and then again, you may *have* blown it. It doesn't matter. Jesus is more than ready to give you a fresh start. He wants you to run to him, not away from him!

Remember when David blew it with Bathsheba? Then he blew it again by having her husband killed. David kept messing up trying to cover his sin. God sent the prophet Nathan to confront him. David's eyes were finally opened, and he repented. God forgave David, and he later was known as the kind of man God wants (Acts 13:22). If David can be forgiven, so can you. But the key is this: David repented. He didn't just apologize. He was truly sorry in his heart. To repent means to turn from sin and go the other direction. Whatever it is that you need to be forgiven for, give it to God right now. Ask for forgiveness: tell him you're sorry, repent, and move on.

Even good people may fall many times, but they will get back up! God is the One who will always forgive, no matter what you've done. He loves you!

"GOD LOVES YOU AND WANTS TO FORGIVE YOU."

notes

5:9 Legion Means very many. A legion was about five thousand men in the Roman army. **5:20 Ten Towns** In Greek, called "Decapolis." It was an area east of Lake Galilee that once had ten main towns.

TOPten
RANDOM WAYS TO HAVE FUN ON A DATE

01 **Make homemade ice cream.**

02 **Go on a double date with your parents.**

03 **Go roller-skating.**

04 **Volunteer at a homeless shelter together.**

05 **Order food from a fancy restaurant and take it on a picnic.**

06 **The classic: dinner and a movie.**

07 **Pick five of your fave games and have a tournament.**

08 **Cook dinner for your friends.**

09 **Take cookies to a nursing home.**

10 **Go for a long walk.**

are made well because you believed. Go in
peace; be healed of your disease."
[35]While Jesus was still speaking, some people came from the house of the synagogue
leader. They said, "Your daughter is dead. There
is no need to bother the teacher anymore."
[36]But Jesus paid no attention to what they
said. He told the synagogue leader, "Don't be
afraid; just believe."
[37]Jesus let only Peter, James, and John the
brother of James go with him. [38]When they
came to the house of the synagogue leader,
Jesus found many people there making lots of
noise and crying loudly. [39]Jesus entered the
house and said to them, "Why are you crying
and making so much noise? The child is not
dead, only asleep." [40]But they laughed at him.
So, after throwing them out of the house, Jesus
took the child's father and mother and his
three followers into the room where the child
was. [41]Taking hold of the girl's hand, he said to
her, "Talitha, koum!" (This means, "Young girl,
I tell you to stand up!") [42]At once the girl stood
right up and began walking. (She was twelve
years old.) Everyone was completely amazed.
[43]Jesus gave them strict orders not to tell people about this. Then he told them to give the
girl something to eat.

JESUS GOES TO HIS HOMETOWN

6 Jesus left there and went to his hometown, and his followers went with him.
[2]On the Sabbath day he taught in the synagogue. Many people heard him and were
amazed, saying, "Where did this man get these
teachings? What is this wisdom that has been
given to him? And where did he get the power
to do miracles? [3]He is just the carpenter, the
son of Mary and the brother of James, Joseph,
Judas, and Simon. And his sisters are here
with us." So the people were upset with Jesus.
[4]Jesus said to them, "A prophet is honored
everywhere except in his hometown and with
his own people and in his own home." [5]So
Jesus was not able to work any miracles there
except to heal a few sick people by putting his
hands on them. [6]He was amazed at how many
people had no faith.
Then Jesus went to other villages in that
area and taught. [7]He called his twelve followers
together and got ready to send them out two
by two and gave them authority over evil spirits. [8]This is what Jesus commanded them:
"Take nothing for your trip except a walking
stick. Take no bread, no bag, and no money in
your pockets. [9]Wear sandals, but take only the
clothes you are wearing. [10]When you enter a
house, stay there until you leave that town. [11]If
the people in a certain place refuse to welcome
you or listen to you, leave that place. Shake its
dust off your feet[n] as a warning to them."
[12]So the followers went out and preached
that people should change their hearts and lives.
[13]They forced many demons out and put olive
oil on many sick people and healed them.

HOW JOHN THE BAPTIST WAS KILLED

[14]King Herod heard about Jesus, because he
was now well known. Some people said, "He is
John the Baptist, who has risen from the dead.
That is why he can work these miracles."
[15]Others said, "He is Elijah."[n]
Other people said, "Jesus is a prophet, like
the prophets who lived long ago."
[16]When Herod heard this, he said, "I killed
John by cutting off his head. Now he has risen
from the dead!"
[17]Herod himself had ordered his soldiers to
arrest John and put him in prison in order to
please his wife, Herodias. She had been the

DIDYA KNOW → **61% OF YOUNG ADULTS SAY THEY ARE FINANCIALLY COMFORTABLE.**

notes

6:11 Shake . . . feet A warning. It showed that they were rejecting these people. **6:15 Elijah** A great prophet who spoke for God and who lived hundreds of years before Christ. See 1 Kings 17.

WHAT KIND OF FRIEND ARE YOU?

YOUR FRIEND CATHERINE BORROWED YOUR FRIEND AMELIA'S FAVORITE BLUE SWEATER WITHOUT ASKING. AMELIA IS ANGRY AND SHE CAME TO TELL YOU ABOUT IT. WHAT DO YOU DO?

A. GO TO CATHERINE AND TRY TO FIX THE PROBLEM YOURSELF.
B. TELL AMELIA, "SHE WAS IN A HURRY, AND SHE DIDN'T MEAN TO MAKE YOU MAD," AND THEN STAY OUT OF IT.
C. TRY TO GET AMELIA AND CATHERINE TOGETHER SO THEY CAN WORK IT OUT.
D. SAY, "WHATEVER! IT'S JUST A SWEATER!"

YOU AND YOUR FRIENDS ARE TRYING TO DECIDE WHERE TO EAT DINNER. EVERYONE IS DISAGREEING. YOU WANT TO GO TO CHING CHONG CHINESE FOOD. WHAT DO YOU SAY?

A. "I THINK WE SHOULD JUST GO TO CHING CHONG."
B. "I REALLY WANT TO GO TO CHING CHONG, BUT WHEREVER WE GO IS FINE."
C. "WELL, LAST WEEK WE WENT TO MCDONALD'S, SO THIS WEEK, LET'S GO TO CHING CHONG."
D. "IT DOESN'T MATTER; WE'LL HAVE FUN GOING ANYWHERE!"

YOU AND YOUR FRIEND KATIE LIKE THE SAME BOY. DO YOU:

A. TAKE HIM. YOU'RE NOT GOING TO GIVE HIM UP WITHOUT A FIGHT.
B. SAY, "GO AHEAD AND HAVE HIM, KATIE." BUT THEN FLIRT WITH HIM LIKE CRAZY.
C. LET HER HAVE HIM IF SHE WANTS HIM SO BADLY, AND GO FIND SOMEONE BETTER.
D. SAY, "LET'S JUST ALL HANG OUT TOGETHER. IF SOMETHING HAPPENS, IT HAPPENS!"

YOUR FRIEND KARI IS VERY UPSET AND WANTS TO TALK TO YOU. YOU'VE BEEN LOOKING FORWARD TO GOING TO THE MALL WITH YOUR FRIEND EMILY. WHAT DO YOU DO?

A. TELL KARI THAT YOU'RE SORRY, BUT YOU ALREADY MADE PLANS AND YOU'LL TALK TO HER LATER.
B. DROP YOUR PLANS WITH EMILY AND TELL KARI TO COME OVER TO TALK.
C. GO TO THE MALL FOR A LITTLE WHILE WITH EMILY, AND THEN GO TALK TO KARI.
D. SAY, "LET'S ALL GO TO THE MALL!"

SOME BOYS ARE TEASING YOUR FRIEND BETH BECAUSE SHE GOT A BAD HAIRCUT. WHAT DO YOU SAY?

A. "GUYS, BE QUIET. SHE LOOKS FINE."
B. "BETH, I THINK YOU LOOK BEAUTIFUL."
C. "BETH, THEY'RE JUST BEING GUYS. AND, GUYS, PLEASE TRY TO BE MORE SENSITIVE!"
D. "THEY'RE JUST BEING FUNNY, BETH! DON'T LET IT HURT YOUR FEELINGS."

NOW ADD UP YOUR A's, B's, C's, AND D's.

IF YOU PICKED MOSTLY A's, YOU ARE A LEADER FRIEND.

You are independent, strong, and assertive. Your friends know exactly what you think all the time, and you aren't afraid to make your opinions known to everyone. You are good at making decisions, moving the group along, and your friends probably look to you for help when they need to get something done. You can be overbearing and insensitive at times, so try to work on being a caring and encouraging listener to your friends.

IF YOU PICKED MOSTLY B's, YOU ARE A SUPPORTIVE FRIEND.

Your friends love coming to you when they need support. You are compassionate and kind, and you genuinely love spending quality time with your friends. You hate fights, you want the approval of others, and you want everyone to get along. However, you're not a pushover deep down inside. One of the reasons you can be so supportive is because you are so strong!

IF YOU PICKED MOSTLY C's, YOU ARE A PEACE-KEEPING FRIEND.

You are a diplomat, a negotiator, and you keep your friends on their toes. You love to take care of your friends by making sure everything is running smoothly in your friendships. Sometimes you are more of a leader, and sometimes you are more of a follower, whatever the situation calls for. Your friends look to you to keep things steady and controlled.

IF YOU PICKED MOSTLY D's, YOU ARE A FUN-LOVING FRIEND.

People love having you around because you are all about having fun, all the time. You are always up for a good time, and you think all your friends should be too. You tend to believe that the best way to be a friend is to have fun together. You are the life of the party! But don't forget that sometimes a good friend needs to take the time to slow down and just listen.

Blab

Q. I go to public school and am made fun of because of my looks and beliefs. I am a Christian. I know God says to "stick up for your beliefs" but sometimes it's tough. Am I alone?

A. You aren't alone in feeling like this. In fact, for centuries believers have gone through pain for their faith and had to figure out the same stuff you are. God wants to use this time as an opportunity to draw you closer to him and to grow you into an amazing person. Get excited from the challenges God has for you. And let them grow you to completeness. You are very special.

Q. My best friend died a couple of months back. She was only eighteen and not a Christian. I'm still struggling with it and am drifting further and further from God. Help!

A. You are going through the grieving process. It's normal to be mad when someone you love dies. You need to talk to a grief counselor to help you through this time. God is your refuge and strength. He is there for you to run to, and he provides other people to be his arms around you. He will lift you up and provide you with comfort.

Q. A member of my family recently molested me. I am very confused. I think it's my fault. I need all the help I can get.

A. It is not your fault. Please find someone to tell. You need to talk to a counselor or pastor. Cling to God and he will see you through. Don't despise your life, because this episode does not define you. The first steps in dealing with this are forgiveness. Let Jesus show you how to forgive him and yourself. If you've been molested, you should call your pastor or local police office to talk about it right away.

wife of Philip, Herod's brother, but then Herod had married her. [18]John had been telling Herod, "It is not lawful for you to be married to your brother's wife." [19]So Herodias hated John and wanted to kill him. But she couldn't, [20]because Herod was afraid of John and protected him. He knew John was a good and holy man. Also, though John's preaching always bothered him, he enjoyed listening to John.

[21]Then the perfect time came for Herodias to cause John's death. On Herod's birthday, he gave a dinner party for the most important government leaders, the commanders of his army, and the most important people in Galilee. [22]When the daughter of Herodias came in and danced, she pleased Herod and the people eating with him.

So King Herod said to the girl, "Ask me for anything you want, and I will give it to you." [23]He promised her, "Anything you ask for I will give to you—up to half of my kingdom."

"THE APOSTLES GATHERED AROUND JESUS AND TOLD HIM ABOUT ALL THE THINGS THEY HAD DONE AND TAUGHT."

[24]The girl went to her mother and asked, "What should I ask for?"

Her mother answered, "Ask for the head of John the Baptist."

[25]At once the girl went back to the king and said to him, "I want the head of John the Baptist right now on a platter."

[26]Although the king was very sad, he had made a promise, and his dinner guests had heard it. So he did not want to refuse what she asked. [27]Immediately the king sent a soldier to bring John's head. The soldier went and cut off John's head in the prison [28]and brought it back on a platter. He gave it to the girl, and the girl gave it to her mother. [29]When John's followers heard this, they came and got John's body and put it in a tomb.

MORE THAN FIVE THOUSAND FED

[30]The apostles gathered around Jesus and told him about all the things they had done and taught. [31]Crowds of people were coming and going so that Jesus and his followers did not even have time to eat. He said to them, "Come away by yourselves, and we will go to a lonely place to get some rest."

[32]So they went in a boat by themselves to a lonely place. [33]But many people saw them leave and recognized them. So from all the towns they ran to the place where Jesus was going, and they got there before him. [34]When he arrived, he saw a great crowd waiting. He felt sorry for them, because they were like sheep without a shepherd. So he began to teach them many things.

Song of Solomon 8:7
Even much water cannot put out the flame of love; floods cannot drown love. If a man offered everything in his house for love, people would totally reject it.

[35]When it was late in the day, his followers came to him and said, "No one lives in this place, and it is already very late. [36]Send the people away so they can go to the countryside and towns around here to buy themselves something to eat."

[37]But Jesus answered, "You give them something to eat."

They said to him, "We would all have to work a month to earn enough money to buy that much bread!"

[38]Jesus asked them, "How many loaves of bread do you have? Go and see."

When they found out, they said, "Five loaves and two fish."

[39]Then Jesus told his followers to have the people sit in groups on the green grass. [40]So they sat in groups of fifty or a hundred. [41]Jesus took the five loaves and two fish and, looking up to heaven, he thanked God for the food. He divided the bread and gave it to his followers for them to give to the people. Then he divided the

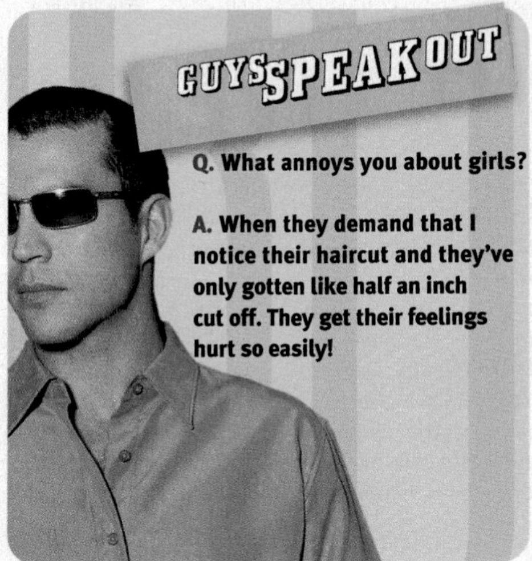

two fish among them all. [42]All the people ate and were satisfied. [43]The followers filled twelve baskets with the leftover pieces of bread and fish. [44]There were five thousand men who ate.

JESUS WALKS ON THE WATER

[45]Immediately Jesus told his followers to get into the boat and go ahead of him to Bethsaida across the lake. He stayed there to send the people home. [46]After sending them away, he went into the hills to pray.

[47]That night, the boat was in the middle of the lake, and Jesus was alone on the land. [48]He saw his followers struggling hard to row the boat, because the wind was blowing against them. Between three and six o'clock in the morning, Jesus came to them, walking on the water, and he wanted to walk past the boat. [49]But when they saw him walking on the water, they thought he was a ghost and cried out. [50]They all saw him and were afraid. But quickly Jesus spoke to them and said, "Have courage! It is I. Do not be afraid." [51]Then he got into the boat with them, and the wind became calm. The followers were greatly amazed. [52]They did not understand about the miracle of the five loaves, because their minds were closed.

[53]When they had crossed the lake, they came to shore at Gennesaret and tied the boat there. [54]When they got out of the boat, people immediately recognized Jesus. [55]They ran everywhere in that area and began to bring sick people on mats wherever they heard he was. [56]And everywhere he went—into towns, cities, or countryside—the people brought the sick to the marketplaces. They begged him to let them touch just the edge of his coat, and all who touched it were healed.

OBEY GOD'S LAW

7 When some Pharisees and some teachers of the law came from Jerusalem, they gathered around Jesus. [2]They saw that some of Jesus' followers ate food with hands that were not clean, that is, they hadn't washed them. [3](The Pharisees and all the Jews never eat before washing their hands in a special way according to their unwritten laws. [4]And when they buy something in the market, they never eat it until they wash themselves in a special way. They also follow many other unwritten laws, such as the washing of cups, pitchers, and pots.)

[5]The Pharisees and the teachers of the law said to Jesus, "Why don't your followers obey the unwritten laws which have been handed down to us? Why do your followers eat their food with hands that are not clean?"

[6]Jesus answered, "Isaiah was right when he spoke about you hypocrites. He wrote,

'These people show honor to me
with words,
but their hearts are far from me.
[7]Their worship of me is worthless.
The things they teach are nothing but
human rules.' *Isaiah 29:13*

[8]You have stopped following the commands of God, and you follow only human teachings."

[9]Then Jesus said to them, "You cleverly ignore the commands of God so you can follow your own teachings. [10]Moses said, 'Honor your father and your mother,'[n] and 'Anyone who says cruel things to his father or mother must be put to death.'[n] [11]But you say a person can tell his father or mother, 'I have something I could use to help you, but it is Corban—a gift to God.' [12]You no longer let that person use that money for his father or his mother. [13]By your own rules, which you teach people, you are rejecting what God said. And you do many things like that."

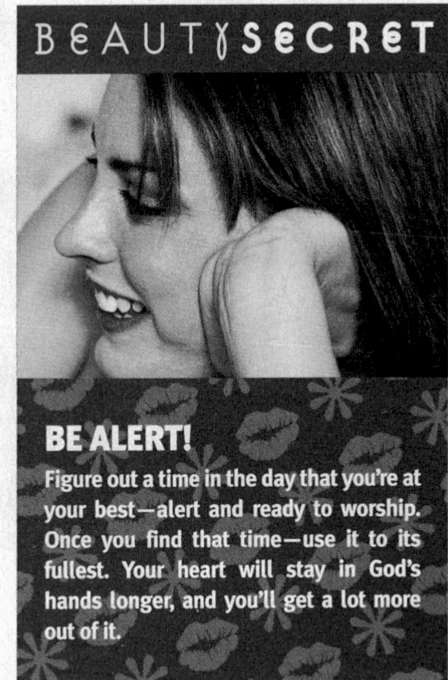

BE ALERT!

Figure out a time in the day that you're at your best—alert and ready to worship. Once you find that time—use it to its fullest. Your heart will stay in God's hands longer, and you'll get a lot more out of it.

[14]After Jesus called the crowd to him again, he said, "Every person should listen to me and understand what I am saying. [15]There is nothing people put into their bodies that makes them unclean. People are made unclean by the things that come out of them." [16n]

[17]When Jesus left the people and went into the house, his followers asked him about this story. [18]Jesus said, "Do you still not understand? Surely you know that nothing that enters someone from the outside can make that person unclean. [19]It does not go into the mind, but into the stomach. Then it goes out of the body." (When Jesus said this, he meant that no longer was any food unclean for people to eat.)

[20]And Jesus said, "The things that come out of people are the things that make them unclean. [21]All these evil things begin inside people, in the mind: evil thoughts, sexual

notes

7:10 'Honor . . . mother' Quotation from Exodus 20:12; Deuteronomy 5:16. **7:10 'Anyone . . . death.'** Quotation from Exodus 21:17.
7:16 Verse 16 Some Greek copies add verse 16: "You people who can hear me, listen!"

LEARN IT & LIVE IT

Luke 12:31:
Learn It: God will take care of you.
Live It: Relax. Don't worry about next week's exam, your prom dress, or your next meal. Trust in the Lord, and he will provide.

Luke 12:34:
Learn It: "Your heart will be where your treasure is."
Live It: Set your mind on heavenly things, not earthly things. Store up treasures in heaven. Value not the things of this world, but the things in the world to come.

Luke 12:48:
Learn It: From everyone who has been given much, much will be demanded.
Live It: Ask yourself what has been given to you. Talents? Money? Brains? Beauty? Use what the Lord has given you according to his good will.

sins, stealing, murder, adultery, 22greed, evil
actions, lying, doing sinful things, jealousy,
speaking evil of others, pride, and foolish living. 23All these evil things come from inside
and make people unclean."

JESUS HELPS A NON-JEWISH WOMAN

24Jesus left that place and went to the area
around Tyre. When he went into a house, he
did not want anyone to know he was there, but
he could not stay hidden. 25A woman whose
daughter had an evil spirit in her heard that he
was there. So she quickly came to Jesus and fell
at his feet. 26She was Greek, born in Phoenicia,
in Syria. She begged Jesus to force the demon
out of her daughter.

27Jesus told the woman, "It is not right to
take the children's bread and give it to the
dogs. First let the children eat all they want."

28But she answered, "Yes, Lord, but even
the dogs under the table can eat the children's
crumbs."

29Then Jesus said, "Because of your answer,
you may go. The demon has left your daughter."

30The woman went home and found her
daughter lying in bed; the demon was gone.

JESUS HEALS A DEAF MAN

31Then Jesus left the area around Tyre and
went through Sidon to Lake Galilee, to the area
of the Ten Towns.[n] 32While he was there, some
people brought a man to him who was deaf
and could not talk plainly. The people begged
Jesus to put his hand on the man to heal him.

33Jesus led the man away from the crowd, by
himself. He put his fingers in the man's ears and
then spit and touched the man's tongue.
34Looking up to heaven, he sighed and said to
the man, "Ephphatha!" (This means, "Be opened.")
35Instantly the man was able to hear and to use
his tongue so that he spoke clearly.

36Jesus commanded the people not to tell
anyone about what happened. But the more he
commanded them, the more they told about it.
37They were completely amazed and said,
"Jesus does everything well. He makes the
deaf hear! And those who can't talk he makes
able to speak."

MORE THAN FOUR THOUSAND PEOPLE FED

8 Another time there was a great crowd
with Jesus that had nothing to eat. So
Jesus called his followers and said, 2"I feel sorry
for these people, because they have already
been with me for three days, and they have
nothing to eat. 3If I send them home hungry,
they will faint on the way. Some of them live a
long way from here."

4Jesus' followers answered, "How can we get
enough bread to feed all these people? We are
far away from any town."

MORE THAN TWICE AS MANY YOUNG ADULTS AS SENIORS INDICATE THAT THEY ARE STRESSED OUT (35% TO 15%, RESPECTIVELY).

RELATIONSHIPS

"In the same way, husbands should love their wives as they love their own bodies" (Ephesians 5:28). Does your guy expect *you* to always jump up and get him a fresh Coke when you're watching the football game with friends? Does he think it's your job to make the popcorn? What about cleaning up around the house—for girls? If he's taking the opportunity to be lazy and is expecting you to do all the work, remember this verse. He's not supposed to be asking you to do things he wouldn't do himself. If he doesn't respect you, end the relationship before it becomes dangerous; he's not husband material.

7:31 Ten Towns In Greek, called "Decapolis." It was an area east of Lake Galilee that once had ten main towns.

[5]Jesus asked, "How many loaves of bread do you have?"

They answered, "Seven."

[6]Jesus told the people to sit on the ground. Then he took the seven loaves, gave thanks to God, and divided the bread. He gave the pieces to his followers to give to the people, and they did so. [7]The followers also had a few small fish. After Jesus gave thanks for the fish, he told his followers to give them to the people also. [8]All the people ate and were satisfied. Then his followers filled seven baskets with the leftover pieces of food. [9]There were about four thousand people who ate. After they had eaten, Jesus sent them home. [10]Then right away he got into a boat with his followers and went to the area of Dalmanutha.

THE LEADERS ASK FOR A MIRACLE

[11]The Pharisees came to Jesus and began to ask him questions. Hoping to trap him, they asked Jesus for a miracle from God. [12]Jesus sighed deeply and said, "Why do you people ask for a miracle as a sign? I tell you the truth, no sign will be given to you." [13]Then Jesus left the Pharisees and went in the boat to the other side of the lake.

GUARD AGAINST WRONG TEACHINGS

[14]His followers had only one loaf of bread with them in the boat; they had forgotten to bring more. [15]Jesus warned them, "Be careful! Beware of the yeast of the Pharisees and the yeast of Herod."

[16]His followers discussed the meaning of this, saying, "He said this because we have no bread."

[17]Knowing what they were talking about, Jesus asked them, "Why are you talking about not having bread? Do you still not see or understand? Are your minds closed? [18]You have eyes, but you don't really see. You have ears, but you don't really listen. Remember when [19]I divided five loaves of bread for the five thousand? How many baskets did you fill with leftover pieces of food?"

They answered, "Twelve."

[20]"And when I divided seven loaves of bread for the four thousand, how many baskets did you fill with leftover pieces of food?"

They answered, "Seven."

[21]Then Jesus said to them, "Don't you understand yet?"

JESUS HEALS A BLIND MAN

[22]Jesus and his followers came to Bethsaida. There some people brought a blind man to Jesus and begged him to touch the man. [23]So Jesus took the blind man's hand and led him out of the village. Then he spit on the man's eyes and put his hands on the man and asked, "Can you see now?"

[24]The man looked up and said, "Yes, I see people, but they look like trees walking around."

[25]Again Jesus put his hands on the man's eyes. Then the man opened his eyes wide and they were healed, and he was able to see everything clearly. [26]Jesus told him to go home, saying, "Don't go into the town."

PETER SAYS JESUS IS THE CHRIST

[27]Jesus and his followers went to the towns around Caesarea Philippi. While they were traveling, Jesus asked them, "Who do people say I am?"

[28]They answered, "Some say you are John the Baptist. Others say you are Elijah,[n] and others say you are one of the prophets."

[29]Then Jesus asked, "But who do you say I am?"

Peter answered, "You are the Christ."

[30]Jesus warned his followers not to tell anyone who he was.

[31]Then Jesus began to teach them that the Son of Man must suffer many things and that he would be rejected by the older Jewish leaders, the leading priests, and the teachers of the law. He told them that the Son of Man

Isaiah 62:5
As a young man marries a woman, so your children will marry your land. As a man rejoices over his new wife, so your God will rejoice over you.

Blab

Q. What about replacement curse words? My church and my parents don't believe in saying "Gosh, darn, or dang." Is that wrong?

A. There is no list of cuss words in the Bible. God wants us to talk nicely to one another, to say stuff that builds people up, not tears them down. But for you, your rules are clear. Your parents lay them out. So if they think they're wrong, you have to stop using them.

Q. How much makeup should a tweener be allowed to wear?

A. Why do you want to wear makeup? This will determine how much you should wear. What do your parents think? This is where you have to start. They make the rules about this kind of stuff and you are called to honor them. So talk to them about it and then decide powder or no powder.

Q. I know that gossiping is wrong, but when I'm with my friends it just seems like what we do. Can I just hang out with them without actually participating in the gossip?

A. No, you can't hang out and just listen. Gossiping takes two people. The talker and the listener. If you are the listener you are a part of the gossip. Gossip hurts the people you are talking about. Don't take part. It will be totally hard, but you have to walk away.

8:28 Elijah A man who spoke for God and who lived hundreds of years before Christ. See 1 Kings 17.

Mark 8:29

When Jesus was born, the Jews were living under the Roman government. They hated it. They had to pay ridiculously high taxes. They had no rights because they weren't Roman citizens.

Israel's prophets had said that a Messiah, God's Chosen One, would come to set the people free. Most of the Jews believed that the Messiah would appear in power and glory, maybe even raise a large army, and overthrow the Roman government that had Israel under its thumb. The Messiah would establish God's kingdom—an independent Jewish nation—on earth.

Jesus didn't exactly fit the bill. He came to set them free—from their sins, their sicknesses, and the oppression of their real enemy (Satan) rather than from the Romans. He never spoke against the Roman government and even suggested that God wanted them to pay taxes to Caesar.

But Peter recognized that Jesus was the Chosen One, even though he may not have understood (yet) that the kingdom Jesus had come to establish was not a political regime, but a kingdom of the heart and of the spirit.

Jesus is the Messiah. Let him be the King of your whole life.

must be killed and then rise from the dead
after three days. 32Jesus told them plainly
what would happen. Then Peter took Jesus
aside and began to tell him not to talk like that.
33But Jesus turned and looked at his followers.
Then he told Peter not to talk that way. He

"SO THE FOLLOWERS OBEYED JESUS, BUT THEY DISCUSSED WHAT HE MEANT ABOUT RISING FROM THE DEAD."

said, "Go away from me, Satan![n] You don't
care about the things of God, but only about
things people think are important."
34Then Jesus called the crowd to him, along
with his followers. He said, "If people want to
follow me, they must give up the things they
want. They must be willing even to give up
their lives to follow me. 35Those who want to
save their lives will give up true life. But those
who give up their lives for me and for the
Good News will have true life. 36It is worth
nothing for them to have the whole world if
they lose their souls. 37They could never pay
enough to buy back their souls. 38The people
who live now are living in a sinful and evil
time. If people are ashamed of me and my
teaching, the Son of Man will be ashamed of
them when he comes with his Father's glory
and with the holy angels."
9 Then Jesus said to the people, "I tell you
the truth, some people standing here will
see the kingdom of God come with power
before they die."

JESUS TALKS WITH MOSES AND ELIJAH

2Six days later, Jesus took Peter, James, and
John up on a high mountain by themselves.
While they watched, Jesus' appearance was
changed. 3His clothes became shining white,
whiter than any person could make them.
4Then Elijah and Moses[n] appeared to them,
talking with Jesus.
5Peter said to Jesus, "Teacher, it is good that
we are here. Let us make three tents—one for
you, one for Moses, and one for Elijah." 6Peter
did not know what to say, because he and the
others were so frightened.
7Then a cloud came and covered them, and
a voice came from the cloud, saying, "This is
my Son, whom I love. Listen to him!"
8Suddenly Peter, James, and John looked
around, but they saw only Jesus there alone with
them.
9As they were coming down the mountain,
Jesus commanded them not to tell anyone
about what they had seen until the Son of Man
had risen from the dead.
10So the followers obeyed Jesus, but they
discussed what he meant about rising from
the dead.
11Then they asked Jesus, "Why do the teachers of the law say that Elijah must come first?"
12Jesus answered, "They are right to say
that Elijah must come first and make everything the way it should be. But why does the
Scripture say that the Son of Man will suffer
much and that people will treat him as if he
were nothing? 13I tell you that Elijah has
already come. And people did to him whatever
they wanted to do, just as the Scriptures said it
would happen."

JESUS HEALS A SICK BOY

14When Jesus, Peter, James, and John came
back to the other followers, they saw a great
crowd around them and the teachers of the law
arguing with them. 15But as soon as the crowd
saw Jesus, the people were surprised and ran
to welcome him.

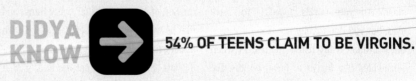

DIDYA KNOW

54% OF TEENS CLAIM TO BE VIRGINS.

8:33 Satan Name for the devil meaning "the enemy." Jesus means that Peter was talking like Satan. **9:4 Elijah and Moses** Two of the most important Jewish leaders in the past. God had given Moses the Law, and Elijah was an important prophet.

16Jesus asked, "What are you arguing about?"
17A man answered, "Teacher, I brought my
son to you. He has an evil spirit in him that stops
him from talking. 18When the spirit
attacks him, it throws him on
the ground. Then my son
foams at the mouth, grinds
his teeth, and becomes very
stiff. I asked your followers
to force the evil spirit out, but they
couldn't."
19Jesus answered, "You people have no faith.
How long must I stay with you? How long
must I put up with you? Bring the boy to me."
20So the followers brought him to Jesus. As
soon as the evil spirit saw Jesus, it made the
boy lose control of himself, and he fell down
and rolled on the ground, foaming at the mouth.
21Jesus asked the boy's father, "How long
has this been happening?"
The father answered, "Since he was very
young. 22The spirit often throws him into a fire
or into water to kill him. If you can do anything
for him, please have pity on us and
help us."
23Jesus said to the father, "You
said, 'If you can!' All things are
possible for the one who
believes."
24Immediately the father cried
out, "I do believe! Help me to believe
more!"
25When Jesus saw that a crowd was quickly
gathering, he ordered the evil spirit, saying, "You
spirit that makes people unable to hear or
speak, I command you to come out of this boy
and never enter him again!"
26The evil spirit screamed and caused the
boy to fall on the ground again. Then the spirit
came out. The boy looked as if he were dead,
and many people said, "He is dead!" 27But Jesus
took hold of the boy's hand and helped him to
stand up.
28When Jesus went into the house, his followers began asking him privately, "Why couldn't
we force that evil spirit out?"
29Jesus answered, "That kind of spirit can
only be forced out by prayer."

Song of Solomon 1:15
My darling, you are beautiful! Oh, you are beautiful, and your eyes are like doves.

JESUS TALKS ABOUT HIS DEATH

30Then Jesus and his followers left that
place and went through Galilee. He didn't
want anyone to know where he was, 31because
he was teaching his followers. He said to them,
"The Son of Man will be handed over to people, and they will kill him. After three days, he
will rise from the dead." 32But the followers
did not understand what Jesus meant, and
they were afraid to ask him.

WHO IS THE GREATEST?

33Jesus and his followers went to Capernaum. When they went into a house there, he
asked them, "What were you arguing about on
the road?" 34But the followers did not answer,
because their argument on the road was about
which one of them was the greatest.
35Jesus sat down and called the twelve apostles to him. He said, "Whoever wants to be the
most important must be last of all and servant
of all."
36Then Jesus took a small child and had him
stand among them. Taking the child in his
arms, he said, 37"Whoever accepts a child like
this in my name accepts me. And whoever
accepts me accepts the One who sent me."

ANYONE NOT AGAINST US IS FOR US

38Then John said, "Teacher, we saw someone
using your name to force demons out of a person. We told him to stop, because he does not
belong to our group."
39But Jesus said, "Don't stop him, because
anyone who uses my name to do powerful
things will not easily say evil things about me.
40Whoever is not against us is with us. 41I tell
you the truth, whoever gives you a drink of

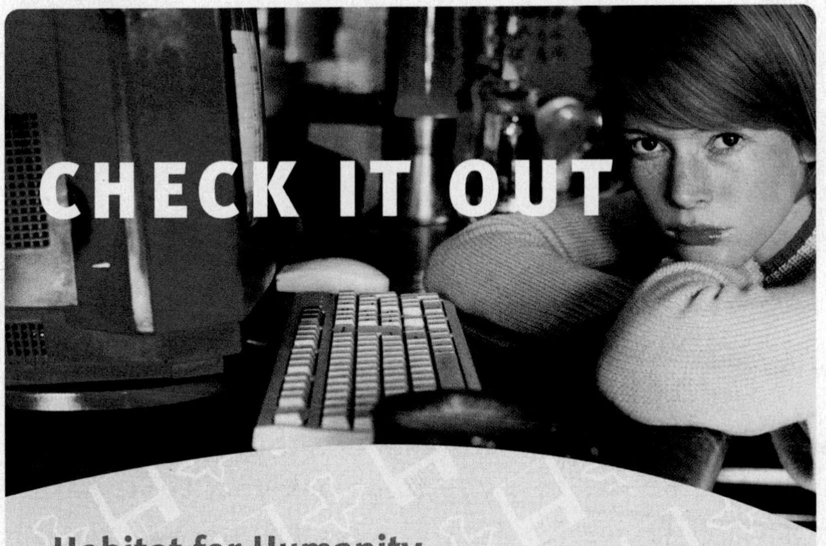

Habitat for Humanity

Habitat for Humanity International is a nonprofit, nondenominational Christian housing organization. We welcome all people to join us as we build simple, decent, affordable houses in partnership with those in need of adequate shelter.

Since 1976, Habitat has built more than 125,000 houses in more than 80 countries, including some 45,000 houses across the United States.

To get involved, go to www.habitat.org.

Mark 9:7

Jesus and God the Father are one. Think about that for a moment. When you see Jesus ministering to the poor, touching the brokenhearted, healing the sick, he is fulfilling the heart of the Father. Just like earthly sons sometimes work for their dads, Jesus works for his Father too.

You have God living on the inside of you—the God who created this earth; the God who made every person who has ever lived on earth; the God who rules the whole universe. When you received Jesus, you received life!

Because of the price that Jesus paid for you on the cross, and because you have received him as your Lord, you have become God's very own child. Wow! Get this now—God is your Father. And the exciting thing is we inherit his characteristics and some of his mannerisms—love, joy, and peace, to name a few (see Galatians 5:22-23).

It's amazing—the more we hang around God, the more of his ways we will pick up! When we look at people from God's perspective, we see them in a completely different light! God has given us a great heritage. We are his children. Remember: "Like Father, like son (daughter)!"

water because you belong to the Christ will
truly get his reward.
42"If one of these little children believes in
me, and someone causes that child to sin, it
would be better for that person to have a large
stone tied around his neck and be drowned in
the sea. 43If your hand causes you to sin, cut it
off. It is better for you to lose part of your body
and live forever than to have two hands and go
to hell, where the fire never goes out. 44[n] 45If
your foot causes you to sin, cut it off. It is better for you to lose part of your body and to live
forever than to have two feet and be thrown
into hell. 46[n] 47If your eye causes you to sin, take
it out. It is better for you to enter the kingdom
of God with only one eye than to have two
eyes and be thrown into hell. 48In hell the
worm does not die; the fire is never put out.
49Every person will be salted with fire.
50"Salt is good, but if the salt loses its salty
taste, you cannot make it salty again. So, be
full of salt, and have peace with each other."

JESUS TEACHES ABOUT DIVORCE

10 Then Jesus left that place and went
into the area of Judea and across
the Jordan River. Again, crowds came to him,
and he taught them as he usually did.
2Some Pharisees came to Jesus and tried to
trick him. They asked, "Is it right for a man to
divorce his wife?"
3Jesus answered, "What did Moses command you to do?"
4They said, "Moses allowed a man to write
out divorce papers and send her away."[n]

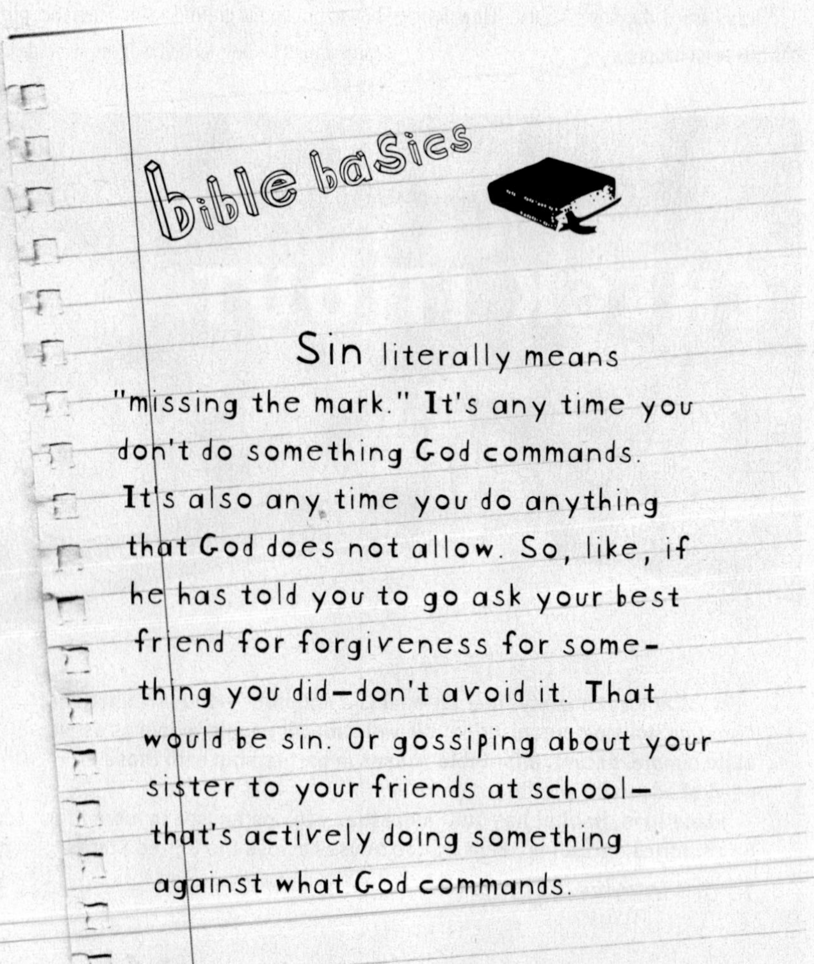

bible basics
Sin literally means "missing the mark." It's any time you don't do something God commands. It's also any time you do anything that God does not allow. So, like, if he has told you to go ask your best friend for forgiveness for something you did—don't avoid it. That would be sin. Or gossiping about your sister to your friends at school—that's actively doing something against what God commands.

9:44 Verse 44 Some Greek copies of Mark add verse 44, which is the same as verse 48. **9:46 Verse 46** Some Greek copies of Mark add verse 46, which is the same as verse 48. **10:4 "Moses . . . away."** Quotation from Deuteronomy 24:1.

5Jesus said, "Moses wrote that command for you because you were stubborn. 6But when God made the world, 'he made them male and female.'[n] 7'So a man will leave his father and mother and be united with his wife, 8and the two will become one body.'[n] So there are not two, but one. 9God has joined the two together, so no one should separate them."

10Later, in the house, his followers asked Jesus again about the question of divorce. 11He answered, "Anyone who divorces his wife and marries another woman is guilty of adultery against her. 12And the woman who divorces her husband and marries another man is also guilty of adultery."

JESUS ACCEPTS CHILDREN

13Some people brought their little children to Jesus so he could touch them, but his followers told them to stop. 14When Jesus saw this, he was upset and said to them, "Let the little children come to me. Don't stop them, because the kingdom of God belongs to

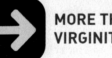

DIDYA KNOW

MORE THAN 50% OF TEEN GIRLS WHO HAVE HAD SEX LOST THEIR VIRGINITY WHEN THEY WERE 15 OR 16 YEARS OLD.

people who are like these children. 15I tell you the truth, you must accept the kingdom of God as if you were a little child, or you will never enter it." 16Then Jesus took the children in his arms, put his hands on them, and blessed them.

A RICH YOUNG MAN'S QUESTION

17As Jesus started to leave, a man ran to him and fell on his knees before Jesus. The man asked, "Good teacher, what must I do to have life forever?"

18Jesus answered, "Why do you call me good? Only God is good. 19You know the commands: 'You must not murder anyone. You must not be guilty of adultery. You must not steal. You must not tell lies about your neighbor. You must not cheat. Honor your father and mother.' "[n]

20The man said, "Teacher, I have obeyed all these things since I was a boy."

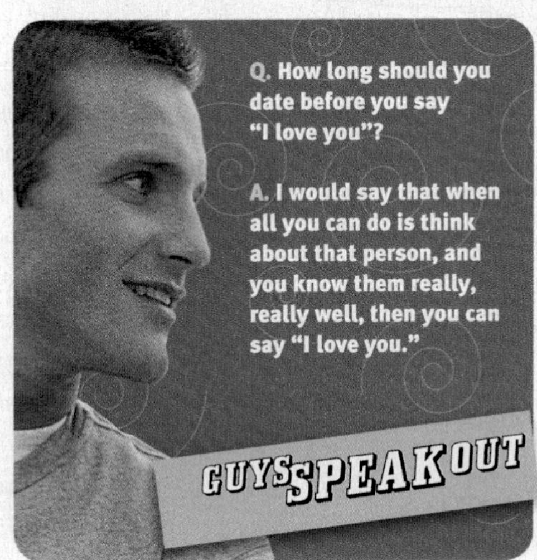

Q. How long should you date before you say "I love you"?
A. I would say that when all you can do is think about that person, and you know them really, really well, then you can say "I love you."
GUYS SPEAK OUT

21Jesus, looking at the man, loved him and said, "There is one more thing you need to do. Go and sell everything you have, and give the money to the poor, and you will have treasure in heaven. Then come and follow me."

22He was very sad to hear Jesus say this, and he left sorrowfully, because he was rich.

23Then Jesus looked at his followers and

"AS JESUS STARTED TO LEAVE, A MAN RAN TO HIM AND FELL ON HIS KNEES BEFORE JESUS."

said, "How hard it will be for the rich to enter the kingdom of God!"

24The followers were amazed at what Jesus said. But he said again, "My children, it is very hard to enter the kingdom of God! 25It is easier for a camel to go through the eye of a needle than for a rich person to enter the kingdom of God."

26The followers were even more surprised and said to each other, "Then who can be saved?"

27Jesus looked at them and said, "This is something people cannot do, but God can. God can do all things."

28Peter said to Jesus, "Look, we have left everything and followed you."

29Jesus said, "I tell you the truth, all those who have left houses, brothers, sisters, mother, father, children, or farms for me and for the Good News 30will get more than they left. Here in this world they will have a hundred times more homes, brothers, sisters, mothers, children, and fields. And with those things, they will also suffer for their belief. But in the age that is coming they will have life forever. 31Many who have the highest place now will have the lowest place in the future. And many who have the lowest place now will have the highest place in the future."

JESUS TALKS ABOUT HIS DEATH

32As Jesus and the people with him were on the road to Jerusalem, he was leading the way. His followers were amazed, but others in the crowd who followed were afraid. Again Jesus took the twelve apostles aside and began to tell them what was about to happen in Jerusalem. 33He said, "Look, we are going to Jerusalem. The Son of Man will be turned over to the leading priests and the teachers of the law. They will say that he must die, and they will turn him over to the non-Jewish people, 34who will laugh at him and spit on him. They will beat him with whips and crucify him. But on the third day, he will rise to life again."

10:6 'he made . . . female.' Quotation from Genesis 1:27. **10:7-8 'So . . . body.'** Quotation from Genesis 2:24. **10:19 'You . . . mother.'** Quotation from Exodus 20:12–16; Deuteronomy 5:16–20.

notes

BIBLE BIOS: DELILAH

Delilah was a cunning and manipulative woman. Samson, a Nazirite, had seemingly supernatural powers. He could kill a lion with his bare hands and break through ropes with amazing strength. The Philistines were curious about this power. How could he do this? Delilah, on behalf of her people, deceptively lured the secret out of Samson: If he cut his hair, his strength would be diminished. One night when Samson was asleep, Delilah told the Philistines Samson's secret in exchange for money, and they came and cut off all Samson's hair. Samson was imprisoned, and years later when he gained his strength back, he brought revenge on the Philistines by pushing the supports out from underneath the porch of a huge party—killing himself and all those there. Delilah manipulated others to their destruction and was not considered an honorable woman. [JUDGES 16]

TWO FOLLOWERS ASK JESUS A FAVOR

35 Then James and John, sons of
Zebedee, came to Jesus and said,
"Teacher, we want to ask you to
do something for us."
36 Jesus asked, "What do
you want me to do for you?"
37 They answered, "Let one of us
sit at your right side and one of us sit at
your left side in your glory in your kingdom."
38 Jesus said, "You don't understand what
you are asking. Can you drink the cup that I
must drink? And can you be bap-
tized with the same kind of
baptism that I must go
through?"[n]
39 They answered, "Yes,
we can."
Jesus said to them, "You will
drink the same cup that I will drink, and
you will be baptized with the same baptism
that I must go through. 40 But I cannot choose
who will sit at my right or my left; those
places belong to those for whom they have
been prepared."
41 When the other ten followers heard this,
they began to be angry with James and John.
42 Jesus called them together and said, "The
other nations have rulers. You know that those
rulers love to show their power over the people,
and their important leaders love to use all their
authority. 43 But it should not be that way among
you. Whoever wants to become great among you
must serve the rest of you like a servant. 44 Whoever wants to become the first among you must
serve all of you like a slave. 45 In the same way, the
Son of Man did not come to be served. He came
to serve others and to give his life as a ransom for
many people."

Song of Solomon 4:7
My darling, everything about you is beautiful, and there is nothing at all wrong with you.

JESUS HEALS A BLIND MAN

46 Then they came to the town of Jericho. As
Jesus was leaving there with his followers
and a great many people, a blind beggar named
Bartimaeus son of Timaeus was sitting by the
road. 47 When he heard that Jesus from Nazareth
was walking by, he began to shout, "Jesus, Son
of David, have mercy on me!"
48 Many people warned the blind man to be
quiet, but he shouted even more, "Son of David,
have mercy on me!"
49 Jesus stopped and said, "Tell the man to
come here."

LEARN IT & LIVE IT

Luke 15:31:
Learn It: All that God has is yours.
Live It: Celebrate tonight the fact that you are a child of God, and you will always be his child.

Luke 18:14:
Learn It: "All who make themselves humble will be made great."
Live It: Eat lunch today with somebody who might typically eat alone, who might not be considered "cool." Humble yourself and know that we are all important in the eyes of God.

John 3:16:
Learn It: All who believe in Jesus will have eternal life.
Live It: If God loved you so much as to give you his Son, what can you give to God? Think of something you can give in return: worship, service, love.

notes

10:38 Can you . . . through? Jesus was asking if they could suffer the same terrible things that would happen to him.

[62]Jesus answered, "I am. And in the future
you will see the Son of Man sitting at the right
hand of God, the Powerful One, and coming
on clouds in the sky."

[63]When the high priest heard this, he tore
his clothes and said, "We don't need any more
witnesses! [64]You all heard him say these
things against God. What do you think?"

They all said that Jesus was guilty and should
die. [65]Some of the people there began to spit at
Jesus. They blindfolded him and beat him with
their fists and said, "Prove you are a prophet!"
Then the guards led Jesus away and beat him.

PETER SAYS HE DOESN'T KNOW JESUS

[66]While Peter was in the courtyard, a servant girl of the high priest came there. [67]She
saw Peter warming himself at the fire and
looked closely at him.

Then she said, "You also were with Jesus,
that man from Nazareth."

[68]But Peter said that he was never with
Jesus. He said, "I don't know or understand
what you are talking about." Then Peter left
and went toward the entrance of the courtyard. And the rooster crowed.[n]

[69]The servant girl saw Peter there, and again
she said to the people who were standing
nearby, "This man is one of those who followed
Jesus." [70]Again Peter said that it was not true.

A short time later, some people were standing
near Peter saying, "Surely you are one of those
who followed Jesus, because you are from
Galilee, too."

[71]Then Peter began to place a curse on himself and swear, "I don't know this man you're
talking about!"

[72]At once, the rooster crowed the second time.
Then Peter remembered what Jesus had told
him: "Before the rooster crows twice, you will
say three times that you don't know me." Then
Peter lost control of himself and began to cry.

PILATE QUESTIONS JESUS

15 Very early in the morning, the leading priests, the older leaders, the
teachers of the law, and all the Jewish council
decided what to do with Jesus. They tied him,
led him away, and turned him over to Pilate,
the governor.

[2]Pilate asked Jesus, "Are you the king of the
Jews?"

Jesus answered, "Those are your words."

[3]The leading priests accused Jesus of many
things. [4]So Pilate asked Jesus another question, "You can see that they are accusing you
of many things. Aren't you going to answer?"

[5]But Jesus still said nothing, so Pilate was
very surprised.

PILATE TRIES TO FREE JESUS

[6]Every year at the time of the Passover the
governor would free one prisoner whom the
people chose. [7]At that time, there was a man
named Barabbas in prison who was a rebel and
had committed murder during a riot. [8]The
crowd came to Pilate and began to ask him to
free a prisoner as he always did.

[9]So Pilate asked them, "Do you want me to
free the king of the Jews?" [10]Pilate knew that
the leading priests had turned Jesus in to him
because they were jealous. [11]But the leading
priests had persuaded the people to ask Pilate
to free Barabbas, not Jesus.

[12]Then Pilate asked the crowd again, "So
what should I do with this man you call the
king of the Jews?"

[13]They shouted, "Crucify him!"

[14]Pilate asked, "Why? What wrong has he
done?"

But they shouted even louder, "Crucify him!"

[15]Pilate wanted to please the crowd, so he
freed Barabbas for them. After having Jesus
beaten with whips, he handed Jesus over to the
soldiers to be crucified.

[16]The soldiers took Jesus into the governor's
palace (called the Praetorium) and called all the
other soldiers together. [17]They put a purple robe
on Jesus and used thorny branches to make a
crown for his head. [18]They began to call out to
him, "Hail, King of the Jews!" [19]The soldiers beat

Blab

Q. I have a question about dating. If I'm going out with a guy, is it bad to make out with him? In other words, is making out a sin?

A. That's a really good question. There is no place in the Bible where it says "making out is a sin." But there are places where you can go to read that you shouldn't let there be even a hint of sexual immorality. Making out is a really dangerous thing. So your best bet is to avoid heavy make-out sessions 'til you are married. It will be so much better then and you won't have to feel any guilt.

Q. I have a question. When you're in a big fight with a friend—what do you do? You want to be mad, but you don't want to upset God. So, what do you do?

A. "A friend loves you all the time, and a brother helps in time of trouble" (Proverbs 17:17). No matter how mad you are at a friend, you have to love them. Live by faith, not feeling. If your friend won't work things out, you have done what God called you to do.

Q. Does the Bible say anything about dating?

A. The Bible does not talk about dating. In fact, it's kind of a new concept. Parents chose your husband or wife for you back then. Nowadays people are a lot more concerned about the emotions related to dating, rather than the choice to love someone. They're both important; you just need to have both.

14:68 And . . . crowed. A few, early Greek copies leave out this phrase.

notes

Jesus on the head many times with a stick. They spit on him and made fun of him by bowing on their knees and worshiping him. 20After they finished, the soldiers took off the purple robe and put his own clothes on him again. Then they led him out of the palace to be crucified.

JESUS IS CRUCIFIED

21A man named Simon from Cyrene, the father of Alexander and Rufus, was coming from the fields to the city. The soldiers forced Simon to carry the cross for Jesus. 22They led Jesus to the place called Golgotha, which means the Place of the Skull. 23The soldiers tried to give Jesus wine mixed with myrrh to drink, but he refused. 24The soldiers crucified Jesus and divided his clothes among themselves, throwing lots to decide what each soldier would get.

25It was nine o'clock in the morning when they crucified Jesus. 26There was a sign with this charge against Jesus written on it: THE KING OF THE JEWS. 27They also put two robbers on crosses beside Jesus, one on the right, and the other on the left. 28[n] 29People walked by and insulted Jesus and shook their heads, saying, "You said you could destroy the Temple and build it again in three days. 30So save yourself! Come down from that cross!"

31The leading priests and the teachers of the law were also making fun of Jesus. They said to each other, "He saved other people, but he can't save himself. 32If he is really the Christ, the king of Israel, let him come down now from the cross. When we see this, we will believe in him." The robbers who were being crucified beside Jesus also insulted him.

JESUS DIES

33At noon the whole country became dark, and the darkness lasted for three hours. 34At three o'clock Jesus cried in a loud voice, "Eloi, Eloi, lama sabachthani." This means, "My God, my God, why have you rejected me?"

35When some of the people standing there heard this, they said, "Listen! He is calling Elijah."

36Someone there ran and got a sponge, filled it with vinegar, tied it to a stick, and gave it to Jesus to drink. He said, "We want to see if Elijah will come to take him down from the cross."

37Then Jesus cried in a loud voice and died.

38The curtain in the Temple[n] was torn into two pieces, from the top to the bottom. 39When the army officer who was standing in front of the cross saw what happened when Jesus died, he said, "This man really was the Son of God!"

40Some women were standing at a distance from the cross, watching; among them were Mary Magdalene, Salome, and Mary the mother of James and Joseph. (James was her youngest son.) 41These women had followed Jesus in Galilee and helped him. Many other women were also there who had come with Jesus to Jerusalem.

JESUS IS BURIED

42This was Preparation Day. (That means the day before the Sabbath day.) That evening, 43Joseph from Arimathea was brave enough to go to Pilate and ask for Jesus' body. Joseph, an important member of the Jewish council, was one of the people who was waiting for the kingdom of God to come. 44Pilate was amazed that Jesus would have already died, so he called the army officer who had guarded Jesus and asked him if Jesus had already died. 45The officer told Pilate that he was dead, so Pilate told Joseph he could have the body. 46Joseph bought some linen cloth, took the body down from the cross, and wrapped it in the linen. He put the body in a tomb that was cut out of a wall of rock. Then he rolled a very large stone

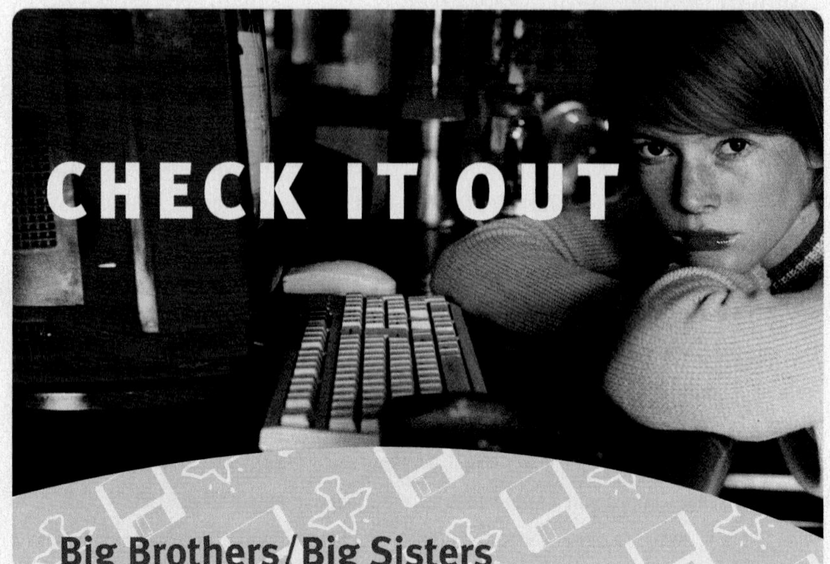

Big Brothers/Big Sisters

Big Brothers/Big Sisters has been the nation's preeminent youth-service organization for nearly a century. We have a proven success in creating and nurturing relationships between adults and children.

Our service is based on our volunteers. Big Brothers and Big Sisters are, foremost, friends to children: They share everyday activities, expand horizons, and experience the joy in even the simplest events. Within those little moments lies the big magic that a Big Brother or Big Sister brings to the life of a young person. Today, Big Brothers/Big Sisters serves hundreds of thousands of children in 5,000 communities across the country.

Nobody else is doing the work that Big Brothers/Big Sisters does in exactly the way we do it. That is why America counts on Big Brothers/Big Sisters.

Get involved by visiting www.bbbsa.org.

15:28 Verse 28 Some Greek copies add verse 28: "And the Scripture came true that says, 'They put him with criminals.'" **15:38 curtain in the Temple** A curtain divided the Most Holy Place from the other part of the Temple. That was the special building in Jerusalem where God commanded the Jewish people to worship him.

Salvation is what all humans need in order to live eternally with God. In the Book of Romans it says that all people have sinned and don't come anywhere close to being as good as God. But when Jesus died on the cross, he took the sinners' places. When we accept Jesus, God forgives all of our faults and sees us as if we had never sinned. That means that when God now looks at a Christian, he sees Jesus. That's how Christians are allowed into heaven.

to block the entrance of the tomb. [47]And Mary Magdalene and Mary the mother of Joseph saw the place where Jesus was laid.

JESUS RISES FROM THE DEAD

16 The day after the Sabbath day, Mary Magdalene, Mary the mother of James, and Salome bought some sweet-smelling spices to put on Jesus' body. [2]Very early on that day, the first day of the week, soon after sunrise, the women were on their way to the tomb. [3]They said to each other, "Who will roll away for us the stone that covers the entrance of the tomb?"

[4]Then the women looked and saw that the stone had already been rolled away, even though it was very large. [5]The women entered the tomb and saw a young man wearing a white robe and sitting on the right side, and they were afraid.

[6]But the man said, "Don't be afraid. You are looking for Jesus from Nazareth, who has been crucified. He has risen from the dead; he is not here. Look, here is the place they laid him. [7]Now go and tell his followers and Peter, 'Jesus is going into Galilee ahead of you, and you will see him there as he told you before.' "

[8]The women were confused and shaking with fear, so they left the tomb and ran away. They did not tell anyone about what happened, because they were afraid.

Verses 9-20 are not included in two of the best and oldest Greek manuscripts of Mark.

SOME FOLLOWERS SEE JESUS

[[9]After Jesus rose from the dead early on the first day of the week, he showed himself first to Mary Magdalene. One time in the past, he had forced seven demons out of her. [10]After Mary saw Jesus, she went and told his followers, who were very sad and were crying. [11]But Mary told them that Jesus was alive. She said that she had seen him, but the followers did not believe her.

[12]Later, Jesus showed himself to two of his followers while they were walking in the country, but he did not look the same as before. [13]These followers went back to the others and told them what had happened, but again, the followers did not believe them.

JESUS TALKS TO THE APOSTLES

[14]Later Jesus showed himself to the eleven apostles while they were eating, and he criticized them because they had no faith. They were stubborn and refused to believe those who had seen him after he had risen from the dead.

[15]Jesus said to his followers, "Go everywhere in the world, and tell the Good News to everyone. [16]Anyone who believes and is baptized will be saved, but anyone who does not believe will be punished. [17]And those who believe will be able to do these things as proof: They will use my name to force out demons. They will speak in new languages.[n] [18]They will pick up snakes and drink poison without being hurt. They will touch the sick, and the sick will be healed."

[19]After the Lord Jesus said these things to his followers, he was carried up into heaven, and he sat at the right side of God. [20]The followers went everywhere in the world and told the Good News to people, and the Lord helped them. The Lord proved that the Good News they told was true by giving them power to work miracles.]

16:17 languages This can also be translated "tongues."

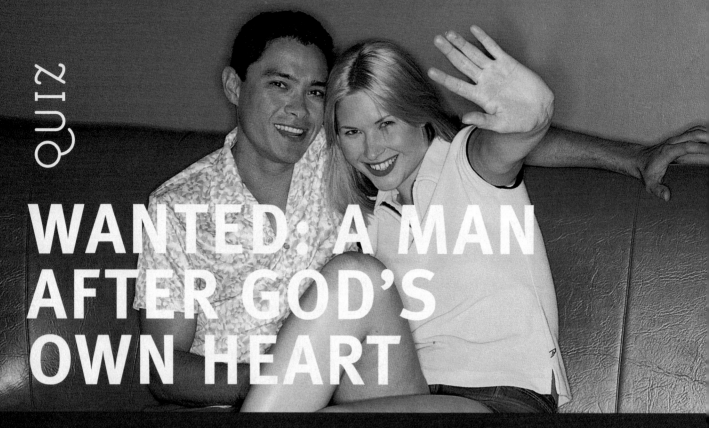

QUIZ

WANTED: A MAN AFTER GOD'S OWN HEART

IS YOUR BOYFRIEND A GODLY MAN-IN-TRAINING?

IT'S LUNCH PERIOD AT SCHOOL. YOUR BOYFRIEND WOULD MOST LIKELY BE FOUND:

A. BULLYING THE CLASS NERD INTO "SHARING" HIS DESSERT.
B. STARTING A FOOD FIGHT.
C. LAUGHING AT A TABLE WITH HIS FRIENDS.
D. SITTING WITH THE LONELY NEW KID.

YOUR SCHOOL HAS AN ALL-STATE BASKETBALL TEAM, AND YOUR BOYFRIEND IS THE POINT GUARD. DURING A CRUCIAL GAME AGAINST YOUR ARCH-RIVALS, THE REFEREE CALLS A FOUL ON YOUR BOYFRIEND. WHAT DOES YOUR BOYFRIEND DO?

A. YELLS AT THE REFEREE, CALLS HIM NAMES, AND EVENTUALLY GETS THROWN OUT OF THE GAME.
B. MARCHES ANGRILY BACK TO THE BENCH AND THROWS HIS TOWEL DOWN IN DISGUST, MUTTERING THINGS UNDER HIS BREATH.
C. LOOKS GLOOMY, BUT RECOVERS AND PLAYS HIS BEST FOR THE REST OF THE GAME.
D. KEEPS ENCOURAGING HIS TEAMMATES TO HAVE GOOD ATTITUDES AND PLAY HARD.

HE'S RUNNING OUT THE DOOR TO GO TO THE MALL WHEN HIS LITTLE SISTER ASKS HIM TO HAVE A TEA PARTY WITH HER.

A. HE TELLS HER THAT HE CAN'T BELIEVE SHE ASKED HIM SUCH A STUPID QUESTION AND THAT HE WOULDN'T BE CAUGHT DEAD HAVING A TEA PARTY WITH HIS BABY SISTER.
B. HE PRETENDS LIKE HE DIDN'T HEAR HER AND RUNS OUT THE DOOR BEFORE SHE CAN SAY ANYTHING ELSE.
C. HE TELLS HER THAT HE'D LOVE TO, AND HE'LL DO IT AS SOON AS HE GETS BACK.
D. HE SITS DOWN RIGHT THEN AND HAS A TEA PARTY WITH HER BEFORE LEAVING.

SOME OF YOUR FRIENDS ARE GOING TO SEE A MOVIE THAT YOU'RE NOT ALLOWED TO SEE. YOU AND YOUR BOYFRIEND WERE BOTH PLANNING TO GO, BUT YOU DON'T WANT TO DISOBEY YOUR PARENTS, SO YOU'RE THINKING ABOUT NOT GOING. WHAT DOES YOUR BOYFRIEND SAY?

A. "AW, COME ON. IT'S NOT LIKE IT'S A REALLY BAD MOVIE, AND YOUR PARENTS WON'T EVER FIND OUT ANYWAY. I DON'T KNOW IF I WANT TO GO OUT WITH YOU IF WE CAN'T EVER HAVE FUN."
B. "YOU'RE OVERREACTING. PLEASE COME. DON'T YOU WANT TO BE WITH ME?"
C. "I THINK YOU'RE RIGHT FOR OBEYING YOUR PARENTS. I'LL MISS YOU, BUT I UNDERSTAND."
D. "I ADMIRE YOU FOR DOING THE RIGHT THING. AND, YOU KNOW, I THINK YOUR PARENTS ARE PROBABLY RIGHT. LET'S GO GET ICE CREAM TOGETHER, INSTEAD."

YOUR BOYFRIEND IS FAMOUS AROUND SCHOOL FOR:

A. THE TIME HE VANDALIZED THE PRINCIPAL'S CAR WITH EGGS AND SHOE POLISH.
B. HIS EGO.
C. HIS KINDNESS TO EVERYONE, ESPECIALLY THE NEW KIDS AND THE PEOPLE WHO DON'T SEEM TO FIT IN.
D. THE BIBLE STUDY HE LEADS ON FRIDAY MORNINGS BEFORE SCHOOL.

IF YOU PICKED MOSTLY A's, RUN AWAY!

This boy is no good for you. Your answers indicate that he is unkind, selfish, rude, irresponsible . . . we could go on. It's time you let him go. You should spend your time with friends who will encourage you and build you up.

IF YOU PICKED MOSTLY B's, WE'RE ASKING, WHERE'S THE FRUIT?

We don't see much fruit of the Spirit in this guy. He doesn't seem to be seeking the Lord. Chances are, he's not a very good influence on you, either. Consider waiting until he shows some spiritual growth before you have a serious relationship with him.

IF YOU PICKED MOSTLY C's, YOU'VE GOT A GOOD GUY.

This boy sounds like he's truly working on being a follower of God. He has many good qualities! He is probably still learning a lot about what it means to follow God, but who isn't still learning, right? Encourage him and pray for him.

IF YOU PICKED MOSTLY D's, YOU'VE GOT A GODLY MAN-IN-TRAINING!

Wow! Where did this guy come from? We'd like to know! He is a great guy who loves the Lord and obeys him. His life shows the fruit of the Spirit, and that means God is working in him! Congratulations on having such good taste!

Notes

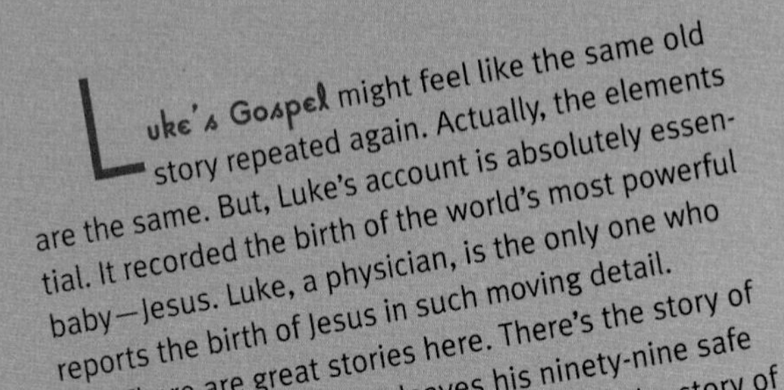

Luke PROCLAIMS WHO JESUS OF NAZARETH WAS

Luke's Gospel might feel like the same old story repeated again. Actually, the elements are the same. But, Luke's account is absolutely essential. It recorded the birth of the world's most powerful baby—Jesus. Luke, a physician, is the only one who reports the birth of Jesus in such moving detail.

There are great stories here. There's the story of the loving shepherd who leaves his ninety-nine safe sheep to look for the one lost sheep. And the story of the prodigal son, squandering his share of the family wealth, then returning home to the open arms of a loving father. And the story of the good Samaritan, a half-breed who shows compassion to an injured man after blue-blooded Jews, supposed men of God, walk on by. In fact, there are fourteen of these stories that are found only in Luke. Oh, yeah . . . there are also six miracles and ten leper healings. Yep . . . lots of stories here. And, all of them point us to Jesus . . . the most powerful baby ever born.

LUKE WRITES ABOUT JESUS' LIFE

1 Many have tried to report on the things that happened among us. [2]They have written the same things that we learned from others—the people who saw those things from the beginning and served God by telling people his message. [3]Since I myself have studied everything carefully from the beginning, most excellent[n] Theophilus, it seemed good for me to write it out for you. I arranged it in order [4]to help you know that what you have been taught is true.

Q. How serious should high school relationships be?
A. Not real serious. That's the time to focus on school.
GUYS SPEAK OUT

ZECHARIAH AND ELIZABETH

[5]During the time Herod ruled Judea, there was a priest named Zechariah who belonged to Abijah's group.[n] Zechariah's wife, Elizabeth, came from the family of Aaron. [6]Zechariah and Elizabeth truly did what God said was good. They did everything the Lord commanded and were without fault in keeping his law. [7]But they had no children, because Elizabeth could not have a baby, and both of them were very old.

[8]One day Zechariah was serving as a priest before God, because his group was on duty. [9]According to the custom of the priests, he was chosen by lot to go into the Temple of the Lord and burn incense. [10]There were a great many people outside praying at the time the incense was offered. [11]Then an angel of the Lord appeared to Zechariah, standing on the right side of the incense table. [12]When he saw the angel, Zechariah was startled and frightened. [13]But the angel said to him, "Zechariah, don't be afraid. God has heard your prayer. Your wife, Elizabeth, will give birth to a son, and you will name him John. [14]He will bring you joy and gladness, and many people will be happy because of his birth. [15]John will be a great man for the Lord. He will never drink wine or beer, and even from birth, he will be filled with the Holy Spirit. [16]He will help many people of Israel return to the Lord their God. [17]He will go before the Lord in spirit and power like Elijah. He will make peace between parents and their children and will bring those who are not obeying God back to the right way of thinking, to make a people ready for the coming of the Lord."

[18]Zechariah said to the angel, "How can I know that what you say is true? I am an old man, and my wife is old, too."

[19]The angel answered him, "I am Gabriel. I stand before God, who sent me to talk to you and to tell you this good news. [20]Now, listen! You will not be able to speak until the day these things happen, because you did not believe what I told you. But they will really happen."

[21]Outside, the people were still waiting for Zechariah and were surprised that he was staying so long in the Temple. [22]When Zechariah came outside, he could not speak to them, and they knew he had seen a vision in the Temple. He could only make signs to them and remained unable to speak. [23]When his time of service at the Temple was finished, he went home.

[24]Later, Zechariah's wife, Elizabeth, became pregnant and did not go out of her house for five months. Elizabeth said, [25]"Look what the Lord has done for me! My people were ashamed[n] of me, but now the Lord has taken away that shame."

AN ANGEL APPEARS TO MARY

[26]During Elizabeth's sixth month of pregnancy, God sent the angel Gabriel to Nazareth,

LEARN IT & LIVE IT

John 10:10:
Learn It: Jesus wants us to live an abundant life.
Live It: Make a list of all the blessings in your life. Go tell one of your "blessings" that they are a part of your abundant life in Jesus.

John 14:1:
Learn It: Do not let your heart be troubled.
Live It: Don't worry. Be happy. The next time you begin to get stressed over a test, a new boyfriend, or problems with your parents, remember that Jesus is always with you.

John 16:20:
Learn It: You will have pain, but your pain will turn into joy.
Live It: Study like you've never studied before for that next biology test. When you get the results, reflect on the pain that led to that joy. What other things in life that bring you joy have been preceded by pain?

notes

1:3 excellent This word was used to show respect to an important person like a king or ruler. **1:5 Abijah's group** The Jewish priests were divided into twenty-four groups. See 1 Chronicles 24. **1:25 ashamed** The Jewish people thought it was a disgrace for women not to have children.

TOPten
RANDOM THINGS TO DO WITH YOUR DAD

01 **Go ice-skating.**

02 **Eat dinner and see a movie.**

03 **Go hear the symphony play.**

04 **Take a walk together.**

05 **Read a book together and meet for coffee to discuss it.**

06 **Organize a family bowling night, with the two of you as cocaptains.**

07 **Go to a fancy restaurant.**

08 **Go to a sporting event, and ask him to teach you the specifics.**

09 **Take a pottery class together.**

10 **Plan a surprise weekend for your mom.**

Song of Solomon 2:2
Among the young women, my darling is like a lily among thorns!

a town in Galilee, 27to a virgin. She
was engaged to marry a man
named Joseph from the family
of David. Her name was Mary.
28The angel came to her and
said, "Greetings! The Lord
has blessed you and is with you."
29But Mary was very startled by
what the angel said and wondered what this
greeting might mean.
30The angel said to her, "Don't be afraid, Mary;
God has shown you his grace. 31Listen! You will
become pregnant and give birth to a son, and
you will name him Jesus. 32He will be great and
will be called the Son of the Most High. The Lord
God will give him the throne of King David,
his ancestor. 33He will rule over the people of
Jacob forever, and his kingdom will never end."
34Mary said to the angel, "How will this
happen since I am a virgin?"
35The angel said to Mary, "The Holy Spirit
will come upon you, and the power of the
Most High will cover you. For this reason the
baby will be holy and will be called the Son of
God. 36Now Elizabeth, your relative, is also
pregnant with a son though she is very old.
Everyone thought she could not have a baby,
but she has been pregnant for six months.
37God can do anything!"
38Mary said, "I am the servant of the Lord.
Let this happen to me as you say!" Then the
angel went away.

MARY VISITS ELIZABETH

39Mary got up and went quickly to a town
in the hills of Judea. 40She came to Zechariah's
house and greeted Elizabeth. 41When Elizabeth
heard Mary's greeting, the unborn baby inside
her jumped, and Elizabeth was filled with the
Holy Spirit. 42She cried out in a loud voice,
"God has blessed you more than any other
woman, and he has blessed the baby to which
you will give birth. 43Why has this good thing
happened to me, that the mother of my Lord
comes to me? 44When I heard your voice, the
baby inside me jumped with joy. 45You
are blessed because you believed
that what the Lord said to you
would really happen."

MARY PRAISES GOD

46Then Mary said,

"My soul praises the Lord;
47 my heart rejoices in God
my Savior,
48because he has shown his concern for his
humble servant girl.
From now on, all people will say that
I am blessed,
49 because the Powerful One has done
great things for me.
His name is holy.
50God will show his mercy forever and ever
to those who worship and serve him.
51He has done mighty deeds by his power.
He has scattered the people who
are proud
and think great things about themselves.
52He has brought down rulers from their
thrones
and raised up the humble.
53He has filled the hungry with good things
and sent the rich away with nothing.
54He has helped his servant, the people
of Israel,
remembering to show them mercy
55as he promised to our ancestors,
to Abraham and to his children forever."

56Mary stayed with Elizabeth for about
three months and then returned home.

THE BIRTH OF JOHN

57When it was time for Elizabeth to give
birth, she had a boy. 58Her neighbors and relatives heard how good the Lord was to her, and
they rejoiced with her.
59When the baby was eight days old, they
came to circumcise him. They wanted to name
him Zechariah because this was his father's
name, 60but his mother said, "No! He will be
named John."

BIBLE BIOS: MARY

Mary faced one of the most daunting tasks and humbling privileges assigned to anyone in human history—to carry the child of God in her womb. We know that Mary and Joseph were poor from the sacrifice they gave at the Temple; we know that Mary was young and unwed when she became pregnant with Jesus. But she demonstrated remarkable courage and faith in the face of crisis. We never hear her complain about her situation. She relied on her family when times became hard for her, and she accomplished her task with grace. She was with Jesus his entire life, watching him die from the foot of the cross. She was an amazing woman, a loving mother, and a devout Christian. Be submissive, obedient, and trusting in your Sovereign God as Mary was.

[MATTHEW 1—2]

61The people said to Elizabeth, "But no one
in your family has this name." 62Then they
made signs to his father to find out what he
would like to name him.

63Zechariah asked for a writing tablet and
wrote, "His name is John," and everyone was
surprised. 64Immediately Zechariah could talk
again, and he began praising God. 65All their
neighbors became alarmed, and in all the
mountains of Judea people continued talking
about all these things. 66The people who heard
about them wondered, saying, "What will this
child be?" because the Lord was with him.

ZECHARIAH PRAISES GOD

67Then Zechariah, John's father, was filled
with the Holy Spirit and prophesied:

68"Let us praise the Lord, the God of Israel,
because he has come to help his people
and has given them freedom.
69He has given us a powerful Savior
from the family of God's servant David.
70He said that he would do this
through his holy prophets who lived
long ago:
71He promised he would save us
from our enemies
and from the power of all those
who hate us.
72He said he would give mercy to our fathers
and that he would remember
his holy promise.
73God promised Abraham, our father,
74 that he would save us from the power
of our enemies
so we could serve him without fear,
75being holy and good before God
as long as we live.

76"Now you, child, will be called a prophet
of the Most High God.
You will go before the Lord to prepare
his way.
77You will make his people know that they
will be saved
by having their sins forgiven.
78With the loving mercy of our God,
a new day from heaven will dawn
upon us.
79It will shine on those who live
in darkness,
in the shadow of death.
It will guide us into the path of peace."

Blab

Q. My friend thinks she is fat but she isn't. She stopped eating, so she lost 25 lbs. in like one or two months. What can I do?

A. Pray. Pray with her. Pray with friends. God sees her and will answer. Anorexia Nervosa is a serious eating disorder that needs to be treated by professional counselors. If you are afraid for her health—physically and mentally—speak first to a guidance counselor, teacher, or parent about your observations. Above all, be her friend through the good times and the bad. This is when she needs you most.

Q. I go to a Christian school, and two of my friends from that school are basically having sex. They are both questioning their faith in God. Sometimes it feels like it's my fault they might be giving up on God, because I can't answer their questions or wasn't helping them enough. Help!

A. It's okay if you don't know all the answers—you're not expected to be perfect. Trust God to take care of all your friends. Your friends' salvation, hopes, problems—none of them is your responsibility. What is your responsibility is to pray for them and leave them with him.

Q. I really, really want to get a tattoo, but what does the Bible say about them. Is it against God?

A. In the Old Testament law tattoos were forbidden. But when Christ came, he redeemed us from the curse of the law (Galatians 3). This means that now God looks at your heart, your motives, when it comes to what you do. Check with your parents, and follow their advice.

BEAUTY SECRET

PAINFUL SIDE-EFFECTS

Next time you say a quick, biting word to a friend, remember the feeling of sunburn pain. Only you can provide the cooling relief that she will need to heal from that. Go to her quickly and apologize, ask her to pray with you, and spend some quality time together. This will help you both heal quickly.

80And so the child grew up and became
strong in spirit. John lived in the desert until
the time when he came out to preach to Israel.

THE BIRTH OF JESUS

2 At that time, Augustus Caesar sent an order
that all people in the countries under
Roman rule must list their names in a register.
2This was the first registration;[n] it was taken
while Quirinius was governor of Syria. 3And
all went to their own towns to be registered.
4So Joseph left Nazareth, a town in Galilee,
and went to the town of Bethlehem in Judea,
known as the town of David. Joseph went
there because he was from the family of
David. 5Joseph registered with Mary, to whom
he was engaged[n] and who was now pregnant.
6While they were in Bethlehem, the time
came for Mary to have the baby, 7and she gave
birth to her first son. Because there were no
rooms left in the inn, she wrapped the baby
with pieces of cloth and laid him in a box
where animals are fed.

SHEPHERDS HEAR ABOUT JESUS

8That night, some shepherds were in the fields
nearby watching their sheep. 9Then an angel
of the Lord stood before them. The glory of the
Lord was shining around them, and they became
very frightened. 10The angel said to them, "Do
not be afraid. I am bringing you good news that
will be a great joy to all the people. 11Today
your Savior was born in the town of David. He
is Christ, the Lord. 12This is how you will
know him: You will find a baby wrapped in
pieces of cloth and lying in a feeding box."
13Then a very large group of angels from
heaven joined the first angel, praising God and
saying:
14"Give glory to God in heaven,
and on earth let there be peace among
the people who please God."
15When the angels left them and went back
to heaven, the shepherds said to each other,
"Let's go to Bethlehem. Let's see this thing
that has happened which the Lord has told us
about."
16So the shepherds went quickly and found
Mary and Joseph and the baby, who was lying
in a feeding box. 17When they had seen him,
they told what the angels had said about this
child. 18Everyone was amazed at what the
shepherds said to them. 19But Mary treasured
these things and continued to think about
them. 20Then the shepherds went back to their
sheep, praising God and thanking him for
everything they had seen and heard. It had
been just as the angel had told them.
21When the baby was eight days old, he was

DIDYA KNOW

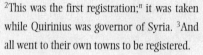

4 IN 5 TEENS SAY THEIR RELATIONSHIP WITH THEIR PARENTS HAS GOTTEN BETTER OR STAYED THE SAME IN THE LAST TWO YEARS.

ISSUES: Friendship

"Make new friends, but keep the old; one is silver and the other gold." That old saying is pretty true. Loyal, old friends are the best kind. You know these friends because they are the ones to whom you tell all your secrets, your problems, your crushes, your anger, your dreams. These are the friends who love you through the thick and thin of it all. They forgive you when you are mean, and they support you when you are having hard times. But, don't discount new friends. New friends can teach you things you never knew! They can show you a whole new world: a new way of seeing life, love, and a way of being. Invite the new friends into your life to meet the old. Learning from each other in a circle of friendship is part of the essence of Christianity.

notes

2:2 registration Census. A counting of all the people and the things they own. **2:5 engaged** For the Jewish people, an engagement was a lasting agreement. It could only be broken by divorce.

Notes

Luke 3:16

God said that in the last days he would pour out his Spirit on all kinds of people. That means on you and me (see Joel 2:28). Just as he did in that upstairs room in Acts 2, he wants to baptize you with the Holy Spirit and with fire. This will give you a new power that you've never had before. Acts 1:8 says, "But when the Holy Spirit comes to you, you will receive power. You will be my witnesses. . . ." The word *power* comes from the Greek word *dunamis,* which is translated as *dynamite!* So the verse actually says that after the Holy Spirit comes upon you, you will receive dynamite power to be witnesses!

This is exactly what happened to Peter. The same Peter who denied Christ three times preached with dynamite power after he received the Holy Spirit and fire as told in Acts 2. In fact, he led 3,000 people to the Lord in one day. Now that's power! That's the same kind of power everyone needs. How do we get it? It's a gift. All we have to do is ask the Lord for it. He wants to baptize us with the Holy Spirit and fire today, so we can receive that dynamite power to be witnesses for him.

circumcised and was named Jesus, the name
given by the angel before the baby began to
grow inside Mary.

JESUS IS PRESENTED IN THE TEMPLE

22 When the time came for Mary and Joseph
to do what the law of Moses taught about being
made pure,[n] they took Jesus to Jerusalem to
present him to the Lord. 23 (It is written in the
law of the Lord: "Every firstborn male shall be
given to the Lord.")[n] 24 Mary and Joseph also
went to offer a sacrifice, as the law of the Lord
says: "You must sacrifice two doves or two
young pigeons."[n]

SIMEON SEES JESUS

25 In Jerusalem lived a man named Simeon
who was a good man and godly. He was waiting for the time when God would take away
Israel's sorrow, and the Holy Spirit was in him.
26 Simeon had been told by the Holy Spirit that
he would not die before he saw the Christ
promised by the Lord. 27 The Spirit led Simeon
to the Temple. When Mary and Joseph
brought the baby Jesus to the Temple to do
what the law said they must do, 28 Simeon
took the baby in his arms and thanked God:

29 "Now, Lord, you can let me, your servant,
die in peace as you said.
30 With my own eyes I have
seen your salvation,
31 which you prepared
before all people.
32 It is a light for the non-
Jewish people to see
and an honor for your people, the
Israelites."

33 Jesus' father and mother were amazed at
what Simeon had said about him. 34 Then
Simeon blessed them and said to Mary, "God
has chosen this child to cause the fall and rise
of many in Israel. He will be a sign from God
that many people will not accept 35 so that the
thoughts of many will be made known. And
the things that will happen will make your
heart sad, too."

ANNA SEES JESUS

36 There was a prophetess, Anna, from the
family of Phanuel in the tribe of Asher. Anna
was very old. She had once been married for
seven years. 37 Then her husband died, and she
was a widow for eighty-four years. Anna never
left the Temple but worshiped God, going
without food and praying day and night.
38 Standing there at that time, she thanked God
and spoke about Jesus to all who were waiting
for God to free Jerusalem.

"EVERY YEAR JESUS' PARENTS WENT TO JERUSALEM FOR THE PASSOVER FEAST."

JOSEPH AND MARY RETURN HOME

39 When Joseph and Mary had done everything the law of the Lord commanded, they
went home to Nazareth, their own town in
Galilee. 40 The little child grew and became
strong. He was filled with wisdom, and God's
goodness was upon him.

JESUS AS A BOY

41 Every year Jesus' parents went to Jerusalem for the Passover Feast.
42 When he was twelve years
old, they went to the feast as
they always did. 43 After the
feast days were over,
they started home. The
boy Jesus stayed behind in Jerusalem,
but his parents did not know it.
44 Thinking that Jesus was with them in the
group, they traveled for a whole day. Then
they began to look for him among their family
and friends. 45 When they did not find him,
they went back to Jerusalem to look for him
there. 46 After three days they found Jesus sitting in the Temple with the teachers, listening
to them and asking them questions. 47 All who
heard him were amazed at his understanding
and answers. 48 When Jesus' parents saw him,

Song of Solomon 4:15
You are like a garden fountain— a well of fresh water flowing down from the mountains of Lebanon.

notes

2:22 pure The Law of Moses said that forty days after a Jewish woman gave birth to a son, she must be cleansed by a ceremony at the Temple. Read Leviticus 12:2-8. **2:23 "Every . . . Lord."** Quotation from Exodus 13:2. **2:24 "You . . . pigeons."** Quotation from Leviticus 12:8.

Luke 4:18

This is such an exciting verse! The Lord has sent you to announce freedom. But not only have you been sent to announce freedom; you can have freedom as well! There is freedom in Jesus—freedom for everyone who struggles or suffers. You've been chosen by God, and you've also been equipped with the power of God to get free, stay free, and bring freedom to anyone and everyone who needs it! Now that's power—power over drugs, alcohol, cigarettes, lust, sex, bitterness, or whatever.

There was a movie about a man who gave up his life just to bring freedom to his people. He was beaten, tortured, and put on a chopping block. All he had to do was simply surrender his freedom, and he would live. His people would remain in bondage, but he could live. Instead, he let out a bloodcurdling cry, "Freeeeeedom!" He lost his life, but his people gained their freedom.

There is another story that hits home for all of us. Jesus died a horrible, shameful death on a cross so we could be free from sin and spend eternity with him. Don't allow yourself to be in bondage over some stupid sin—a sin that Jesus has already paid the price for. Choose freedom today, and watch God work a miracle in your life and in the lives of your friends! He is the One who sets you free!

"THE LORD HAS SENT YOU TO ANNOUNCE FREEDOM."

they were astonished. His mother said to him, "Son, why did you do this to us? Your father and I were very worried about you and have been looking for you."
[49]Jesus said to them, "Why were you looking for me? Didn't you know that I must be in
my Father's house?" [50]But they did not understand the meaning of what he said.
[51]Jesus went with them to Nazareth and was obedient to them. But his mother kept in
her mind all that had happened. [52]Jesus became wiser and grew physically. People liked him, and he pleased God.

THE PREACHING OF JOHN

3 It was the fifteenth year of the rule of Tiberius Caesar. These men were under Caesar: Pontius Pilate, the ruler of Judea; Herod, the ruler of Galilee; Philip, Herod's brother, the ruler of Iturea and Traconitis; and
Lysanias, the ruler of Abilene. [2]Annas and Caiaphas were the high priests. At this time, the word of God came to John son of Zech-
ariah in the desert. [3]He went all over the area around the Jordan River preaching a baptism of changed hearts and lives for the forgiveness
of sins. [4]As it is written in the book of Isaiah the prophet:

"This is a voice of one
 who calls out in the desert:
'Prepare the way for the Lord.
 Make the road straight for him.
[5]Every valley should be filled in,
 and every mountain and hill should
  be made flat.
Roads with turns should be made straight,
 and rough roads should be made
  smooth.
[6]And all people will know about the
  salvation of God!' " *Isaiah 40:3-5*

[7]To the crowds of people who came to be baptized by John, he said, "You are all snakes! Who warned you to run away from God's coming
punishment? [8]Do the things that show you really have changed your hearts and lives.

Luke 4:8

Jesus had been in the desert praying about how to get through to men's hearts. Satan tempted him to take the easy way out—turn stones into bread instead of fasting; serve him in return for glory and power; or jump off the Temple, let the angels miraculously save him, and immediately be accepted by the people. Jesus knew that the only way to win the souls of men was to suffer and go to the cross. It was the harder way, but it was the only right way. Jesus responded to Satan by telling him that only God was to be worshiped and served.

You are going to face incredible temptation in your life. You must know that Jesus has been there. He knows the battles you face. You've got the same spiritual resources that Jesus had. You have prayer and the love of your heavenly Father. The power of the Holy Spirit was with Jesus (4:1), and the Holy Spirit lives in you. Jesus quoted the Word of God to Satan, and you have the complete Word in your hands. Plus, you now have Jesus in heaven, interceding on your behalf. He has dealt with the devil. And he has completely defeated him.

Do not play around with Satan. Stay on your toes. Keep alert. Serve God and flee the devil!

LEARN IT & LIVE IT

John 17:3:
Learn It: Eternal life is knowing God.
Live It: Wake up extra early tomorrow morning to seek the face of God. Take time out to meditate and talk to him.

Acts 10:34:
Learn It: God shows no partiality.
Live It: In your next class, choose to sit by someone who may be different from you by race, class, or gender. Get to know them, to understand them.

Romans 1:12:
Learn It: We can mutually encourage one another's faith.
Live It: Pay a compliment to a friend when you see the fruits of the Spirit in their lives. Encourage one another in love.

Don't begin to say to yourselves, 'Abraham is
our father.' I tell you that God could make children for Abraham from these rocks. [9]The ax is
now ready to cut down the trees, and every
tree that does not produce good fruit will be
cut down and thrown into the fire."[n]
[10]The people asked John, "Then what should
we do?"

DIDYA KNOW  **3 IN 4 TEENS HAVE TOLD THEIR PARENTS THEY LOVE THEM RECENTLY.**

[11]John answered, "If you have two shirts,
share with the person who does not have one.
If you have food, share that also."
[12]Even tax collectors came to John to be
baptized. They said to him, "Teacher, what
should we do?"
[13]John said to them, "Don't take more
taxes from people than you have been
ordered to take."
[14]The soldiers asked John, "What
about us? What should we do?"
John said to them, "Don't force people
to give you money, and don't lie about
them. Be satisfied with the pay you get."
[15]Since the people were hoping for the
Christ to come, they wondered if John
might be the one.

[16]John answered everyone, "I baptize you
with water, but there is one coming who is
greater than I am. I am not good enough to untie
his sandals. He will baptize you with the Holy
Spirit and fire. [17]He will come ready to clean the
grain, separating the good grain from the chaff.
He will put the good part of the grain into his
barn, but he will burn the chaff with a fire that
cannot be put out."[n] [18]And John continued to
preach the Good News, saying many other
things to encourage the people.

Q. What kind of girls do you prefer to be around?

A. Outgoing girls. There's no need to be shy, and outgoing girls are adventurous and fun.

[19]But John spoke against Herod, the governor, because of his sin with Herodias, the wife
of Herod's brother, and because of the many
other evil things Herod did. [20]So Herod did
something even worse: He put John in prison.

JESUS IS BAPTIZED BY JOHN

[21]When all the people were being baptized
by John, Jesus also was baptized. While Jesus
was praying, heaven opened [22]and the Holy
Spirit came down on him in the form of a dove.
Then a voice came from heaven, saying, "You
are my Son, whom I love, and I am very
pleased with you."

THE FAMILY HISTORY OF JESUS

[23]When Jesus began his ministry, he was
about thirty years old. People thought that Jesus
was Joseph's son.
Joseph was the son[n] of Heli.
[24]Heli was the son of Matthat.
Matthat was the son of Levi.
Levi was the son of Melki.
Melki was the son of Jannai.
Jannai was the son of Joseph.
[25]Joseph was the son of Mattathias.
Mattathias was the son of Amos.
Amos was the son of Nahum.
Nahum was the son of Esli.
Esli was the son of Naggai.
[26]Naggai was the son of Maath.
Maath was the son of Mattathias.

notes

3:9 The ax . . . fire. This means that God is ready to punish his people who do not obey him. **3:17 He will . . . out.** This means that Jesus will come to separate good people from bad people, saving the good and punishing the bad. **3:23 son** "Son" in Jewish lists of ancestors can sometimes mean grandson or more distant relative.

Mattathias was the son of Semein.
Semein was the son of Josech.
Josech was the son of Joda.
27Joda was the son of Joanan.
Joanan was the son of Rhesa.
Rhesa was the son of Zerubbabel.
Zerubbabel was the grandson of Shealtiel.
Shealtiel was the son of Neri.
28Neri was the son of Melki.
Melki was the son of Addi.
Addi was the son of Cosam.
Cosam was the son of Elmadam.
Elmadam was the son of Er.
29Er was the son of Joshua.
Joshua was the son of Eliezer.
Eliezer was the son of Jorim.
Jorim was the son of Matthat.
Matthat was the son of Levi.
30Levi was the son of Simeon.
Simeon was the son of Judah.
Judah was the son of Joseph.
Joseph was the son of Jonam.
Jonam was the son of Eliakim.
31Eliakim was the son of Melea.
Melea was the son of Menna.
Menna was the son of Mattatha.
Mattatha was the son of Nathan.

Song of Solomon 6:12
Before I realized it, my desire for you made me feel like a prince in a chariot.

Arni was the son of Hezron.
Hezron was the son of Perez.
Perez was the son of Judah.
34Judah was the son of Jacob.
Jacob was the son of Isaac.
Isaac was the son of Abraham.
Abraham was the son of Terah.
Terah was the son of Nahor.
35Nahor was the son of Serug.
Serug was the son of Reu.
Reu was the son of Peleg.
Peleg was the son of Eber.
Eber was the son of Shelah.
36Shelah was the son of Cainan.
Cainan was the son of Arphaxad.
Arphaxad was the son of Shem.
Shem was the son of Noah.
Noah was the son of Lamech.
37Lamech was the son of Methuselah.
Methuselah was the son of Enoch.
Enoch was the son of Jared.
Jared was the son of Mahalalel.
Mahalalel was the son of Kenan.
38Kenan was the son of Enosh.
Enosh was the son of Seth.
Seth was the son of Adam.
Adam was the son of God.

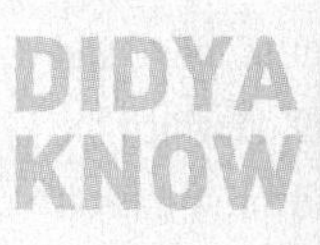

4 IN 5 TEENS SAY THEIR PARENTS HAVE TOLD THEM THEY LOVE THEM RECENTLY.

Nathan was the son of David.
32David was the son of Jesse.
Jesse was the son of Obed.
Obed was the son of Boaz.
Boaz was the son of Salmon.
Salmon was the son of Nahshon.
33Nahshon was the son of Amminadab.
Amminadab was the son of Admin.
Admin was the son of Arni.

JESUS IS TEMPTED BY THE DEVIL

4 Jesus, filled with the Holy Spirit, returned
from the Jordan River. The Spirit led
Jesus into the desert 2where the devil tempted
Jesus for forty days. Jesus ate nothing during that time, and when those days were ended, he was very hungry.

3The devil said to Jesus, "If you are the Son of God, tell this rock to become bread."

Luke 5:24

Some schools have a wall in the school post office where they post the exam grades. Students sometimes affectionately refer to those places as "the wailing walls." One semester, a young man neglected to study for a particular exam and his test grade reflected it! They left the grades of that test up the entire semester. It was a continual reminder to him of how he had messed up. You can imagine what a happy day it was for him when they finally took down the grades at the end of the term. He could have tried covering up that exam with a black marker (which, by the way, he did). But every time he went into the school post office, there was that big black mark reminding him of his failure.

Jesus is the only One who has the right to forgive your sins. John 1:29 says that he takes them away—completely. When he forgives your sins and takes them away, it's like you never sinned at all. What freedom this understanding brings to our lives!

So if you've been struggling with something, confess your sins to him right now. Jesus is not only going to forgive you of your sins; he is going to see to it that they are taken away! After all, he is the One who forgives, forgets, and removes!

"JESUS IS THE ONLY ONE WHO HAS THE RIGHT TO FORGIVE YOUR SINS."

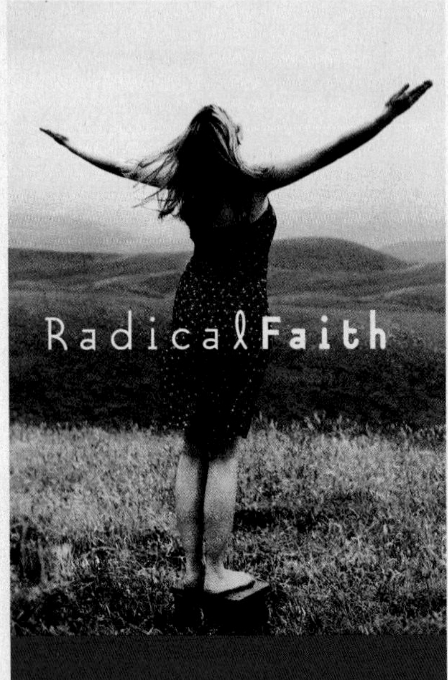

Luke 6:28, 35

Luke says, "Welcome to the club." People who love God have been lied about since the beginning. He also says that God will bless those who have been mistreated because of him. Proverbs 25:18-22 gives us some wisdom about friends who tell lies about us or treat us badly. The advice is to do exactly the opposite of what your friends do. Even when you're disappointed and angry, you are supposed to be Christlike. Matthew 5:11 says, "People will insult you and hurt you. They will lie and say all kinds of evil things about you because you follow me. But when they do, you will be happy" because you love Jesus. When you love a person who hurts you, it "will be like pouring burning coals on his head" (Proverbs 25:22).

Wow—that's pretty tough advice. When people tell lies or spread rumors about you, your reputation gets shattered, your pride gets wounded, and your heart gets broken. And God wants you to do what? Yep, he says to love them anyway—even give food to them if they are hungry and pray for them too. By doing so you prove the strength of your character and you overcome evil with good. God promises to reward you for that.

4Jesus answered, "It is written in the Scriptures: 'A person does not live by eating only
bread.' "[n]
5Then the devil took Jesus and showed him
all the kingdoms of the world in an instant. 6The
devil said to Jesus, "I will give you all these kingdoms and all their power and glory. It has all been
given to me, and I can give it to anyone I wish. 7If
you worship me, then it will all be yours."
8Jesus answered, "It is written in the Scriptures: 'You must worship the Lord your God
and serve only him.' "[n]
9Then the devil led Jesus to Jerusalem and
put him on a high place of the Temple. He said
to Jesus, "If you are the Son of God, jump
down. 10It is written in the Scriptures:

'He has put his angels in charge of you
to watch over you.' *Psalm 91:11*

11It is also written:

'They will catch you in their hands
so that you will not hit your foot
on a rock.' " *Psalm 91:12*

12Jesus answered, "But it also says in the
Scriptures: 'Do not test the Lord your God.' "[n]
13After the devil had tempted Jesus in every
way, he left him to wait until a better time.

JESUS TEACHES THE PEOPLE

14Jesus returned to Galilee in the power of
the Holy Spirit, and stories about him spread
all through the area. 15He began to teach in
their synagogues, and everyone praised him.
16Jesus traveled to Nazareth, where he had
grown up. On the Sabbath day he went to the
synagogue, as he always did, and stood up to
read. 17The book of Isaiah the prophet was
given to him. He opened the book and found
the place where this is written:

18"The Lord has put his Spirit in me,
because he appointed me to tell the
Good News to the poor.
He has sent me to tell the captives
they are free
and to tell the blind that they can
see again. *Isaiah 61:1*
God sent me to free those who have been
treated unfairly *Isaiah 58:6*
19 and to announce the time when the Lord
will show his kindness." *Isaiah 61:2*

20Jesus closed the book, gave it back to the
assistant, and sat down. Everyone in the synagogue was watching Jesus closely. 21He began
to say to them, "While you heard these words
just now, they were coming true!"
22All the people spoke well of Jesus and
were amazed at the words of grace he spoke.
They asked, "Isn't this Joseph's son?"
23Jesus said to them, "I know that you will
tell me the old saying: 'Doctor, heal yourself.'
You want to say, 'We heard about the things
you did in Capernaum. Do those things here
in your own town!' " 24Then Jesus said, "I tell
you the truth, a prophet is not accepted in his
hometown. 25But I tell you the truth, there
were many widows in Israel during the time of
Elijah. It did not rain in Israel for three and
one-half years, and there was no food anywhere in the whole country. 26But Elijah was
sent to none of those widows, only to a widow
in Zarephath, a town in Sidon. 27And there
were many with skin diseases living in Israel
during the time of the prophet Elisha. But
none of them were healed, only Naaman, who
was from the country of Syria."
28When all the people in the synagogue
heard these things, they became very angry.
29They got up, forced Jesus out of town, and
took him to the edge of the cliff on which the
town was built. They planned to throw him off
the edge, 30but Jesus walked through the crowd
and went on his way.

JESUS FORCES OUT AN EVIL SPIRIT

31Jesus went to Capernaum, a city in Galilee,
and on the Sabbath day, he taught the people.
32They were amazed at his teaching, because
he spoke with authority. 33In the synagogue a
man who had within him an evil spirit shouted
in a loud voice, 34"Jesus of Nazareth! What do
you want with us? Did you come to destroy

4:4 'A person . . . bread.' Quotation from Deuteronomy 8:3. **4:8 'You . . . him.'** Quotation from Deuteronomy 6:13. **4:12 'Do . . . God.'** Quotation from Deuteronomy 6:16.

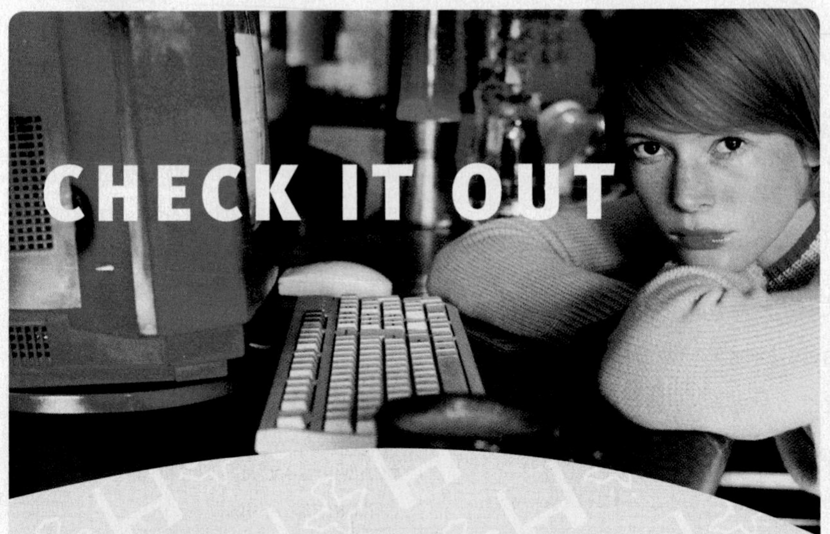

National Institute for Literacy

The National Institute for Literacy (NIFL) was created by the National Literacy Act of 1991, when Congress acted on the literacy field's request for a federal office focused solely on literacy.

The Institute serves as a focal point for public and private activities that support the development of high-quality regional, state, and national literacy services. NIFL's goal is to ensure that all Americans with literacy needs have access to services that can help them gain the basic skills necessary for success in the workplace, family, and community in the 21st century.

To get involved, go to ***www.literacydirectory.org.***

us? I know who you are—God's Holy One!"
35Jesus commanded the evil spirit, "Be quiet! Come out of the man!" The evil spirit threw the man down to the ground before all the people and then left the man without hurting him.
36The people were amazed and said to each other, "What does this mean? With authority and power he commands evil spirits, and they come out."
37And so the news about Jesus spread to every place in the whole area.

JESUS HEALS MANY PEOPLE

38Jesus left the synagogue and went to the home of Simon.[n] Simon's mother-in-law was sick with a high fever, and they asked Jesus to help her.
39He came to her side and commanded the fever to leave. It left her, and immediately she got up and began serving them.
40When the sun went down, the people brought those who were sick to Jesus. Putting his hands on each sick person, he healed every one of them.
41Demons came out of many people, shouting, "You are the Son of God." But Jesus commanded the demons and would not allow them to speak, because they knew Jesus was the Christ.
42At daybreak, Jesus went to a lonely place, but the people looked for him. When they found him, they tried to keep him from leaving.
43But Jesus said to them, "I must preach about God's kingdom to other towns, too. This is why I was sent."
44Then he kept on preaching in the synagogues of Judea.

JESUS' FIRST FOLLOWERS

5 One day while Jesus was standing beside Lake Galilee, many people were pressing

Blab

Q. I have no idea what God thinks about physical relationships—kissing, hand-holding . . . I've consulted the Bible numerous times, but am not having luck finding relationship advice.

A. The Bible specifically says that we are not to have premarital sex. So we know that's off limits. Where most people get confused is the gray areas up to that. For some solid Christian advice you can check out *Too Close Too Soon* by Dr. Jim Talley and Dr. Bobbie Reed. This book might answer some of your questions. Check with your parents and see what they think about it all. Also, see 2 Corinthians 9—10; 1 Peter 1:15-16.

Q. Is something wrong with me? All I think about is sex. I'm only 13. Help!

A. No, nothing is wrong with you. Your hormones are just starting to kick in. That's a wild ride, and part of it is that sex is always on your mind. But don't make it worse by fantasizing and thinking of ways to act on it. When the thoughts come, know they are just human, and go on with your life. You can control your thoughts by not spending hours dreaming about them. Stay in control and you will be fine.

Q. I've always wanted to go to church to learn more about the Lord, but my dad won't let me. Instead of going to church, I've been reading two chapters of the Bible every night. Is this enough?

A. God sees your problem and understands, so yes do your Bible study as much as you can. Are there are any Christian clubs at your school? Join them. Most of all, pray. Ask God to speak to your dad. Be faithful.

notes

4:38 Simon Simon's other name was Peter.

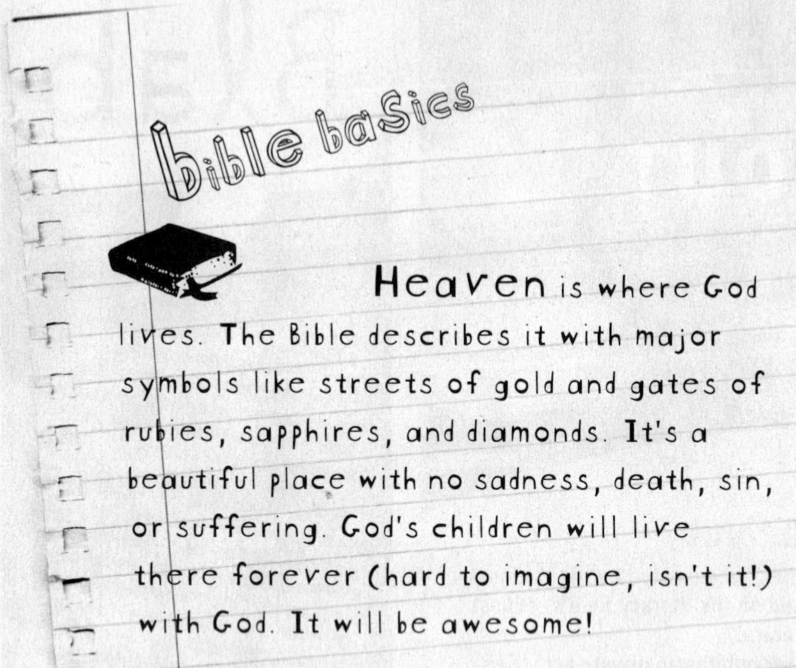

bible basics
Heaven is where God lives. The Bible describes it with major symbols like streets of gold and gates of rubies, sapphires, and diamonds. It's a beautiful place with no sadness, death, sin, or suffering. God's children will live there forever (hard to imagine, isn't it!) with God. It will be awesome!

all around him to hear the word of God. [2]Jesus saw two boats at the shore of the lake. The fishermen had left them and were washing their nets. [3]Jesus got into one of the boats, the one that belonged to Simon,[n] and asked him to push off a little from the land. Then Jesus sat down and continued to teach the people from the boat.

[4]When Jesus had finished speaking, he said to Simon, "Take the boat into deep water, and put your nets in the water to catch some fish."

[5]Simon answered, "Master, we worked hard all night trying to catch fish, and we caught nothing. But you say to put the nets in the water, so I will." [6]When the fishermen did as Jesus told them, they caught so many fish that the nets began to break. [7]They called to their partners in the other boat to come and help them. They came and filled both boats so full that they were almost sinking.

[8]When Simon Peter saw what had happened, he bowed down before Jesus and said, "Go away from me, Lord. I am a sinful man!" [9]He and the other fishermen were amazed at the many fish they caught, as were [10]James and John, the sons of Zebedee, Simon's partners.

Jesus said to Simon, "Don't be afraid. From now on you will fish for people." [11]When the men brought their boats to the shore, they left everything and followed Jesus.

JESUS HEALS A SICK MAN

[12]When Jesus was in one of the towns, there was a man covered with a skin disease. When he saw Jesus, he bowed before him and begged him, "Lord, you can heal me if you will."

[13]Jesus reached out his hand and touched the man and said, "I will. Be healed!" Immediately the disease disappeared. [14]Then Jesus said, "Don't tell anyone about this, but go and show yourself to the priest[n] and offer a gift for your healing, as Moses commanded.[n] This will show the people what I have done."

[15]But the news about Jesus spread even more. Many people came to hear Jesus and to be healed of their sicknesses, [16]but Jesus often slipped away to be alone so he could pray.

JESUS HEALS A PARALYZED MAN

[17]One day as Jesus was teaching the people, the Pharisees and teachers of the law from every town in Galilee and Judea and from Jerusalem were there. The Lord was giving Jesus the power to heal people. [18]Just then, some men were carrying on a mat a man who was paralyzed. They tried to bring him in and put him down before Jesus. [19]But because there were so many people there, they could not find a way in. So they went up on the roof and lowered the man on his mat through the ceiling into the middle of the crowd right before Jesus. [20]Seeing their faith, Jesus said, "Friend, your sins are forgiven."

[21]The Jewish teachers of the law and the Pharisees thought to themselves, "Who is this man who is speaking as if he were God? Only God can forgive sins."

[22]But Jesus knew what they were thinking and said, "Why are you thinking these things? [23]Which is easier: to say, 'Your sins are forgiven,' or to say, 'Stand up and walk'? [24]But I will prove to you that the Son of Man has authority on earth to forgive sins." So Jesus said to the paralyzed man, "I tell you, stand up, take your mat, and go home."

[25]At once the man stood up before them, picked up his mat, and went home, praising God. [26]All the people were fully amazed and began to praise God. They were filled with much respect and said, "Today we have seen amazing things!"

LEVI FOLLOWS JESUS

[27]After this, Jesus went out and saw a tax collector named Levi sitting in the tax collector's booth. Jesus said to him, "Follow me!" [28]So Levi got up, left everything, and followed him.

[29]Then Levi gave a big dinner for Jesus at his house. Many tax collectors and other people were eating there, too. [30]But the Pharisees and the men who taught the law for the Pharisees began to complain to Jesus' followers, "Why do you eat and drink with tax collectors and sinners?"

[31]Jesus answered them, "It is not the healthy people who need a doctor, but the sick. [32]I have not come to invite good people but sinners to change their hearts and lives."

5:3 Simon Simon's other name was Peter. **5:14 show . . . priest** The Law of Moses said a priest must say when a Jewish person with a skin disease was well. **5:14 Moses commanded** Read about this in Leviticus 14:1–32.

JESUS ANSWERS A QUESTION

33They said to Jesus, "John's followers often
give up eating[n] for a certain time and pray, just
as the Pharisees do. But your followers eat and
drink all the time."

34Jesus said to them, "You cannot make the
friends of the bridegroom give up eating while
he is still with them. 35But the time will come
when the bridegroom will be taken away from
them, and then they will give up eating."

36Jesus told them this story: "No one takes
cloth off a new coat to cover a hole in an old
coat. Otherwise, he ruins the new coat, and the
cloth from the new coat will not be the same as
the old cloth. 37Also, no one ever pours new
wine into old leather bags. Otherwise, the new
wine will break the bags, the wine will spill
out, and the leather bags will be ruined. 38New
wine must be put into new leather bags. 39No
one after drinking old wine wants new wine,
because he says, 'The old wine is better.' "

JESUS IS LORD OVER THE SABBATH

6 One Sabbath day Jesus was walking through
some fields of grain. His followers picked
the heads of grain, rubbed them in their hands,
and ate them. 2Some Pharisees said, "Why do
you do what is not lawful on the Sabbath day?"

3Jesus answered, "Have you not read what
David did when he and those with him were
hungry? 4He went into God's house and took
and ate the holy bread, which is lawful only for
priests to eat. And he gave some to the people
who were with him." 5Then Jesus said to the
Pharisees, "The Son of Man is Lord of the
Sabbath day."

JESUS HEALS A MAN'S HAND

6On another Sabbath day Jesus went into
the synagogue and was teaching, and a man
with a crippled right hand was there. 7The
teachers of the law and the Pharisees were
watching closely to see if Jesus would heal on
the Sabbath day so they could accuse him.
8But he knew what they were thinking, and he
said to the man with the crippled hand, "Stand
up here in the middle of everyone." The man
got up and stood there. 9Then Jesus said to
them, "I ask you, which is lawful on the
Sabbath day: to do good or to do evil, to save a
life or to destroy it?" 10Jesus looked around at
all of them and said to the man, "Hold out
your hand." The man held out his hand, and it
was healed.

"AT THAT TIME JESUS WENT OFF TO A MOUNTAIN TO PRAY, AND HE SPENT THE NIGHT PRAYING TO GOD."

11But the Pharisees and the teachers of the
law were very angry and discussed with each
other what they could do to Jesus.

JESUS CHOOSES HIS APOSTLES

12At that time Jesus went off to a mountain
to pray, and he spent the night praying to God.
13The next morning, Jesus called his followers
to him and chose twelve of them, whom he
named apostles: 14Simon (Jesus named him
Peter), his brother Andrew, James, John, Philip,
Bartholomew, 15Matthew, Thomas, James son
of Alphaeus, Simon (called the Zealot), 16Judas
son of James, and Judas Iscariot, who later
turned Jesus over to his enemies.

JESUS TEACHES AND HEALS

17Jesus and the apostles came down from
the mountain, and he stood on level ground. A
large group of his followers was there, as well as
many people from all around Judea, Jerusalem,
and the seacoast cities of Tyre and Sidon. 18They
all came to hear Jesus teach and to be healed of
their sicknesses, and he healed those who
were troubled by evil spirits. 19All the people
were trying to touch Jesus, because power was
coming from him and healing them all.

RELATIONSHIPS

"Love is patient . . ." (1 Corinthians 13). Does your crush get exasperated with you? What about with his best friends? Or does he take the time to wait until you learn how to throw that football, play the newest X-Box game, or whatever? Watch how he acts with those people he's really close to—mom, dad, siblings, best friends. That's how he'll be to you when you guys have been together a while. And since we have a lot of struggles in this life, you're gonna want a guy who loves you enough to be patient with you. It's a sign of maturity, and it really helps as you work through adjusting to marriage!

DIDYA KNOW → **3 IN 5 TEENS EAT DINNER WITH THEIR PARENTS 5 NIGHTS A WEEK OR MORE.**

20Jesus looked at his followers and said,
"You people who are poor are happy,
because the kingdom of God belongs
to you.
21You people who are now hungry are happy,
because you will be satisfied.
You people who are now crying are happy,
because you will laugh with joy.
22"People will hate you, shut you out, insult
you, and say you are evil because you follow the

notes

5:33 give up eating This is called "fasting." The people would give up eating for a special time of prayer and worship to God. It was also done to show sadness and disappointment.

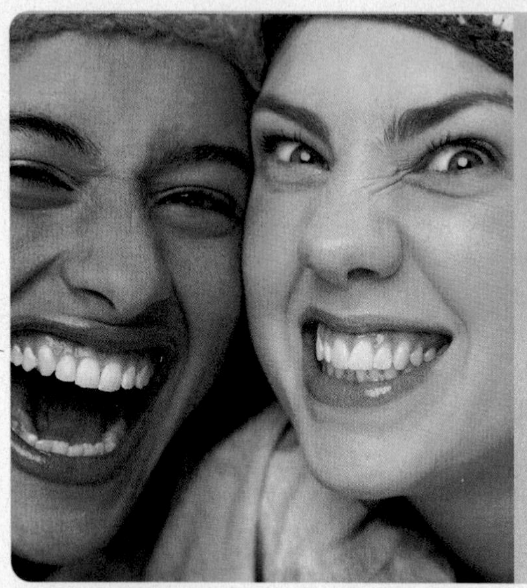

LEARN IT & LIVE IT

Romans 2:4:
Learn It: God's kindness is meant to lead you to repentance.
Live It: There's always that really mean boy in everyone's class. Astound him with a retort of kindness. Ask him with genuine concern, "How are you doing?" three different times.

Romans 3:23:
Learn It: All have sinned and are not good enough for God's glory.
Live It: Forgive your friend for any wrongs in the past month. Tell her you realize we all mess up; no one's perfect.

Romans 5:3-4:
Learn It: Troubles produce patience, which produces character, and character leads to hope.
Live It: Go for a run. Set your goal for two miles (or more if you can!). Afterward, write in your journal how you felt when you finally reached your goal. How did your character change? What else can you accomplish?

Son of Man. But when they do, you will be happy.
23 Be full of joy at that time, because you have
a great reward waiting for you in heaven. Their
ancestors did the same things to the prophets.
24 "But how terrible it will be for you who
are rich,
because you have had your easy life.
25 How terrible it will be for you who are full
now,
because you will be hungry.
How terrible it will be for you who are
laughing now,
because you will be sad and cry.
26 "How terrible when everyone says only
good things about you, because their ancestors
said the same things about the false prophets.

LOVE YOUR ENEMIES

27 "But I say to you who are listening, love
your enemies. Do good to those who hate you,
28 bless those who curse you, pray for those
who are cruel to you. 29 If anyone slaps you on
one cheek, offer him the other cheek, too. If
someone takes your coat, do not stop him
from taking your shirt. 30 Give to everyone
who asks you, and when someone takes something that is yours, don't ask for it back. 31 Do
to others what you would want them to do to
you. 32 If you love only the people who love
you, what praise should you get? Even sinners
love the people who love them. 33 If you do
good only to those who do good to you, what
praise should you get? Even sinners do that!
34 If you lend things to people, always hoping
to get something back, what praise should you
get? Even sinners lend to other sinners so that
they can get back the same amount! 35 But love
your enemies, do good to them, and lend to
them without hoping to get anything back.
Then you will have a great reward,
and you will be children of the
Most High God, because he is
kind even to people who are
ungrateful and full of sin.
36 Show mercy, just as your
Father shows mercy.

LOOK AT YOURSELVES

37 "Don't judge other people, and you will
not be judged. Don't accuse others of being
guilty, and you will not be accused of being
guilty. Forgive, and you will be forgiven. 38 Give,
and you will receive. You will be given much.
Pressed down, shaken together, and running
over, it will spill into your lap. The way you
give to others is the way God will give to you."
39 Jesus told them this story: "Can a blind
person lead another blind person? No! Both of
them will fall into a ditch. 40 A student is not
better than the teacher, but the student who
has been fully trained will be like the teacher.
41 "Why do you notice the little piece of
dust in your friend's eye, but you don't notice
the big piece of wood in your own eye? 42 How
can you say to your friend, 'Friend, let me take
that little piece of dust out of your eye' when
you cannot see that big piece of wood in your
own eye! You hypocrite! First, take the wood
out of your own eye. Then you will
see clearly to take the dust out
of your friend's eye.

Song of Solomon 8:6
Put me like a seal on your heart, like a seal on your arm. Love is as strong as death; jealousy is as strong as the grave. Love bursts into flames and burns like a hot fire.

TWO KINDS OF FRUIT

43 "A good tree does not
produce bad fruit, nor
does a bad tree produce good fruit.
44 Each tree is known by its own fruit.
People don't gather figs from thornbushes,
and they don't get grapes from bushes. 45 Good
people bring good things out of the good they
stored in their hearts. But evil people bring evil
things out of the evil they stored in their hearts.
People speak the things that are in their hearts.

TWO KINDS OF PEOPLE

46 "Why do you call me, 'Lord, Lord,' but do
not do what I say? 47 I will show you what
everyone is like who comes to me and hears

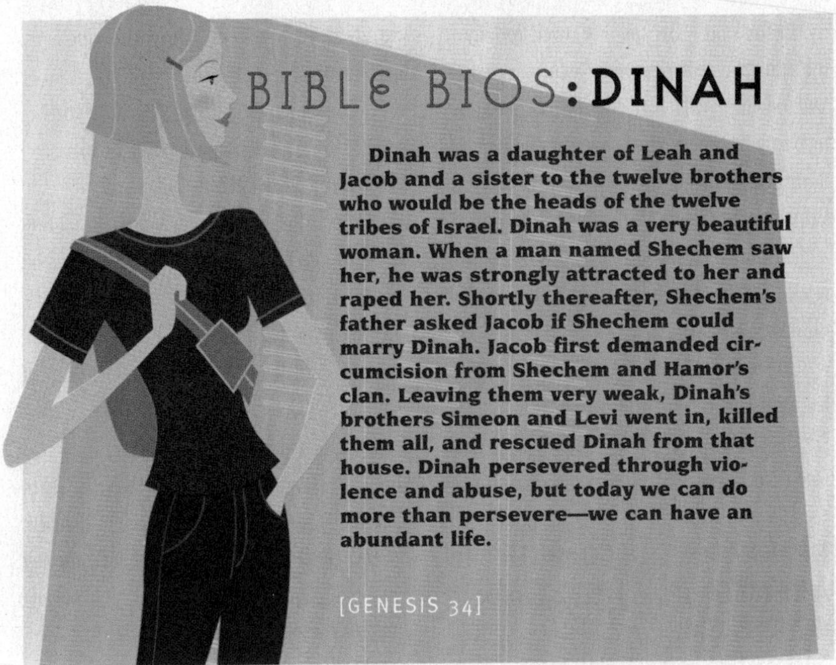

my words and obeys. 48That person is like a man building a house who dug deep and laid the foundation on rock. When the floods came, the water tried to wash the house away, but it could not shake it, because the house was built well. 49But the one who hears my words and does not obey is like a man who built his house on the ground without a foundation. When the floods came, the house quickly fell and was completely destroyed."

BIBLE BIOS: DINAH
Dinah was a daughter of Leah and Jacob and a sister to the twelve brothers who would be the heads of the twelve tribes of Israel. Dinah was a very beautiful woman. When a man named Shechem saw her, he was strongly attracted to her and raped her. Shortly thereafter, Shechem's father asked Jacob if Shechem could marry Dinah. Jacob first demanded circumcision from Shechem and Hamor's clan. Leaving them very weak, Dinah's brothers Simeon and Levi went in, killed them all, and rescued Dinah from that house. Dinah persevered through violence and abuse, but today we can do more than persevere—we can have an abundant life.
[GENESIS 34]

JESUS HEALS A SOLDIER'S SERVANT

7 When Jesus finished saying all these things to the people, he went to Capernaum. 2There was an army officer who had a servant who was very important to him. The servant was so sick he was nearly dead. 3When the officer heard about Jesus, he sent some older Jewish leaders to him to ask Jesus to come and heal his servant. 4The men went to Jesus and begged him, saying, "This officer is worthy of your help. 5He loves our people, and he built us a synagogue."

6So Jesus went with the men. He was getting near the officer's house when the officer sent friends to say, "Lord, don't trouble yourself, because I am not worthy to have you come into my house. 7That is why I did not come to you myself. But you only need to command it, and my servant will be healed. 8I, too, am a man under the authority of others, and I have soldiers under my command. I tell one soldier, 'Go,' and he goes. I tell another soldier, 'Come,' and he comes. I say to my servant, 'Do this,' and my servant does it."

9When Jesus heard this, he was amazed. Turning to the crowd that was following him, he said, "I tell you, this is the greatest faith I have found anywhere, even in Israel."

10Those who had been sent to Jesus went back to the house where they found the servant in good health.

JESUS BRINGS A MAN BACK TO LIFE

11Soon afterwards Jesus went to a town called Nain, and his followers and a large crowd traveled with him. 12When he came near the town gate, he saw a funeral. A mother, who was a widow, had lost her only son. A large crowd from the town was with the mother while her son was being carried out. 13When the Lord saw her, he felt very sorry for her and said, "Don't cry." 14He went up and touched the coffin, and the people who were carrying it stopped. Jesus said, "Young man, I tell you, get up!" 15And the son sat up and began to talk. Then Jesus gave him back to his mother.

16All the people were amazed and began praising God, saying, "A great prophet has come to us! God has come to help his people."

17This news about Jesus spread through all Judea and into all the places around there.

JOHN ASKS A QUESTION

18John's followers told him about all these things. He called for two of his followers 19and sent them to the Lord to ask, "Are you the One who is to come, or should we wait for someone else?"

20When the men came to Jesus, they said, "John the Baptist sent us to you with this question: 'Are you the One who is to come, or should we wait for someone else?' "

21At that time, Jesus healed many people of their sicknesses, diseases, and evil spirits, and he gave sight to many blind people. 22Then Jesus answered John's followers, "Go tell John what you saw and heard here. The blind can see, the crippled can walk, and people with skin diseases are healed. The deaf can hear, the dead are raised to life, and the Good News is preached to the poor. 23Those who do not stumble in their faith because of me are blessed!"

24When John's followers left, Jesus began talking to the people about John: "What did you go out into the desert to see? A reed[n] blown by the wind? 25What did you go out to see? A man dressed in fine clothes? No, people who have fine clothes and much wealth live in kings' palaces. 26But what did you go out to see? A prophet? Yes, and I tell you, John is more than a prophet. 27This was written about him:

'I will send my messenger ahead of you,
who will prepare the way
for you.' *Malachi 3:1*

28I tell you, John is greater than any other person ever born, but even the least important person in the kingdom of God is greater than John."

notes

7:24 reed It means that John was not ordinary or weak like grass blown by the wind.

29(When the people, including the tax collectors, heard this, they all agreed that God's teaching was good, because they had been baptized by John. 30But the Pharisees and experts on the law refused to accept God's plan for themselves; they did not let John baptize them.)

31Then Jesus said, "What shall I say about the people of this time? What are they like? 32They are like children sitting in the marketplace, calling to one another and saying,

'We played music for you, but you did not
dance;
we sang a sad song, but you did not cry.'

33John the Baptist came and did not eat bread or drink wine, and you say, 'He has a demon in him.' 34The Son of Man came eating and drinking, and you say, 'Look at him! He eats too much and drinks too much wine, and he is a friend of tax collectors and sinners!' 35But wisdom is proved to be right by what it does."

A WOMAN WASHES JESUS' FEET

36One of the Pharisees asked Jesus to eat with him, so Jesus went into the Pharisee's house and sat at the table. 37A sinful woman in the town learned that Jesus was eating at the Pharisee's house. So she brought an alabaster jar of perfume 38and stood behind Jesus at his feet, crying. She began to wash his feet with her tears, and she dried them with her hair, kissing them many times and rubbing them with the perfume. 39When the Pharisee who asked Jesus to come to his house saw this, he thought to himself, "If Jesus were a prophet, he would know that the woman touching him is a sinner!"

40Jesus said to the Pharisee, "Simon, I have something to say to you."

Simon said, "Teacher, tell me."

41Jesus said, "Two people owed money to the same banker. One owed five hundred coins[n] and the other owed fifty. 42They had no money to pay what they owed, but the banker told both of them they did not have to pay him. Which person will love the banker more?"

43Simon, the Pharisee, answered, "I think it would be the one who owed him the most money."

Jesus said to Simon, "You are right." 44Then Jesus turned toward the woman and said to Simon, "Do you see this woman? When I came into your house, you gave me no water for my feet, but she washed my feet with her tears and dried them with her hair. 45You gave me no kiss of greeting, but she has been kissing my feet since I came in. 46You did not put oil on my head, but she poured perfume on my feet. 47I tell you that her many sins are forgiven, so she showed great love. But the person who is forgiven only a little will love only a little."

48Then Jesus said to her, "Your sins are forgiven."

49The people sitting at the table began to say among themselves, "Who is this who even forgives sins?"

50Jesus said to the woman, "Because you believed, you are saved from your sins. Go in peace."

THE GROUP WITH JESUS

8 After this, while Jesus was traveling through some cities and small towns, he preached and told the Good News about God's kingdom. The twelve apostles were with him, 2and also some women who had been healed of sicknesses and evil spirits: Mary, called Magdalene, from whom seven demons had gone out; 3Joanna, the wife of Cuza (the manager of Herod's house); Susanna; and many others. These women used their own money to help Jesus and his apostles.

A STORY ABOUT PLANTING SEED

4When a great crowd was gathered, and people were coming to Jesus from every town, he told them this story:

5"A farmer went out to plant his seed. While he was planting, some seed fell by the road. People walked on the seed, and the birds ate it up. 6Some seed fell on rock, and when it began to grow, it died because it had no water. 7Some seed fell among thorny weeds, but the weeds grew up with it and choked the good plants. 8And some seed fell on good ground and grew and made a hundred times more."

As Jesus finished the story, he called out, "You people who can hear me, listen!"

9Jesus' followers asked him what this story meant.

10Jesus said, "You have been chosen to know the secrets about the kingdom of God. But I use stories to speak to other people so that:

'They will look, but they may not see.
They will listen, but they may not
understand.' *Isaiah 6:9*

11"This is what the story means: The seed is God's message. 12The seed that fell beside the road is like the people who hear God's teaching,

DIDYA KNOW → 4 IN 5 TEENS WOULD CONFIDE IN THEIR PARENTS IF THEY HAD A SERIOUS PROBLEM.

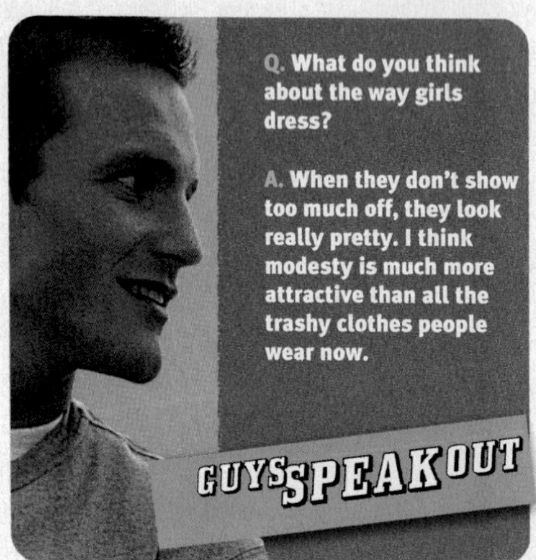
Q. What do you think about the way girls dress?
A. When they don't show too much off, they look really pretty. I think modesty is much more attractive than all the trashy clothes people wear now.
GUYS SPEAK OUT

notes

7:41 coins Roman denarii. One coin was the average pay for one day's work.

but the devil comes and takes it away from them
so they cannot believe it and be saved. 13The
seed that fell on rock is like those who hear
God's teaching and accept it gladly, but they
don't allow the teaching to go deep into their
lives. They believe for a while, but when trouble
comes, they give up. 14The seed that fell among
the thorny weeds is like those who hear God's
teaching, but they let the worries, riches, and
pleasures of this life keep them from growing
and producing good fruit. 15And the seed that
fell on the good ground is like those who hear
God's teaching with good, honest hearts and
obey it and patiently produce good fruit.

USE WHAT YOU HAVE

16"No one after lighting a lamp covers it
with a bowl or hides it under a bed. Instead,
the person puts it on a lampstand so those
who come in will see the light. 17Everything
that is hidden will become clear, and every
secret thing will be made known. 18So be careful how you listen. Those who have understanding will be given more. But those who do
not have understanding, even what they think
they have will be taken away from them."

JESUS' TRUE FAMILY

19Jesus' mother and brothers came to see
him, but there was such a crowd they could
not get to him. 20Someone said to Jesus, "Your
mother and your brothers are standing outside, wanting to see you."

21Jesus answered them, "My mother and
my brothers are those who listen to God's
teaching and obey it!"

JESUS CALMS A STORM

22One day Jesus and his followers got into a
boat, and he said to them, "Let's go across the
lake." And so they started across. 23While they
were sailing, Jesus fell asleep. A very strong
wind blew up on the lake, causing the boat to
fill with water, and they were in danger.

24The followers went to Jesus and woke
him, saying, "Master! Master! We will drown!"

Jesus got up and gave a command to the
wind and the waves. They stopped, and it
became calm. 25Jesus said to his followers,
"Where is your faith?"

The followers were afraid and amazed and
said to each other, "Who is this that commands even the wind and the water, and they
obey him?"

A MAN WITH DEMONS INSIDE HIM

26Jesus and his followers sailed across the
lake from Galilee to the area of the Gerasene
people. 27When Jesus got out on the land, a
man from the town who had demons inside
him came to Jesus. For a long time he had
worn no clothes and had lived in the burial
caves, not in a house. 28When he saw Jesus, he
cried out and fell down before him. He said
with a loud voice, "What do you want with
me, Jesus, Son of the Most High God? I beg
you, don't torture me!" 29He said this because
Jesus was commanding the evil spirit to come
out of the man. Many times it had taken hold
of him. Though he had been kept under guard
and chained hand and foot, he had broken his
chains and had been forced by the demon out
into a lonely place.

30Jesus asked him, "What is your name?"

He answered, "Legion,"*n* because many
demons were in him. 31The demons begged
Jesus not to send them into eternal darkness.*n*
32A large herd of pigs was feeding on a hill, and
the demons begged Jesus to allow them to go
into the pigs. So Jesus allowed them to do this.
33When the demons came out of the man,
they went into the pigs, and the herd ran down
the hill into the lake and was drowned.

34When the herdsmen saw what had happened, they ran away and told about this in
the town and the countryside. 35And people
went to see what had happened. When they
came to Jesus, they found the man sitting at
Jesus' feet, clothed and in his right mind,
because the demons were gone. But the people
were frightened. 36The people who saw this
happen told the others how Jesus had made

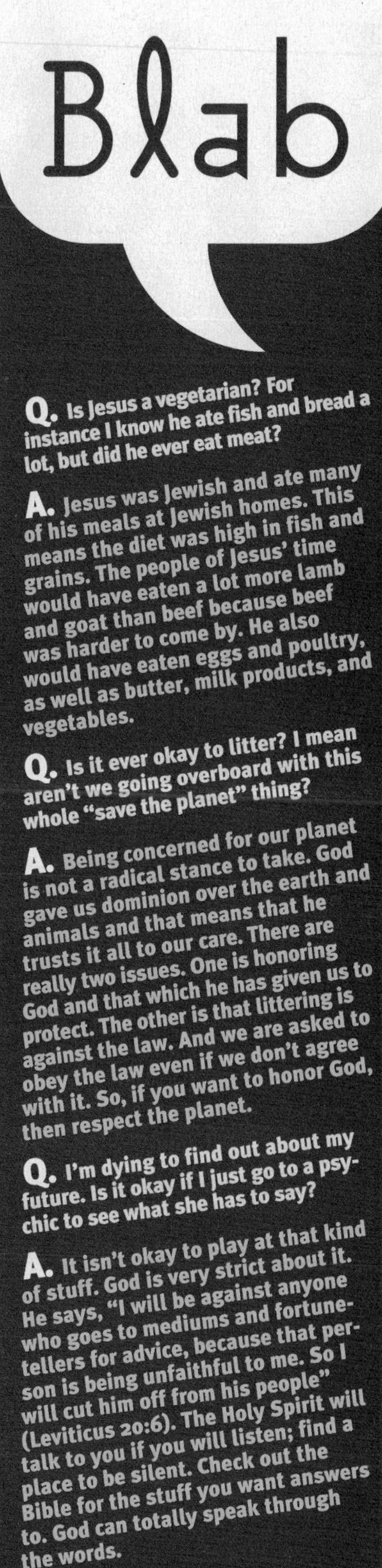
Blab
Q. Is Jesus a vegetarian? For instance I know he ate fish and bread a lot, but did he ever eat meat?
A. Jesus was Jewish and ate many of his meals at Jewish homes. This means the diet was high in fish and grains. The people of Jesus' time would have eaten a lot more lamb and goat than beef because beef was harder to come by. He also would have eaten eggs and poultry, as well as butter, milk products, and vegetables.
Q. Is it ever okay to litter? I mean aren't we going overboard with this whole "save the planet" thing?
A. Being concerned for our planet is not a radical stance to take. God gave us dominion over the earth and animals and that means that he trusts it all to our care. There are really two issues. One is honoring God and that which he has given us to protect. The other is that littering is against the law. And we are asked to obey the law even if we don't agree with it. So, if you want to honor God, then respect the planet.
Q. I'm dying to find out about my future. Is it okay if I just go to a psychic to see what she has to say?
A. It isn't okay to play at that kind of stuff. God is very strict about it. He says, "I will be against anyone who goes to mediums and fortune-tellers for advice, because that person is being unfaithful to me. So I will cut him off from his people" (Leviticus 20:6). The Holy Spirit will talk to you if you will listen; find a place to be silent. Check out the Bible for the stuff you want answers to. God can totally speak through the words.

notes

8:30 "Legion" Means very many. A legion was about five thousand men in the Roman army. **8:31 eternal darkness** Literally, "the abyss," something like a pit or a hole that has no end.

Luke 9:32

Can you imagine waking up and seeing Jesus in his glory? Wow! That would be something—to see the all-powerful and majestic One right there beside you when you wake up!

The fact is, we do serve a glorious God and we have the opportunity to wake up every morning and see "his glory." That's why it's so important to reach over, grab the Word of God, and meditate on it every morning. It gets our thinking headed in the right direction. If we aren't reminded of the glory and power of God every morning, it can be so easy to get caught up in our everyday affairs to the point that we forget that the "all-powerful One" is right beside us!

One thing that will bring us into the presence of his glory is to simply praise the Lord for who he is.

He's the King of glory. He is the Alpha and Omega—the beginning and the end of everything. He's the lily of the valley, the bright and morning star. He's our safe place and our strong place. He's a tower in which we can hide from our enemy. In him we are more than winners. He's the glorious God who is more than enough.

Take time to think about the Lord's glory every day. He is the One who is glorious!

the man well. 37All the people of the Gerasene country asked Jesus to leave, because they were all very afraid. So Jesus got into the boat and went back to Galilee.

38The man whom Jesus had healed begged to go with him, but Jesus sent him away, saying, 39"Go back home and tell people how much God has done for you." So the man went all over town telling how much Jesus had done for him.

"[JESUS] SENT THE APOSTLES OUT TO TELL ABOUT GOD'S KINGDOM AND TO HEAL THE SICK."

JESUS GIVES LIFE TO A DEAD GIRL AND HEALS A SICK WOMAN

40When Jesus got back to Galilee, a crowd welcomed him, because everyone was waiting for him. 41A man named Jairus, a leader of the synagogue, came to Jesus and fell at his feet, begging him to come to his house. 42Jairus' only daughter, about twelve years old, was dying.

While Jesus was on his way to Jairus' house, the people were crowding all around him. 43A woman was in the crowd who had been bleeding for twelve years, but no one was able to heal her. 44She came up behind Jesus and touched the edge of his coat, and instantly her bleeding stopped. 45Then Jesus said, "Who touched me?"

When all the people said they had not touched him, Peter said, "Master, the people are all around you and are pushing against you."

46But Jesus said, "Someone did touch me, because I felt power go out from me." 47When the woman saw she could not hide, she came forward, shaking, and fell down before Jesus. While all the people listened, she told why she had touched him and how she had been instantly healed. 48Jesus said to her, "Dear woman, you are made well because you believed. Go in peace."

49While Jesus was still speaking, someone came from the house of the synagogue leader and said to him, "Your daughter is dead. Don't bother the teacher anymore."

50When Jesus heard this, he said to Jairus, "Don't be afraid. Just believe, and your daughter will be well."

51When Jesus went to the house, he let only Peter, John, James, and the girl's father and mother go inside with him. 52All the people were crying and feeling sad because the girl was dead, but Jesus said, "Stop crying. She is not dead, only asleep."

53The people laughed at Jesus because they knew the girl was dead. 54But Jesus took hold of her hand and called to her, "My child, stand up!" 55Her spirit came back into her, and she stood up at once. Then Jesus ordered that she be given something to eat. 56The girl's parents were amazed, but Jesus told them not to tell anyone what had happened.

JESUS SENDS OUT THE APOSTLES

9 Jesus called the twelve apostles together and gave them power and authority over all demons and the ability to heal sicknesses. 2He sent the apostles out to tell about God's kingdom and to heal the sick. 3He said to them, "Take nothing for your trip, neither a walking stick, bag, bread, money, or extra clothes. 4When you enter a house, stay there until it is time to leave. 5If people do not welcome you, shake the dust off of your feet[n] as you leave the town, as a warning to them."

6So the apostles went out and traveled through all the towns, preaching the Good News and healing people everywhere.

Romans 5:8
But God shows his great love for us in this way: Christ died for us while we were still sinners.

HEROD IS CONFUSED ABOUT JESUS

7Herod, the governor, heard about all the things that were happening and was confused, because some people said, "John the Baptist has risen from the dead." 8Others said, "Elijah

9:5 shake . . . feet A warning. It showed that they had rejected these people.

April

Daylight Saving Time is the first weekend in April.
Turn your clocks forward one hour!

1 April Fool's Day! Play a joke on someone you love!	2	3	4 Pray for a Person of Influence: Heath Ledger's birthday is today.
5	6 Read Psalm 23 and rest with God.	7	8
9 Invite a friend to go to church with you this weekend.	10	11	12 Explore your career options week!
13	14 Pray for a Person of Influence: Today is Sarah Michelle Gellar's birthday.	15 Tax Day!	16
17	18	19 Pray for a Person of Influence: Kate Hudson has a birthday today.	20
21	22	23 Do something sweet for a sister or friend today.	24
25	26	27 Volunteer at a soup kitchen this week!	
28	29 Pray for a Person of Influence: Today is Andre Agassi's birthday.	30	

Easter falls on the first Sunday following the first full moon that occurs on or after March 21—the vernal equinox. Easter can never happen before March 22 or after April 25.

has come to us." And still others said, "One of the prophets who lived long ago has risen from the dead."
9Herod said, "I cut off John's head, so who is this man I hear such things about?" And Herod kept trying to see Jesus.

MORE THAN FIVE THOUSAND FED

10When the apostles returned, they told Jesus everything they had done. Then Jesus took them with him to a town called Bethsaida where they could be alone together.
11But the people learned where Jesus went and followed him. He welcomed them and talked with them about God's kingdom and healed those who needed to be healed.

12Late in the afternoon, the twelve apostles came to Jesus and said, "Send the people away. They need to go to the towns and countryside around here and find places to sleep and something to eat, because no one lives in this place."

13But Jesus said to them, "You give them something to eat."

They said, "We have only five loaves of bread and two fish, unless we go buy food for all these people."
14(There were about five thousand men there.)

Jesus said to his followers, "Tell the people to sit in groups of about fifty people."

15So the followers did this, and all the people sat down.
16Then Jesus took the five loaves of bread and two fish, and looking up to heaven, he thanked God for the food. Then he divided the food and gave it to the followers to give to the people.
17They all ate and were satisfied, and what was left over was gathered up, filling twelve baskets.

JESUS IS THE CHRIST

18One time when Jesus was praying alone, his followers were with him, and he asked them, "Who do the people say I am?"

19They answered, "Some say you are John the Baptist. Others say you are Elijah.[n] And others say you are one of the prophets from long ago who has come back to life."

20Then Jesus asked, "But who do you say I am?"

Peter answered, "You are the Christ from God."

21Jesus warned them not to tell anyone, saying,
22"The Son of Man must suffer many things. He will be rejected by the older Jewish leaders, the leading priests, and the teachers of the law. He will be killed and after three days will be raised from the dead."

23Jesus said to all of them, "If people want to follow me, they must give up the things they want. They must be willing to give up their lives daily to follow me.
24Those who want to save their lives will give up true life. But those who give up their lives for me will have true life.
25It is worth nothing for them to have the whole world if they themselves are destroyed or lost.
26If people are ashamed of me and my teaching, then the Son of Man will be ashamed of them when he comes in his glory and with the glory of the Father and the holy angels.
27I tell you the truth, some people standing here will see the kingdom of God before they die."

BEAUTY SECRET

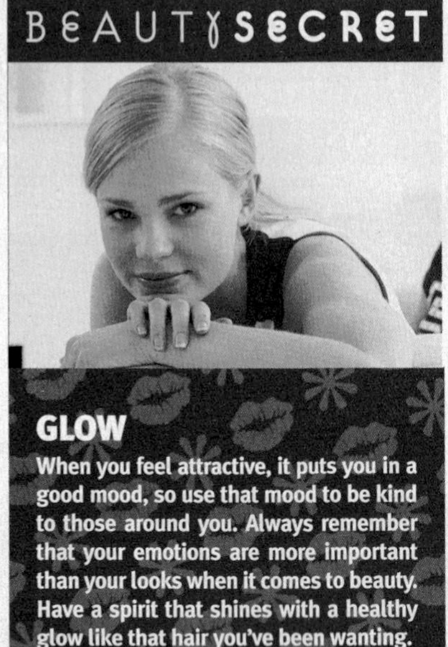

GLOW

When you feel attractive, it puts you in a good mood, so use that mood to be kind to those around you. Always remember that your emotions are more important than your looks when it comes to beauty. Have a spirit that shines with a healthy glow like that hair you've been wanting.

LEARN IT & LIVE IT

Romans 5:21:
Learn It: Where sin increases, grace abounds.
Live It: Forgive the bully at school. Not just this time, but every time they offend you. Keep doing it. Rejoice in the fact that you have an opportunity to share God's grace.

Romans 6:15:
Learn It: Just because we are covered in grace does not mean we should sin.
Live It: Talk to your best friend about being accountability partners. Holding each other "accountable" means that you guys confess your sins to one another, challenge each other to good works, and encourage each other in faith.

Romans 6:23:
Learn It: The free gift of God is eternal life.
Live It: Tell three friends about the free gift of God. Give them a chance to accept the most wonderful gift on earth.

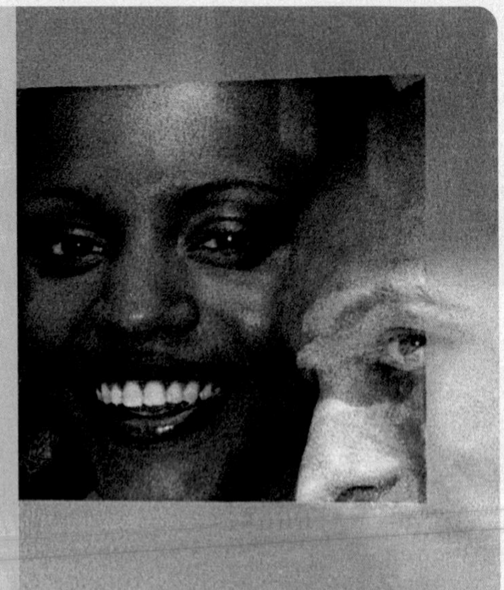

9:19 Elijah A man who spoke for God and who lived hundreds of years before Christ. See 1 Kings 17.

Notes

ARE YOU A LEADER OR A FOLLOWER?

I LIKE TO SPEAK UP IN CLASS.
LOVE IT 1 2 3 4 5 6 7 8 9 10 HATE IT

MY FRIENDS COME TO ME FOR ADVICE.
ALWAYS 1 2 3 4 5 6 7 8 9 10 NEVER

IT'S EASY FOR ME TO MAKE DECISIONS.
ALWAYS 1 2 3 4 5 6 7 8 9 10 NEVER

THE THOUGHT OF RUNNING FOR A SCHOOL OFFICE IS:
GREAT 1 2 3 4 5 6 7 8 9 10 TERRIBLE

I VOLUNTEER FOR THINGS.
ALWAYS 1 2 3 4 5 6 7 8 9 10 NEVER

I LIKE BEING RESPONSIBLE FOR A PROJECT.
LOVE IT 1 2 3 4 5 6 7 8 9 10 HATE IT

I DON'T MIND TELLING OTHERS WHAT I REALLY THINK.
ALWAYS 1 2 3 4 5 6 7 8 9 10 NEVER

IF OTHERS DISAGREE WITH ME, IT CHANGES MY OPINION.
NEVER 1 2 3 4 5 6 7 8 9 10 ALWAYS

IF YOU SCORED BETWEEN 8 AND 24, CONGRATULATIONS, YOU'RE A BORN LEADER!
People look to you for guidance and direction. You are efficient and confident, and people probably love being in your work groups at school because you get things done. Remember to use your leadership skills for good. Jesus was a natural leader too, but he didn't boss others around or ignore their opinions. Use your gifts to lead others to him!

IF YOU SCORED BETWEEN 25 AND 56, YOU ARE A LITTLE OF BOTH A LEADER AND A FOLLOWER.
Most of us probably go back and forth a little between the two. Find more confidence in Christ's purpose for your life, and don't be scared to take the lead if you're called to.

IF YOU SCORED A 57 OR ABOVE, YOU ARE A FOLLOWER.
There's actually nothing wrong with being someone who's in the crowd, putting in the hard work to make something happen. Just make sure you're following the right people. And when it's your turn to lead, don't be afraid of the challenge.

JESUS TALKS WITH MOSES AND ELIJAH

[28]About eight days after Jesus said these things, he took Peter, John, and James and went up on a mountain to pray. [29]While Jesus was praying, the appearance of his face changed, and his clothes became shining white. [30]Then two men, Moses and Elijah,[n] were talking with Jesus. [31]They appeared in heavenly glory, talking about his departure which he would soon bring about in Jerusalem. [32]Peter and the others were very sleepy, but when they awoke fully, they saw the glory of Jesus and the two men standing with him. [33]When Moses and Elijah were about to leave, Peter said to Jesus, "Master, it is good that we are here. Let us make three tents—one for you, one for Moses, and one for Elijah." (Peter did not know what he was talking about.)

[34]While he was saying these things, a cloud came and covered them, and they became afraid as the cloud covered them. [35]A voice came from the cloud, saying, "This is my Son, whom I have chosen. Listen to him!"

[36]When the voice finished speaking, only Jesus was there. Peter, John, and James said nothing and told no one at that time what they had seen.

JESUS HEALS A SICK BOY

[37]The next day, when they came down from the mountain, a large crowd met Jesus. [38]A man in the crowd shouted to him, "Teacher, please come and look at my son, because he is my only child. [39]An evil spirit seizes my son, and suddenly he screams. It causes him to lose control of himself and foam at the mouth. The evil spirit keeps on hurting him and almost never leaves him. [40]I begged your followers to force the evil spirit out, but they could not do it."

[41]Jesus answered, "You people have no faith, and your lives are all wrong. How long must I stay with you and put up with you? Bring your son here."

[42]While the boy was coming, the demon threw him on the ground and made him lose control of himself. But Jesus gave a strong command to the evil spirit and healed the boy and gave him back to his father. [43]All the people were amazed at the great power of God.

JESUS TALKS ABOUT HIS DEATH

While everyone was wondering about all that Jesus did, he said to his followers, [44]"Don't forget what I tell you now: The Son of Man will be handed over to people." [45]But the followers did not understand what this meant; the meaning was hidden from them so they could not understand. But they were afraid to ask Jesus about it.

WHO IS THE GREATEST?

[46]Jesus' followers began to have an argument about which one of them was the greatest. [47]Jesus knew what they were thinking, so he took a little child and stood the child beside him. [48]Then Jesus said, "Whoever accepts this little child in my name accepts me. And whoever accepts me accepts the One who sent me, because whoever is least among you all is really the greatest."

ANYONE NOT AGAINST US IS FOR US

[49]John answered, "Master, we saw someone using your name to force demons out of people. We told him to stop, because he does not belong to our group."

[50]But Jesus said to him, "Don't stop him, because whoever is not against you is for you."

A TOWN REJECTS JESUS

[51]When the time was coming near for Jesus to depart, he was determined to go to Jerusalem. [52]He sent some men ahead of him, who went into a town in Samaria to make everything ready for him. [53]But the people there would not welcome him, because he was set on going to Jerusalem. [54]When James and John, followers of Jesus, saw this, they said, "Lord, do you want us to call fire down from heaven and destroy those people?"[n]

[55]But Jesus turned and scolded them. [56]Then[n] they went to another town.

FOLLOWING JESUS

[57]As they were going along the road, someone said to Jesus, "I will follow you any place you go."

[58]Jesus said to them, "The foxes have holes to live in, and the birds have nests, but the Son of Man has no place to rest his head."

[59]Jesus said to another man, "Follow me!"

But he said, "Lord, first let me go and bury my father."

[60]But Jesus said to him, "Let the people who are dead bury their own dead. You must go and tell about the kingdom of God."

[61]Another man said, "I will follow you, Lord, but first let me go and say good-bye to my family."

[62]Jesus said, "Anyone who begins to plow a field but keeps looking back is of no use in the kingdom of God."

4 IN 5 TEENS THINK THEIR PARENTS ARE AS COOL OR COOLER THAN THEIR FRIENDS' PARENTS.

JESUS SENDS OUT THE SEVENTY-TWO

10 After this, the Lord chose seventy-two[n] others and sent them out in pairs ahead of him into every town and place where he planned to go. [2]He said to them, "There are a great many people to harvest, but there are only a few workers. So pray to God, who owns the harvest, that he will send more workers to help gather his harvest. [3]Go now, but listen! I am sending you out like sheep among wolves. [4]Don't carry a purse, a bag, or sandals, and don't waste time talking with people on

9:30 Moses and Elijah Two of the most important Jewish leaders in the past. God had given Moses the Law, and Elijah was an important prophet. **9:54 Verse 54** Here, some Greek copies add: ". . . as Elijah did." **9:55-56 Verses 55-56** Some copies read: "But Jesus turned and scolded them. And Jesus said, 'You don't know what kind of spirit you belong to. [56]The Son of Man did not come to destroy the souls of people but to save them.' Then. . . ." **10:1 seventy-two** Many Greek copies read seventy.

Blab

Q. My teacher says that the God that Jews and Muslims and all other religions worship is the same as our God. She says there is only one God, and that's from the Bible. Is that true?

A. It's true that there is only one God. But that doesn't mean that the God that other religions worship is the same God. He isn't the same in all religions. Check out what the gods in other religions say, and you'll see their personalities are completely different from that of our God—they can't be the same person.

Q. I want to meditate, but my parents aren't sure it's okay. Is it okay for Christians to meditate?

A. Meditation is a Christian discipline that has been taken on by other non-Christian traditions and changed into different forms. If you're meditating on God and his Word, that's cool. Share that with your parents and let them know what you're thinking about. But be careful to not get involved with other traditions that might become a negative influence on you.

Q. I have a confession. I totally hate my brother. I mean I really hate him. I wish he were never born. How can God expect me to love someone who can be such a jerk?

A. Brothers can act like total jerks and be hard to love, but yep, God does expect you to love him. It might just be that God wants you to learn that love isn't a feeling but a decision. If you want to be holy, you have to practice loving the unlovable. And your brother is the perfect place to start.

the road. [5]Before you go into a house, say, 'Peace be with this house.' [6]If peaceful people live there, your blessing of peace will stay with them, but if not, then your blessing will come back to you. [7]Stay in the peaceful house, eating and drinking what the people there give you. A worker should be given his pay. Don't move from house to house. [8]If you go into a town and the people welcome you, eat what they give you. [9]Heal the sick who live there, and tell them, 'The kingdom of God is near you.' [10]But if you go into a town, and the people don't welcome you, then go into the streets and say, [11]'Even the dirt from your town that sticks to our feet we wipe off against you.[n] But remember that the kingdom of God is near.' [12]I tell you, on the Judgment Day it will be better for the people of Sodom[n] than for the people of that town.

JESUS WARNS UNBELIEVERS

[13]"How terrible for you, Korazin! How terrible for you, Bethsaida! If the miracles I did in you had happened in Tyre and Sidon,[n] those people would have changed their lives long ago. They would have worn rough cloth and put ashes on themselves to show they had changed. [14]But on the Judgment Day it will be better for Tyre and Sidon than for you. [15]And you, Capernaum,[n] will you be lifted up to heaven? No! You will be thrown down to the depths!

[16]"Whoever listens to you listens to me, and whoever refuses to accept you refuses to accept me. And whoever refuses to accept me refuses to accept the One who sent me."

SATAN FALLS

[17]When the seventy-two[n] came back, they were very happy and said, "Lord, even the demons obeyed us when we used your name!"

[18]Jesus said, "I saw Satan fall like lightning from heaven. [19]Listen, I have given you power to walk on snakes and scorpions, power that is greater than the enemy has. So nothing will hurt you. [20]But you should not be happy because the spirits obey you but because your names are written in heaven."

JESUS PRAYS TO THE FATHER

[21]Then Jesus rejoiced in the Holy Spirit and said, "I praise you, Father, Lord of heaven and earth, because you have hidden these things from the people who are wise and smart. But you have shown them to those who are like little children. Yes, Father, this is what you really wanted.

[22]"My Father has given me all things. No one knows who the Son is, except the Father. And no one knows who the Father is, except the Son and those whom the Son chooses to tell."

[23]Then Jesus turned to his followers and said privately, "You are blessed to see what you now see. [24]I tell you, many prophets and kings wanted to see what you now see, but they did not, and they wanted to hear what you now hear, but they did not."

THE GOOD SAMARITAN

[25]Then an expert on the law stood up to test Jesus, saying, "Teacher, what must I do to get life forever?"

[26]Jesus said, "What is written in the law? What do you read there?"

[27]The man answered, "Love the Lord your God with all your heart, all your soul, all your strength, and all your mind."[n] Also, "Love your neighbor as you love yourself."[n]

[28]Jesus said to him, "Your answer is right. Do this and you will live."

[29]But the man, wanting to show the importance of his question, said to Jesus, "And who is my neighbor?"

[30]Jesus answered, "As a man was going down from Jerusalem to Jericho, some robbers attacked him. They tore off his clothes, beat him, and left him lying there, almost dead. [31]It happened that a priest was going down that road. When he saw the man, he walked by on the other side. [32]Next, a Levite[n] came there, and after he went over and looked at the man, he walked by on the other side of the road. [33]Then a Samaritan[n] traveling down the road came to where the hurt man was. When he saw the man, he felt very sorry for him.

notes

10:11 dirt . . . you A warning. It showed that they had rejected these people. **10:12 Sodom** City that God destroyed because the people were so evil. **10:13 Tyre and Sidon** Towns where wicked people lived. **10:13, 15 Korazin, Bethsaida, Capernaum** Towns by Lake Galilee where Jesus preached to the people. **10:17 seventy-two** Many Greek copies read seventy. **10:27 "Love . . . mind."** Quotation from Deuteronomy 6:5. **10:27 "Love . . . yourself."** Quotation from Leviticus 19:18. **10:32 Levite** Levites were members of the tribe of Levi who helped the Jewish priests with their work in the Temple. Read 1 Chronicles 23:24–32. **10:33 Samaritan** Samaritans were people from Samaria. These people were part Jewish, but the Jews did not accept them as true Jews. Samaritans and Jews disliked each other.

34The Samaritan went to him, poured
olive oil and wine[n] on his wounds, and
bandaged them. Then he put the hurt man
on his own donkey and took him to an inn
where he cared for him. 35The next day,
the Samaritan brought out two coins,[n]
gave them to the innkeeper, and said, 'Take
care of this man. If you spend more
money on him, I will pay it back to you
when I come again.' "

36Then Jesus said, "Which one of these
three men do you think was a neighbor to
the man who was attacked by the robbers?"

37The expert on the law answered, "The
one who showed him mercy."

Jesus said to him, "Then go and do what he did."

MARY AND MARTHA

38While Jesus and his followers were traveling, Jesus went into a town. A woman named
Martha let Jesus stay at her house. 39Martha
had a sister named Mary, who was sitting at
Jesus' feet and listening to him teach. 40But
Martha was busy with all the work to be done.
She went in and said, "Lord, don't you care
that my sister has left me alone to
do all the work? Tell her to help
me."

41But the Lord answered
her, "Martha, Martha, you
are worried and upset
about many things. 42Only one
thing is important. Mary has chosen
the better thing, and it will never be taken
away from her."

2 Corinthians 5:14
The love of Christ controls us, because we know that One died for all, so all have died.

JESUS TEACHES ABOUT PRAYER

11 One time Jesus was praying in a certain place. When he finished, one of
his followers said to him, "Lord, teach us to
pray as John taught his followers."

2Jesus said to them, "When you pray, say:
'Father, may your name always be kept holy.
May your kingdom come.
3 Give us the food we need for each day.

GUYS SPEAK OUT
Q. What's the one thing you would tell girls your age if you could?
A. That I like them the way they are—they don't need to try so hard!

4 Forgive us for our sins,
because we forgive everyone who has
done wrong to us.
And do not cause us to be tempted.' "

CONTINUE TO ASK

5Then Jesus said to them, "Suppose one of
you went to your friend's house at midnight
and said to him, 'Friend, loan me three loaves
of bread. 6A friend of mine has come into town
to visit me, but I have nothing for him to eat.'
7Your friend inside the house answers, 'Don't
bother me! The door is already
locked, and my children and I
are in bed. I cannot get up and
give you anything.' 8I tell
you, if friendship is not
enough to make him
get up to give you the bread, your
boldness will make him get up and give
you whatever you need. 9So I tell you, ask, and
God will give to you. Search, and you will find.
Knock, and the door will open for you. 10Yes,
everyone who asks will receive. The one who
searches will find. And everyone who knocks
will have the door opened. 11If your children
ask for a fish, which of you would give them a
snake instead? 12Or, if your children ask for an
egg, would you give them a scorpion? 13Even
though you are bad, you know how to give
good things to your children. How much more
your heavenly Father will give the Holy
Spirit to those who ask him!"

JESUS' POWER IS FROM GOD

14One time Jesus was sending out a
demon that could not talk. When the
demon came out, the man who had been
unable to speak, then spoke. The people
were amazed. 15But some of them said,
"Jesus uses the power of Beelzebul, the ruler
of demons, to force demons out of people."

16Other people, wanting to test Jesus,
asked him to give them a sign from heaven.
17But knowing their thoughts, he said to
them, "Every kingdom that is divided against
itself will be destroyed. And a family that is
divided against itself will not continue. 18So if
Satan is divided against himself, his kingdom
will not continue. You say that I use the power
of Beelzebul to force out demons. 19But if I use
the power of Beelzebul to force out demons,
what power do your people use to force
demons out? So they will be your judges. 20But
if I use the power of God to force out demons,
then the kingdom of God has come to you.

"ANYONE WHO IS NOT WITH ME IS AGAINST ME, AND ANYONE WHO DOES NOT WORK WITH ME IS WORKING AGAINST ME."

21"When a strong person with many weapons
guards his own house, his possessions are
safe. 22But when someone stronger comes and
defeats him, the stronger one will take away
the weapons the first man trusted and will give
away the possessions.

23"Anyone who is not with me is against
me, and anyone who does not work with me is
working against me.

THE EMPTY PERSON

24"When an evil spirit comes out of a person, it travels through dry places, looking for
a place to rest. But when it finds no place, it

notes **10:34 olive oil and wine** Oil and wine were used like medicine to soften and clean wounds. **10:35 coins** Roman denarii. One coin was the average pay for one day's work.

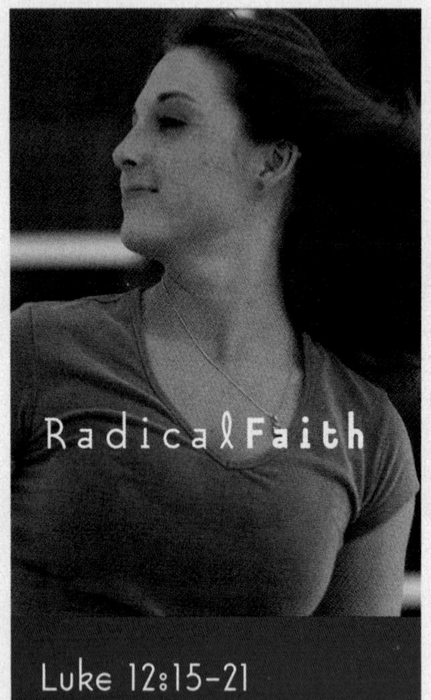

Luke 12:15-21

Jesus makes the point in this parable that things aren't "it." Things don't give you a relationship with God. And things don't make your walk with God any deeper. The rich man in this story thought that he would have an easy life because he had everything he could possibly ever want or need. God called him a fool, because that night when he died, his things could do nothing for him. Where are you spending most of your time? Are you worrying about the next really important "thing" you've got to have and how to get it, or are you thinking about the Lord and how to know and love him more completely?

Jesus says it's foolish to spend your time accumulating stuff that will only rust and decay in the end. Instead, God wants you to concentrate on learning what's really valuable and what isn't; to sacrifice for the good of another person, of yourself, or of the kingdom of God. He promises to provide all you need. But his focus is on the eternal—the souls of men and women. That's what really matters to God.

says, 'I will go back to the house I left.'
[25]And when it comes back, it finds that house
swept clean and made neat. [26]Then the evil
spirit goes out and brings seven other spirits
more evil than it is, and they go in and live
there. So the person has even more trouble
than before."

PEOPLE WHO ARE TRULY HAPPY

[27]As Jesus was saying these things, a woman
in the crowd called out to Jesus, "Happy is the
mother who gave birth to you and nursed you."
[28]But Jesus said, "No, happy are those who
hear the teaching of God and obey it."

THE PEOPLE WANT A MIRACLE

[29]As the crowd grew larger, Jesus said, "The
people who live today are evil. They want to
see a miracle for a sign, but no sign will be
given them, except the sign of Jonah.[n] [30]As
Jonah was a sign for those people who lived in
Nineveh, the Son of Man will be a sign for the
people of this time. [31]On the Judgment Day
the Queen of the South[n] will stand up with the
people who live now. She will show they are
guilty, because she came from far away to listen to Solomon's wise teaching. And I tell you
that someone greater than Solomon is here.
[32]On the Judgment Day the people of Nineveh
will stand up with the people who live now,
and they will show that you are guilty. When
Jonah preached to them, they were sorry and
changed their lives. And I tell you that someone greater than Jonah is here.

BE A LIGHT FOR THE WORLD

[33]"No one lights a lamp and puts it in a
secret place or under a bowl, but on a lampstand so the people who come in can see.
[34]Your eye is a light for the body. When your
eyes are good, your whole body will be full of
light. But when your eyes are evil, your whole
body will be full of darkness. [35]So be careful
not to let the light in you become darkness.
[36]If your whole body is full of light, and none
of it is dark, then you will shine bright, as
when a lamp shines on you."

JESUS ACCUSES THE PHARISEES

[37]After Jesus had finished speaking, a Pharisee
asked Jesus to eat with him. So Jesus went in
and sat at the table. [38]But the Pharisee was
surprised when he saw that Jesus did not wash
his hands[n] before the meal. [39]The Lord said to
him, "You Pharisees clean the outside of the cup
and the dish, but inside you are full of greed
and evil. [40]You foolish people! The same one
who made what is outside also made what is
inside. [41]So give what is in your dishes to the
poor, and then you will be fully clean. [42]How terrible for you Pharisees! You give God one-tenth
of even your mint, your rue, and every other
plant in your garden. But you fail to be fair to
others and to love God. These are the things
you should do while continuing to do those
other things. [43]How terrible for you Pharisees,
because you love to have the most important
seats in the synagogues, and you love to be
greeted with respect in the marketplaces. [44]How
terrible for you, because you are like hidden
graves, which people walk on without knowing."

JESUS TALKS TO EXPERTS ON THE LAW

[45]One of the experts on the law said to
Jesus, "Teacher, when you say these things,
you are insulting us, too."
[46]Jesus answered, "How terrible for you,
you experts on the law! You make strict rules
that are very hard for people to obey, but you
yourselves don't even try to follow those rules.
[47]How terrible for you, because you build
tombs for the prophets whom your ancestors
killed! [48]And now you show that you approve
of what your ancestors did. They killed the
prophets, and you build tombs for them! [49]This
is why in his wisdom God said, 'I will send
prophets and apostles to them. They will kill
some, and they will treat others cruelly.' [50]So
you who live now will be punished for the
deaths of all the prophets who were killed
since the beginning of the world— [51]from the
killing of Abel to the killing of Zechariah,[n]
who died between the altar and the Temple.

notes

11:29 sign of Jonah Jonah's three days in the fish are like Jesus' three days in the tomb. See Matthew 12:40. **11:31 Queen of the South** The Queen of Sheba. She traveled a thousand miles to learn God's wisdom from Solomon. Read 1 Kings 10:1-3. **11:38 wash his hands** This was a Jewish religious custom that the Pharisees thought was very important. **11:51 Abel . . . Zechariah** In the Hebrew Old Testament, the first and last men to be murdered.

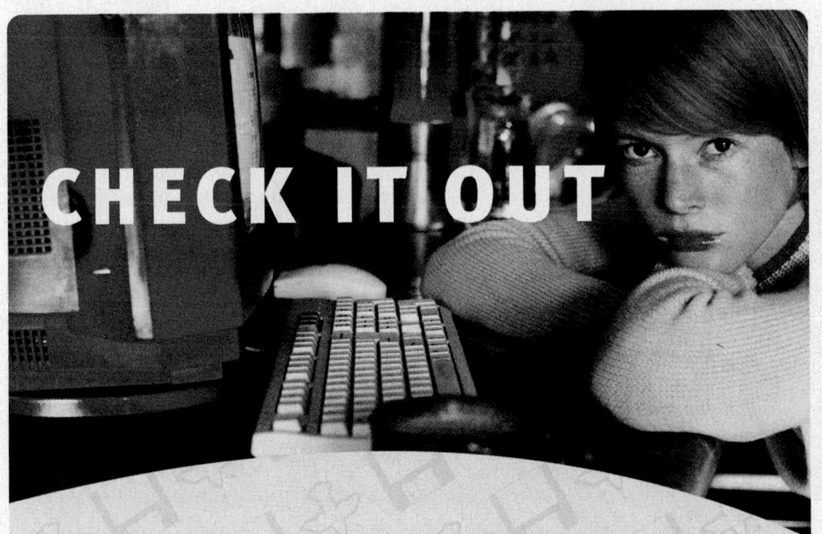

Samaritan's Purse

Samaritan's Purse is a nondenominational evangelical Christian organization providing spiritual and physical aid to hurting people around the world. Since 1970, Samaritan's Purse has helped meet needs of people who are victims of war, poverty, natural disasters, disease, and famine with the purpose of sharing God's love through his Son, Jesus Christ.

The organization serves the church worldwide to promote the Gospel of the Lord Jesus Christ.

*To get involved, visit **www.samaritanspurse.org**.*

Yes, I tell you that you who are alive now will be punished for them all.

52"How terrible for you, you experts on the law. You have taken away the key to learning about God. You yourselves would not learn, and you stopped others from learning, too."

53When Jesus left, the teachers of the law and the Pharisees began to give him trouble, asking him questions about many things, 54trying to catch him saying something wrong.

DON'T BE LIKE THE PHARISEES

12 So many thousands of people had gathered that they were stepping on each other. Jesus spoke first to his followers, saying, "Beware of the yeast of the Pharisees, because they are hypocrites. 2Everything that is hidden will be shown, and everything that is secret will be made known. 3What you have said in the dark will be heard in the light, and what you have whispered in an inner room will be shouted from the housetops.

4"I tell you, my friends, don't be afraid of people who can kill the body but after that can do nothing more to hurt you. 5I will show you the one to fear. Fear the one who has the power to kill you and also to throw you into hell. Yes, this is the one you should fear.

6"Five sparrows are sold for only two pennies, and God does not forget any of them. 7But God even knows how many hairs you have on your head. Don't be afraid. You are worth much more than many sparrows.

DON'T BE ASHAMED OF JESUS

8"I tell you, all those who stand before others and say they believe in me, I, the Son of Man, will say before the angels of God that they belong to me. 9But all who stand before others and say they do not believe in me, I will say before the

TOPten

RANDOM WAYS TO MAKE A DIFFERENCE IN YOUR COMMUNITY

01	**Plant a tree.**
02	**Pick up someone else's litter.**
03	**Smile freely.**
04	**Drop a dollar in charity boxes.**
05	**Offer to baby-sit your neighbors' kids for free.**
06	**Clip the plastic rings on soda six-packs.**
07	**Use washable containers instead of plastic wrap for your lunch.**
08	**Recycle cans and bottles.**
09	**Donate your old clothes to needy families.**
10	**Do yard work for the elderly or sick.**

LEARN IT & LIVE IT

Romans 8:28:
Learn It: All things work together for the good of those who love God.
Live It: Think about a really tough situation in your life. Now, predict the outcome. Was it good? Reflect on how the outcome is good now or could be good five years from now.

Romans 8:31:
Learn It: If God is with us, no one can defeat us.
Live It: Next time you become afraid, repeat this truth to yourself. Think of it as a pregame warm-up against your fear. Say it ten times, and see if you don't feel better.

Romans 10:17:
Learn It: Faith comes from hearing the Good News of Christ.
Live It: Listen to the wind in the trees. Listen to your parents. Listen to your teachers. Listen to your friends. Listen to your pastor. All these (godly) voices can increase your faith.

angels of God that they do not belong to me.

10"Anyone who speaks against the Son of Man can be forgiven, but anyone who speaks against the Holy Spirit will not be forgiven.

11"When you are brought into the synagogues before the leaders and other powerful people, don't worry about how to defend yourself or what to say. 12At that time the Holy Spirit will teach you what you must say."

JESUS WARNS AGAINST SELFISHNESS

13Someone in the crowd said to Jesus, "Teacher, tell my brother to divide with me the property our father left us."

14But Jesus said to him, "Who said I should judge or decide between you?" 15Then Jesus said to them, "Be careful and guard against all kinds of greed. Life is not measured by how much one owns."

16Then Jesus told this story: "There was a rich man who had some land, which grew a good crop. 17He thought to himself, 'What will I do? I have no place to keep all my crops.' 18Then he said, 'This is what I will do: I will tear down my barns and build bigger ones, and there I will store all my grain and other goods. 19Then I can say to myself, "I have enough good things stored to last for many years. Rest, eat, drink, and enjoy life!" '

20"But God said to him, 'Foolish man! Tonight your life will be taken from you. So who will get those things you have prepared for yourself?'

21"This is how it will be for those who store up things for themselves and are not rich toward God."

DON'T WORRY

22Jesus said to his followers, "So I tell you, don't worry about the food you need to live, or about the clothes you need for your body. 23Life is more than food, and the body is more than clothes. 24Look at the birds. They don't plant or harvest, they don't have storerooms or barns, but God feeds them. And you are worth much more than birds. 25You cannot add any time to your life by worrying about it. 26If you cannot do even the little things, then why worry about the big things? 27Consider how the lilies grow; they don't work or make clothes for themselves. But I tell you that even Solomon with his riches was not dressed as beautifully as one of these flowers. 28God clothes the grass in the field, which is alive today but tomorrow is thrown into the fire. So how much more will God clothe you? Don't have so little faith! 29Don't always think about what you will eat or what you will drink, and don't keep worrying. 30All the people in the world are trying to get these things, and your Father knows you need them. 31But seek God's kingdom, and all the other things you need will be given to you.

DON'T TRUST IN MONEY

32"Don't fear, little flock, because your Father wants to give you the kingdom. 33Sell your possessions and give to the poor. Get for yourselves purses that will not wear out, the treasure in heaven that never runs out, where thieves can't steal and moths can't destroy. 34Your heart will be where your treasure is.

ALWAYS BE READY

35"Be dressed, ready for service, and have your lamps shining. 36Be like servants who are waiting for their master to come home from a wedding party. When he comes and knocks, the servants immediately open the door for him. 37They will be blessed when their master comes home, because he sees that they were watching for him. I tell you the truth, the master will dress himself to serve and tell the servants to sit at the table, and he will serve them. 38Those servants will be happy when he comes in and finds them still waiting, even if it is midnight or later.

39"Remember this: If the owner of the house knew what time a thief was coming, he would not allow the thief to enter his house. 40So you also must be ready, because the Son of Man will come at a time when you don't expect him!"

WHO IS THE TRUSTED SERVANT?

41Peter said, "Lord, did you tell this story to us or to all people?"

[42]The Lord said, "Who is the wise and trusted servant that the master trusts to give the other servants their food at the right time? [43]When the master comes and finds the servant doing his work, the servant will be blessed. [44]I tell you the truth, the master will choose that servant to take care of everything he owns. [45]But suppose the servant thinks to himself, 'My master will not come back soon,' and he begins to beat the other servants, men and women, and to eat and drink and get drunk. [46]The master will come when that servant is not ready and is not expecting him. Then the master will cut him in pieces and send him away to be with the others who don't obey.

[47]"The servant who knows what his master wants but is not ready, or who does not do what the master wants, will be beaten with many blows! [48]But the servant who does not know what his master wants and does things that should be punished will be beaten with few blows. From everyone who has been given much, much will be demanded. And from the one trusted with much, much more will be expected.

JESUS CAUSES DIVISION

[49]"I came to set fire to the world, and I wish it were already burning! [50]I have a baptism[n] to suffer through, and I feel very troubled until it is over. [51]Do you think I came to give peace to the earth? No, I tell you, I came to divide it. [52]From now on, a family with five people will be divided, three against two, and two against three. [53]They will be divided: father against son and son against father, mother against daughter and daughter against mother, mother-in-law against daughter-in-law and daughter-in-law against mother-in-law."

UNDERSTANDING THE TIMES

[54]Then Jesus said to the people, "When you see clouds coming up in the west, you say, 'It's going to rain,' and it happens. [55]When you feel the wind begin to blow from the south, you say, 'It will be a hot day,' and it happens. [56]Hypocrites! You know how to understand the appearance of the earth and sky. Why don't you understand what is happening now?

SETTLE YOUR PROBLEMS

[57]"Why can't you decide for yourselves what is right? [58]If your enemy is taking you to court, try hard to settle it on the way. If you don't, your enemy might take you to the judge, and the judge might turn you over to the officer, and the officer might throw you into jail. [59]I tell you, you will not get out of there until you have paid everything you owe."

CHANGE YOUR HEARTS

13 At that time some people were there who told Jesus that Pilate[n] had killed some people from Galilee while they were worshiping. He mixed their blood with the blood of the animals they were sacrificing to God. [2]Jesus answered, "Do you think this happened to them because they were more sinful than all others from Galilee? [3]No, I tell you. But unless you change your hearts and lives, you will be destroyed as they were! [4]What about those eighteen people who died when the tower of Siloam fell on them? Do you think they were more sinful than all the others who live in Jerusalem? [5]No, I tell you. But unless you change your hearts and lives, you will all be destroyed too!"

THE USELESS TREE

[6]Jesus told this story: "A man had a fig tree planted in his vineyard. He came looking for some fruit on the tree, but he found none. [7]So the man said to his gardener, 'I have been looking for fruit on this tree for three years, but I never find any. Cut it down. Why should it waste the ground?' [8]But the servant answered, 'Master, let the tree have one more year to produce fruit. Let me dig up the dirt around it and put on some fertilizer. [9]If the tree produces fruit next year, good. But if not, you can cut it down.' "

JESUS HEALS ON THE SABBATH

[10]Jesus was teaching in one of the synagogues on the Sabbath day. [11]A woman was there who, for eighteen years, had an evil spirit

Q. When I was younger, I did some really bad stuff. Now that I am a Christian I still can't forgive myself. Can God forgive me even if I can't?

A. Yes, that's why he's God and we aren't. God has a totally cool ability to forgive the worst sins in the world. That's what the whole "Christ dying on the cross for all the sins of the world" was about. So even though you can't do it, he can. All you need to do is confess what you did to him and then believe him to forgive.

Q. My parents are getting divorced, and I am worried. Will God hate them if they get married again because he hates divorce?

A. It's true, the Bible does say that God hates divorce. Just like he hates gossip, lying, murder, pride, and all other sins. That doesn't mean he hates the person who commits the sin. God will still love your parents after the divorce. God loves all his children for who they are, not what they do. That is the beauty of God's love in Christ Jesus.

Q. My Dad says he believes in God, but he won't go to church with us. My Mom tells him he's going to hell. That scares me. Is he really going to hell?

A. Not for not going to church. People are saved by faith, not by works. Maybe it's time for a family meeting. See if they will all sit down and talk it out. Does your Dad understand salvation? Does he love God? And can your Mom live with his decision? If your Dad doesn't understand who Christ is, maybe you can help him.

notes

12:50 I . . . baptism Jesus was talking about the suffering he would soon go through. **13:1 Pilate** Pontius Pilate was the Roman governor of Judea from A.D. 26 to A.D. 36.

75% OF TEENS THINK THEIR PARENTS UNDERSTAND THEIR PROBLEMS WELL.

in her that made her crippled. Her back was always bent; she could not stand up straight. 12When Jesus saw her, he called her over and said, "Woman, you are free from your sickness." 13Jesus put his hands on her, and immediately she was able to stand up straight and began praising God.

14The synagogue leader was angry because Jesus healed on the Sabbath day. He said to the people, "There are six days when one has to work. So come to be healed on one of those days, and not on the Sabbath day."

15The Lord answered, "You hypocrites! Doesn't each of you untie your work animals and lead them to drink water every day—even on the Sabbath day? 16This woman that I healed, a daughter of Abraham, has been held by Satan for eighteen years. Surely it is not wrong for her to be freed from her sickness on a Sabbath day!" 17When Jesus said this, all of those who were criticizing him were ashamed, but the entire crowd rejoiced at all the wonderful things Jesus was doing.

STORIES OF MUSTARD SEED AND YEAST

18Then Jesus said, "What is God's kingdom like? What can I compare it with? 19It is like a mustard seed that a man plants in his garden. The seed grows and becomes a tree, and the wild birds build nests in its branches."

20Jesus said again, "What can I compare God's kingdom with? 21It is like yeast that a woman took and hid in a large tub of flour until it made all the dough rise."

THE NARROW DOOR

22Jesus was teaching in every town and village as he traveled toward Jerusalem. 23Someone said to Jesus, "Lord, will only a few people be saved?"

Jesus said, 24"Try hard to enter through the narrow door, because many people will try to enter there, but they will not be able. 25When the owner of the house gets up and closes the door, you can stand outside and knock on the door and say, 'Sir, open the door for us.' But he will answer, 'I don't know you or where you come from.' 26Then you will say, 'We ate and drank with you, and you taught in the streets of our town.' 27But he will say to you, 'I don't know you or where you come from. Go away from me, all you who do evil!' 28You will cry and grind your teeth with pain when you see Abraham, Isaac, Jacob, and all the prophets in God's kingdom, but you yourselves thrown outside. 29People will come from the east, west, north, and south and will sit down at the table in the kingdom of God. 30There are those who have the lowest place in life now who will have the highest place in the future. And there are those who have the highest place now who will have the lowest place in the future."

JESUS WILL DIE IN JERUSALEM

31At that time some Pharisees came to Jesus and said, "Go away from here! Herod wants to kill you!"

32Jesus said to them, "Go tell that fox Herod, 'Today and tomorrow I am forcing demons out and healing people. Then, on the third day, I will reach my goal.' 33Yet I must be on my way today and tomorrow and the next day. Surely it cannot be right for a prophet to be killed anywhere except in Jerusalem.

34"Jerusalem, Jerusalem! You kill the

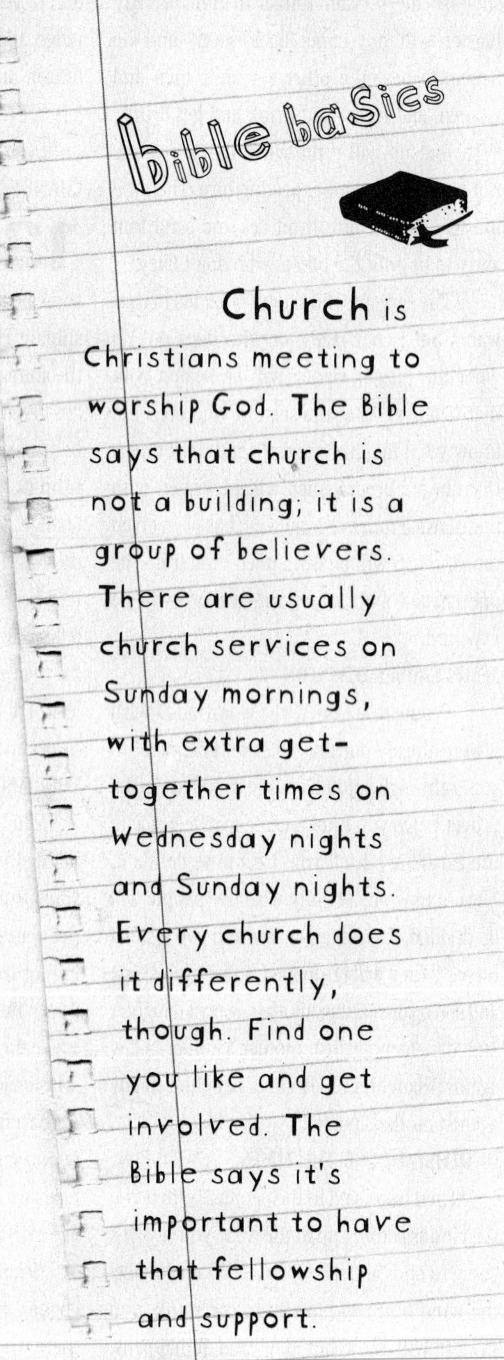

bible basics
Church is Christians meeting to worship God. The Bible says that church is not a building; it is a group of believers. There are usually church services on Sunday mornings, with extra get-together times on Wednesday nights and Sunday nights. Every church does it differently, though. Find one you like and get involved. The Bible says it's important to have that fellowship and support.

prophets and stone to death those who are sent to you. Many times I wanted to gather your people as a hen gathers her chicks under her wings, but you would not let me.
35Now your house is left completely empty. I tell you, you will not see me until that time when you will say, 'God bless the One who comes in the name of the Lord.' "[n]

HEALING ON THE SABBATH

14 On a Sabbath day, when Jesus went to eat at the home of a leading Pharisee, the people were watching Jesus very closely.
2And in front of him was a man with dropsy.[n]
3Jesus said to the Pharisees and experts on the law, "Is it right or wrong to heal on the Sabbath day?"
4But they would not answer his question. So Jesus took the man, healed him, and sent him away.
5Jesus said to the Pharisees and teachers of the law, "If your child or ox falls into a well on the Sabbath day, will you not pull him out quickly?"
6And they could not answer him.

DON'T MAKE YOURSELF IMPORTANT

7When Jesus noticed that some of the guests were choosing the best places to sit, he told this story:
8"When someone invites you to a wedding feast, don't take the most important seat, because someone more important than you may have been invited.
9The host, who invited both of you, will come to you and say, 'Give this person your seat.' Then you will be embarrassed and will have to move to the last place.
10So when you are invited, go sit in a seat that is not important. When the host comes to you, he may say, 'Friend, move up here to a more important place.' Then all the other guests will respect you.
11All who make themselves great will be made humble, but those who make themselves humble will be made great."

Ephesians 3:19
Christ's love is greater than anyone can ever know, but I pray that you will be able to know that love. Then you can be filled with the fullness of God.

YOU WILL BE REWARDED

12Then Jesus said to the man who had invited him, "When you give a lunch or a dinner, don't invite only your friends, your family, your other relatives, and your rich neighbors. At another time they will invite you to eat with them, and you will be repaid.
13Instead, when you give a feast, invite the poor, the crippled, the lame, and the blind.
14Then you will be blessed, because they have nothing and cannot pay you back. But you will be repaid when the good people rise from the dead."

A STORY ABOUT A BIG BANQUET

15One of those at the table with Jesus heard these things and said to him, "Happy are the people who will share in the meal in God's kingdom."

16Jesus said to him, "A man gave a big banquet and invited many people.
17When it was time to eat, the man sent his servant to tell the guests, 'Come. Everything is ready.'

18"But all the guests made excuses. The first one said, 'I have just bought a field, and I must go look at it. Please excuse me.'
19Another said, 'I have just bought five pairs of oxen; I must go and try them. Please excuse me.'
20A third person said, 'I just got married; I can't come.'
21So the servant returned and told his master what had happened. Then the master became angry and said, 'Go at once into the streets and alleys of the town, and bring in the poor, the crippled, the blind, and the lame.'
22Later the servant said to him, 'Master, I did what you commanded, but we still have room.'
23The master said to the servant, 'Go out to the roads and country lanes, and urge the people there to come so my house will be full.
24I tell you, none of those whom I invited first will eat with me.' "

THE COST OF BEING JESUS' FOLLOWER

25Large crowds were traveling with Jesus, and he turned and said to them,
26"If anyone comes to me but loves his father, mother, wife, children, brothers, or sisters—or even life—

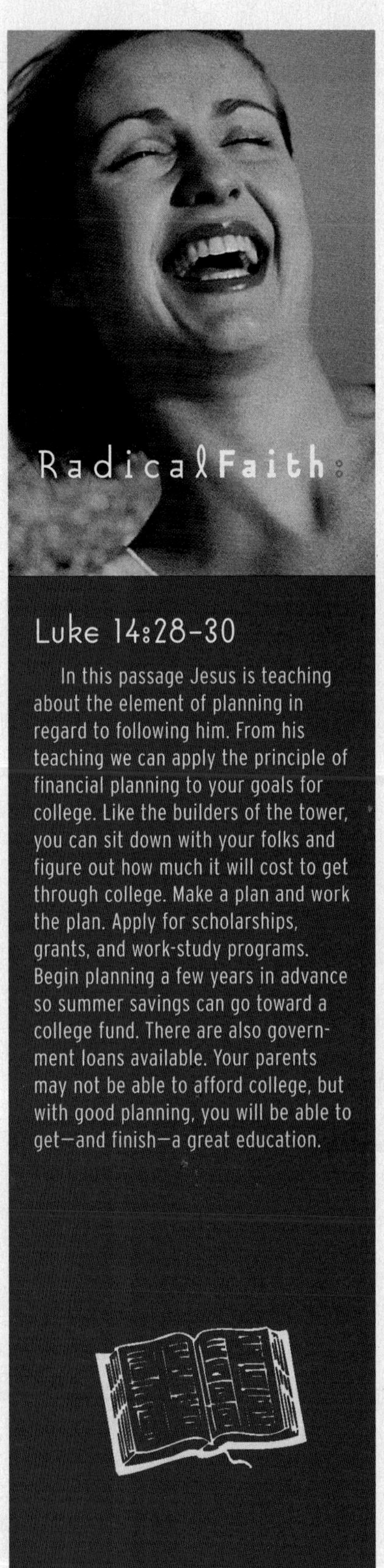

Luke 14:28-30

In this passage Jesus is teaching about the element of planning in regard to following him. From his teaching we can apply the principle of financial planning to your goals for college. Like the builders of the tower, you can sit down with your folks and figure out how much it will cost to get through college. Make a plan and work the plan. Apply for scholarships, grants, and work-study programs. Begin planning a few years in advance so summer savings can go toward a college fund. There are also government loans available. Your parents may not be able to afford college, but with good planning, you will be able to get—and finish—a great education.

notes

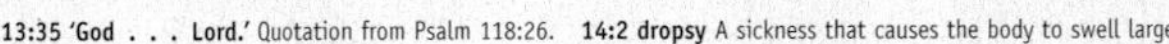

13:35 'God . . . Lord.' Quotation from Psalm 118:26. **14:2 dropsy** A sickness that causes the body to swell larger and larger.

RELATIONSHIPS

"Love is not selfish . . ." (1 Corinthians 13:5). Is your latest crush really popular? Is he a jock? What would you do if he asked you out? Would you freak out? I can't believe it! Why would you react that way? Because now you can tell all your friends you are going out with the coolest guy in school? Because you're now important since he thinks you're so cute? First Corinthians 13 says that love is not self-serving. This means that when you're interested in someone only for what they can do for you—increase your popularity, get you into all the cool parties, whatever—that's selfish. You don't really care about him, just yourself. Check your priorities, sister. They're way off.

more than me, he cannot be my follower. 27Whoever is not willing to carry the cross and follow me cannot be my follower. 28If you want to build a tower, you first sit down and decide how much it will cost, to see if you have enough money to finish the job. 29If you don't, you might lay the foundation, but you would not be able to finish. Then all who would see it would make fun of you, 30saying, 'This person began to build but was not able to finish.'

31"If a king is going to fight another king, first he will sit down and plan. He will decide if he and his ten thousand soldiers can defeat the other king who has twenty thousand soldiers. 32If he can't, then while the other king is still far away, he will send some people to speak to him and ask for peace. 33In the same way, you must give up everything you have to be my follower.

DON'T LOSE YOUR INFLUENCE

34"Salt is good, but if it loses its salty taste, you cannot make it salty again. 35It is no good for the soil or for manure; it is thrown away.

"You people who can hear me, listen."

A LOST SHEEP, A LOST COIN

15 The tax collectors and sinners all came to listen to Jesus. 2But the Pharisees and the teachers of the law began to complain: "Look, this man welcomes sinners and even eats with them."

3Then Jesus told them this story: 4"Suppose one of you has a hundred sheep but loses one of them. Then he will leave the other ninety-nine sheep in the open field and go out and look for the lost sheep until he finds it. 5And when he finds it, he happily puts it on his shoulders 6and goes home. He calls to his friends and neighbors and says, 'Be happy with me because I found my lost sheep.' 7In the same way, I tell you there is more joy in heaven over one sinner who changes his heart and life, than over ninety-nine good people who don't need to change.

8"Suppose a woman has ten silver coins,[n] but loses one. She will light a lamp, sweep the house, and look carefully for the coin until she finds it. 9And when she finds it, she will call her friends and neighbors and say, 'Be happy with me because I have found the coin that I lost.' 10In the same way, there is joy in the presence of the angels of God when one sinner changes his heart and life."

THE SON WHO LEFT HOME

11Then Jesus said, "A man had two sons. 12The younger son said to his father, 'Give me my share of the property.' So the father divided the property between his two sons. 13Then the younger son gathered up all that was his and traveled far away to another country. There he wasted his money in foolish living. 14After he had spent everything, a time came when there was no food anywhere in the country, and the son was poor and hungry. 15So he got a job with one of the citizens there who sent the son into the fields to feed pigs. 16The son was so hungry that he wanted to eat the pods the pigs were eating, but no one gave him anything. 17When he realized what he was doing, he thought, 'All of my father's servants have plenty of food. But I am here, almost dying with hunger. 18I will leave and return to my father and say to him, "Father, I have sinned against God and have done wrong to you. 19I am no longer worthy to be called your son, but let me be like one of your servants." ' 20So the son left and went to his father.

"While the son was still a long way off, his father saw him and felt sorry for his son. So the father ran to him and hugged and kissed him. 21The son said, 'Father, I have sinned against God and have done wrong to you. I am no longer worthy to be called your son.' 22But the father said to his servants, 'Hurry! Bring the best clothes and put them on him. Also, put a ring on his finger and sandals on his feet. 23And get our fat calf and kill it so we can have a feast and celebrate. 24My son was dead, but now he is alive again! He was lost, but now he is found!' So they began to celebrate.

"THE TAX COLLECTORS AND SINNERS ALL CAME TO LISTEN TO JESUS."

25"The older son was in the field, and as he came closer to the house, he heard the sound of music and dancing. 26So he called to one of the servants and asked what all this meant. 27The servant said, 'Your brother has come back, and your father killed the fat calf, because your brother came home safely.' 28The older son was angry and would not go in to the feast. So his father went out and begged him to come in. 29But the older son said to his father, 'I have served you like a slave for many years and have always obeyed your commands. But you never gave me even a young goat to have at a feast with my friends. 30But your other

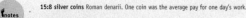

15:8 silver coins Roman denarii. One coin was the average pay for one day's work.

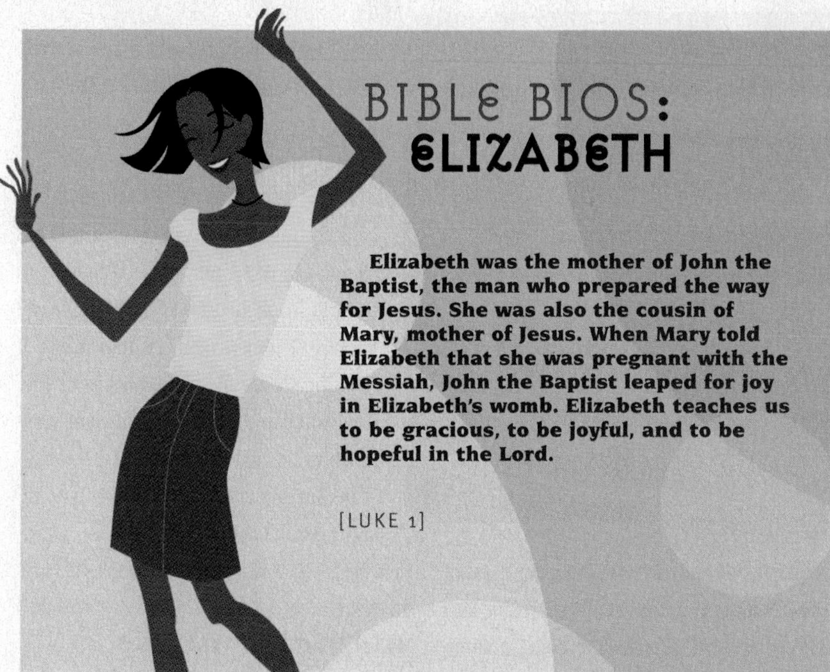
BIBLE BIOS:
ELIZABETH
Elizabeth was the mother of John the Baptist, the man who prepared the way for Jesus. She was also the cousin of Mary, mother of Jesus. When Mary told Elizabeth that she was pregnant with the Messiah, John the Baptist leaped for joy in Elizabeth's womb. Elizabeth teaches us to be gracious, to be joyful, and to be hopeful in the Lord.
[LUKE 1]

son, who wasted all your money on prostitutes, comes home, and you kill the fat calf for him!' 31The father said to him, 'Son, you are always with me, and all that I have is yours. 32We had to celebrate and be happy because your brother was dead, but now he is alive. He was lost, but now he is found.' "

TRUE WEALTH

16 Jesus also said to his followers, "Once there was a rich man who had a manager to take care of his business. This manager was accused of cheating him. 2So he called the manager in and said to him, 'What is this I hear about you? Give me a report of what you have done with my money, because you can't be my manager any longer.' 3The manager thought to himself, 'What will I do since my master is taking my job away from me? I am not strong enough to dig ditches, and I am ashamed to beg. 4I know what I'll do so that when I lose my job people will welcome me into their homes.'

5"So the manager called in everyone who owed the master any money. He asked the first one, 'How much do you owe?' 6He answered, 'Eight hundred gallons of olive oil.' The manager said to him, 'Take your bill, sit down quickly, and write four hundred gallons.' 7Then the manager asked another one, 'How much do you owe?' He answered, 'One thousand bushels of wheat.' Then the manager said to him, 'Take your bill and write eight hundred bushels.' 8So, the master praised the dishonest manager for being smart. Yes, worldly people are smarter with their own kind than spiritual people are.

9"I tell you, make friends for yourselves using worldly riches so that when those riches are gone, you will be welcomed in those homes that continue forever. 10Whoever can be trusted with a little can also be trusted with a lot, and whoever is dishonest with a little is dishonest with a lot. 11If you cannot be trusted with worldly riches, then who will trust you with true riches? 12And if you cannot be trusted with things that belong to someone else, who will give you things of your own?

13"No servant can serve two masters. The servant will hate one master and love the other, or will follow one master and refuse to follow the other. You cannot serve both God and worldly riches."

GOD'S LAW CANNOT BE CHANGED

14The Pharisees, who loved money, were listening to all these things and made fun of Jesus. 15He said to them, "You make yourselves look good in front of people, but God knows what is really in your hearts. What is important to people is hateful in God's sight.

16"The law of Moses and the writings of the prophets were preached until John[n] came. Since then the Good News about the kingdom of God is being told, and everyone tries to enter it by force. 17It would be easier for heaven and earth to pass away than for the smallest part of a letter in the law to be changed.

DIVORCE AND REMARRIAGE

18"If a man divorces his wife and marries another woman, he is guilty of adultery, and the man who marries a divorced woman is also guilty of adultery."

THE RICH MAN AND LAZARUS

19Jesus said, "There was a rich man who always dressed in the finest clothes and lived in luxury every day. 20And a very poor man named Lazarus, whose body was covered with sores, was laid at the rich man's gate. 21He wanted to eat only the small pieces of food that fell from the rich man's table. And the dogs would come and lick his sores. 22Later, Lazarus died, and the angels carried him to the arms of Abraham. The rich man died, too, and was buried. 23In the place of the dead, he was in much pain. The rich man saw Abraham far away with Lazarus at his side. 24He called, 'Father Abraham, have mercy on me! Send Lazarus to dip his finger in water and cool my tongue, because I am suffering in this fire!' 25But Abraham said, 'Child, remember when you were alive you had the good things in life, but bad things happened to Lazarus. Now he is comforted here, and you are suffering. 26Besides, there is a big pit between you and us, so no one can cross over to you, and no one can leave there and come here.' 27The rich man said, 'Father, then please send Lazarus to my

notes

16:16 John John the Baptist, who preached to people about Christ's coming (Matthew 3, Luke 3).

father's house. [28]I have five brothers, and Lazarus could warn them so that they will not come to this place of pain.' [29]But Abraham said, 'They have the law of Moses and the writings of the prophets; let them learn from them.' [30]The rich man said, 'No, father Abraham! If someone goes to them from the dead, they would believe and change their hearts and lives.' [31]But Abraham said to him, 'If they will not listen to Moses and the prophets, they will not listen to someone who comes back from the dead.' "

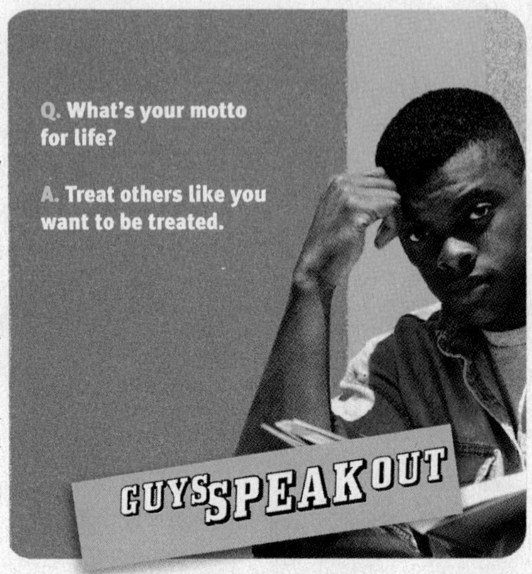

Q. What's your motto for life?
A. Treat others like you want to be treated.
GUYS SPEAK OUT

SIN AND FORGIVENESS

17 Jesus said to his followers, "Things that cause people to sin will happen, but how terrible for the person who causes them to happen! [2]It would be better for you to be thrown into the sea with a large stone around your neck than to cause one of these little ones to sin. [3]So be careful!

"If another follower sins, warn him, and if he is sorry and stops sinning, forgive him. [4]If he sins against you seven times in one day and says that he is sorry each time, forgive him."

AFRICAN AMERICAN TEENS ARE 40% MORE LIKELY TO HAVE HAD SEX THAN CAUCASIAN TEENS.

HOW BIG IS YOUR FAITH?

[5]The apostles said to the Lord, "Give us more faith!"

[6]The Lord said, "If your faith were the size of a mustard seed, you could say to this mulberry tree, 'Dig yourself up and plant yourself in the sea,' and it would obey you.

BE GOOD SERVANTS

[7]"Suppose one of you has a servant who has been plowing the ground or caring for the sheep. When the servant comes in from working in the field, would you say, 'Come in and sit down to eat'? [8]No, you would say to him, 'Prepare something for me to eat. Then get yourself ready and serve me. After I finish eating and drinking, you can eat.' [9]The servant does not get any special thanks for doing what his master commanded. [10]It is the same with you. When you have done everything you are told to do, you should say, 'We are unworthy servants; we have only done the work we should do.' "

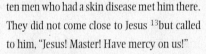

BE THANKFUL

[11]While Jesus was on his way to Jerusalem, he was going through the area between Samaria and Galilee. [12]As he came into a small town, ten men who had a skin disease met him there. They did not come close to Jesus [13]but called to him, "Jesus! Master! Have mercy on us!"

[14]When Jesus saw the men, he said, "Go and show yourselves to the priests."[n]

As the ten men were going, they were healed. [15]When one of them saw that he was healed, he went back to Jesus, praising God in a loud voice. [16]Then he bowed down at Jesus' feet and thanked him. (And this man was a Samaritan.) [17]Jesus said, "Weren't ten men healed? Where are the other nine? [18]Is this Samaritan the only one who came back to thank God?" [19]Then Jesus said to him, "Stand up and go on your way. You were healed because you believed."

GOD'S KINGDOM IS WITHIN YOU

[20]Some of the Pharisees asked Jesus, "When will the kingdom of God come?"

Jesus answered, "God's kingdom is coming, but not in a way that you will be able to see with your eyes. [21]People will not say, 'Look, here it is!' or, 'There it is!' because God's kingdom is within[n] you."

[22]Then Jesus said to his followers, "The time will come when you will want very much to see one of the days of the Son of Man. But you will not see it. [23]People will say to you, 'Look, there he is!' or, 'Look, here he is!' Stay where you are; don't go away and search.

WHEN JESUS COMES AGAIN

[24]"When the Son of Man comes again, he will shine like lightning, which flashes across the sky and lights it up from one side to the other. [25]But first he must suffer many things and be rejected by the people of this time. [26]When the Son of Man comes again, it will be as it was when Noah lived. [27]People were eating, drinking, marrying, and giving their children to be married until the day Noah entered the boat. Then the flood came and killed them all. [28]It will be the same as during the time of Lot. People were eating, drinking, buying, selling, planting, and building. [29]But the day Lot left Sodom,[n] fire and sulfur rained down from the sky and killed them all. [30]This is how it will be when the Son of Man comes again.

[31]"On that day, a person who is on the roof and whose belongings are in the house should not go inside to get them. A person who is in the field should not go back home. [32]Remember Lot's wife.[n] [33]Those who try to keep their lives will lose them. But those who give up their lives will save them. [34]I tell you, on that night two people will be sleeping in one bed; one will be taken and the other will be left. [35]There will be two women grinding grain together; one will be taken, and the other will be left." [36][n]

notes

17:14 show . . . priests The Law of Moses said a priest must say when a person with a skin disease became well. **17:21 within** Or "among." **17:29 Sodom** City that God destroyed because the people were so evil. **17:32 Lot's wife** A story about what happened to Lot's wife is found in Genesis 19:15–17, 26. **17:36 Verse 36** A few Greek copies add verse 36: "Two people will be in the field. One will be taken, and the other will be left."

LEARN IT & LIVE IT

Romans 12:2:
Learn It: Transformation occurs with the renewing of your mind.
Live It: Grab a pen and notepad. Every time you sin, write it down. Be aware of your thought processes. Now, write down a better way of thinking. Allow God to transform you!

Romans 12:6:
Learn It: "We all have different gifts."
Live It: Buy three little gifts for three of your friends. Remind them that we all have different gifts from God too.

Romans 13:11:
Learn it: The time is now for you to awake from sleep.
Live It: Watch the news tonight. What is going on in the world? Who needs your help? Open your eyes to the world around you; pay attention to need.

[37]The followers asked Jesus, "Where will this be, Lord?"

Jesus answered, "Where there is a dead body, there the vultures will gather."

GOD WILL ANSWER HIS PEOPLE

18 Then Jesus used this story to teach his followers that they should always pray and never lose hope. [2]"In a certain town there was a judge who did not respect God or care about people. [3]In that same town there was a widow who kept coming to this judge, saying, 'Give me my rights against my enemy.' [4]For a while the judge refused to help her. But afterwards, he thought to himself, 'Even though I don't respect God or care about people, [5]I will see that she gets her rights. Otherwise she will continue to bother me until I am worn out.' "

[6]The Lord said, "Listen to what the unfair judge said. [7]God will always give what is right to his people who cry to him night and day, and he will not be slow to answer them. [8]I tell you, God will help his people quickly. But when the Son of Man comes again, will he find those on earth who believe in him?"

BEING RIGHT WITH GOD

[9]Jesus told this story to some people who thought they were very good and looked down on everyone else: [10]"A Pharisee and a tax collector both went to the Temple to pray. [11]The Pharisee stood alone and prayed, 'God, I thank you that I am not like other people who steal, cheat, or take part in adultery, or even like this tax collector. [12]I give up eating[n] twice a week, and I give one-tenth of everything I get!'

[13]"The tax collector, standing at a distance, would not even look up to heaven. But he beat on his chest because he was so sad. He said, 'God, have mercy on me, a sinner.' [14]I tell you, when this man went home, he was right with God, but the Pharisee was not. All who make themselves great will be made humble, but all who make themselves humble will be made great."

WHO WILL ENTER GOD'S KINGDOM?

[15]Some people brought even their babies to Jesus so he could touch them. When the followers saw this, they told them to stop. [16]But Jesus called for the children, saying, "Let the little children come to me. Don't stop them, because the kingdom of God belongs to people who are like these children. [17]I tell you the truth, you must accept the kingdom of God as if you were a child, or you will never enter it."

A RICH MAN'S QUESTION

[18]A certain leader asked Jesus, "Good Teacher, what must I do to have life forever?"

[19]Jesus said to him, "Why do you call me good? Only God is good. [20]You know the commands: 'You must not be guilty of adultery. You must not murder anyone. You must not steal. You must not tell lies about your neighbor. Honor your father and mother.' "[n]

[21]But the leader said, "I have obeyed all these commands since I was a boy."

[22]When Jesus heard this, he said to him, "There is still one more thing you need to do. Sell everything you have and give it to the poor, and you will have treasure in heaven. Then come and follow me." [23]But when the man heard this, he became very sad, because he was very rich.

[24]Jesus looked at him and said, "It is very hard for rich people to enter the kingdom of God. [25]It is easier for a camel to go through the eye of a needle than for a rich person to enter the kingdom of God."

WHO CAN BE SAVED?

[26]When the people heard this, they asked, "Then who can be saved?"

[27]Jesus answered, "God can do things that are not possible for people to do."

[28]Peter said, "Look, we have left everything and followed you."

[29]Jesus said, "I tell you the truth, all those who have left houses, wives, brothers, parents, or children for the kingdom of God [30]will get much more in this life. And in the age that is coming, they will have life forever."

JESUS WILL RISE FROM THE DEAD

[31]Then Jesus took the twelve apostles aside

18:12 give up eating This is called "fasting." The people would give up eating for a special time of prayer and worship to God. It was also done to show sadness and disappointment. **18:20 'You . . . mother.'** Quotation from Exodus 20:12–16; Deuteronomy 5:16–20.

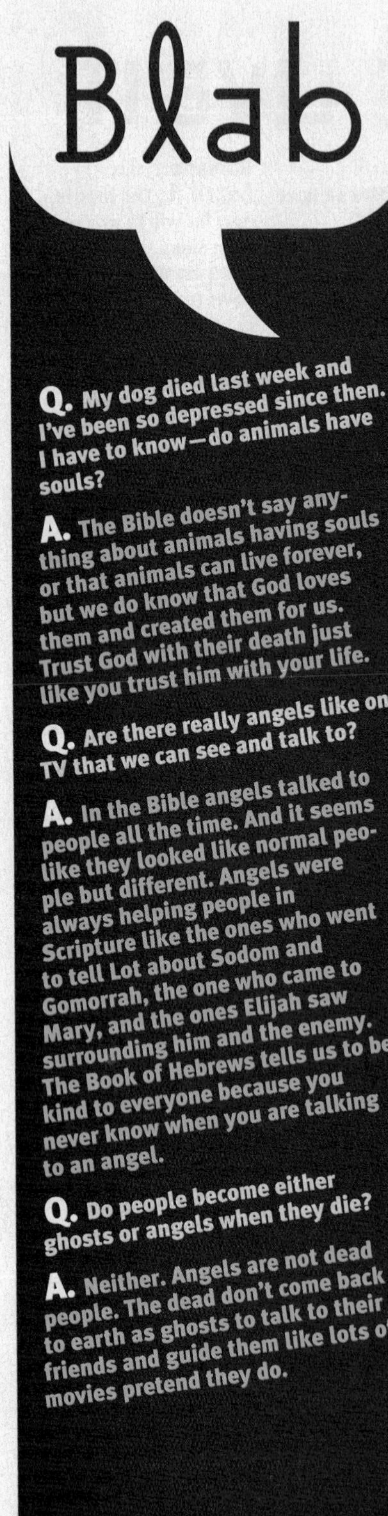

and said to them, "We are going to Jerusalem.
Everything the prophets wrote about the Son
of Man will happen. 32He will be turned over
to those who are evil. They will laugh at him,
insult him, spit on him, 33beat him with whips,
and kill him. But on the third day, he will rise
to life again." 34The apostles did not understand this; the meaning was hidden from them,
and they did not realize what was said.

JESUS HEALS A BLIND MAN

35As Jesus came near the city of Jericho, a
blind man was sitting beside the road, begging.
36When he heard the people coming down the
road, he asked, "What is happening?"

37They told him, "Jesus, from Nazareth, is
going by."

38The blind man cried out, "Jesus, Son of
David, have mercy on me!"

39The people leading the group warned the
blind man to be quiet. But the blind man
shouted even more, "Son of David, have
mercy on me!"

40Jesus stopped and ordered the blind man
to be brought to him. When he came near,
Jesus asked him, 41"What do you want me to
do for you?"

He said, "Lord, I want to see."

42Jesus said to him, "Then see. You are
healed because you believed."

43At once the man was able to see, and he
followed Jesus, thanking God. All the people
who saw this praised God.

ZACCHAEUS MEETS JESUS

19 Jesus was going through the city of
Jericho. 2A man was there named
Zacchaeus, who was a very important tax collector, and he was wealthy. 3He wanted to see
who Jesus was, but he was not able because he
was too short to see above the crowd. 4He ran
ahead to a place where Jesus would come, and
he climbed a sycamore tree so he could see
him. 5When Jesus came to that place, he looked
up and said to him, "Zacchaeus, hurry and
come down! I must stay at your house today."

6Zacchaeus came down quickly and welcomed him gladly. 7All the people saw this
and began to complain, "Jesus is staying with
a sinner!"

"THE BLIND MAN CRIED OUT, 'JESUS, SON OF DAVID, HAVE MERCY ON ME!'"

8But Zacchaeus stood and said to the Lord,
"I will give half of my possessions to the poor.
And if I have cheated anyone, I will pay back
four times more."

9Jesus said to him, "Salvation has come to
this house today, because this man also belongs
to the family of Abraham. 10The Son of Man
came to find lost people and save them."

A STORY ABOUT THREE SERVANTS

11As the people were listening to this, Jesus
told them a story because he was near
Jerusalem and they thought God's kingdom
would appear immediately. 12He said: "A very
important man went to a country far away to
be made a king and then to return home. 13So
he called ten of his servants and gave a coin[n] to
each servant. He said, 'Do business with this
money until I get back.' 14But the people in the
kingdom hated the man. So they sent a group
to follow him and say, 'We don't want this man
to be our king.'

15"But the man became king. When he
returned home, he said, 'Call those servants
who have my money so I can know how much
they earned with it.'

16"The first servant came and said, 'Sir, I
earned ten coins with the one you gave me.'
17The king said to the servant, 'Excellent! You are
a good servant. Since I can trust you with small
things, I will let you rule over ten of my cities.'

18"The second servant said, 'Sir, I earned
five coins with your one.' 19The king said to
this servant, 'You can rule over five cities.'

20"Then another servant came in and said

notes

19:13 coin A Greek "mina." One mina was enough money to pay a person for working three months.

to the king, 'Sir, here is your coin which I wrapped in a piece of cloth and hid. [21]I was afraid of you, because you are a hard man. You even take money that you didn't earn and gather food that you didn't plant.' [22]Then the king said to the servant, 'I will condemn you by your own words, you evil servant. You knew that I am a hard man, taking money that I didn't earn and gathering food that I didn't plant. [23]Why then didn't you put my money in the bank? Then when I came back, my money would have earned some interest.'

[24]"The king said to the men who were standing by, 'Take the coin away from this servant and give it to the servant who earned ten coins.' [25]They said, 'But sir, that servant already has ten coins.' [26]The king said, 'Those who have will be given more, but those who do not have anything will have everything taken away from them. [27]Now where are my enemies who didn't want me to be king? Bring them here and kill them before me.' "

JESUS ENTERS JERUSALEM AS A KING

[28]After Jesus said this, he went on toward Jerusalem. [29]As Jesus came near Bethphage and Bethany, towns near the hill called the Mount of Olives, he sent out two of his followers. [30]He said, "Go to the town you can see there. When you enter it, you will find a colt tied there, which no one has ever ridden. Untie it and bring it here to me. [31]If anyone asks you why you are untying it, say that the Master needs it."

[32]The two followers went into town and found the colt just as Jesus had told them. [33]As they were untying it, its owners came out and asked the followers, "Why are you untying our colt?"

"BUT JESUS ANSWERED, 'I TELL YOU, IF MY FOLLOWERS DIDN'T SAY THESE THINGS, THEN THE STONES WOULD CRY OUT.'"

[34]The followers answered, "The Master needs it." [35]So they brought it to Jesus, threw their coats on the colt's back, and put Jesus on it. [36]As Jesus rode toward Jerusalem, others spread their coats on the road before him.

[37]As he was coming close to Jerusalem, on the way down the Mount of Olives, the whole crowd of followers began joyfully shouting praise to God for all the miracles they had seen. [38]They said,

"God bless the king who comes in the
name of the Lord! *Psalm 118:26*
There is peace in heaven and glory to God!"

[39]Some of the Pharisees in the crowd said to Jesus, "Teacher, tell your followers not to say these things."

[40]But Jesus answered, "I tell you, if my followers didn't say these things, then the stones would cry out."

JESUS CRIES FOR JERUSALEM

[41]As Jesus came near Jerusalem, he saw the city and cried for it, [42]saying, "I wish you knew today what would bring you peace. But now it is hidden from you. [43]The time is coming when your enemies will build a wall around you and will hold you in on all sides. [44]They will destroy you and all your people, and not one stone will be left on another. All this will happen because you did not recognize the time when God came to save you."

JESUS GOES TO THE TEMPLE

[45]Jesus went into the Temple and began to throw out the people who were selling things there. [46]He said, "It is written in the Scriptures, 'My Temple will be a house for prayer.'[n] But you have changed it into a 'hideout for robbers'!"[n]

[47]Jesus taught in the Temple every day. The leading priests, the experts on the law, and some of the leaders of the people wanted to kill Jesus. [48]But they did not know how they could do it, because all the people were listening closely to him.

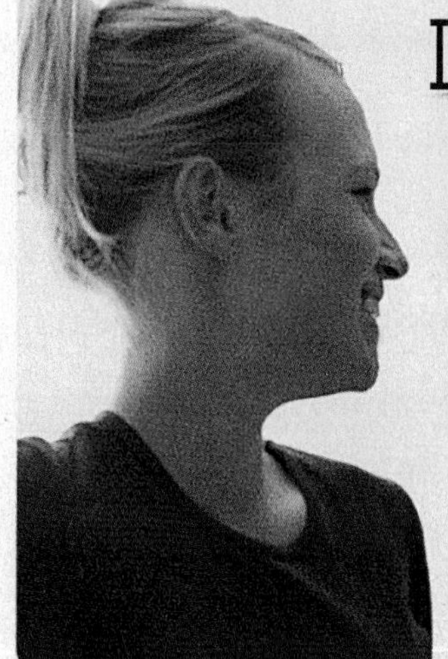

ISSUES: Money

"A penny saved is a penny earned." It's about time for you to be thinking about jobs, money, and how you're going to pay for college! What about a new car? Now your parents may or may not be supporting you, fully or partially. Either way, you still will need to know how to manage your money.
Rule #1: Tithe (give 10 percent of your income to church or charity).
Rule #2: Don't spend what you don't have.
Rule #3: Always save a portion of your check in a savings or investment account.
Rule #4: Create a budget. How much do you spend on your lifestyle?
Rule #5: Alternate money: Focus on scholarships, bargain shopping, inexpensive dates, fun, low-cost outings with friends, and secondhand stuff.
Learning how to save can keep your bank account growing. For more help with money, read *The Big Bucks by Xt4J.*

19:46 'My Temple . . . prayer.' Quotation from Isaiah 56:7. **19:46 'hideout for robbers'** Quotation from Jeremiah 7:11.

JEWISH LEADERS QUESTION JESUS

20 One day Jesus was in the Temple, teaching the people and telling them the Good News. The leading priests, teachers of the law, and older leaders came up to talk with him, [2]saying, "Tell us what authority you have to do these things? Who gave you this authority?"

[3]Jesus answered, "I will also ask you a question. Tell me: [4]When John baptized people, was that authority from God or just from other people?"

[5]They argued about this, saying, "If we answer, 'John's baptism was from God,' Jesus will say, 'Then why did you not believe him?' [6]But if we say, 'It was from other people,' all the people will stone us to death, because they believe John was a prophet." [7]So they answered that they didn't know where it came from.

Ephesians 5:1
You are God's children whom he loves, so try to be like him.

[8]Jesus said to them, "Then I won't tell you what authority I have to do these things."

A STORY ABOUT GOD'S SON

[9]Then Jesus told the people this story: "A man planted a vineyard and leased it to some farmers. Then he went away for a long time. [10]When it was time for the grapes to be picked, he sent a servant to the farmers to get some of the grapes. But they beat the servant and sent him away empty-handed. [11]Then he sent another servant. They beat this servant also, and showed no respect for him, and sent him away empty-handed. [12]So the man sent a third servant. The farmers wounded him and threw him out. [13]The owner of the vineyard said, 'What will I do now? I will send my son whom I love. Maybe they will respect him.' [14]But when the farmers saw the son, they said to each other, 'This son will inherit the vineyard. If we kill him, it will be ours.' [15]So the farmers threw the son out of the vineyard and killed him.

"What will the owner of this vineyard do to them? [16]He will come and kill those farmers and will give the vineyard to other farmers."

When the people heard this story, they said, "Let this never happen!"

[17]But Jesus looked at them and said, "Then what does this verse mean:

'The stone that the builders rejected
became the cornerstone'? *Psalm 118:22*

[18]Everyone who falls on that stone will be broken, and the person on whom it falls, that person will be crushed!"

[19]The teachers of the law and the leading priests wanted to arrest Jesus at once, because they knew the story was about them. But they were afraid of what the people would do.

IS IT RIGHT TO PAY TAXES OR NOT?

[20]So they watched Jesus and sent some spies who acted as if they were sincere. They wanted to trap Jesus in saying something wrong so they could hand him over to the authority and power of the governor. [21]So the spies asked Jesus, "Teacher, we know that what you say and teach is true. You pay no attention to who people are, and you always teach the truth about God's way. [22]Tell us, is it right for us to pay taxes to Caesar or not?"

[23]But Jesus, knowing they were trying to trick him, said, [24]"Show me a coin. Whose image and name are on it?"

They said, "Caesar's."

[25]Jesus said to them, "Then give to Caesar the things that are Caesar's, and give to God the things that are God's."

[26]So they were not able to trap Jesus in anything he said in the presence of the people. And being amazed at his answer, they became silent.

SOME SADDUCEES TRY TO TRICK JESUS

[27]Some Sadducees, who believed people would not rise from the dead, came to Jesus. [28]They asked, "Teacher, Moses wrote that if a man's brother dies and leaves a wife but no children, then that man must marry the widow and have children for his brother. [29]Once there were seven brothers. The first brother married and died, but had no children. [30]Then the second brother married the widow, and he died. [31]And the third brother married the widow, and he died. The same thing happened with all seven brothers; they died and had no children. [32]Finally, the woman died also. [33]Since all seven brothers had married her, whose wife will she be when people rise from the dead?"

[34]Jesus said to them, "On earth, people marry and are given to someone to marry. [35]But those who will be worthy to be raised from the dead and live again will not marry, nor will they be given to someone to marry. [36]In that life they are like angels and cannot die. They are children of God, because they have been raised from the dead. [37]Even Moses clearly showed that the dead are raised to life. When he wrote about the burning bush,[n] he said that the Lord is 'the God of Abraham, the God of Isaac, and the God of Jacob.'[n] [38]God is the God of the living, not the dead, because all people are alive to him."

SPIRITUAL FACIALS

Spiritual cleansing is like a facial cleansing. The fire of God's love burns out the sin the same way the hot steam routs the dirt out of your pores. Then clean your heart with prayer, and cool down in the shade under God's wings. This kind of relationship with God will do more to improve your looks than any amount of facials.

20:37 burning bush Read Exodus 3:1–12 in the Old Testament. **20:37 'the God of . . . Jacob'** These words are taken from Exodus 3:6.

39Some of the teachers of the law said, "Teacher, your answer was good." 40No one was brave enough to ask him another question.

IS THE CHRIST THE SON OF DAVID?

41Then Jesus said, "Why do people say that the Christ is the Son of David? 42In the book of Psalms, David himself says:

'The Lord said to my Lord:
Sit by me at my right side,
43 until I put your enemies under
your control.'[n] *Psalm 110:1*

44David calls the Christ 'Lord,' so how can the Christ be his son?"

JESUS ACCUSES SOME LEADERS

45While all the people were listening, Jesus said to his followers, 46"Beware of the teachers of the law. They like to walk around wearing fancy clothes, and they love for people to greet them with respect in the marketplaces. They love to have the most important seats in the synagogues and at feasts. 47But they cheat widows and steal their houses and then try to make themselves look good by saying long prayers. They will receive a greater punishment."

Q. Describe your ideal girl.
A. Cute, adventurous, athletic, and a great personality.
GUYS SPEAK OUT

DIDYA KNOW

89% OF TEENS HAVE BEEN EDUCATED ABOUT AIDS.

TRUE GIVING

21 As Jesus looked up, he saw some rich people putting their gifts into the Temple money box.[n] 2Then he saw a poor widow putting two small copper coins into the box. 3He said, "I tell you the truth, this poor widow gave more than all those rich people. 4They gave only what they did not need. This woman is very poor, but she gave all she had to live on."

THE TEMPLE WILL BE DESTROYED

5Some people were talking about the Temple and how it was decorated with beautiful stones and gifts offered to God.

But Jesus said, 6"As for these things you are looking at, the time will come when not one stone will be left on another. Every stone will be thrown down."

7They asked Jesus, "Teacher, when will these things happen? What will be the sign that they are about to take place?"

8Jesus said, "Be careful so you are not fooled. Many people will come in my name, saying, 'I am the One' and, 'The time has come!' But don't follow them. 9When you hear about wars and riots, don't be afraid, because these things must happen first, but the end will come later."

10Then he said to them, "Nations will fight against other nations, and kingdoms against other kingdoms. 11In various places there will be great earthquakes, sicknesses, and a lack of food. Fearful events and great signs will come from heaven.

12"But before all these things happen, people will arrest you and treat you cruelly. They will judge you in their synagogues and put you in jail and force you to stand before kings and governors, because you follow me. 13But this will give you an opportunity to tell about me. 14Make up your minds not to worry ahead of time about what you will say. 15I will give you the wisdom to say things that none of your enemies will be able to stand against or prove wrong. 16Even your parents, brothers, relatives, and friends will turn against you, and they will kill some of you. 17All people will hate you because you follow me. 18But none of these things can really harm you. 19By continuing to have faith you will save your lives.

JERUSALEM WILL BE DESTROYED

20"When you see armies all around Jerusalem, you will know it will soon be destroyed. 21At that time, the people in Judea should run away to the mountains. The people in Jerusalem must get out, and those who are near the city should not go in. 22These are the days of punishment to bring about all that is written in the Scriptures. 23How terrible it will be for women who are pregnant or have nursing babies! Great trouble will come upon this land, and God will be angry with these people. 24They will be killed by the sword and taken as prisoners to all nations. Jerusalem will be crushed by non-Jewish people until their time is over.

DON'T FEAR

25"There will be signs in the sun, moon, and stars. On earth, nations will be afraid and confused because of the roar and fury of the sea. 26People will be so afraid they will faint, wondering what is happening to the world, because the powers of the heavens will be shaken. 27Then people will see the Son of Man coming in a cloud with power and great glory. 28When these things begin to happen, look up and hold your heads high, because the time when God will free you is near!"

JESUS' WORDS WILL LIVE FOREVER

29Then Jesus told this story: "Look at the fig tree and all the other trees. 30When their leaves appear, you know that summer is near. 31In the same way, when you see these things happening, you will know that God's kingdom is near.

notes

20:43 until . . . control Literally, "until I make your enemies a footstool for your feet." **21:1 money box** A special box in the Jewish place of worship where people put their gifts to God.

LEARN IT & LIVE IT

Romans 15:5:
Learn It: God calls us to live in harmony with one another.
Live It: Pick a flower on your way to school today. Give it to a friend you have trouble getting along with. Let him or her know that you wish for peace between you.

1 Corinthians 1:5:
Learn It: Speech and knowledge are enriched by Jesus.
Live It: Pick one book of the Bible and read it every day this week. The whole thing. Watch how the things you talk about will start to change by the end of the week.

1 Corinthians 1:9:
Learn It: God is faithful.
Live It: Look at your life really closely and find one thing that you're trying to control. Let go of it. Don't go above and beyond to "make sure it works out." Let God take control of it and see where he takes you.

32"I tell you the truth, all these things will happen while the people of this time are still living. 33Earth and sky will be destroyed, but the words I have spoken will never be destroyed.

BE READY ALL THE TIME

34"Be careful not to spend your time feasting, drinking, or worrying about worldly things. If you do, that day might come on you suddenly, 35like a trap on all people on earth. 36So be ready all the time. Pray that you will be strong enough to escape all these things that will happen and that you will be able to stand before the Son of Man."

37During the day, Jesus taught the people in the Temple, and at night he went out of the city and stayed on the Mount of Olives. 38Every morning all the people got up early to go to the Temple to listen to him.

JUDAS BECOMES AN ENEMY OF JESUS

22 It was almost time for the Feast of Unleavened Bread, called the Passover Feast. 2The leading priests and teachers of the law were trying to find a way to kill Jesus, because they were afraid of the people.

3Satan entered Judas Iscariot, one of Jesus' twelve apostles. 4Judas went to the leading priests and some of the soldiers who guarded the Temple and talked to them about a way to hand Jesus over to them. 5They were pleased and agreed to give Judas money. 6He agreed and watched for the best time to hand Jesus over to them when he was away from the crowd.

JESUS EATS THE PASSOVER MEAL

7The Day of Unleavened Bread came when the Passover lambs had to be sacrificed. 8Jesus said to Peter and John, "Go and prepare the Passover meal for us to eat."

9They asked, "Where do you want us to prepare it?" 10Jesus said to them, "After you go into the city, a man carrying a jar of water will meet you. Follow him into the house that he enters, 11and tell the owner of the house, 'The Teacher says: Where is the guest room in which I may eat the Passover meal with my followers?' 12Then he will show you a large, furnished room upstairs. Prepare the Passover meal there."

13So Peter and John left and found everything as Jesus had said. And they prepared the Passover meal.

THE LORD'S SUPPER

14When the time came, Jesus and the apostles were sitting at the table. 15He said to them, "I wanted very much to eat this Passover meal with you before I suffer. 16I will not eat another Passover meal until it is given its true meaning in the kingdom of God."

17Then Jesus took a cup, gave thanks, and said, "Take this cup and share it among yourselves. 18I will not drink again from the fruit of the vine[n] until God's kingdom comes."

19Then Jesus took some bread, gave thanks, broke it, and gave it to the apostles, saying, "This is my body, which I am giving for you. Do this to remember me." 20In the same way, after supper, Jesus took the cup and said, "This cup is the new agreement that God makes with his people. This new agreement begins with my blood which is poured out for you.

WHO WILL TURN AGAINST JESUS?

21"But one of you will turn against me, and his hand is with mine on the table. 22What God has planned for the Son of Man will happen, but how terrible it will be for that one who turns against the Son of Man."

23Then the apostles asked each other which one of them would do that.

BE LIKE A SERVANT

24The apostles also began to argue about which one of them was the most important. 25But Jesus said to them, "The kings of the non-Jewish people rule over them, and those who have authority over others like to be called 'friends of the people.' 26But you must not be like that. Instead, the greatest among you should be like the youngest, and the leader should be like the servant. 27Who is more important: the one sitting at the table or the one serving? You think the one at the table is more important, but I am like a servant among you.

notes

22:18 fruit of the vine Product of the grapevine; this may also be translated "wine."

28“You have stayed with me through my struggles. 29Just as my Father has given me a kingdom, I also give you a kingdom 30so you may eat and drink at my table in my kingdom. And you will sit on thrones, judging the twelve tribes of Israel.

DON'T LOSE YOUR FAITH!

31“Simon, Simon, Satan has asked to test all of you as a farmer sifts his wheat. 32I have prayed that you will not lose your faith! Help your brothers be stronger when you come back to me.”

Ephesians 5:2
Live a life of love just as Christ loved us and gave himself for us as a sweet-smelling offering and sacrifice to God.

33But Peter said to Jesus, “Lord, I am ready to go with you to prison and even to die with you!”

34But Jesus said, “Peter, before the rooster crows this day, you will say three times that you don't know me.”

BE READY FOR TROUBLE

35Then Jesus said to the apostles, “When I sent you out without a purse, a bag, or sandals, did you need anything?”

They said, “No.”

36He said to them, “But now if you have a purse or a bag, carry that with you. If you don't have a sword, sell your coat and buy one. 37The Scripture says, ‘He was treated like a criminal,’[n] and I tell you this scripture must have its full meaning. It was written about me, and it is happening now.”

38His followers said, “Look, Lord, here are two swords.”

He said to them, “That is enough.”

JESUS PRAYS ALONE

39Jesus left the city and went to the Mount of Olives, as he often did, and his followers went with him. 40When he reached the place, he said to them, “Pray for strength against temptation.”

41Then Jesus went about a stone's throw away from them. He kneeled down and prayed, 42“Father, if you are willing, take away this cup[n] of suffering. But do what you want, not what I want.” 43Then an angel from heaven appeared to him to strengthen him. 44Being full of pain, Jesus prayed even harder. His sweat was like drops of blood falling to the ground. 45When he finished praying, he went to his followers and found them asleep because of their sadness. 46Jesus said to them, “Why are you sleeping? Get up and pray for strength against temptation.”

JESUS IS ARRESTED

47While Jesus was speaking, a crowd came up, and Judas, one of the twelve apostles, was leading them. He came close to Jesus so he could kiss him.

48But Jesus said to him, “Judas, are you using the kiss to give the Son of Man to his enemies?”

49When those who were standing around him saw what was happening, they said, “Lord, should we strike them with our swords?” 50And one of them struck the servant of the high priest and cut off his right ear.

51Jesus said, “Stop! No more of this.” Then he touched the servant's ear and healed him.

52Those who came to arrest Jesus were the leading priests, the soldiers who guarded the Temple, and the older leaders. Jesus said to them, “You came out here with swords and clubs as though I were a criminal. 53I was with you every day in the Temple, and you didn't arrest me there. But this is your time—the time when darkness rules.”

“THEN AN ANGEL FROM HEAVEN APPEARED TO HIM TO STRENGTHEN HIM.”

PETER SAYS HE DOESN'T KNOW JESUS

54They arrested Jesus, and led him away, and brought him into the house of the high priest. Peter followed far behind them. 55After the soldiers started a fire in the middle of the

Luke 22:42

A lot of people have memorized the Bible verse that tells us to obey our parents as the Lord wants—to do what they want (Ephesians 6:1). Do you ever wonder, “What's the big deal?” The big deal is: God's Word says, “It is better to obey than to sacrifice”(1 Samuel 15:22). We can spend all of our time in church and put all of our money in the offering, but if we aren't walking the walk, we're missing the point of what God's Word is saying. Remember that obedience is better than a bunch of rituals. In fact, God's Word says that if we truly love him, we will really do what he says to do (see John 14:15; 15:10). When you obey God, not only does this show the world that you love him, it shows *him* that you love him!

You can study the whole Bible looking at the lives of those who obeyed God and those who didn't. You'll find that the ones who were obedient were the ones who got blessed! Abraham obeyed God. Noah obeyed God. Joseph obeyed God. Daniel obeyed God. Jesus obeyed his Father, God. Paul obeyed God. Every one of those folks reaped the benefits of obedience. Obey God today, and reap the blessings of God tomorrow!

notes

22:37 'He . . . criminal' Quotation from Isaiah 53:12. **22:42 cup** Jesus is talking about the painful things that will happen to him. Accepting these things will be hard, like drinking a cup of something bitter.

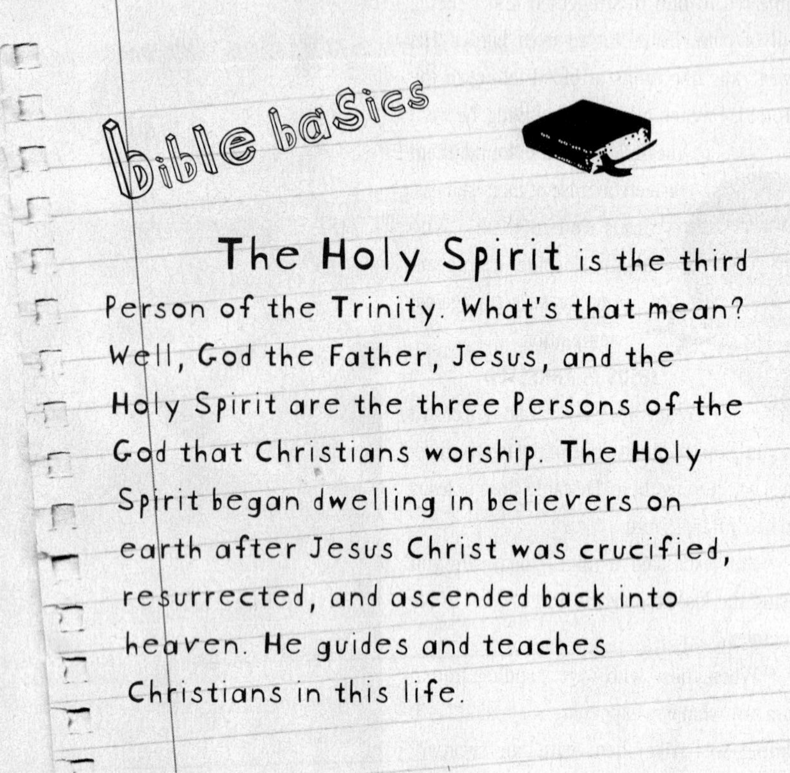

courtyard and sat together, Peter sat with them. 56A servant girl saw Peter sitting there in the firelight, and looking closely at him, she said, "This man was also with him."

bible basics
The Holy Spirit is the third Person of the Trinity. What's that mean? Well, God the Father, Jesus, and the Holy Spirit are the three Persons of the God that Christians worship. The Holy Spirit began dwelling in believers on earth after Jesus Christ was crucified, resurrected, and ascended back into heaven. He guides and teaches Christians in this life.

57But Peter said this was not true; he said, "Woman, I don't know him."

58A short time later, another person saw Peter and said, "You are also one of them."

But Peter said, "Man, I am not!"

59About an hour later, another man insisted, "Certainly this man was with him, because he is from Galilee, too."

60But Peter said, "Man, I don't know what you are talking about!"

At once, while Peter was still speaking, a rooster crowed. 61Then the Lord turned and looked straight at Peter. And Peter remembered what the Lord had said: "Before the rooster crows this day, you will say three times that you don't know me." 62Then Peter went outside and cried painfully.

THE PEOPLE MAKE FUN OF JESUS

63The men who were guarding Jesus began making fun of him and beating him.

64They blindfolded him and said, "Prove that you are a prophet, and tell us who hit you." 65They said many cruel things to Jesus.

JESUS BEFORE THE LEADERS

66When day came, the council of the older leaders of the people, both the leading priests and the teachers of the law, came together and led Jesus to their highest court. 67They said, "If you are the Christ, tell us."

Jesus said to them, "If I tell you, you will not believe me. 68And if I ask you, you will not answer. 69But from now on, the Son of Man will sit at the right hand of the powerful God."

70They all said, "Then are you the Son of God?"

Jesus said to them, "You say that I am."

71They said, "Why do we need witnesses now? We ourselves heard him say this."

PILATE QUESTIONS JESUS

23 Then the whole group stood up and led Jesus to Pilate.[n] 2They began to accuse Jesus, saying, "We caught this man telling things that mislead our people. He says that we should not pay taxes to Caesar, and he calls himself the Christ, a king."

3Pilate asked Jesus, "Are you the king of the Jews?"

Jesus answered, "Those are your words."

4Pilate said to the leading priests and the people, "I find nothing against this man."

5They were insisting, saying, "But Jesus makes trouble with the people, teaching all around Judea. He began in Galilee, and now he is here."

PILATE SENDS JESUS TO HEROD

6Pilate heard this and asked if Jesus was from Galilee. 7Since Jesus was under Herod's authority, Pilate sent Jesus to Herod, who was in Jerusalem at that time. 8When Herod saw

"AT ONCE, WHILE PETER WAS STILL SPEAKING, A ROOSTER CROWED."

Jesus, he was very glad, because he had heard about Jesus and had wanted to meet him for a long time. He was hoping to see Jesus work a miracle. 9Herod asked Jesus many questions, but Jesus said nothing. 10The leading priests and teachers of the law were standing there, strongly accusing Jesus. 11After Herod and his soldiers had made fun of Jesus, they dressed him in a kingly robe and sent him back to Pilate. 12In the past, Pilate and Herod had always been enemies, but on that day they became friends.

JESUS MUST DIE

13Pilate called the people together with the leading priests and the rulers. 14He said to them, "You brought this man to me, saying he makes trouble among the people. But I have questioned him before you all, and I have not found him guilty of what you say. 15Also,

notes

23:1 Pilate Pontius Pilate was the Roman governor of Judea from A.D. 26 to A.D. 36.

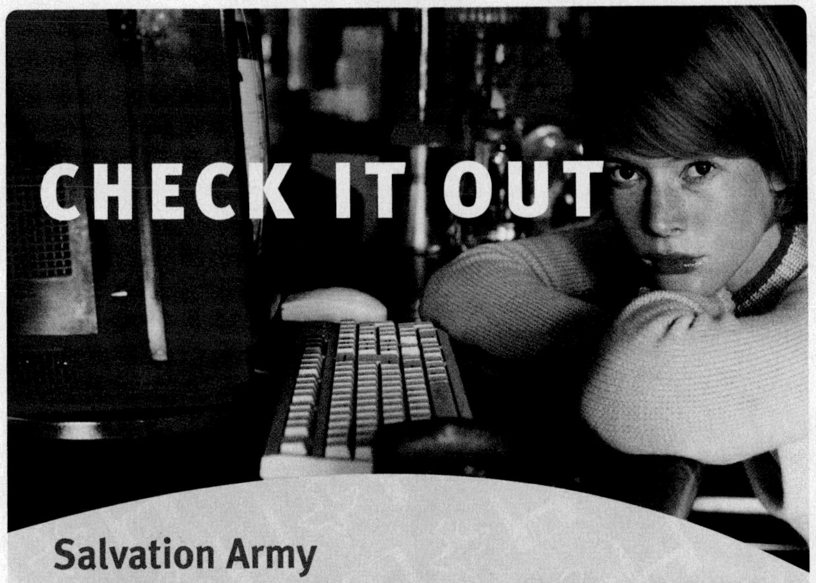

CHECK IT OUT

Salvation Army

Volunteers know the truth of the verse, "It is more blessed to give than to receive." There are few things more rewarding than giving one's time to help someone else.

Approximately one-and-a-half million volunteers throughout the United States dramatically extend The Salvation Army's ability to serve the needy. Volunteers provide assistance in a variety of areas from social services to office work to character building activities. If you have a skill or just the heart to serve, The Salvation Army has a place for you.

Volunteers bring diversity to the Army's work in age, race, social background, and approach. If you would like to volunteer, we need you and appreciate you.

*To help, go to **www.salvationarmyusa.org**.*

Herod found nothing wrong with him; he sent
him back to us. Look, he has done nothing for
which he should die. 16So, after I punish him,
I will let him go free." 17n
18But the people shouted together, "Take this
man away! Let Barabbas go free!" 19(Barabbas
was a man who was in prison for his part in a
riot in the city and for murder.)
20Pilate wanted to let Jesus go free and told
this to the crowd. 21But they shouted again,
"Crucify him! Crucify him!"
22A third time Pilate said to them, "Why?
What wrong has he done? I can find no reason
to kill him. So I will have him punished and
set him free."
23But they continued to shout, demanding
that Jesus be crucified. Their yelling became
so loud that 24Pilate decided to give them
what they wanted. 25He set free the man who
was in jail for rioting and murder, and he
handed Jesus over to them to do with him as
they wished.

JESUS IS CRUCIFIED

26As they led Jesus away, Simon, a man
from Cyrene, was coming in from the fields.
They forced him to carry Jesus' cross and to
walk behind him.
27A large crowd of people was following
Jesus, including some women who were sad
and crying for him. 28But Jesus turned and
said to them, "Women of Jerusalem, don't cry
for me. Cry for yourselves and for your children. 29The time is coming when people will
say, 'Happy are the women who cannot have

Blab

Q. My friend believes in aliens. She is totally convinced they exist. What does the Bible say about aliens? How do I talk to her about them?

A. The Bible doesn't say anything about aliens. Some think that means there aren't any. If God can make people on this planet, there is no reason to think he couldn't make them on other planets and in other galaxies. But don't start arguments about little things that make no difference in your relationship with others. Just don't even concern yourself with it. They might exist; they might not. That doesn't affect your relationship with Christ or his love for the people of this earth.

Q. Does God really know everything?

A. Yep. He knows everything.

Q. Should Christians be in chatrooms?

A. Scripture says everything is permissible but not everything is beneficial. This means there is no hard law about stuff like chatrooms so we have to come to our own conclusions. It comes down to what kind of chatrooms you are in—if they're Christian or family-oriented sites, you're relatively safe from being tempted to sin. Be very careful on the web, however, and never give out ANY personal information.

notes

23:17 Verse 17 A few Greek copies add verse 17: "Every year at the Passover Feast, Pilate had to release one prisoner to the people."

QUIZ

ARE YOU A MARY OR A MARTHA?

QUIET TIMES WITH GOD ARE A PRIORITY FOR ME.
NOT AT ALL TRUE OF ME VERY TRUE OF ME
1 2 3 4 5 6 7 8 9 10

MY LIFE IS CRAZY! I FEEL LIKE I NEVER SLOW DOWN.
VERY TRUE OF ME NOT AT ALL TRUE OF ME
1 2 3 4 5 6 7 8 9 10

I DON'T WORRY MUCH ABOUT THE FUTURE.
NOT AT ALL TRUE OF ME VERY TRUE OF ME
1 2 3 4 5 6 7 8 9 10

I DO A LOT OF VOLUNTEER WORK.
VERY TRUE OF ME NOT AT ALL TRUE OF ME
1 2 3 4 5 6 7 8 9 10

IT IS GOD'S STRENGTH THAT GETS ME THROUGH THE DAY.
NOT AT ALL TRUE OF ME VERY TRUE OF ME
1 2 3 4 5 6 7 8 9 10

I OFTEN GET ANGRY AND STRESSED-OUT ABOUT EVERYTHING.
VERY TRUE OF ME NOT AT ALL TRUE OF ME
1 2 3 4 5 6 7 8 9 10

THE BIBLE IS WHERE I GO WHEN I NEED ADVICE OR ENCOURAGEMENT.
NOT AT ALL TRUE OF ME VERY TRUE OF ME
1 2 3 4 5 6 7 8 9 10

I KNOW HOW IMPORTANT IT IS TO READ THE BIBLE, BUT I JUST DON'T EVER HAVE TIME.
VERY TRUE OF ME NOT AT ALL TRUE OF ME
1 2 3 4 5 6 7 8 9 10

GOD'S TRUTH IS MORE IMPORTANT TO ME THAN WHAT OTHERS THINK.
NOT AT ALL TRUE OF ME VERY TRUE OF ME
1 2 3 4 5 6 7 8 9 10

I AM VERY PROUD OF THE THINGS I'VE ACCOMPLISHED SO FAR IN LIFE.
VERY TRUE OF ME NOT AT ALL TRUE OF ME
1 2 3 4 5 6 7 8 9 10

ADD UP YOUR SCORES AND READ LUKE 10:38-42; THEN CHECK YOUR SCORE BELOW.

IF YOU SCORED LESS THAN 30, YOU ARE A **MARTHA**!

Martha, Martha, you are worried about so many things! Martha's problem was that she was more worried about what was going on around her than what Jesus was teaching. Her focus was not on the things that last. Although she was a talented hostess and welcomed Jesus into her home, she didn't understand that all her significance and her hope for eternal life were found in him. You look a lot like Martha—more concerned about pleasing Christ than with knowing Christ. Take some time today to read what God is saying to you in the Bible, and ask him to help you focus on the truly important things.

IF YOU SCORED BETWEEN 31 AND 70, YOU ARE A **MARY/MARTHA**!

Most of us, if we are honest, probably fall somewhere in this category. We long to spend time with Christ and place our whole trust in him, but we get distracted and busy, and it's hard to make time to read our Bible and pray. Be encouraged that God's love is unfailing, and continue to make him a priority in your life. The blessings are worth it!

IF YOU SCORED MORE THAN 70, YOU ARE A **MARY**!

Jesus praised Mary because she chose "the better thing." She knew that he was her Savior and what he taught was the truth. She placed her trust in him, though it meant leaving the concerns of the world behind. Your answers indicate that God is working in your heart to create the same attitude in you. Thank him for his work in your life!

CHRIST COMES TO THE WORLD

1 In the beginning there was the Word.[n] The Word was with God, and the Word was God. 2 He was with God in the beginning.

EACH YEAR THE GOVERNMENT SPENDS ABOUT $40 BILLION TO HELP FAMILIES THAT BEGAN WITH TEEN BIRTHS.

3 All things were made by him, and nothing was made without him. 4 In him there was life, and that life was the light of all people. 5 The Light shines in the darkness, and the darkness has not overpowered it.

RELATIONSHIPS

Can you tell your guy anything? Can you tell him when he does stuff you don't like without being afraid that he'll get all mad and dump you? Or do you walk on pins and needles around him, making sure he's always happy. It's important to have honest lines of communication in a dating relationship and, more important, in a marriage relationship. Ephesians 4:15 says, "Speaking the truth with love, we will grow up in every way into Christ." Don't you want your dating relationship to grow in Christ? Then be honest with one another—if you don't feel comfortable with something, tell him! Or if there's something you think is awesome about him, tell him that too!

6 There was a man named John[n] who was sent by God. 7 He came to tell people the truth about the Light so that through him all people could hear about the Light and believe. 8 John was not the Light, but he came to tell people the truth about the Light. 9 The true Light that gives light to all was coming into the world!

10 The Word was in the world, and the world was made by him, but the world did not know him. 11 He came to the world that was his own, but his own people did not accept him. 12 But to all who did accept him and believe in him he gave the right to become children of God. 13 They did not become his children in any human way—by any human parents or human desire. They were born of God.

14 The Word became a human and lived among us. We saw his glory—the glory that belongs to the only Son of the Father—and he was full of grace and truth. 15 John tells the truth about him and cries out, saying, "This is the One I told you about: 'The One who comes after me is greater than I am, because he was living before me.' "

16 Because he was full of grace and truth, from him we all received one gift after another. 17 The law was given through Moses, but grace and truth came through Jesus Christ. 18 No one has ever seen God. But God the only Son is very close to the Father,[n] and he has shown us what God is like.

1 John 3:16
This is how we know what real love is: Jesus gave his life for us. So we should give our lives for our brothers and sisters.

JOHN TELLS PEOPLE ABOUT JESUS

19 Here is the truth John[n] told when the leaders in Jerusalem sent priests and Levites to ask him, "Who are you?"

20 John spoke freely and did not refuse to answer. He said, "I am not the Christ."

21 So they asked him, "Then who are you? Are you Elijah?"[n]

He answered, "No, I am not."

"Are you the Prophet?"[n] they asked.

He answered, "No."

22 Then they said, "Who are you? Give us an answer to tell those who sent us. What do you say about yourself?"

23 John told them in the words of the prophet Isaiah:

"I am the voice of one
calling out in the desert:
'Make the road straight for the Lord.' " *Isaiah 40:3*

24 Some Pharisees who had been sent asked John: 25 "If you are not the Christ or Elijah or the Prophet, why do you baptize people?"

"IN THE BEGINNING THERE WAS THE WORD. THE WORD WAS WITH GOD, AND THE WORD WAS GOD."

26 John answered, "I baptize with water, but there is one here with you that you don't know about. 27 He is the One who comes after me. I am not good enough to untie the strings of his sandals."

28 This all happened at Bethany on the other side of the Jordan River, where John was baptizing people.

29 The next day John saw Jesus coming toward him. John said, "Look, the Lamb of God,[n] who takes away the sin of the world! 30 This is the One I was talking about when I said, 'A man will come after me, but he is greater than I am, because he was living before me.' 31 Even I did not know who he was, although I came baptizing with water so that the people of Israel would know who he is."

32-33 Then John said, "I saw the Spirit come down from heaven in the form of a dove and rest on him. Until then I did not know who the Christ was. But the God who sent me to baptize with water told me, 'You will see the Spirit come down and rest on a man; he is the One who will baptize with the Holy Spirit.' 34 I have

1:1 Word The Greek word is "logos," meaning any kind of communication; it could be translated "message." Here, it means Christ, because Christ was the way God told people about himself. **1:6, 19 John** John the Baptist, who preached to people about Christ's coming (Matthew 3, Luke 3). **1:18 But . . . Father** This could be translated, "But the only God is very close to the Father." Also, some Greek copies say, "But the only Son is very close to the Father." **1:21 Elijah** A prophet who spoke for God. He lived hundreds of years before Christ and was expected to return before Christ (Malachi 4:5–6). **1:21 Prophet** They probably meant the prophet that God told Moses he would send (Deuteronomy 18:15–19). **1:29 Lamb of God** Name for Jesus. Jesus is like the lambs that were offered for a sacrifice to God.

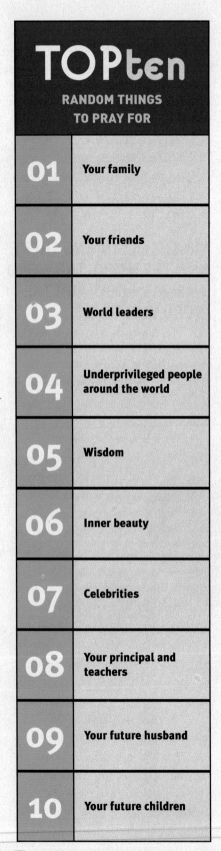

TOPten
RANDOM THINGS TO PRAY FOR

01	Your family
02	Your friends
03	World leaders
04	Underprivileged people around the world
05	Wisdom
06	Inner beauty
07	Celebrities
08	Your principal and teachers
09	Your future husband
10	Your future children

seen this happen, and I tell you the truth: This
man is the Son of God."

THE FIRST FOLLOWERS OF JESUS

35The next day John[n] was there again with
two of his followers. 36When he saw Jesus
walking by, he said, "Look, the Lamb of God!"[n]
37The two followers heard John say this, so
they followed Jesus. 38When Jesus turned and
saw them following him, he asked, "What are
you looking for?"

They said, "Rabbi, where are you staying?"
("Rabbi" means "Teacher.")
39He answered, "Come and see." So the two
men went with Jesus and saw where he was
staying and stayed there with him that day. It
was about four o'clock in the afternoon.
40One of the two men who followed Jesus
after they heard John speak about him was
Andrew, Simon Peter's brother. 41The first thing
Andrew did was to find his brother Simon and
say to him, "We have found the Messiah."
("Messiah" means "Christ.")
42Then Andrew took Simon to Jesus. Jesus
looked at him and said, "You are Simon son of
John. You will be called Cephas." ("Cephas"
means "Peter."[n])
43The next day Jesus decided to go to Galilee.
He found Philip and said to him, "Follow me."
44Philip was from the town of Bethsaida,
where Andrew and Peter lived. 45Philip found
Nathanael and told him, "We have found the
man that Moses wrote about in the law, and
the prophets also wrote about him. He is
Jesus, the son of Joseph, from Nazareth."
46But Nathanael said to Philip, "Can anything good come from Nazareth?"

Philip answered, "Come and see."
47As Jesus saw Nathanael coming toward
him, he said, "Here is truly an Israelite. There
is nothing false in him."
48Nathanael asked, "How do you know me?"

Jesus answered, "I saw you when you were
under the fig tree, before Philip told you
about me."

RadicalFaith

John 1:1

This verse will knock anyone who doesn't believe in the Trinity—that God the Father, God the Son (Jesus), and the Holy Spirit are all three in one—right in the head. Verse 14 says, "The Word became a human and lived among us. We saw his glory—the glory that belongs to the only Son of the Father—and he was full of grace and truth." Jesus is the Word! That's why Hebrews 4:12 says that the Word of God is "alive and working."

If you want to get closer to God, start by spending time in his Word. Not only will you learn about him, but you'll hear from him. Jesus speaks to us through his Word more than any other way. That's why it's so important to read the Bible, study it, and memorize verses.

Did you know that as you spend time in this Book, the Word of God, your faith is being increased? It's vital that you put the Word of God in you when things are going great and you don't think you need it, so it will be there when you do need it. Remember, "Faith comes from hearing the Good News" (Romans 10:17). That message is in the Word of God. Jesus is the Word!

1:35 John John the Baptist, who preached to people about Christ's coming (Matthew 3, Luke 3). **1:36 Lamb of God** Name for Jesus. Jesus is like the lambs that were offered for a sacrifice to God. **1:42 Peter** The Greek name "Peter," like the Aramaic name "Cephas," means "rock."

49Then Nathanael said to Jesus, "Teacher, you are the Son of God; you are the King of Israel."

50Jesus said to Nathanael, "Do you believe simply because I told you I saw you under the fig tree? You will see greater things than that." 51And Jesus said to them, "I tell you the truth, you will all see heaven open and 'angels of God going up and coming down'[n] on the Son of Man."

THE WEDDING AT CANA

2 Two days later there was a wedding in the town of Cana in Galilee. Jesus' mother was there, 2and Jesus and his followers were also invited to the wedding. 3When all the wine was gone, Jesus' mother said to him, "They have no more wine."

4Jesus answered, "Dear woman, why come to me? My time has not yet come."

5His mother said to the servants, "Do whatever he tells you to do."

6In that place there were six stone water jars that the Jews used in their washing ceremony.[n] Each jar held about twenty or thirty gallons.

7Jesus said to the servants, "Fill the jars with water." So they filled the jars to the top.

8Then he said to them, "Now take some out and give it to the master of the feast."

So they took the water to the master. 9When he tasted it, the water had become wine. He did not know where the wine came from, but the servants who had brought the water knew. The master of the wedding called the bridegroom 10and said to him, "People always serve the best wine first. Later, after the guests have been drinking awhile, they serve the cheaper wine. But you have saved the best wine till now."

11So in Cana of Galilee Jesus did his first miracle. There he showed his glory, and his followers believed in him.

JESUS IN THE TEMPLE

12After this, Jesus went to the town of Capernaum with his mother, brothers, and followers. They stayed there for just a few days. 13When it was almost time for the Jewish Passover Feast, Jesus went to Jerusalem. 14In the Temple he found people selling cattle, sheep, and doves. He saw others sitting at tables, exchanging different kinds of money. 15Jesus made a whip out of cords and forced all of them, both the sheep and cattle, to leave the Temple. He turned over the tables and scattered the money of those who were exchanging it. 16Then he said to those who were selling pigeons, "Take these things out of here! Don't make my Father's house a place for buying and selling!"

17When this happened, the followers remembered what was written in the Scriptures: "My strong love for your Temple completely controls me."[n]

18Some of his people said to Jesus, "Show us a miracle to prove you have the right to do these things."

19Jesus answered them, "Destroy this temple, and I will build it again in three days."

20They answered, "It took forty-six years to build this Temple! Do you really believe you can build it again in three days?"

21(But the temple Jesus meant was his own body. 22After Jesus was raised from the dead, his followers remembered that Jesus had said this. Then they believed the Scripture and the words Jesus had said.)

23When Jesus was in Jerusalem for the Passover Feast, many people believed in him because they saw the miracles he did. 24But Jesus did not trust himself to them because he knew them all. 25He did not need anyone to tell him about people, because he knew what was in people's minds.

1 John 4:7
Dear friends, we should love each other, because love comes from God. Everyone who loves has become God's child and knows God.

NICODEMUS COMES TO JESUS

3 There was a man named Nicodemus who was one of the Pharisees and an important Jewish leader. 2One night Nicodemus

John 1:16

Check out what this verse is saying. God has given us "grace and truth." This means he's given us one blessing after another. He is the One who blesses. Notice that the verse doesn't say he *takes* from us.

A lot of people have the idea that God is out to take everything away from them, but that's not true. In fact, his Word says that he has come that we might have life "in all its fullness" (John 10:10). God isn't a taker. He's a giver, and he *wants* to give you the desires of your heart (see Psalm 37:4). So what are you going to do? Make God the joy and the delight of your life—and really mean it—and he will bring to pass your heart's desires.

What's your heart's desire? Tell God! He also says that if we will put him first and do what he wants, he will also add other things to us. What kind of things? Whatever we need. Romans 8:32 sums all of this up: "He did not spare his own Son but gave him for us all. So with Jesus, God will surely give us all things." Don't forget it: he is the One who blesses!

"WHAT'S YOUR HEART'S DESIRE? TELL GOD!"

notes

1:51 'angels . . . down' These words are from Genesis 28:12. **2:6 washing ceremony** The Jewish people washed themselves in special ways before eating, before worshiping in the Temple, and at other special times.
2:17 "My . . . me." Quotation from Psalm 69:9.

Q. What would you tell someone who was hanging on to life by a thread about to break?

A. If you think that someone you know has serious thoughts of suicide, then you have to tell someone. A teacher, a pastor, a parent, an adult who can help them. Suicide isn't the answer to your friend's problems. It only creates more problems and leaves a world of hurt behind it. The best thing you can do for your friend is get them help.

Q. Ever feel like God is pulling you away from you? What did you do to get better?

A. Many people have felt like God was pulling away from them, you aren't alone, but the thing is that God doesn't pull away from us. He is always there, but sometimes he is there in different ways. Faith isn't a feeling, and the way we feel about God shouldn't change what we believe about him. It may take days, it may take months, but your job is to wait and never stop believing.

Q. I have this burning desire for Jesus, and I want to get to know him better. And I want to hear his voice. But sometimes I get frustrated because it seems like I'm not getting the response that I want.

A. Maybe you need to consider what the "response you want" is. We love God not to get something out of it but because we want to give something to him—our love, our worship. If you feel like you are praying with your head and not your spirit, then you might be telling God what you want more than you are loving him for who he is.

came to Jesus and said, "Teacher, we know you are a teacher sent from God, because no one can do the miracles you do unless God is with him."

3Jesus answered, "I tell you the truth, unless one is born again, he cannot be in God's kingdom."

4Nicodemus said, "But if a person is already old, how can he be born again? He cannot enter his mother's body again. So how can a person be born a second time?"

5But Jesus answered, "I tell you the truth, unless one is born from water and the Spirit, he cannot enter God's kingdom. 6Human life comes from human parents, but spiritual life comes from the Spirit. 7Don't be surprised when I tell you, 'You must all be born again.' 8The wind blows where it wants to and you hear the sound of it, but you don't know where the wind comes from or where it is going. It is the same with every person who is born from the Spirit."

9Nicodemus asked, "How can this happen?"

10Jesus said, "You are an important teacher in Israel, and you don't understand these things? 11I tell you the truth, we talk about what we know, and we tell about what we have seen, but you don't accept what we tell you. 12I have told you about things here on earth, and you do not believe me. So you will not believe me if I tell you about things of heaven. 13The only one who has ever gone up to heaven is the One who came down from heaven—the Son of Man.

14"Just as Moses lifted up the snake in the desert,[n] the Son of Man must also be lifted up. 15So that everyone who believes can have eternal life in him.

16"God loved the world so much that he gave his one and only Son so that whoever believes in him may not be lost, but have eternal life. 17God did not send his Son into the world to judge the world guilty, but to save the world through him. 18People who believe in God's Son are not judged guilty. Those who do not believe have already been judged guilty, because they have not believed in God's one and only Son. 19They are judged by this fact: The Light has come into the world, but they did not want light. They wanted darkness, because they were doing evil things. 20All who do evil hate the light and will not come to the light, because it will show all the evil things they do. 21But those who follow the true way come to the light, and it shows that the things they do were done through God."

JESUS AND JOHN THE BAPTIST

22After this, Jesus and his followers went into the area of Judea, where he stayed with his followers and baptized people. 23John was

"JESUS ANSWERED, 'I TELL YOU THE TRUTH, UNLESS ONE IS BORN AGAIN, HE CANNOT BE IN GOD'S KINGDOM.'"

also baptizing in Aenon, near Salim, because there was plenty of water there. People were going there to be baptized. 24(This was before John was put into prison.)

25Some of John's followers had an argument with a Jew about religious washing.[n] 26So they came to John and said, "Teacher, remember the man who was with you on the other side of the Jordan River, the one you spoke about so much? He is baptizing, and everyone is going to him."

27John answered, "A man can get only what God gives him. 28You yourselves heard me say, 'I am not the Christ, but I am the one sent to prepare the way for him.' 29The bride belongs only to the bridegroom. But the friend who helps the bridegroom stands by and listens to him. He is thrilled that he gets to hear the bridegroom's voice. In the same way, I am really happy. 30He must become greater, and I must become less important.

3:14 Moses . . . desert When the Israelites were dying from snakebites, God told Moses to put a brass snake on a pole. The people who looked at the snake were healed (Numbers 21:4–9). **3:25 religious washing** The Jewish people washed themselves in special ways before eating, before worshiping in the Temple, and at other special times.

BEAUTY SECRET

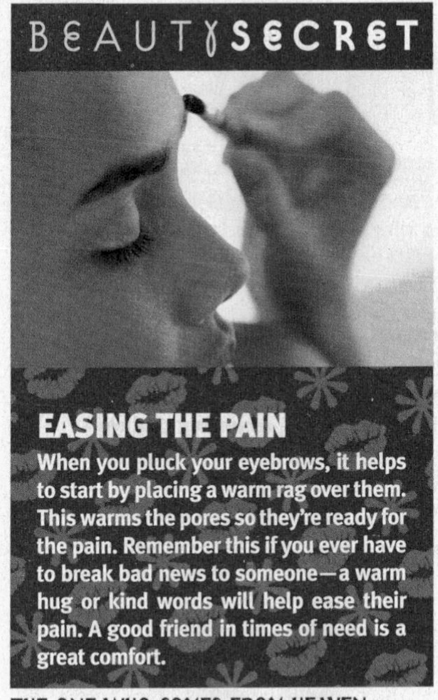

EASING THE PAIN

When you pluck your eyebrows, it helps to start by placing a warm rag over them. This warms the pores so they're ready for the pain. Remember this if you ever have to break bad news to someone—a warm hug or kind words will help ease their pain. A good friend in times of need is a great comfort.

THE ONE WHO COMES FROM HEAVEN

[31]"The One who comes from above is greater than all. The one who is from the earth belongs to the earth and talks about things on the earth. But the One who comes from heaven is greater than all. [32]He tells what he has seen and heard, but no one accepts what he says. [33]Whoever accepts what he says has proven that God is true. [34]The One whom God sent speaks the words of God, because God gives him the Spirit fully. [35]The Father loves the Son and has given him power over everything. [36]Those who believe in the Son have eternal life, but those who do not obey the Son will never have life. God's anger stays on them."

DIDYA KNOW → 63% OF TEENS WHO HAVE HAD SEX SAY THEY WISH THEY HAD WAITED.

JESUS AND A SAMARITAN WOMAN

4 The Pharisees heard that Jesus was making and baptizing more followers than John, [2]although Jesus himself did not baptize people, but his followers did. [3]Jesus knew that the Pharisees had heard about him, so he left Judea and went back to Galilee. [4]But on the way he had to go through the country of Samaria.

[5]In Samaria Jesus came to the town called Sychar, which is near the field Jacob gave to his son Joseph. [6]Jacob's well was there. Jesus was tired from his long trip, so he sat down beside the well. It was about twelve o'clock noon. [7]When a Samaritan woman came to the well to get some water, Jesus said to her, "Please give me a drink." [8](This happened while Jesus' followers were in town buying some food.)

[9]The woman said, "I am surprised that you ask me for a drink, since you are a Jewish man and I am a Samaritan woman." (Jewish people are not friends with Samaritans.[n])

[10]Jesus said, "If you only knew the free gift of God and who it is that is asking you for water, you would have asked him, and he would have given you living water."

[11]The woman said, "Sir, where will you get this living water? The well is very deep, and you have nothing to get water with. [12]Are you greater than Jacob, our father, who gave us this well and drank from it himself along with his sons and flocks?"

[13]Jesus answered, "Everyone who drinks this water will be thirsty again, [14]but whoever drinks the water I give will never be thirsty. The water I give will become a spring of water gushing up inside that person, giving eternal life."

[15]The woman said to him, "Sir, give me this water so I will never be thirsty again and will not have to come back here to get more water."

[16]Jesus told her, "Go get your husband and come back here."

[17]The woman answered, "I have no husband."

Jesus said to her, "You are right to say you have no husband. [18]Really you have had five husbands, and the man you live with now is not your husband. You told the truth."

[19]The woman said, "Sir, I can see that you are a prophet. [20]Our ancestors worshiped on this mountain, but you say that Jerusalem is the place where people must worship."

[21]Jesus said, "Believe me, woman. The time is coming when neither in Jerusalem nor on this mountain will you actually worship the Father. [22]You Samaritans worship something you don't understand. We understand what we worship, because salvation comes from the Jews. [23]The time is coming when the true worshipers will worship the Father in spirit and truth, and that time is here already. You see, the Father too is actively seeking such people to worship him. [24]God is spirit, and those who worship him must worship in spirit and truth."

"GOD IS SPIRIT, AND THOSE WHO WORSHIP HIM MUST WORSHIP IN SPIRIT AND TRUTH."

[25]The woman said, "I know that the Messiah is coming." (Messiah is the One called Christ.) "When the Messiah comes, he will explain everything to us."

[26]Then Jesus said, "I am he—I, the one talking to you."

[27]Just then his followers came back from town and were surprised to see him talking with a woman. But none of them asked, "What do you want?" or "Why are you talking with her?"

[28]Then the woman left her water jar and went back to town. She said to the people, [29]"Come and see a man who told me everything I ever did. Do you think he might be the Christ?" [30]So the people left the town and went to see Jesus.

[31]Meanwhile, his followers were begging him, "Teacher, eat something."

[32]But Jesus answered, "I have food to eat that you know nothing about."

notes

4:9 Jewish people . . . Samaritans This can also be translated "Jewish people don't use things that Samaritans have used."

LEARN IT & LIVE IT

1 Corinthians 6:12:
Learn It: **We are allowed to do all things, but not all things are good for us.**
Live It: **Technically, it's not illegal for you to smoke if you're old enough. But is it good for you? Start to kick the habit today. Find a partner to help you, and make a change!**

1 Corinthians 8:1:
Learn It: **Knowledge puffs us up with pride, but love builds up.**
Live It: **"Actually, it was like this. I was there . . ." Have you ever said those words? Today focus on encouraging others in their accomplishments instead of correcting them on the minor details.**

1 Corinthians 9:25:
Learn It: **Athletes compete to win a perishable award, but we compete for an eternal reward.**
Live It: **Next time you compete at something—your next soccer game, honor roll standing, etc.—remember that we have a much greater prize. Be more gracious in your winning and less devastated in your losses.**

33So the followers asked themselves, "Did somebody already bring him food?"

34Jesus said, "My food is to do what the One who sent me wants me to do and to finish his work. 35You have a saying, 'Four more months till harvest.' But I tell you, open your eyes and look at the fields ready for harvest now. 36Already, the one who harvests is being paid and is gathering crops for eternal life. So the one who plants and the one who harvests celebrate at the same time. 37Here the saying is true, 'One person plants, and another harvests.' 38I sent you to harvest a crop that you did not work on. Others did the work, and you get to finish up their work."[n]

39Many of the Samaritans in that town believed in Jesus because of what the woman said: "He told me everything I ever did." 40When the Samaritans came to Jesus, they begged him to stay with them, so he stayed there two more days. 41And many more believed because of the things he said.

42They said to the woman, "First we believed in Jesus because of your speech, but now we believe because we heard him ourselves. We know that this man really is the Savior of the world."

JESUS HEALS AN OFFICER'S SON

43Two days later, Jesus left and went to Galilee. 44(Jesus had said before that a prophet is not respected in his own country.) 45When Jesus arrived in Galilee, the people there welcomed

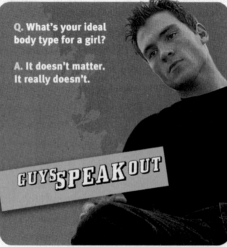

GUYS SPEAK OUT

Q. What's your ideal body type for a girl?

A. It doesn't matter. It really doesn't.

him. They had seen all the things he did at the Passover Feast in Jerusalem, because they had been there, too.

46Jesus went again to visit Cana in Galilee where he had changed the water into wine. One of the king's important officers lived in the city of Capernaum, and his son was sick. 47When he heard that Jesus had come from Judea to Galilee, he went to Jesus and begged him to come to Capernaum and heal his son, because his son was almost dead. 48Jesus said to him, "You people must see signs and miracles before you will believe in me."

49The officer said, "Sir, come before my child dies."

50Jesus answered, "Go. Your son will live."

The man believed what Jesus told him and went home. 51On the way the man's servants came and met him and told him, "Your son is alive."

52The man asked, "What time did my son begin to get well?"

They answered, "Yesterday at one o'clock the fever left him."

53The father knew that one o'clock was the exact time that Jesus had said, "Your son will live." So the man and all the people who lived in his house believed in Jesus.

54That was the second miracle Jesus did after coming from Judea to Galilee.

JESUS HEALS A MAN AT A POOL

5 Later Jesus went to Jerusalem for a special feast. 2In Jerusalem there is a pool with five covered porches, which is called Bethzatha[n] in the Hebrew language.[n] This pool is near the Sheep Gate. 3Many sick people were lying on the porches beside the pool. Some were blind, some were crippled, and some were paralyzed.[n] 5A man was lying there who had been sick for thirty-eight years.

notes

4:38 I . . . their work. As a farmer sends workers to harvest grain, Jesus sends his followers out to bring people to God. **5:2 Bethzatha** Also called Bethsaida or Bethesda, it is a pool of water north of the Temple in Jerusalem. **5:2 Hebrew language** Hebrew or Aramaic, the languages of many people in this region in the first century. **5:3 Verse 3** Some Greek copies add "and they waited for the water to move." A few later copies add verse 4: "Sometimes an angel of the Lord came down to the pool and stirred up the water. After the angel did this, the first person to go into the pool was healed from any sickness he had."

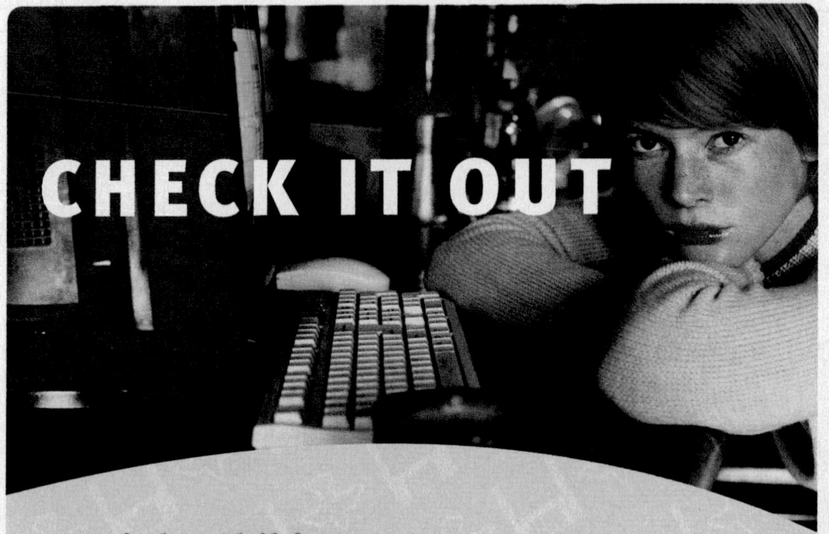

Feed the Children

During our twenty-two-year history, Feed the Children has created and developed one of the world's largest private organizations dedicated to feeding hungry people. Last year, Feed the Children shipped 119 million pounds of food and twenty-one million pounds of other essentials to children and families in all fifty states and in forty-five foreign countries. Feed the Children supplements 1,302,192 meals a day, worldwide.

Our system is fast and efficient. We deliver the food to some 4,900 partner organizations that speed it to over sixty thousand other groups who work with the hungry. The food is provided at no cost to recipients.

For more information, go to ***www.feedthechildren.org.***

[6]When Jesus saw the man and knew that he had been sick for such a long time, Jesus asked him, "Do you want to be well?"

[7]The sick man answered, "Sir, there is no one to help me get into the pool when the water starts moving. While I am coming to the water, someone else always gets in before me."

[8]Then Jesus said, "Stand up. Pick up your mat and walk." [9]And immediately the man was well; he picked up his mat and began to walk.

The day this happened was a Sabbath day. [10]So the Jews said to the man who had been healed, "Today is the Sabbath. It is against our law for you to carry your mat on the Sabbath day."

[11]But he answered, "The man who made me well told me, 'Pick up your mat and walk.' "

[12]Then they asked him, "Who is the man who told you to pick up your mat and walk?"

[13]But the man who had been healed did not know who it was, because there were many people in that place, and Jesus had left.

"WHEN JESUS SAW THE MAN AND KNEW THAT HE HAD BEEN SICK FOR SUCH A LONG TIME, JESUS ASKED HIM, 'DO YOU WANT TO BE WELL?'"

[14]Later, Jesus found the man at the Temple and said to him, "See, you are well now. Stop sinning so that something worse does not happen to you."

[15]Then the man left and told his people that Jesus was the one who had made him well.

[16]Because Jesus was doing this on the Sabbath day, some evil people began to persecute him.

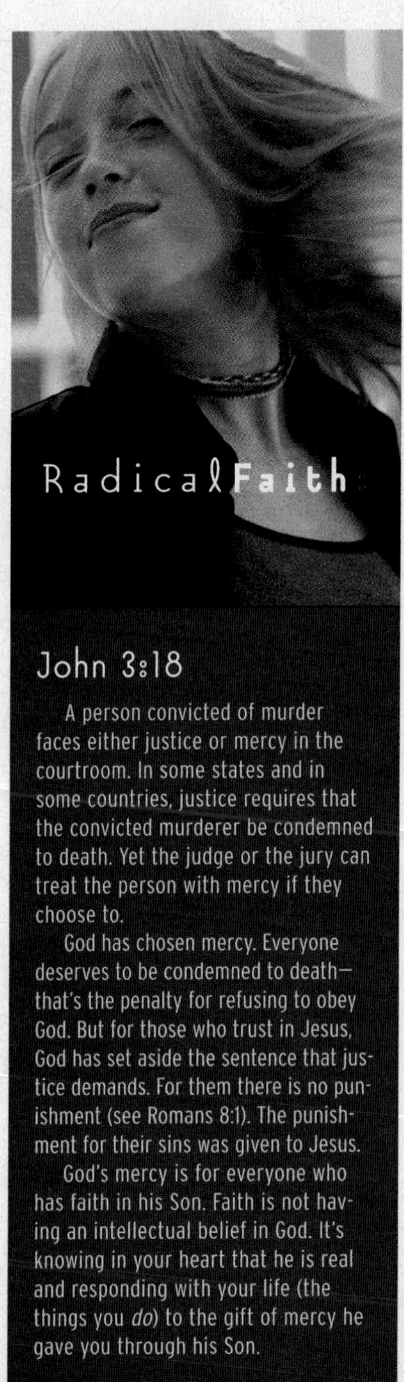

John 3:18

A person convicted of murder faces either justice or mercy in the courtroom. In some states and in some countries, justice requires that the convicted murderer be condemned to death. Yet the judge or the jury can treat the person with mercy if they choose to.

God has chosen mercy. Everyone deserves to be condemned to death—that's the penalty for refusing to obey God. But for those who trust in Jesus, God has set aside the sentence that justice demands. For them there is no punishment (see Romans 8:1). The punishment for their sins was given to Jesus.

God's mercy is for everyone who has faith in his Son. Faith is not having an intellectual belief in God. It's knowing in your heart that he is real and responding with your life (the things you *do*) to the gift of mercy he gave you through his Son.

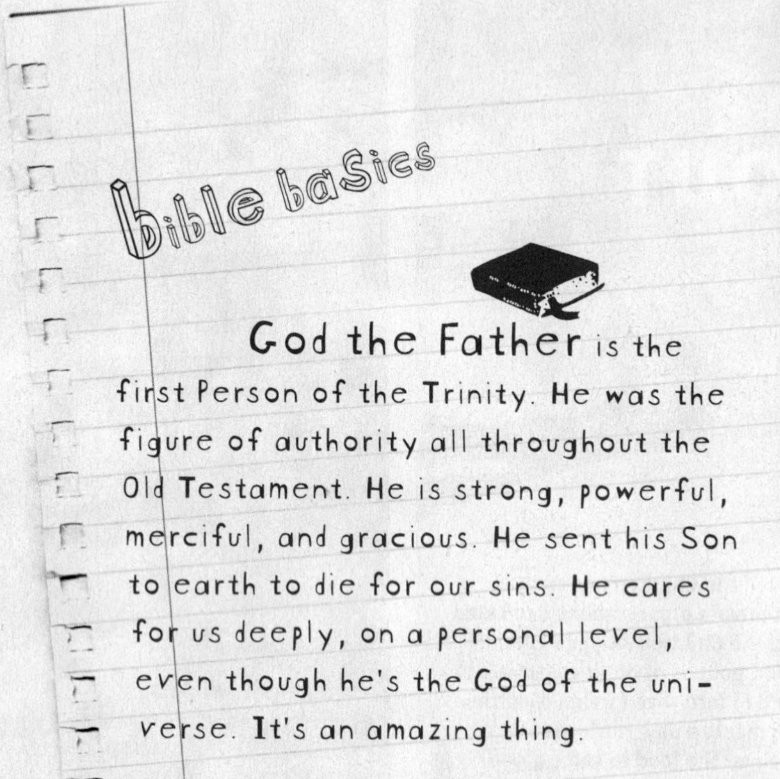

bible basics
God the Father is the
first Person of the Trinity. He was the
figure of authority all throughout the
Old Testament. He is strong, powerful,
merciful, and gracious. He sent his Son
to earth to die for our sins. He cares
for us deeply, on a personal level,
even though he's the God of the universe. It's an amazing thing.

[17]But Jesus said to them, "My Father never
stops working, and so I keep working, too."
[18]This made them try still harder to kill
him. They said, "First Jesus was breaking the
law about the Sabbath day. Now he says that
God is his own Father, making himself equal
with God!"

JESUS HAS GOD'S AUTHORITY

[19]But Jesus said, "I tell you the truth, the
Son can do nothing alone. The Son does only
what he sees the Father doing, because the
Son does whatever the Father does. [20]The
Father loves the Son and shows the Son all the
things he himself does. But the Father will
show the Son even greater things than this so
that you can all be amazed. [21]Just as the Father
raises the dead and gives them life, so also the
Son gives life to those he wants to. [22]In fact, the
Father judges no one, but he has given the Son
power to do all the judging [23]so that all people
will honor the Son as much as they honor the
Father. Anyone who does not honor the Son
does not honor the Father who sent him.
[24]"I tell you the truth, whoever hears what
I say and believes in the One who sent me has
eternal life. That person will not be judged
guilty but has already left death and entered
life. [25]I tell you the truth, the time is coming
and is already here when the dead will hear the
voice of the Son of God, and those who hear
will have life. [26]Life comes from the Father
himself, and he has allowed the Son to have
life in himself as well. [27]And the Father has
given the Son the power to judge, because he
is the Son of Man. [28]Don't be surprised at this:
A time is coming when all who are dead and in
their graves will hear his voice. [29]Then they
will come out of their graves. Those who did
good will rise and have life forever, but those
who did evil will rise to be judged guilty.

JESUS IS GOD'S SON

[30]"I can do nothing alone. I judge only the
way I am told, so my judgment is fair. I don't
try to please myself, but I try to please the One
who sent me.
[31]"If only I tell people about myself, what I
say is not true. [32]But there is another who tells
about me, and I know that the things he says
about me are true.
[33]"You have sent people to John, and he has
told you the truth. [34]It is not that I accept such
human telling; I tell you this so you can be
saved. [35]John was like a burning and shining
lamp, and you were happy to enjoy his light
for a while.
[36]"But I have a proof about myself that is
greater than that of John. The things I do,
which are the things my Father gave me to do,
prove that the Father sent me. [37]And the
Father himself who sent me has given proof
about me. You have never heard his voice or
seen what he looks like. [38]His teaching does not
live in you, because you don't believe in the
One the Father sent. [39]You carefully study the
Scriptures because you think they give you
eternal life. They do in fact tell about me, [40]but
you refuse to come to me to have that life.
[41]"I don't need praise from people. [42]But I
know you—I know that you don't have God's
love in you. [43]I have come from my Father and
speak for him, but you don't accept me. But
when another person comes, speaking only
for himself, you will accept him. [44]You try to
get praise from each other, but you do not try
to get the praise that comes from the only
God. So how can you believe? [45]Don't think
that I will stand before the Father and say you
are wrong. The one who says you are wrong is

APPROXIMATELY 1/3 OF YOUNG SMOKERS WILL DIE OF SMOKING-RELATED DISEASES.

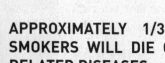

Moses, the one you hoped would save you.
[46]If you really believed Moses, you would
believe me, because Moses wrote about me.
[47]But if you don't believe what Moses wrote,
how can you believe what I say?"

MORE THAN FIVE THOUSAND FED

6 After this, Jesus went across Lake Galilee
(or, Lake Tiberias). [2]Many people followed him because they saw the miracles he
did to heal the sick. [3]Jesus went up on a hill
and sat down there with his followers. [4]It was
almost the time for the Jewish Passover Feast.

"WHEN THEY HAD ROWED THE BOAT ABOUT THREE OR FOUR MILES, THEY SAW JESUS WALKING ON THE WATER, COMING TOWARD THE BOAT."

[5]When Jesus looked up and saw a large
crowd coming toward him, he said to Philip,
"Where can we buy enough bread for all these
people to eat?" [6](Jesus asked Philip this question
to test him, because Jesus already knew what he
planned to do.)

[7]Philip answered, "We would all
have to work a month to buy
enough bread for each person
to have only a little piece."

[8]Another one of his followers, Andrew, Simon Peter's
brother, said, [9]"Here is a boy with
five loaves of barley bread and two little fish, but that is not enough for so many
people."

1 John 4:10
This is what real love is: It is not our love for God; it is God's love for us in sending his Son to be the way to take away our sins.

[10]Jesus said, "Tell the people to sit down."
This was a very grassy place, and about five
thousand men sat down there. [11]Then Jesus
took the loaves of bread, thanked God for
them, and gave them to the people who were
sitting there. He did the same with the fish,
giving as much as the people wanted.

[12]When they had all had enough to eat,
Jesus said to his followers, "Gather the leftover
pieces of fish and bread so that nothing is
wasted." [13]So they gathered up the pieces and
filled twelve baskets with the pieces left from
the five barley loaves.

[14]When the people saw this miracle that
Jesus did, they said, "He must truly be the
Prophet[n] who is coming into the world."

[15]Jesus knew that the people planned to come
and take him by force and make him their
king, so he left and went into the hills alone.

JESUS WALKS ON THE WATER

[16]That evening Jesus' followers went down
to Lake Galilee. [17]It was dark now, and Jesus
had not yet come to them. The followers got into
a boat and started across the lake to Capernaum.
[18]By now a strong wind was blowing, and the
waves on the lake were getting bigger. [19]When
they had rowed the boat about three or four
miles, they saw Jesus walking on the water,
coming toward the boat. The followers were
afraid, [20]but Jesus said to them, "It is I. Do not
be afraid." [21]Then they were glad to take him
into the boat. At once the boat came to land at
the place where they wanted to go.

THE PEOPLE SEEK JESUS

[22]The next day the people who had
stayed on the other side of the
lake knew that Jesus had not
gone in the boat with his followers but that they had left
without him. And they
knew that only one boat had
been there. [23]But then some boats came
from Tiberias and landed near the place
where the people had eaten the bread after the
Lord had given thanks. [24]When the people saw
that Jesus and his followers were not there
now, they got into boats and went to
Capernaum to find Jesus.

JESUS, THE BREAD OF LIFE

[25]When the people found Jesus on the other
side of the lake, they asked him, "Teacher,
when did you come here?"

[26]Jesus answered, "I tell you the truth, you

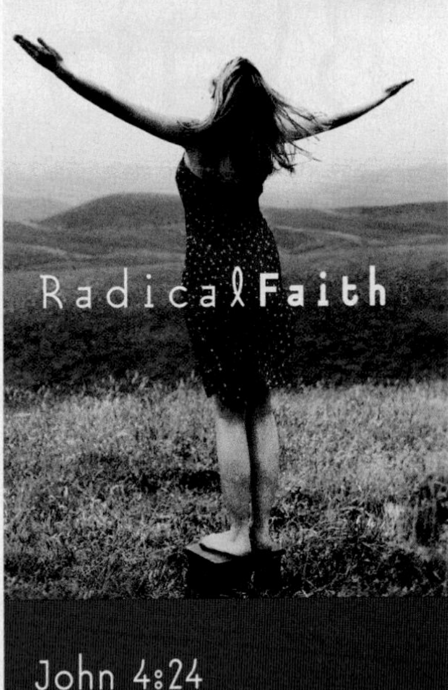

John 4:24

Those who worship God must be led by the Spirit. This verse isn't talking about being led by *a* spirit like the ghosts you see floating around old houses on TV. It's talking about being led by the *Holy Spirit*. The Holy Spirit is part of the Trinity: God the Father, God the Son (Jesus), and God the Holy Spirit. The Holy Spirit has been sent to guide you into all truth (see John 16:13). You are free to make your own choices, but if you're going to be successful in life, you must submit to the Holy Spirit and allow him to guide you.

That's why it's so important to listen to that still, small voice. The next time you're making an important decision or stepping out in a certain direction and you don't feel at peace about it, don't ignore it! That's the Holy Spirit. He wants to lead you. He wants to help you. He wants to see you successful in everything you do. God has given us, as his children, the opportunity and the right to be led by the Holy Spirit. Start being led by the Spirit today, and watch what God will do tomorrow!

notes

6:14 Prophet They probably meant the prophet that God told Moses he would send (Deuteronomy 18:15–19).

Blab

Q. Can people really know they're Christian?

A. Most definitely. God's Word makes it very clear. "If you use your mouth to say, 'Jesus is Lord,' and if you believe in your heart that God raised Jesus from the dead, you will be saved" (Romans 10:9). In order to do those two things, people have to know they are doing them. And once they've done them, they can know they are Christians.

Q. How can we not be part of the world and keep ourselves holy from them but at the same time show them Christ's love and light?

A. To be set apart from the world means that you don't participate in the sinful activity of the world and that you don't envy those who do. It doesn't mean that you remove yourself from the world to protect yourself. Christians are the light of the world; and if they don't go out and light the world, it will stay dark. Hang out with lost people, but show them Christ in the process.

Q. I was saved when I was 11 years old and I am still, but something in my mind saying I'm not saved but I know I am. What do I do or what is happening?

A. The enemy loves to lie to us. He uses these lies to freak us out and keep us from doing anything for God and sometimes from even loving him. There is nothing wrong with you; this happens to a lot of people. Find all the verses you can on how much God loves you and will protect you. These are your weapons. Use them to do what they do—defeat the enemy.

aren't looking for me because you saw me do miracles. You are looking for me because you ate the bread and were satisfied. 27Don't work for the food that spoils. Work for the food that stays good always and gives eternal life. The Son of Man will give you this food, because on him God the Father has put his power."

28The people asked Jesus, "What are the things God wants us to do?"

29Jesus answered, "The work God wants you to do is this: Believe the One he sent."

30So the people asked, "What miracle will you do? If we see a miracle, we will believe you. What will you do? 31Our fathers ate the manna in the desert. This is written in the Scriptures: 'He gave them bread from heaven to eat.' "[n]

32Jesus said, "I tell you the truth, it was not Moses who gave you bread from heaven; it is my Father who is giving you the true bread from heaven. 33God's bread is the One who comes down from heaven and gives life to the world."

34The people said, "Sir, give us this bread always."

35Then Jesus said, "I am the bread that gives life. Whoever comes to me will never be hungry, and whoever believes in me will never be thirsty. 36But as I told you before, you have seen me and still don't believe. 37The Father gives me my people. Every one of them will come to me, and I will always accept them. 38I came down from heaven to do what God wants me to do, not what I want to do. 39Here is what the One who sent me wants me to do: I must not lose even one whom God gave me, but I must raise them all on the last day. 40Those who see the Son and believe in him have eternal life, and I will raise them on the last day. This is what my Father wants."

41Some people began to complain about Jesus because he said, "I am the bread that comes down from heaven." 42They said, "This is Jesus, the son of Joseph. We know his father and mother. How can he say, 'I came down from heaven'?"

43But Jesus answered, "Stop complaining to each other. 44The Father is the One who sent me. No one can come to me unless the Father draws him to me, and I will raise that person up on the last day. 45It is written in the prophets, 'They will all be taught by God.'[n] Everyone who listens to the Father and learns from him comes to me. 46No one has seen the Father except the One who is from God; only he has seen the Father. 47I tell you the truth, whoever believes has eternal life. 48I am the bread that gives life. 49Your ancestors ate the manna in the desert, but still they died. 50Here is the bread that comes down from heaven. Anyone who eats this bread will never die. 51I am the living bread that came down from heaven. Anyone who eats this bread will live forever. This bread is my flesh, which I will give up so that the world may have life."

52Then the evil people began to argue among themselves, saying, "How can this man give us his flesh to eat?"

53Jesus said, "I tell you the truth, you must eat the flesh of the Son of Man and drink his blood. Otherwise, you won't have real life in you. 54Those who eat my flesh and drink my blood have eternal life, and I will raise them

"JESUS ANSWERED, 'THE WORK GOD WANTS YOU TO DO IS THIS: BELIEVE THE ONE HE SENT.'"

up on the last day. 55My flesh is true food, and my blood is true drink. 56Those who eat my flesh and drink my blood live in me, and I live in them. 57The living Father sent me, and I live because of the Father. So whoever eats me will live because of me. 58I am not like the bread your ancestors ate. They ate that bread and still died. I am the bread that came down from heaven, and whoever eats this bread will live forever." 59Jesus said all these things

notes

6:31 'He gave . . . eat.' Quotation from Psalm 78:24. **6:45 'They . . . God.'** Quotation from Isaiah 54:13.

while he was teaching in the synagogue in Capernaum.

THE WORDS OF ETERNAL LIFE

60When the followers of Jesus heard this, many of them said, "This teaching is hard. Who can accept it?"

61Knowing that his followers were complaining about this, Jesus said, "Does this teaching bother you? 62Then will it also bother you to see the Son of Man going back to the place where he came from? 63It is the Spirit that gives life. The flesh doesn't give life. The words I told you are spirit, and they give life. 64But some of you don't believe." (Jesus knew from the beginning who did not believe and who would turn against him.) 65Jesus said, "That is the reason I said, 'If the Father does not bring a person to me, that one cannot come.' "

66After Jesus said this, many of his followers left him and stopped following him.

67Jesus asked the twelve followers, "Do you want to leave, too?"

68Simon Peter answered him, "Lord, where would we go? You have the words that give eternal life. 69We believe and know that you are the Holy One from God."

70Then Jesus answered, "I chose all twelve of you, but one of you is a devil."

71Jesus was talking about Judas, the son of Simon Iscariot. Judas was one of the twelve, but later he was going to turn against Jesus.

DIDYA KNOW → **THERE ARE ONE MILLION MORE TEENS THAN BABY BOOMERS IN AMERICA.**

JESUS' BROTHERS DON'T BELIEVE

7 After this, Jesus traveled around Galilee. He did not want to travel in Judea, because some evil people there wanted to kill him. 2It was time for the Feast of Shelters. 3So Jesus' brothers said to him, "You should leave here and go to Judea so your followers there can see the miracles you do. 4Anyone who wants to be well known does not hide what he does. If you are doing these things, show yourself to the world." 5(Even Jesus' brothers did not believe in him.)

6Jesus said to his brothers, "The right time for me has not yet come, but any time is right for you. 7The world cannot hate you, but it hates me, because I tell it the evil things it does. 8So you go to the feast. I will not go yet to this feast, because the right time for me has not yet come." 9After saying this, Jesus stayed in Galilee.

10But after Jesus' brothers had gone to the feast, Jesus went also. But he did not let people see him. 11At the feast some people were looking for him and saying, "Where is that man?"

12Within the large crowd there, many people were whispering to each other about Jesus. Some said, "He is a good man."

Others said, "No, he fools the people." 13But no one was brave enough to talk about Jesus openly, because they were afraid of the older leaders.

JESUS TEACHES AT THE FEAST

14When the feast was about half over, Jesus went to the Temple and began to teach. 15The people were amazed and said, "This man has never studied in school. How did he learn so much?"

16Jesus answered, "The things I teach are not my own, but they come from him who sent me. 17If people choose to do what God wants, they will know that my teaching comes from God and not from me. 18Those who teach their own ideas are trying to get honor for themselves. But those who try to bring honor to the one who sent him speak the truth, and there is nothing false in them. 19Moses gave you the law,[n] but none of you obeys that law. Why are you trying to kill me?"

20The people answered, "A demon has come into you. We are not trying to kill you."

21Jesus said to them, "I did one miracle, and you are all amazed. 22Moses gave you the law about circumcision. (But really Moses did not give you circumcision; it came from our ancestors.) And yet you circumcise a baby on a

BIBLE BIOS: EVE

Eve is the mother of all humankind. She was the first woman that God created according to Genesis 1. Deceived by a serpent to eat the fruit of the tree of knowledge of good and evil, Eve chose to disobey God. Her husband, Adam, joined with her in this act, and they received a curse from the Lord. Eve's curse was that she would experience pain in childbirth, she would long for her husband, and she was banished from the Garden of Eden. She bravely went out into the world to bear children and live a life of joy and pain. From the first woman, we can learn to have strength and to face suffering with hope.

[GENESIS 1–3]

notes

7:19 law Moses gave God's people the Law that God gave him on Mount Sinai (Exodus 34:29–32).

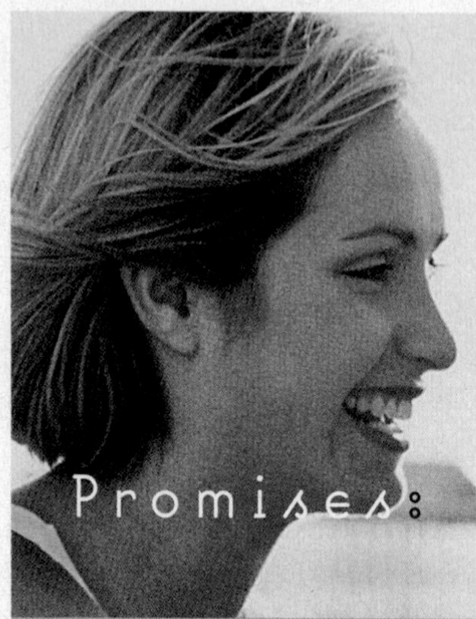

John 6:37

Some people think that they have to have their lives totally together before they turn to God. They think they need to make themselves worthy of Jesus' friendship. This is a lie that suits Satan's purposes pretty well. The problem is that *nobody* will ever be worthy of what God is offering him or her. That's a part of God's truth that's hard to swallow. And if Satan can keep people believing that they have to somehow earn God's favor—that it's even possible—he can keep them from taking the first step toward God's kingdom.

The truth is that God doesn't ask anyone to be worthy of him. If you come to him—without excuses, without trying to justify yourself, just putting your complete trust in him (like putting all of your weight in a chair)—then Jesus promises not to turn you away. He accepts you because he loves you, not because you've earned his friendship.

"GOD DOESN'T ASK ANYONE TO BE WORTHY OF HIM."

Sabbath day. 23If a baby can be circumcised on
a Sabbath day to obey the law of Moses, why
are you angry at me for healing a person's
whole body on the Sabbath day? 24Stop judging by the way things look, but judge by what
is really right."

IS JESUS THE CHRIST?

25Then some of the people who lived in
Jerusalem said, "This is the man they are trying to kill. 26But he is teaching where everyone can see and hear him, and no one is trying
to stop him. Maybe the leaders
have decided he really is the
Christ. 27But we know where
this man is from. And when the
real Christ comes, no one will
know where he comes from."
28Jesus, teaching in the Temple,
cried out, "Yes, you know me, and you know
where I am from. But I have not come by my
own authority. I was sent by the One who is
true, whom you don't know. 29But I know
him, because I am from him, and he sent me."
30When Jesus said this, the people tried to
take him. But no one was able to touch him,
because it was not yet the right time. 31But

"WHEN THE PEOPLE HEARD JESUS' WORDS, SOME OF THEM SAID, 'THIS MAN REALLY IS THE PROPHET.'"

many of the people believed in Jesus. They
said, "When the Christ comes, will he do more
miracles than this man has done?"

THE LEADERS TRY TO ARREST JESUS

32The Pharisees heard the crowd whispering these things about Jesus. So the leading
priests and the Pharisees sent some Temple
guards to arrest him. 33Jesus said, "I will be
with you a little while longer. Then I will go
back to the One who sent me. 34You will look
for me, but you will not find me. And you cannot come where I am."
35Some people said to each other, "Where
will this man go so we cannot find him? Will
he go to the Greek cities where our people live
and teach the Greek people there? 36What did
he mean when he said, 'You will look for me,
but you will not find me,' and 'You cannot
come where I am'?"

JESUS TALKS ABOUT THE SPIRIT

37On the last and most important day of the
feast Jesus stood up and said in a loud voice,
"Let anyone who is thirsty come to me and
drink. 38If anyone believes in me,
rivers of living water will flow
out from that person's heart, as
the Scripture says." 39Jesus
was talking about the
Holy Spirit. The Spirit had
not yet been given, because Jesus had
not yet been raised to glory. But later, those
who believed in Jesus would receive the Spirit.

1 John 4:16
God is love.
Those who live in love
live in God,
and God lives in them.

THE PEOPLE ARGUE ABOUT JESUS

40When the people heard Jesus' words, some
of them said, "This man really is the Prophet."*n*
41Others said, "He is the Christ."
Still others said, "The Christ will not come
from Galilee. 42The Scripture says that the
Christ will come from David's family and from
Bethlehem, the town where David lived." 43So
the people did not agree with each other about
Jesus. 44Some of them wanted to arrest him,
but no one was able to touch him.

SOME LEADERS WON'T BELIEVE

45The Temple guards went back to the leading priests and the Pharisees, who asked,
"Why didn't you bring Jesus?"
46The guards answered, "The words he says
are greater than the words of any other person
who has ever spoken!"
47The Pharisees answered, "So Jesus has
fooled you also! 48Have any of the leaders or
the Pharisees believed in him? No! 49But
these people, who know nothing about the
law, are under God's curse."
50Nicodemus, who had gone to see Jesus

notes
7:40 Prophet They probably meant the prophet God told Moses he would send (Deuteronomy 18:15–19).

before, was in that group.[n] He said, 51“Our law does not judge a man without hearing him and knowing what he has done.”

52They answered, “Are you from Galilee, too? Study the Scriptures, and you will learn that no prophet comes from Galilee.”

Some early Greek manuscripts do not contain 7:53—8:11.

[53And everyone left and went home.

THE WOMAN CAUGHT IN ADULTERY

8 Jesus went to the Mount of Olives. 2But early in the morning he went back to the Temple, and all the people came to him, and he sat and taught them. 3The teachers of the law and the Pharisees brought a woman who had been caught in adultery. They forced her to stand before the people. 4They said to Jesus, “Teacher, this woman was caught having sexual relations with a man who is not her husband. 5The law of Moses commands that we stone to death every woman who does this. What do you say we should do?” 6They were asking this to trick Jesus so that they could have some charge against him.

But Jesus bent over and started writing on the ground with his finger. 7When they continued to ask Jesus their question, he raised up and said, “Anyone here who has never sinned can throw the first stone at her.” 8Then Jesus bent over again and wrote on the ground.

9Those who heard Jesus began to leave one by one, first the older men and then the others. Jesus was left there alone with the woman

“IF YOU KNEW ME, YOU WOULD KNOW MY FATHER, TOO.”

standing before him. 10Jesus raised up again and asked her, “Woman, where are they? Has no one judged you guilty?”

11She answered, “No one, sir.”

Then Jesus said, “I also don’t judge you guilty. You may go now, but don’t sin anymore.”]

JESUS IS THE LIGHT OF THE WORLD

12Later, Jesus talked to the people again, saying, “I am the light of the world. The person who follows me will never live in darkness but will have the light that gives life.”

13The Pharisees said to Jesus, “When you talk about yourself, you are the only one to say these things are true. We cannot accept what you say.”

14Jesus answered, “Yes, I am saying these things about myself, but they are true. I know where I came from and where I am going. But you don’t know where I came from or where I am going. 15You judge by human standards. I am not judging anyone. 16But when I do judge, my judging is true, because I am not alone. The Father who sent me is with me. 17Your own law says that when two witnesses say the same thing, you must accept what they say. 18I am one of the witnesses who speaks about myself, and the Father who sent me is the other witness.”

19They asked, “Where is your father?”

Jesus answered, “You don’t know me or my Father. If you knew me, you would know my Father, too.” 20Jesus said these things while he was teaching in the Temple, near where the money is kept. But no one arrested him, because the right time for him had not yet come.

THE PEOPLE MISUNDERSTAND JESUS

21Again, Jesus said to the people, “I will leave you, and you will look for me, but you will die in your sins. You cannot come where I am going.”

22So the Jews asked, “Will Jesus kill himself? Is that why he said, ‘You cannot come where I am going’?”

LEARN IT & LIVE IT

1 Corinthians 10:13:
Learn It: God will not let you be tested beyond your strength.
Live It: Just do it! It was a huge slogan for Nike, but it applies to your faith too. What trial are you facing right now? It’s not too big for you. You can get through it. Get the focus of an overcomer today.

1 Corinthians 12:12:
Learn It: There is one body with many parts.
Live It: Appreciate the people who are different from you today. I’m not talking about skin color, gender, etc. I’m talking about that person who has to do everything just right, or the one who’s so laid back she drives you nuts! Make an effort to do something nice for her—buy her a Starbucks or make her some cookies.

1 Corinthians 13:4:
Learn It: Love is patient; love is kind.
Live It: Today help someone who is slower than you. This might be someone in a special education class, an elderly lady in a nursing home, or your little brother or sister. Spend at least one hour with them, patiently and kindly. They’ll remember it long after you’ve moved on to other things.

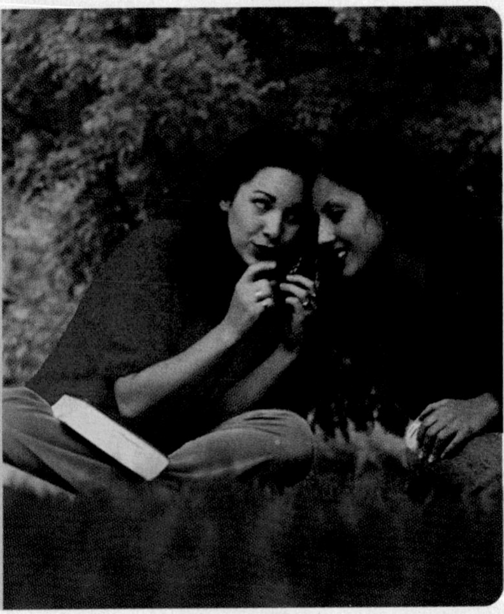

notes

7:50 Nicodemus . . . group. The story about Nicodemus going and talking to Jesus is in John 3:1–21.

23Jesus said, "You people are from here below, but I am from above. You belong to this world, but I don't belong to this world. 24So I told you that you would die in your sins. Yes, you will die in your sins if you don't believe that I am he."

25They asked, "Then who are you?"

Jesus answered, "I am what I have told you from the beginning. 26I have many things to say and decide about you. But I tell people only the things I have heard from the One who sent me, and he speaks the truth."

27The people did not understand that he was talking to them about the Father. 28So Jesus said to them, "When you lift up the Son of Man, you will know that I am he. You will know that these things I do are not by my own authority but that I say only what the Father has taught me. 29The One who sent me is with me. I always do what is pleasing to him, so he has not left me alone." 30While Jesus was saying these things, many people believed in him.

FREEDOM FROM SIN

31So Jesus said to the Jews who believed in him, "If you continue to obey my teaching, you are truly my followers. 32Then you will know the truth, and the truth will make you free."

33They answered, "We are Abraham's children, and we have never been anyone's slaves. So why do you say we will be free?"

"THE PERSON WHO BELONGS TO GOD ACCEPTS WHAT GOD SAYS."

34Jesus answered, "I tell you the truth, everyone who lives in sin is a slave to sin. 35A slave does not stay with a family forever, but a son belongs to the family forever. 36So if the Son makes you free, you will be truly free. 37I know you are Abraham's children, but you want to kill me because you don't accept my teaching. 38I am telling you what my Father has shown me, but you do what your father has told you."

39They answered, "Our father is Abraham."

Jesus said, "If you were really Abraham's children, you would do the things Abraham did. 40I am a man who has told you the truth which I heard from God, but you are trying to kill me. Abraham did nothing like that. 41So you are doing the things your own father did."

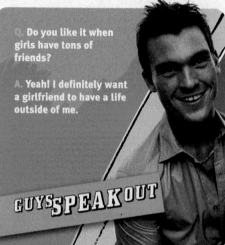

Q. Do you like it when girls have tons of friends?

A. Yeah! I definitely want a girlfriend to have a life outside of me.

GUYS SPEAK OUT

But they said, "We are not like children who never knew who their father was. God is our Father; he is the only Father we have."

42Jesus said to them, "If God were really your Father, you would love me, because I came from God and now I am here. I did not come by my own authority; God sent me. 43You don't understand what I say, because you cannot accept my teaching. 44You belong to your father the devil, and you want to do what he wants. He was a murderer from the beginning and was against the truth, because there is no truth in him. When he tells a lie, he shows what he is really like, because he is a liar and the father of lies. 45But because I speak the truth, you don't believe me. 46Can any of you prove that I am guilty of sin? If I am telling the truth, why don't you believe me? 47The person who belongs to God accepts what God says. But you don't accept what God says, because you don't belong to God."

JESUS IS GREATER THAN ABRAHAM

48They answered, "We say you are a Samaritan and have a demon in you. Are we not right?"

49Jesus answered, "I have no demon in me. I give honor to my Father, but you dishonor me. 50I am not trying to get honor for myself. There is One who wants this honor for me, and he is the judge. 51I tell you the truth, whoever obeys my teaching will never die."

52They said to Jesus, "Now we know that you have a demon in you! Even Abraham and the prophets died. But you say, 'Whoever obeys my teaching will never die.' 53Do you think you are greater than our father Abraham, who died? And the prophets died, too. Who do you think you are?"

54Jesus answered, "If I give honor to myself, that honor is worth nothing. The One who gives me honor is my Father, and you say he is your God. 55You don't really know him, but I know him. If I said I did not know him, I would be a liar like you. But I do know him, and I obey what he says. 56Your father Abraham was very happy that he would see my day. He saw that day and was glad."

57They said to him, "You have never seen Abraham! You are not even fifty years old."

58Jesus answered, "I tell you the truth, before Abraham was even born, I am!" 59When Jesus said this, the people picked up stones to throw at him. But Jesus hid himself, and then he left the Temple.

JESUS HEALS A MAN BORN BLIND

9 As Jesus was walking along, he saw a man who had been born blind. 2His followers asked him, "Teacher, whose sin caused this man to be born blind—his own sin or his parents' sin?"

3Jesus answered, "It is not this man's sin or his parents' sin that made him be blind. This

man was born blind so that God's power could be shown in him. [4]While it is daytime, we must continue doing the work of the One who sent me. Night is coming, when no one can work. [5]While I am in the world, I am the light of the world."

[6]After Jesus said this, he spit on the ground and made some mud with it and put the mud on the man's eyes. [7]Then he told the man, "Go and wash in the Pool of Siloam." (Siloam means Sent.) So the man went, washed, and came back seeing.

[8]The neighbors and some people who had earlier seen this man begging said, "Isn't this the same man who used to sit and beg?"

[9]Some said, "He is the one," but others said, "No, he only looks like him."

The man himself said, "I am the man."

[10]They asked, "How did you get your sight?"

[11]He answered, "The man named Jesus made some mud and put it on my eyes. Then he told me to go to Siloam and wash. So I went and washed, and then I could see."

[12]They asked him, "Where is this man?"

"I don't know," he answered.

PHARISEES QUESTION THE HEALING

[13]Then the people took to the Pharisees the man who had been blind. [14]The day Jesus had made mud and healed his eyes was a Sabbath day. [15]So now the Pharisees asked the man, "How did you get your sight?"

He answered, "He put mud on my eyes, I washed, and now I see."

[16]So some of the Pharisees were saying, "This man does not keep the Sabbath day, so he is not from God."

But others said, "A man who is a sinner can't do miracles like these." So they could not agree with each other.

[17]They asked the man again, "What do you say about him since it was your eyes he opened?"

The man answered, "He is a prophet."

[18]These leaders did not believe that he had been blind and could now see again. So they sent for the man's parents [19]and asked them, "Is this your son who you say was born blind? Then how does he now see?"

[20]His parents answered, "We know that this is our son and that he was born blind. [21]But we don't know how he can now see. We don't know who opened his eyes. Ask him. He is old enough to speak for himself." [22]His parents said this because they were afraid of the older leaders, who had already decided that anyone who said Jesus was the Christ would be avoided. [23]That is why his parents said, "He is old enough. Ask him."

[24]So for the second time, they called the man who had been blind. They said, "You should give God the glory by telling the truth. We know that this man is a sinner."

[25]He answered, "I don't know if he is a sinner. One thing I do know: I was blind, and now I see."

[26]They asked, "What did he do to you? How did he make you see again?"

[27]He answered, "I already told you, and you didn't listen. Why do you want to hear it again? Do you want to become his followers, too?"

[28]Then they insulted him and said, "You are his follower, but we are followers of Moses. [29]We know that God spoke to Moses, but we don't even know where this man comes from."

[30]The man answered, "This is a very strange thing. You don't know where he comes from, and yet he opened my eyes. [31]We all know that God does not listen to sinners, but he listens to anyone who worships and obeys him.

THE AVERAGE TEEN HAS ABOUT $90 A WEEK TO SPEND.

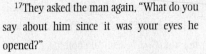

Blab

Q. I would like to know how to pray and why do you pray the way you do?

A. There is no set formula for prayer. When Jesus was asked this question, he spoke the Lord's Prayer. You can find it in Matthew 6.

Q. Why does everyone always refer to God as 'HE'? God is neither male nor female, so why don't people call God 'SHE' instead?

A. We refer to God as he because that is how he most often refers to himself in the Bible. And keep in mind, when Jesus came to earth, he wasn't a girl. This is where we get our most common image of God—in the Person of Jesus Christ.

Q. If you accept Christ but later you turn from him, or start to go down the wrong road, does God stick with you 'til there is no chance of restoration?

A. Scripture tells us that salvation has nothing to do with what we DO but with what we believe, that is, in Christ. But it also says that we should make him Lord of our lives. But if a person claims to be saved but then acts like they are an enemy of God, disobeying him purposefully, then they probably never really made him Lord of their life.

John 7:38

Have you ever been really thirsty—like "walking-across-the-desert-in-search-of-water" thirsty? Then you know that when you get that thirsty, there's nothing better than a nice, long drink of cool, refreshing water! That's the kind of water you need. When you gave your heart to Jesus, you received that refreshing, living water. The question is, What are you going to do with that water? Jesus said it flows from you, not just to you!

Have you ever been for a ride on a scalding hot summer's day and thought you saw a shimmering image that looked like water on the street up ahead? This is called a mirage, and it happens all of the time in the desert. We've all seen it on TV—a person in need of water, crawling across the desert, spots one. Their hopes are dashed as they realize what they had thought was an oasis is really a mirage. Nothing!

That's the question: Are you going to be a mirage or an oasis of life? You have the living water that this world is searching for. Release it today!

"YOU HAVE THE LIVING WATER THAT THIS WORLD IS SEARCHING FOR."

32Nobody has ever heard of anyone giving sight to a man born blind. 33If this man were not from God, he could do nothing."

34They answered, "You were born full of sin! Are you trying to teach us?" And they threw him out.

SPIRITUAL BLINDNESS

35When Jesus heard that they had thrown him out, Jesus found him and said, "Do you believe in the Son of Man?"

36He asked, "Who is the Son of Man, sir, so that I can believe in him?"

37Jesus said to him, "You have seen him. The Son of Man is the one talking with you."

38He said, "Lord, I believe!" Then the man worshiped Jesus.

39Jesus said, "I came into this world so that the world could be judged. I came so that the blind[n] would see and so that those who see will become blind."

40Some of the Pharisees who were nearby heard Jesus say this and asked, "Are you saying we are blind, too?"

41Jesus said, "If you were blind, you would not be guilty of sin. But since you keep saying you see, your guilt remains."

THE SHEPHERD AND HIS SHEEP

10 Jesus said, "I tell you the truth, the person who does not enter the sheepfold by the door, but climbs in some other way, is a thief and a robber. 2The one who enters by the door is the shepherd of the sheep. 3The one who guards the door opens it for him. And the sheep listen to the voice of the shepherd. He calls his own sheep by name and leads them out. 4When he brings all his sheep out, he goes ahead of them, and they follow him because they know his voice. 5But they will never follow a stranger. They will run away from him because they don't know his voice." 6Jesus told the people this story, but they did not understand what it meant.

JESUS IS THE GOOD SHEPHERD

7So Jesus said again, "I tell you the truth, I am the door for the sheep. 8All the people who came before me were thieves and robbers. The sheep did not listen to them. 9I am the door, and the person who enters through me will be saved and will be able to come in and go out and find pasture. 10A thief comes to steal and kill and destroy, but I came to give life—life in all its fullness.

"JESUS SAID, 'I CAME INTO THIS WORLD SO THAT THE WORLD COULD BE JUDGED. I CAME SO THAT THE BLIND WOULD SEE AND SO THAT THOSE WHO SEE WILL BECOME BLIND.'"

11"I am the good shepherd. The good shepherd gives his life for the sheep. 12The worker who is paid to keep the sheep is different from the shepherd who owns them. When the worker sees a wolf coming, he runs away and leaves the sheep alone. Then the wolf attacks the sheep and scatters them. 13The man runs away because he is only a paid worker and does not really care about the sheep.

14-15"I am the good shepherd. I know my sheep, as the Father knows me. And my sheep know me, as I know the Father. I give my life for the sheep. 16I have other sheep that are not in this flock, and I must bring them also. They will listen to my voice, and there will be one flock and one shepherd. 17The Father loves me because I give my life so that I can take it back again. 18No one takes it away from me; I give my own life freely. I have the right to give my life, and I have the right to take it back. This is what my Father commanded me to do."

1 John 4:17
This is how love is made perfect in us: that we can be without fear on the day God judges us, because in this world we are like him.

9:39 blind Jesus is talking about people who are spiritually blind, not physically blind.

QUIZ

WHAT KIND OF SLUMP ARE YOU IN?

1) AFTER A FUN WEEKEND, I DREAD GOING TO SCHOOL.
A. RARELY
B. OCCASIONALLY
C. OFTEN
D. MOST OF THE TIME

2) I TEND TO SLOUCH, OR MY MOM IS ALWAYS SAYING, "SIT UP STRAIGHT!"
A. RARELY
B. OCCASIONALLY
C. OFTEN
D. MOST OF THE TIME

3) I HAVE A NEGATIVE ATTITUDE WHEN I'M HAVING A PROBLEM WITH SOMETHING.
A. RARELY
B. OCCASIONALLY
C. OFTEN
D. MOST OF THE TIME

4) I WANT TO TAKE A NAP WHEN I GET HOME FROM SCHOOL.
A. RARELY
B. OCCASIONALLY
C. OFTEN
D. MOST OF THE TIME

5) I CRAVE JUNK FOOD WHEN I'M SAD OR ANGRY.
A. RARELY
B. OCCASIONALLY
C. OFTEN
D. MOST OF THE TIME

6) I DON'T FEEL EXCITED ABOUT MY SCHOOLWORK.
A. RARELY
B. OCCASIONALLY
C. OFTEN
D. MOST OF THE TIME

7) WHEN MY FRIENDS ASK ME HOW I'M FEELING, I OFTEN SAY "TIRED" OR "OVERWHELMED."
A. RARELY
B. OCCASIONALLY
C. OFTEN
D. MOST OF THE TIME

8) I WONDER HOW SUCCESSFUL I AM AND WHAT VALUE I HAVE.
A. RARELY
B. OCCASIONALLY
C. OFTEN
D. MOST OF THE TIME

9) I EAT MORE THAN I SHOULD, ESPECIALLY LATE IN THE DAY.
A. RARELY
B. OCCASIONALLY
C. OFTEN
D. MOST OF THE TIME

IF YOU ANSWERED C OR D TO QUESTIONS 2, 3, OR 7, YOU'RE IN AN EMOTIONAL SLUMP.

Focus on replacing negative thoughts with positive ones. Try reading through the promises of God in the Bible, and think about God's faithfulness. Then thank him for the ways that he cares for you. Hang out with people who have positive attitudes—laughter is contagious! "A happy heart is like good medicine" (Proverbs 17:22). (If this slump lasts a really long time, you might want to visit a Christian counselor. It could be more than just a slump.)

IF YOU ANSWERED C OR D TO QUESTIONS 1, 6, OR 8, YOU'RE IN A SCHOOL SLUMP.

Define your purpose. Remember that, for right now, school is your calling. It is the job that God has given you to do. Wake up in the morning and remind yourself of this, and be encouraged that he is giving you the best! Create a list of goals and pick one to work toward. For example, your goal might be, "I'm going to make an A in geometry this semester." Then go after it! A little competition against yourself might be just the thing to get your school day jump-started.

IF YOU ANSWERED C OR D TO QUESTIONS 4, 5, OR 9, YOU'RE IN A PHYSICAL SLUMP.

Try changing your eating habits. Eat lunch outside instead of in the cafeteria—the sun will brighten your mood! Also, make sure that you are getting your vitamins. Your body needs complete nutrition to feel its best, and vitamins D, B1, B2, and B6 all help your mind stay positive. Start exercising twenty minutes a day, even if it's just a brisk walk around your neighborhood. It will not only help you stay fit, but you will have more energy and be less tempted to eat junk foods. Your body will thank you! Also, take a visit to the ol' doctor. You might actually have a physical problem, like anemia. By taking care of our bodies we honor God too. Read 1 Corinthians 6:19-20.

IF YOU ANSWERED MOSTLY A OR B, CONGRATULATIONS! YOU'RE PROBABLY SLUMP FREE FOR THE TIME BEING.

19Again the leaders did not agree with each other because of these words of Jesus. 20Many of them said, "A demon has come into him and made him crazy. Why listen to him?"

21But others said, "A man who is crazy with a demon does not say things like this. Can a demon open the eyes of the blind?"

JESUS IS REJECTED

22The time came for the Feast of Dedication at Jerusalem. It was winter, 23and Jesus was walking in the Temple in Solomon's Porch. 24Some people gathered around him and said, "How long will you make us wonder about you? If you are the Christ, tell us plainly."

25Jesus answered, "I told you already, but you did not believe. The miracles I do in my Father's name show who I am. 26But you don't believe, because you are not my sheep. 27My sheep listen to my voice; I know them, and they follow me. 28I give them eternal life, and they will never die, and no one can steal them out of my hand. 29My Father gave my sheep to me. He is greater than all, and no person can steal my sheep out of my Father's hand. 30The Father and I are one."

31Again some of the people picked up stones to kill Jesus. 32But he said to them, "I have done many good works from the Father. Which of these good works are you killing me for?"

33They answered, "We are not killing you because of any good work you did, but because you speak against God. You are only a human, but you say you are the same as God!"

34Jesus answered, "It is written in your law that God said, 'I said, you are gods.'[n] 35This Scripture called those people gods who received God's message, and Scripture is always true. 36So why do you say that I speak against God because I said, 'I am God's Son'? I am the one God chose and sent into the world. 37If I don't do what my Father does, then don't believe me. 38But if I do what my Father does, even though you don't believe in me, believe what I do. Then you will know and understand that the Father is in me and I am in the Father."

39They tried to take Jesus again, but he escaped from them.

40Then he went back across the Jordan River to the place where John had first baptized. Jesus stayed there, 41and many people came to him and said, "John never did a miracle, but everything John said about this man is true." 42And in that place many believed in Jesus.

THE DEATH OF LAZARUS

11 A man named Lazarus was sick. He lived in the town of Bethany, where Mary and her sister Martha lived. 2Mary was the woman who later put perfume on the Lord and wiped his feet with her hair. Mary's brother was Lazarus, the man who was now sick. 3So Mary and Martha sent someone to tell Jesus, "Lord, the one you love is sick."

4When Jesus heard this, he said, "This sickness will not end in death. It is for the glory of God, to bring glory to the Son of God." 5Jesus loved Martha and her sister and Lazarus. 6But when he heard that Lazarus was sick, he stayed where he was for two more days. 7Then Jesus said to his followers, "Let's go back to Judea."

8The followers said, "But Teacher, some people there tried to stone you to death only a short time ago. Now you want to go back there?"

9Jesus answered, "Are there not twelve hours in the day? If anyone walks in the daylight, he will not stumble, because he can see by this world's light. 10But if anyone walks at night, he stumbles because there is no light to help him see."

11After Jesus said this, he added, "Our friend Lazarus has fallen asleep, but I am going there to wake him."

12The followers said, "But Lord, if he is only asleep, he will be all right."

13Jesus meant that Lazarus was dead, but his followers thought he meant Lazarus was really sleeping. 14So then Jesus said plainly, "Lazarus is dead. 15And I am glad for your sakes I was not there so that you may believe. But let's go to him now."

16Then Thomas (the one called Didymus) said to the other followers, "Let us also go so that we can die with him."

JESUS IN BETHANY

17When Jesus arrived, he learned that Lazarus had already been dead and in the tomb for four days. 18Bethany was about two miles from Jerusalem. 19Many of the Jews had come there to comfort Martha and Mary about their brother.

20When Martha heard that Jesus was coming, she went out to meet him, but Mary stayed home. 21Martha said to Jesus, "Lord, if you had been here, my brother would not have died.

48% OF TEENS INFLUENCE FAMILY PURCHASES.

RELATIONSHIPS

Philippians 4:4 says, "Be full of joy in the Lord always. I will say again, be full of joy." Do you have fun with your guy? Real fun? Do you laugh together until your sides hurt and you've got tears streaming down your face? Do you play together—putt-putt, football, board games, whatever? It's really important to have fun in order to make a relationship last. Remember to be friends first; put the romance second. That way you know it will last longer than the come-and-go emotions.

notes

10:34 'I . . . gods.' Quotation from Psalm 82:6.

[22]But I know that even now God will give you anything you ask."

[23]Jesus said, "Your brother will rise and live again."

[24]Martha answered, "I know that he will rise and live again in the resurrection[n] on the last day."

[25]Jesus said to her, "I am the resurrection and the life. Those who believe in me will have life even if they die. [26]And everyone who lives and believes in me will never die. Martha, do you believe this?"

[27]Martha answered, "Yes, Lord. I believe that you are the Christ, the Son of God, the One coming to the world."

JESUS CRIES

[28]After Martha said this, she went back and talked to her sister Mary alone. Martha said, "The Teacher is here and he is asking for you." [29]When Mary heard this, she got up quickly and went to Jesus. [30]Jesus had not yet come into the town but was still at the place where Martha had met him. [31]The Jews were with Mary in the house, comforting her. When they saw her stand and leave quickly, they followed her, thinking she was going to the tomb to cry there.

[32]But Mary went to the place where Jesus was. When she saw him, she fell at his feet and said, "Lord, if you had been here, my brother would not have died."

[33]When Jesus saw Mary crying and the Jews who came with her also crying, he was upset and was deeply troubled. [34]He asked, "Where did you bury him?"

"Come and see, Lord," they said.

[35]Jesus cried.

[36]So the Jews said, "See how much he loved him."

[37]But some of them said, "If Jesus opened the eyes of the blind man, why couldn't he keep Lazarus from dying?"

JESUS RAISES LAZARUS

[38]Again feeling very upset, Jesus came to the tomb. It was a cave with a large stone covering the entrance. [39]Jesus said, "Move the stone away."

Martha, the sister of the dead man, said, "But, Lord, it has been four days since he died. There will be a bad smell."

[40]Then Jesus said to her, "Didn't I tell you that if you believed you would see the glory of God?"

[41]So they moved the stone away from the entrance. Then Jesus looked up and said, "Father, I thank you that you heard me. [42]I know that you always hear me, but I said these things because of the people here around me. I want them to believe that you sent me." [43]After Jesus said this, he cried out in a loud voice, "Lazarus, come out!" [44]The dead man came out, his hands and feet wrapped with pieces of cloth, and a cloth around his face.

"THEN JESUS SAID TO HER, 'DIDN'T I TELL YOU THAT IF YOU BELIEVED YOU WOULD SEE THE GLORY OF GOD?'"

Jesus said to them, "Take the cloth off of him and let him go."

THE PLAN TO KILL JESUS

[45]Many of the people, who had come to visit Mary and saw what Jesus did, believed in him. [46]But some of them went to the Pharisees and told them what Jesus had done. [47]Then the leading priests and Pharisees called a meeting of the council. They asked, "What should we do? This man is doing many miracles. [48]If we let him continue doing these things, everyone will believe in him. Then the Romans will come and take away our Temple and our nation."

[49]One of the men there was Caiaphas, the high priest that year. He said, "You people know nothing! [50]You don't realize that it is better for one man to die for the people than for the whole nation to be destroyed."

[51]Caiaphas did not think of this himself. As high priest that year, he was really prophesying

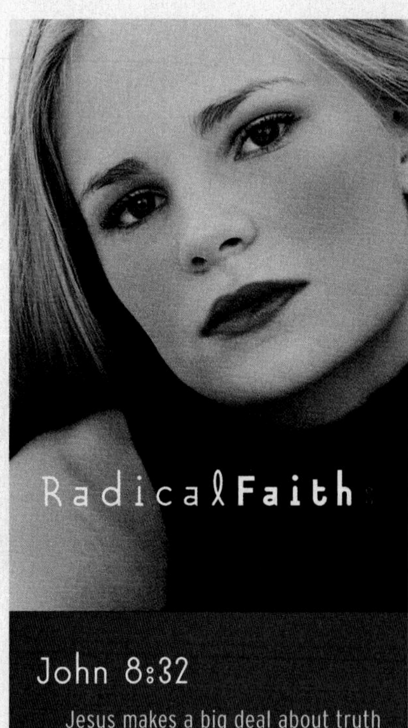

John 8:32

Jesus makes a big deal about truth because only the truth sets you free. Satan is the father of lies, a master deceiver, and he wants you to believe anything other than the teachings of Jesus. The truth is that believing in Jesus saves you from your sin and saves you for eternal life. In this verse Jesus says that the truth will set you free because Jesus frees you from your bondage to sin. Satan will whisper lies to you over and over, hoping you'll believe his tricks and get confused. Remember that confusion is not from God (see 1 Corinthians 14:33).

When you feel confused or overwhelmed, return to Scripture and read the truth of the words of God. From him you will find direction and clear guidance. Meditate on those words. Let his truth come alive in your mind and in your heart.

The Bible makes a big deal about truth because lies will lead you astray. Stay focused on the truth of God's Word. Know the truth, follow the truth, tell the truth. It "will make you free"!

11:24 resurrection Being raised from the dead to live again.

that Jesus would die for their nation 52and for God's scattered children to bring them all together and make them one.

53That day they started planning to kill Jesus. 54So Jesus no longer traveled openly among the people. He left there and went to a place near the desert, to a town called Ephraim and stayed there with his followers.

55It was almost time for the Passover Feast. Many from the country went up to Jerusalem before the Passover to do the special things to make themselves pure. 56The people looked for Jesus and stood in the Temple asking each other, "Is he coming to the Feast? What do you think?" 57But the leading priests and the Pharisees had given orders that if anyone knew where Jesus was, he must tell them. Then they could arrest him.

1 John 4:18
Where God's love is, there is no fear, because God's perfect love drives out fear.

JESUS WITH FRIENDS IN BETHANY

12 Six days before the Passover Feast, Jesus went to Bethany, where Lazarus lived. (Lazarus is the man Jesus raised from the dead.) 2There they had a dinner for Jesus. Martha served the food, and Lazarus was one of the people eating with Jesus. 3Mary brought in a pint of very expensive perfume made from pure nard. She poured the perfume on Jesus' feet, and then she wiped his feet with her hair. And the sweet smell from the perfume filled the whole house.

4Judas Iscariot, one of Jesus' followers who would later turn against him, was there. Judas said, 5"This perfume was worth three hundred coins.[n] Why wasn't it sold and the money given to the poor?" 6But Judas did not really care about the poor; he said this because he was a thief. He was the one who kept the money box, and he often stole from it.

7Jesus answered, "Leave her alone. It was right for her to save this perfume for today, the day for me to be prepared for burial. 8You will always have the poor with you, but you will not always have me."

THE PLOT AGAINST LAZARUS

9A large crowd of people heard that Jesus was in Bethany. So they went there to see not only Jesus but Lazarus, whom Jesus raised from the dead. 10So the leading priests made plans to kill Lazarus, too. 11Because of Lazarus many of the Jews were leaving them and believing in Jesus.

JESUS ENTERS JERUSALEM

12The next day a great crowd who had come to Jerusalem for the Passover Feast heard that Jesus was coming there. 13So they took branches of palm trees and went out to meet Jesus, shouting,

"Praise[n] God!
God bless the One who comes in the name
of the Lord!
God bless the King of Israel!" *Psalm 118:25-26*

"MANY FROM THE COUNTRY WENT UP TO JERUSALEM BEFORE THE PASSOVER TO DO THE SPECIAL THINGS TO MAKE THEMSELVES PURE."

14Jesus found a colt and sat on it. This was as the Scripture says,

15"Don't be afraid, people of Jerusalem!
Your king is coming,
sitting on the colt of a donkey." *Zechariah 9:9*

LEARN IT & LIVE IT

1 Corinthians 14:33:
Learn It: God is a God not of disorder but of peace.
Live It: Are you trying to do your best to work hard for Christ? Is your life a mess—school all day, volunteer in the afternoon, homework 'til 1:00 a.m.? Get your life in order. Set your priorities. Revisit your schedule today.

1 Corinthians 15:58:
Learn It: "Your work in the Lord is never wasted."
Live It: You've worked all week writing your paper for biology when, at the final paragraph, your computer crashes. Classic story. But your work wasn't in vain! Figure out the lesson God has for you in this really frustrating moment.

2 Corinthians 1:3-4:
Learn It: God is the Father of all comfort; he comforts us every time we have trouble.
Live It: Whom do you turn to when things go wrong? Do you immediately call your bff on the cell? When something major happens, stop. Count to ten. Pray, then call your friend for advice. God put these people on earth to walk with us, but he's the One who is our guide.

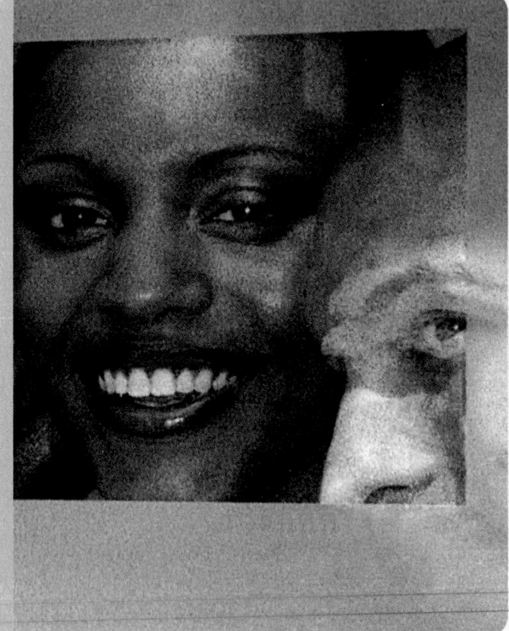

12:5 coins One coin, a denarius, was the average pay for one day's work. **12:13 Praise** Literally, "Hosanna," a Hebrew word used at first in praying to God for help, but at this time it was probably a shout of joy used in praising God or his Messiah.

Notes

Blab

Q. I used to cuss pretty badly. Any tips on how to stop completely?

A. Usually what comes out of our mouths is just the stuff that is overflowing in our heart. Check out your cussing; does it have to do with anger? If so, then ask God to start to work on your anger. Whatever is making you talk this way, get to the root of it. That should help!

Q. A friend of mine has it set in his mind that he wants to take the place of people who are in hell because he doesn't think he deserves to be in heaven. I don't know what to tell him.

A. Your friend has a God complex. God came to earth to die for lost sinners so they wouldn't have to go to hell. God, Jesus, did that once and for all so your friend doesn't have to. In fact, he couldn't even if he wanted to.

Q. I have a friend who has a friend who doesn't believe that once you are saved you are always saved and you don't have to keep doing it over and over again. I was wondering if you could tell me where I could find Bible reference for that.

A. Check out how easy it is: Romans 5:8-11; Ephesians 2:1-22; Romans 10:9, 13; Romans 8:1; Hebrews 7:25; Hebrews 10:11-18; 1 John 5:11-12; Romans 4:13-18; John 1:12.

CHECK IT OUT

Compassion International

Compassion International grew from the desire of one man to help children in need. Rev. Everett Swanson was moved by the plight of Korean orphans as he preached there in the early 1950s. He went on to establish a program through which caring people could sponsor needy Korean children for a few dollars a month. In turn, those children would be provided benefits including food and clothing as needed, education, shelter, health care, and Christian training.

Swanson's program was the basis for what became Compassion International. Compassion's work has since expanded to twenty-two countries—including the United States—providing life-changing benefits for needy children with or without families.

For more information, go to ***www.compassion.com.***

16The followers of Jesus did not understand this at first. But after Jesus was raised to glory, they remembered that this had been written about him and that they had done these things to him.

PEOPLE TELL ABOUT JESUS

17There had been many people with Jesus when he raised Lazarus from the dead and told him to come out of the tomb. Now they were
telling others about what Jesus did. 18Many
people went out to meet Jesus, because they
had heard about this miracle. 19So the Pharisees
said to each other, "You can see that nothing is going right for us. Look! The whole world is following him."

JESUS TALKS ABOUT HIS DEATH

20There were some Greek people, too, who came to Jerusalem to worship at the Passover
Feast. 21They went to Philip, who was from
Bethsaida in Galilee, and said, "Sir, we would
like to see Jesus." 22Philip told Andrew, and
then Andrew and Philip told Jesus.

23Jesus said to them, "The time has come for
the Son of Man to receive his glory. 24I tell you
the truth, a grain of wheat must fall to the ground and die to make many seeds. But if it never dies,
it remains only a single seed. 25Those who love
their lives will lose them, but those who hate their lives in this world will keep true life forever.
26Whoever serves me must follow me. Then my servant will be with me everywhere I am. My Father will honor anyone who serves me.

27"Now I am very troubled. Should I say, 'Father, save me from this time'? No, I came to this time so I could suffer. 28Father, bring glory to your name!"

Then a voice came from heaven, "I have brought glory to it, and I will do it again."

29The crowd standing there, who heard the voice, said it was thunder.

But others said, "An angel has spoken to him."

30Jesus said, "That voice was for your sake, not mine. 31Now is the time for the world to be judged; now the ruler of this world will be thrown down. 32If I am lifted up from the earth, I will draw all people toward me." 33Jesus said this to show how he would die.

34The crowd said, "We have heard from the law that the Christ will live forever. So why do you say, 'The Son of Man must be lifted up'? Who is this 'Son of Man'?"

35Then Jesus said, "The light will be with you for a little longer, so walk while you have the light. Then the darkness will not catch you. If you walk in the darkness, you will not know where you are going. 36Believe in the light while you still have it so that you will become children of light." When Jesus had said this, he left and hid himself from them.

SOME PEOPLE WON'T BELIEVE IN JESUS

37Though Jesus had done many miracles in front of the people, they still did not believe in him. 38This was to bring about what Isaiah the prophet had said:

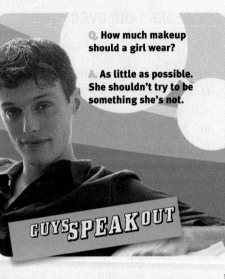

GUYS SPEAK OUT

Q. How much makeup should a girl wear?

A. As little as possible. She shouldn't try to be something she's not.

"Lord, who believed what we told them?
Who saw the Lord's power in this?"

Isaiah 53:1

39This is why the people could not believe: Isaiah also had said,

40"He has blinded their eyes,
and he has closed their minds.
Otherwise they would see with their eyes
and understand in their minds
and come back to me and be healed."

Isaiah 6:10

41Isaiah said this because he saw Jesus' glory and spoke about him.

42But many believed in Jesus, even many of the leaders. But because of the Pharisees, they did not say they believed in him for fear they would be put out of the synagogue. 43They loved praise from people more than praise from God.

44Then Jesus cried out, "Whoever believes in me is really believing in the One who sent me. 45Whoever sees me sees the One who sent me. 46I have come as light into the world so that whoever believes in me would not stay in darkness.

47"Anyone who hears my words and does not obey them, I do not judge, because I did not come to judge the world, but to save the world. 48There is a judge for those who refuse to believe in me and do not accept my words. The word I have taught will be their judge on the last day. 49The things I taught were not from myself. The Father who sent me told me what to say and what to teach. 50And I know that eternal life comes from what the Father commands. So whatever I say is what the Father told me to say."

JESUS WASHES HIS FOLLOWERS' FEET

13 It was almost time for the Passover Feast. Jesus knew that it was time for him to leave this world and go back to the Father. He had always loved those who were his own in the world, and he loved them all the way to the end.

2Jesus and his followers were at the evening meal. The devil had already persuaded Judas Iscariot, the son of Simon, to turn against Jesus. 3Jesus knew that the Father had given him power over everything and that he had come from God and was going back to God. 4So during the meal Jesus stood up and took off his outer clothing. Taking a towel, he wrapped it around his waist. 5Then he poured water into a bowl and began to wash the followers' feet, drying them with the towel that was wrapped around him.

6Jesus came to Simon Peter, who said to him, "Lord, are you going to wash my feet?"

7Jesus answered, "You don't understand now what I am doing, but you will understand later."

8Peter said, "No, you will never wash my feet."

Jesus answered, "If I don't wash your feet, you are not one of my people."

9Simon Peter answered, "Lord, then wash not only my feet, but wash my hands and my head, too!"

BEAUTY SECRET
SUNSCREEN
The Bible is like our spiritual sunscreen. It acts as a filter, letting in the good and keeping out the bad. Keep the Bible close by, especially when it feels as if life's burning rays are beating down on you. And beware those cloudy days: Sin can secretly get in there and burn you when you least expect it!

10Jesus said, "After a person has had a bath, his
whole body is clean. He needs only to wash his
feet. And you men are clean, but not all of you."
11Jesus knew who would turn against him, and
that is why he said, "Not all of you are clean."

37,000 TEENAGERS DIE EVERY YEAR.

12When he had finished washing their feet,
he put on his clothes and sat down again. He
asked, "Do you understand what I have just
done for you? 13You call me 'Teacher' and
'Lord,' and you are right, because that is what I
am. 14If I, your Lord and Teacher, have washed
your feet, you also should wash each other's
feet. 15I did this as an example so that you
should do as I have done for you. 16I tell you
the truth, a servant is not greater than his master. A messenger is not greater than the one
who sent him. 17If you know these things, you
will be happy if you do them.

18"I am not talking about all of you. I
know those I have chosen. But this is to
bring about what the Scripture said: 'The
man who ate at my table has turned against
me.'[n] 19I am telling you this now before it
happens so that when it happens, you will
believe that I am he. 20I tell you the truth,
whoever accepts anyone I send also accepts
me. And whoever accepts me also accepts
the One who sent me."

JESUS TALKS ABOUT HIS DEATH

21After Jesus said this, he was very troubled. He said openly, "I tell you the truth, one
of you will turn against me."

22The followers all looked at each other,
because they did not know whom Jesus was
talking about. 23One of the followers sitting[n]
next to Jesus was the follower Jesus loved.
24Simon Peter motioned to him to ask Jesus
whom he was talking about.

25That follower leaned closer to Jesus and
asked, "Lord, who is it?"

26Jesus answered, "I will dip this bread into
the dish. The man I give it to is the man who will
turn against me." So Jesus took a piece of bread,
dipped it, and gave it to Judas Iscariot, the son
of Simon. 27As soon as Judas took the bread,
Satan entered him. Jesus said to him, "The
thing that you will do—do it quickly." 28No
one at the table understood why Jesus said
this to Judas. 29Since he was the one who kept
the money box, some of the followers thought
Jesus was telling him to buy what was needed
for the feast or to give something to the poor.

"I GIVE YOU A NEW COM-MAND: LOVE EACH OTHER. YOU MUST LOVE EACH OTHER AS I HAVE LOVED YOU."

30Judas took the bread Jesus gave him and
immediately went out. It was night.

31When Judas was gone, Jesus said, "Now
the Son of Man receives his glory, and God
receives glory through him. 32If God receives
glory through him, then God will give glory to
the Son through himself. And God will give
him glory quickly."

33Jesus said, "My children, I will be with
you only a little longer. You will look for me,
and what I told the Jews, I tell you now: Where
I am going you cannot come.

34"I give you a new command: Love each
other. You must love each other as I have loved
you. 35All people will know that you are my
followers if you love each other."

PETER WILL SAY HE DOESN'T KNOW JESUS

36Simon Peter asked Jesus, "Lord, where are
you going?"

Jesus answered, "Where I am going you
cannot follow now, but you will follow later."

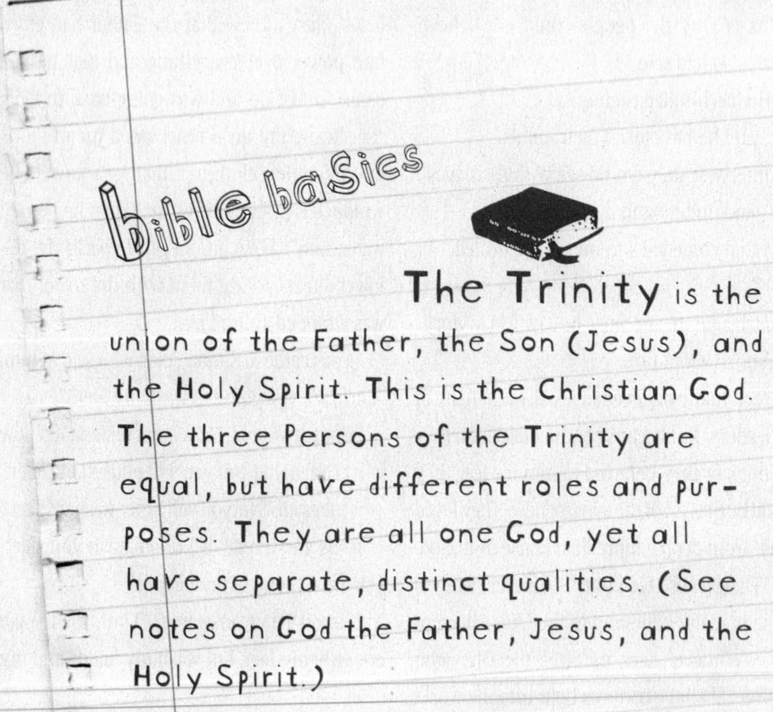

bible basics
The Trinity is the union of the Father, the Son (Jesus), and the Holy Spirit. This is the Christian God. The three Persons of the Trinity are equal, but have different roles and purposes. They are all one God, yet all have separate, distinct qualities. (See notes on God the Father, Jesus, and the Holy Spirit.)

13:18 'The man . . . me.' Quotation from Psalm 41:9. **13:23 sitting** Literally, "lying." The people of that time ate lying down and leaning on one arm.

[37]Peter asked, "Lord, why can't I follow you now? I am ready to die for you!"

[38]Jesus answered, "Are you ready to die for me? I tell you the truth, before the rooster crows, you will say three times that you don't know me."

JESUS COMFORTS HIS FOLLOWERS

14 Jesus said, "Don't let your hearts be troubled. Trust in God, and trust in me. [2]There are many rooms in my Father's house; I would not tell you this if it were not true. I am going there to prepare a place for you. [3]After I go and prepare a place for you, I will come back and take you to be with me so that you may be where I am. [4]You know the way to the place where I am going."

[5]Thomas said to Jesus, "Lord, we don't know where you are going. So how can we know the way?"

[6]Jesus answered, "I am the way, and the truth, and the life. The only way to the Father is through me. [7]If you really knew me, you would know my Father, too. But now you do know him, and you have seen him."

[8]Philip said to him, "Lord, show us the Father. That is all we need."

[9]Jesus answered, "I have been with you a long time now. Do you still not know me, Philip? Whoever has seen me has seen the Father. So why do you say, 'Show us the Father'? [10]Don't you believe that I am in the Father and the Father is in me? The words I say to you don't come from me, but the Father lives in me and does his own work. [11]Believe me when I say that I am in the Father and the Father is in me. Or believe because of the miracles I have done. [12]I tell you the truth, whoever believes in me will do the same things that I do. Those who believe will do even greater things than these, because I am going to the Father. [13]And if you ask for anything in my name, I will do it for you so that the Father's glory will be shown through the Son. [14]If you ask me for anything in my name, I will do it.

THE PROMISE OF THE HOLY SPIRIT

[15]"If you love me, you will obey my commands. [16]I will ask the Father, and he will give you another Helper[n] to be with you forever— [17]the Spirit of truth. The world cannot accept him, because it does not see him or know him. But you know him, because he lives with you and he will be in you.

1 John 4:19
We love because God first loved us.

[18]"I will not leave you all alone like orphans; I will come back to you. [19]In a little while the world will not see me anymore, but you will see me. Because I live, you will live, too. [20]On that day you will know that I am in my Father, and that you are in me and I am in you. [21]Those who know my commands and obey them are the ones who love me, and my Father will love those who love me. I will love them and will show myself to them."

[22]Then Judas (not Judas Iscariot) said, "But, Lord, why do you plan to show yourself to us and not to the rest of the world?"

[23]Jesus answered, "If people love me, they will obey my teaching. My Father will love them, and we will come to them and make our home with them. [24]Those who do not love me do not obey my teaching. This teaching that you hear is not really mine; it is from my Father, who sent me.

[25]"I have told you all these things while I am with you. [26]But the Helper will teach you everything and will cause you to remember all that I told you. This Helper is the Holy Spirit whom the Father will send in my name.

[27]"I leave you peace; my peace I give you. I do not give it to you as the world does. So don't let your hearts be troubled or afraid. [28]You heard me say to you, 'I am going, but I am coming

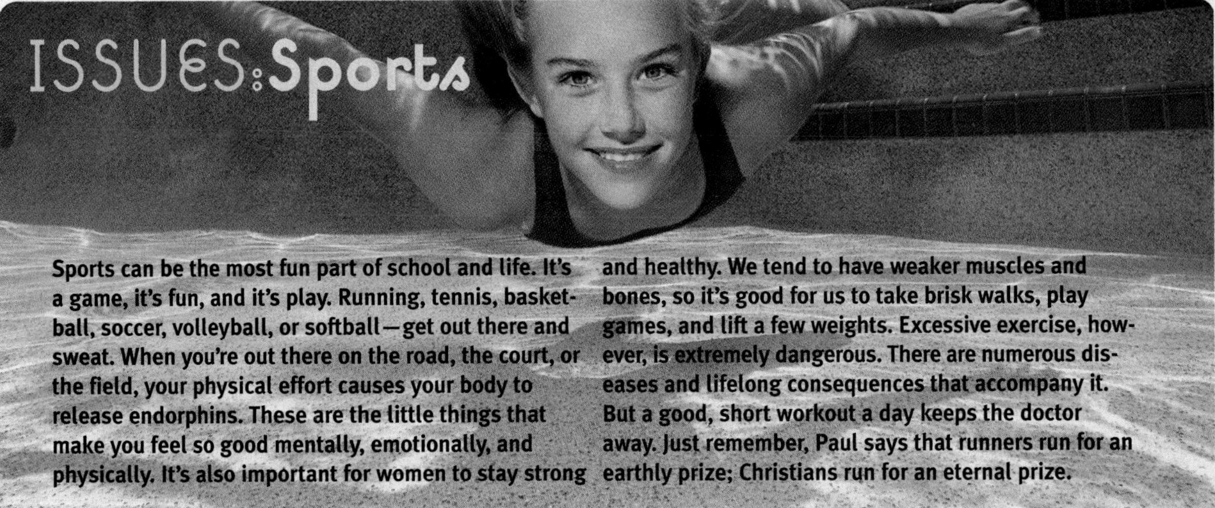

ISSUES: Sports
Sports can be the most fun part of school and life. It's a game, it's fun, and it's play. Running, tennis, basketball, soccer, volleyball, or softball—get out there and sweat. When you're out there on the road, the court, or the field, your physical effort causes your body to release endorphins. These are the little things that make you feel so good mentally, emotionally, and physically. It's also important for women to stay strong and healthy. We tend to have weaker muscles and bones, so it's good for us to take brisk walks, play games, and lift a few weights. Excessive exercise, however, is extremely dangerous. There are numerous diseases and lifelong consequences that accompany it. But a good, short workout a day keeps the doctor away. Just remember, Paul says that runners run for an earthly prize; Christians run for an eternal prize.

notes

14:16 Helper "Counselor" or "Comforter." Jesus is talking about the Holy Spirit.

back to you.' If you loved me, you should be
happy that I am going back to the Father,
because he is greater than I am. [29]I have told
you this now, before it happens, so that when
it happens, you will believe. [30]I will not talk
with you much longer, because the ruler of
this world is coming. He has no power over
me, [31]but the world must know that I love
the Father, so I do exactly what the Father
told me to do.

"Come now, let us go.

JESUS IS LIKE A VINE

15 "I am the true vine; my Father is
the gardener. [2]He cuts off every
branch of mine that does not produce fruit.
And he trims and cleans every branch that
produces fruit so that it will produce even
more fruit. [3]You are already clean because of
the words I have spoken to you. [4]Remain in
me, and I will remain in you. A branch cannot
produce fruit alone but must remain in the
vine. In the same way, you cannot produce
fruit alone but must remain in me.

[5]"I am the vine, and you are the branches. If
any remain in me and I remain in them, they
produce much fruit. But without me they can
do nothing. [6]If any do not remain in me, they
are like a branch that is thrown away and then
dies. People pick up dead branches, throw
them into the fire, and burn them. [7]If you
remain in me and follow my teachings, you
can ask anything you want, and it will be given
to you. [8]You should produce much fruit and
show that you are my followers, which brings
glory to my Father. [9]I loved you as the Father
loved me. Now remain in my love. [10]I have
obeyed my Father's commands, and I remain
in his love. In the same way, if you obey my
commands, you will remain in my love. [11]I
have told you these things so that you can
have the same joy I have and so that your joy
will be the fullest possible joy.

[12]"This is my command: Love each other as
I have loved you. [13]The greatest love a person
can show is to die for his friends. [14]You are my
friends if you do what I command you. [15]I no
longer call you servants, because a servant
does not know what his master is doing. But I
call you friends, because I have made known
to you everything I heard from my Father.
[16]You did not choose me; I chose you. And I

BIBLE BIOS: GOMER

Gomer was a prostitute. But God wanted to use her, like everyone else, in a greater plan. He told Hosea to marry her. Sadly, Gomer was not a faithful wife to Hosea. Just as God loved his people in spite of their unfaithfulness, so did Hosea love Gomer. Through Hosea's love for Gomer, God wanted his people to see his love and learn to have faithful hearts. While Gomer is not a model for Christian women, she teaches us the importance of faithfulness in relationships.

[HOSEA 1–3]

LEARN IT & LIVE IT

2 Corinthians 2:15:
Learn It: We are the fragrance of Christ.
Live It: Put on some deodorant. I'm not talking about Secret; I'm talking about the Spirit of God. Spend twenty-five minutes tomorrow morning before school praying and reading Scripture. Make it a priority, and smell good for goodness' sake!

2 Corinthians 3:18:
Learn It: We are being transformed from one degree of glory to another.
Live It: How are you showing God's glory? Do you have the guts to ask someone for an honest answer? Do you have the guts to ask God?

2 Corinthians 4:16:
Learn It: Our inner nature is being renewed day by day.
Live It: Don't lose hope! Look internally today. Every time you hear a bit of juicy gossip today, take it as a reminder to look into yourself. What needs to be renewed today? Ask God to work on that for you.

gave you this work: to go and produce fruit,
fruit that will last. Then the Father will give
you anything you ask for in my name. [17]This
is my command: Love each other.

JESUS WARNS HIS FOLLOWERS

[18]"If the world hates you, remember that it
hated me first. [19]If you belonged to the world, it
would love you as it loves its own. But I have
chosen you out of the world, so you don't belong to it. That is why the world hates you.
[20]Remember what I told you: A servant is not
greater than his master. If people did wrong to
me, they will do wrong to you, too. And if they
obeyed my teaching, they will obey yours, too.
[21]They will do all this to you on account of me,
because they do not know the One who sent me.
[22]If I had not come and spoken to them, they
would not be guilty of sin, but now they have no
excuse for their sin. [23]Whoever hates me also
hates my Father. [24]I did works among them that
no one else has ever done. If I had not done these
works, they would not be guilty of sin. But now
they have seen what I have done, and yet they
have hated both me and my Father. [25]But this
happened so that what is written in their law
would be true: 'They hated me for no reason.'[n]

[26]"I will send you the Helper[n] from the
Father; he is the Spirit of truth who comes
from the Father. When he comes, he will tell
about me, [27]and you also must tell people
about me, because you have been with me
from the beginning.

16 "I have told you these things to
keep you from giving up. [2]People
will put you out of their synagogues. Yes, the
time is coming when those who kill you will
think they are offering service to God. [3]They
will do this because they have not known the
Father and they have not known me. [4]I have
told you these things now so that when the time
comes you will remember that I warned you.

THE WORK OF THE HOLY SPIRIT

"I did not tell you these things at the beginning, because I was with you then. [5]Now I am
going back to the One who sent me. But none
of you asks me, 'Where are you going?' [6]Your
hearts are filled with sadness because I have
told you these things. [7]But I tell you the truth,
it is better for you that I go away. When I go
away, I will send the Helper[n] to you. If I do not
go away, the Helper will not come. [8]When the
Helper comes, he will prove to the people of
the world the truth about sin, about being
right with God, and about judgment. [9]He will
prove to them that sin is not believing in me.
[10]He will prove to them that being right with
God comes from my going to the Father and
not being seen anymore. [11]And the Helper
will prove to them that judgment happened
when the ruler of this world was judged.

[12]"I have many more things to say to you,
but they are too much for you now. [13]But
when the Spirit of truth comes, he will lead
you into all truth. He will not speak his own
words, but he will speak only what he hears,
and he will tell you what is to come. [14]The
Spirit of truth will bring glory to me, because
he will take what I have to say and tell it to
you. [15]All that the Father has is mine. That is
why I said that the Spirit will take what I have
to say and tell it to you.

SADNESS WILL BECOME HAPPINESS

[16]"After a little while you will not see me, and
then after a little while you will see me again."

[17]Some of the followers said to each other,
"What does Jesus mean when he says, 'After a
little while you will not see me, and then after
a little while you will see me again'? And what
does he mean when he says, 'Because I am
going to the Father'?" [18]They also asked,
"What does he mean by 'a little while'? We
don't understand what he is saying."

[19]Jesus saw that the followers wanted to ask
him about this, so he said to them, "Are you
asking each other what I meant when I said,
'After a little while you will not see me, and
then after a little while you will see me again'?
[20]I tell you the truth, you will cry and be sad,

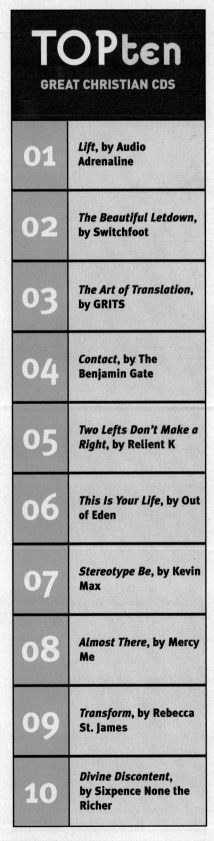

TOPten

GREAT CHRISTIAN CDS

01	***Lift*, by Audio Adrenaline**
02	***The Beautiful Letdown*, by Switchfoot**
03	***The Art of Translation*, by GRITS**
04	***Contact*, by The Benjamin Gate**
05	***Two Lefts Don't Make a Right*, by Relient K**
06	***This Is Your Life*, by Out of Eden**
07	***Stereotype Be*, by Kevin Max**
08	***Almost There*, by Mercy Me**
09	***Transform*, by Rebecca St. James**
10	***Divine Discontent*, by Sixpence None the Richer**

notes

15:25 'They . . . reason.' These words could be from Psalm 35:19 or Psalm 69:4. **15:26; 16:7 Helper** "Counselor" or "Comforter." Jesus is talking about the Holy Spirit.

John 12:46

Have you ever been in a room that was pitch black—no light, no windows, totally dark? What happened when you turned on a flashlight or struck a match? The entire room lit up. You couldn't believe how much light that one match or flashlight gave off. That's exactly the kind of effect you can have in your school and everywhere else in our dark world. The light that Christians give because of Jesus is the only light this world has.

What would you do if you had a friend who was trapped in a cave with a group of people, and they couldn't get out because they couldn't find their way? Let's say that they all died and when their bodies were found, it was discovered that one of the victims had a perfectly good flashlight in his backpack that would have saved all of their lives if it had been used. Wouldn't that upset you?

You know what? You are like that same flashlight that could have saved those lives. Every day you come across the paths of people who desperately need the light of Jesus. Don't hide the light. Use it to impact someone's life forever!

but the world will be happy. You will be sad, but your sadness will become joy. 21When a woman gives birth to a baby, she has pain, because her time has come. But when her baby is born, she forgets the pain, because she is so happy that a child has been born into the world. 22It is the same with you. Now you are sad, but I will see you again and you will be happy, and no one will take away your joy. 23In that day you will not ask me for anything. I tell you the truth, my Father will give you anything you ask for in my name. 24Until now you have not asked for anything in my name. Ask and you will receive, so that your joy will be the fullest possible joy.

VICTORY OVER THE WORLD

25"I have told you these things, using stories that hide the meaning. But the time will come when I will not use stories like that to tell you things; I will speak to you in plain words about the Father. 26In that day you will ask the Father for things in my name. I mean, I will not need to ask the Father for you. 27The Father himself loves you. He loves you because you loved me and believed that I came from God. 28I came from the Father into the world. Now I am leaving the world and going back to the Father."

29Then the followers of Jesus said, "You are speaking clearly to us now and are not using stories that are hard to understand. 30We can see now that you know all things. You can answer a person's question even before it is asked. This makes us believe you came from God."

31Jesus answered, "So now you believe? 32Listen to me; a time is coming when you will be scattered, each to his own home. That time is now here. You will leave me alone, but I am never really alone, because the Father is with me.

33"I told you these things so that you can have peace in me. In this world you will have trouble, but be brave! I have defeated the world."

JESUS PRAYS FOR HIS FOLLOWERS

17 After Jesus said these things, he looked toward heaven and prayed, "Father, the time has come. Give glory to your Son so that the Son can give glory to you. 2You gave the Son power over all people so that the Son could give eternal life to all those you gave him. 3And this is eternal life: that people know you, the only true God, and that they know Jesus Christ, the One you sent. 4Having finished the work you gave me to do, I brought you glory on earth. 5And now, Father, give me glory with you; give me the glory I had with you before the world was made.

Psalm 23:1
The LORD is my shepherd; I have everything I need.

6"I showed what you are like to those you gave me from the world. They belonged to you, and you gave them to me, and they have obeyed your teaching. 7Now they know that everything you gave me comes from you. 8I gave them the teachings you gave me, and they accepted them. They knew that I truly came from you, and they believed that you sent me. 9I am praying for them. I am not praying for people in the world but for those you gave me, because they are yours. 10All I have is yours, and all you have is mine. And my glory is shown through them. 11I am coming to you; I will not stay in the world any longer. But they are still in the world. Holy Father, keep them safe by the power of your

30% OF TEEN DEATHS YEARLY ARE DUE TO ALCOHOL-RELATED CAR CRASHES.

Blab

Q. What if I doubt Jesus? I want to believe in him so bad. I want to be for sure he is real but I just can't understand.

A. It's okay to doubt; in fact, it's normal. But remember you are a believer, not a doubter, so by definition you must say "no" to the doubt and determine in your mind, set your mind, to believe him even if it seems preposterous. Remember, faith is believing in things you can't see.

Q. How can I deal with my parents' divorce? It is hard for me to really trust in God and I even give up on God half the time. How can I trust in God when I think that God did all of this?

A. If you believe that the Bible is true, then you can be sure that God didn't do all of this. He is incapable of doing evil. It really stinks that your parents couldn't work it out, but now you need to figure out what God is going to teach you through this. Remember that the testing of your faith develops perseverance. And perseverance leads to perfection.

Q. Does God always love me?

A. Yes. Read more in Ephesians 3, 1 John 3, Romans 5, and Psalm 36.

name, the name you gave me, so that they will
be one, just as you and I are one. 12While I was
with them, I kept them safe by the power of
your name, the name you gave me. I protected
them, and only one of them, the one worthy of
destruction, was lost so that the Scripture
would come true.

13"I am coming to you now. But I pray these
things while I am still in the world so that these
followers can have all of my joy in them. 14I
have given them your teaching. And the world
has hated them, because they don't belong to
the world, just as I don't belong to the world.
15I am not asking you to take them out of the
world but to keep them safe from the Evil One.
16They don't belong to the world, just as I don't
belong to the world. 17Make them ready for
your service through your truth; your teaching
is truth. 18I have sent them into the world, just
as you sent me into the world. 19For their sake,
I am making myself ready to serve so that they
can be ready for their service of the truth.

20"I pray for these followers, but I am also
praying for all those who will believe in me
because of their teaching. 21Father, I pray that
they can be one. As you are in me and I am in
you, I pray that they can also be one in us. Then
the world will believe that you sent me. 22I
have given these people the glory that you gave
me so that they can be one, just as you and I
are one. 23I will be in them and you will be in
me so that they will be completely one. Then
the world will know that you sent me and that
you loved them just as much as you loved me.

24"Father, I want these people that you gave
me to be with me where I am. I want them to
see my glory, which you gave me because you
loved me before the world was made. 25Father,
you are the One who is good. The world does
not know you, but I know you, and these people know you sent me. 26I showed them what
you are like, and I will show them again. Then
they will have the same love that you have for
me, and I will live in them."

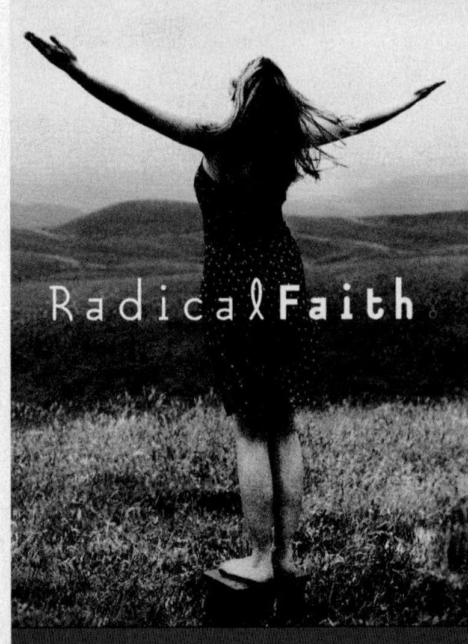

RadicalFaith

John 13:13-15

Jesus gives his apostles a lesson in humility when he washes their feet. He tells them that they are to follow his example. And we, as followers of Christ, are to do the same. Meeting the needs of other people and sacrificing your own is the example of Jesus, and we are to be like him. Did you know that when you feel sorry for yourself, one of the best things to help you feel better is to do something good for somebody else? And if you are acting like Jesus, it may cost you something—some time, some energy, some money, maybe even your pride. Sometimes we can serve others secretly, and God gets all of the glory. Jesus came and humbled himself by being as a servant to others. Being Christlike means that we humble ourselves and do the same. It's the whole point of our time here on earth—following his example, looking more and more like Jesus.

Jun

Father's Day is the third Sunday in June.
Tell your dad you love him!

1 Pray for a Person of Influence: Today is Tim from Delirious?'s birthday!

2 Reflect on God's goodness today as you enjoy the summer.

3

4 Pray for a Person of Influence: Today is Angelina Jolie's birthday.

5

6 National Chocolate Ice Cream Day. Fix yourself a bowl!

7 Pray for a Person of Influence: Today is Martin and Stu from Delirious?'s birthday!

8

9 Pray for a Person of Influence: Natalie Portman's birthday is today.

10

11

12

13

14 National E-mail Week! Write someone you haven't talked to in a while.

15

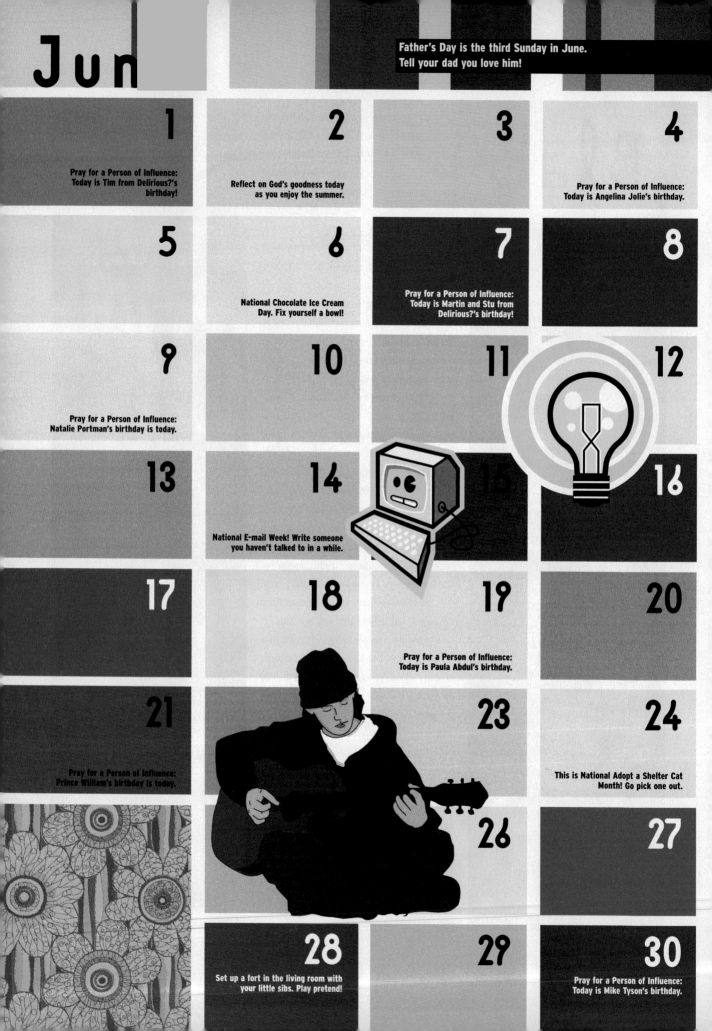

16

17

18

19 Pray for a Person of Influence: Today is Paula Abdul's birthday.

20

21 Pray for a Person of Influence: Prince William's birthday is today.

23

24 This is National Adopt a Shelter Cat Month! Go pick one out.

26

27

28 Set up a fort in the living room with your little sibs. Play pretend!

29

30 Pray for a Person of Influence: Today is Mike Tyson's birthday.

JESUS IS ARRESTED

18 When Jesus finished praying, he
went with his followers across the
Kidron Valley. On the other side there was a garden, and Jesus and his followers went into it.
2Judas knew where this place was, because
Jesus met there often with his followers. Judas
was the one who turned against Jesus. 3So
Judas came there with a group of soldiers and
some guards from the leading priests and the
Pharisees. They were carrying torches, lanterns,
and weapons.
4Knowing everything that would happen to
him, Jesus went out and asked, "Who is it you
are looking for?"
5They answered, "Jesus from Nazareth."
"I am he," Jesus said. (Judas, the one who
turned against Jesus, was standing there with
them.) 6When Jesus said, "I am he," they moved
back and fell to the ground.
7Jesus asked them again, "Who is it you are
looking for?"
They said, "Jesus of Nazareth."
8"I told you that I am he," Jesus
said. "So if you are looking for
me, let the others go." 9This
happened so that the words
Jesus said before would come
true: "I have not lost any of
the ones you gave me."
10Simon Peter, who had a sword,
pulled it out and struck the servant of the
high priest, cutting off his right ear. (The servant's name was Malchus.) 11Jesus said to
Peter, "Put your sword back. Shouldn't I drink
the cup*n* the Father gave me?"

JESUS IS BROUGHT BEFORE ANNAS

12Then the soldiers with their commander
and the guards arrested Jesus. They tied him
13and led him first to Annas, the father-in-law
of Caiaphas, the high priest that year.
14Caiaphas was the one who told the Jews that
it would be better if one man died for all the
people.

PETER SAYS HE DOESN'T KNOW JESUS

15Simon Peter and another one of Jesus' followers went along after Jesus. This follower
knew the high priest, so he went with Jesus
into the high priest's courtyard. 16But Peter
waited outside near the door. The follower
who knew the high priest came back outside,
spoke to the girl at the door, and brought Peter
inside. 17The girl at the door said to Peter,
"Aren't you also one of that man's followers?"
Peter answered, "No, I am not!"
18It was cold, so the servants and guards
had built a fire and were standing around it,
warming themselves. Peter also was standing
with them, warming himself.

THE HIGH PRIEST QUESTIONS JESUS

19The high priest asked Jesus questions
about his followers and his teaching. 20Jesus
answered, "I have spoken openly to everyone.
I have always taught in synagogues and in the
Temple, where all the Jews come together. I
never said anything in secret. 21So why do you
question me? Ask the people who heard my
teaching. They know what I said."
22When Jesus said this, one of
the guards standing there hit
him. The guard said, "Is that
the way you answer the
high priest?"
23Jesus answered him, "If I
said something wrong, then show what it
was. But if what I said is true, why do you hit
me?"
24Then Annas sent Jesus, who was still tied,
to Caiaphas the high priest.

PETER SAYS AGAIN HE DOESN'T KNOW JESUS

25As Simon Peter was standing and warming himself, they said to him, "Aren't you one
of that man's followers?"
Peter said it was not true; he said, "No, I am
not."
26One of the servants of the high priest was
there. This servant was a relative of the man

Psalm 23:4
Even if I walk through
a very dark valley,
I will not be afraid,
because you are with me.

John 14:2-4

This is one of the most awesome promises in all of Scripture. Jesus has gone to heaven to prepare our home—our forever home. A room in our Father's house waits for each one of us. And then, when it is time, Jesus will return to take us there. It's the home your heart has been longing for since the day you were born. It's the place where all your wounds will be healed. All your hopes will be fulfilled. Joy will be complete. Laughter will bounce off the walls. Tears will be banned. Worry won't even be a word. Home. Home at last with Jesus. Everything you've ever thought a home should be, and more than you ever dreamed it could be. Not a day too early, but just in time, Jesus will take us home.

"A ROOM IN OUR FATHER'S HOUSE WAITS FOR EACH ONE OF US."

notes

18:11 cup Jesus is talking about the painful things that will happen to him. Accepting these things will be very hard, like drinking a cup of something bitter.

whose ear Peter had cut off. The servant said, "Didn't I see you with him in the garden?"

[27]Again Peter said it wasn't true. At once a rooster crowed.

JESUS IS BROUGHT BEFORE PILATE

[28]Early in the morning they led Jesus from Caiaphas's house to the Roman governor's palace. They would not go inside the palace, because they did not want to make themselves unclean;[n] they wanted to eat the Passover meal. [29]So Pilate went outside to them and asked, "What charges do you bring against this man?"

[30]They answered, "If he were not a criminal, we wouldn't have brought him to you."

[31]Pilate said to them, "Take him yourselves and judge him by your own law."

"But we are not allowed to put anyone to death," the Jews answered. [32](This happened so that what Jesus said about how he would die would come true.)

[33]Then Pilate went back inside the palace and called Jesus to him and asked, "Are you the king of the Jews?"

[34]Jesus said, "Is that your own question, or did others tell you about me?"

[35]Pilate answered, "I am not one of you. It was your own people and their leading priests who handed you over to me. What have you done wrong?"

[36]Jesus answered, "My kingdom does not belong to this world. If it belonged to this world, my servants would fight so that I would not be given over to the Jews. But my kingdom is from another place."

[37]Pilate said, "So you are a king!"

Jesus answered, "You are the one saying I am a king. This is why I was born and came into the world: to tell people the truth. And everyone who belongs to the truth listens to me."

[38]Pilate said, "What is truth?" After he said this, he went out to the crowd again and said to them, "I find nothing against this man. [39]But it is your custom that I free one prisoner to you at Passover time. Do you want me to free the 'king of the Jews'?"

[40]They shouted back, "No, not him! Let Barabbas go free!" (Barabbas was a robber.)

19 Then Pilate ordered that Jesus be taken away and whipped. [2]The soldiers made a crown from some thorny branches and put it on Jesus' head and put a

purple robe around him. [3]Then they came to him many times and said, "Hail, King of the Jews!" and hit him in the face.

Q. What do you think about girls and guys praying together?

A. It's really important for your relationships to be based on God, not anything else.

GUYS SPEAK OUT

[4]Again Pilate came out and said to them, "Look, I am bringing Jesus out to you. I want you to know that I find nothing against him." [5]So Jesus came out, wearing the crown of thorns and the purple robe. Pilate said to them, "Here is the man!"

[6]When the leading priests and the guards saw Jesus, they shouted, "Crucify him! Crucify him!"

But Pilate answered, "Crucify him yourselves, because I find nothing against him."

[7]The leaders answered, "We have a law that says he should die, because he said he is the Son of God."

[8]When Pilate heard this, he was even more afraid. [9]He went back inside the palace and asked Jesus, "Where do you come from?" But Jesus did not answer him. [10]Pilate said, "You refuse to speak to me? Don't you know I have power to set you free and power to have you crucified?"

[11]Jesus answered, "The only power you have over me is the power given to you by God. The man who turned me in to you is guilty of a greater sin."

[12]After this, Pilate tried to let Jesus go. But some in the crowd cried out, "Anyone who makes himself king is against Caesar. If you let this man go, you are no friend of Caesar."

[13]When Pilate heard what they were saying, he brought Jesus out and sat down on the judge's seat at the place called The Stone Pavement. (In the Hebrew language[n] the name is Gabbatha.) [14]It was about noon on Preparation Day of Passover week. Pilate said to the crowd, "Here is your king!"

[15]They shouted, "Take him away! Take him away! Crucify him!"

Pilate asked them, "Do you want me to crucify your king?"

The leading priests answered, "The only king we have is Caesar."

[16]So Pilate handed Jesus over to them to be crucified.

JESUS IS CRUCIFIED

The soldiers took charge of Jesus. [17]Carrying his own cross, Jesus went out to a place called The Place of the Skull, which in the Hebrew language[n] is called Golgotha. [18]There they crucified Jesus. They also crucified two other men, one on each side, with Jesus in the middle. [19]Pilate wrote a sign and put it on the cross. It read: JESUS OF NAZARETH, THE KING OF THE JEWS. [20]The sign was written in Hebrew, in Latin, and in Greek. Many of the people read the sign, because the place where Jesus was crucified was near the city. [21]The leading priests said to Pilate, "Don't write, 'The King of the Jews.' But write, 'This man said, "I am the King of the Jews."' "

18:28 unclean Going into the Roman palace would make them unfit to eat the Passover Feast, according to their Law. **19:13, 17 Hebrew language** Or Aramaic, the languages of many people in this region in the first century.

Blab

Q. Can someone who has sold their soul to the devil be a Christian?

A. If someone gave her life to Satan, but then rebuked him and gave her life to Christ, Satan can no longer own her. But he can bother her. That is, the demons she allowed to control her could still be hanging around whispering stuff in her ear. If she has a concern that she hasn't gotten rid of all of them, its a good idea for her to talk to a pastor.

Q. Should I be scared about God coming back?

A. No, not if you're a Christian. In the Old Testament, whenever people saw God or his angels, they freaked out. But whenever anybody saw Christ, they were healed, cleansed, and saved. Christ will be the One who will come back for us, and you won't be scared at all. It will probably be the most amazing feeling you have ever felt in your life.

Q. How was God created? How did he get here?

A. Scripture tells us that there was never a time when God wasn't. He has always existed. If he were created, then he wouldn't be God. The one who created him would be God. It's really impossible for us humans to wrap our minds around, isn't it? That's why it takes faith.

22 Pilate answered, "What I have written, I
have written."
23 After the soldiers crucified Jesus, they
took his clothes and divided them into four
parts, with each soldier getting one part. They
also took his long shirt, which was all one
piece of cloth, woven from top to bottom. 24 So
the soldiers said to each other, "We should not
tear this into parts. Let's throw lots to see who
will get it." This happened so that this Scripture
would come true:

"They divided my clothes among them,
and they threw lots for my clothing."

Psalm 22:18

So the soldiers did this.
25 Standing near his cross were Jesus' mother,
his mother's sister, Mary the wife of Clopas,
and Mary Magdalene. 26 When Jesus saw his
mother and the follower he loved standing
nearby, he said to his mother, "Dear woman,
here is your son." 27 Then he said to the follower, "Here is your mother." From that time
on, the follower took her to live in his home.

JESUS DIES

28 After this, Jesus knew that everything had
been done. So that the Scripture would come
true, he said, "I am thirsty."[n] 29 There was a jar
full of vinegar there, so the soldiers soaked a
sponge in it, put the sponge on a branch of a
hyssop plant, and lifted it to Jesus' mouth.
30 When Jesus tasted the vinegar, he said, "It is
finished." Then he bowed his head and died.
31 This day was Preparation Day, and the next
day was a special Sabbath day. Since the religious leaders did not want the bodies to stay
on the cross on the Sabbath day, they asked
Pilate to order that the legs of the men be broken[n] and the bodies be taken away. 32 So the soldiers came and broke the legs of the first man
on the cross beside Jesus. Then they broke the
legs of the man on the other cross beside Jesus.
33 But when the soldiers came to Jesus and saw
that he was already dead, they did not break his
legs. 34 But one of the soldiers stuck his spear

John 14:16

Have you ever needed help? Of course you have. You may need help right now. All of us need help at some time or another. None of us is immune to the storms of life, but the good news is God sent the Holy Spirit to go with us through these storms. Not only did he come to fill us with power, but he was also sent to help us with every trial, every temptation, and every circumstance.

You may be going through something at this very moment, but you know what? The Holy Spirit is there right now ready and willing to help, even as you read this. In fact, if we will become aware of God's presence in us there isn't anything that the devil can throw at us that we can't handle. Jesus, the greater One, lives on the inside! Nothing can stop us now! We have victory! He'll help you!

"THE HOLY SPIRIT IS THERE RIGHT NOW READY AND WILLING TO HELP."

notes

19:28 "I am thirsty." Read Psalms 22:15; 69:21. **19:31 broken** The breaking of their bones would make them die sooner.

John 15:14-15

Jesus called the apostles his *friends*. That word applies to everyone who would ever become his follower. In verse 15, Jesus says, "I no longer call you servants. . . . But I call you friends."

You've probably heard a lot about being Jesus' servant. He's done so much for you! Because of him you're loved more than you can imagine. Because of him you can be strong and confident. Because of him you'll spend eternity with God. So a good response to him is, "Jesus, what can I do for you?" Of course, Jesus wants you to do your best to be a servant who pleases him. But more than that, he wants a friend who loves him more than anyone or anything else. What counts is not wearing yourself out with good deeds, but turning yourself toward him and loving him with your whole heart.

Be careful not to take his friendship for granted. He is God. While you're learning to love him as your best friend, don't ever lose sight of how awesome he is and of all the incredible gifts he gives you. Start to think of yourself as a friend of Jesus.

" BECAUSE OF HIM YOU'RE LOVED MORE THAN YOU CAN IMAGINE."

into Jesus' side, and at once blood and water came out. 35(The one who saw this happen is the one who told us this, and whatever he says is true. And he knows that he tells the truth, and he tells it so that you might believe.) 36These things happened to make the Scripture come true: "Not one of his bones will be broken."[n] 37And another Scripture says, "They will look at the one they stabbed."[n]

JESUS IS BURIED

38Later, Joseph from Arimathea asked Pilate if he could take the body of Jesus. (Joseph was a secret follower of Jesus, because he was afraid of some of the leaders.) Pilate gave his permission, so Joseph came and took Jesus' body away. 39Nicodemus, who earlier had come to Jesus at night, went with Joseph. He brought about seventy-five pounds of myrrh and aloes. 40These two men took Jesus' body and wrapped it with the spices in pieces of linen cloth, which is how they bury the dead. 41In the place where Jesus was crucified, there was a garden. In the garden was a new tomb that had never been used before. 42The men laid Jesus in that tomb because it was nearby, and they were preparing to start their Sabbath day.

JESUS' TOMB IS EMPTY

20 Early on the first day of the week, Mary Magdalene went to the tomb while it was still dark. When she saw that the large stone had been moved away from the tomb, 2she ran to Simon Peter and the follower whom Jesus loved. Mary said, "They have taken the Lord out of the tomb, and we don't know where they have put him."

3So Peter and the other follower started for the tomb. 4They were both running, but the other follower ran faster than Peter and reached the tomb first. 5He bent down and looked in and saw the strips of linen cloth lying there, but he did not go in. 6Then following him, Simon Peter arrived and went into the tomb and saw the strips of linen lying there. 7He also saw the cloth that had been around Jesus'

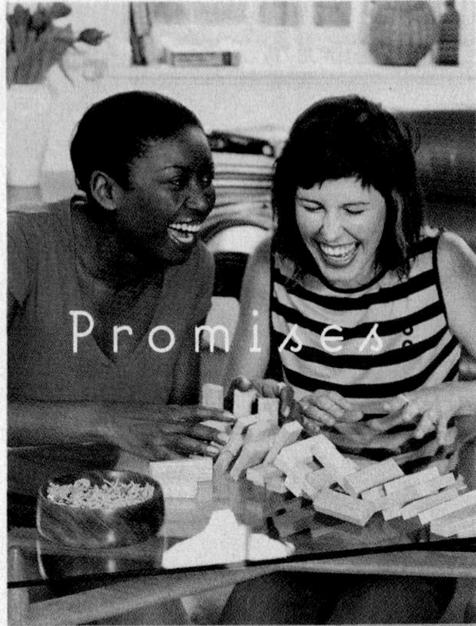

John 16:13

Have you ever had a tough time making a decision? Everybody has. Well, the Holy Spirit has been sent to speak to you at those very moments. And this verse assures you that he will not just spout off on his own, but will only say what God says. He will speak to you and he's going to show you what is true. So make sure you're listening and not ignoring him.

How do you hear the Holy Spirit speak? Second Timothy 2:15 says, "Make every effort to give yourself to God as the kind of person he will accept. Be a worker who is not ashamed and who uses the true teaching in the right way." So what do you do? Begin doing your best and studying the Bible—not just reading words, but really getting into the Word of God. Start out by just reviewing a few verses in your mind—over and over. Begin putting the Word of God inside you by memorizing a verse or two. Read Psalm 119:1-24. Notice how the psalmist felt about God's Word. Whenever you read the words *teachings, demands, rules, orders, commands,* or *word*, you can think of them as the Bible. As you begin to "feed" yourself the Word of God, you'll begin to notice that you are hearing God speak to you in ways and about things you've never heard before. Start doing it now, and let the Holy Spirit lead you "into all truth"!

"LET THE HOLY SPIRIT LEAD YOU 'INTO ALL TRUTH'!"

19:36 "Not one . . . broken." Quotation from Psalm 34:20. The idea is from Exodus 12:46; Numbers 9:12. **19:37 "They . . . stabbed."** Quotation from Zechariah 12:10.

LEARN IT & LIVE IT

2 Corinthians 5:7:
Learn It: We walk by faith, not by sight.
Live It: Do you need proof before you'll act on something? Go ahead and make the leap—sign up for that missions trip, even though you don't know if your best friends will be able to join you. You never know what God might do for you while you're there.

2 Corinthians 5:20:
Learn It: We are ambassadors for Christ.
Live It: Who do you know who doesn't know Christ? Represent him well to that person today. It doesn't mean preaching or giving the five-step plan to salvation, necessarily. It means being a human face of Christ to that person. Act with dignity and not with depravity when you're around him or her today.

2 Corinthians 6:14:
Learn It: Do not be mismatched with unbelievers.
Live It: Break up with your boyfriend if he's not a Christian. It's *that* black-and-white. Do it today.

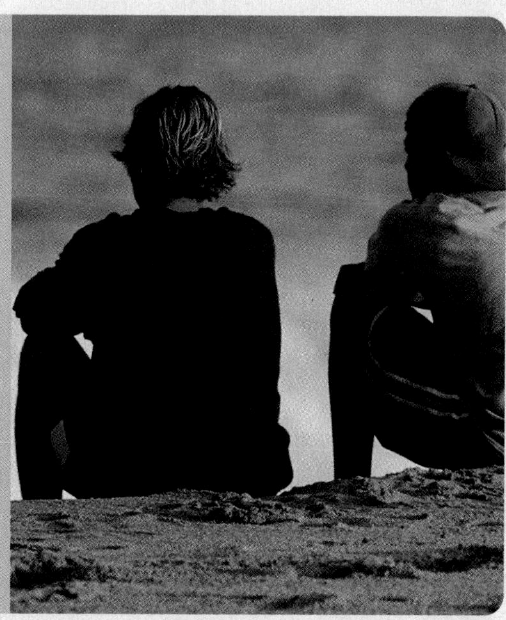

head, which was folded up and laid in a different place from the strips of linen. [8]Then the
other follower, who had reached the tomb
first, also went in. He saw and believed. [9](They
did not yet understand from the Scriptures
that Jesus must rise from the dead.)

JESUS APPEARS TO MARY MAGDALENE

[10]Then the followers went back home.
[11]But Mary stood outside the tomb, crying. As
she was crying, she bent down and looked
inside the tomb. [12]She saw two angels dressed
in white, sitting where Jesus' body had been,
one at the head and one at the feet.

[13]They asked her, "Woman, why are you
crying?"

She answered, "They have taken away my
Lord, and I don't know where they have put
him." [14]When Mary said this, she turned around
and saw Jesus standing there, but she did not
know it was Jesus.

[15]Jesus asked her, "Woman, why are you
crying? Whom are you looking for?"

Thinking he was the gardener, she said to
him, "Did you take him away, sir? Tell me
where you put him, and I will get him."

[16]Jesus said to her, "Mary."

Mary turned toward Jesus and said in
Hebrew,[n] "Rabboni." (This means Teacher.)

[17]Jesus said to her, "Don't hold on to me,
because I have not yet gone up to the Father.
But go to my brothers and tell them, 'I am
going back to my Father and your Father, to
my God and your God.' "

[18]Mary Magdalene went and said to the followers, "I saw the Lord!" And she told them
what Jesus had said to her.

JESUS APPEARS TO HIS FOLLOWERS

[19]When it was evening on the first day of
the week, the followers were together. The
doors were locked, because they were afraid of
the older leaders. Then Jesus came and stood
right in the middle of them and said, "Peace be
with you." [20]After he said this, he showed
them his hands and his side. The followers
were thrilled when they saw the Lord.

[21]Then Jesus said again, "Peace be with
you. As the Father sent me, I now send you."
[22]After he said this, he breathed on them and
said, "Receive the Holy Spirit. [23]If you forgive
anyone his sins, they are forgiven. If you don't
forgive them, they are not forgiven."

JESUS APPEARS TO THOMAS

[24]Thomas (called Didymus), who was one
of the twelve, was not with them when Jesus
came. [25]The other followers kept telling
Thomas, "We saw the Lord."

But Thomas said, "I will not believe it until
I see the nail marks in his hands and put my
finger where the nails were and put my hand
into his side."

[26]A week later the followers were in the
house again, and Thomas was with them. The
doors were locked, but Jesus came in and stood
right in the middle of them. He said, "Peace be
with you." [27]Then he said to Thomas, "Put

BEAUTY SECRET

SHOPPING TIPS

Make sure that Jesus would be pleased with what you wear. You don't have to look frumpy; just make sure you look like a child of God. Imagine him close by as you shop. Would he be pleased with the outfit you're about to buy?

notes

20:16 Hebrew language Or Aramaic, the languages of many people in this region in the first century.

your finger here, and look at my hands. Put your hand here in my side. Stop being an unbeliever and believe."

[28]Thomas said to him, "My Lord and my God!"

[29]Then Jesus told him, "You believe because you see me. Those who believe without seeing me will be truly happy."

WHY JOHN WROTE THIS BOOK

[30]Jesus did many other miracles in the presence of his followers that are not written in this book. [31]But these are written so that you may believe that Jesus is the Christ, the Son of God. Then, by believing, you may have life through his name.

JESUS APPEARS TO SEVEN FOLLOWERS

21 Later, Jesus showed himself to his followers again—this time at Lake Galilee.[n] This is how he showed himself: [2]Some of the followers were together: Simon Peter, Thomas (called Didymus), Nathanael from Cana in Galilee, the two sons of Zebedee, and two other followers. [3]Simon Peter said, "I am going out to fish."

The others said, "We will go with you." So they went out and got into the boat. They fished that night but caught nothing.

[4]Early the next morning Jesus stood on the shore, but the followers did not know it was Jesus. [5]Then he said to them, "Friends, did you catch any fish?"

They answered, "No."

[6]He said, "Throw your net on the right side of the boat, and you will find some." So they did, and they caught so many fish they could not pull the net back into the boat.

[7]The follower whom Jesus loved said to Peter, "It is the Lord!" When Peter heard him say this, he wrapped his coat around himself. (Peter had taken his clothes off.) Then he jumped into the water. [8]The other followers went to shore in the boat, dragging the net full of fish. They were not very far from shore, only about a hundred yards. [9]When the followers stepped out of the boat and onto the shore, they saw a fire of hot coals. There were fish on the fire, and there was bread.

[10]Then Jesus said, "Bring some of the fish you just caught."

[11]Simon Peter went into the boat and pulled the net to the shore. It was full of big fish, one hundred fifty-three in all, but even though there were so many, the net did not tear. [12]Jesus said to them, "Come and eat." None of the followers dared ask him, "Who are you?" because they knew it was the Lord. [13]Jesus came and took the bread and gave it to them, along with the fish.

[14]This was now the third time Jesus showed himself to his followers after he was raised from the dead.

JESUS TALKS TO PETER

[15]When they finished eating, Jesus said to Simon Peter, "Simon son of John do you love me more than these?"

He answered, "Yes, Lord, you know that I love you."

Jesus said, "Feed my lambs."

[16]Again Jesus said, "Simon son of John do you love me?"

He answered, "Yes, Lord, you know that I love you."

Jesus said, "Take care of my sheep."

[17]A third time he said, "Simon son of John do you love me?"

Peter was hurt because Jesus asked him the third time, "Do you love me?" Peter said, "Lord, you know everything; you know that I love you!"

He said to him, "Feed my sheep. [18]I tell you the truth, when you were younger, you tied your own belt and went where you wanted. But when you are old, you will put out your hands and someone else will tie you and take you where you don't want to go." [19](Jesus said this to show how Peter would die to give glory to God.) Then Jesus said to Peter, "Follow me!"

[20]Peter turned and saw that the follower Jesus loved was walking behind them. (This was the follower who had leaned against Jesus at the supper and had said, "Lord, who will turn against you?") [21]When Peter saw him behind them, he asked Jesus, "Lord, what about him?"

[22]Jesus answered, "If I want him to live until I come back, that is not your business. You follow me."

[23]So a story spread among the followers that this one would not die. But Jesus did not say he would not die. He only said, "If I want him to live until I come back, that is not your business."

[24]That follower is the one who is telling these things and who has now written them down. We know that what he says is true.

[25]There are many other things Jesus did. If every one of them were written down, I suppose the whole world would not be big enough for all the books that would be written.

RELATIONSHIPS

In today's world *family* has a ton of different meanings for everyone. Some people have huge families with lots of get-togethers throughout the year. It's really important for them to be together—they make it a priority. For others, family is just kinda something you're born into and it's not a huge influence on your day-to-day life. When you decide to start dating a guy seriously, make sure you take a look at his family. Do they treat each other the way you want to be treated? Do they have the kind of relationship you want to have with your family? How different is his family from yours? All that will be really important one day. But for now, if you're still not that serious, don't get too caught up with his family. And don't let him get too involved with yours. It makes it a lot easier when you break up.

21:1 Lake Galilee Literally, "Sea of Tiberias."

Acts: THE EXTRAORDINARY ACTS OF ORDINARY PEOPLE

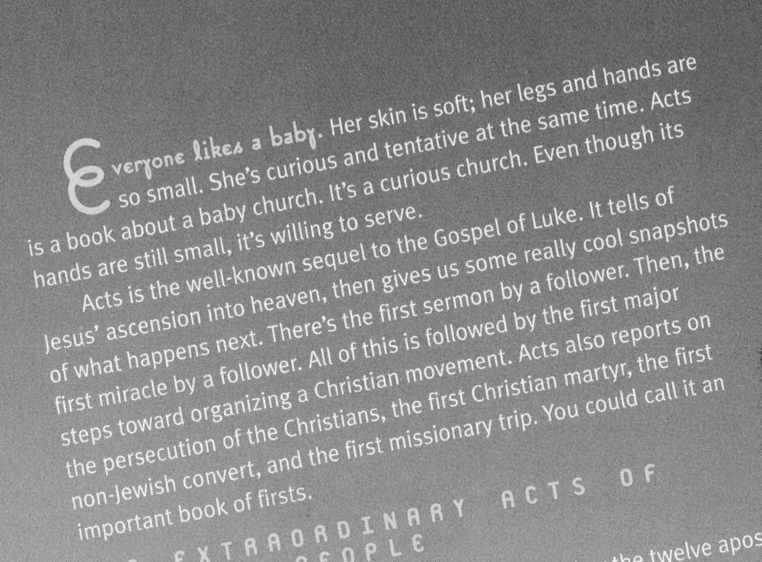

Everyone likes a baby. Her skin is soft; her legs and hands are so small. She's curious and tentative at the same time. Acts is a book about a baby church. It's a curious church. Even though its hands are still small, it's willing to serve.

Acts is the well-known sequel to the Gospel of Luke. It tells of Jesus' ascension into heaven, then gives us some really cool snapshots of what happens next. There's the first sermon by a follower. Then, the first miracle by a follower. All of this is followed by the first major steps toward organizing a Christian movement. Acts also reports on the persecution of the Christians, the first Christian martyr, the first non-Jewish convert, and the first missionary trip. You could call it an important book of firsts.

And there's really cool stuff here too. Remember the twelve apostles? In the Gospels they were really important figures. Well, in Acts, they're almost invisible. The Twelve are still respected, but other leaders become well known and begin leading the church. Acts introduces these leaders, like Paul. It also introduces us to the miracles believers can do through the Holy Spirit. God's Spirit making bold witnesses out of ordinary people is the reason behind the phenomenal success of the first-generation church. And, hey, don't forget that this same God who did all this in Acts does it for us today. He's behind our success. He's with us, just like he was with the baby church.

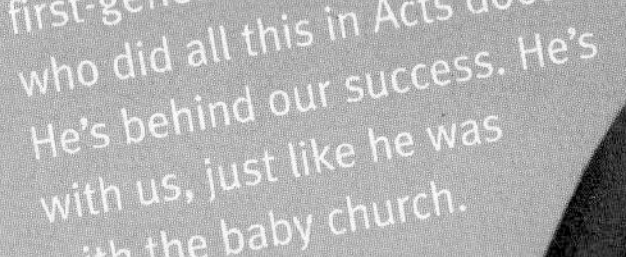

Acts 1:8-9

Just think of it—your favorite teacher calls a class meeting. He or she says, "This is the last time you will ever see me. I'm leaving for heaven in a matter of minutes. Before I go, I have one last thing to say to you." You listen intently. Nothing else matters at this moment. How long will you remember your teacher's last words to you? Probably until the day you die.

That's what's happening here. Jesus leaves his followers with this final word. He tells them that the Holy Spirit is coming after him. The Holy Spirit is going to give them power. He'll give them the strength they need to do everything Jesus wants them to do.

As a Christian, you have that same power. The Holy Spirit lives inside of you to give you the power you need to do everything Jesus wants you to do. One thing you know is that he wants you to go out and spread the Good News about his love and forgiveness. He's the power for shaky voices, weak knees, butterflies in your stomach. He's the giver of abundant life, the supplier of words, the revealer of truth, and the protector of courageous hearts. He's the One who always loves you and will never leave you. He gives you comfort and good advice. He gives you the power to know what to do in every situation. That's power!

LUKE WRITES ANOTHER BOOK

1 To Theophilus.

The first book I wrote was about everything Jesus began to do and teach [2]until the day he was taken up into heaven. Before this, with the help of the Holy Spirit, Jesus told the apostles he had chosen what they should do. [3]After his death, he showed himself to them and proved in many ways that he was alive. The apostles saw Jesus during the forty days after he was raised from the dead, and he spoke to them about the kingdom of God. [4]Once when he was eating with them, he told them not to leave Jerusalem. He said, "Wait here to receive the promise from the Father which I told you about. [5]John baptized people with water, but in a few days you will be baptized with the Holy Spirit."

JESUS IS TAKEN UP INTO HEAVEN

[6]When the apostles were all together, they asked Jesus, "Lord, are you now going to give the kingdom back to Israel?"

[7]Jesus said to them, "The Father is the only One who has the authority to decide dates and times. These things are not for you to know. [8]But when the Holy Spirit comes to you, you will receive power. You will be my witnesses—in Jerusalem, in all of Judea, in Samaria, and in every part of the world."

[9]After he said this, as they were watching, he was lifted up, and a cloud hid him from their sight. [10]As he was going, they were looking into the sky. Suddenly, two men wearing white clothes stood beside them. [11]They said, "Men of Galilee, why are you standing here looking into the sky? Jesus, whom you saw taken up from you into heaven, will come back in the same way you saw him go."

A NEW APOSTLE IS CHOSEN

[12]Then they went back to Jerusalem from the Mount of Olives. (This mountain is about half a mile from Jerusalem.) [13]When they entered the city, they went to the upstairs room where they were staying. Peter, John, James, Andrew, Philip, Thomas, Bartholomew, Matthew, James son of Alphaeus, Simon (known as the Zealot), and Judas son of James were there. [14]They all continued praying together with some women, including Mary the mother of Jesus, and Jesus' brothers.

[15]During this time there was a meeting of the believers (about one hundred twenty of them). Peter stood up and said, [16-17]"Brothers and sisters,[n] in the Scriptures the Holy Spirit said through David something that must happen involving Judas. He was one of our own group and served together with us. He led those who arrested Jesus." [18](Judas bought a field with the money he got for his evil act. But he fell to his death, his body burst open, and all his intestines poured out. [19]Everyone in Jerusalem learned about this so they named this place Akeldama. In their language Akeldama means "Field of Blood.") [20]"In the Book of Psalms," Peter said, "this is written:

'May his place be empty;
leave no one to live in it.' *Psalm 69:25*

And it is also written:

'Let another man replace him as leader.' *Psalm 109:8*

[21-22]"So now a man must become a witness with us of Jesus' being raised from the dead. He must be one of the men who were part of our group during all the time the Lord Jesus was among us—from the time John was baptizing people until the day Jesus was taken up from us to heaven."

[23]They put the names of two men before the group. One was Joseph Barsabbas, who was also called Justus. The other was Matthias. [24-25]The apostles prayed, "Lord, you know the thoughts of everyone. Show us which one of

Psalm 29:11
The LORD gives strength to his people; the LORD blesses his people with peace.

1:16-17 Brothers and sisters Although the Greek text says "Brothers" here and throughout this book, the words of the speakers were meant for the entire church, including men and women.

WHAT'S YOUR LOVE LANGUAGE*?

YOU HAVE THE FLU AND HAD TO MISS SCHOOL TODAY. YOUR BEST FRIEND COMES BY TO CHEER YOU UP. SHE MAKES YOU FEEL SO MUCH BETTER BECAUSE:

A. SHE SAYS THAT SCHOOL JUST WASN'T THE SAME WITHOUT YOU TODAY, AND SHE LOVES THOSE CUTE COW PAJAMAS YOU'RE WEARING!
B. SHE SPENDS THE WHOLE AFTERNOON PLAYING MONOPOLY WITH YOU AND CATCHING YOU UP ON ALL THE NEWS FROM SCHOOL.
C. SHE BRINGS YOU A FUNNY "GET WELL" BALLOON AND A BAG OF YOUR FAVORITE CANDY—MMM!
D. SHE COPIED HER NOTES FOR YOU, GOT YOUR HOMEWORK ASSIGNMENTS, AND BROUGHT YOU THE BOOKS YOU NEED FROM SCHOOL.
E. SHE GAVE YOU A BIG HUG—SHE KNOWS THAT HUGS HELP EVERYONE FEEL BETTER!

IT'S YOUR LITTLE BROTHER'S BIRTHDAY. SURE, HE'S ANNOYING SOMETIMES, BUT WHAT LITTLE BROTHERS AREN'T? YOU WANT TO MAKE SURE HE HAS A GREAT BIRTHDAY, SO YOU:

A. TELL HIM HOW GLAD YOU ARE THAT HE'S YOUR BROTHER, AND THAT YOU THINK HE'S THE GREATEST.
B. OFFER TO HELP HIM PUT TOGETHER HIS NEW SCOOTER WHILE GIVING HIM ADVICE ON BEING IN THE FOURTH GRADE (FROM YOUR OLDER, WISER SELF).
C. USE WHAT YOU'VE LEARNED IN ART CLASS AND MAKE HIM A REALLY COOL BIRTHDAY CARD THAT YOU KNOW HE'LL LOVE.
D. DO HIS CHORES FOR THE DAY—EVERY KID NEEDS A DAY OFF!
E. TICKLE HIM ON THE FLOOR AND SING "HAPPY BIRTHDAY" WHILE HE LAUGHS HYSTERICALLY.

YOUR BOYFRIEND (HE'S SOOOOOO WONDERFUL!) REMEMBERED YOUR THREE-MONTH ANNIVERSARY TODAY. YOU FEEL LIKE YOU'RE WALKING ON CLOUDS BECAUSE HE:

TOLD YOU HOW SPECIAL AND BEAUTIFUL YOU ARE TO HIM, AND THAT THE LAST THREE MONTHS HAVE BEEN THE BEST OF HIS LIFE.
B. TOOK YOU ON A HIKE TO THAT BEAUTIFUL OVERLOOK, WHERE YOU SAT AND TALKED FOR HOURS AS THE SUN SET.
C. SURPRISED YOU WITH FLOWERS AND THAT SILVER CROSS NECKLACE HE KNEW YOU WANTED.
D. CARRIED YOUR BOOKS AT SCHOOL, WASHED YOUR CAR, AND MADE YOU BROWNIES.
E. GAVE YOU A BIG HUG AND A SMILE BETWEEN EACH CLASS PERIOD AT SCHOOL TODAY.

YOU KNOW THAT YOUR FANTASTIC MOM HAS HAD A TOUGH WEEK AT WORK, AND SHE NEEDS ENCOURAGEMENT. (YES, EVEN SUPER-MOMS GET DISCOURAGED!) WHEN FRIDAY NIGHT ROLLS AROUND, YOU SHOW HER SHE'S SPECIAL BY:

A. READING PROVERBS 31 OUT LOUD TO HER, TELLING HER THAT SHE HAS BEEN AN EXAMPLE OF A GODLY WOMAN TO YOU, AND THAT YOU HOPE TO BE LIKE HER SOMEDAY.
B. RENT HER FAVORITE MOVIE AND STAY HOME TO WATCH IT WITH HER. (DON'T FORGET THE POPCORN!)
C. GIVE HER A GIFT CERTIFICATE TO GET A SPA PEDICURE AT THE NEW SALON IN TOWN.
D. GIVE HER A WELL-DESERVED BREAK AND COOK DINNER FOR THE FAMILY—NOT FORGETTING TO CLEAN UP AFTERWARD.
E. OFFER HER ONE OF YOUR FAMOUS BACKRUBS TO RELAX HER.

THE MOST ROMANTIC THING YOU CAN IMAGINE YOUR FUTURE HUSBAND DOING IS:

A. LOOKING YOU IN THE EYES AND TELLING YOU HOW MUCH HE LOVES YOU—EVERY SINGLE DAY OF YOUR LIFE TOGETHER.
B. OFTEN TAKING A DAY OFF WORK JUST TO STAY AT HOME AND BE WITH YOU.
C. BRINGING YOU FLOWERS SPONTANEOUSLY AND ALWAYS THINKING OF A SPECIAL GIFT ON YOUR ANNIVERSARY.
D. ALWAYS LOOKING FOR WAYS HE CAN SERVE YOU BY HELPING AROUND THE HOUSE, MAKING YOU BREAKFAST, ETC.—AND ALWAYS DOING IT GLADLY.
E. GIVING YOU LOTS AND LOTS OF HUGS AND KISSES!

IF YOU PICKED MOSTLY A's, YOUR PRIMARY LOVE LANGUAGE IS WORDS OF AFFIRMATION.

Verbal compliments and words of appreciation powerfully communicate love to you. You probably glow when people give you compliments, your boyfriend tells you how he cares about you, or your dad praises you. It means a lot when others say encouraging and uplifting words to you. You probably tend to show others love with words also. Proverbs 16:24 says, "Pleasant words are like a honeycomb, making people happy and healthy."

IF YOU PICKED MOSTLY B's, YOUR PRIMARY LOVE LANGUAGE IS QUALITY TIME.

When people spend special, quality time with you, they are communicating love to you. You probably enjoy spending time just hanging out with your best friend, going shopping with your mom, and making cookies with your grandmother. An important part of quality time is togetherness. You feel loved when people enjoy spending time with you. You show others how much you care by investing quality time in them, too. Read Psalm 139 to see how God knows you, loves you, and never leaves you—now *that's* quality time!

IF YOU PICKED MOSTLY C's, YOUR PRIMARY LOVE LANGUAGE IS RECEIVING GIFTS.

Now, I know what you're thinking: *Everybody likes getting presents!* That's true, but if this is your love language, gifts mean even more. You probably love it when your baby sister draws you a picture, your best friend gives you her lucky pen, or your parents get you those earrings you really wanted. The price doesn't matter to you—it is truly the thought that counts. Gifts are visual symbols of love that have emotional value. You often show affection through giving gifts of all kinds as well. Remember that God shows us his love by giving us the Ultimate Gift, the gift of his Son, so that we may have eternal life (John 3:16).

IF YOU PICKED MOSTLY D's, YOUR PRIMARY LOVE LANGUAGE IS ACTS OF SERVICE.

When people do special things for you—things like helping you clean your room, making you breakfast, walking your dog when it's raining, or helping you carry your big science project to fifth period—you feel loved and appreciated. These acts of service communicate love to you because they require thought, planning, time, effort, and energy. You probably love to serve others whom you love too. Serving others imitates Christ, who said that he came to serve, not to be served. "Serve each other with love" (Galatians 5:13).

IF YOU PICKED MOSTLY E's, YOUR PRIMARY LOVE LANGUAGE IS PHYSICAL TOUCH.

The average person needs seven hugs or touches of some kind a day to be healthy. You probably keep all your family and friends hug-healthy! You love it when your dad gives you a big bear hug, your friends give you encouraging pats on the back, and your boyfriend holds your hand. Physical touch is a way of communicating all kinds of love. It is a tangible way that we can feel that others care about us. The New Testament is full of stories about Jesus' touching people with powerful love—forgiving them, making them clean, healing them, and even giving them life. We can't do miracles, but we can remember the power of touch and make someone's day with a hug!

*Note: Credit to Gary Chapman for the term *Love Language*.

these two you have chosen to do this work. Show us who should be an apostle in place of Judas, who turned away and went where he belongs." 26 Then they used lots to choose between them, and the lots showed that Matthias was the one. So he became an apostle with the other eleven.

THE COMING OF THE HOLY SPIRIT

2 When the day of Pentecost came, they were all together in one place. 2 Suddenly a noise like a strong, blowing wind came from heaven and filled the whole house where they were sitting. 3 They saw something like flames of fire that were separated and stood over each person there. 4 They were all filled with the Holy Spirit, and they began to speak different languages[n] by the power the Holy Spirit was giving them.

5 There were some religious Jews staying in Jerusalem who were from every country in the world. 6 When they heard this noise, a crowd came together. They were all surprised, because each one heard them speaking in his own language. 7 They were completely amazed at this. They said, "Look! Aren't all these people that we hear speaking from Galilee? 8 Then how is it possible that we each hear them in our own languages? We are from different places: 9 Parthia, Media, Elam, Mesopotamia, Judea, Cappadocia, Pontus, Asia, 10 Phrygia, Pamphylia, Egypt, the areas of Libya near Cyrene, Rome 11 (both Jews and those who had become Jews), Crete, and Arabia. But we hear them telling in our own languages about the great things God has done!" 12 They were all amazed and confused, asking each other, "What does this mean?"

13 But others were making fun of them, saying, "They have had too much wine."

GUYS SPEAK OUT
Q. What's your ideal date?
A. Dinner, and something where we can really get to talk, get to know each other.

PETER SPEAKS TO THE PEOPLE

14 But Peter stood up with the eleven apostles, and in a loud voice he spoke to the crowd: "My fellow Jews, and all of you who are in Jerusalem, listen to me. Pay attention to what I have to say. 15 These people are not drunk, as you think; it is only nine o'clock in the morning! 16 But Joel the prophet wrote about what is happening here today:

17 'God says: In the last days
  I will pour out my Spirit on all kinds
    of people.
 Your sons and daughters will prophesy.
  Your young men will see visions,
  and your old men will dream dreams.
18 At that time I will pour out my Spirit
  also on my male slaves and female slaves,
  and they will prophesy.
19 I will show miracles
  in the sky and on the earth:
  blood, fire, and thick smoke.
20 The sun will become dark,
  the moon red as blood,
  before the overwhelming and glorious
    day of the Lord will come.
21 Then anyone who calls on the Lord
    will be saved.' *Joel 2:28-32*

22 "People of Israel, listen to these words: Jesus from Nazareth was a very special man. God clearly showed this to you by the miracles, wonders, and signs he did through Jesus. You all know this, because it happened right here among you. 23 Jesus was given to you, and with the help of those who don't know the law, you put him to death by nailing him to a cross. But this was God's plan which he had made long ago; he knew all this would happen. 24 God raised Jesus from the dead and set him free from the pain of death, because death could not hold him. 25 For David said this about him:

'I keep the Lord before me always.
  Because he is close by my side,
  I will not be hurt.
26 So I am glad, and I rejoice.
  Even my body has hope,
27 because you will not leave me in
    the grave.
  You will not let your Holy One rot.
28 You will teach me how to live a holy life.
  Being with you will fill me with joy.' *Psalm 16:8-11*

29 "Brothers and sisters, I can tell you truly that David, our ancestor, died and was buried. His grave is still here with us today. 30 He was a prophet and knew God had promised him that he would make a person from David's family a king just as he was.[n] 31 Knowing this before it happened, David talked about the Christ rising from the dead. He said:

'He was not left in the grave.
  His body did not rot.'

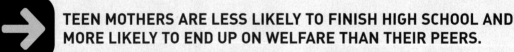

DIDYA KNOW  **TEEN MOTHERS ARE LESS LIKELY TO FINISH HIGH SCHOOL AND MORE LIKELY TO END UP ON WELFARE THAN THEIR PEERS.**

 notes

2:4 languages This can also be translated "tongues." **2:30 God . . . was** See 2 Samuel 7:13; Psalm 132:11.

32 So Jesus is the One whom God raised from the dead. And we are all witnesses to this. 33 Jesus was lifted up to heaven and is now at God's right side. The Father has given the Holy Spirit to Jesus as he promised. So Jesus has poured out that Spirit, and this is what you now see and hear. 34 David was not the one who was lifted up to heaven, but he said:

'The Lord said to my Lord,
"Sit by me at my right side,
35 until I put your enemies under your
control." '[n] *Psalm 110:1*

36 "So, all the people of Israel should know this truly: God has made Jesus—the man you nailed to the cross—both Lord and Christ."

37 When the people heard this, they felt guilty and asked Peter and the other apostles, "What shall we do?"

38 Peter said to them, "Change your hearts

"BY THE POWER OF JESUS CHRIST FROM NAZARETH, STAND UP AND WALK!"

and lives and be baptized, each one of you, in the name of Jesus Christ for the forgiveness of your sins. And you will receive the gift of the Holy Spirit. 39 This promise is for you, for your children, and for all who are far away. It is for everyone the Lord our God calls to himself."

40 Peter warned them with many other words. He begged them, "Save yourselves from the evil of today's people!" 41 Then those people who accepted what Peter said were baptized. About three thousand people were added to the number of believers that day. 42 They spent their time learning the apostles' teaching, sharing, breaking bread,[n] and praying together.

THE BELIEVERS SHARE

43 The apostles were doing many miracles and signs, and everyone felt great respect for God. 44 All the believers were together and shared everything. 45 They would sell their land and the things they owned and then divide the money and give it to anyone who needed it. 46 The believers met together in the Temple every day. They ate together in their homes, happy to share their food with joyful hearts. 47 They praised God and were liked by all the people. Every day the Lord added those who were being saved to the group of believers.

PETER HEALS A CRIPPLED MAN

3 One day Peter and John went to the Temple at three o'clock, the time set each day for the afternoon prayer service. 2 There, at the Temple gate called Beautiful Gate, was a man who had been crippled all his life. Every day he was carried to this gate to beg for money from the people going into the Temple. 3 The man saw Peter and John going into the Temple and asked them for money. 4 Peter and John looked straight at him and said, "Look at us!" 5 The man looked at them, thinking they were going to give him some money. 6 But Peter said, "I don't have any silver or gold, but I do have something else I can give you. By the power of Jesus Christ from Nazareth, stand up and walk!" 7 Then Peter took the man's right hand and lifted him up. Immediately the man's feet and ankles became strong. 8 He jumped up, stood on his feet, and began to walk. He went into the Temple with them, walking and jumping and praising God. 9-10 All the people recognized

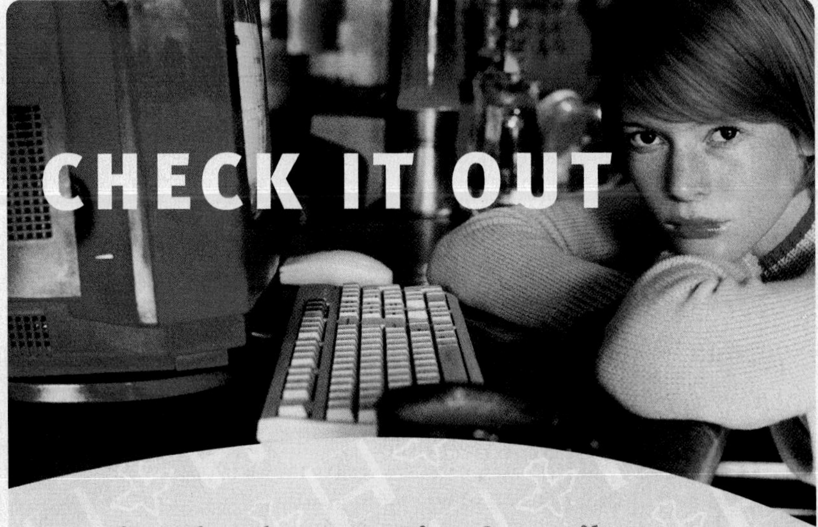

National Volunteer Fire Council

The National Volunteer Fire Council (NVFC) is a nonprofit membership association representing the interests of the volunteer fire, EMS, and rescue services. The NVFC serves as the information source regarding legislation, standards, and regulatory issues.

The NVFC mission is to provide a unified voice for volunteer Fire/EMS organizations.

This Mission will be accomplished by: Representing the interests of the volunteer Fire/EMS organizations at the U.S. congress and federal agencies; Promoting the interests of the state and local organizations at the national level; Promoting and providing education and training for the volunteer Fire/EMS organizations; Providing representation on national standards setting committees and projects; and Gathering information from and disseminating information to the volunteer Fire/EMS organizations.

To become a volunteer firefighter, go to ***www.nvfc.org.***

notes

2:35 until . . . control Literally, "until I make your enemies a footstool for your feet." **2:42 breaking bread** This may mean a meal as in verse 46, or the Lord's Supper, the special meal Jesus told his followers to eat to remember him (Luke 22:14–20).

bible basics

Reading the Bible is not as scary as it seems. The Bible is God's love letter to us and an instruction manual and answer book for life, so we should read it with the same passion we'd have when we read a letter from our biggest crush. Start anywhere you want; read as much or as little as you want. The Gospels (Matthew, Mark, Luke, and John) are a great place to start if you feel lost. They tell the story of Jesus' life. Or the Book of Romans is a good one to read if you just want to know what faith is all about.

him as the crippled man who always sat by
the Beautiful Gate begging for money. Now
they saw this same man walking and praising God, and they were amazed. They wondered how this could happen.

PETER SPEAKS TO THE PEOPLE

11While the man was holding on to
Peter and John, all the people were amazed
and ran to them at Solomon's Porch.
12When Peter saw this, he said to them,
"People of Israel, why are you surprised?
You are looking at us as if it were our own
power or goodness that made this man
walk. 13The God of Abraham, Isaac, and
Jacob, the God of our ancestors, gave glory
to Jesus, his servant. But you handed him
over to be killed. Pilate decided to let him
go free, but you told Pilate you did not
want Jesus. 14You did not want the One
who is holy and good but asked Pilate to
give you a murderer[n] instead. 15And so you
killed the One who gives life, but God raised
him from the dead. We are witnesses to this.
16It was faith in Jesus that made this crippled man well. You can see this
man, and you know him. He
was made completely well
because of trust in Jesus,
and you all saw it happen!
17"Brothers and sis-
ters, I know you did those things
to Jesus because neither you nor
your leaders understood what you were
doing. 18God said through the prophets
that his Christ would suffer and die. And
now God has made these things come true
in this way. 19So you must change your
hearts and lives! Come back to God, and he
will forgive your sins. Then the Lord will
send the time of rest. 20And he will send
Jesus, the One he chose to be the Christ.
21But Jesus must stay in heaven until the
time comes when all things will be made
right again. God told about this time long
ago when he spoke through his holy prophets.
22Moses said, 'The Lord your God will give
you a prophet like me, who is one of your own
people. You must listen to everything he tells
you. 23Anyone who does not listen to that
prophet will die, cut off from God's people.'[n]
24Samuel, and all the other prophets who
spoke for God after Samuel, told about this
time now. 25You are descendants of the
prophets. You have received the agreement
God made with your ancestors. He said to
your father Abraham, 'Through your descendants all the nations on the earth will be
blessed.'[n] 26God has raised up his servant Jesus
and sent him to you first to bless you by turning each of you away from doing evil."

PETER AND JOHN AT THE COUNCIL

4 While Peter and John were speaking to
the people, priests, the captain of the
soldiers that guarded the Temple, and
Sadducees came up to them. 2They were upset
because the two apostles were teaching the
people and were preaching that people will
rise from the dead through the power of Jesus.
3The older leaders grabbed Peter
and John and put them in jail.
Since it was already night, they
kept them in jail until the
next day. 4But many of
those who had heard
Peter and John preach believed the
things they said. There were now about
five thousand in the group of believers.
5The next day the rulers, the older leaders,
and the teachers of the law met in Jerusalem.
6Annas the high priest, Caiaphas, John, and
Alexander were there, as well as everyone
from the high priest's family. 7They made
Peter and John stand before them and then
asked them, "By what power or authority did
you do this?"
8Then Peter, filled with the Holy Spirit, said
to them, "Rulers of the people and you older
leaders, 9are you questioning us about a good

Psalm 30:11
You changed my sorrow into dancing. You took away my clothes of sadness, and clothed me in happiness.

notes

3:14 murderer Barabbas, the man the crowd asked Pilate to set free instead of Jesus (Luke 23:18). **3:22-23 'The Lord . . . people.'** Quotation from Deuteronomy 18:15, 19. **3:25 'Through . . . blessed.'** Quotation from Genesis 22:18; 26:4.

thing that was done to a crippled man? Are you asking us who made him well? [10]We want all of you and all the people to know that this man was made well by the power of Jesus Christ from Nazareth. You crucified him, but God raised him from the dead. This man was crippled, but he is now well and able to stand here before you because of the power of Jesus. [11]Jesus is

'the stone[n] that you builders rejected,
which has become the cornerstone.'
Psalm 118:22

[12]Jesus is the only One who can save people. His name is the only power in the world that has been given to save people. We must be saved through him."

[13]The leaders saw that Peter and John were not afraid to speak, and they understood that these men had no special training or education. So they were amazed. Then they realized that Peter and John had been with Jesus. [14]Because they saw the healed man standing there beside the two apostles, they could say nothing against them. [15]After the leaders ordered them to leave the meeting, they began to talk to each other. [16]They said, "What shall we do with these men? Everyone in Jerusalem knows they have done a great miracle, and we cannot say it is not true. [17]But to keep it from spreading among the people, we must warn them not to talk to people anymore using that name."

[18]So they called Peter and John in again and told them not to speak or to teach at all in the name of Jesus. [19]But Peter and John answered them, "You decide what God would want. Should we obey you or God? [20]We cannot keep quiet. We must speak about what we have seen and heard." [21]The leaders warned the apostles again and let them go free. They could not find a way to punish them, because all the people were praising God for what had been done. [22]The man who received the miracle of healing was more than forty years old.

THE BELIEVERS PRAY

[23]After Peter and John left the meeting of leaders, they went to their own group and told them everything the leading priests and the older leaders had said to them. [24]When the believers heard this, they prayed to God together, "Lord, you are the One who made the sky, the earth, the sea, and everything in them. [25]By the Holy Spirit, through our father David your servant, you said:

'Why are the nations so angry?
Why are the people making useless plans?
[26]The kings of the earth prepare to fight,
and their leaders make plans together
against the Lord
and his Christ.'
Psalm 2:1-2

[27]These things really happened when Herod, Pontius Pilate, and some of the people all came together against Jesus here in Jerusalem. Jesus is your holy servant, the One you made to be the Christ. [28]These people made your plan happen because of your power and your will. [29]And now, Lord, listen to their threats. Lord, help us, your servants, to speak your word without fear. [30]Help us to be brave by showing us your power to heal. Give proofs and make miracles happen by the power of Jesus, your holy servant."

[31]After they had prayed, the place where they were meeting was shaken. They were all filled with the Holy Spirit, and they spoke God's word without fear.

THE BELIEVERS SHARE

[32]The group of believers were united in their hearts and spirit. All those in the group acted as though their private property belonged to everyone in the group. In fact, they shared everything. [33]With great power the apostles were telling people that the Lord Jesus was truly raised from the dead. And God blessed all the believers very much. [34]No one in the group needed anything. From time to time those who owned fields or houses sold

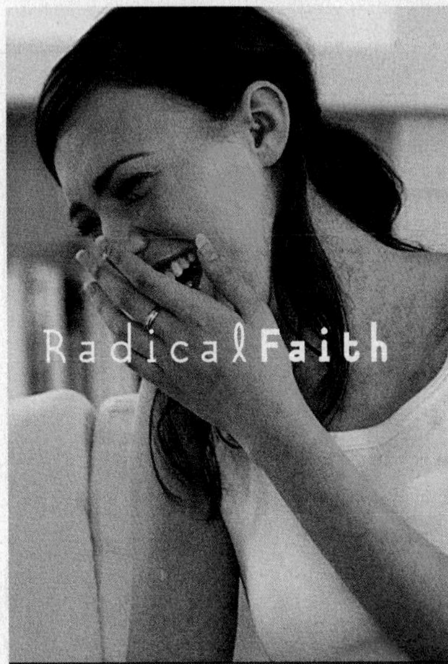

Acts 1:18–19

Mike started telling his friends that he didn't have anything to live for. He wanted to stay in bed all day. He talked a lot about a girl from school who had killed herself. He was so serious all the time. He began to give some of his clothes and stuff away. He withdrew from everybody. He didn't want to go out or to ball games. He seemed depressed. His family thought it was a phase and overlooked it. His friends thought he needed some space and left him alone. He died in his parents' car in their garage one afternoon after school. The note he left said he was just too lonely. Life was too hard. No one seemed to care.

If your friend mentions suicide, talks about not having anything to live for, distances himself/herself from everyone, or shows any other suspicious behavior, take that person seriously. Always take suicide threats seriously. Your friend needs help—quick. Talk to his or her parents, your pastor, a teacher, or counselor until you find someone who cares about your friend and is willing to help. Your job as a friend is to get qualified help. Don't try to handle this one alone. Whatever you do, believe that your friend is hurting, pray for him or her and for wisdom, and get help immediately.

notes

4:11 stone A symbol meaning Jesus.

Acts 2:21

Salvation is a one-time thing. You make the decision to *become* a Christian one time. You make decisions to *live* like a Christian daily — sometimes even moment by moment. Sometimes people are insecure about their salvation. They keep wondering if they "did it right" the first time. So they wind up raising their hand to accept Christ every time the offer is made.

Jesus promises that when you call out to him and ask him to save you, he does. It's that simple. You give your heart to him, ask him to forgive your sins, and make him the Lord and Savior of your life. You are saved from that moment until forever. So nail it down. If you've accepted Jesus Christ as your Savior, then you are saved. It's time to move on and grow up in Christ. If you are still unsure, then turn to Acts 16:30-31 and find out what you need to do in order to be saved. Salvation isn't a tricky thing. The Lord sees your heart and knows your sincerity. The right attitude is more important than the right words. Jesus' promise is strong — call out to him, and you will be saved.

"JESUS' PROMISE IS STRONG—CALL OUT TO HIM, AND YOU WILL BE SAVED."

them, brought the money, 35and gave it to the apostles. Then the money was given to anyone who needed it.

36One of the believers was named Joseph, a Levite born in Cyprus. The apostles called him Barnabas (which means "one who encourages"). 37Joseph owned a field, sold it, brought the money, and gave it to the apostles.

ANANIAS AND SAPPHIRA DIE

5 But a man named Ananias and his wife Sapphira sold some land. 2He kept back part of the money for himself; his wife knew about this and agreed to it. But he brought the rest of the money and gave it to the apostles. 3Peter said, "Ananias, why did you let Satan rule your thoughts to lie to the Holy Spirit and to keep for yourself part of the money you received for the land? 4Before you sold the land, it belonged to you. And even after you sold it, you could have used the money any way you wanted. Why did you think of doing this? You lied to God, not to us!" 5-6When Ananias heard this, he fell down and died. Some young men came in, wrapped up his body, carried it out, and buried it. And everyone who heard about this was filled with fear.

7About three hours later his wife came in, but she did not know what had happened. 8Peter said to her, "Tell me, was the money you got for your field this much?"

Sapphira answered, "Yes, that was the price."

9Peter said to her, "Why did you and your husband agree to test the Spirit of the Lord? Look! The men who buried your husband are at the door, and they will carry you out." 10At that moment Sapphira fell down by his feet and died. When the young men came in and saw that she was dead, they carried her out and buried her beside her husband. 11The whole church and all the others who heard about these things were filled with fear.

THE APOSTLES HEAL MANY

12The apostles did many signs and miracles among the people. And they would all meet together on Solomon's Porch. 13None of the others dared to join them, but all the people respected them. 14More and more men and women believed in the Lord and were added to the group of believers. 15The people placed their sick on beds and mats in the streets, hoping that when Peter passed by at least his shadow might fall on them. 16Crowds came from all the towns around Jerusalem, bringing their sick and those who were bothered by evil spirits, and all of them were healed.

LEADERS TRY TO STOP THE APOSTLES

17The high priest and all his friends (a group called the Sadducees) became very jealous. 18They took the apostles and put them in jail. 19But during the night, an angel of the Lord opened the doors of the jail and led the apostles outside. The angel said, 20"Go stand in the Temple and tell the people everything about this new life." 21When the apostles heard this, they obeyed and went into the Temple early in the morning and continued teaching.

"THE ANGEL SAID, 'GO STAND IN THE TEMPLE AND TELL THE PEOPLE EVERYTHING ABOUT THIS NEW LIFE.'"

When the high priest and his friends arrived, they called a meeting of the leaders and all the important older men. They sent some men to the jail to bring the apostles to them. 22But, upon arriving, the officers could not find the apostles. So they went back and reported to the leaders. 23They said, "The jail was closed and locked, and the guards were standing at the doors. But when we opened the doors, the jail was empty!" 24Hearing this, the captain of the Temple guards and the leading priests were confused and wondered what was happening.

25Then someone came and told them, "Listen! The men you put in jail are standing in the Temple teaching the people." 26Then the captain and his men went out and brought the apostles back. But the soldiers did not use force, because they were afraid the people would stone them to death.

[27]The soldiers brought the apostles to the meeting and made them stand before the leaders. The high priest questioned them, [28]saying, "We gave you strict orders not to continue teaching in that name. But look, you have filled Jerusalem with your teaching and are trying to make us responsible for this man's death."

[29]Peter and the other apostles answered, "We must obey God, not human authority! [30]You killed Jesus by hanging him on a cross. But God, the God of our ancestors, raised Jesus up from the dead! [31]Jesus is the One whom God raised to be on his right side, as Leader and Savior. Through him, all people could change their hearts and lives and have their sins forgiven. [32]We saw all these things happen. The Holy Spirit, whom God has given to all who obey him, also proves these things are true."

[33]When the leaders heard this, they became angry and wanted to kill them. [34]But a Pharisee named Gamaliel stood up in the meeting. He was a teacher of the law, and all the people respected him. He ordered the apostles to leave the meeting for a little while. [35]Then he said, "People of Israel, be careful what you are planning to do to these men. [36]Remember when Theudas appeared? He said he was a great man, and about four hundred men joined him. But he was killed, and all his followers were scattered; they were able to do nothing. [37]Later, a man named Judas came from Galilee at the time of the registration.[n] He also led a group of followers and was killed, and all his followers were scattered. [38]And so now I tell you: Stay away from these men, and leave them alone. If their plan comes from human authority, it will fail. [39]But if it is from God, you will not be able to stop them. You might even be fighting against God himself!"

The leaders agreed with what Gamaliel said. [40]They called the apostles in, beat them, and told them not to speak in the name of Jesus again. Then they let them go free. [41]The apostles left the meeting full of joy because they were given the honor of suffering disgrace for Jesus. [42]Every day in the Temple and in people's homes they continued teaching the people and telling the Good News—that Jesus is the Christ.

SEVEN LEADERS ARE CHOSEN

6 The number of followers was growing. But during this same time, the Greek-speaking followers had an argument with the other followers. The Greek-speaking widows were not getting their share of the food that was given out every day. [2]The twelve apostles called the whole group of followers together and said, "It is not right for us to stop our work of teaching God's word in order to serve tables. [3]So, brothers and sisters, choose seven of your own men who are good, full of the Spirit and full of wisdom. We will put them in charge of this work. [4]Then we can continue to pray and to teach the word of God."

[5]The whole group liked the idea, so they chose these seven men: Stephen (a man with great faith and full of the Holy Spirit), Philip,[n] Procorus, Nicanor, Timon, Parmenas, and Nicolas (a man from Antioch who had become a follower of the Jewish religion). [6]Then they put these men before the apostles, who prayed and laid their hands[n] on them.

[7]The word of God was continuing to spread. The group of followers in Jerusalem increased, and a great number of the Jewish priests believed and obeyed.

STEPHEN IS ACCUSED

[8]Stephen was richly blessed by God who gave him the power to do great miracles and signs among the people. [9]But some people were against him. They belonged to the synagogue of Free Men[n] (as it was called), which included people from Cyrene, Alexandria, Cilicia, and

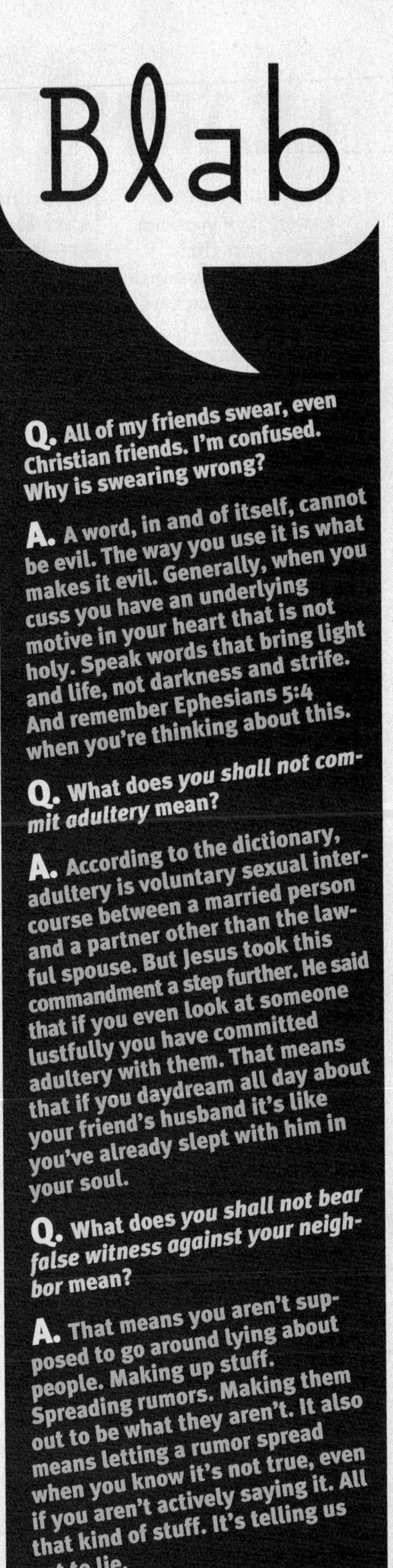
Blab
Q. All of my friends swear, even Christian friends. I'm confused. Why is swearing wrong?
A. A word, in and of itself, cannot be evil. The way you use it is what makes it evil. Generally, when you cuss you have an underlying motive in your heart that is not holy. Speak words that bring light and life, not darkness and strife. And remember Ephesians 5:4 when you're thinking about this.
Q. What does you shall not commit adultery mean?
A. According to the dictionary, adultery is voluntary sexual intercourse between a married person and a partner other than the lawful spouse. But Jesus took this commandment a step further. He said that if you even look at someone lustfully you have committed adultery with them. That means that if you daydream all day about your friend's husband it's like you've already slept with him in your soul.
Q. What does you shall not bear false witness against your neighbor mean?
A. That means you aren't supposed to go around lying about people. Making up stuff. Spreading rumors. Making them out to be what they aren't. It also means letting a rumor spread when you know it's not true, even if you aren't actively saying it. All that kind of stuff. It's telling us not to lie.

notes

5:37 registration Census. A counting of all the people and the things they own. **6:5 Philip** Not the apostle named Philip. **6:6 laid their hands** The laying on of hands had many purposes, including the giving of a blessing, power, or authority. **6:9 Free Men** Jewish people who had been slaves or whose fathers had been slaves, but were now free.

LEARN IT & LIVE IT

2 Corinthians 8:12:
Learn It: If you want to give, your gift is acceptable according to what talents you have to work with.
Live It: Just because you aren't a famous rock star doesn't mean you can't fight for your favorite cause. Join a local chapter of whatever organization you feel led to champion, and get going. You'll be amazed at how much you can accomplish even without the fame!

2 Corinthians 9:6:
Learn It: You reap what you sow.
Live It: Think about the consequences today. Did you just spill the beans about the secret you were supposed to be keeping? You just lost some trust points with your friend. Did you help out someone in need? You gained a bit of happiness and peace from it.

2 Corinthians 10:5:
Learn It: We hold every thought captive to obey Christ.
Live It: Refuse to let your mind get carried away with negative thoughts. *Oh, he thinks I'm such a loser. This test is going to be really scary. I hate that teacher.* Refuse to think thoughts like this, and your spirit will really take off. It's amazing how much peace you'll find from those simple changes.

Asia. They all came and argued with Stephen.
10But the Spirit was helping him to speak
with wisdom, and his words were so strong
that they could not argue with him. 11So they
secretly urged some men to say, "We heard
Stephen speak against Moses and against God."
12This upset the people, the older leaders,
and the teachers of the law. They came and
grabbed Stephen and brought him to a meeting of the leaders. 13They brought in some
people to tell lies about Stephen, saying, "This
man is always speaking against this holy place
and the law of Moses. 14We heard him say that
Jesus from Nazareth will destroy this place
and that Jesus will change the customs Moses
gave us." 15All the people in the meeting were
watching Stephen closely and saw that his face
looked like the face of an angel.

STEPHEN'S SPEECH

7The high priest said to Stephen, "Are
these things true?"
2Stephen answered, "Brothers and fathers,
listen to me. Our glorious God appeared to
Abraham, our ancestor, in Mesopotamia before
he lived in Haran. 3God said to Abraham,
'Leave your country and your relatives, and go
to the land I will show you.'[n] 4So Abraham left
the country of Chaldea and went to live in
Haran. After Abraham's father died, God sent
him to this place where you now live. 5God
did not give Abraham any of this land, not
even a foot of it. But God promised that he
would give this land to him and his descendants, even before Abraham had a child. 6This
is what God said to him: 'Your descendants
will be strangers in a land they don't own. The
people there will make them slaves and will
mistreat them for four hundred years. 7But I
will punish the nation where they are slaves.
Then your descendants will leave that land
and will worship me in this place.'[n] 8God made
an agreement with Abraham, the sign of which
was circumcision. And so when Abraham had
his son Isaac, Abraham circumcised him when
he was eight days old. Isaac also circumcised
his son Jacob, and Jacob did the same for his
sons, the twelve ancestors[n] of our people.
9"Jacob's sons became jealous of Joseph
and sold him to be a slave in Egypt. But God
was with him 10and saved him from all his
troubles. The king of Egypt liked Joseph and
respected him because of the wisdom God gave
him. The king made him governor of Egypt
and put him in charge of all the people in his
palace.
11"Then all the land of Egypt and Canaan
became so dry that nothing would grow, and
the people suffered very much. Jacob's sons,
our ancestors, could not find anything to eat.
12But when Jacob heard there was grain in
Egypt, he sent his sons there. This was their
first trip to Egypt. 13When they went there a
second time, Joseph told his brothers who he

DIDYA KNOW  **70% OF TEENS SAID THEY WERE READY TO LISTEN TO THINGS THEIR PARENTS THOUGHT THEY WERE NOT READY TO HEAR.**

 notes

7:3 'Leave . . . you.' Quotation from Genesis 12:1. **7:6-7 'Your descendants . . . place.'** Quotation from Genesis 15:13-14 and Exodus 3:12. **7:8 twelve ancestors** Important ancestors of the people of Israel; the leaders of the twelve tribes of Israel.

Notes

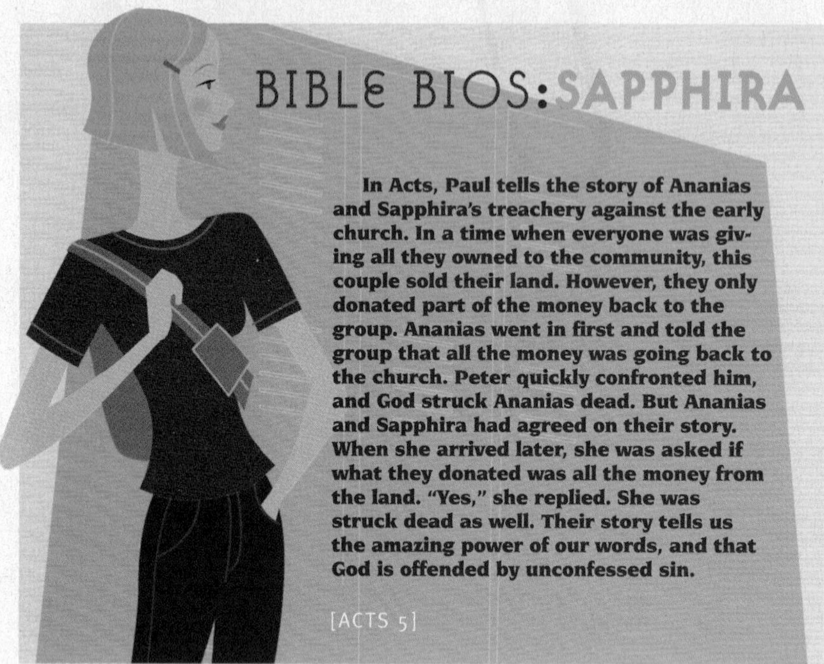

was, and the king learned about Joseph's family. [14]Then Joseph sent messengers to invite Jacob, his father, to come to Egypt along with all his relatives (seventy-five persons altogether). [15]So Jacob went down to Egypt, where he and his sons died. [16]Later their bodies were moved to Shechem and put in a grave there. (It was the same grave Abraham had bought for a sum of money from the sons of Hamor in Shechem.)

BIBLE BIOS: SAPPHIRA
In Acts, Paul tells the story of Ananias and Sapphira's treachery against the early church. In a time when everyone was giving all they owned to the community, this couple sold their land. However, they only donated part of the money back to the group. Ananias went in first and told the group that all the money was going back to the church. Peter quickly confronted him, and God struck Ananias dead. But Ananias and Sapphira had agreed on their story. When she arrived later, she was asked if what they donated was all the money from the land. "Yes," she replied. She was struck dead as well. Their story tells us the amazing power of our words, and that God is offended by unconfessed sin.
[ACTS 5]

[17]"The promise God made to Abraham was soon to come true, and the number of people in Egypt grew large. [18]Then a new king, who did not know who Joseph was, began to rule Egypt. [19]This king tricked our people and was cruel to our ancestors, forcing them to leave their babies outside to die. [20]At this time Moses was born, and he was very beautiful. For three months Moses was cared for in his father's house. [21]When they put Moses outside, the king's daughter adopted him and raised him as if he were her own son. [22]The Egyptians taught Moses everything they knew, and he was a powerful man in what he said and did.

[23]"When Moses was about forty years old, he thought it would be good to visit his own people, the people of Israel. [24]Moses saw an Egyptian mistreating one of his people, so he defended the Israelite and punished the Egyptian by killing him. [25]Moses thought his own people would understand that God was using him to save them, but they did not. [26]The next day when Moses saw two men of Israel fighting, he tried to make peace between them. He said, 'Men, you are brothers. Why are you hurting each other?' [27]The man who was hurting the other pushed Moses away and said, 'Who made you our ruler and judge? [28]Are you going to kill me as you killed the Egyptian yesterday?'[n] [29]When Moses heard him say this, he left Egypt and went to live in the land of Midian where he was a stranger. While Moses lived in Midian, he had two sons.

[30]"Forty years later an angel appeared to Moses in the flames of a burning bush as he was in the desert near Mount Sinai. [31]When Moses saw this, he was amazed and went near to look closer. Moses heard the Lord's voice say, [32]'I am the God of your ancestors, the God of Abraham, Isaac, and Jacob.'[n] Moses began to shake with fear and was afraid to look. [33]The Lord said to him, 'Take off your sandals, because you are standing on holy ground. [34]I have seen the troubles my people have suffered in Egypt. I have heard their cries and have come down to save them. And now, Moses, I am sending you back to Egypt.'[n]

Psalm 31:21
Praise the LORD. His love to me was wonderful when my city was attacked.

[35]"This Moses was the same man the two men of Israel rejected, saying, 'Who made you a ruler and judge?'[n] Moses is the same man God sent to be a ruler and savior, with the help of the angel that Moses saw in the burning bush. [36]So Moses led the people out of Egypt. He worked miracles and signs in Egypt, at the Red Sea, and then in the desert for forty years. [37]This is the same Moses that said to the people of Israel, 'God will give you a prophet like me, who is one of your own people.'[n] [38]This is the Moses who was with the gathering of the Israelites in the desert. He was with the angel that spoke to him at Mount Sinai, and he was with our ancestors. He received commands from God that give life, and he gave those commands to us.

[39]"But our ancestors did not want to obey Moses. They rejected him and wanted to go back to Egypt. [40]They said to Aaron, 'Make us gods who will lead us. Moses led us out of Egypt, but we don't know what has happened to him.'[n] [41]So the people made an idol that looked like a calf. Then they brought sacrifices to it and were proud of what they had made with their own hands. [42]But God turned against them and did not try to stop them from worshiping the sun, moon, and stars. This is what is written in the book of the prophets: God says,

'People of Israel, you did not bring me
sacrifices and offerings
while you traveled in the desert for
forty years.
[43]You have carried with you

notes

7:27-28 **'Who . . . yesterday?'** Quotation from Exodus 2:14. 7:32 **'I am . . . Jacob.'** Quotation from Exodus 3:6. 7:33-34 **'Take . . . Egypt.'** Quotation from Exodus 3:5-10. 7:35 **'Who . . . judge?'** Quotation from Exodus 2:14. 7:37 **'God . . . people.'** Quotation from Deuteronomy 18:15. 7:40 **'Make . . . him.'** Quotation from Exodus 32:1.

LEARN IT & LIVE IT

2 Corinthians 10:17:
Learn It: Let the one who boasts, boast about the Lord.
Live It: Are you really proud of some huge accomplishment you just achieved? Tell others how amazing God is for letting you have the opportunity!

2 Corinthians 12:10:
Learn It: When we are weak, we are strong.
Live It: Do you like people who come across like they can do everything and are proud of it? Probably not. Be vulnerable. Let others see your weaknesses, and they'll really see the strength of your character.

2 Corinthians 13:5:
Learn It: Jesus Christ is in you.
Live It: Do you really believe that? You represent the God of the universe in your body. Respect yourself, dress appropriately, eat healthy, and live like God is in you.

the tent to worship Molech
and the idols of the star god Rephan that
you made to worship.
So I will send you away beyond Babylon.'
Amos 5:25-27

44"The Holy Tent where God spoke to our
ancestors was with them in the desert. God
told Moses how to make this Tent, and he
made it like the plan God showed him. 45Later,
Joshua led our ancestors to capture the lands
of the other nations. Our people went in, and
God forced the other people out. When our
people went into this new land, they took with
them this same Tent they had received from
their ancestors. They kept it until the time of
David, 46who pleased God and asked God to
let him build a house for him, the God of
Jacob. 47But Solomon was the one who
built the Temple.

48"But the Most High does not live in
houses that people build with their hands.
As the prophet says:
49'Heaven is my throne,
and the earth is my footstool.
So do you think you can build a house
for me? says the Lord.
Do I need a place to rest?
50Remember, my hand made all these
things!' "
Isaiah 66:1-2

51Stephen continued speaking: "You
stubborn people! You have not given your
hearts to God, nor will you listen to him! You
are always against what the Holy Spirit is trying to tell you, just as your ancestors were.
52Your ancestors tried to hurt every prophet
who ever lived. Those prophets said long ago
that the One who is good would come, but
your ancestors killed them. And now you have
turned against and killed the One who is good.
53You received the law of Moses, which God
gave you through his angels, but you haven't
obeyed it."

STEPHEN IS KILLED

54When the leaders heard this, they became
furious. They were so mad they were grinding
their teeth at Stephen. 55But Stephen was full of
the Holy Spirit. He looked up to heaven and saw
the glory of God and Jesus standing at God's
right side. 56He said, "Look! I see heaven open
and the Son of Man standing at God's right side."

57Then they shouted loudly and covered
their ears and all ran at Stephen. 58They took
him out of the city and began to throw stones
at him to kill him. And those who told lies
against Stephen left their coats with a young
man named Saul. 59While they were throwing
stones, Stephen prayed, "Lord Jesus, receive
my spirit." 60He fell on his knees and cried in a
loud voice, "Lord, do not hold this sin against
them." After Stephen said this, he died.

8 Saul agreed that the killing of Stephen
was good.

TROUBLES FOR THE BELIEVERS

On that day the church of Jerusalem
began to be persecuted, and all the believers, except the apostles, were scattered
throughout Judea and Samaria.

2And some religious people buried
Stephen and cried loudly for him. 3Saul
was also trying to destroy the church,
going from house to house, dragging out
men and women and putting them in jail.
4And wherever they were scattered, they
told people the Good News.

PHILIP PREACHES IN SAMARIA

5Philip went to the city of Samaria and

Q. Do you ever think about getting married?
A. Yep. I just wonder who she is and if I know her now.
GUYS SPEAK OUT

preached about the Christ. 6When the people there heard Philip and saw the miracles he was doing, they all listened carefully to what he said. 7Many of these people had evil spirits in

75% OF TEENS WHO SMOKE STARTED WHEN THEY WERE IN NINTH GRADE.

them, but Philip made the evil spirits leave. The spirits made a loud noise when they came out. Philip also healed many weak and crippled people there. 8So the people in that city were very happy.

9But there was a man named Simon in that city. Before Philip came there, Simon had practiced magic and amazed all the people of Samaria. He bragged and called himself a great man. 10All the people—the least important and the most important—paid attention to Simon, saying, "This man has the power of God, called 'the Great Power'!" 11Simon had amazed them with his magic so long that the people became his followers. 12But when Philip told them the Good News about the kingdom of God and the power of Jesus Christ, men and women believed Philip and were baptized. 13Simon himself believed, and after he was baptized, he stayed very close to Philip. When he saw the miracles and the powerful things Philip did, Simon was amazed.

14When the apostles who were still in Jerusalem heard that the people of Samaria had accepted the word of God, they sent Peter and John to them. 15When Peter and John arrived, they prayed that the Samaritan believers might receive the Holy Spirit. 16These people had been baptized in the name of the Lord Jesus, but the Holy Spirit had not yet come upon any of them. 17Then, when the two apostles began laying their hands on the people, they received the Holy Spirit.

18Simon saw that the Spirit was given to people when the apostles laid their hands on them. So he offered the apostles money, 19saying, "Give me also this power so that anyone on whom I lay my hands will receive the Holy Spirit."

20Peter said to him, "You and your money should both be destroyed, because you thought you could buy God's gift with money. 21You cannot share with us in this work since your heart is not right before God. 22Change your heart! Turn away from this evil thing you have done, and pray to the Lord. Maybe he will forgive you for thinking this. 23I see that you are full of bitter jealousy and ruled by sin."

24Simon answered, "Both of you pray for me to the Lord so the things you have said will not happen to me."

25After Peter and John told the people what they had seen Jesus do and after they had spoken the message of the Lord, they went back to Jerusalem. On the way, they went through many Samaritan towns and preached the Good News to the people.

PHILIP TEACHES AN ETHIOPIAN

26An angel of the Lord said to Philip, "Get ready and go south to the road that leads down to Gaza from Jerusalem—the desert road." 27So Philip got ready and went. On the road he saw a man from Ethiopia, a eunuch. He was an important officer in the service of Candace, the queen of the Ethiopians; he was responsible for taking care of all her money. He had gone to Jerusalem to worship. 28Now, as he was on his way home, he was sitting in his chariot reading from the Book of Isaiah, the prophet. 29The Spirit said to Philip, "Go to that chariot and stay near it."

30So when Philip ran toward the chariot, he heard the man reading from Isaiah the prophet. Philip asked, "Do you understand what you are reading?"

31He answered, "How can I understand unless someone explains it to me?" Then he invited Philip to climb in and sit with him. 32The portion of Scripture he was reading was this:

"He was like a sheep being led to be killed.
He was quiet, as a lamb is quiet while
its wool is being cut;
he never opened his mouth.
33 He was shamed and was treated unfairly.
He died without children to continue his
family.
His life on earth has ended." *Isaiah 53:7-8*

34The officer said to Philip, "Please tell me, who is the prophet talking about—himself or someone else?" 35Philip began to speak, and starting with this same Scripture, he told the man the Good News about Jesus.

36While they were traveling down the road, they came to some water. The officer said, "Look, here is water. What is stopping me from being baptized?" 37*n* 38Then the officer commanded the chariot to stop. Both Philip and the officer went down into the water, and Philip baptized him. 39When they came up out of the

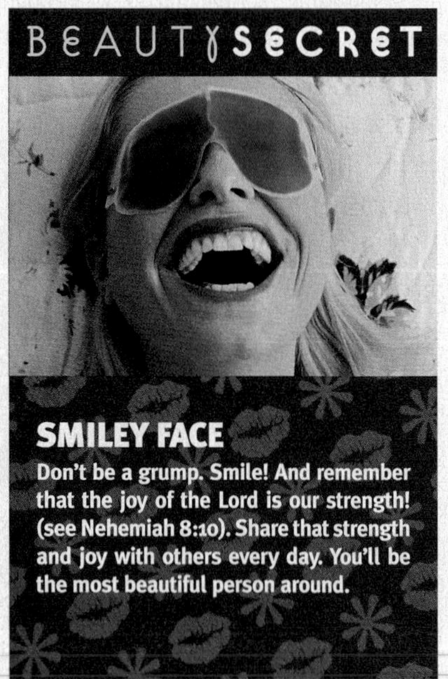

BEAUTY SECRET
SMILEY FACE
Don't be a grump. Smile! And remember that the joy of the Lord is our strength! (see Nehemiah 8:10). Share that strength and joy with others every day. You'll be the most beautiful person around.

notes

8:37 Verse 37 Some late copies of Acts add verse 37: "Philip answered, 'If you believe with all your heart, you can.' The officer said, 'I believe that Jesus Christ is the Son of God.' "

water, the Spirit of the Lord took Philip away; the officer never saw him again. And the officer continued on his way home, full of joy. [40]But Philip appeared in a city called Azotus and preached the Good News in all the towns on the way from Azotus to Caesarea.

SAUL IS CONVERTED

9 In Jerusalem Saul was still threatening the followers of the Lord by saying he would kill them. So he went to the high priest [2]and asked him to write letters to the synagogues in the city of Damascus. Then if Saul found any followers of Christ's Way, men or women, he would arrest them and bring them back to Jerusalem.

Psalm 31:23
Love the LORD, all you who belong to him. The LORD protects those who truly believe, but he punishes the proud as much as they have sinned.

[3]So Saul headed toward Damascus. As he came near the city, a bright light from heaven suddenly flashed around him. [4]Saul fell to the ground and heard a voice saying to him, "Saul, Saul! Why are you persecuting me?"

[5]Saul said, "Who are you, Lord?"

The voice answered, "I am Jesus, whom you are persecuting. [6]Get up now and go into the city. Someone there will tell you what you must do."

[7]The people traveling with Saul stood there but said nothing. They heard the voice, but

"I AM JESUS, WHOM YOU ARE PERSECUTING."

they saw no one. [8]Saul got up from the ground and opened his eyes, but he could not see. So those with Saul took his hand and led him into Damascus. [9]For three days Saul could not see and did not eat or drink.

[10]There was a follower of Jesus in Damascus named Ananias. The Lord spoke to Ananias in a vision, "Ananias!"

Ananias answered, "Here I am, Lord."

[11]The Lord said to him, "Get up and go to Straight Street. Find the house of Judas,[n] and ask for a man named Saul from the city of Tarsus. He is there now, praying. [12]Saul has seen a vision in which a man named Ananias comes to him and lays his hands on him. Then he is able to see again."

[13]But Ananias answered, "Lord, many people have told me about this man and the terrible things he did to your holy people in Jerusalem. [14]Now he has come here to Damascus, and the leading priests have given him the power to arrest everyone who worships you."

[15]But the Lord said to Ananias, "Go! I have chosen Saul for an important work. He must tell about me to those who are not Jews, to kings, and to the people of Israel. [16]I will show him how much he must suffer for my name."

[17]So Ananias went to the house of Judas. He laid his hands on Saul and said, "Brother Saul, the Lord Jesus sent me. He is the one you saw on the road on your way here. He sent me so that you can see again and be filled with the Holy Spirit." [18]Immediately, something that looked like fish scales fell from Saul's eyes, and he was able to see again! Then Saul got up and was baptized. [19]After he ate some food, his strength returned.

SAUL PREACHES IN DAMASCUS

Saul stayed with the followers of Jesus in Damascus for a few days. [20]Soon he began to preach about Jesus in the synagogues, saying, "Jesus is the Son of God."

[21]All the people who heard him were amazed. They said, "This is the man who was in Jerusalem trying to destroy those who trust in this name! He came here to arrest the followers of Jesus and take them back to the leading priests."

Blab
Q. What does you shall not covet anything of your neighbor's mean?
A. It means you aren't supposed to sit around all day thinking about what other people have, wishing you could have it.
Q. What does remember the Sabbath day and keep it holy mean?
A. God wants us to take at least one day a week and set it aside for him. He's not just talking about church. He's talking about taking an entire day and dedicating it to him. In the Old Testament, the Israelites were commanded not to do a thing on that day but love God. They couldn't cook, or work, or climb a mountain. It was God's day and they were commanded to keep it holy.
Q. Can you tell me anything about the signs of a messed-up church? Like some verse or something?
A. There really isn't such a thing as a church that's not messed up. You know why? Because it is made up of humans and we are all messed up. Every church you go to will have some kind of problem or other. That's human.

[22]But Saul grew more powerful. His proofs that Jesus is the Christ were so strong that his own people in Damascus could not argue with him.

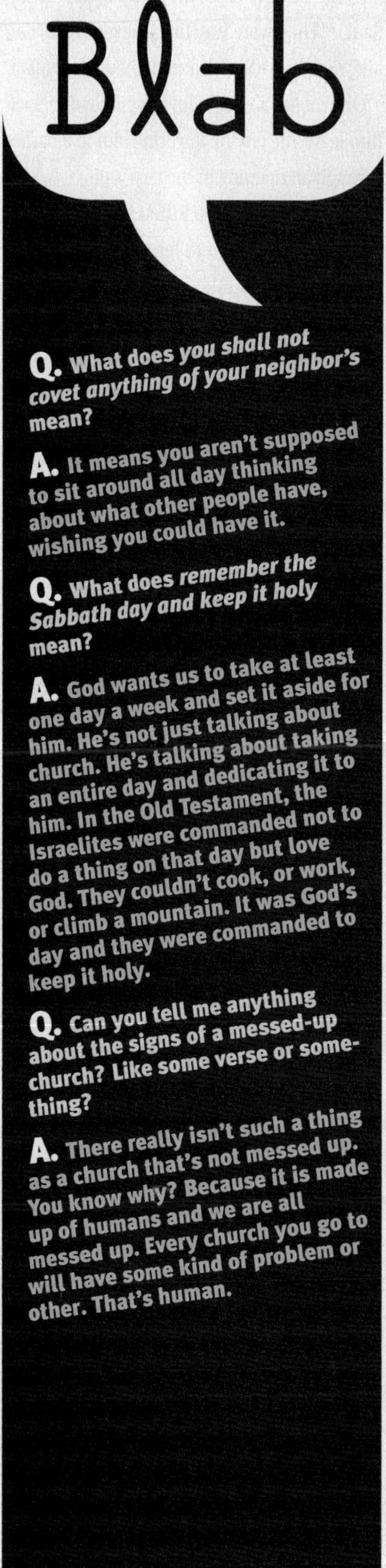

notes

9:11 Judas This is not either of the apostles named Judas.

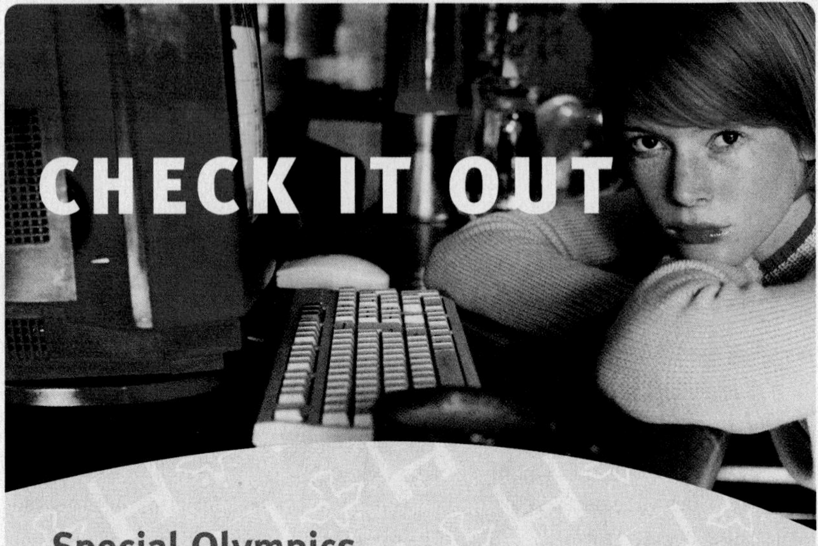

Special Olympics

Special Olympics is an international organization dedicated to empowering individuals with mental retardation to become physically fit, productive, and respected members of society through sports training and competition. Special Olympics offers children and adults with mental retardation year-round training and competition in twenty-six Olympic-type summer and winter sports. There is no cost to participate in Special Olympics.

Today Special Olympics serves one million people with mental retardation through more than two hundred programs in more than 150 countries. And the movement continues to reach out to the 170 million individuals with mental retardation around the world. Special Olympics has launched an ambitious worldwide growth campaign to double the number of athletes involved in the movement to two million by 2005.

To get involved, go to ***www.specialolympics.org.***

23 After many days, they made plans to kill
Saul. 24 They were watching the city gates day
and night, but Saul learned about their plan.
25 One night some followers of Saul helped
him leave the city by lowering him in a basket
through an opening in the city wall.

SAUL PREACHES IN JERUSALEM

26 When Saul went to Jerusalem, he tried to
join the group of followers, but they were all
afraid of him. They did not believe he was
really a follower. 27 But Barnabas accepted Saul
and took him to the apostles. Barnabas
explained to them that Saul had seen the Lord
on the road and the Lord had spoken to Saul.
Then he told them how boldly Saul had
preached in the name of Jesus in Damascus.

28 And so Saul stayed with the followers,
going everywhere in Jerusalem, preaching
boldly in the name of the Lord. 29 He would
often talk and argue with the Jewish people
who spoke Greek, but they were trying to kill
him. 30 When the followers learned about this,
they took Saul to Caesarea and from there sent
him to Tarsus.

31 The church everywhere in Judea, Galilee,
and Samaria had a time of peace and became
stronger. Respecting the Lord by the way they
lived, and being encouraged by the Holy Spirit,
the group of believers continued to grow.

PETER HEALS AENEAS

32 As Peter was traveling through all the
area, he visited God's people who lived in
Lydda. 33 There he met a man named Aeneas,
who was paralyzed and had not been able to
leave his bed for the past eight years. 34 Peter
said to him, "Aeneas, Jesus Christ heals you.
Stand up and make your bed." Aeneas stood up
immediately. 35 All the people living in Lydda
and on the Plain of Sharon saw him and turned
to the Lord.

PETER HEALS TABITHA

36 In the city of Joppa there was a follower
named Tabitha (whose Greek name was Dorcas).
She was always doing good deeds and kind
acts. 37 While Peter was in Lydda, Tabitha
became sick and died. Her body was washed
and put in a room upstairs. 38 Since Lydda is
near Joppa and the followers in Joppa heard that
Peter was in Lydda, they sent two messengers
to Peter. They begged him, "Hurry, please come
to us!" 39 So Peter got ready and went with them.
When he arrived, they took him to the
upstairs room where all the widows stood
around Peter, crying. They showed him the
shirts and coats Tabitha had made when she
was still alive. 40 Peter sent everyone out of the
room and kneeled and prayed. Then he turned
to the body and said, "Tabitha, stand up." She
opened her eyes, and when she saw Peter, she
sat up. 41 He gave her his hand and helped her
up. Then he called the saints and the widows
into the room and showed them that Tabitha
was alive. 42 People everywhere in Joppa
learned about this, and many believed in the
Lord. 43 Peter stayed in Joppa for many days
with a man named Simon who was a tanner.

PETER TEACHES CORNELIUS

10 At Caesarea there was a man named
Cornelius, an officer in the Italian
group of the Roman army. 2 Cornelius was a
religious man. He and all the other people who
lived in his house worshiped the true God. He
gave much of his money to the poor and prayed
to God often. 3 One afternoon about three
o'clock, Cornelius clearly saw a vision. An angel
of God came to him and said, "Cornelius!"

4Cornelius stared at the angel. He became afraid and said, "What do you want, Lord?"

The angel said, "God has heard your prayers. He has seen that you give to the poor, and he remembers you. 5Send some men now to Joppa to bring back a man named Simon who is also called Peter. 6He is staying with a man, also named Simon, who is a tanner and has a house beside the sea." 7When the angel who spoke to Cornelius left, Cornelius called two of his servants and a soldier, a religious man who worked for him. 8Cornelius explained everything to them and sent them to Joppa.

9About noon the next day as they came near Joppa, Peter was going up to the roof[n] to pray. 10He was hungry and wanted to eat, but while the food was being prepared, he had a vision. 11He saw heaven opened and something coming down that looked like a big sheet being lowered to earth by its four corners. 12In it were all kinds of animals, reptiles, and birds. 13Then a voice said to Peter, "Get up, Peter; kill and eat."

14But Peter said, "No, Lord! I have never eaten food that is unholy or unclean."

15But the voice said to him again, "God has made these things clean so don't call them 'unholy'!" 16This happened three times, and at once the sheet was taken back to heaven.

17While Peter was wondering what this vision meant, the men Cornelius sent had found Simon's house and were standing at the gate. 18They asked, "Is Simon Peter staying here?"

19While Peter was still thinking about the vision, the Spirit said to him, "Listen, three men are looking for you. 20Get up and go downstairs. Go with them without doubting, because I have sent them to you."

21So Peter went down to the men and said, "I am the one you are looking for. Why did you come here?"

22They said, "A holy angel spoke to Cornelius, an army officer and a good man; he worships God. All the people respect him. The angel told Cornelius to ask you to come to his house so that he can hear what you have to say." 23So Peter asked the men to come in and spend the night.

The next day Peter got ready and went with them, and some of the followers from Joppa joined him. 24On the following day they came to Caesarea. Cornelius was waiting for them and had called together his relatives and close friends. 25When Peter entered, Cornelius met him, fell at his feet, and worshiped him. 26But Peter helped him up, saying, "Stand up. I too am only a human." 27As he talked with Cornelius, Peter went inside where he saw many people gathered. 28He said, "You people understand that it is against our law for Jewish people to associate with or visit anyone who is not Jewish. But God has shown me that I should not call any person 'unholy' or 'unclean.' 29That is why I did not argue when I was asked to come here. Now, please tell me why you sent for me."

30Cornelius said, "Four days ago, I was praying in my house at this same time—three o'clock in the afternoon. Suddenly, there was a man standing before me wearing shining clothes. 31He said, 'Cornelius, God has heard your prayer and has seen that you give to the poor and remembers you. 32So send some men to Joppa and ask Simon Peter to come. Peter is staying in the house of a man, also named Simon, who is a tanner and has a house beside the sea.' 33So I sent for you immediately, and it was very good of you to come. Now we are all here before God to hear everything the Lord has commanded you to tell us."

TEENS WHO SMOKE ARE MORE LIKELY TO BECOME DRUG ABUSERS.

bible basics

Witnessing means sharing the truth about God with other people. In the Bible, Jesus tells his followers to share the news about him with the entire world. Today, we have missionaries who go all over the place sharing the Good News. You can witness through a relationship you have with a person, by sitting down and telling someone exactly what you believe, or by preaching in a crowded place.

notes

10:9 roof In Bible times houses were built with flat roofs. The roof was used for drying things such as flax and fruit. And it was used as an extra room, as a place for worship, and as a cool place to sleep in the summer.

TOPten

GREAT CHRISTIAN BOOKS

01	***Witnessing 101,*** **by Tim Baker**
02	***The Rules: Ten to Live By,*** **by M. Nicholas**
03	***Mission: Africa,*** **by various contemporary music artists**
04	***Wait for Me,*** **by Rebecca St. James**
05	***I Can Only Imagine,*** **by Mercy Me**
06	***The Big Bucks,*** **by Elizabeth Patton**
07	***Unfinished Work,*** **by Kevin Max**
08	***Why So Many Gods?,*** **by Tim Baker and Kate Etue**
09	***Diary of an Anorexic Girl,*** **by Morgan Menzie**
10	***Now What?,*** **by Loretta Andrews**

34Peter began to speak: "I really understand
now that to God every person is the same. 35In
every country God accepts anyone who worships him and does what is right. 36You know
the message that God has sent to the people of
Israel is the Good News that peace has come
through Jesus Christ. Jesus is the Lord of all
people! 37You know what has happened all
over Judea, beginning in Galilee after John[n]
preached to the people about baptism. 38You
know about Jesus from Nazareth, that God
gave him the Holy Spirit and power. You know
how Jesus went everywhere doing good and
healing those who were ruled by the devil,
because God was with him. 39We saw what
Jesus did in Judea and in Jerusalem, but the
Jews in Jerusalem killed him by hanging him
on a cross. 40Yet, on the third day, God raised
Jesus to life and caused him to be seen, 41not
by all the people, but only by the witnesses
God had already chosen. And we are those witnesses who ate and drank with him after he
was raised from the dead. 42He told us to
preach to the people and to tell them that he is
the one whom God chose to be the judge of
the living and the dead. 43All the prophets say
it is true that all who believe in Jesus will be
forgiven of their sins through Jesus' name."

44While Peter was still saying this, the Holy
Spirit came down on all those who were listening. 45The Jewish believers who came with
Peter were amazed that the gift of the Holy
Spirit had been given even to the nations.
46These believers heard them speaking in different languages[n] and praising God. Then
Peter said, 47"Can anyone keep these people
from being baptized with water? They have
received the Holy Spirit just as we did!" 48So
Peter ordered that they be baptized in the
name of Jesus Christ. Then they asked Peter to
stay with them for a few days.

PETER RETURNS TO JERUSALEM

11 The apostles and the believers in
Judea heard that some who were
not Jewish had accepted God's teaching too.
2But when Peter came to Jerusalem, some people argued with him. 3They said, "You went
into the homes of people who are not circumcised and ate with them!"

4So Peter explained the whole story to
them. 5He said, "I was in the city of Joppa, and
while I was praying, I had a vision. I saw something that looked like a big sheet being lowered from heaven by its four corners. It came
very close to me. 6I looked inside it and saw animals, wild beasts, reptiles, and birds. 7I heard a
voice say to me, 'Get up, Peter. Kill and eat.' 8But
I said, 'No, Lord! I have never eaten anything that
is unholy or unclean.' 9But the voice from
heaven spoke again, 'God has made these things
clean, so don't call them unholy.' 10This happened three times. Then the whole thing was
taken back to heaven. 11Right then three men
who were sent to me from Caesarea came to the
house where I was staying. 12The Spirit told me
to go with them without doubting. These six
believers here also went with me, and we entered

RELATIONSHIPS

Are you on the same page spiritually as your guy? How important is your relationship with God to you, on a scale of one to ten (with one being the most important)? How important is it for him? Do you want to go to church every week? Does he? Does he like to pray over every meal, and you get embarrassed in restaurants? This kind of thing is real important if you're thinking long-term about this crush. Make sure you're able to pray together and for each other. Your spiritual life should always be your priority—make sure God's okay with the relationship before you pursue it further.

notes

10:37 John John the Baptist, who preached to people about Christ's coming (Luke 3). **10:46 languages** This can also be translated "tongues."

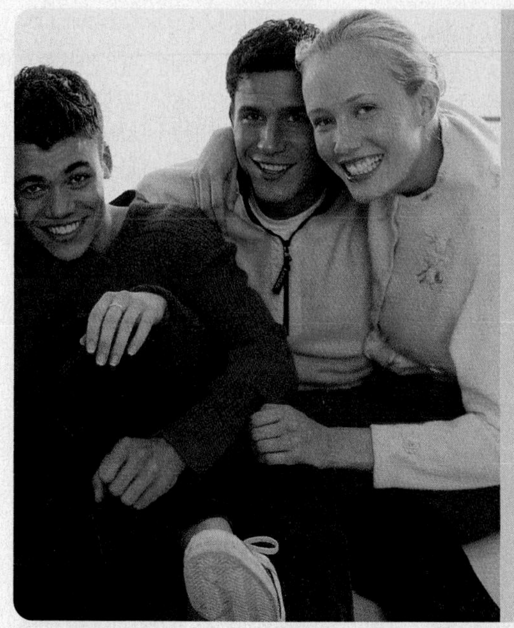

LEARN IT & LIVE IT

Galatians 1:12:
Learn It: The gospel is received through the revelation of Jesus Christ.
Live It: Do you know someone who needs to hear the gospel? Then they need to hear about Jesus. Share the story tactfully and casually, without making it come across like an intervention. The person will be much more willing to receive Jesus' love this way.

Galatians 2:21:
Learn It: Christ died for nothing if the law could make us right with God.
Live It: Don't stress if you mess up today. You're bound to because you're human. Just run to Christ and receive his forgiveness. We aren't saved by doing everything perfectly, but by Christ's gracious work on the cross.

Galatians 3:28:
Learn It: There is no longer black or white; there is no longer poor or rich; there is no longer male or female; for we are all the same in Christ Jesus.
Live It: When you look at people today, look for their soul. Try to get to the point where you don't even notice the color of their skin or hair, but be able to give details about their personality, hopes, dreams, etc.

the house of Cornelius. [13]He told us about the
angel he saw standing in his house. The angel
said to him, 'Send some men to Joppa and
invite Simon Peter to come. [14]By the words he
will say to you, you and all your family will be
saved.' [15]When I began my speech, the Holy
Spirit came on them just as he came on us
at the beginning. [16]Then I remembered the
words of the Lord. He said, 'John baptized
with water, but you will be baptized with
the Holy Spirit.' [17]Since God gave them
the same gift he gave us who believed in
the Lord Jesus Christ, how could I stop the
work of God?"

[18]When the believers heard this, they
stopped arguing. They praised God and
said, "So God is allowing even other
nations to turn to him and live."

THE GOOD NEWS COMES TO ANTIOCH

[19]Many of the believers were scattered
when they were persecuted after Stephen
was killed. Some of them went as far as
Phoenicia, Cyprus, and Antioch telling the
message to others, but only to Jews. [20]Some of
these believers were people from Cyprus and
Cyrene. When they came to Antioch, they
spoke also to Greeks, telling them the Good
News about the Lord Jesus. [21]The Lord was
helping the believers, and a large group of people believed and turned to the Lord.

[22]The church in Jerusalem heard about all
of this, so they sent Barnabas to Antioch.
[23-24]Barnabas was a good man, full of the Holy
Spirit and full of faith. When he reached
Antioch and saw how God had blessed the
people, he was glad. He encouraged all the
believers in Antioch always to obey the Lord
with all their hearts, and many people
became followers of the Lord.

GUYS SPEAK OUT

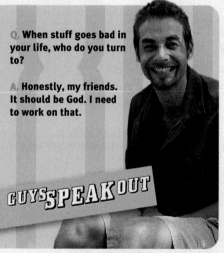

Q. When stuff goes bad in your life, who do you turn to?

A. Honestly, my friends. It should be God. I need to work on that.

[25]Then Barnabas went to the city of Tarsus
to look for Saul, [26]and when he found Saul, he
brought him to Antioch. For a whole year Saul
and Barnabas met with the church and taught
many people there. In Antioch the followers
were called Christians for the first time.

[27]About that time some prophets came
from Jerusalem to Antioch. [28]One of them,
named Agabus, stood up and spoke with
the help of the Holy Spirit. He said, "A
very hard time is coming to the whole
world. There will be no food to eat." (This
happened when Claudius ruled.) [29]The
believers all decided to help the followers
who lived in Judea, as much as each one
could. [30]They gathered the money and
gave it to Barnabas and Saul, who brought
it to the elders in Judea.

HEROD AGRIPPA HURTS THE CHURCH

12 During that same time King
Herod began to mistreat some
who belonged to the church. [2]He ordered
James, the brother of John, to be killed by the
sword. [3]Herod saw that some of the people
liked this, so he decided to arrest Peter, too.
(This happened during the time of the Feast of
Unleavened Bread.)

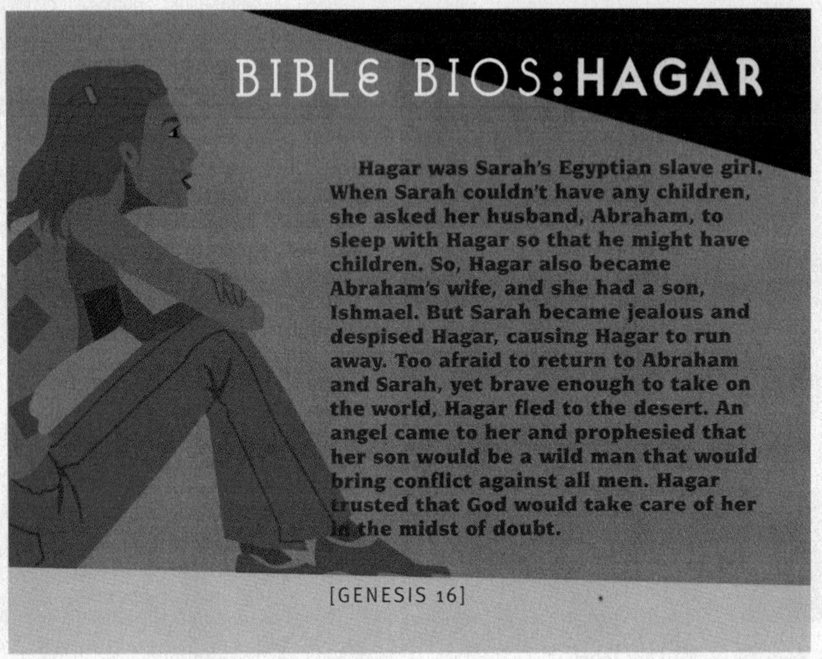

BIBLE BIOS:HAGAR
Hagar was Sarah's Egyptian slave girl. When Sarah couldn't have any children, she asked her husband, Abraham, to sleep with Hagar so that he might have children. So, Hagar also became Abraham's wife, and she had a son, Ishmael. But Sarah became jealous and despised Hagar, causing Hagar to run away. Too afraid to return to Abraham and Sarah, yet brave enough to take on the world, Hagar fled to the desert. An angel came to her and prophesied that her son would be a wild man that would bring conflict against all men. Hagar trusted that God would take care of her in the midst of doubt.
[GENESIS 16]

[4]After Herod arrested Peter, he put him in
jail and handed him over to be guarded by six-
teen soldiers. Herod planned to bring Peter
before the people for trial after the Passover
Feast. [5]So Peter was kept in jail, but the church
prayed earnestly to God for him.

PETER LEAVES THE JAIL

[6]The night before Herod was to bring him
to trial, Peter was sleeping between two soldiers, bound with two chains. Other soldiers
were guarding the door of the jail. [7]Suddenly,
an angel of the Lord stood there, and a light
shined in the cell. The angel struck Peter on
the side and woke him up. "Hurry! Get up!"
the angel said. And the chains fell off Peter's
hands. [8]Then the angel told him, "Get dressed
and put on your sandals." And Peter did. Then
the angel said, "Put on your coat and follow
me." [9]So Peter followed him out, but he did not
know if what the angel was doing was real; he
thought he might be seeing a vision. [10]They
went past the first and second guards and came
to the iron gate that separated them from the
city. The gate opened by itself for them, and
they went through it. When they had walked
down one street, the angel suddenly left him.

[11]Then Peter realized what had happened.
He thought, "Now I know that the Lord really
sent his angel to me. He rescued me from
Herod and from all the things the people
thought would happen."

[12]When he considered this, he went to the
home of Mary, the mother of John Mark. Many
people were gathered there, praying. [13]Peter
knocked on the outside door, and a servant girl
named Rhoda came to answer it. [14]When she
recognized Peter's voice, she was so happy she
forgot to open the door. Instead, she ran inside
and told the group, "Peter is at the door!"

[15]They said to her, "You are crazy!" But she
kept on saying it was true, so they said, "It
must be Peter's angel."

[16]Peter continued to knock, and when they
opened the door, they saw him and were
amazed. [17]Peter made a sign with his hand to
tell them to be quiet. He explained how the
Lord led him out of the jail, and he said, "Tell
James and the other believers what happened." Then he left to go to another place.

[18]The next day the soldiers were very upset
and wondered what had happened to Peter.
[19]Herod looked everywhere for him but could
not find him. So he questioned the guards and
ordered that they be killed.

THE DEATH OF HEROD AGRIPPA

Later Herod moved from Judea and went to
the city of Caesarea, where he stayed. [20]Herod
was very angry with the people of Tyre and
Sidon, but the people of those cities all came
in a group to him. After convincing Blastus,
the king's personal servant, to be on their side,
they asked Herod for peace, because their
country got its food from his country.

[21]On a chosen day Herod put on his royal
robes, sat on his throne, and made a speech to
the people. [22]They shouted, "This is the voice
of a god, not a human!" [23]Because Herod did
not give the glory to God, an angel of the Lord
immediately caused him to become sick, and
he was eaten by worms and died.

[24]God's message continued to spread and
reach people.

[25]After Barnabas and Saul finished their
task in Jerusalem, they returned to Antioch,
taking John Mark with them.

BARNABAS AND SAUL ARE CHOSEN

13 In the church at Antioch there
were these prophets and teachers:
Barnabas, Simeon (also called Niger), Lucius
(from the city of Cyrene), Manaen (who had
grown up with Herod, the ruler), and Saul.
[2]They were all worshiping the Lord and giving
up eating for a certain time.[n] During this time
the Holy Spirit said to them, "Set apart for me
Barnabas and Saul to do a special work for
which I have chosen them."

57% OF TEENS LIVE WITH BOTH THEIR PARENTS.

notes

13:2 giving up . . . time This is called "fasting." The people would give up eating for a special time of prayer and worship to God. It was also done sometimes to show sadness and disappointment.

3So after they gave up eating and prayed, they laid their hands on[n] Barnabas and Saul and sent them out.

BARNABAS AND SAUL IN CYPRUS

4Barnabas and Saul, sent out by the Holy Spirit, went to the city of Seleucia. From there they sailed to the island of Cyprus. 5When they came to Salamis, they preached the Good News of God in the synagogues. John Mark was with them to help.

6They went across the whole island to Paphos where they met a magician named Bar-Jesus. He was a false prophet 7who always stayed close to Sergius Paulus, the governor and a smart man. He asked Barnabas and Saul to come to him, because he wanted to hear the message of God. 8But Elymas, the magician, was against them. (Elymas is the name for Bar-Jesus in the Greek language.) He tried to stop the governor from believing in Jesus. 9But Saul, who was also called Paul, was filled with the Holy Spirit. He looked straight at Elymas 10and said, "You son of the devil! You are an enemy of everything that is right! You are full of evil tricks and lies, always trying to change the Lord's truths into lies. 11Now the Lord will touch you, and you will be blind. For a time you will not be able to see anything—not even the light from the sun."

Then everything became dark for Elymas, and he walked around, trying to find someone to lead him by the hand. 12When the governor saw this, he believed because he was amazed at the teaching about the Lord.

PAUL AND BARNABAS LEAVE CYPRUS

13Paul and those with him sailed from Paphos and came to Perga, in Pamphylia. There John Mark left them to return to Jerusalem. 14They continued their trip from Perga and went to Antioch, a city in Pisidia. On the Sabbath day they went into the synagogue and sat down. 15After the law of Moses and the writings of the prophets were read, the leaders of the synagogue sent a message to Paul and Barnabas: "Brothers, if you have any message that will encourage the people, please speak."

16Paul stood up, raised his hand, and said, "You Israelites and you who worship God, please listen! 17The God of the Israelites chose our ancestors. He made the people great during the time they lived in Egypt, and he brought them out of that country with great power. 18And he was patient with them for forty years in the desert. 19God destroyed seven nations in the land of Canaan and gave the land to his people. 20All this happened in about four hundred fifty years.

"After this, God gave them judges until the time of Samuel the prophet. 21Then the people asked for a king, so God gave them Saul son of Kish. Saul was from the tribe of Benjamin and was king for forty years. 22After God took him away, God made David their king. God said about him: 'I have found in David son of Jesse the kind of man I want. He will do all I want him to do.' 23So God has brought Jesus, one of David's descendants, to Israel to be its Savior, as he promised. 24Before Jesus came, John[n] preached to all the people of Israel about a baptism of changed hearts and lives. 25When he was finishing his work, he said, 'Who do you think I am? I am not the Christ. He is coming later, and I am not worthy to untie his sandals.'

26"Brothers, sons of the family of Abraham, and others who worship God, listen! The news about this salvation has been sent to us. 27Those who live in Jerusalem and their leaders did not realize that Jesus was the Savior. They did not understand the words that the prophets wrote, which are read every Sabbath day. But they made them come true when they said Jesus was guilty. 28They could not find

Psalm 36:5
LORD, your love reaches to the heavens, your loyalty to the skies.

Blab

Q. **In the Bible God tells us not to be jealous because it is a sin, but at the same time the Bible says that God is very jealous. How can this be?**

A. **When humans are jealous it is sinful because it is out of rivalry, envy, competition, or anger that we are jealous. We covet what sinners have and get to do. We are sinful. But with God his jealousy is righteous. In most instances *jealous*, for God, means "provoked to anger," or "to be zealous." His holiness does not tolerate competing idols or gods, or sin. He's protective in his jealousy not envious or covetous.**

Q. **Having sex at a young age—is it bad? Will God still accept you?**

A. **God will always accept you, but that isn't the real question. The real question is, *Do you love God?* When people love someone they want to do things to please them. Having sex when you are young and unmarried doesn't please God. You can never get back what you have given away. It is a gift from God intended only for you and your husband. Wait for marriage to open that precious gift.**

Q. **I wonder if mythology is against the Lord?**

A. **A myth is a traditional story about what people believe. Jesus also used stories when he preached. We call them parables. He used story to explain his worldview to the people of his time. There's nothing sinful about it as long as it is taken in context, as with most things; it needs to be seen for what it is—a story—and enjoyed as such.**

notes

13:3 laid their hands on The laying on of hands had many purposes, including the giving of a blessing, power, or authority. **13:24 John** John the Baptist, who preached to people about Christ's coming (Luke 3).

ISSUES: School

You may think, *Sometimes I wonder why I'm going to all this trouble to learn geometry. I'm never going to use it in my real life anyway. It's just a waste of time.* Well, that's not true. The Bible says to do whatever you do to the glory of God. Why? Because he put you on this earth and has ordained the steps you will take. There's a reason he wants you to learn the things you're learning. Trust him, and do your best. Take pride in becoming an intelligent, educated woman.

any real reason for Jesus to be put to death, but
they asked Pilate to have him killed. 29When
they had done to him all that the Scriptures
had said, they took him down from the cross
and laid him in a tomb. 30But God raised him
up from the dead! 31After this, for many days,
those who had gone with Jesus from Galilee to
Jerusalem saw him. They are now his witnesses
to the people. 32We tell you the Good News
about the promise God made to our ancestors.
33God has made this promise come true for us,
his children, by raising Jesus from the dead.
We read about this also in Psalm 2:

'You are my Son.
Today I have become your Father.' *Psalm 2:7*

34God raised Jesus from the dead, and he will
never go back to the grave and become dust.
So God said:

'I will give you the holy and sure blessings
that I promised to David.' *Isaiah 55:3*

35But in another place God says:

'You will not let your Holy One rot.' *Psalm 16:10*

36David did God's will during his lifetime.
Then he died and was buried beside his ancestors, and his body did rot in the grave. 37But
the One God raised from the dead did not rot
in the grave. 38-39Brothers, understand what
we are telling you: You can have forgiveness of
your sins through Jesus. The law of Moses
could not free you from your sins. But through
Jesus everyone who believes is free from all
sins. 40Be careful! Don't let what the prophets
said happen to you:

41'Listen, you people who doubt!
You can wonder, and then die.
I will do something in your lifetime
that you won't believe even when you
are told about it!' " *Habakkuk 1:5*

42While Paul and Barnabas were leaving
the synagogue, the people asked them to tell
them more about these things on the next
Sabbath. 43When the meeting was over, many
people with those who had changed to worship God followed Paul and Barnabas from
that place. Paul and Barnabas were persuading
them to continue trusting in God's grace.

44On the next Sabbath day, almost everyone in the city came to hear the word of the
Lord. 45Seeing the crowd, the Jewish people
became very jealous and said insulting things
and argued against what Paul said. 46But Paul
and Barnabas spoke very boldly, saying, "We
must speak the message of God to you first.
But you refuse to listen. You are
judging yourselves not worthy
of having eternal life! So we
will now go to the people of
other nations. 47This is
what the Lord told us to do, saying:

'I have made you a light for the
nations;
you will show people all over the world
the way to be saved.' " *Isaiah 49:6*

48When those who were not Jewish heard
Paul say this, they were happy and gave honor
to the message of the Lord. And the people
who were chosen to have life forever believed
the message.

49So the message of the Lord was spreading
through the whole country. 50But the Jewish
people stirred up some of the important religious women and the leaders of the city. They
started trouble against Paul and Barnabas and
forced them out of their area. 51So Paul and
Barnabas shook the dust off their feet[n] and
went to Iconium. 52But the followers were
filled with joy and the Holy Spirit.

Psalm 36:7
God, your love is so precious! You protect people in the shadow of your wings.

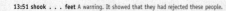

PAUL AND BARNABAS IN ICONIUM

14 In Iconium, Paul and Barnabas
went as usual to the synagogue.
They spoke so well that a great many Jews and
Greeks believed. 2But some people who did
not believe excited the others and turned
them against the believers. 3Paul and
Barnabas stayed in Iconium a long time and
spoke bravely for the Lord. He
showed that their message
about his grace was true by
giving them the power to
work miracles and signs.
4But the city was divided.
Some of the people agreed with the
Jews, and others believed the apostles.

5Some who were not Jews, some Jews, and
some of their rulers wanted to mistreat Paul
and Barnabas and to stone them to death.
6When Paul and Barnabas learned about this,
they ran away to Lystra and Derbe, cities in

notes

13:51 shook . . . feet A warning. It showed that they had rejected these people.

July

1

Pray for a Person of Influence: Today is Liv Tyler's birthday.

2

4

Independence Day: celebrate with those you love.

5

6

Today write a letter to someone you care about.

7

8

9

Read the paper today and pray for those God shows to you.

10

11

Eric Liddell—see *Chariots of Fire*—won the Olympic gold for the 400-meter race in 1924.

12

Pray for a Person of Influence: Today is Adrienne Liesching's (from The Benjamin Gate) birthday!

13

14

Buy a sibling an ice-cream cone today to show them that you care.

15

16

17

18

Pray that God will show you something wonderful through your Bible reading today.

19

Elizabeth Cady Stanton led the first women's rights conference in 1848.

20

First moon landing—ask your mom where she was that day.

21

22

23

Catch a firefly tonight and pray for someone special as you let it go.

24

25

26

Pray for a Person of Influence: Rebecca St. James's birthday.

27

28

29

Before you go to sleep tonight, pray for God to be in your thoughts.

30

31

Clean your room today without having to be asked.

Lycaonia, and to the areas around those cities.
[7]They announced the Good News there, too.

PAUL IN LYSTRA AND DERBE

[8]In Lystra there sat a man who had been
born crippled; he had never walked. [9]As this
man was listening to Paul speak, Paul looked
straight at him and saw that he believed God
could heal him. [10]So he cried out, "Stand up
on your feet!" The man jumped up and began
walking around. [11]When the crowds saw what
Paul did, they shouted in the Lycaonian language, "The gods have become like humans
and have come down to us!" [12]Then the people began to call Barnabas "Zeus"[n] and Paul
"Hermes,"[n] because he was the main speaker.
[13]The priest in the temple of Zeus, which was
near the city, brought some bulls and flowers
to the city gates. He and the people wanted to
offer a sacrifice to Paul and Barnabas. [14]But
when the apostles, Barnabas and Paul, heard
about it, they tore their clothes. They ran in
among the people, shouting, [15]"Friends, why
are you doing these things? We are only
human beings like you. We are bringing you
the Good News and are telling you to turn
away from these worthless things and turn to
the living God. He is the One who made the
sky, the earth, the sea, and everything in them.
[16]In the past, God let all the nations do what
they wanted. [17]Yet he proved he is real by
showing kindness, by giving you rain from
heaven and crops at the right times, by giving
you food and filling your hearts with joy."
[18]Even with these words, they were barely
able to keep the crowd from offering sacrifices
to them.

[19]Then some evil people came from Antioch
and Iconium and persuaded the people to turn
against Paul. So they threw stones at him and
dragged him out of town, thinking they had
killed him. [20]But the followers gathered
around him, and he got up and went back into
the town. The next day he and Barnabas left
and went to the city of Derbe.

THE RETURN TO ANTIOCH IN SYRIA

[21]Paul and Barnabas told the Good News in
Derbe, and many became followers. Paul and
Barnabas returned to Lystra, Iconium, and
Antioch, [22]making the followers of Jesus
stronger and helping them stay in the faith. They
said, "We must suffer many things to enter God's
kingdom." [23]They chose elders for each church,
by praying and giving up eating for a certain
time.[n] These elders had trusted the Lord, so
Paul and Barnabas put them in the Lord's care.

[24]Then they went through Pisidia and came
to Pamphylia. [25]When they had preached the
message in Perga, they went down to Attalia.
[26]And from there they sailed away to Antioch
where the believers had put them into God's
care and had sent them out to do this work.
Now they had finished.

[27]When they arrived in Antioch, Paul and
Barnabas gathered the church together. They
told the church all about what God had done
with them and how God had made it possible

43% OF TEENS TALK ABOUT RELIGION IN A TYPICAL DAY.

LEARN IT & LIVE IT

Galatians 4:4-5:
Learn It: God sent his Son so that we could become his.
Live It: Did you know that in Bible times adopted children could not be cut off from the family? Children born into the family could, but adopted children couldn't. This is another example of God's love for us. Meditate on that for fifteen minutes today.

Galatians 5:6:
Learn It: The only thing that counts is faith working through love.
Live It: What are you striving so hard to achieve? Is it faith? Look at your calendar today and make sure that your priorities are in line with Scripture. Faith and love should be at the top of the list. Are they?

Galatians 5:26:
Learn It: Let us not become conceited, competing against one another, envying one another.
Live It: Are you a toxic person? Do you constantly try to be better, prettier, and smarter than everyone else around? 'Cause if that is your goal, it's gonna show in the way you act. Be gracious today. Make an effort to let someone else get the attention.

notes

14:12 "Zeus" The Greeks believed in many false gods, of whom Zeus was most important. **14:12 "Hermes"** The Greeks believed he was a messenger for the other gods. **14:23 giving . . . time** This is called "fasting." The people would give up eating for a special time of prayer and worship to God. It was also done sometimes to show sadness and disappointment.

for those who were not Jewish to believe.
28 And they stayed there a long time with the
followers.

THE MEETING AT JERUSALEM

15 Then some people came to Antioch
from Judea and began teaching the
non-Jewish believers: "You cannot be
saved if you are not circumcised as Moses
taught us." 2 Paul and Barnabas were
against this teaching and argued with
them about it. So the church decided to
send Paul, Barnabas, and some others to
Jerusalem where they could talk more
about this with the apostles and elders.

3 The church helped them leave on the
trip, and they went through the countries
of Phoenicia and Samaria, telling all about
how the other nations had turned to God.
This made all the believers very happy.
4 When they arrived in Jerusalem, they
were welcomed by the apostles, the elders,
and the church. Paul, Barnabas, and the others
told about everything God had done with them.
5 But some of the believers who belonged to the
Pharisee group came forward and said, "The
non-Jewish believers must be circumcised. They
must be told to obey the law of Moses."

6 The apostles and the elders gathered to
consider this problem. 7 After a long debate,
Peter stood up and said to them, "Brothers,
you know that in the early days God chose me
from among you to preach the Good News to
the nations. They heard the Good News from
me, and they believed. 8 God, who knows the
thoughts of everyone, accepted them. He
showed this to us by giving them the Holy
Spirit, just as he did to us. 9 To God, those people are not different from us. When they
believed, he made their hearts pure. 10 So now
why are you testing God by putting a heavy
load around the necks of the non-Jewish
believers? It is a load that neither we nor our
ancestors were able to carry. 11 But we believe
that we and they too will be saved by the grace
of the Lord Jesus."

GUYS SPEAK OUT
Q. How serious should high school relationships be?
A. They should not be too serious—there's much more important stuff to focus on at that point in life.

12 Then the whole group became quiet.
They listened to Paul and Barnabas tell about
all the miracles and signs that God did through
them among the people. 13 After they finished
speaking, James said, "Brothers, listen to me.
14 Simon has told us how God showed his love
for those people. For the first time he is accepting from among them a people to be his own.
15 The words of the prophets agree with this too:
16 'After these things I will return.

The kingdom of David is like a fallen tent.
But I will rebuild its ruins,
and I will set it up.
17 Then those people who are left alive may
ask the Lord for help,
and the other nations that belong to me,
says the Lord,
who will make it happen.
18 And these things have been known for a
long time.' *Amos 9:11-12*

19 "So I think we should not bother the other
people who are turning to God. 20 Instead, we
should write a letter to them telling them these
things: Stay away from food that has been
offered to idols (which makes it unclean),
any kind of sexual sin, eating animals that
have been strangled, and blood. 21 They
should do these things, because for a long
time in every city the law of Moses has
been taught. And it is still read in the synagogue every Sabbath day."

LETTER TO NON-JEWISH BELIEVERS

22 The apostles, the elders, and the whole
church decided to send some of their men
with Paul and Barnabas to Antioch. They
chose Judas Barsabbas and Silas, who
were respected by the believers. 23 They
sent the following letter with them:

From the apostles and elders, your
brothers.

To all the non-Jewish believers in
Antioch, Syria, and Cilicia:

Greetings!

24 We have heard that some of our group
have come to you and said things that trouble and upset you. But we did not tell them
to do this. 25 We have all agreed to choose
some messengers and send them to you
with our dear friends Barnabas and Paul—
26 people who have given their lives to serve
our Lord Jesus Christ. 27 So we are sending
Judas and Silas, who will tell you the same
things. 28 It has pleased the Holy Spirit that
you should not have a heavy load to carry,
and we agree. You need to do only these
things: 29 Stay away from any food that
has been offered to idols, eating any animals that have been strangled, and blood,
and any kind of sexual sin. If you stay
away from these things, you will do well.

Good-bye.

41% OF TEENS TALK ABOUT POLITICS IN A TYPICAL DAY.

Acts 11:26

After Jesus returned to heaven, the apostles and other followers became known as Christians. It literally means "belonging to the party of Jesus." At a restaurant, you may wait with a group until the host calls "table for the Smith party." Everyone who is with your group gets up to be seated. Each one of you is different, but you all belong together. You are recognized as a distinct group. Your party is separate from all the other people in the restaurant. In Antioch, the followers of Christ had become recognized as a separate group of people who belonged together. Followers today are still called Christians, meaning that we belong with all the others who believe in Christ. It is a high privilege to carry the banner of Christ along with those who have gone before us.

30So they left Jerusalem and went to Antioch where they gathered the church and gave them the letter. 31When they read it, they were very happy because of the encouraging message. 32Judas and Silas, who were also prophets, said many things to encourage the believers and make them stronger. 33After some time Judas and Silas were sent off in peace by the believers, and they went back to those who had sent them. 34[n]

Psalm 40:11
LORD, do not hold back your mercy from me; let your love and truth always protect me.

35But Paul and Barnabas stayed in Antioch and, along with many others, preached the Good News and taught the people the message of the Lord.

PAUL AND BARNABAS SEPARATE

36After some time, Paul said to Barnabas, "We should go back to all those towns where we preached the message of the Lord. Let's visit the believers and see how they are doing."

"THAT NIGHT PAUL SAW IN A VISION A MAN FROM MACEDONIA."

37Barnabas wanted to take John Mark with them, 38but he had left them at Pamphylia; he did not continue with them in the work. So Paul did not think it was a good idea to take him. 39Paul and Barnabas had such a serious argument about this that they separated and went different ways. Barnabas took Mark and sailed to Cyprus, 40but Paul chose Silas and left. The believers in Antioch put Paul into the Lord's care, 41and he went through Syria and Cilicia, giving strength to the churches.

TIMOTHY GOES WITH PAUL

16 Paul came to Derbe and Lystra, where a follower named Timothy lived. Timothy's mother was Jewish and a believer, but his father was a Greek.

2The believers in Lystra and Iconium respected Timothy and said good things about him. 3Paul wanted Timothy to travel with him, but all the people living in that area knew that Timothy's father was Greek. So Paul circumcised Timothy to please his mother's people. 4Paul and those with him traveled from town to town and gave the decisions made by the apostles and elders in Jerusalem for the people to obey. 5So the churches became stronger in the faith and grew larger every day.

PAUL IS CALLED OUT OF ASIA

6Paul and those with him went through the areas of Phrygia and Galatia since the Holy Spirit did not let them preach the Good News in the country of Asia. 7When they came near the country of Mysia, they tried to go into Bithynia, but the Spirit of Jesus did not let them. 8So they passed by Mysia and went to Troas. 9That night Paul saw in a vision a man from Macedonia. The man stood and begged, "Come over to Macedonia and help us." 10After Paul had seen the vision, we immediately prepared to leave for Macedonia, understanding that God had called us to tell the Good News to those people.

LYDIA BECOMES A CHRISTIAN

11We left Troas and sailed straight to the island of Samothrace. The next day we sailed to Neapolis.[n] 12Then we went by land to Philippi, a Roman colony[n] and the leading city in that part of Macedonia. We stayed there for several days.

13On the Sabbath day we went outside the city gate to the river where we thought we would find a special place for prayer. Some women had gathered there, so we sat down and talked with them. 14One of the listeners was a woman named Lydia from the city of Thyatira whose job was selling purple cloth. She worshiped God, and he opened her mind to pay attention to what Paul was saying. 15She and all the people in her house were

15:34 Verse 34 Some Greek copies add verse 34: ". . . but Silas decided to remain there." **16:11 Neapolis** City in Macedonia. It was the first city Paul visited on the continent of Europe. **16:12 Roman colony** A town begun by Romans with Roman laws, customs, and privileges.

QUIZ

WHAT'S YOUR SPIRITUAL GIFT?

RATE YOURSELF FROM 1 (REALLY *NOT* ME) TO 10 (DEFINITELY ME) ON EACH OF THE FOLLOWING STATEMENTS.

1. I'M GONNA STAND UP FOR WHAT I BELIEVE, EVEN IF NO ONE ELSE BACKS ME UP. ____
2. I'M WILLING TO WORK ON A PROJECT UNTIL IT'S DONE AND DONE WELL. ____
3. I'M USUALLY THE LEADER IN THE GROUP—CHEERLEADING CAPTAIN, MOVIE PICKER, PARTY PLANNER. ____
4. I DON'T SPEND A LOT OF MONEY ON MYSELF.
5. I REALLY LOVE HELPING OUT PEOPLE WHO HAVE PROBLEMS—LIKE ADDICTIONS OR DISEASES. ____
6. I THINK IT'S MORE IMPORTANT TO LIVE OUT WHAT YOU BELIEVE THAN TO KNOW ALL THE TECHNICAL STUFF. ____
7. I LOVE READING MY BIBLE—IT'S HONESTLY MY FAVORITE BOOK. ____
8. I LIKE TO TELL PEOPLE AT SCHOOL ABOUT MY FAITH—LIKE, TALK TO THEM ABOUT IT. ____
9. I'M PRETTY GOOD ABOUT ALWAYS REMEMBERING TO TITHE. ____
10. I'M A TRENDSETTER; I PLAN FOR THE FUTURE AND PEOPLE FOLLOW ME. ____
11. IT'S REALLY IMPORTANT TO ME THAT MY FRIENDS ALL BECOME REALLY STRONG CHRISTIANS. ____
12. I HAVE VOLUNTEERED TO LEAD SOME BIBLE STUDIES AT SCHOOL OR CHURCH 'CAUSE I LOVE TO SHARE WHAT I KNOW ABOUT THE BIBLE WITH OTHERS. ____
13. AS LONG AS WHAT I'M DOING HELPS OUT THE CAUSE, I REALLY DON'T CARE WHO GETS THE CREDIT. ____
14. I GET UPSET WHEN THE PASTOR AT CHURCH DOESN'T TALK ABOUT THE SINS THAT ARE OBVIOUSLY GOING ON IN OUR CHURCH. ____
15. I'M GOOD AT GETTING OTHER PEOPLE TO HELP OUT WHEN THERE'S A CHARITY EVENT OR MISSIONS TRIP. ____
16. I TRY TO FIND WAYS TO SAVE MY MONEY SO I CAN GIVE MORE TO GOD. ____
17. I DON'T MIND DOING GRUNT WORK IF IT MEANS THAT GOD'S WORD WILL REACH MORE PEOPLE. ____
18. I WANT PEOPLE TO BECOME CHRISTIANS SO BAD THAT I'LL TELL THEM ABOUT GOD EVEN IF THEY DON'T WANT TO HEAR ABOUT IT. ____

RESULTS:

Add together your rating from questions:

a) 1 and 14: ________

b) 2 and 13: ________

c) 6 and 15: ________

d) 7 and 12: ________

e) 9 and 16: ________

f) 4 and 10: ________

g) 5 and 17: ________

h) 8 and 18: ________

i) 3 and 11: ________

WHICHEVER GROUP GIVES YOU THE HIGHEST NUMBER IS YOUR STRONGEST SPIRITUAL GIFT.

a) PROPHECY—ability to see the influence of evil and warn other Christians

b) HELPING—ability to help without needing to get credit

c) EXHORTATION—ability to show others practical ways to serve God

d) TEACHING—desire to study the Bible and share knowledge with others

e) GIVING—desire to give your things for God's work

f) ADMINISTRATION—ability to manage resources efficiently

g) SHOWING MERCY—ability to show comfort and support to people who need help

h) EVANGELISM—ability to lead unbelievers to Christ

i) SHEPHERDING—ability to lead a group of Christians

Q. Should cloning be allowed?

A. Cloning is a pretty sticky situation. The first animal cloned was Dolly, a sheep. This was a pretty celebrated event in the world of science. It marked man's achievement like never before. When Dolly was cloned, however, it brought up the possibility of cloning people. Many people believe that this is unethical. This is man trying to be God. Man is deciding when to bring life into the world and when to make it leave. This is clearly God's job.

Q. What do I do if my parents only let me use KJV? They say the modern versions aren't accurate, but I can't understand it!

A. Grab a couple of different versions of the Bible and sit down with your parents. In the front of any translation, it should explain to you how the translation was written. In most any modern translation the scholars did extensive research in the original languages. They are very accurate. But the thing here is that you have to honor your parents. So sit and talk with them, explain to them that you'd like to deepen your Bible study, and see what they say.

Q. I really want to be closer to the Lord! I know I have to read the Bible and everything and pray, but I also want something more! I want to feel him reach down on me! And talk to me!

A. What you're looking for is an emotional relationship with God. Sometimes we feel him really intensely. It's like he's right there with us, touching us like you said. But sometimes, we don't feel him. It's like we don't even know he's there. What you need to do is stay immersed in the Scripture and keep praying your heart out. Eventually, you will be at a point where you can feel him again. But 'til then, understand that those desert times where you can't feel him don't mean you aren't close to him. He's just taking you on a different path for a while.

baptized. Then she invited us to her home, saying, "If you think I am truly a believer in the Lord, then come stay in my house." And she persuaded us to stay with her.

PAUL AND SILAS IN JAIL

[16]Once, while we were going to the place for prayer, a servant girl met us. She had a special spirit[n] in her, and she earned a lot of money for her owners by telling fortunes. [17]This girl followed Paul and us, shouting, "These men are servants of the Most High God. They are telling you how you can be saved."

[18]She kept this up for many days. This bothered Paul, so he turned and said to the spirit, "By the power of Jesus Christ, I command you to come out of her!" Immediately, the spirit came out.

[19]When the owners of the servant girl saw this, they knew that now they could not use her to make money. So they grabbed Paul and Silas and dragged them before the city rulers in the marketplace. [20]They brought Paul and Silas to the Roman rulers and said, "These men are Jews and are making trouble in our city. [21]They are teaching things that are not right for us as Romans to do."

[22]The crowd joined the attack against them. The Roman officers tore the clothes of Paul and Silas and had them beaten with rods. [23]Then Paul and Silas were thrown into jail, and the jailer was ordered to guard them carefully. [24]When he heard this order, he put them far inside the jail and pinned their feet down between large blocks of wood.

[25]About midnight Paul and Silas were praying and singing songs to God as the other prisoners listened. [26]Suddenly, there was a strong earthquake that shook the foundation of the jail. Then all the doors of the jail broke open, and all the prisoners were freed from their chains. [27]The jailer woke up and saw that the jail doors were open. Thinking that the prisoners had already escaped, he got his sword and was about to kill himself.[n] [28]But Paul shouted, "Don't hurt yourself! We are all here."

[29]The jailer told someone to bring a light. Then he ran inside and, shaking with fear, fell down before Paul and Silas. [30]He brought them outside and said, "Men, what must I do to be saved?"

[31]They said to him, "Believe in the Lord Jesus and you will be saved—you and all the people in your house." [32]So Paul and Silas told the message of the Lord to the jailer and all the people in his house. [33]At that hour of the night the jailer took Paul and Silas and washed their wounds. Then he and all his people were baptized immediately. [34]After this the jailer took Paul and Silas home and gave them food. He and his family were very happy because they now believed in God.

[35]The next morning, the Roman officers sent the police to tell the jailer, "Let these men go free."

[36]The jailer said to Paul, "The officers have sent an order to let you go free. You can leave now. Go in peace."

[37]But Paul said to the police, "They beat us in public without a trial, even though we are Roman citizens.[n] And they threw us in jail. Now they want to make us go away quietly. No! Let them come themselves and bring us out."

[38]The police told the Roman officers what Paul said. When the officers heard that Paul and Silas were Roman citizens, they were afraid. [39]So they came and told Paul and Silas they were sorry and took them out of jail and asked them to leave the city. [40]So when they came out of the jail, they went to Lydia's house where they saw some of the believers and encouraged them. Then they left.

PAUL AND SILAS IN THESSALONICA

17 Paul and Silas traveled through Amphipolis and Apollonia and came to Thessalonica where there was a synagogue. [2]Paul went into the synagogue as he always did, and on each Sabbath day for three weeks, he talked with his fellow Jews about

notes

16:16 spirit This was a spirit from the devil, which caused her to say she had special knowledge. **16:27 kill himself** He thought the leaders would kill him for letting the prisoners escape. **16:37 Roman citizens** Roman law said that Roman citizens must not be beaten before they had a trial.

70% OF TEENS HAVE DAILY CONVERSATIONS WITH THEIR MOTHERS ABOUT AN IMPORTANT ISSUE IN THEIR LIFE.

the Scriptures. 3He explained and proved that the Christ must die and then rise from the dead. He said, "This Jesus I am telling you about is the Christ." 4Some of them were convinced and joined Paul and Silas, along with many of the Greeks who worshiped God and many of the important women.

5But some others became jealous. So they got some evil men from the marketplace, formed a mob, and started a riot. They ran to Jason's house, looking for Paul and Silas, wanting to bring them out to the people. 6But when they did not find them, they dragged Jason and some other believers to the leaders of the city. The people were yelling, "These people have made trouble everywhere in the world, and now they have come here too! 7Jason is keeping them in his house. All of them do things against the laws of Caesar, saying there is another king, called Jesus."

"THE GOD WHO MADE THE WHOLE WORLD AND EVERYTHING IN IT IS THE LORD OF THE LAND AND THE SKY."

8When the people and the leaders of the city heard these things, they became very upset. 9They made Jason and the others put up a sum of money. Then they let the believers go free.

PAUL AND SILAS GO TO BEREA

10That same night the believers sent Paul and Silas to Berea where they went to the synagogue. 11These people were more willing to listen than the people in Thessalonica. The Bereans were eager to hear what Paul and Silas said and studied the Scriptures every day to find out if these things were true. 12So, many of them believed, as well as many important Greek women and men. 13But the people in Thessalonica learned that Paul was preaching the word of God in Berea, too. So they came there, upsetting the people and making trouble. 14The believers quickly sent Paul away to the coast, but Silas and Timothy stayed in Berea. 15The people leading Paul went with him to Athens. Then they carried a message from Paul back to Silas and Timothy for them to come to him as soon as they could.

PAUL PREACHES IN ATHENS

16While Paul was waiting for Silas and Timothy in Athens, he was troubled because he saw that the city was full of idols. 17In the synagogue, he talked with the Jews and the Greeks who worshiped God. He also talked every day with people in the marketplace.

18Some of the Epicurean and Stoic philosophers[n] argued with him, saying, "This man doesn't know what he is talking about. What is he trying to say?" Others said, "He seems to be telling us about some other gods," because Paul was telling them about Jesus and his rising from the dead. 19They got Paul and took him to a meeting of the Areopagus,[n] where they said, "Please explain to us this new idea you have been teaching. 20The things you are saying are new to us, and we want to know what this teaching means." 21(All the people of Athens and those from other countries who lived there always used their time to talk about the newest ideas.)

22Then Paul stood before the meeting of the Areopagus and said, "People of Athens, I can see you are very religious in all things. 23As I was going through your city, I saw the objects you worship. I found an altar that had these words written on it: TO A GOD WHO IS NOT KNOWN. You worship a god that you don't know, and this is the God I am telling you about! 24The God who made the whole world and everything in it is the Lord of the land and the sky. He does not live in temples built by human hands. 25This God is the One who gives life, breath, and everything else to people. He does not need any help from them; he has everything he needs. 26God began by making one person, and from him came all the different people who live everywhere in the world. God decided exactly when and where they must live. 27God wanted them to look for him and perhaps search all around for him and find him, though he is not far from any of us: 28'We live in him. We walk in him. We are in

RELATIONSHIPS

"Children, obey your parents as the Lord wants, because this is the right thing to do" (Ephesians 6:1). We all know that this is easier said than done. Say your parents decide to ground you from the phone for the next two weeks. Not fair! So maybe you got a D on your algebra test . . . it's not the end of the world. They are *way* overreacting. Read that verse above again. Does it say, "Obey your parents when they are being reasonable"? Nope. If you really think they're being unreasonable, try discussing it with them. But no matter what happens, remember that God has put your parents in authority over you and you have to trust that they are doing their best.

notes

17:18 Epicurean and Stoic philosophers Philosophers were those who searched for truth. Epicureans believed that pleasure, especially pleasures of the mind, were the goal of life. Stoics believed that life should be without feelings of joy or grief. **17:19 Areopagus** A council or group of important leaders in Athens. They were like judges.

him.' Some of your own poets have said: 'For
we are his children.' 29Since we are God's children, you must not think that God is like
something that people imagine or make from
gold, silver, or rock. 30In the past, people did
not understand God, and he ignored this. But
now, God tells all people in the world to change
their hearts and lives. 31God has set a day that
he will judge all the world with fairness, by the
man he chose long ago. And God has proved this
to everyone by raising that man from the dead!"
32When the people heard about Jesus being
raised from the dead, some of them laughed.
But others said, "We will hear more about this
from you later." 33So Paul went away from
them. 34But some of the people believed Paul
and joined him. Among those who believed
was Dionysius, a member of the Areopagus, a
woman named Damaris, and some others.

PAUL IN CORINTH

18 Later Paul left Athens and went to
Corinth. 2Here he met a Jew named
Aquila who had been born in the country of
Pontus. But Aquila and his wife, Priscilla, had
recently moved to Corinth from Italy, because
Claudius[n] commanded that all Jews must leave
Rome. Paul went to visit Aquila and Priscilla.
3Because they were tentmakers, just as he was,
he stayed with them and worked with them.
4Every Sabbath day he talked with the Jews
and Greeks in the synagogue, trying to persuade them to believe in Jesus.
5Silas and Timothy came from Macedonia
and joined Paul in Corinth. After this, Paul
spent all his time telling people the Good
News, showing them that Jesus is the Christ.
6But they would not accept Paul's teaching
and said some evil things. So he shook off the
dust from his clothes[n] and said to them, "If
you are not saved, it will be your own fault! I
have done all I can do! After this, I will go only
to other nations." 7Paul left the synagogue and
moved into the home of Titius Justus, next to
the synagogue. This man worshiped God.
8Crispus was the leader of that synagogue, and
he and all the people living in his house believed
in the Lord. Many others in Corinth also listened
to Paul and believed and were baptized.
9During the night, the Lord told Paul in a
vision: "Don't be afraid. Continue talking to
people and don't be quiet. 10I am with you, and
no one will hurt you because many of my people
are in this city." 11Paul stayed there for a year
and a half, teaching God's word to the people.

PAUL IS BROUGHT BEFORE GALLIO

12When Gallio was the governor of the country of Southern Greece, some people came
together against Paul and took him to the court.
13They said, "This man is teaching people to
worship God in a way that is against our law."
14Paul was about to say something, but

"WHEN THE PEOPLE HEARD ABOUT JESUS BEING RAISED FROM THE DEAD, SOME OF THEM LAUGHED."

Gallio spoke, saying, "I would listen to you if
you were complaining about a crime or some
wrong. 15But the things you are saying are
only questions about words and names—
arguments about your own law. So you must
solve this problem yourselves. I don't want to

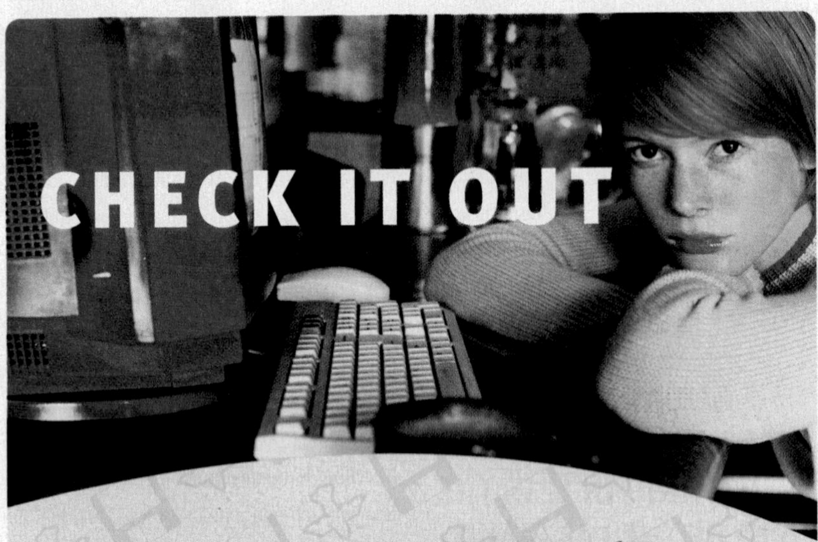

National Coalition for the Homeless

Our Mission is to end homelessness. Toward this end, the National Coalition for the Homeless (NCH) engages in public education, policy advocacy, and grassroots organizing. We focus our work in the following four areas: housing justice, economic justice, health care justice, and civil rights.

Volunteering your time to work directly with people experiencing homelessness is one of the best ways to learn about homelessness and help to meet immediate needs at the same time. There is a lot of "behind-the-scenes" work (filing, sorting clothes, cutting vegetables, etc.) to be done at shelters and other direct service agencies. Think about what you do best and the kind of setting in which you work most effectively—with individuals or groups, with men, women, or children, and so on. Then call a few places, ask what help they need, and arrange for a visit.

For more information,
go to www.nationalhomeless.org/local/local.html.

notes **18:2 Claudius** The emperor (ruler) of Rome, A.D. 41–54. **18:6 shook . . . clothes** This was a warning to show that Paul was finished talking to the people in that city.

32"Now I am putting you in the care of God
and the message about his grace. It is able to
give you strength, and it will give you the
blessings God has for all his holy people.
33When I was with you, I never wanted anyone's money or fine clothes. 34You know I
always worked to take care of my own needs
and the needs of those who were with me. 35I
showed you in all things that you should work
as I did and help the weak. I taught you to
remember the words Jesus said: 'It is more
blessed to give than to receive.' "
36When Paul had said this, he knelt down
with all of them and prayed. 37-38And they all
cried because Paul had said they would never
see him again. They put their arms around
him and kissed him. Then they went with him
to the ship.

PAUL GOES TO JERUSALEM

21 After we all said good-bye to them,
we sailed straight to the island of
Cos. The next day we reached Rhodes, and
from there we went to Patara. 2There we found
a ship going to Phoenicia, so we went aboard
and sailed away. 3We sailed near the island of
Cyprus, seeing it to the north, but we sailed on
to Syria. We stopped at Tyre because the ship
needed to unload its cargo there. 4We found
some followers in Tyre and stayed with them
for seven days. Through the Holy Spirit they
warned Paul not to go to Jerusalem. 5When we
finished our visit, we left and continued our
trip. All the followers, even the women and
children, came outside the city with us. After
we all knelt on the beach and prayed, 6we said
good-bye and got on the ship, and the followers
went back home.
7We continued our trip from Tyre and arrived
at Ptolemais, where we greeted the believers
and stayed with them for a day. 8The next day we
left Ptolemais and went to the city of Caesarea.
There we went into the home of Philip the
preacher, one of the seven helpers,[n] and stayed
with him. 9He had four unmarried daughters
who had the gift of prophesying. 10After we
had been there for some time, a prophet named
Agabus arrived from Judea. 11He came to us
and borrowed Paul's belt and used it to tie his
own hands and feet. He said, "The Holy Spirit
says, 'This is how evil people in Jerusalem will
tie up the man who wears this belt. Then they
will give him to the older leaders.' "
12When we all heard this, we and the people
there begged Paul not to go to Jerusalem. 13But
he said, "Why are you crying and making me
so sad? I am not only ready to be tied up in
Jerusalem, I am ready to die for the Lord Jesus!"
14We could not persuade him to stay away
from Jerusalem. So we stopped begging him
and said, "We pray that what the Lord wants
will be done."
15After this, we got ready and started on our
way to Jerusalem. 16Some of the followers from
Caesarea went with us and took us to the home
of Mnason, where we would stay. He was from
Cyprus and was one of the first followers.

PAUL VISITS JAMES

17In Jerusalem the believers were glad to see
us. 18The next day Paul went with us to visit
James, and all the elders were there. 19Paul
greeted them and told them everything God
had done among the other nations through
him. 20When they heard this, they praised
God. Then they said to Paul, "Brother, you can
see that many thousands of our people have
become believers. And they think it is very
important to obey the law of Moses. 21They
have heard about your teaching, that you tell
our people who live among the nations to
leave the law of Moses. They have heard that
you tell them not to circumcise their children
and not to obey customs. 22What should we
do? They will learn that you have come. 23So
we will tell you what to do: Four of our men
have made a promise to God. 24Take these
men with you and share in their cleansing ceremony.[n] Pay their expenses so they can shave
their heads.[n] Then it will prove to everyone

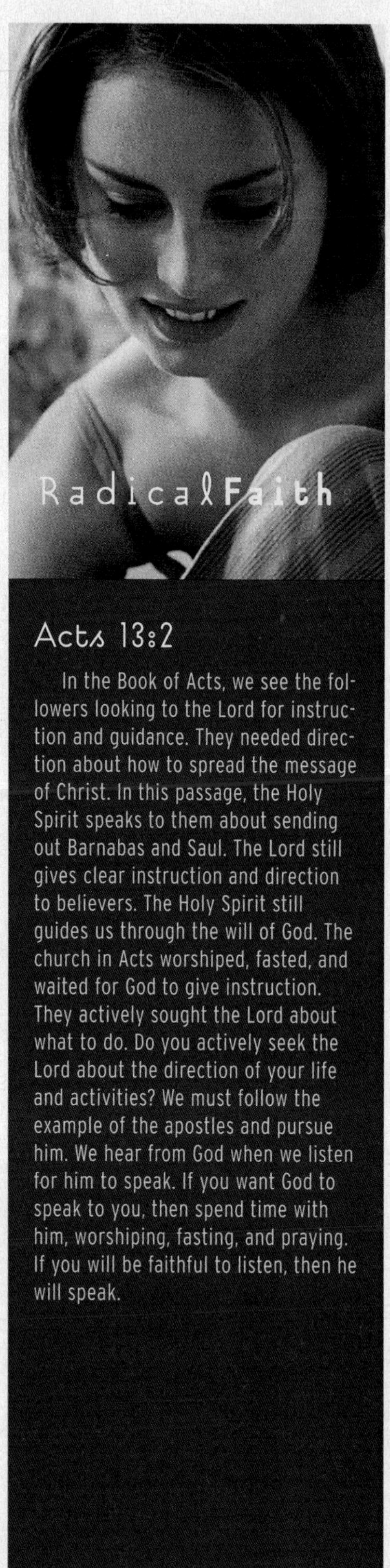

Acts 13:2

In the Book of Acts, we see the followers looking to the Lord for instruction and guidance. They needed direction about how to spread the message of Christ. In this passage, the Holy Spirit speaks to them about sending out Barnabas and Saul. The Lord still gives clear instruction and direction to believers. The Holy Spirit still guides us through the will of God. The church in Acts worshiped, fasted, and waited for God to give instruction. They actively sought the Lord about what to do. Do you actively seek the Lord about the direction of your life and activities? We must follow the example of the apostles and pursue him. We hear from God when we listen for him to speak. If you want God to speak to you, then spend time with him, worshiping, fasting, and praying. If you will be faithful to listen, then he will speak.

notes

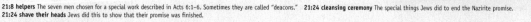

21:8 helpers The seven men chosen for a special work described in Acts 6:1–6. Sometimes they are called "deacons." **21:24 cleansing ceremony** The special things Jews did to end the Nazirite promise.
21:24 shave their heads Jews did this to show that their promise was finished.

Q. I am trying to decide whether I should go to a Christian high school or not. If anyone has any pros or cons for me, please let me know!

A. Where to go to high school is a really big decision. Some pros for a Christian high school are that it is often easier to find Christian friends to be a support, you have support from teachers and staff in your faith, and you often have teachers who are educated in the Christian faith teaching you. However, a public high school can be a great place to challenge yourself in your faith. You have to be a little bit bolder about it. It might be harder to find Christian friends, but you also get a better perspective on how God's love needs to be shown in the world.

Q. My crush likes me back, but my friend has a major problem with it! I would like to know a godly way to approach her about this.

A. Talk to your friend and find out what's bugging her. Maybe she has a good reason. If you two just can't see eye-to-eye on it, it's time to make a decision. Friend or Crush. You have two options. Choose the crush, and you might lose a friend forever for a crush that won't last very long. These kinds of things don't often work out. So make your choice, but choose wisely.

Q. What do you think about boyfriends tickling their girlfriends?

A. Tickling = Foreplay. That is straight from a guy's perspective. It is sexual. Girls can call it flirting, playing, or whatever. Guys want to be able to touch your body. And they are going to let their hands tickle you everywhere they can touch. Because "Hey, we were just playing. It was no big deal."

that what they have heard about you is not
true and that you follow the law of Moses in
your own life. 25We have already sent a letter
to the non-Jewish believers. The letter said:
'Do not eat food that has been offered to idols,
or blood, or animals that have been strangled.
Do not take part in sexual sin.' "

26The next day Paul took the four men and
shared in the cleansing ceremony with them.
Then he went to the Temple and announced
the time when the days of the cleansing ceremony would be finished. On the last day an
offering would be given for each of the men.

27When the seven days were almost over,
some of his people from Asia saw Paul at the
Temple. They caused all the people to be upset
and grabbed Paul. 28They shouted, "People of
Israel, help us! This is the man who goes everywhere teaching against the law of Moses, against
our people, and against this Temple. Now he has
brought some Greeks into the Temple and has
made this holy place unclean!" 29(They said this
because they had seen Trophimus, a man from
Ephesus, with Paul in Jerusalem. They thought
that Paul had brought him into the Temple.)

30All the people in Jerusalem became
upset. Together they ran, took Paul, and
dragged him out of the Temple. The Temple
doors were closed immediately. 31While they
were trying to kill Paul, the commander of the
Roman army in Jerusalem learned that there
was trouble in the whole city. 32Immediately
he took some officers and soldiers and ran to
the place where the crowd was gathered.
When the people saw them, they stopped
beating Paul. 33The commander went to Paul
and arrested him. He told his soldiers to tie
Paul with two chains. Then he asked who he
was and what he had done wrong. 34Some in
the crowd were yelling one thing, and some
were yelling another. Because of all this confusion and shouting, the commander could not
learn what had happened. So he ordered the
soldiers to take Paul to the army building.
35When Paul came to the steps, the soldiers
had to carry him because the people were
ready to hurt him. 36The whole mob was following them, shouting, "Kill him!"

37As the soldiers were about to take Paul
into the army building, he spoke to the commander, "May I say something to you?"

The commander said, "Do you speak Greek?
38I thought you were the Egyptian who
started some trouble against the government
not long ago and led four thousand killers out
to the desert."

39Paul said, "No, I am a Jew from Tarsus in the
country of Cilicia. I am a citizen of that important city. Please, let me speak to the people."

40The commander gave permission, so Paul
stood on the steps and waved his hand to quiet
the people. When there was silence, he spoke
to them in the Hebrew language.

"ALL THE PEOPLE IN JERUSALEM BECAME UPSET."

PAUL SPEAKS TO THE PEOPLE

22 Paul said, "Friends, fellow Jews,
listen to my defense to you."
2When they heard him speaking the Hebrew
language,[n] they became very quiet. Paul said,
3"I am a Jew, born in Tarsus in the country of
Cilicia, but I grew up in this city. I was a student of Gamaliel,[n] who carefully taught me
everything about the law of our ancestors. I
was very serious about serving God, just as are
all of you here today. 4I persecuted the people
who followed the Way of Jesus, and some of
them were even killed. I arrested men and
women and put them in jail. 5The high priest
and the whole council of older leaders can tell
you this is true. They gave me letters to the
brothers in Damascus. So I was going there to
arrest these people and bring them back to
Jerusalem to be punished.

6"About noon when I came near Damascus,

notes

22:2 Hebrew language Or Aramaic, the languages of many people in this region in the first century. **22:3 Gamaliel** A very important teacher of the Pharisees, a Jewish religious group (Acts 5:34).

a bright light from heaven suddenly flashed all around me. 7I fell to the ground and heard a voice saying, 'Saul, Saul, why are you persecuting me?' 8I asked, 'Who are you, Lord?' The voice said, 'I am Jesus from Nazareth whom you are persecuting.' 9Those who were with me did not hear the voice, but they saw the light. 10I said, 'What shall I do, Lord?' The Lord answered, 'Get up and go to Damascus. There you will be told about all the things I have planned for you to do.' 11I could not see, because the bright light had made me blind. So my companions led me into Damascus.

12"There a man named Ananias came to me. He was a religious man; he obeyed the law of Moses, and all the Jews who lived there respected him. 13He stood by me and said, 'Brother Saul, see again!' Immediately I was able to see him. 14He said, 'The God of our ancestors chose you long ago to know his plan, to see the Righteous One, and to hear words from him. 15You will be his witness to all people, telling them about what you have seen and heard. 16Now, why wait any longer? Get up, be baptized, and wash your sins away, trusting in him to save you.'

17"Later, when I returned to Jerusalem, I was praying in the Temple, and I saw a vision. 18I saw the Lord saying to me, 'Hurry! Leave Jerusalem now! The people here will not accept the truth about me.' 19But I said, 'Lord, they know that in every synagogue I put the believers in jail and beat them. 20They also know I was there when Stephen, your witness, was killed. I stood there agreeing and holding the coats of those who were killing him!' 21But the Lord said to me, 'Leave now. I will send you far away to the other nations.' "

22The crowd listened to Paul until he said this. Then they began shouting, "Kill him! Get him out of the world! He should not be allowed to live!" 23They shouted, threw off their coats,[n] and threw dust into the air.[n]

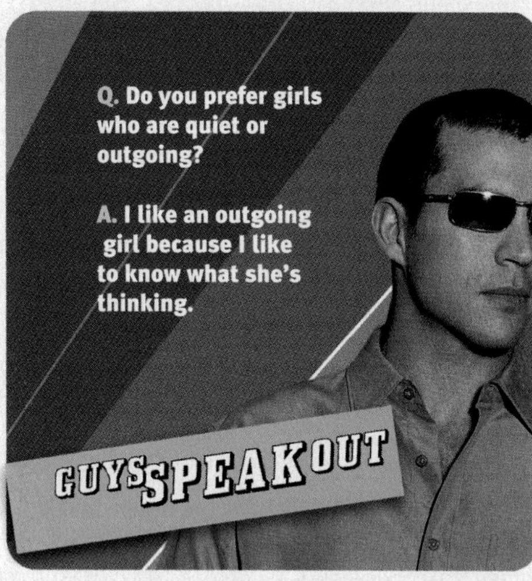

Q. Do you prefer girls who are quiet or outgoing?
A. I like an outgoing girl because I like to know what she's thinking.
GUYS SPEAK OUT

24Then the commander ordered the soldiers to take Paul into the army building and beat him. He wanted to make Paul tell why the people were shouting against him like this. 25But as the soldiers were tying him up, preparing to beat him, Paul said to an officer nearby, "Do you have the right to beat a Roman citizen[n] who has not been proven guilty?"

26When the officer heard this, he went to the commander and reported it. The officer said, "Do you know what you are doing? This man is a Roman citizen."

27The commander came to Paul and said, "Tell me, are you really a Roman citizen?"

He answered, "Yes."

28The commander said, "I paid a lot of money to become a Roman citizen."

But Paul said, "I was born a citizen."

29The men who were preparing to question Paul moved away from him immediately. The commander was frightened because he had already tied Paul, and Paul was a Roman citizen.

DIDYA KNOW

53% OF TEENS HAVE DAILY CONVERSATIONS WITH THEIR FATHERS ABOUT AN IMPORTANT ISSUE IN THEIR LIFE.

PAUL SPEAKS TO LEADERS

30The next day the commander decided to learn why the Jews were accusing Paul. So he ordered the leading priests and the council to meet. The commander took Paul's chains off. Then he brought Paul out and stood him before their meeting.

23 Paul looked at the council and said, "Brothers, I have lived my life without guilt feelings before God up to this day." 2Ananias,[n] the high priest, heard this and told the men who were standing near Paul to hit him on the mouth. 3Paul said to Ananias, "God will hit you, too! You are like a wall that has been painted white. You sit there and judge me, using the law of Moses, but you are telling them to hit me, and that is against the law."

4The men standing near Paul said to him, "You cannot insult God's high priest like that!"

5Paul said, "Brothers, I did not know this man was the high priest. It is written in the Scriptures, 'You must not curse a leader of your people.' "[n]

6Some of the men in the meeting were Sadducees, and others were Pharisees. Knowing this, Paul shouted to them, "My brothers, I am a Pharisee, and my father was a Pharisee. I am on trial here because I believe that people will rise from the dead."

7When Paul said this, there was an argument between the Pharisees and the Sadducees, and the group was divided. 8(The Sadducees do not believe in angels or spirits or that people will rise from the dead. But the Pharisees believe in them all.) 9So there was a great uproar. Some of the teachers of the law, who were Pharisees, stood up and argued, "We find nothing wrong with this man. Maybe an angel or a spirit did speak to him."

notes

22:23 threw off their coats This showed that the people were very angry with Paul. **22:23 threw dust into the air** This showed even greater anger. **22:25 Roman citizen** Roman law said that Roman citizens must not be beaten before they had a trial. **23:2 Ananias** This is not the same man named Ananias in Acts 22:12. **23:5 'You . . . people.'** Quotation from Exodus 22:28.

10The argument was beginning to turn into such a fight that the commander was afraid some evil people would tear Paul to pieces. So he told the soldiers to go down and take Paul away and put him in the army building.

11The next night the Lord came and stood by Paul. He said, "Be brave! You have told people in Jerusalem about me. You must do the same in Rome."

12In the morning some evil people made a plan to kill Paul, and they took an oath not to eat or drink anything until they had killed him. 13There were more than forty men who made this plan. 14They went to the leading priests and the older leaders and said, "We have taken an oath not to eat or drink until we have killed Paul. 15So this is what we want you to do: Send a message to the commander to bring Paul out to you as though you want to ask him more questions. We will be waiting to kill him while he is on the way here."

16But Paul's nephew heard about this plan and went to the army building and told Paul. 17Then Paul called one of the officers and said, "Take this young man to the commander. He has a message for him."

18So the officer brought Paul's nephew to the commander and said, "The prisoner, Paul, asked me to bring this young man to you. He wants to tell you something."

19The commander took the young man's hand and led him to a place where they could be alone. He asked, "What do you want to tell me?"

20The young man said, "The Jews have decided to ask you to bring Paul down to their council meeting tomorrow. They want you to think they are going to ask him more questions. 21But don't believe them! More than forty men are hiding and waiting to kill Paul. They have all taken an oath not to eat or drink until they have killed him. Now they are waiting for you to agree."

22The commander sent the young man away, ordering him, "Don't tell anyone that you have told me about their plan."

Psalm 59:10
My God loves me, and he goes in front of me. He will help me defeat my enemies.

PAUL IS SENT TO CAESAREA

23Then the commander called two officers and said, "I need some men to go to Caesarea. Get two hundred soldiers, seventy horsemen, and two hundred men with spears ready to leave at nine o'clock tonight. 24Get some horses for Paul to ride so he can be taken to Governor Felix safely." 25And he wrote a letter that said:

> 26From Claudius Lysias.
> To the Most Excellent Governor Felix:
> Greetings.
>
> 27Some of the Jews had taken this man and planned to kill him. But I learned that he is a Roman citizen, so I went with my soldiers and saved him. 28I wanted to know why they were accusing him, so I brought him before their council meeting. 29I learned that these people said Paul did some things that were wrong by their own laws, but no charge was worthy of jail or death. 30When I was told that some of them were planning to kill Paul, I sent him to you at once. I also told them to tell you what they have against him.

31So the soldiers did what they were told and took Paul and brought him to the city of Antipatris that night. 32The next day the horsemen went with Paul to Caesarea, but the other soldiers went back to the army building in Jerusalem. 33When the horsemen came to Caesarea and gave the letter to the governor, they turned Paul over to him. 34The governor read the letter and asked Paul, "What area are you from?" When he learned that Paul was from Cilicia, 35he said, "I will hear your case when those who are against you come here, too." Then the governor gave orders for Paul to be kept under guard in Herod's palace.

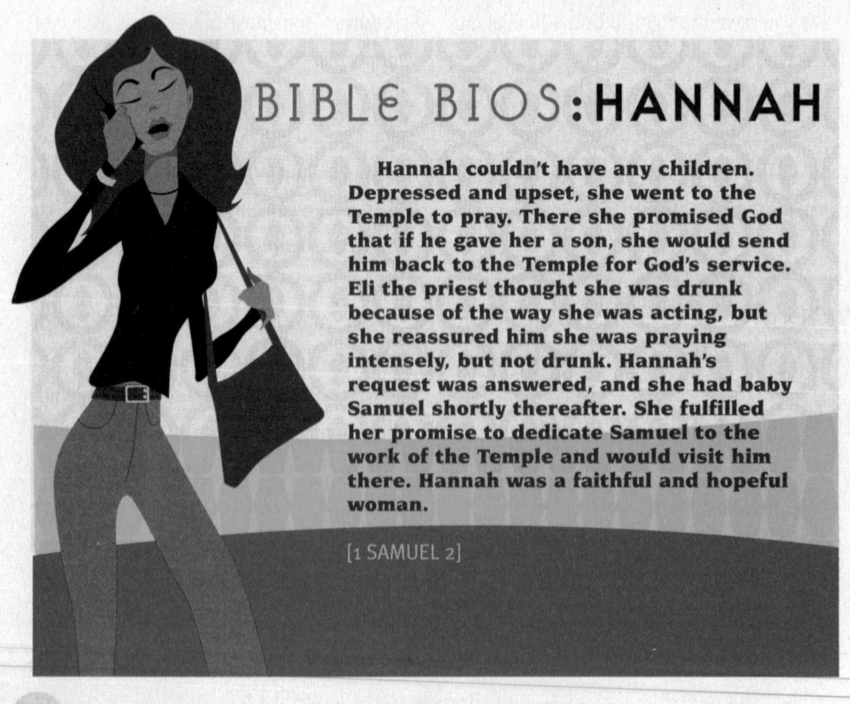

BIBLE BIOS: HANNAH
Hannah couldn't have any children. Depressed and upset, she went to the Temple to pray. There she promised God that if he gave her a son, she would send him back to the Temple for God's service. Eli the priest thought she was drunk because of the way she was acting, but she reassured him she was praying intensely, but not drunk. Hannah's request was answered, and she had baby Samuel shortly thereafter. She fulfilled her promise to dedicate Samuel to the work of the Temple and would visit him there. Hannah was a faithful and hopeful woman.
[1 SAMUEL 2]

PAUL IS ACCUSED

24 Five days later Ananias, the high priest, went to the city of Caesarea with some of the older leaders and a lawyer

LEARN IT & LIVE IT

Ephesians 4:8:
Learn It: Each of us was given grace according to the measure of God's gift.
Live It: Do you know where God's given you grace in your life? Find it today. And celebrate the gift of grace.

Ephesians 5:21:
Learn It: Be subject to one another out of reverence for Christ.
Live It: Volunteer for the job nobody wants. "Yes, I'd love to clean the toilets, Mom!" This will honor Christ.

Ephesians 6:2-3:
Learn It: Honor your father and mother is the first commandment, with a promise of long life.
Live It: Treat your parents to a special night out one night this week. Promise to baby-sit and feed your siblings, and let them go out to a nice dinner. If their relationship is good, everyone will feel better.

named Tertullus. They had come to make
charges against Paul before the governor. [2]Paul
was called into the meeting, and Tertullus
began to accuse him, saying, "Most Excellent
Felix! Our people enjoy much peace because
of you, and many wrong things in our country
are being made right through your wise help.
[3]We accept these things always and in
every place, and we are thankful for them.
[4]But not wanting to take any more of your
time, I beg you to be kind and listen to our
few words. [5]We have found this man to be
a troublemaker, stirring up his people
everywhere in the world. He is a leader of
the Nazarene group. [6]Also, he was trying
to make the Temple unclean, but we
stopped him.[n] [8]By asking him questions
yourself, you can decide if all these things
are true." [9]The others agreed and said that
all of this was true.

[10]When the governor made a sign for
Paul to speak, Paul said, "Governor Felix, I
know you have been a judge over this nation
for a long time. So I am happy to defend myself
before you. [11]You can learn for yourself that I
went to worship in Jerusalem only twelve days
ago. [12]Those who are accusing me did not find
me arguing with anyone in the Temple or stirring up the people in the synagogues or in the
city. [13]They cannot prove the things they are
saying against me now. [14]But I will tell you
this: I worship the God of our ancestors as a
follower of the Way of Jesus. The others say
that the Way of Jesus is not the right way. But
I believe everything that is taught in the law of
Moses and that is written in the books of the
Prophets. [15]I have the same hope in God that
they have—the hope that all people, good and
bad, will surely be raised from the dead. [16]This
is why I always try to do what I believe is right
before God and people.

[17]"After being away from Jerusalem for several years, I went back to bring money to my
people and to offer sacrifices. [18]I was doing
this when they found me in the Temple. I had
finished the cleansing ceremony and had not
made any trouble; no people were gathering
around me. [19]But there were some people
from the country of Asia who should be here,
standing before you. If I have really done anything wrong, they are the ones who should
accuse me. [20]Or ask these people here if
they found any wrong in me when I stood
before the council in Jerusalem. [21]But I did
shout one thing when I stood before them:
'You are judging me today because I believe
that people will rise from the dead!' "

[22]Felix already understood much about
the Way of Jesus. He stopped the trial and
said, "When commander Lysias comes
here, I will decide your case." [23]Felix told
the officer to keep Paul guarded but to give
him some freedom and to let his friends
bring what he needed.

PAUL SPEAKS TO FELIX AND HIS WIFE

[24]After some days Felix came with his wife,
Drusilla, who was Jewish, and asked for Paul
to be brought to him. He listened to Paul talk
about believing in Christ Jesus. [25]But Felix
became afraid when Paul spoke about living
right, self-control, and the time when God will
judge the world. He said, "Go away now.

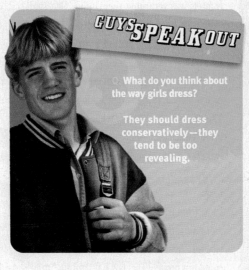

GUYS SPEAK OUT

Q. What do you think about the way girls dress?

A. They should dress conservatively—they tend to be too revealing.

notes

24:6 Verse 6 Some Greek copies add 6b-8a: "And we wanted to judge him by our own law. [7]But the officer Lysias came and used much force to take him from us. [8]And Lysias commanded those who wanted to accuse Paul to come to you."

Q. My friend just broke up with her boyfriend after almost a year. She is really heartbroken, so what should I say to her that will help her get over him?

A. The answer is time. There is no way to hurry up and get over someone. It really hurts and it takes time for the pain to go away. The best counsel is Scripture. Search it out and find passages that talk about trusting God with our lives.

Q. Is it bad for me to have a boyfriend right now at my age? I'm 14. Is there anything in the Bible about when it's okay to date?

A. There is not one mention of dating in the Bible. And no, it's not wrong for you to date if you are looking for a husband. You have to know a person before you marry them and dating is one way to do that. At 14 you are not ready to be married. So my suggestion would be put off the dating stuff 'til you are ready for what it leads to, marriage.

Q. If you really like a guy and you know that he doesn't like you and everything, is it wrong to pray about it?

A. It's never wrong to pray for God's will to be done. And it's not wrong to talk to God about things that are important to you. What is wrong is when you start to spend so much time praying to God about him that what you are really doing is fantasizing about the guy. You have to guard your heart and the best way to do that is to ask God to give you his best.

When I have more time, I will call for you."
26At the same time Felix hoped that Paul
would give him some money, so he often sent
for Paul and talked with him.

27But after two years, Felix was replaced by
Porcius Festus as governor. But Felix had left
Paul in prison to please the Jews.

PAUL ASKS TO SEE CAESAR

25 Three days after Festus became
governor, he went from Caesarea
to Jerusalem. 2There the leading priests and
the important leaders made charges against
Paul before Festus. 3They asked Festus to do
them a favor. They wanted him to send Paul
back to Jerusalem, because they had a plan to
kill him on the way. 4But Festus answered that
Paul would be kept in Caesarea and that he
himself was returning there soon. 5He said,
"Some of your leaders should go with me.
They can accuse the man there in Caesarea, if
he has really done something wrong."

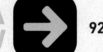

6Festus stayed in Jerusalem another eight
or ten days and then went back to Caesarea.
The next day he told the soldiers to
bring Paul before him. Festus
was seated on the judge's seat
7when Paul came into the
room. The people who had
come from Jerusalem stood
around him, making serious
charges against him, which they
could not prove. 8This is what Paul said to
defend himself: "I have done nothing wrong
against the law, against the Temple, or against
Caesar."

9But Festus wanted to please the people. So
he asked Paul, "Do you want to go to Jerusalem
for me to judge you there on these
charges?"

10Paul said, "I am standing at Caesar's judgment
seat now, where I should be judged. I
have done nothing wrong to them; you know
this is true. 11If I have done something wrong
and the law says I must die, I do not ask to be
saved from death. But if these charges are not
true, then no one can give me to them. I want
Caesar to hear my case!"

12Festus talked about this with his advisers.
Then he said, "You have asked to see Caesar,
so you will go to Caesar!"

DIDYA KNOW  **92% OF TEENS SAY THEY ARE HAPPY.**

Deuteronomy 7:9
So know that the LORD your God is God, the faithful God. He will keep his agreement of love for a thousand lifetimes for people who love him and obey his commands.

PAUL BEFORE KING AGRIPPA

13A few days later King Agrippa and
Bernice came to Caesarea to visit Festus.
14They stayed there for some time, and Festus
told the king about Paul's case. Festus said,
"There is a man that Felix left in prison.
15When I went to Jerusalem, the leading priests
and the older leaders there made charges
against him, asking me to sentence him to
death. 16But I answered, 'When a man is
accused of a crime, Romans do not hand him
over until he has been allowed to face his accusers
and defend himself against their
charges.' 17So when these people
came here to Caesarea for the
trial, I did not waste time. The
next day I sat on the
judge's seat and commanded
that the man be
brought in. 18They stood up and accused
him, but not of any serious crime as I thought
they would. 19The things they said were about
their own religion and about a man named Jesus
who died. But Paul said that he is still alive. 20Not
knowing how to find out about these questions,
I asked Paul, 'Do you want to go to Jerusalem
and be judged there?' 21But he asked to be kept
in Caesarea. He wants a decision from the

emperor.[n] So I ordered that he be held until I could send him to Caesar."

[22]Agrippa said to Festus, "I would also like to hear this man myself."

Festus said, "Tomorrow you will hear him."

[23]The next day Agrippa and Bernice appeared with great show, acting like very important people. They went into the judgment room with the army leaders and the important men of Caesarea. Then Festus ordered the soldiers to bring Paul in. [24]Festus said, "King Agrippa and all who are gathered here with us, you see this man. All the people, here and in Jerusalem, have complained to me about him, shouting that he should not live any longer. [25]When I judged him, I found no reason to order his death. But since he asked to be judged by Caesar, I decided to send him. [26]But I have nothing definite to write the emperor about him. So I have brought him before all of you—especially you, King Agrippa. I hope you can question him and give me something to write. [27]I think it is foolish to send a prisoner to Caesar without telling what charges are against him."

PAUL DEFENDS HIMSELF

26 Agrippa said to Paul, "You may now speak to defend yourself."

Then Paul raised his hand and began to speak. [2]He said, "King Agrippa, I am very happy to stand before you and will answer all the charges the evil people make against me. [3]You know so much about all the customs and the things they argue about, so please listen to me patiently.

[4]"All my people know about my whole life, how I lived from the beginning in my own country and later in Jerusalem. [5]They have known me for a long time. If they want to, they can tell you that I was a good Pharisee. And the Pharisees obey the laws of my tradition more carefully than any other group. [6]Now I am on trial because I hope for the promise that God made to our ancestors. [7]This is the promise that the twelve tribes of our people hope to receive as they serve God day and night. My king, they have accused me because I hope for this same promise! [8]Why do any of you people think it is impossible for God to raise people from the dead?

[9]"I, too, thought I ought to do many things against Jesus from Nazareth. [10]And that is what I did in Jerusalem. The leading priests gave me the power to put many of God's people in jail, and when they were being killed, I agreed it was a good thing. [11]In every synagogue, I often punished them and tried to make them speak against Jesus. I was so angry against them I even went to other cities to find them and punish them.

[12]"One time the leading priests gave me permission and the power to go to Damascus. [13]On the way there, at noon, I saw a light from heaven. It was brighter than the sun and flashed all around me and those who were traveling with me. [14]We all fell to the ground. Then I heard a voice speaking to me in the Hebrew language,[n] saying, 'Saul, Saul, why are you persecuting me? You are only hurting yourself by fighting me.' [15]I said, 'Who are you, Lord?' The Lord said, 'I am Jesus, the one you are persecuting. [16]Stand up! I have chosen you to be my servant and my witness—you will tell people the things that you have seen and the things that I will show you. This is why I have come to you today. [17]I will keep you safe from your own people and also from the others. I am sending you to them [18]to open their eyes so that they may turn away from darkness to the light, away from the power of Satan and to God. Then their sins can be forgiven, and they can have a place with those people who have been made holy by believing in me.'

[19]"King Agrippa, after I had this vision from heaven, I obeyed it. [20]I began telling people that they should change their hearts and lives and turn to God and do things to show they really had changed. I told this first to those in

TOPten

RANDOM THINGS TO LOOK FOR IN A GODLY GUY

01	Respect
02	Honesty
03	Leadership
04	Integrity
05	Humor
06	Friendship
07	Loyalty
08	Self-Control
09	Strength
10	Gentleness

notes

25:21 emperor The ruler of the Roman Empire, which was almost all the known world. **26:14 Hebrew language** Hebrew or Aramaic, the languages of many people in this region in the first century.

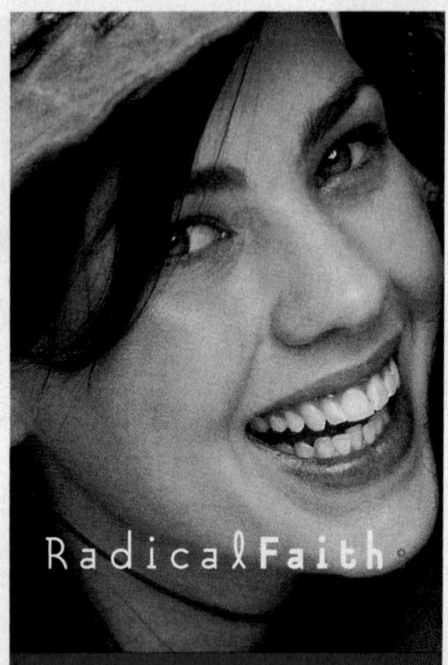

Acts 16:30-31

Tommy thought that since his family went to church every Sunday and he knew the words to the hymns that he must be saved. Alexa goes to a church where they don't talk about being saved. She's heard other people talk about it, but she's confused. Every night she begs God to take her to heaven if she dies in her sleep. Every time she thinks about this "saved" thing, she gets scared. No one has ever explained it to her, and she's too proud to ask. Joey heard from a friend that God loves everybody, and that God would let everyone into heaven. Sounds great.

Tommy, Alexa, and Joey aren't saved. Here's the answer for them and for you: "Believe in the Lord Jesus and you will be saved." When you decide that you believe in God and in his Son, Jesus, and in the fact that Jesus died on a cross for you, then you are saved from an eternity away from God. That's salvation. Your faith in Jesus saves you. Nothing more. Nothing less. It's a matter of believing so much that you commit your life to him.

Ask the Lord to show you how to live what you have decided to believe. He is waiting for you to choose him. Long ago—way before you were born—he chose you. He loves you and wants to spend forever with you.

Damascus, then in Jerusalem, and in every part of Judea, and also to the other people. 21This is why the Jews took me and were trying to kill me in the Temple. 22But God has helped me, and so I stand here today, telling all people, small and great, what I have seen. But I am saying only what Moses and the prophets said would happen— 23that the Christ would die, and as the first to rise from the dead, he would bring light to all people."

PAUL TRIES TO PERSUADE AGRIPPA

24While Paul was saying these things to defend himself, Festus said loudly, "Paul, you are out of your mind! Too much study has driven you crazy!"

25Paul said, "Most excellent Festus, I am not crazy. My words are true and sensible. 26King Agrippa knows about these things, and I can speak freely to him. I know he has heard about all of these things, because they did not happen off in a corner. 27King Agrippa, do you believe what the prophets wrote? I know you believe."

28King Agrippa said to Paul, "Do you think you can persuade me to become a Christian in such a short time?"

29Paul said, "Whether it is a short or a long time, I pray to God that not only you but every person listening to me today would be saved and be like me—except for these chains I have."

30Then King Agrippa, Governor Festus, Bernice, and all the people sitting with them stood up 31and left the room. Talking to each other, they said, "There is no reason why this man should die or be put in jail." 32And Agrippa said to Festus, "We could let this man go free, but he has asked Caesar to hear his case."

Job 5:11
He makes the humble person important and lifts the sad to places of safety.

PAUL SAILS FOR ROME

27 It was decided that we would sail for Italy. An officer named Julius, who served in the emperor's[n] army, guarded Paul and some other prisoners. 2We got on a ship that was from the city of Adramyttium and was about to sail to different ports in the country of Asia. Aristarchus, a man from the city of Thessalonica in Macedonia, went with us. 3The next day we came to Sidon. Julius was very good to Paul and gave him freedom to go visit his friends, who took care of his needs. 4We left Sidon and sailed close to the island of Cyprus, because the wind was blowing against us. 5We went across the sea by Cilicia and Pamphylia and landed at the city of Myra, in Lycia. 6There the officer found a ship from Alexandria that was going to Italy, so he put us on it.

7We sailed slowly for many days. We had a hard time reaching Cnidus because the wind was blowing against us, and we could not go any farther. So we sailed by the south side of the island of Crete near Salmone. 8Sailing past it was hard. Then we came to a place called Fair Havens, near the city of Lasea.

9We had lost much time, and it was now dangerous to sail, because it was already after the Day of Cleansing.[n] So Paul warned them, 10"Men, I can see there will be a lot of trouble on this trip. The ship, the cargo, and even our lives may be lost." 11But the captain and the owner of the ship did not agree with Paul, and the officer believed what the captain and owner of the ship said. 12Since that harbor was not a good place for the ship to stay for the winter, most of the men decided that the ship should leave. They hoped we could go to Phoenix and stay there for the winter. Phoenix, a city on the island of Crete, had a harbor which faced southwest and northwest.

THE STORM

13When a good wind began to blow from the south, the men on the ship thought, "This is the wind we wanted, and now we have it." So they pulled up the anchor, and we sailed very close to the island of Crete. 14But then a very

27:1 emperor The ruler of the Roman Empire, which was almost all the known world. **27:9 Day of Cleansing** An important Jewish holy day in the fall of the year. This was the time of year that bad storms arose on the sea.

strong wind named the "northeaster" came from the island. 15The ship was caught in it and could not sail against it. So we stopped trying and let the wind carry us. 16When we went below a small island named Cauda, we were barely able to bring in the lifeboat. 17After the men took the lifeboat in, they tied ropes around the ship to hold it together. The men were afraid that the ship would hit the sandbanks of Syrtis,[n] so they lowered the sail and let the wind carry the ship. 18The next day the storm was blowing us so hard that the men threw out some of the cargo. 19A day later with their own hands they threw out the ship's equipment. 20When we could not see the sun or the stars for many days, and the storm was very bad, we lost all hope of being saved.

21After the men had gone without food for a long time, Paul stood up before them and said, "Men, you should have listened to me. You should not have sailed from Crete. Then you would not have all this trouble and loss. 22But now I tell you to cheer up because none of you will die. Only the ship will be lost. 23Last night an angel came to me from the God I belong to and worship. 24The angel said, 'Paul, do not be afraid. You must stand before Caesar. And God has promised you that he will save the lives of everyone sailing with you.' 25So men, have courage. I trust in God that everything will happen as his angel told me. 26But we will crash on an island."

27On the fourteenth night we were still being carried around in the Adriatic Sea.[n] About midnight the sailors thought we were close to land, 28so they lowered a rope with a weight on the end of it into the water. They found that the water was one hundred twenty feet deep. They went a little farther and lowered the rope again. It was ninety feet deep. 29The sailors were afraid that we would hit the rocks, so they threw four anchors into the water and prayed for daylight to come. 30Some of the sailors wanted to leave the ship, and they lowered the lifeboat, pretending they were throwing more anchors from the front of the ship. 31But Paul told the officer and the other soldiers, "If these men do not stay in the ship, your lives cannot be saved." 32So the soldiers cut the ropes and let the lifeboat fall into the water.

"WHEN DAYLIGHT CAME, THE SAILORS SAW LAND."

33Just before dawn Paul began persuading all the people to eat something. He said, "For the past fourteen days you have been waiting and watching and not eating. 34Now I beg you to eat something. You need it to stay alive. None of you will lose even one hair off your heads." 35After he said this, Paul took some bread and thanked God for it before all of them. He broke off a piece and began eating. 36They all felt better and started eating, too. 37There were two hundred seventy-six people on the ship. 38When they had eaten all they wanted, they began making the ship lighter by throwing the grain into the sea.

THE SHIP IS DESTROYED

39When daylight came, the sailors saw land. They did not know what land it was, but they saw a bay with a beach and wanted to sail the ship to the beach if they could. 40So they cut the ropes to the anchors and left the anchors in the sea. At the same time, they untied the ropes that were holding the rudders. Then they raised the front sail into the wind and sailed toward the beach. 41But the ship hit a sandbank. The front of the ship stuck there and could not move, but the back of the ship began to break up from the big waves.

42The soldiers decided to kill the prisoners so none of them could swim away and escape. 43But Julius, the officer, wanted to let Paul live and did not allow the soldiers to kill the prisoners. Instead he ordered everyone who could swim to jump into the water first and swim to land. 44The rest were to follow using wooden

Acts 17:28

Ever feel like you're expected to be somebody you're not? Straight-A student? Club president? Perfect little angel? Sure, there are times when you need to venture out of your comfort zone and expect more of yourself than what comes easily for you. And God has given you natural, inborn abilities that (as you begin to spot them) will shape the person you are. He didn't just bundle up a bunch of leftovers and throw them in your direction. He knew what he wanted to do in you, what he wanted you to accomplish, what he wanted you to be good at. And he knew exactly what you'd need in order to pull it off.

He's placed spiritual gifts in you, unique and powerful tools that shape the way you serve him and relate to others—as a peacemaker, an encourager, a leader.

You're not an afterthought, but a complete package of Christlike potential, waiting to be discovered and put into practice. And you can start living it today right where you are, with the people right around you. You'll be miserable being anybody else.

"YOU'LL BE MISERABLE BEING ANYBODY ELSE."

notes

27:17 Syrtis Shallow area in the sea near the Libyan coast. **27:27 Adriatic Sea** The sea between Greece and Italy, including the central Mediterranean.

boards or pieces of the ship. And this is how all the people made it safely to land.

PAUL ON THE ISLAND OF MALTA

28 When we were safe on land, we learned that the island was called Malta. 2The people who lived there were very good to us. Because it was raining and very cold, they made a fire and welcomed all of us. 3Paul gathered a pile of sticks and was putting them on the fire when a poisonous snake came out because of the heat and bit him on the hand. 4The people living on the island saw the snake hanging from Paul's hand and said to each other, "This man must be a murderer! He did not die in the sea, but Justice[n] does not want him to live." 5But Paul shook the snake off into the fire and was not hurt. 6The people thought that Paul would swell up or fall down dead. They waited and watched him for a long time, but nothing bad happened to him. So they changed their minds and said, "He is a god!"

91% OF TEENS SAY THEY ARE RESPONSIBLE.

"I WANT YOU TO KNOW THAT GOD HAS ALSO SENT HIS SALVATION TO ALL NATIONS, AND THEY WILL LISTEN!"

7There were some fields around there owned by Publius, an important man on the island. He welcomed us into his home and was very good to us for three days. 8Publius' father was sick with a fever and dysentery.[n] Paul went to him, prayed, and put his hands on the man and healed him. 9After this, all the other sick people on the island came to Paul, and he healed them, too. 10-11The people on the island gave us many honors. When we were ready to leave, three months later, they gave us the things we needed.

PAUL GOES TO ROME

We got on a ship from Alexandria that had stayed on the island during the winter. On the front of the ship was the sign of the twin gods.[n] 12We stopped at Syracuse for three days. 13From there we sailed to Rhegium. The next day a wind began to blow from the south, and a day later we came to Puteoli. 14We found some believers there who asked us to stay with them for a week. Finally, we came to Rome. 15The believers in Rome heard that we were there and came out as far as the Market of Appius[n] and the Three Inns[n] to meet us. When Paul saw them, he was encouraged and thanked God.

PAUL IN ROME

16When we arrived at Rome, Paul was allowed to live alone, with the soldier who guarded him.

17Three days later Paul sent for the leaders there. When they came together, he said, "Brothers, I have done nothing against our people or the customs of our ancestors. But I was arrested in Jerusalem and given to the Romans. 18After they asked me many questions, they could find no reason why I should be killed. They wanted to let me go free, 19but the evil people there argued against that. So I had to ask to come to Rome to have my trial before Caesar. But I have no charge to bring against my own people. 20That is why I wanted to see you and talk with you. I am bound with this chain because I believe in the hope of Israel."

21They answered Paul, "We have received no letters from Judea about you. None of our Jewish brothers who have come from there brought news or told us anything bad about you. 22But we want to hear your ideas, because we know that people everywhere are speaking against this religious group."

23Paul and the people chose a day for a meeting and on that day many more of the Jews met with Paul at the place he was staying. He spoke to them all day long. Using the law of Moses and the prophets' writings, he explained the kingdom of God, and he tried to persuade them to believe these things about Jesus. 24Some believed what Paul said, but others did not. 25So they argued and began leaving after Paul said one more thing to them: "The Holy Spirit spoke the truth to your ancestors through Isaiah the prophet, saying,

26'Go to this people and say:
You will listen and listen, but you will
not understand.
You will look and look, but you will
not learn,
27because these people have become
stubborn.
They don't hear with their ears,
and they have closed their eyes.
Otherwise, they might really understand
what they see with their eyes
and hear with their ears.
They might really understand in their minds
and come back to me and be healed.'

Isaiah 6:9-10

28"I want you to know that God has also sent his salvation to all nations, and they will listen!" 29[n]

30Paul stayed two full years in his own rented house and welcomed all people who came to visit him. 31He boldly preached about the kingdom of God and taught about the Lord Jesus Christ, and no one tried to stop him.

notes

28:4 Justice The people thought there was a god named Justice who would punish bad people. **28:8 dysentery** A sickness like diarrhea. **28:10-11 twin gods** Statues of Castor and Pollux, gods in old Greek tales. **28:15 Market of Appius** A town about twenty-seven miles from Rome. **28:15 Three Inns** A town about thirty miles from Rome. **28:29 Verse 29** Some late Greek copies add verse 29: "After Paul said this, the Jews left. They were arguing very much with each other."

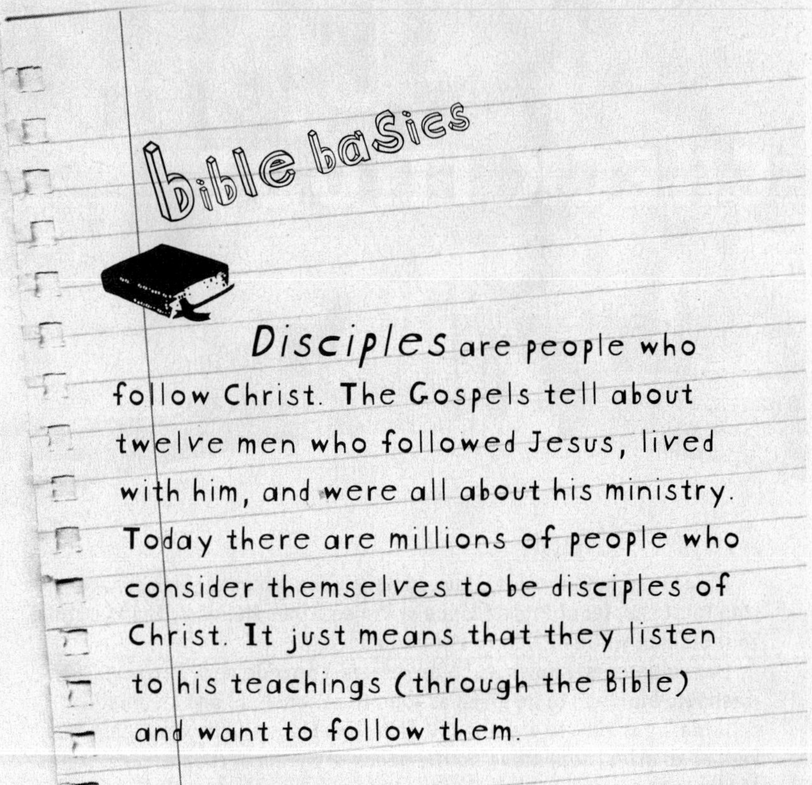

bible basics
Disciples are people who follow Christ. The Gospels tell about twelve men who followed Jesus, lived with him, and were all about his ministry. Today there are millions of people who consider themselves to be disciples of Christ. It just means that they listen to his teachings (through the Bible) and want to follow them.

1 From Paul, a servant of Christ Jesus. God called me to be an apostle and chose me to tell the Good News.

2God promised this Good News long ago through his prophets, as it is written in the Holy Scriptures. 3-4The Good News is about God's Son, Jesus Christ our Lord. As a man, he was born from the family of David. But through the Spirit of holiness he was appointed to be God's Son with great power by rising from the dead. 5Through Christ, God gave me the special work of an apostle, which was to lead people of all nations to believe and obey. I do this work for him. 6And you who are in Rome are also called to belong to Jesus Christ.

7To all of you in Rome whom God loves and has called to be his holy people:

Grace and peace to you from God our Father and the Lord Jesus Christ.

A PRAYER OF THANKS

8First I want to say that I thank my God through Jesus Christ for all of you, because people everywhere in the world are talking about your faith. 9God, whom I serve with my whole heart by telling the Good News about his Son, knows that I always mention you 10every time I pray. I pray that I will be allowed to come to you, and this will happen if God wants it. 11I want very much to see you, to give you some spiritual gift to make you strong. 12I mean that I want us to help each other with the faith we have. Your faith will help me, and my faith will help you. 13Brothers and sisters,[n] I want you to know that I planned many times to come to you, but this has not been possible. I wanted to come so that I could help you grow spiritually as I have helped the other non-Jewish people.

14I have a duty to all people—Greeks and those who are not Greeks, the wise and the foolish. 15That is why I want so much to preach the Good News to you in Rome.

16I am proud of the Good News, because it is the power God uses to save everyone who believes—to save the Jews first, and also to save those who are not Jews. 17The Good News shows how God makes people right with himself—that it begins and ends with faith. As the Scripture says, "But those who are right with God will live by trusting in him."[n]

ALL PEOPLE HAVE DONE WRONG

18God's anger is shown from heaven against all the evil and wrong things people do. By their own evil lives they hide the truth. 19God shows his anger because some knowledge of him has been made clear to them. Yes, God has shown himself to them. 20There are things about him that people cannot see—his eternal power and all the things that make him God. But since the beginning of the world those things have been easy to understand by what God has made. So people have no excuse for the bad things they do. 21They knew God, but they did not give glory to God or thank him. Their thinking became useless. Their foolish minds were filled with darkness. 22They said they were wise, but they became fools. 23They traded the glory of God who lives forever for the worship of idols made to look like earthly people, birds, animals, and snakes.

24Because they did these things, God left them and let them go their sinful way, wanting only to do evil. As a result, they became full of sexual sin, using their bodies wrongly with each

"GOD PROMISED THIS GOOD NEWS LONG AGO THROUGH HIS PROPHETS, AS IT IS WRITTEN IN THE HOLY SCRIPTURES."

other. 25They traded the truth of God for a lie. They worshiped and served what had been created instead of the God who created those things, who should be praised forever. Amen.

26Because people did those things, God left them and let them do the shameful things they wanted to do. Women stopped having

1:13 Brothers and sisters Although the Greek text says "Brothers" here and throughout this book, Paul's words were meant for the entire church, including men and women. **1:17 "But those . . . him."** Quotation from Habakkuk 2:4.

Romans 1:17

Most people want to do something so that God will like them. They think that if they're really good, if they do everything—or most things—right, then God will accept them. It makes people feel really good to think there's something so neat about them that they can earn a spot in heaven.

The truth is that no one can be *that* good. But "the Good News shows how God makes people right with himself—that it begins and ends with faith." In other words, God accepts those who come to him in faith. Now *that's* good news. It's not being good that gets God to accept you; it's having faith in his Son. You can have a faith so strong, so alive that you can't wait to commit your whole life to Jesus. Then, as Romans 1:17 says, you will live—not just physically, but live with strength and power because you're trusting in him.

Keep renewing your mind with God's Word. That's how you build faith. Do your best to live the way God wants you to just because you love him and you want to please him. Faith sets you free from the vicious cycle of constantly trying to work your way into God's good graces.

"GOD ACCEPTS THOSE WHO COME TO HIM IN FAITH."

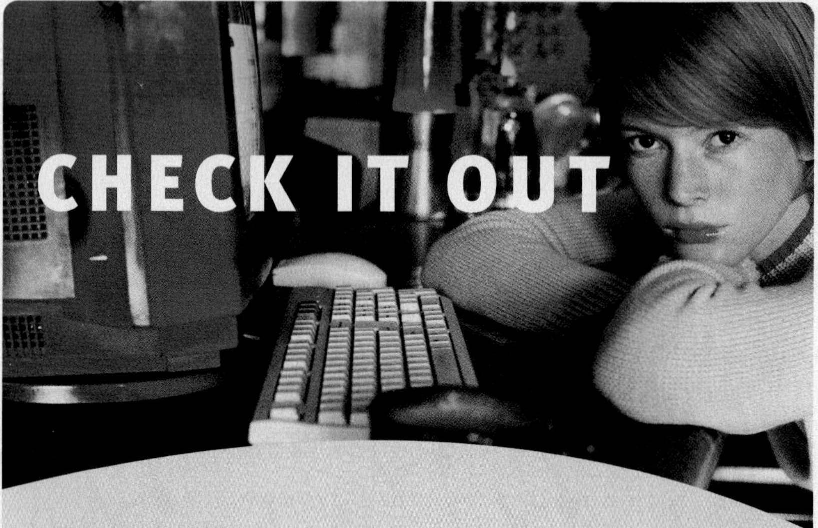

Project Linus

It's easy to help Project Linus. Simply make a blanket and donate it to your local chapter of Project Linus or Project Linus National Headquarters. Your blanket will be given to a child in need.

Our volunteers, known as "blanketeers," provide new, handmade, washable blankets to be given as gifts to seriously ill and traumatized children, ages zero to eighteen. It is Project Linus's policy to accept blankets of all sizes, depending on the needs of the local chapters. All styles of blankets are welcome, including quilts, tied comforters, fleece blankets, crocheted or knitted afghans, and receiving blankets in child-friendly colors. The site has patterns for blankets to get you started!

For more info, go to ***www.projectlinus.org/blanketeer.htm.***

natural sex and started having sex with other
women. 27In the same way, men stopped having natural sex and began wanting each other.
Men did shameful things with
other men, and in their bodies
they received the punishment
for those wrongs.
28People did not think it
was important to have a true
knowledge of God. So God left them
and allowed them to have their own
worthless thinking and to do things they
should not do. 29They are filled with every
kind of sin, evil, selfishness, and hatred. They
are full of jealousy, murder, fighting, lying, and
thinking the worst about each other. They gossip 30and say evil things about each other.
They hate God. They are rude and conceited
and brag about themselves. They invent ways
of doing evil. They do not obey their parents.
31They are foolish, they do not
keep their promises, and they
show no kindness or mercy to
others. 32They know God's
law says that those who
live like this should die.
But they themselves not only continue to do these evil things, they applaud
others who do them.

Psalm 5:11
But let everyone who trusts you be happy; let them sing glad songs forever. Protect those who love you and who are happy because of you.

YOU PEOPLE ALSO ARE SINFUL

2 If you think you can judge others, you
are wrong. When you judge them, you
are really judging yourself guilty, because you
do the same things they do. 2God judges those

who do wrong things, and we know that his
judging is right. [3]You judge those who do
wrong, but you do wrong yourselves. Do you
think you will be able to escape the judgment
of God? [4]He has been very kind and patient,
waiting for you to change, but you think nothing of his kindness. Perhaps you do not understand that God is kind to you so you will
change your hearts and lives. [5]But you are
stubborn and refuse to change, so you are
making your own punishment even greater on
the day he shows his anger. On that day everyone will see God's right judgments. [6]God will
reward or punish every person for what that
person has done. [7]Some people, by always
continuing to do good, live for God's glory, for
honor, and for life that has no end. God will
give them life forever. [8]But other people are
selfish. They refuse to follow truth and, instead,
follow evil. God will give them his punishment and anger. [9]He will give trouble and suffering to everyone who does evil—to the Jews
first and also to those who are not Jews. [10]But
he will give glory, honor, and peace to everyone who does good—to the Jews first and also
to those who are not Jews. [11]For God judges all
people in the same way.

[12]People who do not have the law and who
are sinners will be lost, although they do not
have the law. And, in the same way, those who
have the law and are sinners will be judged by
the law. [13]Hearing the law does not make people right with God. It is those who obey the
law who will be right with him. [14](Those who
are not Jews do not have the law, but when
they freely do what the law commands, they
are the law for themselves. This is true even
though they do not have the law. [15]They show
that in their hearts they know what is right
and wrong, just as the law commands. And they
show this by their consciences. Sometimes
their thoughts tell them they did wrong, and
sometimes their thoughts tell them they did
right.) [16]All these things will happen on the
day when God, through Christ Jesus, will
judge people's secret thoughts. The Good
News that I preach says this.

THE JEWS AND THE LAW

[17]What about you? You call yourself a Jew.
You trust in the law of Moses and brag that you
are close to God. [18]You know what he wants
you to do and what is important, because you
have learned the law. [19]You think you are a
guide for the blind and a light for those who

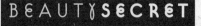

BEAUTY SECRET

EXERCISING TO THE GLORY OF GOD

Looking for ways to stay in shape? How about incorporating a compassionate heart into your workout? Do a car wash for charity. Paint a house of someone less fortunate than yourself. Walk in the local heart, cancer, or AIDS walk. Give back to the community—that's the sign of true beauty!

are in darkness. [20]You think you can show
foolish people what is right and teach those
who know nothing. You have the law; so you
think you know everything and have all truth.
[21]You teach others, so why don't you teach
yourself? You tell others not to steal, but you
steal. [22]You say that others must not take part
in adultery, but you are guilty of that sin. You

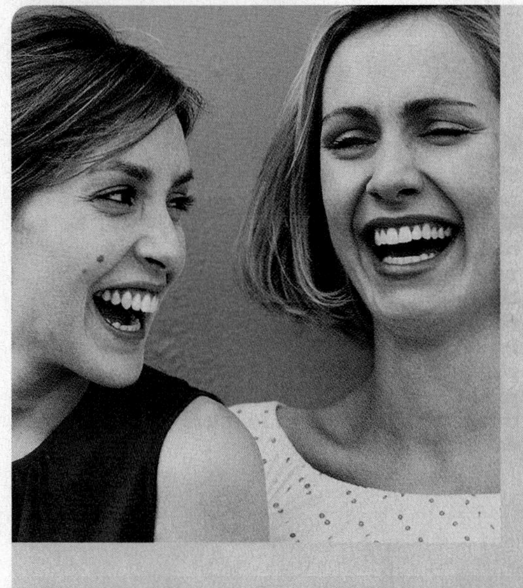

LEARN IT & LIVE IT

Philippians 1:6:
Learn It: The One who began a good work in you will be faithful to complete it.
Live It: Don't give up on Christ. If you're in the middle of a long journey, sit down, take a rest, and worship God. He is walking with you. Imagine yourself in a field with him, just resting and enjoying a beautiful day. Then gain courage to fight the good fight 'til the end.

Philippians 2:4:
Learn It: We need to be interested in others' lives.
Live It: Sacrifice your schedule for someone else's. If you've got a big football game to attend this Friday and your parents have tickets to the play and need you to watch the kids, do it. Give up the game. Enjoy your time with your family—soon you'll be out of the house and will miss them terribly.

Philippians 3:14:
Learn It: Keep your eyes on Jesus.
Live It: Set your watch to beep or vibrate every ten minutes today. It will be a reminder to think about Christ again. It's hard to stay focused with such a busy life; reminders like this help us every once in a while.

Romans 3:24

Hate to break it to you this way, but pockets of sin have been discovered in numerous places on your body—some leading all the way down to your heart—and your track record certainly bears out the fact that you do indeed have a serious problem. So . . . your file's being turned over to the justice department.

In all the time that God's been handling cases like this, only one Person has ever been cleared of the death sentence on the first try. Just one. Fellow from Nazareth by the name of Jesus. But ever since then, before these cases can be properly executed, convicted lawbreakers like you have the right to pursue one final route of appeal.

It goes something like this. If you'll deliver an honest confession to God that your personal performance has been a dismal failure, and that you are willing to let Jesus' innocence stand in the place of all your hard work and effort at passing the grade . . . well, let's just say no one has ever been turned down yet.

Are you ready to exercise your option? Go for it!

"YOU HAVE THE RIGHT TO PURSUE ONE FINAL ROUTE TO APPEAL."

hate idols, but you steal from temples. [23]You brag about having God's law, but you bring shame to God by breaking his law, [24]just as the Scriptures say: "Those who are not Jews speak against God's name because of you."[n]

[25]If you follow the law, your circumcision has meaning. But if you break the law, it is as if you were never circumcised. [26]People who are not Jews are not circumcised, but if they do what the law says, it is as if they were circumcised. [27]You Jews have the written law and circumcision, but you break the law. So those who are not circumcised in their bodies, but still obey the law, will show that you are guilty. [28]They can do this because a person is not a true Jew if he is only a Jew in his physical body; true circumcision is not only on the outside of the body. [29]A person is a Jew only if he is a Jew inside; true circumcision is done in the heart by the Spirit, not by the written law. Such a person gets praise from God rather than from people.

3 So, do Jews have anything that other people do not have? Is there anything special about being circumcised? [2]Yes, of course, there is in every way. The most important thing is this: God trusted the Jews with his teachings. [3]If some Jews were not faithful to him, will that stop God from doing what he promised? [4]No! God will continue to be true even when every person is false. As the Scriptures say:

> "So you will be shown to be right
> when you speak,
> and you will win your case." *Psalm 51:4*

[5]When we do wrong, that shows more clearly that God is right. So can we say that God is wrong to punish us? (I am talking as people might talk.) [6]No! If God could not punish us, he could not judge the world.

[7]A person might say, "When I lie, it really gives him glory, because my lie shows God's truth. So why am I judged a sinner?" [8]It would be the same to say, "We should do evil so that good will come." Some people find fault with us and say we teach this, but they are wrong and deserve the punishment they will receive.

ALL PEOPLE ARE GUILTY

[9]So are we Jews better than others? No! We have already said that Jews and those who are

BIBLE BIOS: JAEL

Jael was the woman about whom Deborah prophesied. One day, General Sisera, an enemy of the Lord, came to the tent of Jael and asked for water. She gave him a cup of milk and a blanket. When he had fallen fast asleep, Jael took a tent peg and drove it through his head into the ground. She had killed him. After this, Deborah rejoiced and the land of Israel enjoyed forty years of peace. Jael played a key role in God's will for the people of Israel at that time. Jael shows us the greater truth that God has a role for each of our lives.

[JUDGES 4]

notes

2:24 "Those . . . you." Quotation from Isaiah 52:5; Ezekiel 36:20.

not Jews are all guilty of sin. [10]As the Scriptures say:

"There is no one who always does
what is right,
not even one.
[11]There is no one who understands.
There is no one who looks to God
for help.
[12]All have turned away.
Together, everyone has become useless.
There is no one who does anything good;
there is not even one." *Psalm 14:1-3*
[13]"Their throats are like open graves;
they use their tongues for
telling lies." *Psalm 5:9*
"Their words are like snake poison."
Psalm 140:3
[14] "Their mouths are full of cursing
and hate." *Psalm 10:7*
[15]"They are always ready to kill people.
[16] Everywhere they go they cause ruin
and misery.
[17]They don't know how to live in peace."
Isaiah 59:7-8
[18] "They have no fear of God." *Psalm 36:1*

[19]We know that the law's commands are for those who have the law. This stops all excuses and brings the whole world under God's judgment, [20]because no one can be made right with God by following the law. The law only shows us our sin.

HOW GOD MAKES PEOPLE RIGHT

[21]But God has a way to make people right with him without the law, and he has now shown us that way which the law and the prophets told us about. [22]God makes people right with himself through their faith in Jesus Christ. This is true for all who believe in Christ, because all people are the same: [23]All have sinned and are not good enough for God's glory, [24]and all need to be made right with God by his grace, which is a free gift. They need to be made free from sin through Jesus Christ. [25]God gave him as a way to forgive sin through faith in the blood of Jesus' death. This showed that God always does what is right and fair, as in the past when he was patient and did not punish people for their sins. [26]And God gave Jesus to show today that he does what is right. God did this so he could judge rightly and so he could make right any person who has faith in Jesus.

[27]So do we have a reason to brag about ourselves? No! And why not? It is the way of faith that stops all bragging, not the way of trying to obey the law. [28]A person is made right with God through faith, not through obeying the law. [29]Is God only the God of the Jews? Is he not also the God of those who are not Jews? [30]Of course he is, because there is only one God. He will make Jews right with him by their faith, and he will also make those who are not Jews right with him through their faith. [31]So do we destroy the law by following the way of faith? No! Faith causes us to be what the law truly wants.

THE EXAMPLE OF ABRAHAM

4 So what can we say that Abraham,[n] the father of our people, learned about faith? [2]If Abraham was made right by the things he did, he had a reason to brag. But this is not God's view, [3]because the Scripture says, "Abraham believed God, and God accepted Abraham's faith, and that faith made him right with God."[n]

[4]When people work, their pay is not given as a gift, but as something earned. [5]But people cannot do any work that will make them right with God. So they must trust in him, who makes even evil people right in his sight. Then God accepts their faith, and that makes them right with him. [6]David said the same thing. He said that people are truly blessed when God, without paying attention to good deeds, makes people right with himself.

[7]"Happy are they
whose sins are forgiven,
whose wrongs are pardoned.
[8]Happy is the person
whom the Lord does not consider
guilty." *Psalm 32:1-2*

Blab

Q. **My friend uses laxatives or throws up once in a while, like if she wants to lose five pounds for a date. That's not so bad, is it?**

A. Your friend probably has a problem with an eating disorder. She might not be telling you everything, but even if she is, this is dangerous behavior. Obviously her body is something she feels like she can control with violence. Forcing yourself to throw up is an attack against your body. It is not healthy and is incredibly destructive. You need to talk with her about seeing a counselor or nurse about her disease.

Q. **This guy that I don't like keeps asking me for sex. What should I do? The only way to stop him from asking is to have sex with him. What should I do?**

A. If this guy has some kind of control over you that would force you to have sex with him, then that is rape and you need to tell someone right away. But if all he is doing is asking, then he has no control over you. You are the only one who has control over whether or not you say yes. If he keeps bothering you, you have to tell someone. It's called stalking, and he could end up being a danger to you.

Q. **I did something that I shouldn't have and now I think I have lost a friend. I asked her to forgive me but she won't talk to me. What do I do?**

A. Honestly, now your friend's being the jerk. You did your job. You asked for forgiveness. You can't force her to forgive you. Sorry.

notes

4:1 Abraham Most respected ancestor of the Jews. Every Jew hoped to see Abraham. **4:3 "Abraham . . . God."** Quotation from Genesis 15:6.

Romans 5:1

Now that you are a believer, the battle for your spirit is over. You chose the path of victory when you chose Jesus. When you trusted him, God gave you peace. Are you enjoying the peace you have, or are you trying to fight a battle that's already been won? God wants to come into your life and bring calm to the chaos. He wants you to let him be the light that shatters your darkest storm. A lot of people give their hearts to Jesus and then keep on fighting the same old way they used to. With the peace of God, you can let go of some of your anxiety about grades, college, finances, family, whatever. Do everything you know to do and trust God. You don't have to manipulate decisions and worry about things you can't see. You don't have to go through life by yourself anymore. Rest in the peace God brings. Maybe, if we could hear him, he would be saying, "Stop fighting that battle. I've already done that for you. Be still. Rest. Open your eyes. My love for you has cast out all fear. Look at what I've done. Stop wringing your hands in worry. I love you. I want you to experience the peace I've given you."

[9]Is this blessing only for those who are circumcised or also for those who are not circumcised? We have already said that God accepted Abraham's faith and that faith made him right with God. [10]So how did this happen? Did God accept Abraham before or after he was circumcised? It was before his circumcision. [11]Abraham was circumcised to show that he was right with God through faith before he was circumcised. So Abraham is the father of all those who believe but are not circumcised; he is the father of all believers who are accepted as being right with God. [12]And Abraham is also the father of those who have been circumcised and who live following the faith that our father Abraham had before he was circumcised.

86% OF TEENS SAY THEY ARE SELF-RELIANT.

GOD KEEPS HIS PROMISE

[13]Abraham[n] and his descendants received the promise that they would get the whole world. He did not receive that promise through the law, but through being right with God by

"ABRAHAM AND HIS DESCENDANTS RECEIVED THE PROMISE THAT THEY WOULD GET THE WHOLE WORLD."

his faith. [14]If people could receive what God promised by following the law, then faith is worthless. And God's promise to Abraham is worthless, [15]because the law can only bring God's anger. But if there is no law, there is nothing to disobey.

[16]So people receive God's promise by having faith. This happens so the promise can be a free gift. Then all of Abraham's children can have that promise. It is not only for those who live under the law of Moses but for anyone who lives with faith like that of Abraham, who is the father of us all. [17]As it is written in the Scriptures: "I am making you a father of many nations."[n] This is true before God, the God Abraham believed, the God who gives life to the dead and who creates something out of nothing.

[18]There was no hope that Abraham would have children. But Abraham believed God and continued hoping, and so he became the father of many nations. As God told him, "Your descendants also will be too many to count."[n] [19]Abraham was almost a hundred years old, much past the age for having children, and Sarah could not have children. Abraham thought about all this, but his faith in God did not become weak. [20]He never doubted that God would keep his promise, and he never stopped believing. He grew stronger in his faith and gave praise to God. [21]Abraham felt sure that God was able to do what he had promised. [22]So, "God accepted Abraham's faith, and that faith made him right with God."[n] [23]Those words ("God accepted Abraham's faith") were written not only for Abraham [24]but also for us. God will accept us also because we believe in the One who raised Jesus our Lord from the dead. [25]Jesus was given to die for our sins, and he was raised from the dead to make us right with God.

RIGHT WITH GOD

5 Since we have been made right with God by our faith, we have peace with God. This happened through our Lord Jesus Christ, [2]who has brought us into that blessing of God's grace that we now enjoy. And we are happy because of the hope we have of sharing God's glory. [3]We also have joy with our troubles, because we know that these troubles produce patience. [4]And patience produces character,

notes

4:13 Abraham Most respected ancestor of the Jews. Every Jew hoped to see Abraham. **4:17 "I . . . nations."** Quotation from Genesis 17:5. **4:18 "Your . . . count."** Quotation from Genesis 15:5. **4:22 "God . . . God."** Quotation from Genesis 15:6.

and character produces hope. 5And this hope
will never disappoint us, because God has
poured out his love to fill our hearts. He gave
us his love through the Holy Spirit, whom God
has given to us.

6When we were unable to help ourselves, at the moment of our need, Christ
died for us, although we were living
against God. 7Very few people will die to
save the life of someone else. Although
perhaps for a good person someone
might possibly die. 8But God shows his
great love for us in this way: Christ died
for us while we were still sinners.

9So through Christ we will surely be
saved from God's anger, because we have
been made right with God by the blood of
Christ's death. 10While we were God's enemies, he made friends with us through the
death of his Son. Surely, now that we are his
friends, he will save us through his Son's life.
11And not only that, but now we are also very
happy in God through our Lord Jesus Christ.
Through him we are now God's friends again.

ADAM AND CHRIST COMPARED

12Sin came into the world because of what
one man did, and with sin came death. This is
why everyone must die—because everyone
sinned. 13Sin was in the world before the law
of Moses, but sin is not counted against us as
breaking a command when there is no law. 14But
from the time of Adam to the time of Moses,
everyone had to die, even those who had not
sinned by breaking a command, as Adam had.

Q. How "real" are you at school?
A. Everybody knows that I'm a Christian. If they ask, I tell. I don't try to hide it because I'm not ashamed of it.
GUYS SPEAK OUT

Adam was like the One who was coming in
the future. 15But God's free gift is not like
Adam's sin. Many people died because of the
sin of that one man. But the grace from God
was much greater; many people received God's
gift of life by the grace of the one man, Jesus
Christ. 16After Adam sinned once, he was judged
guilty. But the gift of God is different. God's free
gift came after many sins, and it makes people
right with God. 17One man sinned, and so
death ruled all people because of that one
man. But now those people who accept God's
full grace and the great gift of being made right
with him will surely have true life and rule
through the one man, Jesus Christ.

18So as one sin of Adam brought the
punishment of death to all people, one
good act that Christ did makes all people
right with God. And that brings true life for
all. 19One man disobeyed God, and many
became sinners. In the same way, one man
obeyed God, and many will be made right.
20The law came to make sin worse. But
when sin grew worse, God's grace increased.
21Sin once used death to rule us, but God
gave people more of his grace so that grace
could rule by making people right with
him. And this brings life forever through
Jesus Christ our Lord.

DEAD TO SIN BUT ALIVE IN CHRIST

6 So do you think we should continue sinning so that God will give us even more
grace? 2No! We died to our old sinful lives, so
how can we continue living with sin? 3Did
you forget that all of us became part of Christ
when we were baptized? We shared his death
in our baptism. 4When we were baptized, we
were buried with Christ and shared his death.
So, just as Christ was raised from the dead by
the wonderful power of the Father, we also can
live a new life.

LEARN IT & LIVE IT

Philippians 4:5:
Learn It: The Lord is near.
Live It: Act like you believe that. He's right there next to you, listening to you, watching you. How much will you change the way you behave because of this truth?

Colossians 1:15:
Learn It: Jesus is the image of the invisible God.
Live It: Be Jesus' representative to those who don't know God. Today, find one person who isn't a Christian and do something merciful or kind for them—buy their lunch, no strings attached.

Colossians 2:2-3:
Learn It: Jesus Christ holds all the treasures of wisdom and knowledge.
Live It: If you are looking for advice on how to act, go to God. Pray, talk with him. He'll direct you to scripture that will help you know what to do.

QUIZ

ARE YOU CRUSHING TOO HARD?

1. YOU SPEND YOUR EVENINGS:

A. ON THE PHONE WITH GIRLFRIENDS, CHATTING EXCLUSIVELY ABOUT YOUR LATEST FLAME
B. HANGING OUT WITH YOUR FAMILY
C. WITH FRIENDS, ALWAYS WITH FRIENDS, LOOKING FOR THE GUYS
D. CALLING YOUR CRUSH AND HANGING UP

2. HOW FAR WOULD YOU GO TO SPOT YOUR CRUSH?

A. BE SURE TO TAKE THE LONG ROUTE TO CLASS, CHECKING OUT HIS LOCKER
B. DRIVE THE LONG WAY HOME FROM SCHOOL, PAST HIS HOUSE OR FOOTBALL PRACTICE
C. BUY TICKETS TO A CONCERT YOU KNOW HE'S GONNA BE AT
D. NOT MUCH, MAYBE JUST SIT AT HIS TABLE AT LUNCH

3. HOW MANY TIMES HAVE YOU LOOKED AT WEDDING MAGAZINES IN THE LAST YEAR?

A. LESS THAN 3
B. 3-10
C. 11-15
D. MORE THAN 15

4. HAVE YOU PRACTICED WRITING YOUR NAME WITH HIS BEFORE?

A. YES
B. NO

5. HAVE YOU PRAYED FOR HIM?

A. YES, ON MY OWN
B. YES, AT A SMALL GROUP
C. NO

ANSWERS:

1. a = 5; b = 0; c = 2; d = 4
2. a = 2; b = 5; c = 3; d = 0
3. a = 1; b = 2; c = 3; d = 4
4. a = 5; b = 0
5. a = 3; b = 5; c = 0

IF YOU SCORED BETWEEN 17 AND 24, YOU ARE TOTALLY CRUSHED OUT!

Chill out, girl. God's gonna provide a man when the time is right. No need to become a stalker. Check your priorities.

IF YOU SCORED BETWEEN 10 AND 16, YOU ARE BOY-CRAZY!

Okay, you're a little boy-crazy, but not abnormal. Still, you might want to get in the Scripture and refocus on God. Remember, all your fulfillment is in him.

IF YOU SCORED BETWEEN 0 AND 9, YOU ARE LEVEL HEADED!

Right on. You're not carried away about guys. Sounds like you've got your priorities in order!

5 Christ died, and we have been joined with him by dying too. So we will also be joined with him by rising from the dead as he did. 6 We know that our old life died with Christ on the cross so that our sinful selves would have no power over us and we would not be slaves to sin. 7 Anyone who has died is made free from sin's control.

8 If we died with Christ, we know we will also live with him. 9 Christ was raised from the dead, and we know that he cannot die again. Death has no power over him now. 10 Yes, when Christ died, he died to defeat the power of sin one time—enough for all time. He now has a new life, and his new life is with God. 11 In the same way, you should see yourselves as being dead to the power of sin and alive with God through Christ Jesus.

12 So, do not let sin control your life here on earth so that you do what your sinful self wants to do. 13 Do not offer the parts of your body to serve sin, as things to be used in doing evil. Instead, offer yourselves to God as people who have died and now live. Offer the parts of your body to God to be used in doing good. 14 Sin will not be your master, because you are not under law but under God's grace.

BE SLAVES OF RIGHTEOUSNESS

15 So what should we do? Should we sin because we are under grace and not under law? No! 16 Surely you know that when you give yourselves like slaves to obey someone, then you are really slaves of that person. The person you obey is your master. You can follow sin, which brings spiritual death, or you can obey God, which makes you right with him. 17 In the past you were slaves to sin—sin controlled you. But thank God, you fully obeyed the things that you were taught. 18 You were made free from sin, and now you are slaves to goodness. 19 I use this example because this is hard for you to understand. In the past you offered the parts of your body to be slaves to sin and evil; you lived only for evil. In the same way now you must give yourselves to be slaves of goodness. Then you will live only for God.

20 In the past you were slaves to sin, and goodness did not control you. 21 You did evil things, and now you are ashamed of them. Those things only bring death. 22 But now you are free from sin and have become slaves of God. This brings you a life that is only for God, and this gives you life forever. 23 When people sin, they earn what sin pays—death. But God gives us a free gift—life forever in Christ Jesus our Lord.

AN EXAMPLE FROM MARRIAGE

7 Brothers and sisters, all of you understand the law of Moses. So surely you know that the law rules over people only while they are alive. 2 For example, a woman must stay married to her husband as long as he is alive. But if her husband dies, she is free from the law of marriage. 3 But if she marries another man while her husband is still alive, the law says she is guilty of adultery. But if her husband dies, she is free from the law of marriage. Then if she marries another man, she is not guilty of adultery.

4 In the same way, my brothers and sisters, your old selves died, and you became free from the law through the body of Christ. This happened so that you might belong to someone else—the One who was raised from the dead—and so that we might be used in service to God. 5 In the past, we were ruled by our sinful selves. The law made us want to do sinful things that controlled our bodies, so the things we did were bringing us death. 6 In the past,

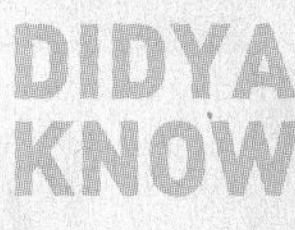

82% OF TEENS SAY THEY ARE OPTIMISTIC ABOUT THEIR FUTURES.

Romans 8:14

When you put your faith in God's Son, his Spirit became part of your life. God knew that you would need his Spirit to help you live the way he wants you to live. People who haven't trusted Jesus don't have God's Spirit. They have no choice but to live life to please themselves or to get on the good side of other people. But you don't have to live that way. You can let God's Spirit choose the road you're going to take. Living that way pleases God. And it has a fringe benefit for you too. "If people's thinking is controlled by the sinful self, there is death. But if their thinking is controlled by the Spirit, there is life and peace" (8:6).

In order for your mind to be ruled by his Spirit, you've got to stay tight with God. Spend time in prayer, in worship, and in his Word. Really work these things into your life—so much that they become a part of you. Then you'll know when the Spirit is leading you, and you'll be able to follow.

August

1
Anne Frank wrote the last entry in her diary—pray for those who are still persecuted.

2

3
Hug the first person you see when you wake up.

4

5
Write a letter to yourself that you'll open five years from now.

6

7
Read your favorite psalm.

8

9

10
Spend an entire day outside enjoying God's creation.

11

12

13
International Lefthanders Day—shake hands the lefty way.

14
Pray for a Person of Influence: Today is Ben from Audio Adrenaline's birthday.

15
Reread your favorite verse today and search for new meaning.

16

17
Pray for a Person of Influence: Today is Kevin Max's birthday!

18
Tell yourself that whatever you do today, you do for the Lord.

19
Pray for a Person of Influence: It's Matthew Perry's birthday.

20

21

22
Tell your brother or sister that you love them today—no matter how they act.

23
Martin Luther King delivered his "I have a dream . . ." speech—pray for unity in our country.

24

26
Women earned the right to vote on this day in 1920—thank God for the rights won by women of the past.

27

28
Volunteer at a nursing home or soup kitchen to show those in need God's love.

29

30
Pray for a Person of Influence: Wish Cameron Diaz a happy birthday.

31

the law held us like prisoners, but our old selves died, and we were made free from the law. So now we serve God in a new way with the Spirit, and not in the old way with written rules.

OUR FIGHT AGAINST SIN

7You might think I am saying that sin and the law are the same thing. That is not true. But the law was the only way I could learn what sin meant. I would never have known what it means to want to take something belonging to someone else if the law had not said, "You must not want to take your neighbor's things."*n* 8And sin found a way to use that command and cause me to want all kinds of things I should not want. But without the law,

"THOSE WHO LIVE FOLLOWING THEIR SINFUL SELVES THINK ONLY ABOUT THINGS THAT THEIR SINFUL SELVES WANT."

sin has no power. 9I was alive before I knew the law. But when the law's command came to me, then sin began to live, 10and I died. The command was meant to bring life, but for me it brought death. 11Sin found a way to fool me by using the command to make me die.

12So the law is holy, and the command is holy and right and good. 13Does this mean that something that is good brought death to me? No! Sin used something that is good to bring death to me. This happened so that I could see what sin is really like; the command was used to show that sin is very evil.

THE WAR WITHIN US

14We know that the law is spiritual, but I am not spiritual since sin rules me as if I were its slave. 15I do not understand the things I do. I do not do what I want to do, and I do the things I hate. 16And if I do not want to do the hated things I do, that means I agree that the law is good. 17But I am not really the one who is doing these hated things; it is sin living in me that does them. 18Yes, I know that nothing good lives in me—I mean nothing good lives in the part of me that is earthly and sinful. I want to do the things that are good, but I do not do them. 19I do not do the good things I want to do, but I do the bad things I do not want to do. 20So if I do things I do not want to do, then I am not the one doing them. It is sin living in me that does those things.

21So I have learned this rule: When I want to do good, evil is there with me. 22In my mind, I am happy with God's law. 23But I see another law working in my body, which makes war against the law that my mind accepts. That other law working in my body is the law of sin, and it makes me its prisoner. 24What a miserable man I am! Who will save me from this body that brings me death? 25I thank God for saving me through Jesus Christ our Lord!

So in my mind I am a slave to God's law, but in my sinful self I am a slave to the law of sin.

BE RULED BY THE SPIRIT

8 So now, those who are in Christ Jesus are not judged guilty. 2Through Christ Jesus the law of the Spirit that brings life made me free from the law that brings sin and death. 3The law was without power, because the law was made weak by our sinful selves. But God did what the law could not do. He sent his own Son to earth with the same human life that others use for sin. By sending his Son to be an offering for sin, God used a human life to destroy sin. 4He did this so that we could be the kind of people the law correctly wants us to be. Now we do not live following our sinful selves, but we live following the Spirit.

5Those who live following their sinful selves think only about things that their sinful selves want. But those who live following the Spirit are thinking about the things the Spirit wants them to do. 6If people's thinking is controlled by the sinful self, there is death. But if their thinking is controlled by the Spirit, there is life and peace. 7When people's thinking is

RELATIONSHIPS

Here's a way for you to challenge yourself for the next week: Think of ways that you can show your family members you appreciate them. Maybe it means taking out the garbage or setting the table for your mom without being asked. Or maybe it means calling your dad at work to see how his day is going. Or it could mean going to your little brother's baseball game, even if it's early on a Saturday morning. Get creative. There are acts of kindness galore that you could do to show your family how you appreciate them.

controlled by the sinful self, they are against God, because they refuse to obey God's law and really are not even able to obey God's law. 8Those people who are ruled by their sinful selves cannot please God.

9But you are not ruled by your sinful selves. You are ruled by the Spirit, if that Spirit of God really lives in you. But the person who does not have the Spirit of Christ does not belong to Christ. 10Your body will always be dead because of sin. But if Christ is in you, then the Spirit gives you life, because Christ made you right with God. 11God raised Jesus from the dead, and if God's Spirit is living in you, he will also give life to your bodies that die. God is the One who raised Christ from the dead, and he will give life through his Spirit that lives in you.

12So, my brothers and sisters, we must not be ruled by our sinful selves or live the way our sinful selves want. 13If you use your lives to do the wrong things your sinful selves want, you will die spiritually. But if you use the Spirit's help to stop doing the wrong things you do with your body, you will have true life.

notes

7:7 "You . . . things." Quotation from Exodus 20:17.

Blab

Q. I found out that my friend, who is 15, sells and smokes weed. What should I say? Should I try to help him?

A. Your best bet is to find out more about him. What's up in his life? Does he have problems? Does he know that God has a purpose for his life and pot will destroy that? Love him like Jesus would. Be there for him, but you can't hang out with him and get involved in this stuff. Talk to a pastor and have him talk with your friend. It's better for a guy to talk to him than you, as a girl.

Q. If I have sex with my boyfriend and I'm not saved, will God forgive me when I get saved? I'm waiting to get saved so that I can have sex with my boyfriend.

A. You obviously know that sex outside marriage is wrong or you wouldn't be asking about forgiveness. So let me ask you this, why are you having sex with this guy? Figure out why you are doing something that you know is wrong. You're worth far more than that in God's eyes. And whether you're saved or not, God's Word is still true. Sex outside of marriage is sinful. But remember, none of us are guaranteed another breath. You may not get the chance to be saved later. Don't procrastinate when it comes to your eternity.

Q. My boyfriend wants me to have sex with him. I know I should say no, but if I do he will dump me. I really like him, and I don't want to break up with him. What should I tell him?

A. You need to tell him that you two just aren't meant for each other because you thought you were dating a godly guy, and a godly guy wouldn't obey his feelings over his God. Some men think about sex all the time. But you, if you want a relationship that honors God, need to find a guy that doesn't. If a man is pressuring you to do anything immoral, is God pleased?

[14]The true children of God are those who
let God's Spirit lead them. [15]The Spirit we
received does not make us slaves again to fear;
it makes us children of God. With that Spirit
we cry out, "Father."[n] [16]And the Spirit himself
joins with our spirits to say we are God's children. [17]If we are God's children, we will receive
blessings from God together with Christ. But
we must suffer as Christ suffered so that we
will have glory as Christ has glory.

OUR FUTURE GLORY

[18]The sufferings we have now are nothing
compared to the great glory that will be shown
to us. [19]Everything God made is waiting with
excitement for God to show his children's
glory completely. [20]Everything God made was
changed to become useless, not by its own
wish but because God wanted it and because
all along there was this hope: [21]that everything God made would be set free from ruin to
have the freedom and glory that belong to
God's children.

[22]We know that everything God made has
been waiting until now in pain, like a woman
ready to give birth. [23]Not only the world, but we
also have been waiting with pain inside us. We
have the Spirit as the first part of God's promise. So we are waiting for God to finish making
us his own children, which means our bodies
will be made free. [24]We were saved, and we
have this hope. If we see what we are waiting
for, that is not really hope. People do not hope
for something they already have. [25]But we are
hoping for something we do not have yet, and
we are waiting for it patiently.

[26]Also, the Spirit helps us with our weakness.
We do not know how to pray as we should. But
the Spirit himself speaks to God for us, even
begs God for us with deep feelings that words
cannot explain. [27]God can see what is in people's hearts. And he knows what is in the mind
of the Spirit, because the Spirit speaks to God
for his people in the way God wants.

[28]We know that in everything God works
for the good of those who love him. They are
the people he called, because that was his
plan. [29]God knew them before he made the
world, and he decided that they would be like
his Son so that Jesus would be the firstborn[n] of
many brothers. [30]God planned for them to be
like his Son; and those he planned to be like
his Son, he also called; and those he called, he
also made right with him; and those he made
right, he also glorified.

DIDYA KNOW

80% OF TEENS SAY THEY TRUST OTHER PEOPLE.

GOD'S LOVE IN CHRIST JESUS

[31]So what should we say about this? If God
is with us, no one can defeat us. [32]He did not
spare his own Son but gave him for us all. So
with Jesus, God will surely give us all things.
[33]Who can accuse the people God has chosen?
No one, because God is the One who makes
them right. [34]Who can say God's people are
guilty? No one, because Christ Jesus died, but
he was also raised from the dead, and now he
is on God's right side, begging God for us. [35]Can
anything separate us from the love Christ has
for us? Can troubles or problems or sufferings
or hunger or nakedness or danger or violent
death? [36]As it is written in the Scriptures:

"For you we are in danger of death
all the time.
People think we are worth no more than
sheep to be killed." *Psalm 44:22*

[37]But in all these things we have full victory through God who showed his love for us.
[38]Yes, I am sure that neither death, nor life,
nor angels, nor ruling spirits, nothing now,
nothing in the future, no powers, [39]nothing

notes

8:15 "Father" Literally, "Abba, Father." Jewish children called their fathers "Abba." **8:29 firstborn** Here this probably means that Christ was the first in God's family to share God's glory.

above us, nothing below us, nor anything else in the whole world will ever be able to separate us from the love of God that is in Christ Jesus our Lord.

GOD AND THE JEWISH PEOPLE

9 I am in Christ, and I am telling you the truth; I do not lie. My conscience is ruled by the Holy Spirit, and it tells me I am not lying. [2]I have great sorrow and always feel much sadness. [3]I wish I could help my Jewish brothers and sisters, my people. I would even wish that I were cursed and cut off from Christ if that would help them. [4]They are the people of Israel, God's chosen children. They have seen the glory of God, and they have the agreements that God made between himself and his people. God gave them the law of Moses and the right way of worship and his promises. [5]They are the descendants of our great ancestors, and they are the earthly family into which Christ was born, who is God over all. Praise him forever![n] Amen.

[6]It is not that God failed to keep his promise to them. But only some of the people of Israel are truly God's people,[n] [7]and only some of Abraham's[n] descendants are true children of Abraham. But God said to Abraham: "The descendants I promised you will be from Isaac."[n] [8]This means that not all of Abraham's descendants are God's true children. Abraham's true children are those who become God's children because of the promise God made to Abraham. [9]God's promise to Abraham was this: "At the right time I will return, and Sarah will have a son."[n] [10]And that is not all. Rebekah's sons had the same father, our father Isaac. [11-12]But before the two boys were born, God told Rebekah, "The older will serve the younger."[n] This was before the boys had done anything good or bad. God said this so that the one chosen would be chosen because of God's own plan. He was chosen because he was the one God wanted to call, not because of anything he did. [13]As the Scripture says, "I loved Jacob, but I hated Esau."[n]

> **Jeremiah 33:11**
> There will be sounds of joy and gladness and the happy sounds of brides and bridegrooms. . . . They will say, "Praise the LORD All-Powerful, because the LORD is good! His love continues forever!"

[14]So what should we say about this? Is God unfair? In no way. [15]God said to Moses, "I will show kindness to anyone to whom I want to show kindness, and I will show mercy to anyone to whom I want to show mercy."[n] [16]So God will choose the one to whom he decides to show mercy; his choice does not depend on what people want or try to do. [17]The Scripture says to the king of Egypt: "I made you king for this reason: to show my power in you so that my name will be talked about in all the earth."[n] [18]So God shows mercy where he wants to show mercy, and he makes stubborn the people he wants to make stubborn.

[19]So one of you will ask me: "Then why does God blame us for our sins? Who can fight his will?" [20]You are only human, and human beings have no right to question God. An object should not ask the person who made it, "Why did you make me like this?" [21]The potter can make anything he wants to make. He can use the same clay to make one thing for special use and another thing for daily use.

[22]It is the same way with God. He wanted to show his anger and to let people see his power. But he patiently stayed with those people he was angry with—people who were made ready to be destroyed. [23]He waited with patience so that he could make known his rich glory to the people who receive his mercy. He has prepared these people to have his glory, [24]and we are those people whom God called. He called us not from the Jews only but also from those who are not Jews. [25]As the Scripture says in Hosea:

"I will say, 'You are my people'
to those I had called 'not my people.'
And I will show my love
to those people I did not love." *Hosea 2:1, 23*

[26]"They were called,
'You are not my people,'
but later they will be called
'children of the living God.' " *Hosea 1:10*

[27]And Isaiah cries out about Israel:
"The people of Israel are many,
like the grains of sand by the sea.
But only a few of them will be saved,
[28]because the Lord will quickly and
completely punish the people
on the earth." *Isaiah 10:22-23*

[29]It is as Isaiah said:
"The Lord All-Powerful
allowed a few of our descendants
to live.
Otherwise we would have been completely
destroyed
like the cities of Sodom and
Gomorrah."[n] *Isaiah 1:9*

[30]So what does all this mean? Those who are not Jews were not trying to make themselves right with God, but they were made right with God because of their faith. [31]The people of Israel tried to follow a law to make themselves right with God. But they did not succeed, [32]because they tried to make themselves right by the things they did instead of trusting in God to make them right. They stumbled over the stone that causes people to stumble. [33]As it is written in the Scripture:

"I will put in Jerusalem a stone that causes
people to stumble,
a rock that makes them fall.
Anyone who trusts in him will never be
disappointed." *Isaiah 8:14; 28:16*

10 Brothers and sisters, the thing I want most is for all the Jews to be saved. That is my prayer to God. [2]I can say this about them: They really try to follow God, but they do not know the right way. [3]Because they did not know the way that God makes people right with him, they tried to make themselves right in their own way. So they did not accept God's way of making people right. [4]Christ

notes

9:5 born . . . forever! This can also mean "born. May God, who rules over all things, be praised forever!" **9:6 God's people** Literally, "Israel," the people God chose to bring his blessings to the world. **9:7 Abraham** Most respected ancestor of the Jews. Every Jew hoped to see Abraham. **9:7 "The descendants . . . Isaac."** Quotation from Genesis 21:12. **9:9 "At . . . son."** Quotation from Genesis 18:10, 14. **9:11-12 "The older . . . younger."** Quotation from Genesis 25:23. **9:13 "I . . . Esau."** Quotation from Malachi 1:2–3. **9:15 "I . . . mercy."** Quotation from Exodus 33:19. **9:17 "I . . . earth."** Quotation from Exodus 9:16. **9:29 Sodom and Gomorrah** Two cities that God destroyed because the people were so evil.

ended the law so that everyone who believes in him may be right with God.

[5]Moses writes about being made right by following the law. He says, "A person who obeys these things will live because of them."[n] [6]But this is what the Scripture says about being made right through faith: "Don't say to yourself, 'Who will go up into heaven?' " (That means, "Who will go up to heaven and bring Christ down to earth?") [7]"And do not say, 'Who will go down into the world below?' " (That means, "Who will go down and bring Christ up from the dead?") [8]This is what the Scripture says: "The word is near you; it is in your mouth and in your heart."[n] That is the teaching of faith that we are telling. [9]If you use your mouth to say, "Jesus is Lord," and if you believe in your heart that God raised Jesus from the dead, you will be saved. [10]We believe with our hearts, and so we are made right with God. And we use our mouths to say that we believe, and so we are saved. [11]As the Scripture says, "Anyone who trusts in him will never be disappointed."[n] [12]That Scripture says "anyone" because there is no difference between those who are Jews and those who are not. The same Lord is the Lord of all and gives many blessings to all who trust in him, [13]as the Scripture says, "Anyone who calls on the Lord will be saved."[n]

[14]But before people can ask the Lord for help, they must believe in him; and before they can believe in him, they must hear about him; and for them to hear about the Lord, someone must tell them; [15]and before someone can go and tell them, that person must be sent. It is written, "How beautiful is the person who comes to bring good news."[n] [16]But not all the Jews accepted the good news. Isaiah said, "Lord, who believed what we told them?"[n] [17]So faith comes from hearing the Good News, and people hear the Good News when someone tells them about Christ.

[18]But I ask: Didn't people hear the Good News? Yes, they heard—as the Scripture says:

"Their message went out through all the world;
their words go everywhere on earth."
Psalm 19:4

Do you prefer to hang out with girls or guys?
Girls, because they don't care about who you are as much as guys do.
GUYS SPEAK OUT

[19]Again I ask: Didn't the people of Israel understand? Yes, they did understand. First, Moses says:

"I will use those who are not a nation to
make you jealous.
I will use a nation that does not
understand to make you angry."
Deuteronomy 32:21

[20]Then Isaiah is bold enough to say:

"I was found by those who were not asking
me for help.
I made myself known to people who
were not looking for me." *Isaiah 65:1*

[21]But about Israel God says,

"All day long I stood ready to accept
people who disobey and are
stubborn." *Isaiah 65:2*

GOD SHOWS MERCY TO ALL PEOPLE

11 So I ask: Did God throw out his people? No! I myself am an Israelite from the family of Abraham, from the tribe of Benjamin. [2]God chose the Israelites to be his people before they were born, and he has not thrown his people out. Surely you know what the Scripture says about Elijah, how he prayed to God against the people of Israel. [3]"Lord," he said, "they have killed your prophets, and they have destroyed your altars. I am the only prophet left, and now they are trying to kill me, too."[n] [4]But what answer did God give Elijah? He said, "But I have left seven thousand people in Israel who have never bowed down before Baal."[n] [5]It is the same now. There are a few people that God has chosen by his grace. [6]And if he chose them by grace, it is not for the things they have done. If they could be made God's people by what they did, God's gift of grace would not really be a gift.

[7]So this is what has happened: Although the Israelites tried to be right with God, they did not succeed, but the ones God chose did become right with him. The others were made stubborn and refused to listen to God. [8]As it is written in the Scriptures:

"God gave the people a dull mind so they
could not understand." *Isaiah 29:10*
"He closed their eyes so they could not see
and their ears so they could not hear.
This continues until today." *Deuteronomy 29:4*

[9]And David says:

"Let their own feasts trap them and cause
their ruin;
let their feasts cause them to stumble
and be paid back.
[10]Let their eyes be closed so they cannot see
and their backs be forever weak from
troubles." *Psalm 69:22-23*

[11]So I ask: When the Jews fell, did that fall destroy them? No! But their mistake brought salvation to those who are not Jews, in order to make the Jews jealous. [12]The Jews' mistake brought rich blessings for the world, and the Jews' loss brought rich blessings for the non-Jewish people. So surely the world will receive much richer blessings when enough Jews become the kind of people God wants.

notes

10:5 "A person . . . them." Quotation from Leviticus 18:5. **10:6-8 Verses 6-8** Quotations from Deuteronomy 9:4; 30:12–14; Psalm 107:26. **10:11 "Anyone . . . disappointed."** Quotation from Isaiah 28:16. **10:13 "Anyone . . . saved."** Quotation from Joel 2:32. **10:15 "How . . . news."** Quotation from Isaiah 52:7. **10:16 "Lord, . . . them?"** Quotation from Isaiah 53:1. **11:3 "They . . . too."** Quotation from 1 Kings 19:10, 14. **11:4 "But . . . Baal."** Quotation from 1 Kings 19:18.

13Now I am speaking to you who are not Jews.
I am an apostle to those who are not Jews, and
since I have that work, I will make the most of
it. 14I hope I can make my own people jealous
and, in that way, help some of them to be saved.
15When God turned away from the Jews, he
became friends with other people in the world.
So when God accepts the Jews, surely that will
bring them life after death.

16If the first piece of bread is offered to God,
then the whole loaf is made holy. If the roots of
a tree are holy, then the tree's branches are
holy too.

17It is as if some of the branches from an
olive tree have been broken off. You non-
Jewish people are like the branch of a wild
olive tree that has been joined to that first tree.
You now share the strength and life of the first
tree, the Jews. 18So do not brag about those
branches that were broken off. If you brag,
remember that you do not support the root,
but the root supports you. 19You will say,
"Branches were broken off so that I could be
joined to their tree." 20That is true. But those
branches were broken off because they did not
believe, and you continue to be part of the tree
only because you believe. Do not be proud,
but be afraid. 21If God did not let the natural
branches of that tree stay, then he will not let
you stay if you don't believe.

22So you see that God is kind and also very
strict. He punishes those who stop following

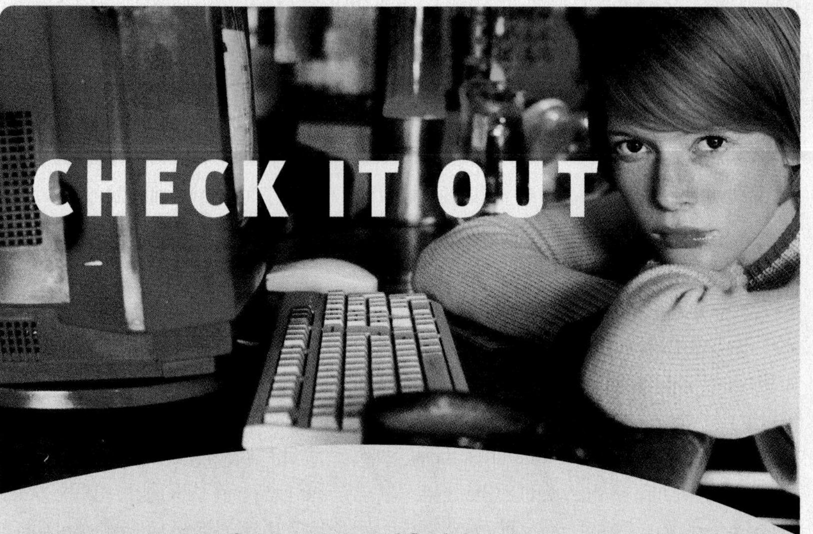

Keep America Beautiful

Keep America Beautiful (KAB) is a national nonprofit public education organization dedicated since 1953 to empowering individuals to take greater responsibility for enhancing their local community environment. Our programs are focused on enabling volunteers to acquire the skills, tools, and resources to work together to create more beautiful and better quality communities. KAB advocates positive environmental action, not finger-pointing or blame-placing.

By turning their attention to litter prevention, beautification, and community improvement, the minimization of the impact of waste on communities, and the improvement of public places like parks, downtowns, roadways, and waterfronts, KAB's more than five hundred community affiliates across the country and twenty-two state affiliates lead the way in protecting and enhancing local environments.

To get involved, go to ***www.kab.org***.

Romans 10:9-13

Know any people who think they're too far gone for Jesus? Maybe they think their sins are too big or their lives too ugly. They think God couldn't possibly save them. They think God's probably mad or that he's given up on them by now or that he's too holy to want them around.

Well, this passage is for the hopeless. God delights in saving the unlovable and the lost and the ones who think they could never be saved. To think that God couldn't save you because you're too far gone is to say, "I'm bigger than God. I can do something so evil that he can't forgive me. I have more power than God." The truth is that *everyone* is hopelessly lost without him and every sin is repulsive to him. But Jesus died for everybody—no exceptions. Anyone who calls out to him will be saved.

"BUT JESUS DIED FOR EVERYBODY—NO EXCEPTIONS."

Romans 12:4-5

You have a destiny that God has designed for you. He wants you to live in a way that honors him, to be part of his plan to bring other people to know him, and eventually to have the same character traits that Jesus has. But part of God's plan is that you wouldn't be able to accomplish any of this by yourself. Of course, you need his Spirit, and he's given you that. But you also need other people.

God wants his people to care about each other and to be able to depend on each other. Your strengths and weaknesses are different from another person's. That person may be able to help you with an area of your life that gives you a lot of trouble. Or you may be able to help someone else see clearly in a situation that is really confusing to him.

Everyone has to trust Jesus as an individual. But once you become a Christian, your life and your relationship with God is connected to other people. You need other Christians! And they need you.

him. But God is kind to you, if you continue following in his kindness. If you do not, you will be cut off from the tree. 23And if the Jews will believe in God again, he will accept them back. God is able to put them back where they were. 24It is not natural for a wild branch to be part of a good tree. And you who are not Jews are like a branch cut from a wild olive tree and joined to a good olive tree. But since those Jews are like a branch that grew from the good tree, surely they can be joined to their own tree again.

25I want you to understand this secret, brothers and sisters, so you will understand that you do not know everything: Part of Israel has been made stubborn, but that will change when many who are not Jews have come to God. 26And that is how all Israel will be saved. It is written in the Scriptures:

"The Savior will come from Jerusalem;
he will take away all evil from the
family of Jacob.[n]
27And I will make this agreement with
those people
when I take away their sins."

Isaiah 59:20-21; 27:9

28The Jews refuse to accept the Good News, so they are God's enemies. This has happened to help you who are not Jews. But the Jews are still God's chosen people, and he loves them very much because of the promises he made to their ancestors. 29God never changes his mind about the people he calls and the things he gives them. 30At one time you refused to obey God. But now you have received mercy, because those people refused to obey. 31And now the Jews refuse to obey, because God showed mercy to you. But this happened so that they also can receive mercy from him. 32God has given all people over to their stubborn ways so that he can show mercy to all.

PRAISE TO GOD

33Yes, God's riches are very great, and his wisdom and knowledge have no end! No one can explain the things God decides or understand his ways. 34As the Scripture says,

"Who has known the mind of the Lord,
or who has been able to give him
advice?" *Isaiah 40:13*

35"No one has ever given God anything
that he must pay back." *Job 41:11*

36Yes, God made all things, and everything continues through him and for him. To him be the glory forever! Amen.

GIVE YOUR LIVES TO GOD

12 So brothers and sisters, since God has shown us great mercy, I beg you to offer your lives as a living sacrifice to him. Your offering must be only for God and pleasing to him, which is the spiritual way for you to worship. 2Do not change yourselves to be like the people of this world, but be changed within by a new way of thinking. Then you will be able to decide what God wants for you; you will know what is good and pleasing to him and what is perfect. 3Because God has given me a special gift, I have something to say to everyone among you. Do not think you are better than you are. You must decide what you really are by the amount of faith God has given you. 4Each one of us has a body with many parts, and these parts all have different uses. 5In the same way, we are many, but in Christ we are all one body. Each one is a part of that body, and each part belongs to all the other parts. 6We all have different gifts, each of which came because of the grace God gave us. The person who has the gift of prophecy should use that gift in agreement with the faith. 7Anyone who has the gift of serving should serve. Anyone who has the gift of teaching should teach. 8Whoever has the gift of encouraging others should encourage. Whoever has the gift of giving to others should give freely. Anyone who has the gift of being a leader should try hard when he leads. Whoever has the gift of showing mercy to others should do so with joy.

9Your love must be real. Hate what is evil, and hold on to what is good. 10Love each other

11:26 Jacob Father of the twelve family groups of Israel, the people God chose to be his people.

ISSUES: Religion

You probably encounter tons of different religions every day on your school campus. What are they all about? Why do they all exist? Those details are important, and you should know what the people you spend time with believe. There's a cool book called *Why So Many Gods?* that will explain a lot of it for you. But until you know the details, don't try to argue with people. Be respectful. Appreciate them for who they are. Become their friend first, and then lead them to the truth of the Good News.

like brothers and sisters. Give each other more
honor than you want for yourselves. 11Do not
be lazy but work hard, serving the Lord with all
your heart. 12Be joyful because you have hope.
Be patient when trouble comes, and pray at all
times. 13Share with God's people who need
help. Bring strangers in need into your homes.

14Wish good for those who harm you; wish
them well and do not curse them. 15Be happy
with those who are happy, and be sad with
those who are sad. 16Live in peace with each
other. Do not be proud, but make friends with
those who seem unimportant. Do not think
how smart you are.

17If someone does wrong to you, do not pay
him back by doing wrong to him. Try to do
what everyone thinks is right. 18Do your best
to live in peace with everyone. 19My friends,
do not try to punish others when they wrong
you, but wait for God to punish them with his
anger. It is written: "I will punish those who
do wrong; I will repay them,"[n] says the Lord.
20But you should do this:

"If your enemy is hungry, feed him;
if he is thirsty, give him a drink.
Doing this will be like pouring burning
coals on his head." *Proverbs 25:21-22*

21Do not let evil defeat you, but defeat evil by
doing good.

CHRISTIANS SHOULD OBEY THE LAW

13 All of you must yield to the government rulers. No one rules unless
God has given him the power to rule, and no
one rules now without that power from God.
2So those who are against the government are
really against what God has commanded. And
they will bring punishment on themselves.
3Those who do right do not have to fear the
rulers; only those who do wrong fear them. Do
you want to be unafraid of the rulers? Then do
what is right, and they will praise you. 4The
ruler is God's servant to help you. But if you
do wrong, then be afraid. He has the power to
punish; he is God's servant to punish those
who do wrong. 5So you must yield to the government, not only because you might be punished, but because you know it is right.

6This is also why you pay taxes. Rulers are
working for God and give their time to their
work. 7Pay everyone, then, what you owe. If
you owe any kind of tax, pay it. Show respect
and honor to them all.

LOVING OTHERS

8Do not owe people anything, except always
owe love to each other, because the person
who loves others has obeyed all the law. 9The
law says, "You must not be guilty of adultery.
You must not murder anyone. You must not
steal. You must not want to take your neighbor's things."[n] All these commands and all others are really only one rule: "Love your neighbor as you love yourself."[n] 10Love never hurts
a neighbor, so loving is obeying all the law.

11Do this because we live in an important
time. It is now time for you to wake up from
your sleep, because our salvation is nearer
now than when we first believed. 12The
"night"[n] is almost finished, and the "day"[n] is
almost here. So we should stop doing things
that belong to darkness and take up the
weapons used for fighting in the light. 13Let us
live in a right way, like people who belong to

"WISH GOOD FOR THOSE WHO HARM YOU; WISH THEM WELL AND DO NOT CURSE THEM."

the day. We should not have wild parties or get
drunk. There should be no sexual sins of any
kind, no fighting or jealousy. 14But clothe
yourselves with the Lord Jesus Christ and forget about satisfying your sinful self.

DO NOT CRITICIZE OTHER PEOPLE

14 Accept into your group someone
who is weak in faith, and do not
argue about opinions. 2One person believes it

notes

12:19 "I . . . them" Quotation from Deuteronomy 32:35. **13:9 "You . . . things."** Quotation from Exodus 20:13–15, 17. **13:9 "Love . . . yourself."** Quotation from Leviticus 19:18. **13:12 "night"** This is used as a symbol of the sinful world we live in. This world will soon end. **13:12 "day"** This is used as a symbol of the good time that is coming, when we will be with God.

BEAUTY SECRET

STAYING HYDRATED

Chug that water down and you'll notice a remarkable difference in the way that you feel. But don't wait until you're feeling thirsty. That means you're already dehydrated. Keep this in mind when you feel a little low on God. Jesus is our living water; we'll never get thirsty after tasting him. Keep a regular dose of Scripture in your diet to stay on top of your game.

is right to eat all kinds of food.[n] But another, who is weak, believes it is right to eat only vegetables. [3]The one who knows that it is right to eat any kind of food must not reject the one who eats only vegetables. And the person who eats only vegetables must not think that the one who eats all foods is wrong, because God has accepted that person. [4]You cannot judge another person's servant. The master decides if the servant is doing well or not. And the Lord's servant will do well because the Lord helps him do well.

[5]Some think that one day is more important than another, and others think that every day is the same. Let all be sure in their own mind. [6]Those who think one day is more important than other days are doing that for the Lord. And those who eat all kinds of food are doing that for the Lord, and they give thanks to God. Others who refuse to eat some foods do that for the Lord, and they give thanks to God. [7]We do not live or die for ourselves. [8]If we live, we are living for the Lord, and if we die, we are dying for the Lord. So living or dying, we belong to the Lord.

[9]The reason Christ died and rose from the dead to live again was so he would be Lord over both the dead and the living. [10]So why do you judge your brothers or sisters in Christ? And why do you think you are better than they are? We will all stand before God to be judged, [11]because it is written in the Scriptures:

" 'As surely as I live,' says the Lord,
'Everyone will bow before me;
everyone will say that I am God.' "

Isaiah 45:23

[12]So each of us will have to answer to God.

DO NOT CAUSE OTHERS TO SIN

[13]For that reason we should stop judging each other. We must make up our minds not to do anything that will make another Christian sin. [14]I am in the Lord Jesus, and I know that there is no food that is wrong to eat. But if a person believes something is wrong, that thing is wrong for him. [15]If you hurt your brother's or sister's faith because of something you eat, you are not really following the way of love. Do not destroy someone's faith by eating food he thinks is wrong, because Christ died for him. [16]Do not allow what you think is good to become what others say is evil. [17]In the kingdom of God, eating and drinking are not important. The important things are living right with God, peace, and joy in the Holy Spirit. [18]Anyone who serves Christ by living this way is pleasing God and will be accepted by other people.

[19]So let us try to do what makes peace and helps one another. [20]Do not let the eating of food destroy the work of God. All foods are all right to eat, but it is wrong to eat food that causes someone else to sin. [21]It is better not to eat meat or drink wine or do anything that will cause your brother or sister to sin.

[22]Your beliefs about these things should be kept secret between you and God. People are happy if they can do what they think is right without feeling guilty. [23]But those who eat something without being sure it is right are wrong because they did not believe it was right. Anything that is done without believing it is right is a sin.

15 We who are strong in faith should help the weak with their weaknesses, and not please only ourselves. [2]Let each of us please our neighbors for their good, to help them be stronger in faith. [3]Even Christ

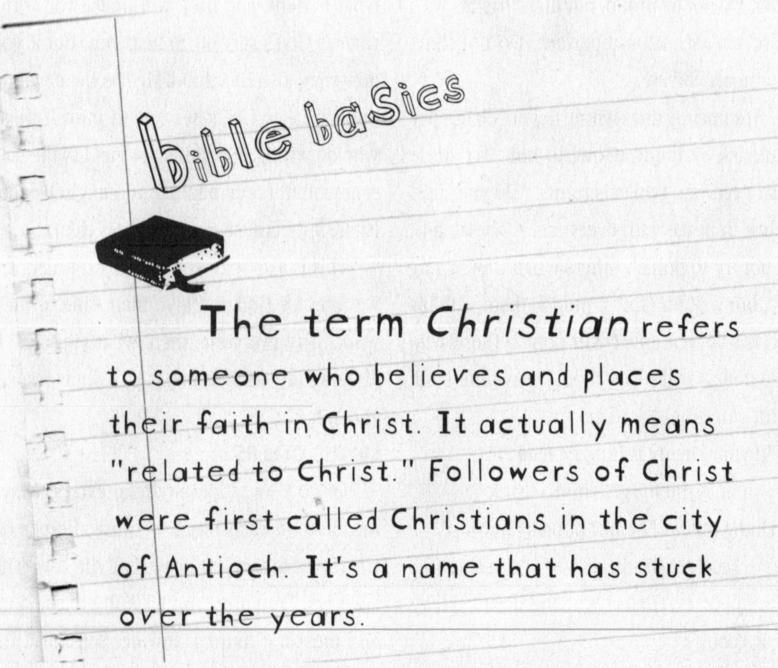

bible basics
The term Christian refers to someone who believes and places their faith in Christ. It actually means "related to Christ." Followers of Christ were first called Christians in the city of Antioch. It's a name that has stuck over the years.

14:2 all . . . food The Jewish law said there were some foods Jews should not eat. When Jews became Christians, some of them did not understand they could now eat all foods.

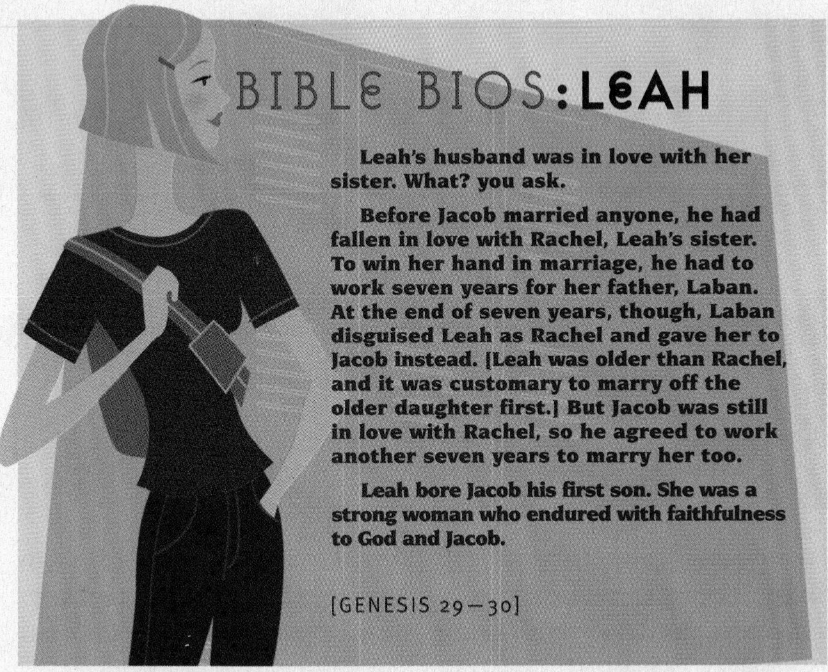
BIBLE BIOS: LEAH
Leah's husband was in love with her sister. What? you ask.
Before Jacob married anyone, he had fallen in love with Rachel, Leah's sister. To win her hand in marriage, he had to work seven years for her father, Laban. At the end of seven years, though, Laban disguised Leah as Rachel and gave her to Jacob instead. [Leah was older than Rachel, and it was customary to marry off the older daughter first.] But Jacob was still in love with Rachel, so he agreed to work another seven years to marry her too.
Leah bore Jacob his first son. She was a strong woman who endured with faithfulness to God and Jacob.
[GENESIS 29—30]

did not live to please himself. It was as the
Scriptures said: "When people insult you, it
hurts me."[n] 4Everything that was written in the
past was written to teach us. The Scriptures
give us patience and encouragement so that
we can have hope. 5Patience and encouragement come from God. And I pray that God will
help you all agree with each other the way
Christ Jesus wants. 6Then you will all be joined
together, and you will give glory to God the
Father of our Lord Jesus Christ. 7Christ accepted
you, so you should accept each other, which
will bring glory to God. 8I tell you that Christ
became a servant of the Jews to show that God's
promises to the Jewish ancestors are true.
9And he also did this so that those who are not
Jews could give glory to God for the mercy he
gives to them. It is written in the Scriptures:

"So I will praise you among the non-Jewish
people.
I will sing praises to your name."
Psalm 18:49

10The Scripture also says,

"Be happy, you who are not Jews, together
with his people." *Deuteronomy 32:43*

11Again the Scripture says,

"All you who are not Jews, praise the Lord.
All you people, sing praises
to him." *Psalm 117:1*

12And Isaiah says,

"A new king will come from the family
of Jesse.[n]
He will come to rule over the
non-Jewish people,
and they will have hope because
of him." *Isaiah 11:10*

13I pray that the God who gives hope will
fill you with much joy and peace while you
trust in him. Then your hope will overflow by
the power of the Holy Spirit.

PAUL TALKS ABOUT HIS WORK

14My brothers and sisters, I am sure that you
are full of goodness. I know that you have all
the knowledge you need and that you are able
to teach each other. 15But I have written to you
very openly about some things I wanted you to
remember. I did this because God gave me this
special gift: 16to be a minister of Christ Jesus to
those who are not Jews. I served God by teaching his Good News, so that the non-Jewish people
could be an offering that God would accept—
an offering made holy by the Holy Spirit.

17So I am proud of what I have done for God
in Christ Jesus. 18I will not talk about anything
except what Christ has done through me in
leading those who are not Jews to obey God.
They have obeyed God because of what I have
said and done, 19because of the power of miracles and the great things they saw, and because
of the power of the Holy Spirit. I preached the
Good News from Jerusalem all the way around
to Illyricum, and so I have finished that part of
my work. 20I always want to preach the Good
News in places where people have never heard
of Christ, because I do not want to build on the
work someone else has already started. 21But
it is written in the Scriptures:

"Those who were not told about him
will see,
and those who have not heard about
him will understand." *Isaiah 52:15*

PAUL'S PLAN TO VISIT ROME

22This is the reason I was stopped many
times from coming to you. 23Now I have finished my work here. Since for many years I
have wanted to come to you, 24I hope to visit
you on my way to Spain. After I enjoy being
with you for a while, I hope you can help me
on my trip. 25Now I am going to Jerusalem to
help God's people. 26The believers in Macedonia
and Southern Greece were happy to give their
money to help the poor among God's people at
Jerusalem. 27They were happy to do this, and
really they owe it to them. These who are not
Jews have shared in the Jews' spiritual blessings, so they should use their material possessions to help the Jews. 28After I am sure the
poor in Jerusalem get the money that has been
given for them, I will leave for Spain and stop
and visit you. 29I know that when I come to
you I will bring Christ's full blessing.

30Brothers and sisters, I beg you to help me
in my work by praying to God for me. Do this
because of our Lord Jesus and the love that the
Holy Spirit gives us. 31Pray that I will be saved
from the nonbelievers in Judea and that this

notes

15:3 "When . . . me." Quotation from Psalm 69:9. **15:12 Jesse** Jesse was the father of David, king of Israel. Jesus was from their family.

LEARN IT & LIVE IT

Colossians 3:10:
Learn It: You have clothed yourself with a new self in Christ Jesus.
Live It: As you get dressed this morning, think about the fact that you're a Christian. Does that influence your choices at all? It should.

Colossians 4:6:
Learn It: "When you talk, you should always be kind and pleasant."
Live It: Say only nice things today. If you feel the urge to gossip, resist. If you feel the urge to say something bratty or sassy, resist. You can do it for one day. People will notice a difference.

1 Thessalonians 2:4:
Learn It: God tests our hearts.
Live It: Think about the biggest challenge you're facing right now. Now what will you do to overcome it in Christ? Come up with a strategy, write it down, and act on it.

help I bring to Jerusalem will please God's people there. 32Then, if God wants me to, I will come to you with joy, and together you and I will have a time of rest. 33The God who gives peace be with you all. Amen.

GREETINGS TO THE CHRISTIANS

16 I recommend to you our sister Phoebe, who is a helper[n] in the church in Cenchrea. 2I ask you to accept her in the Lord in the way God's people should. Help her with anything she needs, because she has helped me and many other people also.

3Give my greetings to Priscilla and Aquila, who work together with me in Christ Jesus 4and who risked their own lives to save my life. I am thankful to them, and all the non-Jewish churches are thankful as well. 5Also, greet for me the church that meets at their house.

Greetings to my dear friend Epenetus, who was the first person in the country of Asia to follow Christ. 6Greetings to Mary, who worked very hard for you. 7Greetings to Andronicus and Junia, my relatives, who were in prison with me. They are very important apostles. They were believers in Christ before I was. 8Greetings to Ampliatus, my dear friend in the Lord. 9Greetings to Urbanus, a worker together with me for Christ. And greetings to my dear friend Stachys. 10Greetings to Apelles, who was tested and proved that he truly loves Christ. Greetings to all those who are in the family of Aristobulus. 11Greetings to Herodion, my fellow citizen. Greetings to all those in the family of Narcissus who belong to the Lord. 12Greetings to Tryphena and Tryphosa, women who work very hard for the Lord. Greetings to my dear friend Persis, who also has worked very hard for the Lord. 13Greetings to Rufus, who is a special person in the Lord, and to his mother, who has been like a mother to me also. 14Greetings to Asyncritus, Phlegon, Hermes, Patrobas, Hermas, and all the brothers who are with them. 15Greetings to Philologus and Julia, Nereus and his sister, and Olympas, and to all God's people with them. 16Greet each other with a holy kiss. All of Christ's churches send greetings to you.

17Brothers and sisters, I ask you to look out for those who cause people to be against each other and who upset other people's faith. They are against the true teaching you learned, so stay away from them. 18Such people are not serving our Lord Christ but are only doing what pleases themselves. They use fancy talk and fine words to fool the minds of those who do not know about evil. 19All the believers have heard that you obey, so I am very happy because of you. But I want you to be wise in what is good and innocent in what is evil.

20The God who brings peace will soon defeat Satan and give you power over him.

The grace of our Lord Jesus be with you.

21Timothy, a worker together with me, sends greetings, as well as Lucius, Jason, and Sosipater, my relatives.

22I am Tertius, and I am writing this letter from Paul. I send greetings to you in the Lord.

23Gaius is letting me and the whole church here use his home. He also sends greetings to you, as do Erastus, the city treasurer, and our brother Quartus. 24[n]

25Glory to God who can make you strong in faith by the Good News that I tell people and by the message about Jesus Christ. The message about Christ is the secret that was hidden for long ages past but is now made known. 26It has been made clear through the writings of the prophets. And by the command of the eternal God it is made known to all nations that they might believe and obey.

27To the only wise God be glory forever through Jesus Christ! Amen.

16:1 helper Literally, "deaconess." This might mean the same as one of the special women helpers in 1 Timothy 3:11. **16:24 Verse 24** Some Greek copies add verse 24: "The grace of our Lord Jesus Christ be with all of you. Amen."

1 Corinthians

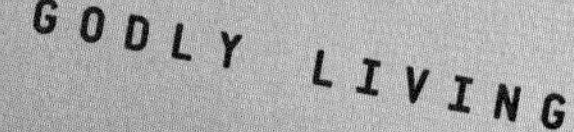

BUILDING MATERIALS FOR GODLY LIVING

There is no such thing as the perfect church. Period. End of story. As long as human beings are involved in running the show, there will never ever be a perfect church. Consider the church founded by the most notable, influential, successful Christian minister of first-generation believers. Paul didn't stay in Corinth just a few days or weeks as he did in most cities he visited. He stayed there for two years, training and nurturing these spiritual infants. Yet, it took only a couple of years before these Corinthians were behaving like disobedient, rebellious kids who didn't know any better.

Take a look at what was going on: They were arguing over who in the church was most important; suing each other in court; turning a blind eye to incest among the congregation; and showing that they were thoroughly confused about key Christian beliefs, such as the Resurrection. In a blunt but loving letter, Paul replies to an array of practical questions the Corinthians raised in a letter to him. But he also confronts issues they were apparently too embarrassed to mention.

This is not a boring letter. First Corinthians cuts to the heart of these issues. And it's timely because, unfortunately, there's a little bit of Corinth in every church—and a lot of Corinth in some.

1 Corinthians 1:9

Paul says that God chose you to "share everything" with Jesus, to be his partner. Being his partner is an honor you don't deserve, but neither does anyone else. But God, because of his kindness and love, chose you for the job even though you aren't qualified for it.

What does it mean to be Jesus' partner? Partners work together toward a common goal. Think about what that goal might be for you and Jesus. Don't just think about your own life—Jesus isn't your genie-in-a-bottle helping you get the things you want. Instead, think about other people. Ask yourself, What does Jesus want to do in my sister's life, my dad's life? What does he want to do for my friends? Ask Jesus those questions too, and ask him what you can do to make that happen. He'll answer you.

It's an awesome privilege to be chosen as Jesus' partner, to work with him to change the lives of people you care about—and maybe even some people you haven't met yet. Make up your mind to be the kind of partner Jesus can be proud of.

1 From Paul. God called me to be an apostle of Christ Jesus because that is what God wanted. Also from Sosthenes, our brother in Christ.

2To the church of God in Corinth, to you who have been made holy in Christ Jesus. You were called to be God's holy people with all people everywhere who pray in the name of the Lord Jesus Christ—their Lord and ours:

3Grace and peace to you from God our Father and the Lord Jesus Christ.

DIDYA KNOW  **74% OF TEENS SAY THEY ARE PHYSICALLY ATTRACTIVE.**

PAUL GIVES THANKS TO GOD

4I always thank my God for you because of the grace God has given you in Christ Jesus. 5I thank God because in Christ you have been made rich in every way, in all your speaking and in all your knowledge. 6Just as our witness about Christ has been guaranteed to you, 7so you have every gift from God while you wait for our Lord Jesus Christ to come again. 8Jesus will keep you strong until the end so that there will be no wrong in you on the day our Lord Jesus Christ comes again. 9God, who has called you to share everything with his Son, Jesus Christ our Lord, is faithful.

PROBLEMS IN THE CHURCH

10I beg you, brothers and sisters,[n] by the name of our Lord Jesus Christ that all of you agree with each other and not be split into groups. I beg that you be completely joined together by having the same kind of thinking and the same purpose. 11My brothers and sisters, some people from Chloe's family have told me quite plainly that there are quarrels among you. 12This is what I mean: One of you says, "I follow Paul"; another says, "I follow Apollos"; another says, "I follow Peter"; and another says, "I follow Christ." 13Christ has been divided up into different groups! Did Paul die on the cross for you? No! Were you baptized in the name of Paul? No! 14I thank God I did not baptize any of you except Crispus and Gaius 15so that now no one can say you were baptized in my name. 16(I also baptized the family of Stephanas, but I do not remember that I baptized anyone else.) 17Christ did not send me to baptize people but to preach the Good News. And he sent me to preach the Good News without using words of human wisdom so that the cross[n] of Christ would not lose its power.

CHRIST IS GOD'S POWER AND WISDOM

18The teaching about the cross is foolishness to those who are being lost, but to us who are being saved it is the power of God. 19It is written in the Scriptures:

"I will cause the wise men to lose their
wisdom;
I will make the wise men unable to
understand." *Isaiah 29:14*

20Where is the wise person? Where is the educated person? Where is the skilled talker of this world? God has made the wisdom of the world foolish. 21In the wisdom of God the world did not know God through its own wisdom. So God chose to use the message that sounds foolish to save those who believe. 22The Jews ask for miracles, and the Greeks want wisdom. 23But we preach a crucified Christ. This is a big problem to the Jews, and it is foolishness to those who are not Jews. 24But Christ is the power of God and the wisdom of God to those people God has called—Jews and Greeks. 25Even the foolishness of God is wiser than human wisdom, and the weakness of God is stronger than human strength.

26Brothers and sisters, look at what you were when God called you. Not many of you were wise in the way the world judges wisdom. Not

1:10 brothers and sisters Although the Greek text says "brothers" here and throughout this book, Paul's words were meant for the entire church, including men and women. **1:17 cross** Paul uses the cross as a picture of the Good News, the story of Christ's death and rising from the dead for people's sins. The cross, or Christ's death, was God's way to save people.

many of you had great influence. Not many of you came from important families. [27]But God chose the foolish things of the world to shame the wise, and he chose the weak things of the world to shame the strong. [28]He chose what the world thinks is unimportant and what the world looks down on and thinks is nothing in order to destroy what the world thinks is important. [29]God did this so that no one can brag in his presence. [30]Because of God you are in Christ Jesus, who has become for us wisdom from God. In Christ we are put right with God, and have been made holy, and have been set free from sin. [31]So, as the Scripture says, "If someone wants to brag, he should brag only about the Lord."[n]

Revelation 19:7
Let us rejoice and be happy and give God glory, because the wedding of the Lamb has come, and the Lamb's bride has made herself ready.

THE MESSAGE OF CHRIST'S DEATH

2 Dear brothers and sisters, when I came to you, I did not come preaching God's secret with fancy words or a show of human wisdom. [2]I decided that while I was with you I would forget about everything except Jesus Christ and his death on the cross. [3]So when I came to you, I was weak and fearful and trembling. [4]My teaching and preaching were not with words of human wisdom that persuade people but with proof of the power that the Spirit gives. [5]This was so that your faith would be in God's power and not in human wisdom.

GOD'S WISDOM

[6]However, I speak a wisdom to those who are mature. But this wisdom is not from this world or from the rulers of this world, who are losing their power. [7]I speak God's secret wisdom, which he has kept hidden. Before the world began, God planned this wisdom for our glory. [8]None of the rulers of this world understood it. If they had, they would not have crucified the Lord of glory. [9]But as it is written in the Scriptures:

"No one has ever seen this,
and no one has ever heard about it.
No one has ever imagined
what God has prepared for those
who love him." *Isaiah 64:4*

[10]But God has shown us these things through the Spirit.

The Spirit searches out all things, even the deep secrets of God. [11]Who knows the thoughts that another person has? Only a person's spirit that lives within him knows his thoughts. It is the same with God. No one knows the thoughts of God except the Spirit of God. [12]Now we did not receive the spirit of the world, but we received the Spirit that is from God so that we can know all that God has given us. [13]And we speak about these things, not with words taught us by human wisdom but with words taught us by the Spirit. And so we explain spiritual truths to spiritual people. [14]A person who does not have the Spirit does not accept the truths that come from the Spirit of God. That person thinks they are foolish and cannot understand them, because they can only be judged to be true by the Spirit. [15]The spiritual person is able to judge all things, but no one can judge him. The Scripture says:

[16]"Who has known the mind of the Lord?
Who has been able to teach him?" *Isaiah 40:13*

But we have the mind of Christ.

FOLLOWING PEOPLE IS WRONG

3 Brothers and sisters, in the past I could not talk to you as I talk to spiritual people. I had to talk to you as I would to people without the Spirit—babies in Christ. [2]The teaching I gave you was like milk, not solid food, because you were not able to take solid food. And even now you are not ready. [3]You are still not spiritual, because there is jealousy and quarreling among you, and this shows that you are not spiritual. You are acting like people of the world. [4]One of you says, "I belong to Paul,"

TOPten
RANDOM BEAUTY SECRETS

01 **Be joyful always.**

02 **Be on time.**

03 **Don't complain.**

04 **Smile, a lot!**

05 **Be modest.**

06 **Don't wear too much makeup.**

07 **Classic style is always best.**

08 **Listen to your mother's advice.**

09 **Befriend the friendless.**

10 **Help other people.**

notes

1:31 "If . . . Lord." Quotation from Jeremiah 9:24.

and another says, "I belong to Apollos." When you say things like this, you are acting like people of the world.

[5]Is Apollos important? No! Is Paul important? No! We are only servants of God who helped you believe. Each one of us did the work God gave us to do. [6]I planted the seed, and Apollos watered it. But God is the One who made it grow. [7]So the one who plants is not important, and the one who waters is not important. Only God, who makes things grow, is important. [8]The one who plants and the one who waters have the same purpose, and each will be rewarded for his own work. [9]We are God's workers, working together; you are like God's farm, God's house.

[10]Using the gift God gave me, I laid the foundation of that house like an expert builder. Others are building on that foundation, but all people should be careful how they build on it. [11]The foundation that has already been laid is Jesus Christ, and no one can lay down any other foundation. [12]But if people build on that foundation, using gold, silver, jewels, wood, grass, or straw, [13]their work will be clearly seen, because the Day of Judgment[n] will make it visible. That Day will appear with fire, and the fire will test everyone's work to show what sort of work it was. [14]If the building that has been put on the foundation still stands, the builder will get a reward. [15]But if the building is burned up, the builder will suffer loss. The builder will be saved, but it will be as one who escaped from a fire.

[16]Don't you know that you are God's temple and that God's Spirit lives in you? [17]If anyone destroys God's temple, God will destroy that person, because God's temple is holy and you are that temple.

[18]Do not fool yourselves. If you think you are wise in this world, you should become a fool so that you can become truly wise, [19]because the wisdom of this world is foolishness with God. It is written in the Scriptures, "He catches those who are wise in their own clever traps."[n] [20]It is also written in the Scriptures, "The Lord knows what wise people think. He knows their thoughts are just a puff of wind."[n] [21]So

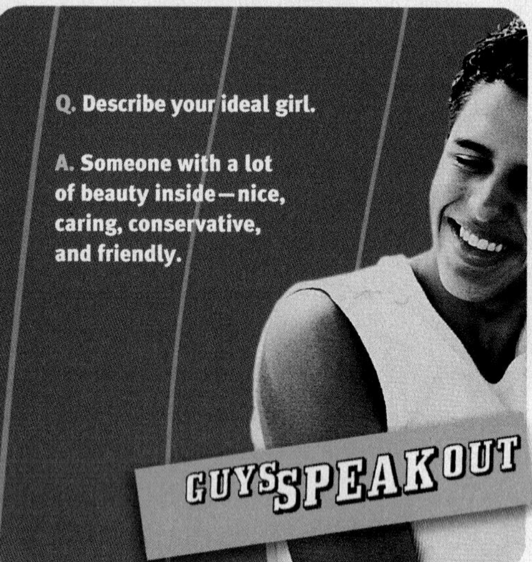
Q. Describe your ideal girl.
A. Someone with a lot of beauty inside—nice, caring, conservative, and friendly.
GUYS SPEAK OUT

you should not brag about human leaders. All things belong to you: [22]Paul, Apollos, and Peter; the world, life, death, the present, and the future—all these belong to you. [23]And you belong to Christ, and Christ belongs to God.

APOSTLES ARE SERVANTS OF CHRIST

4 People should think of us as servants of Christ, the ones God has trusted with his secrets. [2]Now in this way those who are trusted with something valuable must show they are worthy of that trust. [3]As for myself, I do not care if I am judged by you or by any human court. I do not even judge myself. [4]I know of no wrong I have done, but this does not make me right before the Lord. The Lord is the One who judges me. [5]So do not judge before the right time; wait until the Lord comes. He will bring to light things that are now hidden in darkness, and will make known the secret purposes of people's hearts. Then God will praise each one of them.

[6]Brothers and sisters, I have used Apollos and myself as examples so you could learn through us the meaning of the saying, "Follow only what is written in the Scriptures." Then you will not be more proud of one person than another. [7]Who says you are better than others? What do you have that was not given to you? And if it was given to you, why do you brag as if you did not receive it as a gift?

[8]You think you already have everything you need. You think you are rich. You think you have become kings without us. I wish you really were kings so we could be kings together with you. [9]But it seems to me that God has put us apostles in last place, like those sentenced to die. We are like a show for the whole world to see—angels and people. [10]We are fools for Christ's sake, but you are very wise in Christ. We are weak, but you are strong. You receive honor, but we are shamed. [11]Even to this very hour we do not have enough to eat or drink or to wear. We are often beaten, and we have no homes in which to live. [12]We work hard with our own hands for our food. When people curse us, we bless them. When they hurt us, we put up with it. [13]When they tell evil lies about us, we speak nice words about them. Even today, we are treated as though we were the garbage of the world—the filth of the earth.

[14]I am not trying to make you feel ashamed. I am writing this to give you a warning as my own dear children. [15]For though you may have ten thousand teachers in Christ, you do not have many fathers. Through the Good News I became your father in Christ Jesus, [16]so I beg you, please follow my example. [17]That is why I am sending to you Timothy, my son in the Lord. I love Timothy, and he is faithful. He will help you remember my way of life in Christ Jesus, just as I teach it in all the churches everywhere.

[18]Some of you have become proud, thinking that I will not come to you again. [19]But I will come to you very soon if the Lord wishes. Then I will know what the proud ones do, not what they say, [20]because the kingdom of God is present not in talk but in power. [21]Which do

notes

3:13 Day of Judgment The day Christ will come to judge all people and take his people home to live with him. **3:19 "He . . . traps."** Quotation from Job 5:13. **3:20 "The Lord . . . wind."** Quotation from Psalm 94:11.

you want: that I come to you with punishment or with love and gentleness?

WICKEDNESS IN THE CHURCH

5 It is actually being said that there is sexual sin among you. And it is a kind that does not happen even among people who do not know God. A man there has his father's wife. 2And you are proud! You should have been filled with sadness so that the man who did this should be put out of your group. 3I am not there with you in person, but I am with you in spirit. And I have already judged the man who did that sin as if I were really there. 4When you meet together in the name of our Lord Jesus, and I meet with you in spirit with the power of our Lord Jesus, 5then hand this man over to Satan. So his sinful self[n] will be destroyed, and his spirit will be saved on the day of the Lord.

6Your bragging is not good. You know the saying, "Just a little yeast makes the whole batch of dough rise." 7Take out all the old yeast so that you will be a new batch of dough without yeast, which you really are. For Christ, our Passover lamb, has been sacrificed. 8So let us celebrate this feast, but not with the bread that has the old yeast—the yeast of sin and wickedness. Let us celebrate this feast with the bread that has no yeast—the bread of goodness and truth.

9I wrote you in my earlier letter not to associate with those who sin sexually. 10But I did not mean you should not associate with those of this world who sin sexually, or with the greedy, or robbers, or those who worship idols. To get away from them you would have to leave this world. 11I am writing to tell you that you must not associate with those who call themselves believers in Christ but who sin sexually, or are greedy, or worship idols, or abuse others with words, or get drunk, or cheat people. Do not even eat with people like that.

12-13It is not my business to judge those who are not part of the church. God will judge them. But you must judge the people who are part of the church. The Scripture says, "You must get rid of the evil person among you."[n]

JUDGING PROBLEMS AMONG CHRISTIANS

6 When you have something against another Christian, how can you bring yourself to go before judges who are not right with God? Why do you not let God's people decide who is right? 2Surely you know that God's people will judge the world. So if you are to judge the world, are you not able to judge small cases as well? 3You know that in the future we will judge angels, so surely we can judge the ordinary things of this life. 4If you have ordinary cases that must be judged, are you going to appoint people as judges who mean nothing to the church? 5I say this to shame you. Surely there is someone among you wise enough to judge a complaint between believers. 6But now one believer goes to court against another believer—and you do this in front of unbelievers!

7The fact that you have lawsuits against each other shows that you are already defeated. Why not let yourselves be wronged? Why not let yourselves be cheated? 8But you yourselves do wrong and cheat, and you do this to other believers!

9-10Surely you know that the people who do wrong will not inherit God's kingdom. Do not be fooled. Those who sin sexually, worship idols, take part in adultery, those who are male prostitutes, or men who have sexual relations with other men, those who steal, are greedy, get drunk, lie about others, or rob—these people will not inherit God's kingdom. 11In the past, some of you were like that, but you were washed clean. You were made holy, and you were made right with God in the name of the Lord Jesus Christ and in the Spirit of our God.

USE YOUR BODIES FOR GOD'S GLORY

12"I am allowed to do all things," but all things are not good for me to do. "I am allowed to do all things," but I will not let anything make me its slave. 13"Food is for the stomach, and the stomach for food," but God will destroy them

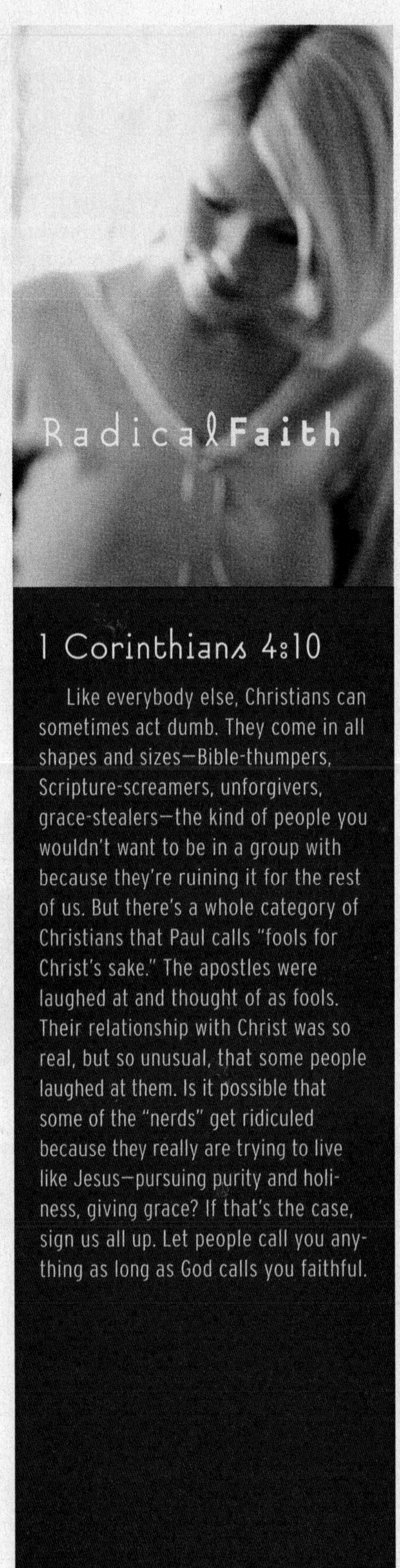

1 Corinthians 4:10

Like everybody else, Christians can sometimes act dumb. They come in all shapes and sizes—Bible-thumpers, Scripture-screamers, unforgivers, grace-stealers—the kind of people you wouldn't want to be in a group with because they're ruining it for the rest of us. But there's a whole category of Christians that Paul calls "fools for Christ's sake." The apostles were laughed at and thought of as fools. Their relationship with Christ was so real, but so unusual, that some people laughed at them. Is it possible that some of the "nerds" get ridiculed because they really are trying to live like Jesus—pursuing purity and holiness, giving grace? If that's the case, sign us all up. Let people call you anything as long as God calls you faithful.

notes

5:5 sinful self Literally, "flesh." This could also mean his body. **5:12-13 "You . . . you."** Quotation from Deuteronomy 17:7; 19:19; 22:21, 24; 24:7.

LEARN IT & LIVE IT

1 Thessalonians 4:17:
Learn It: Christians who are living when the Lord comes again will meet the Lord in the air.
Live It: Do you know someone who might not be with us in the clouds on that day? Share the message of the gospel with them today.

2 Thessalonians 1:5:
Learn It: God is right in his judgment.
Live It: Try to go one entire day without complaining about anything. Remember that everything you face is for a reason.

2 Thessalonians 1:6:
Learn It: God will do what is right.
Live It: Are you scared of something you have to face? Sit down, take three minutes, and focus on the fact that God has designed this especially for you, and it is right. Don't be afraid.

both. The body is not for sexual sin but for the Lord, and the Lord is for the body. 14By his power God has raised the Lord from the dead and will also raise us from the dead. 15Surely you know that your bodies are parts of Christ himself. So I must never take the parts of Christ and join them to a prostitute! 16It is written in the Scriptures, "The two will become one body."[n] So you should know that anyone who joins with a prostitute becomes one body with the prostitute. 17But the one who joins with the Lord is one spirit with the Lord.

18So run away from sexual sin. Every other sin people do is outside their bodies, but those who sin sexually sin against their own bodies. 19You should know that your body is a temple for the Holy Spirit who is in you. You have received the Holy Spirit from God. So you do not belong to yourselves, 20because you were bought by God for a price. So honor God with your bodies.

Song of Solomon 2:4
He brought me to the banquet room, and his banner over me is love.

ABOUT MARRIAGE

7 Now I will discuss the things you wrote me about. It is good for a man not to have sexual relations with a woman. 2But because sexual sin is a danger, each man should have his own wife, and each woman should have her own husband. 3The husband should give his wife all that he owes her as his wife. And the wife should give her husband all that she owes him as her husband. 4The wife does not have full rights over her own body; her husband shares them. And the husband does not have full rights over his own body; his wife shares them. 5Do not refuse to give your bodies to each other, unless you both agree to stay away from sexual relations for a time so you can give your time to prayer. Then come together again so Satan cannot tempt you because of a lack of self-control. 6I say this to give you permission to stay away from sexual relations for a time. It is not a command to do so. 7I wish that everyone were like me, but each person has his own gift from God. One has one gift, another has another gift.

8Now for those who are not married and for the widows I say this: It is good for them to stay unmarried as I am. 9But if they cannot control themselves, they should marry. It is better to marry than to burn with sexual desire.

10Now I give this command for the married people. (The command is not from me; it is from the Lord.) A wife should not leave her husband. 11But if she does leave, she must not marry again, or she should make up with her husband. Also the husband should not divorce his wife.

12For all the others I say this (I am saying this, not the Lord): If a Christian man has a wife who is not a believer, and she is happy to live with him, he must not divorce her. 13And if a Christian woman has a husband who is not a believer, and he is happy to live with her, she must not divorce him. 14The husband who is not a believer is made holy through his believing wife. And the wife who is not a believer is made holy through her believing husband. If this were not true, your children would not be clean, but now your children are holy.

15But if those who are not believers decide to leave, let them leave. When this happens, the Christian man or woman is free. But God called us to live in peace. 16Wife, you don't know; maybe you will save your husband. And husband, you don't know; maybe you will save your wife.

LIVE AS GOD CALLED YOU

17But in any case each one of you should continue to live the way God has given you to live—the way you were when God called you. This is a rule I make in all the churches. 18If a man was already circumcised when he was called, he should not undo his circumcision. If a man was without circumcision when he was called, he should not be circumcised. 19It is

6:16 "The two . . . body." Quotation from Genesis 2:24.

Blab

Q. My spiritual life just seems so dull and boring, almost like there's a cloud and God's behind it, ya know?

A. You are in a place called the desert. We all go through it. It's dry, dull, and lifeless. Seems like God isn't there. But don't let feelings be your guide. You have a job to do in the desert. It's the place where your faith is tested. Do you only love God because you feel him or because you know him? Are you still reading the Bible? Still praying? Keep going strong!

Q. What is appropriate for girls to wear? I've been told I can't wear tube tops and mini skirts. But is it okay to wear a tankini-top bathing suit that hardly shows your belly button? What is going too far?

A. You've got to look at your motive when it comes to clothes. If your motive is to get guys to like you because of your body, your dress will be more revealing. If your goal is to worship God in everything you do, your clothes will naturally be more modest. You can't decide item by item—it's a lifestyle decision.

Q. What if you were a younger girl who liked real older guys? What do you think God would think?

A. As you get older, age becomes less of a problem, because you are both adults and have lots of life experiences. But if you are still pretty young and the guy you like is an adult, then there is something wrong. A man should not want to hang out with a girl. If he wants to, then he probably has some issues.

not important if a man is circumcised or not.
The important thing is obeying God's commands. 20Each one of you should stay the way
you were when God called you. 21If you were
a slave when God called you, do not let that
bother you. But if you can be free, then make
good use of your freedom. 22Those who were
slaves when the Lord called them are free persons who belong to the Lord. In the same way,
those who were free when they were called are
now Christ's slaves. 23You all were bought at a
great price, so do not become slaves of people.
24Brothers and sisters, each of you should stay
as you were when you were called, and stay
there with God.

QUESTIONS ABOUT GETTING MARRIED

25Now I write about people who are not married. I have no command from the Lord about
this; I give my opinion. But I can be trusted,
because the Lord has shown me mercy. 26The
present time is a time of trouble, so I think it is
good for you to stay the way you are. 27If you
have a wife, do not try to become free from
her. If you are not married, do not try to find a
wife. 28But if you decide to marry, you have
not sinned. And if a girl who has never married decides to marry, she has not sinned. But
those who marry will have trouble in this life,
and I want you to be free from trouble.

29Brothers and sisters, this is what I mean:
We do not have much time left. So starting now,
those who have wives should live as if they had
no wives. 30Those who are crying should live
as if they were not crying. Those who are happy
should live as if they were not happy. Those who
buy things should live as if they own nothing.
31Those who use the things of the world should
live as if they were not using them, because
this world in its present form will soon be gone.

32I want you to be free from worry. A man
who is not married is busy with the Lord's
work, trying to please the Lord. 33But a man
who is married is busy with things of the
world, trying to please his wife. 34He must

1 Corinthians 6:19

A temple is a place where God is worshiped. God says that your body is a temple for him. Think about what you do to your body. If you could see God dwelling inside you, would you treat your body the same? Doing drugs turns the temple into a haunted house. Not only are you tearing down the place God lives, you're making a mockery of his home and his creation. Would you go to an actual temple and mess it all up? No. Neither should you throw trash into your own temple, turn it into a house of prostitution, or cover it with graffiti.

The God who loves you deserves better than a crack house for a temple. He wants to glorify himself in you. Drugs are stupid and kill. You already know that. But did you know that Satan uses drugs to destroy as many temples as possible? Don't do drugs. Practice self-control and keep your temple pure and holy and healthy. Ask God to dwell richly in you and commit to being a good temple for him.

notes

QUIZ

WHAT'S YOUR FRUIT OF THE SPIRIT?

1) IT'S CHRISTMAS EVE AND YOUR LITTLE SISTER THROWS A FIT BECAUSE SHE WANTS TO WAIT UP FOR SANTA. YOU:

A. ALMOST LOSE IT—IT'S CHRISTMAS FOR CRYING OUT LOUD, CAN'T SHE BEHAVE JUST ONCE—BUT STOP YOURSELF BEFORE YOU SAY SOMETHING YOU'LL REGRET.
B. JUST SMILE AND HELP YOUR MOM—KIDS WILL BE KIDS.
C. GET HER ALONE AND SWEETLY REMIND HER ABOUT HONORING YOUR PARENTS.

2) ON A DATE WITH A GUY, YOU:

A. ENJOY A NICE DINNER WITH CONVERSATION—LEARNING ABOUT HIM AND HIS BACKGROUND.
B. GO TO A FOOTBALL GAME—NOTHING LIKE THAT KIND OF ACTION.
C. VOLUNTEER TOGETHER AT THE SOUP KITCHEN. YOU LOVE HELPING PEOPLE OUT.

3) DURING A THUNDERSTORM, YOU:

A. CUDDLE UP WITH A BOOK AND READ WITH YOUR FLASHLIGHT.
B. HIDE IN THE BASEMENT—SAFETY FIRST.
C. GO MAKE SURE YOUR LITTLE BRO AND SIS AREN'T SCARED.

4) YOUR TWO BEST FRIENDS ARE IN A FIGHT AND WANT YOUR ADVICE. YOU TELL THEM:

A. "BITE YOUR TONGUE. COOL OFF BEFORE YOU TRY TO WORK IT OUT."
B. "Y'ALL ARE SUCH GOOD FRIENDS. DON'T WASTE TIME ARGUING OVER SOMETHING SO PETTY."
C. "DON'T GET SO WORKED UP. WHY DON'T YOU TAKE SOME TIME TO PRAY ABOUT IT?"

5) WHAT DO YOU WANT TO BE WHEN YOU GROW UP?

A. A DOCTOR.
B. A CHARITY WORKER.
C. A PASTOR'S WIFE.
D. A LAWYER.
E. A MOM.

ANSWERS:

1) a = self-control; b = patience; c = goodness
2) a = gentleness; b = joy; c = kindness
3) a = peace; b = patience; c = love
4) a = self-control; b = joy; c = peace
5) a = gentleness; b = goodness; c = kindness; d = patience; e = love

WHICHEVER QUALITY YOU SCORE THE MOST OF, THAT'S YOUR STRONGEST!

16Some people may still want to argue about this, but I would add that neither we nor the churches of God have any other practice.

THE LORD'S SUPPER

17In the things I tell you now I do not praise you, because when you come together you do more harm than good. 18First, I hear that when you meet together as a church you are divided, and I believe some of this. 19(It is necessary to have differences among you so that it may be clear which of you really have God's approval.) 20When you come together, you are not really eating the Lord's Supper.[n] 21This is because when you eat, each person eats without waiting for the others. Some people do not get enough to eat, while others have too much to drink. 22You can eat and drink in your own homes! You seem to think God's church is not important, and you embarrass those who are poor. What should I tell you? Should I praise you? I do not praise you for doing this.

23The teaching I gave you is the same teaching I received from the Lord: On the night when the Lord Jesus was handed over to be killed, he took bread 24and gave thanks for it. Then he broke the bread and said, "This is my body; it is for you. Do this to remember me." 25In the same way, after they ate, Jesus took the cup. He said, "This cup is the new agreement that is sealed with the blood of my death. When you drink this, do it to remember me." 26Every time you eat this bread and drink this cup you are telling others about the Lord's death until he comes.

27So a person who eats the bread or drinks the cup of the Lord in a way that is not worthy of it will be guilty of sinning against the body and the blood of the Lord. 28Look into your own hearts before you eat the bread and drink the cup, 29because all who eat the bread and drink the cup without recognizing the body eat and drink judgment against themselves. 30That is why many in your group are sick and weak, and many have died. 31But if we judged ourselves in the right way, God would not judge us. 32But when the Lord judges us, he punishes us so that we will not be destroyed along with the world.

Song of Solomon 4:3
Your lips are like red silk thread, and your mouth is lovely.

33So my brothers and sisters, when you come together to eat, wait for each other. 34Anyone who is too hungry should eat at home so that in meeting together you will not bring God's judgment on yourselves. I will tell you what to do about the other things when I come.

GIFTS FROM THE HOLY SPIRIT

12 Now, brothers and sisters, I want you to understand about spiritual gifts. 2You know the way you lived before you were believers. You let yourselves be influenced and led away to worship idols—things that could not speak. 3So I want you to understand that no one who is speaking with the help of God's Spirit says, "Jesus be cursed." And no one can say, "Jesus is Lord," without the help of the Holy Spirit.

4There are different kinds of gifts, but they are all from the same Spirit. 5There are different ways to serve but the same Lord to serve. 6And there are different ways that God works through people but the same God. God works in all of us in everything we do. 7Something from the Spirit can be seen in each person, for the common good. 8The Spirit gives one person the ability to speak with wisdom, and the same Spirit gives another the ability to speak with knowledge. 9The same Spirit gives faith to one person. And, to another, that one Spirit gives gifts of healing. 10The Spirit gives to another person the power to do miracles, to another the ability to prophesy. And he gives to another the ability to know the difference between good and evil spirits. The Spirit gives one person the ability to speak in different kinds of languages[n] and to another the ability to interpret those languages. 11One Spirit, the same Spirit, does all these things, and the Spirit decides what to give each person.

THE BODY OF CHRIST WORKS TOGETHER

12A person's body is only one thing, but it has many parts. Though there are many parts to a body, all those parts make only one body. Christ is like that also. 13Some of us are Jews, and some are Greeks. Some of us are slaves, and some are free. But we were all baptized into one body through one Spirit. And we were all made to share in the one Spirit.

14The human body has many parts. 15The foot might say, "Because I am not a hand, I am not part of the body." But saying this would not stop the foot from being a part of the body. 16The ear might say, "Because I am not an eye, I am not part of the body." But saying this would not stop the ear from being a part of the body. 17If the whole body were an eye, it would not be able to hear. If the whole body were an ear, it would not be able to smell. 18-19If each part of the body were the same part, there would be no body. But truly God put all the parts, each one of them, in the body as he wanted them. 20So then there are many parts, but only one body.

21The eye cannot say to the hand, "I don't need you!" And the head cannot say to the foot, "I don't need you!" 22No! Those parts of the body that seem to be the weaker are really necessary. 23And the parts of the body we

70% OF TEENS SAY ADULTS WOULD DESCRIBE YOUNG ADULTS AS SLOPPY.

notes

11:20 Lord's Supper The meal Jesus told his followers to eat to remember him (Luke 22:14–20). **12:10 languages** This can also be translated "tongues."

Q. What do you think about human cloning. I'm totally against it, how 'bout you?

A. Human cloning is indicative of man's desire to prove that we don't need God. We are strong enough and smart enough to make life on our own. Scientists are using cloning to create better and safer products for us. They are using what they learn right now, for good, but it could be perverted when we try to make human clones. The moral dilemma comes when we try to create a human race to our liking. We determine what traits are best and make people in our image. It is a very dangerous toy to play with.

Q. Did God make the world in six literal days?

A. We don't have a solid answer. It is a matter of faith and science. Some choose to believe that every word in the English Bible is literal. Therefore, a day equals twenty-four hours. And why can't God create the earth in just seven days? He's God! Others say that in the original language a day could have been a longer time.

Q. What is the point of life? Isn't being a Christian just meant to benefit you after you die?

A. Once we fall in love with God we start to realize that it's not just about us and our eternity. The real point of life is for us to fall in love with God: to love God and to love others.

think are less deserving are the parts to which
we give the most honor. We give special
respect to the parts we want to hide. 24The
more respectable parts of our body need no
special care. But God put the body together and
gave more honor to the parts that need it 25so
our body would not be divided. God wanted
the different parts to care the same for each other.
26If one part of the body suffers, all the other
parts suffer with it. Or if one part of our body
is honored, all the other parts share its honor.

27Together you are the body of Christ, and
each one of you is a part of that body. 28In the
church God has given a place first to apostles,
second to prophets, and third to teachers.
Then God has given a place to those who do
miracles, those who have gifts of healing,
those who can help others, those who are able
to govern, and those who can speak in different
languages.[n] 29Not all are apostles. Not all
are prophets. Not all are teachers. Not all do
miracles. 30Not all have gifts of healing. Not all
speak in different languages. Not all interpret
those languages. 31But you should truly want
to have the greater gifts.

LOVE IS THE GREATEST GIFT

And now I will show you the best way of all.

13 I may speak in different languages[n]
of people or even angels. But if I do
not have love, I am only a noisy bell or a crash-
ing cymbal. 2I may have the gift of prophecy. I
may understand all the secret things of God
and have all knowledge, and I may have faith
so great I can move mountains. But even with
all these things, if I do not have love, then I
am nothing. 3I may give away everything I
have, and I may even give my body as an
offering to be burned.[n] But I gain nothing if I
do not have love.

4Love is patient and kind. Love is not jealous, it does not brag, and it is not proud. 5Love
is not rude, is not selfish, and does not get upset
with others. Love does not count up wrongs
that have been done. 6Love is not happy with
evil but is happy with the truth. 7Love patiently
accepts all things. It always trusts, always
hopes, and always remains strong.

8Love never ends. There are gifts of prophecy,
but they will be ended. There are gifts of speaking in different languages, but those gifts will
stop. There is the gift of knowledge, but it will
come to an end. 9The reason is that our knowledge and our ability to prophesy are not perfect. 10But when perfection comes, the things
that are not perfect will end. 11When I was a
child, I talked like a child, I thought like a child,
I reasoned like a child. When I became a man,
I stopped those childish ways. 12It is the same
with us. Now we see a dim reflection, as if we
were looking into a mirror, but then we shall
see clearly. Now I know only a part, but then I
will know fully, as God has known me. 13So
these three things continue forever: faith, hope,
and love. And the greatest of these is love.

DESIRE SPIRITUAL GIFTS

14 You should seek after love, and you
should truly want to have the spiri-
tual gifts, especially the gift of prophecy. 2I will
explain why. Those who have the gift of speaking in different languages[n] are not speaking to

BEAUTY SECRET

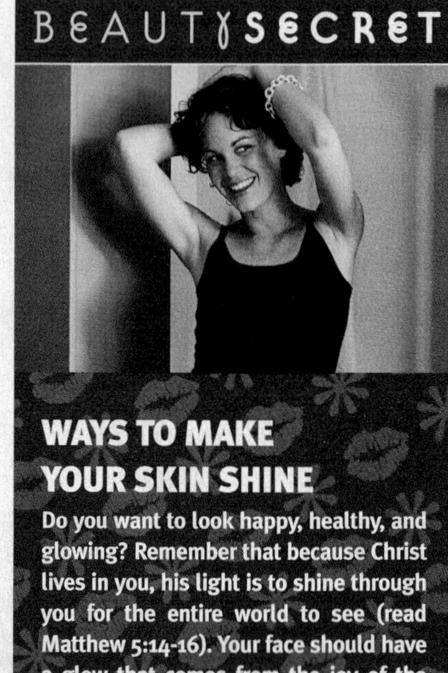

WAYS TO MAKE YOUR SKIN SHINE

Do you want to look happy, healthy, and glowing? Remember that because Christ lives in you, his light is to shine through you for the entire world to see (read Matthew 5:14-16). Your face should have a glow that comes from the joy of the Lord, a glow that is beyond compare!

12:28; 13:1 languages This can also be translated "tongues." **13:3 Verse 3** Other Greek copies read: "hand over my body in order that I may brag." **14:2 languages** This can also be translated "tongues."

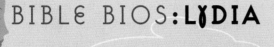

BIBLE BIOS: LYDIA

Lydia was from Thyatira, in Macedonia. She spent her time making purple cloth, which means she probably dealt with the wealthy quite a bit. She was a businesswoman, an entrepreneur. She didn't expect her life to be changed radically, but little did she know that Paul was given a vision to come preach in her hometown. He preached the good news of salvation there, and Lydia and her family heard him speak. They were converted to Christianity, and Lydia became one of the pioneers of the faith in Macedonia. Lydia's heart was open to the will of God.

[ACTS 16]

people; they are speaking to God. No one understands them; they are speaking secret things through the Spirit.
3But those who prophesy are speaking to people to give them strength, encouragement, and comfort.
4The ones who speak in different languages are helping only themselves, but those who prophesy are helping the whole church.
5I wish all of you had the gift of speaking in different kinds of languages, but more, I wish you would prophesy. Those who prophesy are greater than those who can only speak in different languages—unless someone is there who can explain what is said so that the whole church can be helped.

6Brothers and sisters, will it help you if I come to you speaking in different languages? No! It will help you only if I bring you a new truth or some new knowledge, or prophecy, or teaching.
7It is the same as with lifeless things that make sounds—like a flute or a harp. If they do not make clear musical notes, you will not know what is being played.
8And in a war, if the trumpet does not give a clear sound, who will prepare for battle?
9It is the same with you. Unless you speak clearly with your tongue, no one can understand what you are saying. You will be talking into the air!
10It may be true that there are all kinds of sounds in the world, and none is without meaning.
11But unless I understand the meaning of what someone says to me, I will be a foreigner to him, and he will be a foreigner to me.
12It is the same with you. Since you want spiritual gifts very much, seek most of all to have the gifts that help the church grow stronger.

13The one who has the gift of speaking in a different language should pray for the gift to interpret what is spoken.
14If I pray in a different language, my spirit is praying, but my mind does nothing.
15So what should I do? I will pray with my spirit, but I will also pray with my mind. I will sing with my spirit, but I will also sing with my mind.
16If you praise God with your spirit, those persons there without understanding cannot say amen[n] to your prayer of thanks, because they do not know what you are saying.
17You may be thanking God in a good way, but the other person is not helped.

18I thank God that I speak in different kinds of languages more than all of you.
19But in the church meetings I would rather speak five words I understand in order to teach others

RadicalFaith:

1 Corinthians 13:4-5

A wise mom once said, "Take it as a compliment that other girls think your guy is great too." Be secure enough to acknowledge their good taste. If your relationship is about love, then jealousy can't be part of it. Paul spends this whole chapter defining love. He is clear to point out that true love is not jealous. Somehow we've confused this and begun to think that if you love someone, you are supposed to act jealous and possessive. Love is about serving, selflessness, and caring. Arrogance and jealousy are for the insecure. Have faith in Jesus. He will bring the perfect mate for you. Learning to love and trust someone means that you don't worry about who he talks to, or who he's in the same room with. If your guy isn't trustworthy, then he's definitely not the one for you. Don't even start a romantic relationship with him. Start making friendships instead of dating. That way you can spend time with different people until you find the one who lines up with your beliefs and values, the one you have fun with, the one you love, the one you trust completely.

When it's really about love, jealousy will lose out and trust will win.

notes

14:16 amen To say amen means to agree with the things that were said.

than thousands of words in a different language.

[20]Brothers and sisters, do not think like children. In evil things be like babies, but in your thinking you should be like adults. [21]It is written in the Scriptures:

"With people who use strange words and
foreign languages
I will speak to these people.
But even then they will not listen to me,"

Isaiah 28:11-12

says the Lord.

[22]So the gift of speaking in different kinds of languages is a proof for those who do not believe, not for those who do believe. And prophecy is for people who believe, not for those who do not believe. [23]Suppose the whole church meets together and everyone speaks in different languages. If some people come in who do not understand or do not believe, they will say you are crazy. [24]But suppose everyone is prophesying and some people come in who do not believe or do not understand. If everyone is prophesying, their sin will be shown to them, and they will be judged by all that they hear. [25]The secret things in their hearts will be made known. So they will bow down and worship God saying, "Truly, God is with you."

Song of Solomon 4:12
My sister, my bride, you are like a garden locked up, like a walled-in spring, a closed-up fountain.

MEETINGS SHOULD HELP THE CHURCH

[26]So, brothers and sisters, what should you do? When you meet together, one person has a song, and another has a teaching. Another has a new truth from God. Another speaks in a different language,[n] and another person interprets that language. The purpose of all these things should be to help the church grow strong. [27]When you meet together, if anyone speaks in a different language, it should be only two, or not more than three, who speak. They should speak one after the other, and someone else should interpret. [28]But if there is no interpreter, then those who speak in a different language should be quiet in the church meeting. They should speak only to themselves and to God.

[29]Only two or three prophets should speak, and the others should judge what they say. [30]If a message from God comes to another person who is sitting, the first speaker should stop. [31]You can all prophesy one after the other. In this way all the people can be taught and encouraged. [32]The spirits of prophets are under the control of the prophets themselves. [33]God is not a God of confusion but a God of peace.

As is true in all the churches of God's people, [34]women should keep quiet in the church meetings. They are not allowed to speak, but they must yield to this rule as the law says. [35]If they want to learn something, they should ask their own husbands at home. It is shameful for a woman to speak in the church meeting. [36]Did God's teaching come from you? Or are you the only ones to whom it has come?

[37]Those who think they are prophets or spiritual persons should understand that what I am writing to you is the Lord's command. [38]Those who ignore this will be ignored by God.

[39]So my brothers and sisters, you should truly want to prophesy. But do not stop people from using the gift of speaking in different kinds of languages. [40]But let everything be done in a right and orderly way.

THE GOOD NEWS ABOUT CHRIST

15 Now, brothers and sisters, I want you to remember the Good News I brought to you. You received this Good News and continue strong in it. [2]And you are being saved by it if you continue believing what I told you. If you do not, then you believed for nothing.

[3]I passed on to you what I received, of which this was most important: that Christ died for our sins, as the Scriptures say; [4]that he was buried and was raised to life on the third day as the Scriptures say; [5]and that he was seen by Peter and then by the twelve apostles. [6]After that, Jesus was seen by more than five hundred of the believers at the same time. Most of them are still living today, but some have died. [7]Then he was seen by James and later by all the apostles. [8]Last of all he was seen by me—as by a person not born at the normal time.

"NOW, BROTHERS AND SISTERS, I WANT YOU TO REMEMBER THE GOOD NEWS I BROUGHT TO YOU."

[9]All the other apostles are greater than I am. I am not even good enough to be called an apostle, because I persecuted the church of God. [10]But God's grace has made me what I am, and his grace to me was not wasted. I worked harder than all the other apostles. (But it was not I really; it was God's grace that was with me.) [11]So if I preached to you or the other apostles preached to you, we all preach the same thing, and this is what you believed.

WE WILL BE RAISED FROM THE DEAD

[12]Now since we preached that Christ was raised from the dead, why do some of you say that people will not be raised from the dead? [13]If no one is ever raised from the dead, then Christ has not been raised. [14]And if Christ has not been raised, then our preaching is worth nothing, and your faith is worth nothing. [15]And also, we are guilty of lying about God, because we testified of him that he raised Christ from the dead. But if people are not raised from the dead, then God never raised Christ. [16]If the dead are not raised, Christ has not been raised either. [17]And if Christ has not been raised, then your faith has nothing to it; you are still guilty of your sins. [18]And those in Christ who have already died are lost. [19]If our hope in Christ is for this life only, we should be pitied more than anyone else in the world.

[20]But Christ has truly been raised from the dead—the first one and proof that those who

14:26 language This can also be translated "tongue."

Notes

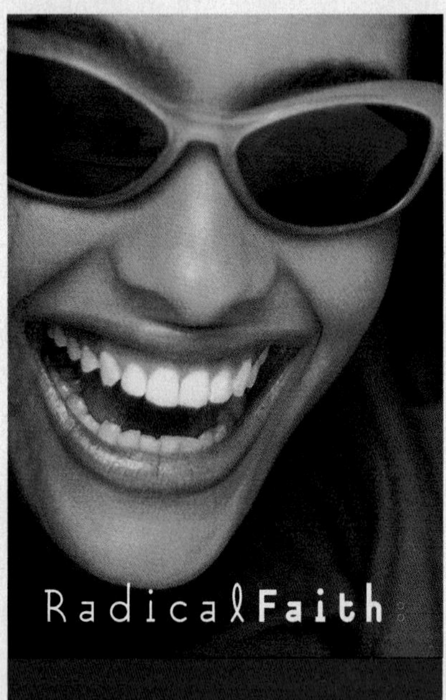

1 Corinthians 15:47-48

Call it amazing. God takes a handful of dirt and makes a man. Very humble beginnings for people who think so highly of themselves. Have you felt jealous of anyone lately? Do you think you deserve more than you have? Are you mad at God because your family doesn't have some of the comforts other families do? Maybe it's time to remember where you came from—dust. Yep, you (and all the people you're jealous of) are just a bunch of dust.

Your life is a gift. It's a blessing to be on earth and to be able to enjoy life. You've got the freedom to choose what you're going to do with your life. The point is to make something out of the gifts God has given you. Your body, mind, emotions, and personality are specially crafted by God for his purpose. God wants you to use the time you've got on earth and the gifts you've been given to glorify him. Your glory comes later. Paul says that everyone in heaven will have a body like the glorified Christ. There's a lot to do between now and the time you get to heaven, so get that old, dusty body in gear. God has great things for you!

sleep in death will also be raised. [21]Death has come because of what one man did, but the rising from death also comes because of one man. [22]In Adam all of us die. In the same way, in Christ all of us will be made alive again. [23]But everyone will be raised to life in the right order. Christ was first to be raised. When Christ comes again, those who belong to him

DIDYA KNOW  **65% OF TEENS SAY ADULTS WOULD DESCRIBE YOUNG ADULTS AS DISHONEST.**

will be raised to life, [24]and then the end will come. At that time Christ will destroy all rulers, authorities, and powers, and he will hand over the kingdom to God the Father. [25]Christ must rule until he puts all enemies under his control. [26]The last enemy to be destroyed will be death. [27]The Scripture says that God put all things under his control.[n] When it says "all things" are under him, it is clear this does not include God himself. God is the One who put everything under his control. [28]After everything has been put under the Son, then he will put himself under God, who had put all things under him. Then God will be the complete ruler over everything.

[29]If the dead are never raised, what will people do who are being baptized for the dead? If the dead are not raised at all, why are people being baptized for them?

[30]And what about us? Why do we put ourselves in danger every hour? [31]I die every day. That is true, brothers and sisters, just as it is true that I brag about you in Christ Jesus our Lord. [32]If I fought wild animals in Ephesus only with human hopes, I have gained nothing. If the dead are not raised, "Let us eat and drink, because tomorrow we will die."[n]

[33]Do not be fooled: "Bad friends will ruin good habits." [34]Come back to your right way of thinking and stop sinning. Some of you do not know God—I say this to shame you.

WHAT KIND OF BODY WILL WE HAVE?

[35]But someone may ask, "How are the dead raised? What kind of body will they have?" [36]Foolish person! When you sow a seed, it must die in the ground before it can live and grow. [37]And when you sow it, it does not have the same "body" it will have later. What you sow is only a bare seed, maybe wheat or something else. [38]But God gives it a body that he has planned for it, and God gives each kind of seed its own body. [39]All things made of flesh are not the same: People have one kind of flesh, animals have another, birds have another, and fish have another. [40]Also there are heavenly bodies and earthly bodies. But the beauty of the heavenly bodies is one kind, and the beauty of the earthly bodies is another. [41]The sun has one kind of beauty, the moon has another beauty, and the stars have another. And each star is different in its beauty.

[42]It is the same with the dead who are raised to life. The body that is "planted" will ruin and decay, but it is raised to a life that cannot be destroyed. [43]When the body is "planted," it is without honor, but it is raised in glory. When the body is "planted," it is weak, but when it is raised, it is powerful. [44]The body that is "planted" is a physical body. When it is raised, it is a spiritual body.

There is a physical body, and there is also a spiritual body. [45]It is written in the Scriptures: "The first man, Adam, became a living person."[n] But the last Adam became a spirit that gives life. [46]The spiritual did not come first, but the physical and then the spiritual. [47]The first man came from the dust of the earth. The second man came from heaven. [48]People who belong to the earth are like the first man of earth. But those people who belong to heaven

notes **15:27 God put . . . control.** From Psalm 8:6. **15:32 "Let us . . . die."** Quotation from Isaiah 22:13; 56:12. **15:45 "The first . . . person."** Quotation from Genesis 2:7.

are like the man of heaven. 49Just as we were made like the man of earth, so we will also be made like the man of heaven.

50I tell you this, brothers and sisters: Flesh and blood cannot have a part in the kingdom of God. Something that will ruin cannot have a part in something that never ruins. 51But look! I tell you this secret: We will not all sleep in death, but we will all be changed. 52It will take only a second—as quickly as an eye blinks—when the last trumpet sounds. The trumpet will sound, and those who have died will be raised to live forever, and we will all be changed. 53This body that can be destroyed must clothe itself with something that can never be destroyed. And this body that dies must clothe itself with something that can never die. 54So this body that can be destroyed will clothe itself with that which can never be destroyed, and this body that dies will clothe itself with that which can never die. When this happens, this Scripture will be made true:

"Death is destroyed forever in victory." *Isaiah 25:8*

55"Death, where is your victory?
Death, where is your pain?" *Hosea 13:14*

56Death's power to hurt is sin, and the power of sin is the law. 57But we thank God! He gives us the victory through our Lord Jesus Christ.

58So my dear brothers and sisters, stand strong. Do not let anything change you. Always give yourselves fully to the work of the Lord, because you know that your work in the Lord is never wasted.

THE GIFT FOR OTHER BELIEVERS

16 Now I will write about the collection of money for God's people. Do the same thing I told the Galatian churches to do: 2On the first day of every week, each one of you should put aside money as you have been blessed. Save it up so you will not have to collect money after I come. 3When I arrive, I will send whomever you approve to take your gift to Jerusalem. I will send them with letters of introduction, 4and if it seems good for me to go also, they will go along with me.

GUYS SPEAK OUT
Q. How much makeup should a girl wear?
A. I like the natural look—as little makeup as possible.

PAUL'S PLANS

5I plan to go through Macedonia, so I will come to you after I go through there. 6Perhaps I will stay with you for a time or even all winter. Then you can help me on my trip, wherever I go. 7I do not want to see you now just in passing. I hope to stay a longer time with you if the Lord allows it. 8But I will stay at Ephesus until Pentecost, 9because a good opportunity for a great and growing work has been given to me now. And there are many people working against me.

10If Timothy comes to you, see to it that he has nothing to fear with you, because he is working for the Lord just as I am. 11So none of you should treat Timothy as unimportant, but help him on his trip in peace so that he can come back to me. I am expecting him to come with the brothers.

12Now about our brother Apollos: I strongly encouraged him to visit you with the other brothers. He did not at all want to come now; he will come when he has the opportunity.

PAUL ENDS HIS LETTER

13Be alert. Continue strong in the faith. Have courage, and be strong. 14Do everything in love.

15You know that the family of Stephanas were the first believers in Southern Greece and that they have given themselves to the service of God's people. I ask you, brothers and sisters, 16to follow the leading of people like these and anyone else who works and serves with them.

17I am happy that Stephanas, Fortunatus, and Achaicus have come. You are not here, but they have filled your place. 18They have refreshed my spirit and yours. You should recognize the value of people like these.

19The churches in the country of Asia send greetings to you. Aquila and Priscilla greet you in the Lord, as does the church that meets in their house. 20All the brothers and sisters here send greetings. Give each other a holy kiss when you meet.

"BE ALERT. CONTINUE STRONG IN THE FAITH. HAVE COURAGE, AND BE STRONG."

21I, Paul, am writing this greeting with my own hand.

22If anyone does not love the Lord, let him be separated from God—lost forever!

Come, O Lord!

23The grace of the Lord Jesus be with you.

24My love be with all of you in Christ Jesus.

2 Corinthians

PAUL'S HEART AND GOD'S WORD TO A STRUGGLING CHURCH

When we first meet the church at Corinth, it is in crisis mode. Paul, who has started and trained the church, has been gone for several years and the church is in chaos. Arguments have broken out about who was in church, how Christians should behave, and how they should worship. Paul does some emergency church triage by sending a letter and making a personal visit to address the problems.

It's a year later, and the church at Corinth is facing yet another crisis. Some men who claim to be apostles arrive in Corinth and begin enticing the church leaders away from Paul's leadership. The letter never mentions the specifics of what these false apostles are teaching, but Paul accuses the impostors of repackaging the Good News with a different Jesus, spirit, and gospel (11:4).

When Paul catches wind of what's going on in Corinth, he goes on the attack. He battles for the hearts and minds of the Corinthians, knowing full well that it's a fight he may lose. Someone concerned about his or her reputation or personal pride might walk away from this one. But not Paul. He refuses to back off. He genuinely cares about the Corinthian people. And he'll do whatever it takes—regardless of the heartache or humiliation—to win them back to the true Jesus, the true Spirit, and the genuine message.

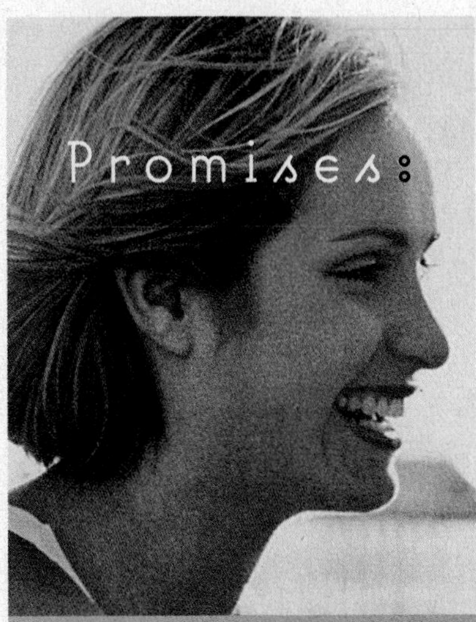

2 Corinthians 1:3-4

Trouble can come in all sizes. There's the kind you get yourself into, like staying out too late or tossing water balloons at passing cars. There's the kind that other people cause for you, like when somebody tells somebody else something you said when you said something totally different. And there's also the kind that just sort of hits you out of the blue, like when your best friend gets hurt in a car wreck or your grandmother dies on an operating table.

But God's comfort comes in colors to match every problem. It fits every hole left behind by someone you love. It soothes every wound that's opened by the daggers of jealousy and anger. It covers every sin with the hope that Christ's blood can forgive completely—and his discipline can keep you from ever visiting this awful place again.

God's comfort—so real, so refreshing—can appear in a Bible verse, a mom's tender arm around your shoulder, a series of events. But it's always there. And it's always yours. And it's always God.

"GOD'S COMFORT COMES IN COLORS TO MATCH EVERY PROBLEM."

1 From Paul, an apostle of Christ Jesus. I
am an apostle because that is what God
wanted. Also from Timothy our brother in Christ.
To the church of God in Corinth, and to all of
God's people everywhere in Southern Greece:
2Grace and peace to you from God our Father and the Lord Jesus Christ.

PAUL GIVES THANKS TO GOD

3Praise be to the God and Father of our
Lord Jesus Christ. God is the Father who is
full of mercy and all comfort. 4He comforts us
every time we have trouble, so when others
have trouble, we can comfort them with the
same comfort God gives us. 5We share in the
many sufferings of Christ. In the same way,
much comfort comes to us through Christ. 6If
we have troubles, it is for your comfort and
salvation, and if we have comfort, you also
have comfort. This helps you to accept patiently the same sufferings we have. 7Our hope
for you is strong, knowing that you share in our
sufferings and also in the comfort we receive.
8Brothers and sisters,[n] we want you to know
about the trouble we suffered in Asia. We had
great burdens there that were beyond our
own strength. We even gave up hope of living.
9Truly, in our own hearts we believed we
would die. But this happened so we would not
trust in ourselves but in God, who raises people from the dead. 10God saved us from these
great dangers of death, and he will continue to
save us. We have put our hope in him, and he
will save us again. 11And you can help us with
your prayers. Then many people will give
thanks for us—that God blessed us because of
their many prayers.

THE CHANGE IN PAUL'S PLANS

12This is what we are proud of, and I can say
it with a clear conscience: In everything we have
done in the world, and especially with you, we
have had an honest and sincere heart from
God. We did this by God's grace, not by the
kind of wisdom the world has. 13-14We write to
you only what you can read and understand.

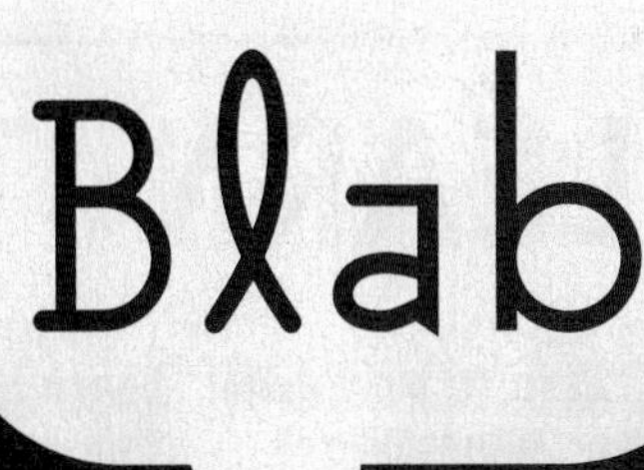

Q. My friends say that Ecstasy is a safe drug. Does that mean that it's okay for me to take it?

A. Even if something were safe that wouldn't necessarily make it right. So safety isn't the question, even though drugs are totally unsafe. Taking drugs is always about feeling good. It's always self-absorbed. Ecstasy can seriously hurt you physically, emotionally, and spiritually. Stay away from the stuff if you want a decent life!

Q. When you repent, do you have to cry and stuff?

A. Repenting of a sin is a tricky thing to understand. You have to understand and accept that what you've done is wrong, and you have to be willing to stop doing it. But check this, when you repent, it doesn't mean you are suddenly perfect. It just means you're doing what God said to do today. So don't get all teary-eyed; just get over it and get on with life.

Q. I have been gay a long time, and it seems I can't shake it. I mean I know the Lord wants me to be free, but I don't think he is showing me a way to get out of all this.

A. Homosexuality is clearly sinful, according to the Bible. If you are a Christian, God says that you are not a slave to sin. This means that you don't have to be a slave to your desires for a gay relationship. Pray a lot. Ask God to give you repentance for your sin. And go talk to a Christian counselor—this is a big deal.

notes

1:8 Brothers and sisters Although the Greek text says "Brothers" here and throughout this book, Paul's words were meant for the entire church, including men and women.

LEARN IT & LIVE IT

1 Timothy 1:4:
Learn It: Don't waste your time talking all about yourself.
Live It: Refuse to go on and on about yourself today. In fact, only talk about yourself if asked. Don't volunteer stories about "me" and "my" and "I" . . . it gets old. Talk about other people—praise their accomplishments and honor their hard work.

1 Timothy 1:12:
Learn It: Our work is from Jesus.
Live It: Jesus has given you the work you have to do. So? Act like it. Do your homework with honor; serve that coffee with dignity. Jesus is your boss.

1 Timothy 1:15:
Learn It: Jesus came to save sinners.
Live It: So what? What does that mean for you? Tell two people about Jesus' love today. Others need to know he came to save them.

And I hope that as you have understood some things about us, you may come to know everything about us. Then you can be proud of us, as we will be proud of you on the day our Lord Jesus Christ comes again.

[15]I was so sure of all this that I made plans to visit you first so you could be blessed twice. [16]I planned to visit you on my way to Macedonia and again on my way back. I wanted to get help from you for my trip to Judea. [17]Do you think that I made these plans without really meaning it? Or maybe you think I make plans as the world does, so that I say yes, yes and at the same time no, no.

[18]But if you can believe God, you can believe that what we tell you is never both yes and no. [19]The Son of God, Jesus Christ, that Silas and Timothy and I preached to you, was not yes and no. In Christ it has always been yes. [20]The yes to all of God's promises is in Christ, and through Christ we say yes to the glory of God. [21]Remember, God is the One who makes you and us strong in Christ. God made us his chosen people. [22]He put his mark on us to show that we are his, and he put his Spirit in our hearts to be a guarantee for all he has promised.

[23]I tell you this, and I ask God to be my witness that this is true: The reason I did not come back to Corinth was to keep you from being punished or hurt. [24]We are not trying to control your faith. You are strong in faith. But we are workers with you for your own joy.

2 So I decided that my next visit to you would not be another one to make you sad. [2]If I make you sad, who will make me glad? Only you can make me glad—particularly the person whom I made sad. [3]I wrote you a letter for this reason: that when I came to you I would not be made sad by the people who should make me happy. I felt sure of all of you, that you would share my joy. [4]When I wrote to you before, I was very troubled and unhappy in my heart, and I wrote with many tears. I did not write to make you sad, but to let you know how much I love you.

FORGIVE THE SINNER

[5]Someone there among you has caused sadness, not to me, but to all of you. I mean he caused sadness to all in some way. (I do not want to make it sound worse than it really is.) [6]The punishment that most of you gave him is enough for him. [7]But now you should forgive him and comfort him to keep him from having too much sadness and giving up completely. [8]So I beg you to show that you love him. [9]I wrote you to test you and to see if you obey in everything. [10]If you forgive someone, I also forgive him. And what I have forgiven—if I had anything to forgive—I forgave it for you, as if Christ were with me. [11]I did this so that Satan would not win anything from us, because we know very well what Satan's plans are.

PAUL'S CONCERN IN TROAS

[12]When I came to Troas to preach the Good News of Christ, the Lord gave me a good opportunity there. [13]But I had no peace, because I did not find my brother Titus. So I said goodbye to them at Troas and went to Macedonia.

VICTORY THROUGH CHRIST

[14]But thanks be to God, who always leads us in victory through Christ. God uses us to spread his knowledge everywhere like a sweet-smelling perfume. [15]Our offering to God is this: We are the sweet smell of Christ among those who are being saved and among those who are being lost. [16]To those who are lost, we are the smell of death that brings death, but to those who are being saved, we are the smell of life that brings life.

Song of Solomon 6:5
Turn your eyes from me, because they excite me too much.

So who is able to do this work? 17We do not sell the word of God for a profit as many other people do. But in Christ we speak the truth before God, as messengers of God.

SERVANTS OF THE NEW AGREEMENT

3 Are we starting to brag about ourselves again? Do we need letters of introduction to you or from you, like some other people? 2You yourselves are our letter, written on our hearts, known and read by everyone. 3You show that you are a letter from Christ sent through us. This letter is not written with ink but with the Spirit of the living God. It is not written on stone tablets*n* but on human hearts.

4We can say this, because through Christ we feel certain before God. 5We are not saying that we can do this work ourselves. It is God who makes us able to do all that we do. 6He made us able to be servants of a new agreement from himself to his people. This new agreement is not a written law, but it is of the Spirit. The written law brings death, but the Spirit gives life.

7The law that brought death was written in words on stone. It came with God's glory, which made Moses' face so bright that the Israelites could not continue to look at it. But that glory later disappeared. 8So surely the new way that brings the Spirit has even more glory. 9If the law that judged people guilty of sin had glory, surely the new way that makes people right with God has much greater glory. 10That old law had glory, but it really loses its glory when it is compared to the much greater glory of this new way. 11If that law which disappeared came with glory, then this new way which continues forever has much greater glory.

12We have this hope, so we are very bold. 13We are not like Moses, who put a covering over his face so the Israelites would not see it. The glory was disappearing, and Moses did not want them to see it end. 14But their minds were closed, and even today that same covering hides the meaning when they read the old agreement. That covering is taken away only through Christ. 15Even today, when they read the law of Moses, there is a covering over their minds. 16But when a person changes and follows the Lord, that covering is taken away. 17The Lord is the Spirit, and where the Spirit of the Lord is, there is freedom. 18Our faces, then, are not covered. We all show the Lord's glory, and we are being changed to be like him. This change in us brings ever greater glory, which comes from the Lord, who is the Spirit.

PREACHING THE GOOD NEWS

4 God, with his mercy, gave us this work to do, so we don't give up. 2But we have turned away from secret and shameful ways. We use no trickery, and we do not change the teaching of God. We teach the truth plainly, showing everyone who we are. Then they can know in their hearts what kind of people we are in God's sight. 3If the Good News that we preach is hidden, it is hidden only to those who are lost. 4The devil who rules this world has blinded the minds of those who do not believe. They cannot see the light of the Good News—the Good News about the glory of Christ, who is exactly like God. 5We do not preach about ourselves, but we preach that Jesus Christ is Lord and that we are your servants for Jesus. 6God once said, "Let the light

"THE WRITTEN LAW BRINGS DEATH, BUT THE SPIRIT GIVES LIFE."

DIDYA KNOW

57% OF TEENS SAY ADULTS WOULD DESCRIBE YOUNG ADULTS AS VIOLENT.

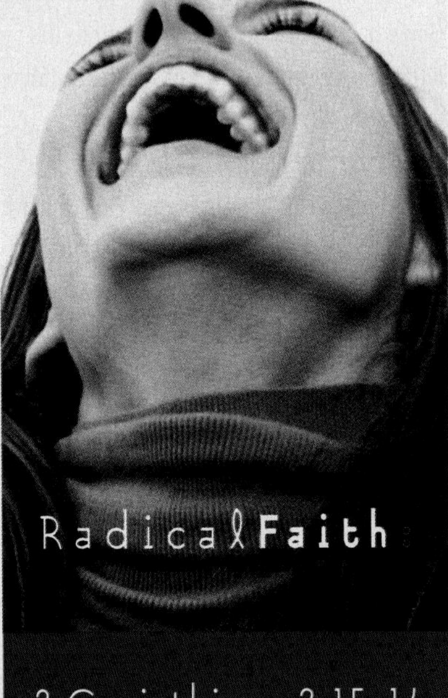

RadicalFaith

2 Corinthians 2:15-16

When you do what God wants instead of acting like all the people around you, Paul says that you are, figuratively speaking, a perfume. For some people that perfume smells wonderful. These people are inspired by your relationship with Jesus. If they haven't met him, they see the peace you have, the way it really makes you happy to follow him, and they want what you have. If they do know Jesus, your example encourages them to keep getting closer to him.

Unfortunately, there are others who think your life really stinks. The fact that you do things they wouldn't do—take up for someone who everyone else is picking on, stay straight-faced when you hear a dirty joke, refuse to drink at a party—that bugs them a lot. They can make things pretty unpleasant for you, but they're hurting themselves more than they hurt you and they don't even realize it. By giving you a hard time, they're pushing away Jesus—and knowing him is the whole reason they were born!

notes

3:3 stone tablets Meaning the Law of Moses that was written on stone tablets (Exodus 24:12; 25:16).

shine out of the darkness!" This is the same God who made his light shine in our hearts by letting us know the glory of God that is in the face of Christ.

SPIRITUAL TREASURE IN CLAY JARS

7We have this treasure from God, but we are like clay jars that hold the treasure. This shows that the great power is from God, not from us. 8We have troubles all around us, but we are not defeated. We do not know what to do, but we do not give up the hope of living. 9We are persecuted, but God does not leave us. We are hurt sometimes, but we are not destroyed. 10We carry the death of Jesus in our own bodies so that the life of Jesus can also be seen in our bodies. 11We are alive, but for Jesus we are always in danger of death so that the life of Jesus can be seen in our bodies that die. 12So death is working in us, but life is working in you.

13It is written in the Scriptures, "I believed, so I spoke."[n] Our faith is like this, too. We believe, and so we speak. 14God raised the Lord Jesus from the dead, and we know that God will also raise us with Jesus. God will bring us together with you, and we will stand before him. 15All these things are for you. And so the grace of God that is being given to more and more people will bring increasing thanks to God for his glory.

LIVING BY FAITH

16So we do not give up. Our physical body is becoming older and weaker, but our spirit inside us is made new every day. 17We have small troubles for a while now, but they are helping us gain an eternal glory that is much greater than the troubles. 18We set our eyes not on what we see but on what we cannot see. What we see will last only a short time, but what we cannot see will last forever.

5 We know that our body—the tent we live in here on earth—will be destroyed. But when that happens, God will have a house for us. It will not be a house made by human hands; instead, it will be a home in heaven that will last forever. 2But now we groan in this tent. We want God to give us our heavenly home, 3because it will clothe us so we will not be naked. 4While we live in this body,

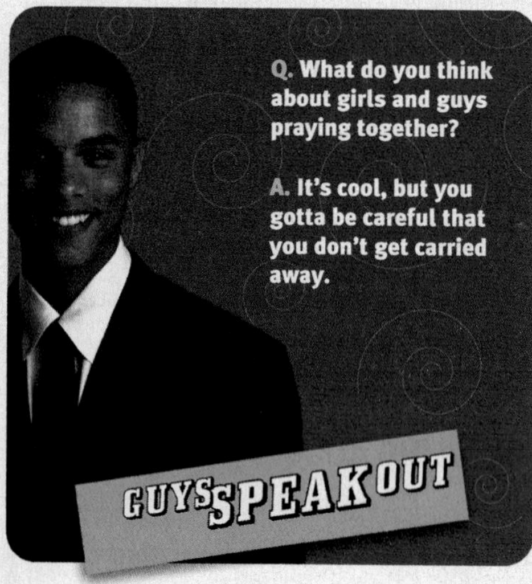

we have burdens, and we groan. We do not want to be naked, but we want to be clothed with our heavenly home. Then this body that dies will be fully covered with life. 5This is what God made us for, and he has given us the Spirit to be a guarantee for this new life.

Q. What do you think about girls and guys praying together?
A. It's cool, but you gotta be careful that you don't get carried away.
GUYS SPEAK OUT

6So we always have courage. We know that while we live in this body, we are away from the Lord. 7We live by what we believe, not by what we can see. 8So I say that we have courage. We really want to be away from this body and be at home with the Lord. 9Our only goal is to please God whether we live here or there, 10because we must all stand before Christ to be judged. Each of us will receive what we should get—good or bad—for the things we did in the earthly body.

John 13:34
I give you a new command: Love each other. You must love each other as I have loved you.

BECOMING FRIENDS WITH GOD

11Since we know what it means to fear the Lord, we try to help people accept the truth about us. God knows what we really are, and I hope that in your hearts you know, too. 12We are not trying to prove ourselves to you again, but we are telling you about ourselves so you will be proud of us. Then you will have an answer for those who are proud about things that can be seen rather than what is in the heart. 13If we are out of our minds, it is for God. If we have our right minds, it is for you. 14The love of Christ controls us, because we know that One died for all, so all have died. 15Christ died for all so that those who live would not continue to live for themselves. He died for them and was raised from the dead so that they would live for him.

16From this time on we do not think of anyone as the world does. In the past we thought of Christ as the world thinks, but we no longer think of him in that way. 17If anyone belongs to Christ, there is a new creation. The old things have gone; everything is made new! 18All this is from God. Through Christ, God made peace between us and himself, and God gave us the work of telling everyone about the peace we can have with him. 19God was in Christ, making peace between the world and himself. In Christ, God did not hold the world guilty of its sins. And he gave us this message of peace. 20So we have been sent to speak for Christ. It is as if God is calling to you through us. We speak for Christ when we beg you to be at peace with God. 21Christ had no sin, but God made him become sin so that in Christ we could become right with God.

6 We are workers together with God, so we beg you: Do not let the grace that you received from God be for nothing. 2God says,

"At the right time I heard your prayers.
On the day of salvation I helped you."

Isaiah 49:8

I tell you that the "right time" is now, and the "day of salvation" is now.

4:13 "I . . . spoke." Quotation from Psalm 116:10.

[3]We do not want anyone to find fault with
our work, so nothing we do will be a problem
for anyone. [4]But in every way we show we are
servants of God: in accepting many hard
things, in troubles, in difficulties, and in great
problems. [5]We are beaten and thrown into
prison. We meet those who become upset
with us and start riots. We work hard, and
sometimes we get no sleep or food. [6]We show
we are servants of God by our pure lives, our
understanding, patience, and kindness, by the
Holy Spirit, by true love, [7]by speaking the truth,
and by God's power. We use our right living
to defend ourselves against everything. [8]Some
people honor us, but others blame us. Some
people say evil things about us, but others say
good things. Some people say we are liars, but
we speak the truth. [9]We are not known, but
we are well known. We seem to be dying, but
we continue to live. We are punished, but we
are not killed. [10]We have much sadness, but
we are always rejoicing. We are poor, but we
are making many people rich in faith. We
have nothing, but really we have everything.

[11]We have spoken freely to you in Corinth
and have opened our hearts to you. [12]Our
feelings of love for you have not stopped, but
you have stopped your feelings of love for us.

63% OF TEENS SAY ADULTS WOULD DESCRIBE YOUNG ADULTS AS FRIENDLY.

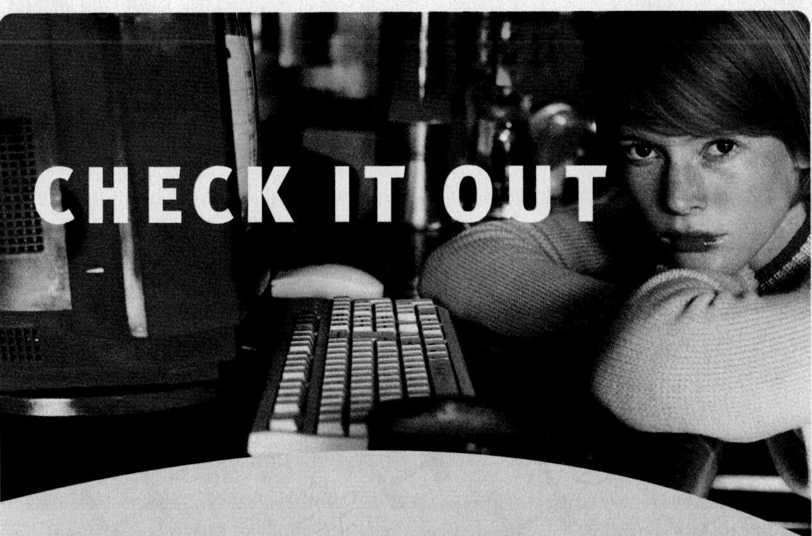

Second Harvest Food Bank

America's Second Harvest is the nation's largest domestic hunger relief organization. Through a network of over two hundred food banks and food-rescue programs, we provide emergency food assistance to more than twenty-three million hungry Americans each year, eight million of whom are children.

Last year, America's Second Harvest distributed 1.7 billion pounds of food to needy Americans, serving all fifty states and Puerto Rico. Our goal is to end hunger in America.

To find out how to volunteer, go to ***www.secondharvest.org/foodbanks/volunteer.html.***

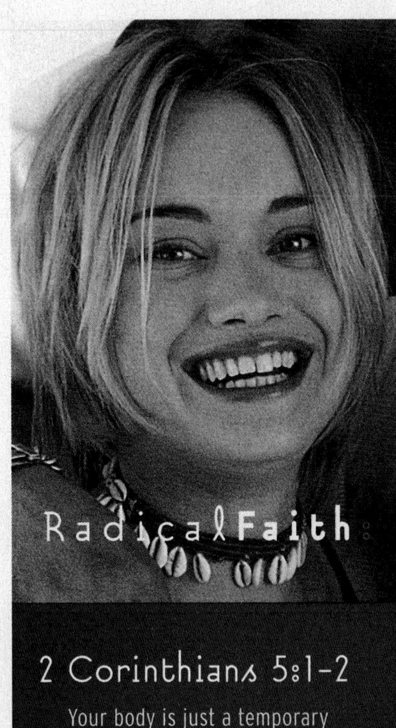

2 Corinthians 5:1-2

Your body is just a temporary home. That's right, it's just like a tent—a place for the real you, your spirit, to live. It's important to exercise, eat right, and take care of your body, but someday your tent is going to check out of here. That's just the natural cycle of life. Your body cannot live forever, but, thank God, death is not the end. You're on your way to a much greater place—a place where there's no more sadness, a place we've all heard about, a place called heaven!

Your body may be like a tent down here on earth, but someday you're going to live in a home that God himself has prepared just for you. Just think—he made the whole world in seven days, but he's still working on your eternal home. Your mind can't even imagine how awesome that place will be! So don't be discouraged with your home here on earth. It won't be long, and you'll be walking those streets of gold!

2 Corinthians 7:6

Paul is so honest. He wasn't always standing on a spiritual mountaintop, and he doesn't mind admitting it. He spends a lot of time in this book talking about his suffering, worry, tears, and broken heart. He doesn't try to pretend that just because he loves Jesus, nothing hard ever happens. He admits to his struggles and hardships. He talks about the troubles he's faced. He is real and vulnerable.

Somehow over time, Christians have lost sight of Paul's example. Somehow we've replaced honesty with pretending. Too many Christians pretend that their lives are happy and suffer in total silence. They won't admit to their own needs and weaknesses, yet wonder why God doesn't do something. God will bring cheer and comfort to those who are in need. Do you need God to comfort you? Do you need some cheering up? Then talk to the Lord. Be honest with some people who are close to you. Be brave enough to say, "I love God, but life is tough right now." God may use the Holy Spirit, or the body of believers, or the truth of his Word—but he will bring cheer to people in need.

"SOMEHOW WE'VE REPLACED HONESTY WITH PRETENDING."

13I speak to you as if you were my children. Do to us as we have done—open your hearts to us.

WARNING ABOUT NON-CHRISTIANS

14You are not the same as those who do not believe. So do not join yourselves to them. Good and bad do not belong together. Light and darkness cannot share together. 15How can Christ and Belial, the devil, have any agreement? What can a believer have together with a nonbeliever? 16The temple of God cannot have any agreement with idols, and we are the temple of the living God. As God said: "I will live with them and walk with them. And I will be their God, and they will be my people."[n]

17"Leave those people,
and be separate, says the Lord.
Touch nothing that is unclean,
and I will accept you."

Isaiah 52:11; Ezekiel 20:34, 41

18"I will be your father,
and you will be my sons and daughters,
says the Lord Almighty."

2 Samuel 7:14

7 Dear friends, we have these promises from God, so we should make ourselves pure—free from anything that makes body or soul unclean. We should try to become holy in the way we live, because we respect God.

PAUL'S JOY

2Open your hearts to us. We have not done wrong to anyone, we have not ruined the faith of anyone, and we have not cheated anyone. 3I do not say this to blame you. I told you before that we love you so much we would live or die with you. 4I feel very sure of you and am very proud of you. You give me much comfort, and in all of our troubles I have great joy.

5When we came into Macedonia, we had no rest. We found trouble all around us. We had fighting on the outside and fear on the inside. 6But God, who comforts those who are troubled, comforted us when Titus came. 7We were comforted, not only by his coming but also by the comfort you gave him. Titus told us about your wish to see me and that you are very sorry for what you did. He also told me about your great care for me, and when I heard this, I was much happier.

8Even if my letter made you sad, I am not sorry I wrote it. At first I was sorry, because it made you sad, but you were sad only for a short time. 9Now I am happy, not because you were made sad, but because your sorrow made you change your lives. You became sad in the way God wanted you to, so you were not hurt by us in any way. 10The kind of sorrow God wants makes people change their hearts and lives. This leads to salvation, and you cannot be sorry for that. But the kind of sorrow the world has brings death. 11See what this sorrow—the sorrow God wanted you to have—has done to you: It has made you very serious. It made you want to prove you were not wrong. It made you angry and afraid. It made you want to see me. It made you care. It made you want the right thing to be done. You proved you were innocent in the problem. 12I wrote that letter, not because of the one who did the wrong or because of the person who was hurt. I wrote the letter so you could see, before God, the great care you have for us. 13That is why we were comforted.

Not only were we very comforted, we were even happier to see that Titus was so happy. All of you made him feel much better. 14I bragged to Titus about you, and you showed that I was right. Everything we said to you was true, and you have proved that what we bragged about to Titus is true. 15And his love for you is stronger when he remembers that you were all ready to obey. You welcomed him with respect and fear. 16I am very happy that I can trust you fully.

CHRISTIAN GIVING

8 And now, brothers and sisters, we want you to know about the grace God gave the churches in Macedonia. 2They have been tested by great troubles, and they are very poor.

6:16 "I . . . people." Quotation from Leviticus 26:11-12; Jeremiah 32:38; Ezekiel 37:27.

But they gave much because of their great joy. [3]I can tell you that they gave as much as they were able and even more than they could afford. No one told them to do it. [4]But they begged and pleaded with us to let them share in this service for God's people. [5]And they gave in a way we did not expect: They first gave themselves to the Lord and to us. This is what God wants. [6]So we asked Titus to help you finish this special work of grace since he is the one who started it. [7]You are rich in everything—in faith, in speaking, in knowledge, in truly wanting to help, and in the love you learned from us. In the same way, be strong also in the grace of giving.

[8]I am not commanding you to give. But I want to see if your love is true by comparing you with others that really want to help. [9]You know the grace of our Lord Jesus Christ. You know that Christ was rich, but for you he became poor so that by his becoming poor you might become rich.

[10]This is what I think you should do: Last year you were the first to want to give, and you were the first who gave. [11]So now finish the work you started. Then your "doing" will be equal to your "wanting to do." Give from what you have. [12]If you want to give, your gift will be accepted. It will be judged by what you have, not by what you do not have. [13]We do not want you to have troubles while other people are at ease, but we want everything to be equal. [14]At this time you have plenty. What you have can help others who are in need. Then later, when they have plenty, they can help you when you are in need, and all will be equal. [15]As it is written in the Scriptures, "The person who gathered more did not have too much, nor did the person who gathered less have too little."[n]

"WE ARE TRYING HARD TO DO WHAT THE LORD ACCEPTS AS RIGHT AND ALSO WHAT PEOPLE THINK IS RIGHT."

TITUS AND HIS COMPANIONS HELP

[16]I thank God because he gave Titus the same love for you that I have. [17]Titus accepted what we asked him to do. He wanted very much to go to you, and this was his own idea. [18]We are sending with him the brother who is praised by all the churches because of his service in preaching the Good News. [19]Also, this brother was chosen by the churches to go with us when we deliver this gift of money. We are doing this service to bring glory to the Lord and to show that we really want to help.

[20]We are being careful so that no one will criticize us for the way we are handling this large gift. [21]We are trying hard to do what the Lord accepts as right and also what people think is right.

[22]Also, we are sending with them our brother, who is always ready to help. He has proved this to us in many ways, and he wants to help even more now, because he has much faith in you.

[23]Now about Titus—he is my partner who is working with me to help you. And about the other brothers—they are sent from the churches, and they bring glory to Christ. [24]So show these men the proof of your love and the reason we are proud of you. Then all the churches can see it.

HELP FOR FELLOW CHRISTIANS

9 I really do not need to write you about this help for God's people. [2]I know you want to help. I have been bragging about this to the people in Macedonia, telling them that you in Southern Greece have been ready to give since last year. And your desire to give has made most of them ready to give also. [3]But I am sending the brothers to you so that our bragging about you in this will not be empty words. I want you to be ready, as I said you would be. [4]If any of the people from Macedonia come with me and find that you are not ready,

LEARN IT & LIVE IT

1 Timothy 2:1:
Learn It: We should pray for all people.
Live It: Spend thirty minutes praying today. Pray for your family, friends, teachers, the president, and others you can think of.

1 Timothy 2:9:
Learn It: We should dress modestly.
Live It: Go through your closet today and donate to Goodwill anything that isn't modest. Be honest about it. If you get rid of it, you won't be tempted to wear it.

1 Timothy 3:11:
Learn It: You should be respected by others.
Live It: Do you do things that make people respect you? Find one respect-worthy cause to get behind this week, and go for it full-speed ahead.

notes

8:15 "The person . . . little." Quotation from Exodus 16:18.

RELATIONSHIPS

Your sister has done the unforgivable. She borrowed your favorite dress without asking and then returned it with a mustard stain! That's it. You'll never ever let her borrow anything again. She'll be lucky if you even speak to her after this. Okay, time to get off your high horse. How about checking out Matthew 18:21-35, the parable of the unforgiving servant? Jesus says to forgive not seven times, but seventy times seven. In other words, forgive over and over again as Christ forgave you. Maybe you should give your sister another chance. She'll probably mess up again at some point, but that'll just give you another chance to show her the love of Christ by forgiving her.

bible basics

Baptism is another public acknowledgment of Jesus Christ. A person is covered with water—through sprinkling, pouring, or full immersion—as a symbol of their commitment to God. This comes from the New Testament. Even before Christ began his ministry, John the Baptist was baptizing people in the wilderness. Jesus himself was actually baptized by John. **It's** a public way to show your belief in God, and it symbolizes death to your old self by leaving it behind as you come up with a new life.

we will be ashamed that we were so sure of you.
(And you will be ashamed, too!) 5So I thought
I should ask these brothers to go to you before
we do. They will finish getting in order the
generous gift you promised so it will be ready
when we come. And it will be a generous
gift—not one that you did not want to give.

6Remember this: The person who plants a
little will have a small harvest, but the person
who plants a lot will have a big harvest. 7Each
one should give as you have decided in your
heart to give. You should not be sad when you
give, and you should not give because you feel
forced to give. God loves the person who gives
happily. 8And God can give you more blessings
than you need. Then you will always have
plenty of everything—enough to give to every
good work. 9It is written in the Scriptures:

"He gives freely to the poor.
The things he does are right and will
continue forever." *Psalm 112:9*

10God is the One who gives seed to the
farmer and bread for food. He will give you all
the seed you need and make it grow so there
will be a great harvest from your goodness.
11He will make you rich in every way so that
you can always give freely. And your giving
through us will cause many to give thanks to
God. 12This service you do not only helps the
needs of God's people, it also brings many
more thanks to God. 13It is a proof of your
faith. Many people will praise God because
you obey the Good News of Christ—the
gospel you say you believe—and because you
freely share with them and with all others.
14And when they pray, they will wish they
could be with you because of the great grace
that God has given you. 15Thanks be to God
for his gift that is too wonderful for words.

PAUL DEFENDS HIS MINISTRY

10 I, Paul, am begging you with the
gentleness and the kindness of
Christ. Some people say that I am easy on
you when I am with you and bold when I am
away. 2They think we live in a worldly way,
and I plan to be very bold with them when I
come. I beg you that when I come I will not
need to use that same boldness with you. 3We
do live in the world, but we do not fight in the
same way the world fights. 4We fight with
weapons that are different from those the
world uses. Our weapons have power from
God that can destroy the enemy's strong
places. We destroy people's arguments 5and
every proud thing that raises itself against the
knowledge of God. We capture every thought
and make it give up and obey Christ. 6We are
ready to punish anyone there who does not
obey, but first we want you to obey fully.

7You must look at the facts before you. If
you feel sure that you belong to Christ, you
must remember that we belong to Christ just
as you do. 8It is true that we brag freely about

Blab

Q. I'm tempted to have sex, and I was wondering if I do would I be forgiven afterwards?

A. What you are asking is the same as if someone planned to walk up and spit in your face and say "I'm sorry." Will that be okay? No, it's not okay! Deal with the real issue. Take control of this area of your life and you will see other areas where you will gain control.

Q. I am scared to walk into rooms with people in them. I am always self-conscious. How can I be confident?

A. Okay, it's time to renew your mind. Stop spending so much time looking at all the negatives. We're supposed to think about stuff that is cool, awesome, exciting, and all that good stuff (read Philippians 4). You have to take the negative thinking out of your head. Try this: Whenever you start to think these stupid thoughts, literally say "No," and start thinking about something good. Change the cycle. Renew your mind, because you are not living a life of faith right now.

Q. How modestly should people dress?

A. The way you dress influences the way you are treated. If you dress modestly, you will be treated like you are valuable and have important, interesting stuff inside you. If you dress like a tramp, you will get treated like a tramp.

the authority the Lord gave us. But this authority is to build you up, not to tear you down. So I
will not be ashamed. 9I do not want you to
think I am trying to scare you with my letters.
10Some people say, "Paul's letters are powerful
and sound important, but when he is with us,
he is weak. And his speaking is nothing." 11They
should know this: We are not there with you
now, so we say these things in letters. But
when we are there with you, we will show the
same authority that we show in our letters.
12We do not dare to compare ourselves
with those who think they are very important.
They use themselves to measure themselves,
and they judge themselves by what they themselves are. This shows that they know nothing.
13But we will not brag about things outside
the work that was given us to do. We will limit
our bragging to the work that God gave us,
and this includes our work with you. 14We are
not bragging too much, as we would be if we
had not already come to you. But we have
come to you with the Good News of Christ.
15We limit our bragging to the work that is
ours, not what others have done. We hope that
as your faith continues to grow, you will help
our work to grow much larger. 16We want to
tell the Good News in the areas beyond your
city. We do not want to brag about work that
has already been done in another person's
area. 17But, "If someone wants to brag, he
should brag only about the Lord."*n* 18It is not
those who say they are good who are accepted
but those who the Lord thinks are good.

PAUL AND THE FALSE APOSTLES

11 I wish you would be patient with
me even when I am a little foolish,
but you are already doing that. 2I am jealous
over you with a jealousy that comes from
God. I promised to give you to Christ, as your
only husband. I want to give you as his pure
bride. 3But I am afraid that your minds will be
led away from your true and pure following of
Christ just as Eve was tricked by the snake

2 Corinthians 8:9

Jesus had it all. In heaven, he had angels singing his praises all day long. He'd been sitting at God's right hand ever since the beginning of time. He ruled the whole universe and walked on streets of gold—comfortable, adored, worshiped. Then, one day, it was decision time. Someone had to go to earth. God loved his people so much that he couldn't stand to watch them suffer and wander. The humans needed someone like them to explain God's plan and purpose. So God sent Jesus to be like the people and to live among them on earth. He poured his glorious body into one like ours, gave up all the magnificence of heaven just to help us learn how to live and be right with God. He became poor so that we could know the riches of heaven—joy in a busted world, love when hearts are broken, peace when chaos is reigning, and other blessings. Jesus said that his riches have become ours by our faith in him. That's great news—you're rich!

notes

10:17 "If . . . Lord." Quotation from Jeremiah 9:24.

BEAUTY SECRET

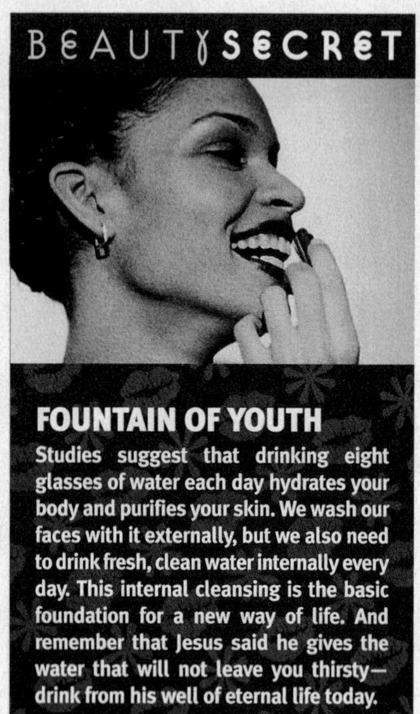

FOUNTAIN OF YOUTH

Studies suggest that drinking eight glasses of water each day hydrates your body and purifies your skin. We wash our faces with it externally, but we also need to drink fresh, clean water internally every day. This internal cleansing is the basic foundation for a new way of life. And remember that Jesus said he gives the water that will not leave you thirsty—drink from his well of eternal life today.

with his evil ways. 4You are very patient with anyone who comes to you and preaches a different Jesus from the one we preached. You are very willing to accept a spirit or gospel that is different from the Spirit and Good News you received from us.

5I do not think that those "great apostles" are any better than I am. 6I may not be a trained speaker, but I do have knowledge. We have shown this to you clearly in every way.

DIDYA KNOW

58% OF TEENS SAY ADULTS WOULD DESCRIBE YOUNG ADULTS AS INTELLIGENT.

7I preached God's Good News to you without pay. I made myself unimportant to make you important. Do you think that was wrong? 8I accepted pay from other churches, taking their money so I could serve you. 9If I needed something when I was with you, I did not trouble any of you. The brothers who came from Macedonia gave me all that I needed. I did not allow myself to depend on you in any way, and I will never depend on you. 10No one in Southern Greece will stop me from bragging about that. I say this with the truth of Christ in me. 11And why do I not depend on you? Do you think it is because I do not love you? God knows that I love you.

12And I will continue doing what I am doing now, because I want to stop those people from having a reason to brag. They would like to say that the work they brag about is the same as ours. 13Such men are not true apostles but are workers who lie. They change themselves to look like apostles of Christ. 14This does not surprise us. Even Satan changes himself to look like an angel of light.[n] 15So it does not surprise us if Satan's servants also make themselves look like servants who work for what is right. But in the end they will be punished for what they do.

Romans 5:10
While we were God's enemies, he made friends with us through the death of his Son. Surely, now that we are his friends, he will save us through his Son's life.

PAUL TELLS ABOUT HIS SUFFERINGS

16I tell you again: No one should think I am a fool. But if you think so, accept me as you would accept a fool. Then I can brag a little, too. 17When I brag because I feel sure of myself, I am not talking as the Lord would talk but as a fool. 18Many people are bragging about their lives in the world. So I will brag too. 19You are wise, so you will gladly be patient with fools! 20You are even patient with those who order you around, or use you, or trick you, or think they are better than you, or hit you in the face. 21It is shameful to me to say this, but we were too "weak" to do those things to you!

But if anyone else is brave enough to brag, then I also will be brave and brag. (I am talking as a fool.) 22Are they Hebrews?[n] So am I. Are they Israelites? So am I. Are they from Abraham's family? So am I. 23Are they serving Christ? I am serving him more. (I am crazy to talk like this.) I have worked much harder than they. I have been in prison more often. I have been hurt more in beatings. I have been near death many times. 24Five times the Jews have given me their punishment of thirty-nine lashes with a whip. 25Three different times I was beaten with rods. One time I was almost stoned to death. Three times I was in ships that wrecked, and one of those times I spent a night and a day in the sea. 26I have gone on many travels and have been in danger from rivers, thieves, my own people, the Jews, and those who are not Jews. I have been in danger in cities, in places where no one lives, and on the sea. And I have been in danger with false Christians. 27I have done hard and tiring work, and many times I did not sleep. I have been hungry and thirsty, and many times I have been without food. I have been cold and without clothes. 28Besides all this, there is on me every day the load of my concern for all the churches. 29I feel weak every time someone is weak, and I feel upset every time someone is led into sin.

30If I must brag, I will brag about the things that show I am weak. 31God knows I am not lying. He is the God and Father of the Lord Jesus Christ, and he is to be praised forever. 32When I was in Damascus, the governor under King Aretas wanted to arrest me, so he put guards around the city. 33But my friends lowered me in a basket through a hole in the city wall. So I escaped from the governor.

A SPECIAL BLESSING IN PAUL'S LIFE

12 I must continue to brag. It will do no good, but I will talk now about visions and revelations[n] from the Lord. 2I know a man in Christ who was taken up to the third heaven fourteen years ago. I do not

notes **11:14 angel of light** Messenger from God. The devil fools people so that they think he is from God. **11:22 Hebrews** A name for the Jews that some Jews were very proud of. **12:1 revelations** Revelation is making known a truth that was hidden.

know whether the man was in his body or out
of his body, but God knows. [3-4]And I know
that this man was taken up to paradise.[n] I
don't know if he was in his body or away from
his body, but God knows. He heard things he is
not able to explain, things that no human is allowed to tell. [5]I will brag about a man like that,
but I will not brag about myself, except about
my weaknesses. [6]But if I wanted to brag about
myself, I would not be a fool, because I would
be telling the truth. But I will not brag about
myself. I do not want people to think more of
me than what they see me do or hear me say.

[7]So that I would not become too proud of
the wonderful things that were shown to me,
a painful physical problem[n] was given to me.
This problem was a messenger from Satan,
sent to beat me and keep me from being too
proud. [8]I begged the Lord three times to take
this problem away from me. [9]But he said to
me, "My grace is enough for you. When you
are weak, my power is made perfect in you."
So I am very happy to brag about my weaknesses. Then Christ's power can live in me.
[10]For this reason I am happy when I have
weaknesses, insults, hard times, sufferings,
and all kinds of troubles for Christ. Because
when I am weak, then I am truly strong.

PAUL'S LOVE FOR THE CHRISTIANS

[11]I have been talking like a fool, but you
made me do it. You are the ones who should
say good things about me. I am worth nothing, but those "great apostles" are not worth
any more than I am!

[12]When I was with you, I patiently did the
things that prove I am an apostle—signs, wonders, and miracles. [13]So you received everything that the other churches have received.
Only one thing was different: I was not a burden to you. Forgive me for this!

[14]I am now ready to visit you the third time,
and I will not be a burden to you. I want nothing from you, except you. Children should not
have to save up to give to their parents. Parents
should save to give to their children. [15]So I am
happy to give everything I have for you, even
myself. If I love you more, will you love me less?

[16]It is clear I was not a burden to you, but
you think I was tricky and lied to catch you.
[17]Did I cheat you by using any of the messengers I sent to you? No, you know I did not. [18]I
asked Titus to go to you, and I sent our brother

BIBLE BIOS:
MARY & MARTHA
Mary and Martha were sisters, but they were exact opposites. We usually see them together in the Scriptures, and they were close friends of Jesus and his followers. Martha is the very practical extrovert of the pair; Mary is the more reflective introvert. Their classic story is told when Jesus meets the two women at their home and confronts Martha about her reluctance to rest at his feet. We should learn from these women how opposites can love each other and work together well, and that there is also a time for rest and relaxation at the feet of Jesus.
[LUKE 10; JOHN 11—12]

TOPten
RANDOM THINGS TO KNOW ABOUT BEING A REVOLVE GIRL

01	**Revolve girls don't call guys.**
02	**Revolve girls don't talk with food in their mouths.**
03	**Revolve girls have good posture.**
04	**Revolve girls are not argumentative.**
05	**Revolve girls should never gossip.**
06	**Revolve girls know their bodies are temples of God.**
07	**Revolve girls are respectful of others.**
08	**Revolve girls enjoy spending time with family.**
09	**Revolve girls don't kiss and tell.**
10	**Revolve girls are fabulous friends.**

notes

12:3-4 paradise Another word for heaven. **12:7 painful physical problem** Literally, "thorn in the flesh."

with him. Titus did not cheat you, did he? No, you know that Titus and I did the same thing and with the same spirit.

"YOU ARE OUR DEAR FRIENDS, AND EVERYTHING WE DO IS TO MAKE YOU STRONGER."

19Do you think we have been defending
ourselves to you all this time? We have been
speaking in Christ and before God. You are
our dear friends, and everything we do is to
make you stronger. 20I am afraid that when I
come, you will not be what I want you to be,
and I will not be what you want me to be. I
am afraid that among you there may be arguing, jealousy, anger, selfish fighting, evil talk,
gossip, pride, and confusion. 21I am afraid that
when I come to you again, my God will make
me ashamed before you. I may be saddened
by many of those who have sinned because they have not changed their hearts or turned from their sexual sins and the shameful things they have done.

FINAL WARNINGS AND GREETINGS

13 I will come to you for the third
time. "Every case must be proved
by two or three witnesses."[n] 2When I was
with you the second time, I gave a warning to
those who had sinned. Now I am away from
you, and I give a warning to all the others.
When I come to you again, I will not be easy
with them. 3You want proof that Christ is
speaking through me. My proof is that he is
not weak among you, but he is powerful. 4It is
true that he was weak when he was killed on
the cross, but he lives now by God's power. It
is true that we are weak in Christ, but for you
we will be alive in Christ by God's power.
5Look closely at yourselves. Test yourselves
to see if you are living in the faith. You know
that Jesus Christ is in you—unless you fail the
test. 6But I hope you will see that we ourselves
have not failed the test. 7We pray to God that
you will not do anything wrong. It is not important to see that we have passed the test, but it is
important that you do what is right, even if it
seems we have failed. 8We cannot do anything
against the truth, but only for the truth. 9We
are happy to be weak, if you are strong, and we
pray that you will become complete. 10I am
writing this while I am away from you so that
when I come I will not have to be harsh in my
use of authority. The Lord gave me this authority to build you up, not to tear you down.
11Now, brothers and sisters, I say good-bye.
Try to be complete. Do what I have asked you
to do. Agree with each other, and live in peace.
Then the God of love and peace will be with you.
12Greet each other with a holy kiss. 13All of
God's holy people send greetings to you.
14The grace of the Lord Jesus Christ, the
love of God, and the fellowship of the Holy
Spirit be with you all.

Notes

notes

13:1 **"Every . . . witnesses."** Quotation from Deuteronomy 19:15.

Labor Day is always on the first Monday of September. Take advantage of the opportunity for one last summer party!

September

1 This month is National Courtesy Month—turn it into a habit!

2

3

4 Pray for a Person of Influence: Beyonce Knowles celebrates her b-day.

5

6 The *Mayflower* sailed for the New World in 1620—thank the Lord for your country today.

7

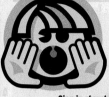

8 Sing in church without worrying who's listening—see what happens.

9

10

11 Pray for all the families of the victims in the WTC bombing—pray that they will encounter peace today.

12 Little Rock High School was ordered to admit black students in 1958—love others without prejudice today/for life.

13

14 Hug your parents a little longer today.

15 Pray for a Person of Influence: Happy Birthday to Prince Harry!

16 Pray for the president today.

17 Sit with someone you don't know very well today at lunch.

18 Cook dinner tonight and give your parents a rest—tell them how grateful you are for all they do.

19

20

21 Pray for a Person of Influence: Happy birthday to Faith Hill!

22

23 Look for the first autumn leaf—put it in your Bible and let it remind you of God's creativity.

24 Pray for a Person of Influence: Today is Will Smith's birthday.

25

26

27 Go to a football game tonight and worship God through your cheering and joy!

28

29

30 The Frisbee was invented today in 1958—play a little Ultimate with friends.

Galatians

Remember the Good News of Amazing Grace and Freedom

Sometimes it might feel as if the Bible is devoid of emotion. The cold, hard facts of history barely leap off the page. There's little to move your emotion. Well, if you've ever felt that way . . . try this book. It's the most emotionally charged book of the Bible. You can almost see the thick purple veins popping out on Paul's neck as he unloads on the misguided Christians of Galatia.

What's the big deal? Well, for starters, Paul has taught them God saves them by trusting in Christ alone, not in doing religious things. The people obviously don't buy it. Instead, they've bought into the message of some missionaries who are teaching that Christians have to obey the Jewish laws. Paul is adamant that the Law has nothing to do with salvation now that Jesus has come. So, with an emotionally charged response, Paul reminds the Galatians of the miracles and the gift of the Holy Spirit they experienced when Paul was still in the area. He fires away . . . asking them how they actually received God's Spirit. Did they have to work to get it? Nope. How in the world can they be so stupid? (Hey . . . those are Paul's words!)

It's hard to understand the rage and intensity that drive Paul to say what he does. Paul uses some of the most harsh language in Scripture. Yet in an oddly familiar way, when he detonates his anger all over the Galatians and the people leading them in the wrong direction, he sounds like a furious but loving parent reading the riot act to a child who just did something incredibly stupid and nearly got killed. Sometimes love is silent. But sometimes love is a vein-popping scream, calling one back from the brink of disaster.

LEARN IT & LIVE IT

1 Timothy 4:1:
Learn It: Follow the teaching of the Holy Spirit.
Live It: How do you know if what you feel called to do is of God or of the devil? Read Scripture. You'll know it lines up with what God wants if it is biblical.

1 Timothy 4:7:
Learn It: You should train yourself to serve God.
Live It: How are you training for your spiritual calling? Is your gift hospitality? Take some cooking classes. Is it evangelism? Take a public speaking course. Learn to be better at what God has called you to do.

1 Timothy 5:3:
Learn It: We need to take care of widows.
Live It: Log on to www.worldvision.org today and find out how you can help widows and orphans worldwide. Many people around the world have been devastated by disease, drought, or other calamities. Help them.

1 From Paul, an apostle. I was not chosen
to be an apostle by human beings, nor
was I sent from human beings. I was made an
apostle through Jesus Christ and God the
Father who raised Jesus from the dead. [2]This
letter is also from all those of God's family[n]
who are with me.

To the churches in Galatia:[n]

[3]Grace and peace to you from God our Father
and the Lord Jesus Christ. [4]Jesus gave himself
for our sins to free us from this evil world we
live in, as God the Father planned. [5]The glory
belongs to God forever and ever. Amen.

THE ONLY GOOD NEWS

[6]God, by his grace through Christ, called
you to become his people. So I am amazed that
you are turning away so quickly and believing
something different than the Good News.
[7]Really, there is no other Good News. But some
people are confusing you; they want to change
the Good News of Christ. [8]We preached to you
the Good News. So if we ourselves, or even an
angel from heaven, should preach to you something different, we should be judged guilty! [9]I
said this before, and now I say it again: You
have already accepted the Good News. If anyone is preaching something different to you,
he should be judged guilty!

[10]Do you think I am trying to make people
accept me? No, God is the One I am trying to
please. Am I trying to please people? If I still
wanted to please people, I would not be a servant of Christ.

PAUL'S AUTHORITY IS FROM GOD

[11]Brothers and sisters,[n] I want you to know
that the Good News I preached to you was not
made up by human beings. [12]I did not get it
from humans, nor did anyone teach it to me,
but Jesus Christ showed it to me.

[13]You have heard about my past life in the
Jewish religion. I attacked the church of God
and tried to destroy it. [14]I was becoming a
leader in the Jewish religion, doing better than
most other Jews of my age. I tried harder than
anyone else to follow the teachings handed
down by our ancestors.

[15]But God had special plans for me and set
me apart for his work even before I was born.
He called me through his grace [16]and showed
his son to me so that I might tell the Good
News about him to those who are not Jewish.
When God called me, I did not get advice or
help from any person. [17]I did not go to Jerusalem
to see those who were apostles before I was. But,
without waiting, I went away to Arabia and
later went back to Damascus.

[18]After three years I went to Jerusalem to
meet Peter and stayed with him for fifteen
days. [19]I met no other apostles, except James,
the brother of the Lord. [20]God knows that
these things I write are not lies. [21]Later, I went
to the areas of Syria and Cilicia.

[22]In Judea the churches in Christ had never
met me. [23]They had only heard it said, "This man
who was attacking us is now preaching the
same faith that he once tried to destroy." [24]And
these believers praised God because of me.

OTHER APOSTLES ACCEPTED PAUL

2 After fourteen years I went to Jerusalem
again, this time with Barnabas. I also took
Titus with me. [2]I went because God showed me
I should go. I met with the believers there, and
in private I told their leaders the Good News
that I preach to the non-Jewish people. I did not
want my past work and the work I am now doing
to be wasted. [3]Titus was with me, but he was
not forced to be circumcised, even though he was
a Greek. [4]We talked about this problem because
some false believers had come into our group
secretly. They came in like spies to overturn the
freedom we have in Christ Jesus. They wanted
to make us slaves. [5]But we did not give in to
those false believers for a minute. We wanted
the truth of the Good News to continue for you.

[6]Those leaders who seemed to be important
did not change the Good News that I preach. (It
doesn't matter to me if they were "important"
or not. To God everyone is the same.) [7]But
these leaders saw that I had been given the
work of telling the Good News to those who

notes

1:2 those . . . family The Greek text says "brothers." **1:2 Galatia** Probably the same country where Paul preached and began churches on his first missionary trip. Read the Book of Acts, chapters 13 and 14.
1:11 Brothers and sisters Although the Greek text says "Brothers" here and throughout this book, Paul's words were meant for the entire church, including men and women.

Galatians 3:26

You are God's child, and he is your Father. But how? Because you put your faith in Jesus. What is faith? Belief without proof. Hebrews 11:1 says, "Faith means being sure of the things we hope for and knowing that something is real even if we do not see it." Even though you've never seen God, you know he exists. Because you know he exists, you put your faith in him.

God cares for you the same way an earthly father takes care of his children, only better. God is concerned with every detail of your life. He wants to give you good things. He wants to see you grow up and be everything he's designed you to be. He really wants you to know him—deeply and powerfully. How can you get to know your Father better? By spending time with him in prayer and by studying his Word.

You're God's child. You're a princess in his kingdom because the King is your Dad! He loves you so much that he's adopted you as his very own. By faith, take your place as a child of God.

"YOU'RE GOD'S CHILD."

are not Jewish, just as Peter had the work of telling the Jews. 8God gave Peter the power to work as an apostle for the Jewish people. But he also gave me the power to work as an apostle for those who are not Jews. 9James, Peter, and John, who seemed to be the leaders, understood that God had given me this special grace, so they accepted Barnabas and me. They agreed that they would go to the Jewish people and that we should go to those who are not Jewish. 10The only thing they asked us was to remember to help the poor—something I really wanted to do.

PAUL SHOWS THAT PETER WAS WRONG

11When Peter came to Antioch, I challenged him to his face, because he was wrong. 12Peter ate with the non-Jewish people until some Jewish people sent from James came to Antioch. When they arrived, Peter stopped eating with those who weren't Jewish, and he separated himself from them. He was afraid of the Jews. 13So Peter was a hypocrite, as were the other Jewish believers who joined with him. Even Barnabas was influenced by what these Jewish believers did. 14When I saw they were not following the truth of the Good News, I spoke to Peter in front of them all. I said, "Peter, you are a Jew, but you are not living like a Jew. You are living like those who are not Jewish. So why do you now try to force those who are not Jewish to live like Jews?"

15We were not born as non-Jewish "sinners," but as Jews. 16Yet we know that a person is made right with God not by following the law, but by trusting in Jesus Christ. So we, too, have put our faith in Christ Jesus, that we might be made right with God because we trusted in Christ. It is not because we followed the law, because no one can be made right with God by following the law.

17We Jews came to Christ, trying to be made right with God, and it became clear that we are sinners, too. Does this mean that Christ encourages sin? No! 18But I would really be wrong to begin teaching again those things that I gave up. 19It was the law that put me to death, and I died to the law so that I can now live for God. 20I was put to death on the cross with Christ, and I do not live anymore—it is Christ who lives in me. I still live in my body, but I live by faith in the Son of God who loved me and gave himself to save me. 21By saying these things I am not going against God's grace. Just the opposite, if the law could make us right with God, then Christ's death would be useless.

BLESSING COMES THROUGH FAITH

3 You people in Galatia were told very clearly about the death of Jesus Christ on the cross. But you were foolish; you let someone trick you. 2Tell me this one thing: How did you receive the Holy Spirit? Did you receive the Spirit by following the law? No, you received the Spirit because you heard the Good News and believed it. 3You began your life in Christ by the Spirit. Now are you trying to make it complete by your own power? That is foolish. 4Were all your experiences wasted? I hope not! 5Does God give you the Spirit and work miracles among you because you follow the law? No, he does these things because you heard the Good News and believed it.

6The Scriptures say the same thing about Abraham: "Abraham believed God, and God accepted Abraham's faith, and that faith made him right with God."[n] 7So you should know that the true children of Abraham are those who have faith. 8The Scriptures, telling what would happen in the future, said that God would make the non-Jewish people right through their faith. This Good News was told to Abraham beforehand, as the Scripture says: "All nations will be blessed through you."[n] 9So all who believe as Abraham believed are blessed just as Abraham was. 10But those who depend on following the law to make them right are under a curse, because the Scriptures say, "Anyone will be cursed who does not always obey what is written in the Book of the Law."[n] 11Now it is clear that no one can be made right

notes

3:6 "Abraham . . . God." Quotation from Genesis 15:6. **3:8 "All . . . you."** Quotation from Genesis 12:3 and 18:18. **3:10 "Anyone . . . Law."** Quotation from Deuteronomy 27:26.

ISSUES: Race

When you look at a person, do you see their skin color? Do you find yourself expressing signs of racism? Just little things, like being surprised to see an affluent African-American or Hispanic person; or feeling a little more nervous when you pass a man from a minority race on the street at night? You may not think so, but this is racism. The Bible says that there is neither slave nor free, Jew nor Greek. This means that God doesn't see race—he sees souls. Start looking for people's souls when you meet them, not the color of their skin. You might be surprised to find out who you become friends with.

with God by the law, because the Scriptures say, "Those who are right with God will live by trusting in him."[n] 12The law is not based on faith. It says, "A person who obeys these things will live because of them."[n] 13Christ took away the curse the law put on us. He changed places with us and put himself under that curse. It is written in the Scriptures, "Anyone whose body is displayed on a tree[n] is cursed." 14Christ did this so that God's blessing promised to Abraham might come through Jesus Christ to those who are not Jews. Jesus died so that by our believing we could receive the Spirit that God promised.

THE LAW AND THE PROMISE

15Brothers and sisters, let us think in human terms: Even an agreement made between two persons is firm. After that agreement is accepted by both people, no one can stop it or add anything to it. 16God made promises both to Abraham and to his descendant. God did not say, "and to your descendants." That would mean many people. But God said, "and to your descendant." That means only one person; that person is Christ. 17This is what I mean: God had an agreement with Abraham and promised to keep it. The law, which came four hundred thirty years later, cannot change that agreement and so destroy God's promise to Abraham. 18If the law could give us Abraham's blessing, then the promise would not be necessary. But that is not possible, because God freely gave his blessings to Abraham through the promise he had made.

Q. What's your ideal date?
A. Goin' out and doing something where we can talk—bowling, putt-putt, dinner. Something like that.
GUYS SPEAK OUT

19So what was the law for? It was given to show that the wrong things people do are against God's will. And it continued until the special descendant, who had been promised, came. The law was given through angels who used Moses for a mediator[n] to give the law to people. 20But a mediator is not needed when there is only one side, and God is only one.

THE PURPOSE OF THE LAW OF MOSES

21Does this mean that the law is against God's promises? Never! That would be true only if the law could make us right. But God did not give a law that can bring life. 22Instead, the Scriptures showed that the whole world is bound by sin. This was so the promise would be given through faith to people who believe in Jesus Christ.

23Before this faith came, we were all held prisoners by the law. We had no freedom until God showed us the way of faith that was coming. 24In other words, the law was our guardian leading us to Christ so that we could be made right with God through faith. 25Now the way of faith has come, and we no longer live under a guardian.

26-27You were all baptized into Christ, and so you were all clothed with Christ. This means that you are all children of God through faith in Christ Jesus. 28In Christ, there is no difference between Jew and Greek, slave and free person, male and female. You are all the same in Christ Jesus. 29You belong to Christ, so you are Abraham's descendants. You will inherit all of God's blessings because of the promise God made to Abraham.

4 I want to tell you this: While those who will inherit their fathers' property are

3:11 "Those . . . him." Quotation from Habakkuk 2:4. **3:12 "A person . . . them."** Quotation from Leviticus 18:5. **3:13 displayed on a tree** Deuteronomy 21:22–23 says that when a person was killed for doing wrong, the body was hung on a tree to show shame. Paul means that the cross of Jesus was like that. **3:19 mediator** A person who helps one person talk to or give something to another person.

Blab

Q. I go to public school and am made fun of because of my looks and beliefs. I am a Christian. I know God says to "stick up for your beliefs" but sometimes it's tough. What do I do?

A. Try being a contagious Christian. Figure out how to be so appealing to everyone that they want to know you and not dis' you. Get really good at loving people. Learn to care about them, not preach at them. Ask questions about their lives and don't judge their responses. Remember, it's not your job to fix them, just to show them God's love.

Q. My friend just told me that she was sexually abused by her uncle when she was younger. What can I tell her to help her?

A. If her uncle is still a threat, she should report him to authorities. She should probably also meet with a Christian counselor to discuss all the issues she's going to deal with. If she doesn't find a way to get over it all, she will be her entire life as "an abused little kid." The way she does this is by forgiveness. She has to forgive her uncle, even if he doesn't deserve it. Then she has to get on with her life. God has cleansed her. She is a new creation and needs to act and think like it. God makes all things new.

Q. My dad drinks like three or four beers every night. Is that a sin? How much can you drink before it is a sin?

A. 1.5 cups. Wouldn't you love it if someone could tell you that easily. There is no easy answer. Drinking alcohol is not a sin in Scripture. Even Jesus turned water into wine at a party. But getting drunk is a different story.

still children, they are no different from slaves.
It does not matter that the children own everything. 2While they are children, they must obey
those who are chosen to care for them. But
when the children reach the age set by their
fathers, they are free. 3It is the same for us. We
were once like children, slaves to the useless
rules of this world. 4But when the right time
came, God sent his Son who was born of a
woman and lived under the law. 5God did this so
he could buy freedom for those who were under
the law and so we could become his children.

6Since you are God's children, God sent the
Spirit of his Son into your hearts, and the Spirit
cries out, "Father."[n] 7So now you are not a slave;
you are God's child, and God will give you the
blessing he promised, because you are his child.

PAUL'S LOVE FOR THE CHRISTIANS

8In the past you did not know God. You
were slaves to gods that were not real. 9But
now you know the true God. Really, it is God
who knows you. So why do you turn back to
those weak and useless rules you followed
before? Do you want to be slaves to those
things again? 10You still follow teachings
about special days, months, seasons, and
years. 11I am afraid for you, that my work for
you has been wasted.

12Brothers and sisters, I became like you, so
I beg you to become like me. You were very
good to me before. 13You remember that it was
because of an illness that I came to you the
first time, preaching the Good News. 14Though
my sickness was a trouble for you, you did not
hate me or make me leave. But you welcomed
me as an angel from God, as if I were Jesus
Christ himself! 15You were very happy then,
but where is that joy now? I am ready to testify
that you would have taken out your eyes and
given them to me if that were possible. 16Now
am I your enemy because I tell you the truth?

17Those people[n] are working hard to persuade you, but this is not good for you. They
want to persuade you to turn against us and
follow only them. 18It is good for people to
show interest in you, but only if their purpose
is good. This is always true, not just when I am
with you. 19My little children, again I feel the
pain of childbirth for you until you truly
become like Christ. 20I wish I could be with
you now and could change the way I am talking to you, because I do not know what to
think about you.

THE EXAMPLE OF HAGAR AND SARAH

21Some of you still want to be under the
law. Tell me, do you know what the law says?
22The Scriptures say that Abraham had two
sons. The mother of one son was a slave
woman, and the mother of the other son was a
free woman. 23Abraham's son from the slave
woman was born in the normal human way.
But the son from the free woman was born
because of the promise God made to Abraham.
24This story teaches something else: The
two women are like the two agreements between
God and his people. One agreement is the law
that God made on Mount Sinai,[n] and the people
who are under this agreement are like slaves.
The mother named Hagar is like that agreement. 25She is like Mount Sinai in Arabia and is
a picture of the earthly Jewish city of Jerusalem.
This city and its people, the Jews, are slaves to
the law. 26But the heavenly Jerusalem, which
is above, is like the free woman. She is our
mother. 27It is written in the Scriptures:

"Be happy, Jerusalem.
You are like a woman who never gave
birth to children.
Start singing and shout for joy.
You never felt the pain of giving birth,
but you will have more children
than the woman who has a husband."

Isaiah 54:1

28My brothers and sisters, you are God's
children because of his promise, as Isaac was
then. 29The son who was born in the normal
way treated the other son badly. It is the same
today. 30But what does the Scripture say?

notes

4:6 "Father" Literally, "Abba, Father." Jewish children called their fathers "Abba." **4:17 Those people** They are the false teachers who were bothering the believers in Galatia (Galatians 1:7). **4:24 Mount Sinai** Mountain in Arabia where God gave his Law to Moses (Exodus 19 and 20).

"Throw out the slave woman and her son. The
son of the slave woman should not inherit
anything. The son of the free woman should
receive it all."[n] 31So, my brothers and sisters,
we are not children of the slave woman, but of
the free woman.

KEEP YOUR FREEDOM

5 We have freedom now, because Christ
made us free. So stand strong. Do not
change and go back into the slavery of the law.
2Listen, I Paul tell you that if you go back to the
law by being circumcised, Christ does you no
good. 3Again, I warn every man: If you allow
yourselves to be circumcised, you must follow
all the law. 4If you try to be made right with
God through the law, your life with Christ is
over—you have left God's grace. 5But we have
the true hope that comes from being made
right with God, and by the Spirit we wait
eagerly for this hope. 6When we are in Christ
Jesus, it is not important if we are circumcised
or not. The important thing is faith—the kind
of faith that works through love.

7You were running a good race. Who stopped
you from following the true way? 8This change
did not come from the One who chose you.
9Be careful! "Just a little yeast makes the whole
batch of dough rise." 10But I trust in the Lord
that you will not believe those different ideas.
Whoever is confusing you with such ideas will
be punished.

11My brothers and sisters, I do not teach
that a man must be circumcised. If I teach circumcision, why am I still being attacked? If I
still taught circumcision, my preaching about
the cross would not be a problem. 12I wish the
people who are bothering you would castrate[n]
themselves!

13My brothers and sisters, God called you
to be free, but do not use your freedom as an
excuse to do what pleases your sinful self.
Serve each other with love. 14The whole law is
made complete in this one command: "Love
your neighbor as you love yourself."[n] 15If you
go on hurting each other and tearing each
other apart, be careful, or you will completely
destroy each other.

THE SPIRIT AND HUMAN NATURE

16So I tell you: Live by following the Spirit.
Then you will not do what your sinful selves
want. 17Our sinful selves want what is against
the Spirit, and the Spirit wants what is against
our sinful selves. The two are against each
other, so you cannot do just what you please.
18But if the Spirit is leading you, you are not
under the law.

19The wrong things the sinful self does are
clear: being sexually unfaithful, not being pure,
taking part in sexual sins, 20worshiping gods,
doing witchcraft, hating, making trouble, being
jealous, being angry, being selfish, making people angry with each other, causing divisions
among people, 21feeling envy, being drunk,
having wild and wasteful parties, and doing
other things like these. I warn you now as I
warned you before: Those who do these things
will not inherit God's kingdom. 22But the Spirit
produces the fruit of love, joy, peace, patience,
kindness, goodness, faithfulness, 23gentleness,
self-control. There is no law that says these
things are wrong. 24Those who belong to Christ
Jesus have crucified their own sinful selves.
They have given up their old selfish feelings and
the evil things they wanted to do. 25We get our
new life from the Spirit, so we should follow the
Spirit. 26We must not be proud or make trouble
with each other or be jealous of each other.

HELP EACH OTHER

6 Brothers and sisters, if someone in your
group does something wrong, you who
are spiritual should go to that person and gently help make him right again. But be careful,
because you might be tempted to sin, too. 2By
helping each other with your troubles, you
truly obey the law of Christ. 3If anyone thinks
he is important when he really is not, he is only
fooling himself. 4Each person should judge his
own actions and not compare himself with

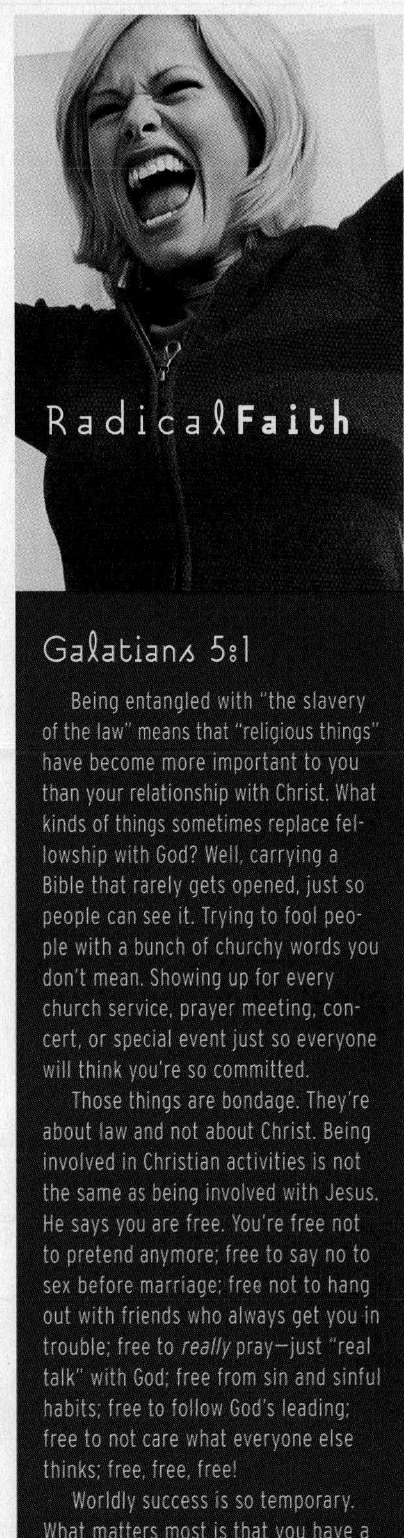

Galatians 5:1

Being entangled with "the slavery of the law" means that "religious things" have become more important to you than your relationship with Christ. What kinds of things sometimes replace fellowship with God? Well, carrying a Bible that rarely gets opened, just so people can see it. Trying to fool people with a bunch of churchy words you don't mean. Showing up for every church service, prayer meeting, concert, or special event just so everyone will think you're so committed.

Those things are bondage. They're about law and not about Christ. Being involved in Christian activities is not the same as being involved with Jesus. He says you are free. You're free not to pretend anymore; free to say no to sex before marriage; free not to hang out with friends who always get you in trouble; free to *really* pray—just "real talk" with God; free from sin and sinful habits; free to follow God's leading; free to not care what everyone else thinks; free, free, free!

Worldly success is so temporary. What matters most is that you have a relationship with God and that you do what he tells you to do. Love God and be free in him.

notes

4:30 "Throw . . . all." Quotation from Genesis 21:10. **5:12 castrate** To cut off part of the male sex organ. Paul uses this word because it is similar to "circumcision." Paul wanted to show that he is very upset with the false teachers. **5:14 "Love . . . yourself."** Quotation from Leviticus 19:18.

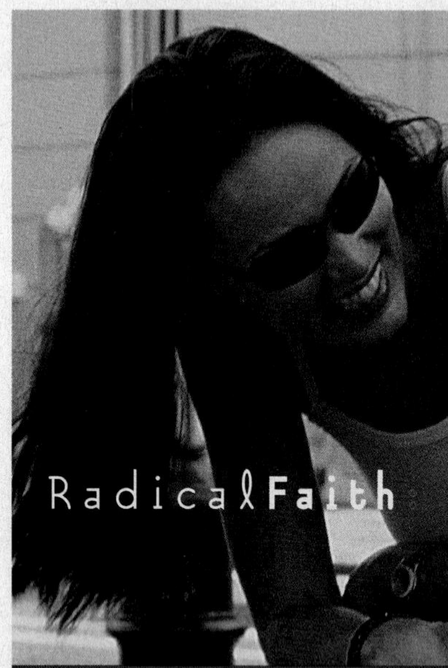

Galatians 5:17

God's Word tells us to love the Lord with all of our heart, with all of our soul, and with all of our strength (see Deuteronomy 6:4-5). When you first got saved, you gave your heart to Jesus first. You didn't give him your soul or your strength first. You gave him your heart.

Satan will always counterfeit what God does, and do the exact opposite. He'll always go after your mind first, because he knows that if he can get something into your mind and get you to think continually about it, then he can get you to do it. That's why it's so important to realize that you can control your thoughts and desires.

Sin always starts in the mind. It's not sin to have an evil thought—that's temptation; but it is wrong to dwell on and entertain those thoughts. To make it simpler: A bird can lay an egg on your head, but only you can let him build a nest in your hair!

James 1:13-15 reminds us that if we think about sin long enough, we'll desire to sin. If we want to sin, we will eventually sin. After sin is done, it will leave us dead. That's why it's so important to walk in the Spirit and feed your mind with the Word of God.

others. Then he can be proud for what he himself has done. 5Each person must be responsible
for himself.

6Anyone who is learning the teaching of
God should share all the good things he has
with his teacher.

LIFE IS LIKE PLANTING A FIELD

7Do not be fooled: You cannot cheat God.
People harvest only what they plant. 8If they
plant to satisfy their sinful selves, their sinful
selves will bring them ruin. But if they plant to
please the Spirit, they will receive eternal life
from the Spirit. 9We must not become tired of
doing good. We will receive our harvest of eternal
life at the right time if we do not give up. 10When
we have the opportunity to help anyone, we
should do it. But we should give special attention to those who are in the family of believers.

PAUL ENDS HIS LETTER

11See what large letters I use to write this
myself. 12Some people are trying to force you
to be circumcised so the Jews will accept them.
They are afraid they will be attacked if they follow only the cross of Christ.[n] 13Those who are
circumcised do not obey the law themselves,
but they want you to be circumcised so they
can brag about what they forced you to do. 14I
hope I will never brag about things like that.
The cross of our Lord Jesus Christ is my only
reason for bragging. Through the cross of Jesus
my world was crucified, and I died to the world.
15It is not important if a man is circumcised or
uncircumcised. The important thing is being
the new people God has made. 16Peace and
mercy to those who follow this rule—and to
all of God's people.

17So do not give me any more trouble. I
have scars on my body that show[n] I belong to
Christ Jesus.

18My brothers and sisters, the grace of our
Lord Jesus Christ be with your spirit. Amen.

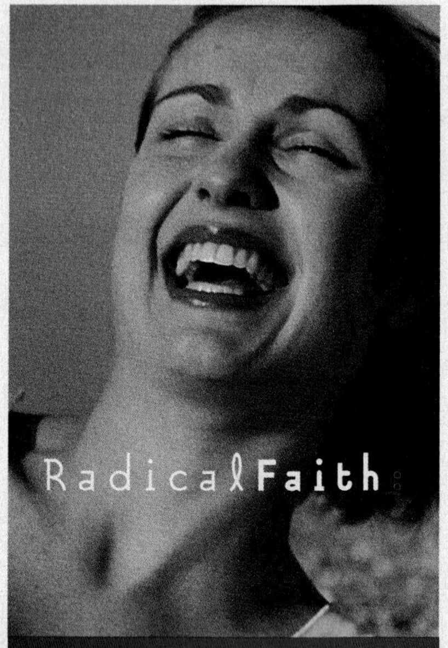

Galatians 5:22-25

The Spirit of God lives in each believer and is the agent of change. He brings power to our lives that we would otherwise be without. Because he is in us, we have the ability to change and become more Christlike. Verses 22 and 23 list some of the areas that the Holy Spirit can change in your life. In which of these areas could you use some help? Find a specific Scripture and use it to renew your mind. Memorize it; meditate on it; say it in your sleep! Then pray for the Holy Spirit to begin working. The most important part is that you cooperate with the Holy Spirit when he reminds you to be gentle instead of whining. It's called obedience. Eventually, little by little, the whining will be replaced and you will have begun to make some changes in your life.

6:12 cross of Christ Paul uses the cross as a picture of the Good News, the story of Christ's death and rising from the dead to pay for our sins. The cross, or Christ's death, was God's way to save us. **6:17 that show** Many times Paul was beaten and whipped by people who were against him because he was teaching about Christ. The scars were from these beatings.

ARE YOU A GOOD DAUGHTER?

1) IT'S 3:00 A.M. AND YOU HEAR YOUR MOM OUTSIDE YELLING FOR THE DOG. YOU:

A. PRAY FOR HER THAT SHE'LL BE ABLE TO GET THE DOG IN QUICKLY AND GO BACK TO SLEEP.
B. GET UP EARLY AND MAKE HER BREAKFAST AS A TREAT.
C. GET UP THEN AND GO HELP HER.
D. PRETEND LIKE YOU NEVER HEARD IT.

2) IN THE CAR ON THE WAY TO SCHOOL, YOU:

A. LISTEN TO YOUR MOM'S OR DAD'S RADIO STATION AND TALK ABOUT THE NEWS.
B. ASK THEM TO CHANGE THE STATION TO WHAT YOU LIKE TO LISTEN TO IN THE MORNINGS.
C. A LITTLE OF A AND A LITTLE OF B.
D. WEAR HEADPHONES—THAT WAY EVERYONE IS HAPPY.

3) IT'S YOUR DAD'S BIRTHDAY. YOU:

A. COOK A NICE DINNER FOR THE FAMILY, THEN GO SEE A MOVIE WITH FRIENDS.
B. GO OUT OF TOWN ON A ONCE-IN-A-LIFETIME VACATION TO THE MOUNTAINS WITH FRIENDS.
C. ARRANGE A NIGHT OF FAMILY FUN—MOVIES, GAMES, DINNER, THE WORKS.
D. MEET THE FAM AT A RESTAURANT, THEN HEAD YOUR OWN WAY AFTER THAT.

4) HOW OFTEN DO YOU HAVE A FIVE-MINUTE (OR LONGER) CONVERSATION WITH YOUR PARENTS?

A. ONCE A WEEK
B. ONCE A MONTH
C. AT LEAST ONCE A DAY
D. CAN'T REMEMBER THE LAST TIME YOU TALKED THAT LONG

5) WHEN YOU GROW UP, YOU WANT TO BE:

A. JUST LIKE YOUR MOM—Y'ALL ARE BEST FRIENDS.
B. NOTHING LIKE YOUR PARENTS—YOU CAN'T STAND THEM.
C. AN INDIVIDUAL, BUT YOU IMAGINE YOU'LL END UP EXACTLY LIKE YOUR MOTHER.
D. VERY COOL; VERY NOT LIKE YOUR PARENTS—GOD LOVE 'EM.

ANSWER

1) a=3; b=2; c=1; d=4
2) a=1; b=3; c=2; d=4
3) a=2; b=4; c=1; d=3
4) a=2; b=3; c=1; d=4
5) a=1; b=4; c=2; d=3

IF YOU SCORED BETWEEN 5 AND 8, YOU ARE THE WORLD'S BEST DAUGHTER!

You're a great daughter who loves spending time with her parents. Some people may consider you kinda a dork for it, but you're not. You're so cool in God's eyes. This is what he was talking about when he said, "Honor your father and mother." You've become friends with your parents and don't mind hanging with them. You want to know who they really are. Keep it up. This will be a huge blessing for you later in life.

IF YOU SCORED BETWEEN 9 AND 14, YOU ARE A TYPICAL TEENAGER.

You're a little embarrassed by the parents, but you want to do the right thing. Sometimes you need to be willing to take the hard road. Go out of your way for your parents; realize everything they've done for you. Give them an extra-long hug today, and tell them that you love them.

IF YOU SCORED BETWEEN 15 AND 20, YOU ARE TOO SELFISH!

Okay, you need to check your priorities. It looks like you're being a little selfish with your life. You don't have much time left living in the same house with your parents. This is a real treasure—wake up to it. Make a decision to spend some major quality time with the 'rents soon—like this week. They'll really appreciate it, and it might even help things on the home front get a little better.

Ephesians

A Word to the Ultimate New Testament Church

Paul had a vision for the church. He intended for it to have a lot of meetings. His hopes were that our churches would be bogged down with heavy agendas. He hoped that someday we'd give 100 percent of our time to counting the number of warm bodies in the church.

Not really. Actually Paul *does* lay out the job of the church in this book, and it has nothing to do with agendas or number-crunching. The church's job is to be the people of faith—God's people. So, how do we measure our success? The measuring is God's job. But the goals before us, Paul says, are unity among believers, following the Spirit within us, maturing our faith, defeating spiritual forces allied against us, and (maybe the hardest job of all) getting along with the people we live with every day. Can the church ever hope to accomplish all of this? Oh yeah! But only with God's help.

Ephesians 2:4-6

A prince is tragically separated from his parents at birth. For years they search for him, sending out soldiers to every region to look for the one who belongs to them. Finally, the boy is found, living in poverty, robbing for food, and acting like a savage. A soldier tells the boy about his father. His father is king of the entire country. In an instant, the beggar child has a new position. He is the son of a king. The one who thought he had no family has become royalty. He has a new life, new power, and a new home. He even has a place to sit beside his father's throne. You too are the child of a King. God has been merciful. He knew that you were dead in your sins, ruled by selfish desires, and destined for eternal punishment. He loved you and graciously gave you new life. With your new life has come new power and a new home with Christ in heaven.

1 From Paul, an apostle of Christ Jesus. I
am an apostle because that is what God
wanted.

To God's holy people living in Ephesus,
believers in Christ Jesus:

[2]Grace and peace to you from God our
Father and the Lord Jesus Christ.

"IN CHRIST WE WERE CHOSEN TO BE GOD'S PEOPLE, BECAUSE FROM THE VERY BEGINNING GOD HAD DECIDED THIS IN KEEPING WITH HIS PLAN."

SPIRITUAL BLESSINGS IN CHRIST

[3]Praise be to the God and Father of our Lord
Jesus Christ. In Christ, God has given us every
spiritual blessing in the heavenly world. [4]That
is, in Christ, he chose us before the world was
made so that we would be his holy people—
people without blame before him. [5]Because of
his love, God had already decided to make us his
own children through Jesus Christ. That was
what he wanted and what pleased him, [6]and it
brings praise to God because of his wonderful
grace. God gave that grace to us freely, in Christ,
the One he loves. [7]In Christ we are set free by
the blood of his death, and so we have forgiveness of sins. How rich is God's grace, [8]which
he has given to us so fully and freely. God,
with full wisdom and understanding, [9]let us
know his secret purpose. This was what God
wanted, and he planned to do it through
Christ. [10]His goal was to carry out his plan,
when the right time came, that all things in
heaven and on earth would be joined together
in Christ as the head.

[11]In Christ we were chosen to be God's people,
because from the very beginning God had
decided this in keeping with his plan. And he is

Ephesians 2:10

Most days just seem to go by like every other day. Same old stuff. Same old everything. Blah blah blah. One day runs into another one. You close your eyes and wake up to do it all over again. Doesn't seem like much of a plan, does it?

Maybe not. But God has an exciting plan for your life—a plan that will give you purpose and fulfillment beyond your wildest dreams. Following God's plan takes commitment from you. You don't just accidentally fulfill what he's planned for you to do. You've got to seek God and ask him to reveal his plan to you and to give you understanding about how you can fulfill it. Then, you've got to determine to make every day count for him and for his plan.

Pay attention to every decision you face—even the ones that seem so insignificant. Take seriously every person you meet—even the ones you don't like. Embrace every situation you find yourself in—even the ones that seem to make no sense at all. They're shaping you, molding you, preparing you for the next decision, the next person, the next situation.

Lose yourself in doing what God wants with every aspect of your life. Live your life in light of his plan!

"FOLLOWING GOD'S PLAN TAKES COMMITMENT FROM YOU."

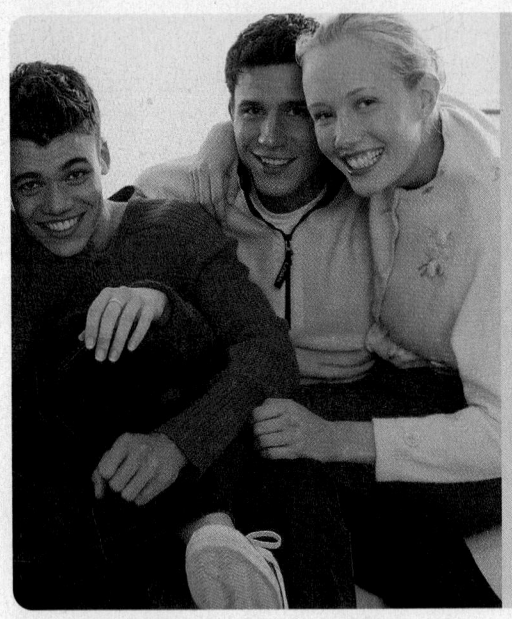

LEARN IT & LIVE IT

1 Timothy 5:19:
Learn It: Don't listen to accusations against your superiors that are without witnesses.
Live It: Is your friend complaining about a teacher who just isn't fair? Tell her you're sorry, but you just can't listen to her unless she's willing to go to the teacher and confront him or her on his unfairness. You'll find out if she's serious or not.

1 Timothy 6:7:
Learn It: We brought nothing into the world, and we can take nothing out.
Live It: What are you obsessing over? A new car? That awesome sweater you just got? Give it up. It's not important. Refocus; think about the people who have nothing. Remember the stuff in life that really matters.

2 Timothy 1:6:
Learn It: We should let our gifts grow.
Live It: Don't hide your gifts because you might be embarrassed of them. God gave them to you for a purpose. Get them out in the open, practice them freely, and let them grow. You are becoming the woman God wants you to be.

the One who makes everything agree with what
he decides and wants. [12]We are the first people
who hoped in Christ, and we were chosen so
that we would bring praise to God's glory. [13]So
it is with you. When you heard the true teaching—the Good News about your salvation—
you believed in Christ. And in Christ, God put
his special mark of ownership on you by giving you the Holy Spirit that he had promised.
[14]That Holy Spirit is the guarantee that we will
receive what God promised for his people
until God gives full freedom to those who are
his—to bring praise to God's glory.

PAUL'S PRAYER

[15]That is why since I heard about your faith
in the Lord Jesus and your love for all God's
people, [16]I have not stopped giving thanks to
God for you. I always remember you in my
prayers, [17]asking the God of our Lord Jesus
Christ, the glorious Father, to give you a spirit
of wisdom and revelation so that you will
know him better. [18]I pray also that you will
have greater understanding in your heart so
you will know the hope to which he has called
us and that you will know how rich and glorious are the blessings God has promised his
holy people. [19]And you will know that God's
power is very great for us who believe. That
power is the same as the great strength [20]God
used to raise Christ from the dead and put him
at his right side in the heavenly world. [21]God
has put Christ over all rulers, authorities, powers, and kings, not only in this world but also
in the next. [22]God put everything under his
power and made him the head over everything
for the church, [23]which is Christ's body. The
church is filled with Christ, and Christ fills
everything in every way.

WE NOW HAVE LIFE

2 In the past you were spiritually dead
because of your sins and the things you
did against God. [2]Yes, in the past you lived the
way the world lives, following the ruler of the
evil powers that are above the earth. That
same spirit is now working in those who
refuse to obey God. [3]In the past all of us lived
like them, trying to please our sinful selves
and doing all the things our bodies and minds
wanted. We should have suffered God's anger
because of the way we were. We were the
same as all other people.

[4]But God's mercy is great, and he loved us
very much. [5]Though we were spiritually dead
because of the things we did against God, he
gave us new life with Christ. You have been
saved by God's grace. [6]And he raised us up
with Christ and gave us a seat with him in the
heavens. He did this for those in Christ Jesus
[7]so that for all future time he could show the
very great riches of his grace by being kind to
us in Christ Jesus. [8]I mean that you have been
saved by grace through believing. You did not
save yourselves; it was a gift from God. [9]It was
not the result of your own efforts, so you cannot brag about it. [10]God has made us what we
are. In Christ Jesus, God made us to do good
works, which God planned in advance for us to
live our lives doing.

"BUT GOD'S MERCY IS GREAT, AND HE LOVED US VERY MUCH."

ONE IN CHRIST

[11]You were not born Jewish. You are the
people the Jews call "uncircumcised."[n] Those
who call you "uncircumcised" call themselves
"circumcised." (Their circumcision is only
something they themselves do on their bodies.) [12]Remember that in the past you were
without Christ. You were not citizens of Israel,

2:11 uncircumcised People not having the mark of circumcision as the Jews had.

without fault, with no evil or sin or any other wrong thing in it. [28]In the same way, husbands should love their wives as they love their own bodies. The man who loves his wife loves himself. [29]No one ever hates his own body, but feeds and takes care of it. And that is what Christ does for the church, [30]because we are parts of his body. [31]The Scripture says, "So a man will leave his father and mother and be united with his wife, and the two will become one body."[n] [32]That secret is very important—I am talking about Christ and the church. [33]But each one of you must love his wife as he loves himself, and a wife must respect her husband.

CHILDREN AND PARENTS

6 Children, obey your parents as the Lord wants, because this is the right thing to do. [2]The command says, "Honor your father and mother."[n] This is the first command that has a promise with it— [3]"Then everything will be well with you, and you will have a long life on the earth."[n]

[4]Fathers, do not make your children angry, but raise them with the training and teaching of the Lord.

SLAVES AND MASTERS

[5]Slaves, obey your masters here on earth with fear and respect and from a sincere heart, just as you obey Christ. [6]You must do this not only while they are watching you, to please them. With all your heart you must do what God wants as people who are obeying Christ. [7]Do your work with enthusiasm. Work as if you were serving the Lord, not as if you were serving only men and women. [8]Remember that the Lord will give a reward to everyone, slave or free, for doing good.

[9]Masters, in the same way, be good to your slaves. Do not threaten them. Remember that the One who is your Master and their Master is in heaven, and he treats everyone alike.

WEAR THE FULL ARMOR OF GOD

[10]Finally, be strong in the Lord and in his great power. [11]Put on the full armor of God so that you can fight against the devil's evil tricks. [12]Our fight is not against people on earth but against the rulers and authorities and the powers of this world's darkness, against the spiritual powers of evil in the heavenly world. [13]That is why you need to put on God's full armor. Then on the day of evil you will be able to stand strong. And when you have finished the whole fight, you will still be standing. [14]So stand strong, with the belt of truth tied around your waist and the protection of right living on your chest. [15]On your feet wear the Good News of peace to help you stand strong. [16]And also use the shield of faith with which you can stop all the burning arrows of the Evil One. [17]Accept God's salvation as your helmet, and take the sword of the Spirit, which is the word of God. [18]Pray in the Spirit at all times with all kinds of prayers, asking for everything you need. To do this you must always be ready and never give up. Always pray for all God's people.

[19]Also pray for me that when I speak, God will give me words so that I can tell the secret of the Good News without fear. [20]I have been sent to preach this Good News, and I am doing that now, here in prison. Pray that when I preach the Good News I will speak without fear, as I should.

FINAL GREETINGS

[21]I am sending to you Tychicus, our brother whom we love and a faithful servant of the Lord's work. He will tell you everything that is happening with me. Then you will know how I am and what I am doing. [22]I am sending him to you for this reason—so that you will know how we are, and he can encourage you.

[23]Peace and love with faith to you from God the Father and the Lord Jesus Christ. [24]Grace to all of you who love our Lord Jesus Christ with love that never ends.

notes

5:31 "So . . . body." Quotation from Genesis 2:24. **6:2 "Honor . . . mother."** Quotation from Exodus 20:12; Deuteronomy 5:16. **6:3 "Then . . . earth."** Quotation from Exodus 20:12; Deuteronomy 5:16.

Philippians

Imagine this: You're locked up in prison. The conditions are rotten. The food stinks. It's dark. Rats crawl over you at night, keeping you awake. You get a chance to write your friends a letter. What will you say? Guess what Paul writes about. How happy he is!

Nope. Paul isn't nuts. He says he's happy that he has such caring friends. He's even happy that he's suffering for Christ because his suffering is inspiring other Christians to preach more boldly. And he says if need be, he will be happy to die because he will go to be with Christ, which is a much better place than where he is now.

A LETTER OF JOY BETWEEN TRUE FRIENDS

Paul wants the Philippians to experience this same peaceful joy when they reflect on their lives. So, he advises them to discover one of the things it means to be saved. So, what does it mean . . . according to Paul? It means . . . be happy. No matter what. No matter where you are. Locked up in prison? Living a terrible life? On the brink of death? Be happy. Shine as a light in a darkened world. Never mind the rats. Smile.

1 From Paul and Timothy, servants of
Christ Jesus.

To all of God's holy people in Christ Jesus who live in Philippi, including your elders and deacons:

[2]Grace and peace to you from God our
Father and the Lord Jesus Christ.

[7]And I know that I am right to think like this
about all of you, because I have you in my
heart. All of you share in God's grace with me
while I am in prison and while I am defending
and proving the truth of the Good News. [8]God
knows that I want to see you very much, because
I love all of you with the love of Christ Jesus.

82% OF TEENS SAY THEIR PARENTS HAVE BEEN GOOD ROLE MODELS FOR THEM.

PAUL'S PRAYER

[3]I thank my God every time I remember
you, [4]always praying with joy for all of you. [5]I
thank God for the help you gave me while I
preached the Good News—help you gave
from the first day you believed until now.
[6]God began doing a good work in you, and I
am sure he will continue it until it is finished
when Jesus Christ comes again.

[9]This is my prayer for you: that your love
will grow more and more; that you will have
knowledge and understanding with your love;
[10]that you will see the difference between
good and bad and will choose the good; that
you will be pure and without wrong for the
coming of Christ; [11]that you will do many
good things with the help of Christ to bring
glory and praise to God.

PAUL'S TROUBLES HELP THE WORK

[12]I want you brothers and sisters[n] to know
that what has happened to me has helped to
spread the Good News. [13]All the palace guards
and everyone else knows that I am in prison
because I am a believer in Christ. [14]Because I am
in prison, most of the believers have become
more bold in Christ and are not afraid to speak
the word of God.

[15]It is true that some preach about Christ
because they are jealous and ambitious, but
others preach about Christ because they want
to help. [16]They preach because they have love,
and they know that God gave me the work of
defending the Good News. [17]But the others
preach about Christ for selfish and wrong reasons, wanting to make trouble for me in prison.

[18]But it doesn't matter. The important thing
is that in every way, whether for right or wrong
reasons, they are preaching about Christ. So I
am happy, and I will continue to be happy.

1:12 brothers and sisters Although the Greek text says "brothers" here and throughout this book, Paul's words were meant for the entire church, including men and women.

[19]Because you are praying for me and the Spirit of Jesus Christ is helping me, I know this trouble will bring my freedom. [20]I expect and hope that I will not fail Christ in anything but that I will have the courage now, as always, to show the greatness of Christ in my life here on earth, whether I live or die. [21]To me the only important thing about living is Christ, and dying would be profit for me. [22]If I continue living in my body, I will be able to work for the Lord. I do not know what to choose—living or dying. [23]It is hard to choose between the two. I want to leave this life and be with Christ, which is much better, [24]but you need me here in my body. [25]Since I am sure of this, I know I will stay with you to help you grow and have joy in your faith. [26]You will be very happy in Christ Jesus when I am with you again.

[27]Only one thing concerns me: Be sure that you live in a way that brings honor to the Good News of Christ. Then whether I come and visit you or am away from you, I will hear that you are standing strong with one purpose, that you work together as one for the faith of the Good News, [28]and that you are not afraid of those who are against you. All of this is proof that your enemies will be destroyed but that you will be saved by God. [29]God gave you the honor not only of believing in Christ but also of suffering for him, both of which bring glory to Christ. [30]When I was with you, you saw the struggles I had, and you hear about the struggles I am having now. You yourselves are having the same kind of struggles.

2 Does your life in Christ give you strength? Does his love comfort you? Do we share together in the spirit? Do you have mercy and kindness? [2]If so, make me very happy by having the same thoughts, sharing the same love, and having one mind and purpose. [3]When you do things, do not let selfishness or pride be your guide. Instead, be humble and give more honor to others than to yourselves. [4]Do not be interested only in your own life, but be interested in the lives of others.

"WHEN YOU DO THINGS, DO NOT LET SELFISHNESS OR PRIDE BE YOUR GUIDE."

BE UNSELFISH LIKE CHRIST

[5]In your lives you must think and act like Christ Jesus.

[6]Christ himself was like God in everything.
But he did not think that being equal
with God was something to be used
for his own benefit.
[7]But he gave up his place with God and
made himself nothing.
He was born to be a man
and became like a servant.
[8]And when he was living as a man,
he humbled himself and was fully
obedient to God,
even when that caused his death—
death on a cross.

RELATIONSHIPS

"Wise children take their parents' advice, but whoever makes fun of wisdom won't listen to correction" (Proverbs 13:1). You may not always like or agree with what your parents say, but for the time being, they are in charge of raising you. They want what is best for you and sometimes that means disciplining you. In the same way God, who is our heavenly Father, disciplines his children whom he loves. Rather than complaining and grumbling, how about being thankful for parents who care enough about you to steer you in the right direction?

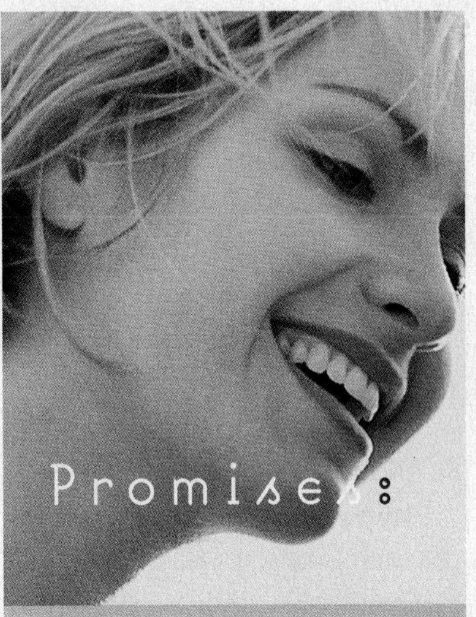

Promises:

Philippians 1:6

Have you heard? Jesus is coming back again. No, really. It may seem highly unlikely from where you're sitting. But one day, in some heart-pounding way where no one in the world will have to wonder what's happening, he's going to step back in here and finish some business. One of those little unfinished matters . . . is you. Don't sweat it, though. If you're one of his, he won't be coming back to pull the curtain down on your performance, but to raise the blinds and allow you to see what he's been doing in your life. And one day—one great, big, glorious day—he'll let you know what was going on. God finishes what he starts. Give him permission to get started with you.

"GOD FINISHES WHAT HE STARTS."

9So God raised him to the highest place.
God made his name greater than every
other name
10so that every knee will bow to the name
of Jesus—
everyone in heaven, on earth,
and under the earth.
11And everyone will confess that Jesus Christ
is Lord
and bring glory to God the Father.

BE THE PEOPLE GOD WANTS YOU TO BE

12My dear friends, you have always obeyed
God when I was with you. It is even more
important that you obey now while I am away
from you. Keep on working to complete your
salvation with fear and trembling, 13because
God is working in you to help you want to do
and be able to do what pleases him.

14Do everything without complaining or
arguing. 15Then you will be innocent and
without any wrong. You will be God's children
without fault. But you are living with crooked
and mean people all around you, among
whom you shine like stars in the dark world.
16You offer the teaching that gives life. So
when Christ comes again, I can be happy
because my work was not wasted. I ran the
race and won.

17Your faith makes you offer your lives as a
sacrifice in serving God. If I have to offer my
own blood with your sacrifice, I will be happy
and full of joy with all of you. 18You also
should be happy and full of joy with me.

TIMOTHY AND EPAPHRODITUS

19I hope in the Lord Jesus to send Timothy
to you soon. I will be happy to learn how you
are. 20I have no one else like Timothy, who truly
cares for you. 21Other people are interested
only in their own lives, not in the work of Jesus
Christ. 22You know the kind of person Timothy
is. You know he has served with me in telling
the Good News, as a son serves his father. 23I
plan to send him to you quickly when I know
what will happen to me. 24I am sure that the
Lord will help me to come to you soon.

25Epaphroditus, my brother in Christ, works
and serves with me in the army of Christ. When
I needed help, you sent him to me. I think now
that I must send him back to you, 26because
he wants very much to see all of you. He is
worried because you heard that he was sick.
27Yes, he was sick, and nearly died, but God
had mercy on him and me too so that I would
not have more sadness. 28I want very much to
send him to you so that when you see him you
can be happy, and I can stop worrying about
you. 29Welcome him in the Lord with much
joy. Give honor to people like him, 30because
he almost died for the work of Christ. He
risked his life to give me the help you could
not give in your service to me.

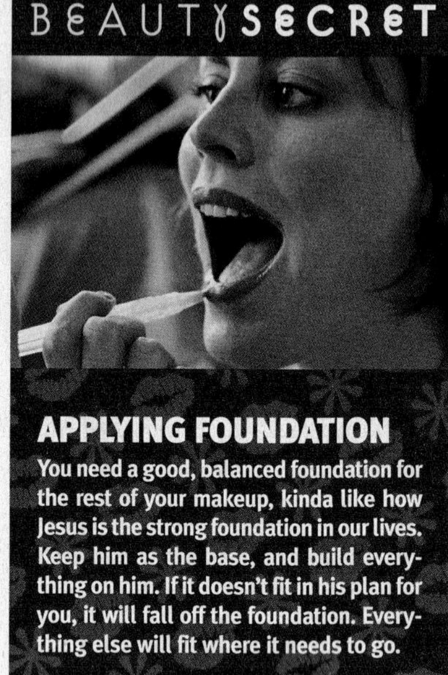

BEAUTY SECRET
APPLYING FOUNDATION
You need a good, balanced foundation for the rest of your makeup, kinda like how Jesus is the strong foundation in our lives. Keep him as the base, and build everything on him. If it doesn't fit in his plan for you, it will fall off the foundation. Everything else will fit where it needs to go.

THE IMPORTANCE OF CHRIST

3 My brothers and sisters, be full of joy in
the Lord. It is no trouble for me to write
the same things to you again, and it will help
you to be more ready. 2Watch out for those
who do evil, who are like dogs, who demand
to cut[n] the body. 3We are the ones who are
truly circumcised. We worship God through
his Spirit, and our pride is in Christ Jesus. We
do not put trust in ourselves or anything we
can do, 4although I might be able to put trust
in myself. If anyone thinks he has a reason to
trust in himself, he should know that I have
greater reason for trusting in myself. 5I was circumcised eight days after my birth. I am from
the people of Israel and the tribe of Benjamin.
I am a Hebrew, and my parents were Hebrews.
I had a strict view of the law, which is why I

notes

3:2 cut The word in Greek is like the word "circumcise," but it means "to cut completely off."

became a Pharisee. [6]I was so enthusiastic I tried to hurt the church. No one could find fault with the way I obeyed the law of Moses. [7]Those things were important to me, but now I think they are worth nothing because of Christ. [8]Not only those things, but I think that

"BROTHERS AND SISTERS, THINK ABOUT THE THINGS THAT ARE GOOD AND WORTHY OF PRAISE."

all things are worth nothing compared with the greatness of knowing Christ Jesus my Lord. Because of him, I have lost all those things, and now I know they are worthless trash. This allows me to have Christ [9]and to belong to him. Now I am right with God, not because I followed the law, but because I believed in Christ. God uses my faith to make me right with him. [10]I want to know Christ and the power that raised him from the dead. I want to share in his sufferings and become like him in his death. [11]Then I have hope that I myself will be raised from the dead.

CONTINUING TOWARD OUR GOAL

[12]I do not mean that I am already as God wants me to be. I have not yet reached that goal, but I continue trying to reach it and to make it mine. Christ wants me to do that, which is the reason he made me his. [13]Brothers and sisters, I know that I have not yet reached that goal, but there is one thing I always do. Forgetting the past and straining toward what is ahead, [14]I keep trying to reach the goal and get the prize for which God called me through Christ to the life above.

[15]All of us who are spiritually mature should think this way, too. And if there are things you do not agree with, God will make them clear to you. [16]But we should continue following the truth we already have.

[17]Brothers and sisters, all of you should try to follow my example and to copy those who live the way we showed you. [18]Many people live like enemies of the cross of Christ. I have often told you about them, and it makes me cry to tell you about them now. [19]In the end, they will be destroyed. They do whatever their bodies want, they are proud of their shameful acts, and they think only about earthly things. [20]But our homeland is in heaven, and we are waiting for our Savior, the Lord Jesus Christ, to come from heaven. [21]By his power to rule all things, he will change our simple bodies and make them like his own glorious body.

WHAT THE CHRISTIANS ARE TO DO

4 My dear brothers and sisters, I love you and want to see you. You bring me joy and make me proud of you, so stand strong in the Lord as I have told you.

[2]I ask Euodia and Syntyche to agree in the Lord. [3]And I ask you, my faithful friend, to help these women. They served with me in telling the Good News, together with Clement and others who worked with me, whose names are written in the book of life.[n]

[4]Be full of joy in the Lord always. I will say again, be full of joy.

[5]Let everyone see that you are gentle and kind. The Lord is coming soon. [6]Do not worry about anything, but pray and ask God for everything you need, always giving thanks. [7]And God's peace, which is so great we cannot understand it, will keep your hearts and minds in Christ Jesus.

[8]Brothers and sisters, think about the things that are good and worthy of praise. Think about the things that are true and honorable and right and pure and beautiful and respected. [9]Do what you learned and received from me, what I told you, and what you saw me do. And the God who gives peace will be with you.

PAUL THANKS THE CHRISTIANS

[10]I am very happy in the Lord that you have shown your care for me again. You continued

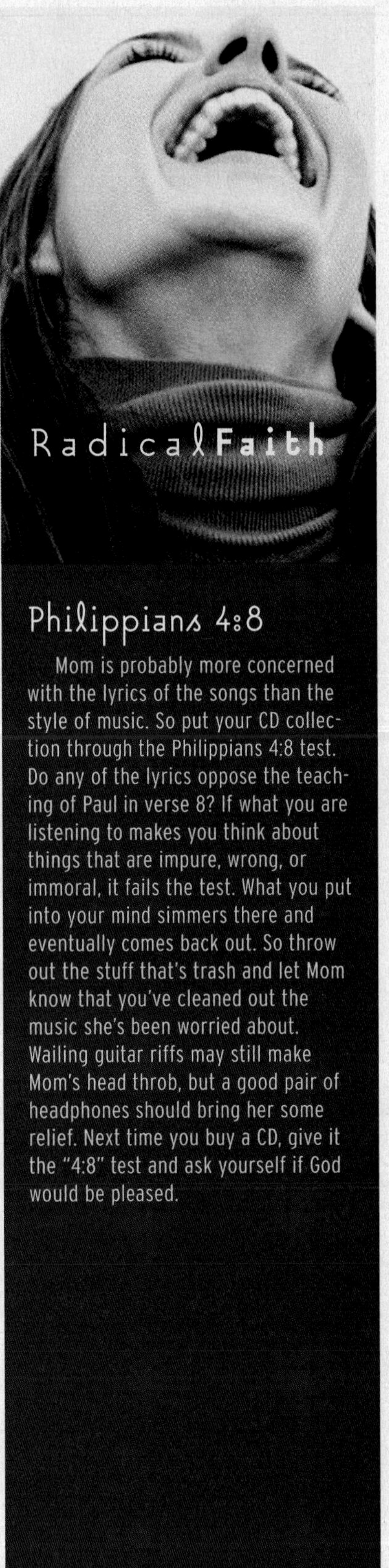

RadicalFaith

Philippians 4:8

Mom is probably more concerned with the lyrics of the songs than the style of music. So put your CD collection through the Philippians 4:8 test. Do any of the lyrics oppose the teaching of Paul in verse 8? If what you are listening to makes you think about things that are impure, wrong, or immoral, it fails the test. What you put into your mind simmers there and eventually comes back out. So throw out the stuff that's trash and let Mom know that you've cleaned out the music she's been worried about. Wailing guitar riffs may still make Mom's head throb, but a good pair of headphones should bring her some relief. Next time you buy a CD, give it the "4:8" test and ask yourself if God would be pleased.

notes

4:3 book of life God's book that has the names of all God's chosen people (Revelation 3:5; 21:27).

LEARN IT & LIVE IT

2 Timothy 1:8:
Learn It: We should not be ashamed of the Good News.
Live It: Tell three people the story of the Good News today.

2 Timothy 2:22:
Learn It: We should run away from evil.
Live It: The next time you're out with friends, and they're all wanting to do something you know is wrong—just leave. There's nothing to be embarrassed about. Use the time to just relax, enjoy time alone, pray, and rejuvenate. And if your friends don't respect you for it, it's time for new friends.

2 Timothy 3:14:
Learn It: The Scriptures are true.
Live It: Follow the Scriptures with confidence today. Do not be ashamed of them. Share them with others, for they are truth.

to care about me, but there was no way for you
to show it. 11I am not telling you this because

"GLORY TO OUR GOD AND FATHER FOREVER AND EVER! AMEN."

I need anything. I have learned to be satisfied
with the things I have and with everything
that happens. 12I know how to live when I am
poor, and I know how to live when I have
plenty. I have learned the secret of being
happy at any time in everything that happens,
when I have enough to eat and when I go hungry, when I have more than I need and when I
do not have enough. 13I can do all things
through Christ, because he gives me strength.

14But it was good that you helped me when
I needed it. 15You Philippians remember
when I first preached the Good News there.
When I left Macedonia, you were the only
church that gave me help. 16Several times you
sent me things I needed when I was in
Thessalonica. 17Really, it is not that I want to
receive gifts from you, but I want you to have
the good that comes from giving. 18And now I
have everything, and more. I have all I need,
because Epaphroditus brought your gift to me.
It is like a sweet-smelling sacrifice offered to
God, who accepts that sacrifice and is pleased
with it. 19My God will use his wonderful
riches in Christ Jesus to give you everything
you need. 20Glory to our God and Father forever and ever! Amen.

21Greet each of God's people in Christ.
Those who are with me send greetings to you.
22All of God's people greet you, particularly
those from the palace of Caesar.

23The grace of the Lord Jesus Christ be with
you all.

Colossians

JESUS IS THE PREEMINENT LORD OF THE UNIVERSE

This letter was written to warn followers of Christ to stay clear of this deceptive religion.

Paul's facing a real challenge. He's discovering a new religion popping up that approaches its beliefs like many of us hit the buffet. It takes a little truth from Christianity, and some stuff from other religions too. This religion looks kind of familiar to the people in the area. It teaches that angels exist, it honors religious holidays, and it urges people to seek God. All this looks so familiar, in fact, that it makes the Christians of Colossae begin to wonder if this new teaching is simply a more insightful way of interpreting old truths.

Paul insists that this isn't a good religion. It's actually just another set of human teachings. For the people who are getting confused about this new religion, Paul has this advice: Follow Jesus. Simple truth . . . but often so very difficult to do.

1 From Paul, an apostle of Christ Jesus. I am an apostle because that is what God wanted. Also from Timothy, our brother.

[2]To the holy and faithful brothers and sisters[n] in Christ that live in Colossae:

Grace and peace to you from God our Father.

88% OF TEENS WANT A COLLEGE DEGREE.

[3]In our prayers for you we always thank God, the Father of our Lord Jesus Christ, [4]because we have heard about the faith you have in Christ Jesus and the love you have for all of God's people. [5]You have this faith and love because of your hope, and what you hope for is kept safe for you in heaven. You learned about this hope when you heard the message about the truth, the Good News [6]that was told to you. Everywhere in the world that Good News is bringing blessings and is growing. This has happened with you, too, since you heard the Good News and understood the truth about the grace of God. [7]You learned about God's grace from Epaphras, whom we love. He works together with us and is a faithful servant of Christ for us. [8]He also told us about the love you have from the Holy Spirit.

[9]Because of this, since the day we heard about you, we have continued praying for you, asking God that you will know fully what he wants. We pray that you will also have great wisdom and understanding in spiritual things [10]so that you will live the kind of life that honors and pleases the Lord in every way. You will produce fruit in every good work and grow in the knowledge of God. [11]God will strengthen you with his own great power so that you will not give up when troubles come, but you will be patient. [12]And you will joyfully give thanks to the Father who has made you able to have a share in all that he has prepared for his people in the kingdom of light. [13]God has freed us from the power of darkness, and he brought us into the kingdom of his dear Son. [14]The Son paid for our sins, and in him we have forgiveness.

THE IMPORTANCE OF CHRIST

[15]No one can see God, but Jesus Christ is exactly like him. He ranks higher than everything that has been made. [16]Through his power all things were made—things in heaven and on earth, things seen and unseen, all powers, authorities, lords, and rulers. All things were made through Christ and for Christ. [17]He was there before anything was made, and all things continue because of him. [18]He is the head of the body, which is the church. Everything comes

notes

1:2 brothers and sisters Although the Greek text says "brothers" here and throughout this book, Paul's words were meant for the entire church, including men and women.

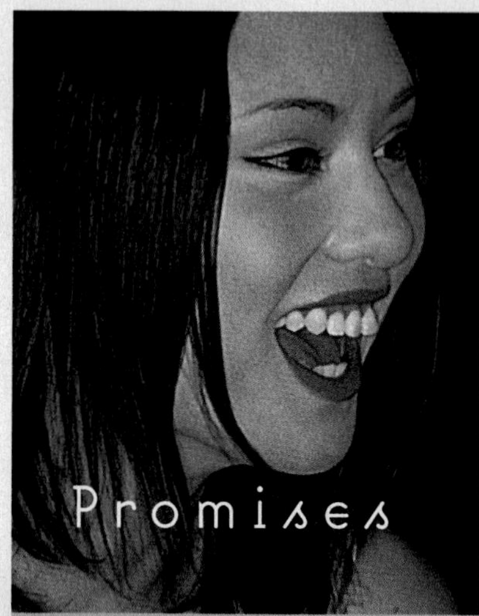

Colossians 1:21-23

It seems like people are always dividing up. Teams, clubs, cliques, or groups. With everyone taking sides, there are a lot of ways you can be left out. Your grades might keep you from the Honor Society or your first-choice college. Lack of skill keeps you off the basketball team. Your friends plan a party and forget to call you. Being left out will happen for all kinds of reasons for the rest of your life. But Jesus promises that, one day in heaven, he will call your name, and you will never be left out again. You won't have to watch while everyone else has all the fun. You won't have to congratulate everyone else on their great accomplishments. Because of Christ, you will be made perfect enough to stand with him—holy, sinless, and free from the guilt of your sin. You'll be first-team, first-pick, forever included with Jesus and all the saints of heaven.

"WITH EVERYONE TAKING SIDES, THERE ARE A LOT OF WAYS YOU CAN BE LEFT OUT."

from him. He is the first one who was raised
from the dead. So in all things Jesus has first
place. 19God was pleased for all of himself to
live in Christ. 20And through Christ, God has
brought all things back to himself again—
things on earth and things in heaven. God
made peace through the blood of Christ's
death on the cross.

21At one time you were separated from
God. You were his enemies in your minds, and
the evil things you did were against God. 22But
now God has made you his friends again. He
did this through Christ's death in the body so
that he might bring you into God's presence as
people who are holy, with no wrong, and with
nothing of which God can judge you guilty.
23This will happen if you continue strong and
sure in your faith. You must not be moved
away from the hope brought to you by the
Good News that you heard. That same Good
News has been told to everyone in the world,
and I, Paul, help in preaching that Good News.

PAUL'S WORK FOR THE CHURCH

24I am happy in my sufferings for you.
There are things that Christ must still suffer
through his body, the church. I am accepting,
in my body, my part of these things that must
be suffered. 25I became a servant of the church
because God gave me a special work to do that
helps you, and that work is to tell fully the
message of God. 26This message is the secret
that was hidden from everyone since the
beginning of time, but now it is made known
to God's holy people. 27God decided to let his
people know this rich and glorious secret
which he has for all people. This secret is
Christ himself, who is in you. He is our only
hope for glory. 28So we continue to preach
Christ to each person, using all wisdom to
warn and to teach everyone, in order to bring
each one into God's presence as a mature person in Christ. 29To do this, I work and struggle,
using Christ's great strength that works so
powerfully in me.

Colossians 2:13-14

We think we're pretty slick with our big-screen TVs and surround-sound systems. But wonder what God's got in store for the day of judgment, when every person who's ever lived has to stand before him and give account of their lives?

This is just a wild guess—highly unproven—but can't you just imagine some gigantic movie screen, out in the middle of this huge mass of people, playing surveillance camera footage of their secret sins, their bad thoughts, their evil intentions—right there in front of their mamas and everybody?

If that scenario is even remotely true, what do you think would be on your tape? The time you let your sister's pet mouse loose? The day you got mad and told your dad you hated him—and thought something worse?

If you've asked Christ into your heart, your own personal private showing will have been somehow, mysteriously erased . . . deleted from memory by a nail-scarred hand.

"WE THINK WE'RE PRETTY SLICK WITH OUR BIG-SCREEN TVS AND SURROUND-SOUND SYSTEMS."

2 I want you to know how hard I work for you, those in Laodicea, and others who have never seen me. [2]I want them to be strengthened and joined together with love so that they may be rich in their understanding. This leads to their knowing fully God's secret, that is, Christ himself. [3]In him all the treasures of wisdom and knowledge are safely kept.

"GOD STRIPPED THE SPIRITUAL RULERS AND POWERS OF THEIR AUTHORITY."

[4]I say this so that no one can fool you by arguments that seem good, but are false. [5]Though I am absent from you in my body, my heart is with you, and I am happy to see your good lives and your strong faith in Christ.

CONTINUE TO LIVE IN CHRIST

[6]As you received Christ Jesus the Lord, so continue to live in him. [7]Keep your roots deep in him and have your lives built on him. Be strong in the faith, just as you were taught, and always be thankful.

Job 34:19
He is not nicer to princes than other people, nor kinder to rich people than poor people, because he made them all with his own hands.

[8]Be sure that no one leads you away with false and empty teaching that is only human, which comes from the ruling spirits of this world, and not from Christ. [9]All of God lives in Christ fully (even when Christ was on earth), [10]and you have a full and true life in Christ, who is ruler over all rulers and powers.

[11]Also in Christ you had a different kind of circumcision, a circumcision not done by hands. It was through Christ's circumcision, that is, his death, that you were made free from the power of your sinful self. [12]When you were baptized, you were buried with Christ, and you were raised up with him through your faith in God's power that was shown when he raised Christ from the dead. [13]When you were spiritually dead because of your sins and because you were not free from the power of your sinful self, God made you alive with Christ, and he forgave all our sins. [14]He canceled the debt, which listed all the rules we failed to follow. He took away that record with its rules and nailed it to the cross. [15]God stripped the spiritual rulers and powers of their authority. With the cross, he won the victory and showed the world that they were powerless.

DON'T FOLLOW PEOPLE'S RULES

[16]So do not let anyone make rules for you about eating and drinking or about a religious feast, a New Moon Festival, or a Sabbath day. [17]These things were like a shadow of what was to come. But what is true and real has come and is found in Christ. [18]Do not let anyone disqualify you by making you humiliate yourself and worship angels. Such people enter into visions, which fill them with foolish pride because of their human way of thinking. [19]They do not hold tightly to Christ, the head. It is from him that all the parts of the body are cared for and held together. So it grows in the way God wants it to grow.

[20]Since you died with Christ and were made free from the ruling spirits of the world, why do you act as if you still belong to this world by following rules like these: [21]"Don't eat this," "Don't taste that," "Don't even touch that thing"? [22]These rules refer to earthly things that are gone as soon as they are used. They are only man-made commands and teachings. [23]They seem to be wise, but they are only part of a man-made religion. They make people pretend not to be proud and make them punish their bodies, but they do not really control the evil desires of the sinful self.

YOUR NEW LIFE IN CHRIST

3 Since you were raised from the dead with Christ, aim at what is in heaven,

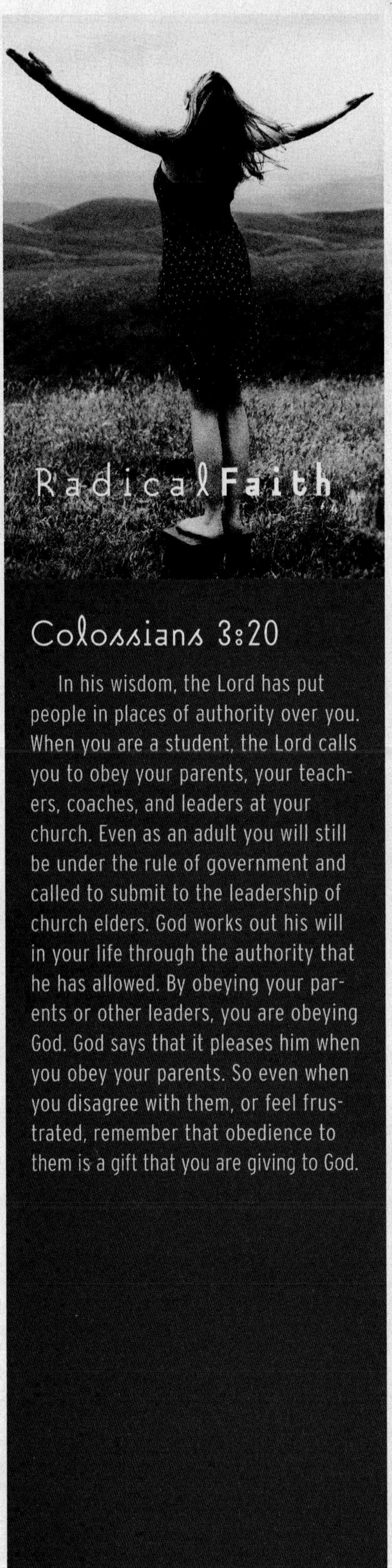

Colossians 3:20

In his wisdom, the Lord has put people in places of authority over you. When you are a student, the Lord calls you to obey your parents, your teachers, coaches, and leaders at your church. Even as an adult you will still be under the rule of government and called to submit to the leadership of church elders. God works out his will in your life through the authority that he has allowed. By obeying your parents or other leaders, you are obeying God. God says that it pleases him when you obey your parents. So even when you disagree with them, or feel frustrated, remember that obedience to them is a gift that you are giving to God.

October

Switch to Standard Time on the last Sunday of October—turn your clocks back one hour!

1	2	3 Pray for a Person of Influence: Today is Gwen Stefanie's birthday.	4
5 Make a card for your mom or dad today. Tell them you love them.	6	7 Pray for a Person of Influence: Happy Birthday to Desmond Tutu.	8
9 Do your part to help campaign for world peace today.	10	11 Read the Book of John today. Meditate on Jesus' love for you.	12 Columbus Day. Read up on what it was like for those guys coming across the Atlantic.
13	14	15	16 Boss's Day. Do something special for the guy or gal who writes the check.
17 Pray for a Person of Influence: Eminem celebrates his b-day today!		19 Treat your best friend extra special today.	20 Pray for a Person of Influence: Danielle Kimmey's birthday, from Out of Eden!
21	22 Pray for a Person of Influence: Toby Mac's birthday is today!	23	24 Go collect some leaves for a fun fall wreath today. Praise God for his creation while you're doing it.
25	26	27 Pray for a Person of Influence: Kelly Osbourne turns one year older today.	28
	29 Read the Book of Jude today.	30	31 Halloween. Find a fun way to honor and glorify God today.

you will be holy and without fault before our
God and Father when our Lord Jesus comes
with all his holy ones.

A LIFE THAT PLEASES GOD

4 Brothers and sisters, we taught you how
to live in a way that will please God, and
you are living that way. Now we ask and
encourage you in the Lord Jesus to live that
way even more. [2]You know what we told you
to do by the authority of the Lord Jesus. [3]God
wants you to be holy and to stay away from
sexual sins. [4]He wants each of you to learn to
control your own body[n] in a way that is holy
and honorable. [5]Don't use your body for sexual sin like the people who do not know God.
[6]Also, do not wrong or cheat another Christian
in this way. The Lord will punish people who
do those things as we have already told you
and warned you. [7]God called us to be holy and
does not want us to live in sin. [8]So the person
who refuses to obey this teaching is disobeying God, not simply a human teaching. And
God is the One who gives us his Holy Spirit.

[9]We do not need to write you about having
love for your Christian family, because God
has already taught you to love each other.
[10]And truly you do love the Christians in all of
Macedonia. Brothers and sisters, now we
encourage you to love them even more.

[11]Do all you can to live a peaceful life. Take
care of your own business, and do your own
work as we have already told you. [12]If you do,
then people who are not believers will respect
you, and you will not have to depend on others for what you need.

THE LORD'S COMING

[13]Brothers and sisters, we want you to
know about those Christians who have died so
you will not be sad, as others who have no
hope. [14]We believe that Jesus died and that he
rose again. So, because of him, God will raise
with Jesus those who have died. [15]What we
tell you now is the Lord's own message. We
who are living when the Lord comes again will
not go before those who have already died.
[16]The Lord himself will come down from
heaven with a loud command, with the voice
of the archangel,[n] and with the trumpet call of
God. And those who have died believing in
Christ will rise first. [17]After that, we who are
still alive will be gathered up with them in the
clouds to meet the Lord in the air. And we will
be with the Lord forever. [18]So encourage each
other with these words.

BE READY FOR THE LORD'S COMING

5 Now, brothers and sisters, we do not
need to write you about times and dates.
[2]You know very well that the day the Lord comes
again will be a surprise, like a thief that comes
in the night. [3]While people are saying, "We have
peace and we are safe," they will be destroyed
quickly. It is like pains that come quickly to a
woman having a baby. Those people will not
escape. [4]But you, brothers and sisters, are not
living in darkness, and so that day will not surprise you like a thief. [5]You are all people who
belong to the light and to the day. We do not
belong to the night or to darkness. [6]So we
should not be like other people who are sleeping, but we should be alert and have self-control.
[7]Those who sleep, sleep at night. Those who
get drunk, get drunk at night. [8]But we belong
to the day, so we should control ourselves. We
should wear faith and love to protect us, and
the hope of salvation should be our helmet.
[9]God did not choose us to suffer his anger but to
have salvation through our Lord Jesus Christ.
[10]Jesus died for us so that we can live together
with him, whether we are alive or dead when
he comes. [11]So encourage each other and give
each other strength, just as you are doing now.

LEARN IT & LIVE IT

2 Timothy 4:2:
Learn It: We must preach the Good News of Scripture.
Live It: Tell five people something you learned from the Bible this week.

2 Timothy 4:16:
Learn It: We should forgive those who abandon us.
Live It: Make a conscious effort not to hold a grudge against someone who has abandoned you. Resentment means actually feeling the pain from the wound over and over again. This isn't healthy for you, and it's not what God wants from you. It may still hurt, but you can't dwell on being mad at the person.

Titus 1:2:
Learn It: God promised us eternal life before time began.
Live It: Reflect on your destiny for thirty minutes today. You are like a princess, a child of the King. Your destiny has been in place since before time began. What does God have planned for you?

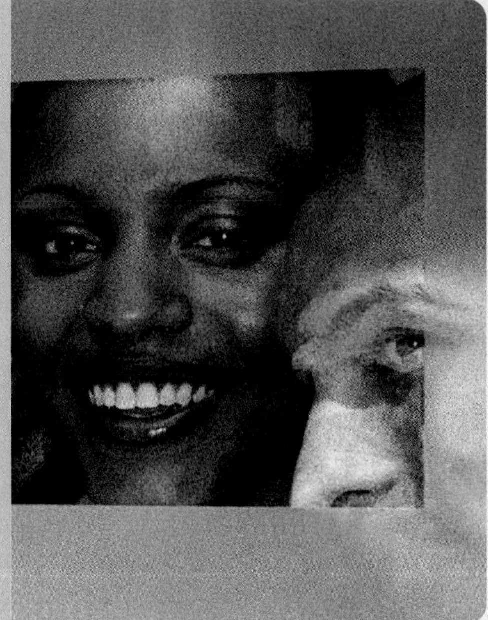

notes

4:4 learn . . . body This might also mean "learn to live with your own wife." **4:16 archangel** The leader among God's angels or messengers.

1 Thessalonians 4:4-5

According to the Bible, the requirement for sex is *marriage*, not just love. God gave sex to marriage as a gift. Two people have made a permanent commitment to each other and God gives them the privilege and gift of sex.

If you play the dating game, you may love many times and date many people. But those who are wise choose friendships that lead to holy courtships. That kind of relationship reserves sex for the lifelong bond of marriage. Sex outside of marriage can have so many hard consequences. You know what they are—diseases that can kill you, babies you aren't ready to have, stress like you've never known, horrible guilt or shame. The list goes on. Sex as a part of marriage is good and blessed.

Don't have sex with the person you're dating because dating is not marriage. There is no commitment. There is no blessing from God. The consequences could be damaging and even deadly. God's advice is perfect and it's perfectly right and good for you. Take his advice and wait. You'll be so glad you did.

Neighborhood Watch

In a society where both parents work, many neighborhoods are deserted during the day. Criminals notice this and take advantage of the situation. Law Enforcement also noticed and realized that the communities in which citizens observed and reported suspicious activity had lower crime rates. As a result, police chiefs and sheriffs around the country implemented a program that incorporated neighborhood involvement in hopes that it would lower the crime rate. In 1972 the National Sheriffs' Association started the National Neighborhood Watch program. As communities began adopting the program and reporting success, the Neighborhood Watch's popularity grew.

To hand out flyers about Neighborhood Watch, go to ***www.usaonwatch.org/locate.asp.***

FINAL INSTRUCTIONS AND GREETINGS

12Now, brothers and sisters, we ask you to
appreciate those who work hard among you,
who lead you in the Lord and teach you.
13Respect them with a very special love because
of the work they do.

Live in peace with each other. 14We ask you,
brothers and sisters, to warn those who do not
work. Encourage the people who are afraid.
Help those who are weak. Be patient with
everyone. 15Be sure that no one pays back
wrong for wrong, but always try to do what is
good for each other and for all people.

16Always be joyful. 17Pray continually, 18and
give thanks whatever happens. That is what
God wants for you in Christ Jesus.

19Do not hold back the work of the Holy Spirit.
20Do not treat prophecy as if it were unimportant. 21But test everything. Keep what is good,
22and stay away from everything that is evil.

23Now may God himself, the God of peace,
make you pure, belonging only to him. May
your whole self—spirit, soul, and body—be
kept safe and without fault when our Lord
Jesus Christ comes. 24You can trust the One
who calls you to do that for you.

25Brothers and sisters, pray for us.

26Give each other a holy kiss when you
meet. 27I tell you by the authority of the Lord
to read this letter to all the believers.

28The grace of our Lord Jesus Christ be
with you.

In 2 Thessalonians, Paul threw cold water on a bunch of people who quit their jobs and were just hanging out at church waiting around for Jesus. Once Paul had their attention (cold water does that), he basically told them that while it's a good thing to look forward to Christ's return, they all needed to get a life, quit waiting around, and get on with living and serving God. Paul teaches us that we don't know the day or the hour of Christ's return, so we should stop waiting around and get on with our lives and our work. Paul doesn't seem to be a fan of laziness. He calls the Thessalonians to get out there and work for a living. In this way, Christians can be respected as hard workers and lawful people. Good call, Paul.

2 Thessalonians

GET ON WITH LIVING AND SERVING GOD

1 From Paul, Silas, and Timothy.
To the church in Thessalonica in God
our Father and the Lord Jesus Christ:
2Grace and peace to you from God the
Father and the Lord Jesus Christ.

PAUL TALKS ABOUT GOD'S JUDGMENT

3We must always thank God for you, brothers and sisters.[n] This is only right, because
your faith is growing more and more, and the
love that every one of you has for each
other is increasing. 4So we brag about you
to the other churches of God. We tell
them about the way you continue to be
strong and have faith even though you are
being treated badly and are suffering
many troubles.
5This is proof that God is right in his
judgment. He wants you to be counted
worthy of his kingdom for which you are
suffering. 6God will do what is right. He
will give trouble to those who trouble
you. 7And he will give rest to you who are
troubled and to us also when the Lord
Jesus appears with burning fire from heaven
with his powerful angels. 8Then he will punish
those who do not know God and who do not
obey the Good News about our Lord Jesus
Christ. 9Those people will be punished with a
destruction that continues forever. They will
be kept away from the Lord and from his great
power. 10This will happen on the day when
the Lord Jesus comes to receive glory because
of his holy people. And all the people who
have believed will be amazed at Jesus. You will
be in that group, because you believed what
we told you.
11That is why we always pray for you, asking our God to help you live the kind of life he
called you to live. We pray that with his power
God will help you do the good things you want
and perform the works that come from your
faith. 12We pray all this so that the name of
our Lord Jesus Christ will have glory in
you, and you will have glory in him. That
glory comes from the grace of our God and
the Lord Jesus Christ.

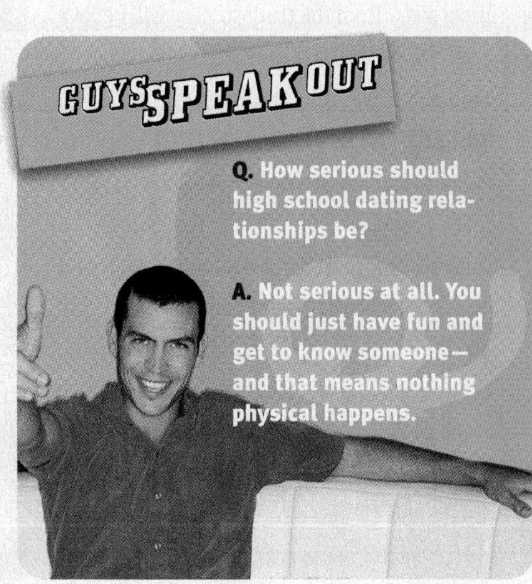

GUYS SPEAK OUT
Q. How serious should high school dating relationships be?
A. Not serious at all. You should just have fun and get to know someone—and that means nothing physical happens.

EVIL THINGS WILL HAPPEN

2 Brothers and sisters, we have something to say about the coming of our
Lord Jesus Christ and the time when we will
meet together with him. 2Do not become
easily upset in your thinking or afraid if you
hear that the day of the Lord has already
come. Someone may say this in a prophecy
or in a message or in a letter as if it came

notes

1:3 brothers and sisters Although the Greek text says "brothers" here and throughout this book, Paul's words were meant for the entire church, including men and women.

2 Thessalonians 1:6-8

Been laughed at lately? Taken any jabs for being a Christian? Been made fun of because you did the right thing? Take heart, because relief is on its way. When Jesus comes, he promises to give you rest from your troubles. You won't have to fight anymore. Jesus will take over with his powerful angels and a flaming fire. He will take care of your enemies and all who would persecute you. Sometimes the battle is bigger than you are. The trouble seems overwhelming. Be courageous enough to know which battles belong to the Lord, and leave them for him to fight.

"SOMETIMES THE BATTLE IS BIGGER THAN YOU ARE."

from us. 3Do not let anyone fool you in any
way. That day of the Lord will not come until the
turning away[n] from God happens and the Man
of Evil, who is on his way to hell, appears. 4He
will be against and put himself above anything
called God or anything that people worship.
And that Man of Evil will even go into God's
Temple and sit there and say that he is God.

5I told you when I was with you that all this
would happen. Do you not remember? 6And
now you know what is stopping that Man of
Evil so he will appear at the right time. 7The
secret power of evil is already working in the
world, but there is one who is stopping that
power. And he will continue to stop it until he
is taken out of the way. 8Then that Man of Evil

"STAND STRONG AND CONTINUE TO BELIEVE."

will appear, and the Lord Jesus will kill him
with the breath that comes from his mouth
and will destroy him with the glory of his coming.
9The Man of Evil will come by the power
of Satan. He will have great power, and he will
do many different false miracles, signs, and
wonders. 10He will use every kind of evil to
trick those who are lost. They will die, because
they refused to love the truth. (If they loved the
truth, they would be saved.) 11For this reason
God sends them something powerful that leads
them away from the truth so they will believe
a lie. 12So all those will be judged guilty who did
not believe the truth, but enjoyed doing evil.

YOU ARE CHOSEN FOR SALVATION

13Brothers and sisters, whom the Lord
loves, God chose you from the beginning to be
saved. So we must always thank God for you.
You are saved by the Spirit that makes you holy
and by your faith in the truth. 14God used the
Good News that we preached to call you to be
saved so you can share in the glory of our Lord
Jesus Christ. 15So, brothers and sisters, stand
strong and continue to believe the teachings
we gave you in our speaking and in our letter.

2 Thessalonians 2:13

When you gave your heart to Jesus, you became a new person—"a new creation" (see 2 Corinthians 5:17). The old you disappeared, and you were transformed from darkness to light—from death to life! Now God wants you to be changed into his likeness, and he has equipped you to do this by his Spirit. The Holy Spirit puts in you the desire not to sin—not just the desire, but also the ability. Sin doesn't have authority over you anymore. You are free! We all need to submit ourselves to God, by remaining set apart for him. As you begin to do this, it will become easier to walk in his will.

Walking in God's will is nothing more than walking in obedience to him and to his Word. That's when the true blessings of God will begin to flow in your life. When Paul writes you are chosen to be "saved by the Spirit that makes you holy," he is telling you that the Holy Spirit has given you the power to live a holy life—a life that pleases and serves God. He is the One who makes you holy.

notes

2:3 **turning away** Or "the rebellion."

Blab

Q. My friend says he's a Christian, but he goes to church on Saturdays. Aren't we supposed to go on Sunday? Does God care what day you do church?

A. No. The Sabbath is a day set aside when all you do is worship God, hang out with him, pray to him and think about him. It's all God, all day. So pick the day that's best for you and honor him on it. That's the most important thing.

Q. If God made pot, why can't I smoke it?

A. The Bible says that everything is permissible but not everything is beneficial. God made pot, and some people say that's a reason to smoke it. The trouble with pot is this: 1. It is illegal, and we have to obey the law. 2. It controls you. 3. It's bad for your health. It kills brain cells. So yes, God made pot, but he also made poison ivy; you gonna smoke that too?

Q. My best friend fasts all the time. She says she is doing it because she wants to get close to God, but I think she's doing it to lose weight. What can I do?

A. Your friend has issues. Killing yourself and pretending like it's all for God is mixed up. Fasting is cool when God calls you to it. But if she's doing it all the time, it's probably anorexia. Help her get counseling. Anorexics don't know when they are anorexic, so friends have to help point it out.

[16-17]May our Lord Jesus Christ himself and
God our Father encourage you and strengthen
you in every good thing you do and say. God
loved us, and through his grace he gave us a
good hope and encouragement that continues
forever.

PRAY FOR US

3 And now, brothers and sisters, pray for
us that the Lord's teaching will continue
to spread quickly and that people will give
honor to that teaching, just as happened with
you. [2]And pray that we will be protected from
stubborn and evil people, because not all people believe.

[3]But the Lord is faithful and will give you
strength and will protect you from the Evil
One. [4]The Lord makes us feel sure that you are
doing and will continue to do the things we
told you. [5]May the Lord lead your hearts into
God's love and Christ's patience.

THE DUTY TO WORK

[6]Brothers and sisters, by the authority of
our Lord Jesus Christ we command you to stay
away from any believer who refuses to work
and does not follow the teaching we gave you.
[7]You yourselves know that you should live as
we live. We were not lazy when we were with

"THE LORD IS FAITHFUL AND WILL GIVE YOU STRENGTH."

you. [8]And when we ate another person's food,
we always paid for it. We worked very hard
night and day so we would not be an expense
to any of you. [9]We had the right to ask you to
help us, but we worked to take care of ourselves so we would be an example for you to
follow. [10]When we were with you, we gave
you this rule: "Anyone who refuses to work
should not eat."

[11]We hear that some people in your group
refuse to work. They do nothing but busy
themselves in other people's lives. [12]We com-

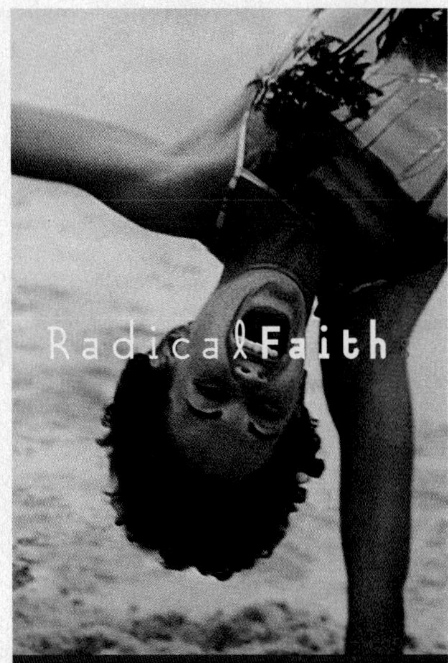

2 Thessalonians 3:13

"So why have I kept my heart pure? Why have I kept my hands from doing wrong?" (Psalm 73:13). Can you relate to this person's frustration? You tell the truth, even when it costs you, because you trust God to reward you for it. You help other people to try to make their lives better. Those are good reasons, but sometimes you just don't see those things happening. It's enough to make you want to give up.

Paul says you *must not* give up. How can you keep from getting tired of doing the right thing when it seems like it's getting you nowhere? Well, it takes some faith. You have to believe that God's going to do what he promised he would—even when his timetable is different from yours (and it usually is). You also have to continually fill up with God's Spirit. If you don't do that, you're like a car that's about to run out of gas. He keeps you going—you can't do it yourself.

Finally, you have to have your priorities straight. Ask yourself: Am I doing this to get results or am I doing it to please God? The answer makes all the difference.

LEARN IT & LIVE IT

Titus 1:16:
Learn It: Our actions must reflect our claim to know God.
Live It: Ask someone (who doesn't know you're a Christian) what kind of faith they think you follow. Do your actions show others that you believe in God?

Titus 2:7:
Learn It: We are to be an example of good deeds.
Live It: Get to be buddies with a little kid. Be an example to him or her of how a person should act.

Titus 2:15:
Learn It: We are not to let anyone treat us as if we are unimportant.
Live It: Don't be a doormat. Don't let people walk all over you and push you around. Don't be aggressive and pushy yourself, but be humbly assertive.

mand those people and beg them in the Lord Jesus Christ to work quietly and earn their own food.
13But you, brothers and sisters, never become tired of doing good.

14If some people do not obey what we tell you in this letter, then take note of them. Have nothing to do with them so they will feel ashamed.
15But do not treat them as enemies. Warn them as fellow believers.

"NEVER BECOME TIRED OF DOING GOOD."

FINAL WORDS

16Now may the Lord of peace give you peace at all times and in every way. The Lord be with all of you.

17I, Paul, end this letter now in my own handwriting. All my letters have this to show they are from me. This is the way I write.

18The grace of our Lord Jesus Christ be with you all.

bible basics

The Garden of Eden is where the first people lived. In the Old Testament, the first chapter of Genesis tells us about God creating mankind and placing them in the garden. The garden was perfect paradise. There was no sin, and Adam and Eve (the first people) were in perfect relationship with God. But Adam and Eve didn't follow God's rules, so they were banished from the garden.

Timothy was like a son to Paul. Paul loved
him and took him on trips and talked to
him about things that mattered. Together
they hit the road and spread the Good News in
Turkey, Greece, and Italy (sounds like a band on
tour). While Paul spent two years getting the church
going in Corinth, Timothy was right there as his assistant pastor. But Timothy had a lot to learn, and Paul
had a lot to teach. God used their relationship to
teach us about instructions for church life, being
faithful to your calling, and following Christ. In his
1 Timothy
A PRACTICAL MANUAL
FOR CHURCH LIFE
first letter to Timothy, Paul had two agendas: to offer
guidance for church administration and to oppose
false teachings in the seemingly "goody-goodies."
He accomplishes both with suggestions for regular
worship as well as a mandatory resume for leadership.

1 From Paul, an apostle of Christ Jesus, by
the command of God our Savior and
Christ Jesus our hope.
2To Timothy, a true child to me because you
believe:
Grace, mercy, and peace from God the Father
and Christ Jesus our Lord.

WARNING AGAINST FALSE TEACHING

3I asked you to stay longer in Ephesus when
I went into Macedonia so you could command
some people there to stop teaching false things.
4Tell them not to spend their time on stories
that are not true and on long lists of names in
family histories. These things only bring arguments; they do not help God's work, which is
done in faith. 5The purpose of this command
is for people to have love, a love that comes
from a pure heart and a good conscience and a
true faith. 6Some people have missed these
things and turned to useless talk. 7They want
to be teachers of the law, but they do not understand either what they are talking about or
what they are sure about.
8But we know that the law is good if someone uses it lawfully. 9We also know that the
law is not made for good people but for those
who are against the law and for those who
refuse to follow it. It is for people who are
against God and are sinful, who are not holy
and have no religion, who kill their fathers and
mothers, who murder, 10who take part in sexual sins, who have sexual relations with people of the same sex, who sell slaves, who tell
lies, who speak falsely, and who do anything
against the true teaching of God. 11That teaching is part of the Good News of the blessed
God that he gave me to tell.

THANKS FOR GOD'S MERCY

12I thank Christ Jesus our Lord, who gave
me strength, because he trusted me and gave
me this work of serving him. 13In the past I
spoke against Christ and persecuted him and
did all kinds of things to hurt him. But God
showed me mercy, because I did not know
what I was doing. I did not believe. 14But the
grace of our Lord was fully given to me, and
with that grace came the faith and love that are
in Christ Jesus.
15What I say is true, and you should fully
accept it: Christ Jesus came into the world to
save sinners, of whom I am the worst. 16But I
was given mercy so that in me, the worst of all
sinners, Christ Jesus could show that he has
patience without limit. His patience with me
made me an example for those who would
believe in him and have life forever. 17To the
King that rules forever, who will never die,
who cannot be seen, the only God, be honor
and glory forever and ever. Amen.
18Timothy, my child, I am giving you a
command that agrees with the prophecies that
were given about you in the past. I tell you this
so you can follow them and fight the good
fight. 19Continue to have faith and do what
you know is right. Some people have rejected
this, and their faith has been shipwrecked.
20Hymenaeus and Alexander have done that,
and I have given them to Satan so they will
learn not to speak against God.

Blab

Q. I get porn sites on my computer every day! Is there anything that I can do?

A. Unfortunately, there is no way to get rid of all that junk mail that comes into your account. There are some service providers that can block some of it but not all. Give your parents a heads up. Tell them you get it but you don't want to. Ask if they can help block it.

Q. My parents are getting divorced, and I have to choose which one to move in with. What do I do?

A. Go to the house where you'll get to spend the most time with your parent, where you'll be spiritually nourished, and you'll get to be in Christian fellowship. If this is both, then pray real hard. God will let you know.

Q. Why is a religion—the set of rules, traditions, and rituals—necessary if you have an individual faith in God that you feel content with?

A. Religion is not necessary. That's like saying, Why are the rules, traditions, and rituals necessary to play basketball? They're not. But they help the game move smoother and faster and they give you a guide. That is like with the whole religion thing. It helps give you some direction on how to create a deep relationship with God the Father without getting majorly sidetracked.

SOME RULES FOR MEN AND WOMEN

2 First, I tell you to pray for all people, asking God for what they need and being
thankful to him. 2Pray for rulers and for all
who have authority so that we can have quiet
and peaceful lives full of worship and respect
for God. 3This is good, and it pleases God our
Savior, 4who wants all people to be saved and
to know the truth. 5There is one God and one
way human beings can reach God. That way is
through Christ Jesus, who is himself human.
6He gave himself as a payment to free all people.
He is proof that came at the right time. 7That
is why I was chosen to tell the Good News and
to be an apostle. (I am telling the truth; I am
not lying.) I was chosen to teach those who are
not Jews to believe and to know the truth.

8So, I want the men everywhere to pray, lift-
ing up their hands in a holy manner, without
anger and arguments.

9Also, women should wear proper clothes
that show respect and self-control, not using
braided hair or gold or pearls or expensive
clothes. 10Instead, they should do good
deeds, which is right for women who say
they worship God.

11Let a woman learn by listening quietly
and being ready to cooperate in everything.
12But I do not allow a woman to teach or to
have authority over a man, but to listen quietly, 13because Adam was formed first and
then Eve. 14And Adam was not tricked, but the
woman was tricked and became a sinner. 15But
she will be saved through having children if
they continue in faith, love, and holiness, with
self-control.

ELDERS IN THE CHURCH

3 What I say is true: Anyone wanting to
become an elder desires a good work.
2An elder must not give people a reason to
criticize him, and he must have only one wife.
He must be self-controlled, wise, respected by
others, ready to welcome guests, and able to
teach. 3He must not drink too much wine or
like to fight, but rather be gentle and peace-
able, not loving money. 4He must be a good
family leader, having children who cooperate
with full respect. 5(If someone does not know
how to lead the family, how can that person
take care of God's church?) 6But an elder must
not be a new believer, or he might be too
proud of himself and be judged guilty just as

BIBLE BIOS: MIRIAM

Miriam was Moses' courageous older sister. When he was born, his mother put him in a reed basket and floated him down the Nile River to save him from the king of Egypt's death sentence. Miriam followed the baby right into the palace of the king. She approached the princess, who had found the baby Moses, and told her she knew of a nursemaid for the baby, her own mother. Miriam's actions saved Moses' life and reunited mother and child. May we be as courageous as this young woman.

[EXODUS 2; 15; NUMBERS 12]

MOISTURIZER

David, in the Psalms, cried out to the Lord for this kind of spiritual renewal. As you feel the fresh cleansing of your skin, imagine God doing the same to your soul every morning. Remember, God's faithfulness is great and his mercies are new every morning.

the devil was. 7An elder must also have the respect of people who are not in the church so he will not be criticized by others and caught in the devil's trap.

DEACONS IN THE CHURCH

8In the same way, deacons must be respected by others, not saying things they do not mean. They must not drink too much wine or try to get rich by cheating others. 9With a clear conscience they must follow the secret of the faith that God made known to us. 10Test them first. Then let them serve as deacons if you find nothing wrong in them. 11In the same way, women[n] must be respected by others. They must not speak evil of others. They must be self-controlled and trustworthy in everything. 12Deacons must have only one wife and be good leaders of their children and their own families. 13Those who serve well as deacons are making an honorable place for themselves, and they will be very bold in their faith in Christ Jesus.

THE SECRET OF OUR LIFE

14Although I hope I can come to you soon, I am writing these things to you now. 15Then, even if I am delayed, you will know how to live in the family of God. That family is the church of the living God, the support and foundation of the truth. 16Without doubt, the secret of our life of worship is great:

He was shown to us in a human body,
proved right in spirit,
and seen by angels.
He was preached to those who
are not Jews,
believed in by the world,
and taken up in glory.

A WARNING ABOUT FALSE TEACHERS

4 Now the Holy Spirit clearly says that in the later times some people will stop believing the faith. They will follow spirits that lie and teachings of demons. 2Such teachings come from the false words of liars whose consciences are destroyed as if by a hot iron. 3They forbid people to marry and tell them not to eat certain foods which God created to be eaten with thanks by people who believe and know the truth. 4Everything God made is good, and nothing should be refused if it is accepted with thanks, 5because it is made holy by what God has said and by prayer.

Isaiah 49:13
Heavens and earth, be happy. Mountains, shout with joy, because the LORD comforts his people and will have pity on those who suffer.

BE A GOOD SERVANT OF CHRIST

6By telling these things to the brothers and sisters,[n] you will be a good servant of Christ Jesus. You will be made strong by the words of the faith and the good teaching which you have been following. 7But do not follow foolish stories that disagree with God's truth, but train yourself to serve God. 8Training your body helps you in some ways, but serving God helps you in every way by bringing you blessings in this life and in the future life, too. 9What I say is true, and you should fully accept it. 10This is why we work and struggle: We hope in the living God who is the Savior of all people, especially of those who believe.

11Command and teach these things. 12Do not let anyone treat you as if you are unimportant because you are young. Instead, be an example to the believers with your words, your actions, your love, your faith, and your pure life. 13Until I come, continue to read the Scriptures to the people, strengthen them, and teach them. 14Use the gift you have, which was given to you through prophecy when the group of elders laid their hands on[n] you. 15Continue to do those things; give your life to doing them so your progress may be seen by everyone. 16Be careful in your life and in your teaching. If you

56% OF TEENS WANT TO MAKE A DIFFERENCE IN THE WORLD.

RELATIONSHIPS

How often do you take time to sit down and thank God for your family? Do you take for granted that you have parents who love you? Do you think your siblings are more pains-in-the-neck than they are actual human beings? Try dwelling on the positive aspects of your family for a change. Think about how your brother makes you laugh. Think about how your mom takes care of you when you're sick. Make a list of specific things that you appreciate about your family. You'll be surprised at how your perspective will change!

3:11 women This might mean the wives of the deacons, or it might mean women who serve in the same way as deacons. **4:6 brothers and sisters** Although the Greek text says "brothers" here and throughout this book, Paul's words refer to the entire church, including men and women. **4:14 laid their hands on** The laying on of hands had many purposes, including the giving of a blessing, power, or authority.

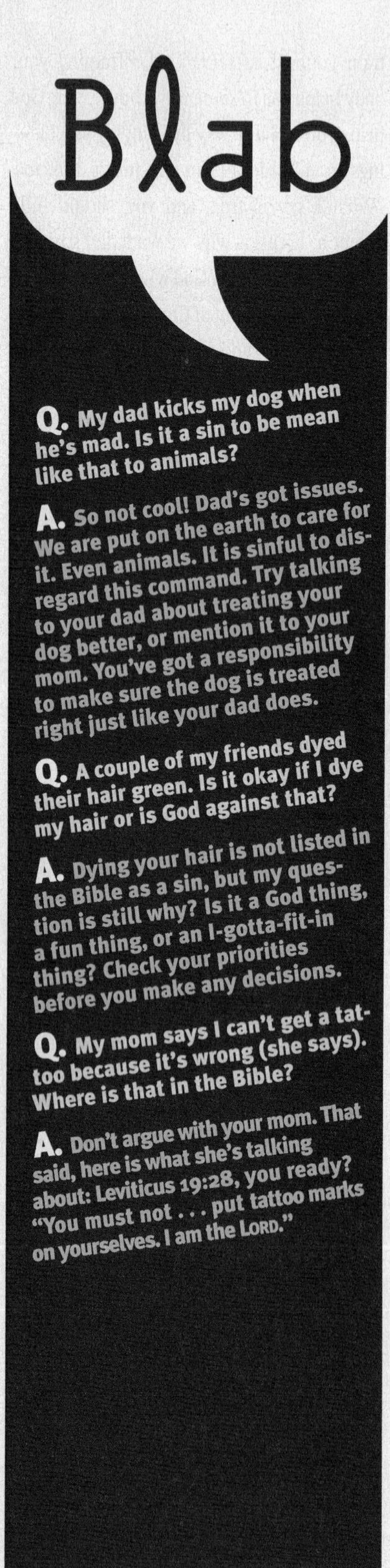

continue to live and teach rightly, you will save both yourself and those who listen to you.

Blab
Q. My dad kicks my dog when he's mad. Is it a sin to be mean like that to animals?
A. So not cool! Dad's got issues. We are put on the earth to care for it. Even animals. It is sinful to disregard this command. Try talking to your dad about treating your dog better, or mention it to your mom. You've got a responsibility to make sure the dog is treated right just like your dad does.
Q. A couple of my friends dyed their hair green. Is it okay if I dye my hair or is God against that?
A. Dying your hair is not listed in the Bible as a sin, but my question is still why? Is it a God thing, a fun thing, or an I-gotta-fit-in thing? Check your priorities before you make any decisions.
Q. My mom says I can't get a tattoo because it's wrong (she says). Where is that in the Bible?
A. Don't argue with your mom. That said, here is what she's talking about: Leviticus 19:28, you ready? "You must not . . . put tattoo marks on yourselves. I am the LORD."

RULES FOR LIVING WITH OTHERS

5 Do not speak angrily to an older man, but plead with him as if he were your father. Treat younger men like brothers, [2]older women like mothers, and younger women like sisters. Always treat them in a pure way.

[3]Take care of widows who are truly widows. [4]But if a widow has children or grandchildren, let them first learn to do their duty to their own family and to repay their parents or grandparents. That pleases God. [5]The true widow, who is all alone, puts her hope in God and continues to pray night and day for God's help. [6]But the widow who uses her life to please herself is really dead while she is alive. [7]Tell the believers to do these things so that no one can criticize them. [8]Whoever does not care for his own relatives, especially his own family members, has turned against the faith and is worse than someone who does not believe in God.

Psalm 11:7
The LORD does what is right, and he loves justice, so honest people will see his face.

[9]To be on the list of widows, a woman must be at least sixty years old. She must have been faithful to her husband. [10]She must be known for her good works—works such as raising her children, welcoming strangers, washing the feet of God's people, helping those in trouble, and giving her life to do all kinds of good deeds.

[11]But do not put younger widows on that list. After they give themselves to Christ, they are pulled away from him by their physical needs, and then they want to marry again. [12]They will be judged for not doing what they first promised to do. [13]Besides that, they learn to waste their time, going from house to house. And they not only waste their time but also begin to gossip and busy themselves with other people's lives, saying things they should not say. [14]So I want the younger widows to marry, have children, and manage their homes. Then no enemy will have any reason to criticize them. [15]But some have already turned away to follow Satan.

[16]If any woman who is a believer has widows in her family, she should care for them herself. The church should not have to care for them. Then it will be able to take care of those who are truly widows.

[17]The elders who lead the church well should receive double honor, especially those who work hard by speaking and teaching, [18]because the Scripture says: "When an ox is working in the grain, do not cover its mouth to keep it from eating,"[n] and "A worker should be given his pay."[n]

[19]Do not listen to someone who accuses an elder, without two or three witnesses. [20]Tell those who continue sinning that they are wrong. Do this in front of the whole church so that the others will have a warning.

[21]Before God and Christ Jesus and the chosen angels, I command you to do these things without showing favor of any kind to anyone.

DIDYA KNOW → 55% OF TEENS WANT A HIGH PAYING JOB.

[22]Think carefully before you lay your hands on[n] anyone, and don't share in the sins of others. Keep yourself pure.

[23]Stop drinking only water, but drink a little wine to help your stomach and your frequent sicknesses.

[24]The sins of some people are easy to see even before they are judged, but the sins of others are seen only later. [25]So also good deeds are

notes

5:18 "When . . . eating," Quotation from Deuteronomy 25:4. **5:18 "A worker . . . pay."** Quotation from Luke 10:7. **5:22 lay your hands on** The laying on of hands had many purposes, including the giving of a blessing, power, or authority.

easy to see, but even those that are not easily seen cannot stay hidden.

6 All who are slaves under a yoke should show full respect to their masters so no one will speak against God's name and our
teaching. 2The slaves whose masters are believ-
ers should not show their masters any less respect because they are believers. They should serve their masters even better, because they are helping believers they love.

You must teach and preach these things.

FALSE TEACHING AND TRUE RICHES

3Anyone who has a different teaching does not agree with the true teaching of our Lord Jesus Christ and the teaching that shows the
true way to serve God. 4This person is full of
pride and understands nothing, but is sick with a love for arguing and fighting about words. This brings jealousy, fighting, speaking against
others, evil mistrust, 5and constant quarrels
from those who have evil minds and have lost the truth. They think that serving God is a way to get rich.

6Serving God does make us very rich, if we
are satisfied with what we have. 7We brought
nothing into the world, so we can take nothing
out. 8But, if we have food and clothes, we will
be satisfied with that. 9Those who want to
become rich bring temptation to themselves and are caught in a trap. They want many foolish and harmful things that ruin and destroy
people. 10The love of money causes all kinds of evil. Some people have left the faith, because they wanted to get more money, but they have caused themselves much sorrow.

SOME THINGS TO REMEMBER

11But you, man of God, run away from all those things. Instead, live in the right way, serve God, have faith, love, patience, and gentleness.
12Fight the good fight of faith, grabbing hold of the life that continues forever. You were called to have that life when you confessed the good
confession before many witnesses. 13In the
sight of God, who gives life to everything, and of Christ Jesus, I give you a command. Christ Jesus made the good confession when he stood before
Pontius Pilate. 14Do what you were commanded to do without wrong or blame until our
Lord Jesus Christ comes again. 15God will make
that happen at the right time. He is the blessed and only Ruler, the King of all kings and the Lord
of all lords. 16He is the only One who never dies.
He lives in light so bright no one can go near it. No one has ever seen God, or can see him. May honor and power belong to God forever. Amen.

17Command those who are rich with things
of this world not to be proud. Tell them to hope in God, not in their uncertain riches. God richly
gives us everything to enjoy. 18Tell the rich
people to do good, to be rich in doing good deeds,
to be generous and ready to share. 19By doing
that, they will be saving a treasure for themselves as a strong foundation for the future. Then they will be able to have the life that is true life.

20Timothy, guard what God has trusted to
you. Stay away from foolish, useless talk and from the arguments of what is falsely called
"knowledge." 21By saying they have that
"knowledge," some have missed the true faith.

Grace be with you.

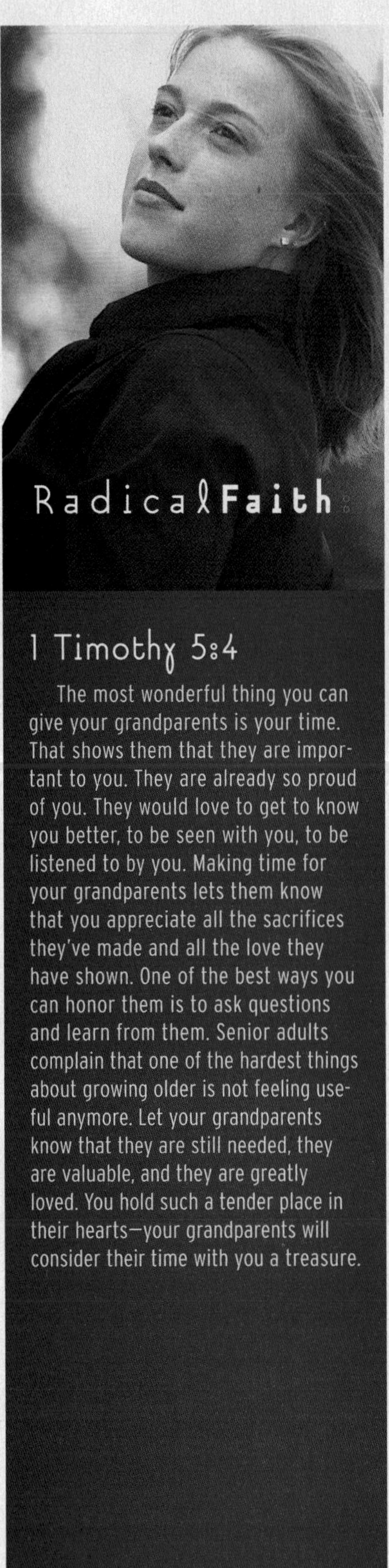

1 Timothy 5:4

The most wonderful thing you can give your grandparents is your time. That shows them that they are important to you. They are already so proud of you. They would love to get to know you better, to be seen with you, to be listened to by you. Making time for your grandparents lets them know that you appreciate all the sacrifices they've made and all the love they have shown. One of the best ways you can honor them is to ask questions and learn from them. Senior adults complain that one of the hardest things about growing older is not feeling useful anymore. Let your grandparents know that they are still needed, they are valuable, and they are greatly loved. You hold such a tender place in their hearts—your grandparents will consider their time with you a treasure.

2 Timothy

Encouragement to be strong in the faith

This letter is a follow-up to the first letter—probably from within the walls of a jail! Of all the Pastoral Epistles, this one is the most personal. Paul wrote his friend Timothy a second letter of advice to renew the importance of commitment to Scripture and to remind him that holy living is essential. Paul warns Timothy that times of trouble are on the way both from forces outside the church and from false teachers within the church. He encourages Timothy to endure throughout these times with faithfulness as he leads the church with fortitude in the face of imminent martyrdom. As Timothy perseveres, Paul teaches him how to combat false teachers, keep on preaching the Good News, and handle suffering as a believer in Jesus Christ. Like a good coach, Paul takes Timothy under his wing and tells him how to win the second half of the ball game.

1 From Paul, an apostle of Christ Jesus by
the will of God. God sent me to tell about
the promise of life that is in Christ Jesus.
[2]To Timothy, a dear child to me:
Grace, mercy, and peace to you from God
the Father and Christ Jesus our Lord.

ENCOURAGEMENT FOR TIMOTHY

[3]I thank God as I always mention you in
my prayers, day and night. I serve him, doing
what I know is right as my ancestors did.
[4]Remembering that you cried for me, I
want very much to see you so I can be
filled with joy. [5]I remember your true faith.
That faith first lived in your grandmother
Lois and in your mother Eunice, and I
know you now have that same faith.
[6]This is why I remind you to keep using
the gift God gave you when I laid my
hands on[n] you. Now let it grow, as a small
flame grows into a fire. [7]God did not give
us a spirit that makes us afraid but a spirit
of power and love and self-control.
[8]So do not be ashamed to tell people
about our Lord Jesus, and do not be ashamed
of me, in prison for the Lord. But suffer with
me for the Good News. God, who gives us the
strength to do that, [9]saved us and made us his
holy people. That was not because of anything
we did ourselves but because of God's
purpose and grace. That grace was given to us
through Christ Jesus before time began, [10]but
it is now shown to us by the coming of our
Savior Christ Jesus. He destroyed death, and
through the Good News he showed us the
way to have life that cannot be destroyed. [11]I
was chosen to tell that Good News and to be
an apostle and a teacher. [12]I am suffering now
because I tell the Good News, but I am not
ashamed, because I know Jesus, the One in
whom I have believed. And I am sure he is able
to protect what he has trusted me with until
that day.[n] [13]Follow the pattern of true
teachings that you heard from me in faith
and love, which are in Christ Jesus. [14]Protect
the truth that you were given; protect
it with the help of the Holy Spirit who
lives in us.
[15]You know that everyone in the country
of Asia has left me, even Phygelus and
Hermogenes. [16]May the Lord show mercy
to the family of Onesiphorus, who has often
helped me and was not ashamed that I
was in prison. [17]When he came to Rome,
he looked eagerly for me until he found me.
[18]May the Lord allow him to find mercy

Q. Do you prefer quiet girls or outgoing girls?
A. Quiet. I mean, they need to be not *painfully* shy, but I don't like it when girls are too aggressive or pushy.
GUYS SPEAK OUT

notes

1:6 laid my hands on The laying on of hands had many purposes, including the giving of a blessing, power, or authority.
1:12 day The day Christ will come to judge all people and take his people to live with him.

from the Lord on that day. You know how
many ways he helped me in Ephesus.

A LOYAL SOLDIER OF CHRIST JESUS

2 You then, Timothy, my child, be strong
in the grace we have in Christ Jesus.
2You should teach people whom you can trust
the things you and many others have heard
me say. Then they will be able to teach others.
3Share in the troubles we have like a good soldier of Christ Jesus. 4A soldier wants to please
the enlisting officer, so no one serving in the
army wastes time with everyday matters. 5Also
an athlete who takes part in a contest must
obey all the rules in order to win. 6The farmer
who works hard should be the first person to
get some of the food that was grown. 7Think
about what I am saying, because the Lord will
give you the ability to understand everything.

8Remember Jesus Christ, who was raised
from the dead, who is from the family of
David. This is the Good News I preach, 9and I
am suffering because of it to the point of being bound with chains like a criminal. But
God's teaching is not in chains. 10So I patiently accept all these troubles so that those

"THE LORD WILL GIVE YOU THE ABILITY TO UNDERSTAND EVERYTHING."

whom God has chosen can have the salvation that is in Christ Jesus. With that salvation comes glory that never ends.

11This teaching is true:

If we died with him, we will also live
with him.
12If we accept suffering, we will also rule
with him.
If we refuse to accept him, he will refuse
to accept us.
13If we are not faithful, he will still be
faithful,
because he cannot be false to himself.

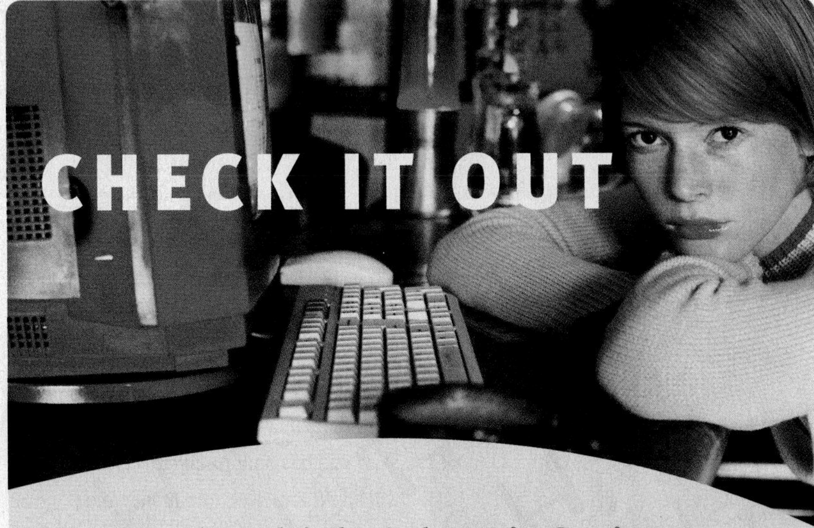

National Multiple Sclerosis Society

Volunteers at the National Multiple Sclerosis Society are integral partners in our fight against MS. Throughout the United States, volunteers contribute valuable resources (time, knowledge, skills, and leadership), infusing our organization with the energy and passion necessary to end the devastating effects of multiple sclerosis.

The National MS Society strives to be known and respected for excellence in volunteerism among the country's voluntary health agencies. We envision an organization in which volunteers work as partners at all levels; an environment that embraces, values, and recognizes every contribution.

Volunteer involvement is continually expanded and enhanced through exemplary training programs and tools. Our organization welcomes the diversity that individuals bring to our efforts and is dedicated to providing growth and development to everyone involved with our programs.

*For more info, go to **www.nationalmssociety.org**.*

A WORKER PLEASING TO GOD

14Continue teaching these things, warning
people in God's presence not to argue about
words. It does not help anyone, and it ruins
those who listen. 15Make every effort to give
yourself to God as the kind of person he will
accept. Be a worker who is not ashamed and
who uses the true teaching in the right way.
16Stay away from foolish, useless talk, because
that will lead people further away from God.
17Their evil teaching will spread like a sickness
inside the body. Hymenaeus and Philetus are
like that. 18They have left the true teaching,
saying that the rising from the dead has already taken place, and so they are destroying
the faith of some people. 19But God's strong
foundation continues to stand. These words
are written on the seal: "The Lord knows those
who belong to him,"[n] and "Everyone who wants
to belong to the Lord must stop doing wrong."

20In a large house there are not only things
made of gold and silver, but also things made
of wood and clay. Some things are used for
special purposes, and others are made for ordinary jobs. 21All who make themselves clean
from evil will be used for special purposes.
They will be made holy, useful to the Master,
ready to do any good work.

22But run away from the evil young people
like to do. Try hard to live right and to have
faith, love, and peace, together with those who
trust in the Lord from pure hearts. 23Stay away

notes

2:19 "The Lord . . . him" Quotation from Numbers 16:5.

2 Timothy 3:15-17

The Bible is an awesome book. It's full of answers and advice and wisdom. It's full of war and deceit and natural disasters and family squabbles. It tells you how to live and be successful, and it tells you what to look out for. It's the richest piece of literature ever written.

But beyond all of that, the Bible is the Word of God. It's the letter that God has personally written to you. God's got some things to say and they're all together in this one incredible book. When Jesus lived on earth, he prayed to God one day and said, "Make them ready for your service through your truth; your teaching is truth" (John 17:17). Are you a follower of Jesus? Then this prayer is for you. Jesus says that God's Word is truth. And what does truth do for you? It makes you free (see John 8:32). The Bible has the power to give you freedom from whatever has got you down—family, school, depression, confusion, guilt, stress, frustration, bad self-image, loneliness, lack of direction, apathy, boredom. You name it.

So spend time in reading the Bible. Get it into your head and into your heart. Nothing else will make you free.

from foolish and stupid arguments, because
you know they grow into quarrels. 24And a
servant of the Lord must not quarrel but must
be kind to everyone, a good teacher, and patient. 25The Lord's servant must gently teach
those who disagree. Then maybe God will let
them change their minds so they can accept
the truth. 26And they may wake up and escape from the trap of the devil, who catches
them to do what he wants.

THE LAST DAYS

3 Remember this! In the last days there
will be many troubles, 2because people
will love themselves, love money, brag, and be
proud. They will say evil things against others
and will not obey their parents or be thankful
or be the kind of people God wants. 3They will
not love others, will refuse to forgive, will gossip, and will not control themselves. They will
be cruel, will hate what is good, 4will turn
against their friends, and will do foolish things
without thinking. They will be conceited, will
love pleasure instead of God, 5and will act as if
they serve God but will not have his power.

"TRY HARD TO LIVE RIGHT AND TO HAVE FAITH, LOVE, AND PEACE."

Stay away from those people. 6Some of them
go into homes and get control of silly women
who are full of sin and are led by many evil
desires. 7These women are always learning
new teachings, but they are never able to understand the truth fully. 8Just as Jannes and
Jambres were against Moses, these people are
against the truth. Their thinking has been ruined, and they have failed in trying to follow
the faith. 9But they will not be successful in
what they do, because as with Jannes and Jambres, everyone will see that they are foolish.

OBEY THE TEACHINGS

10But you have followed what I teach, the
way I live, my goal, faith, patience, and love.

Blab

Q. What is God and the church's view on homosexuality and its place in our world?

A. You want God's view, or the church's? Start with God. Romans chapter 1 says that it is impurity. It's a sin, just like gossiping about your best friend is a sin. You need to stop acting on your impulses. Sometimes the church's view can be a little harsher. Many people in the church see it like the worst of all evils. But they are looking at it through human eyes. God says it's a sin: It's not how he made you, so stop.

Q. I am a little unsure of what, specifically, the Original Sin was and why we should feel accountable.

A. Original Sin is the concept that when you're born, you're sinful. From the minute you start to exist, you desperately need God.

Q. I have had a lot of trouble lately. I am a born Catholic but I don't exactly agree with everything that we are supposed to believe. What am I supposed to do? I am so lost.

A. Sounds like you just need to do a little research. Start reading the Bible. Get a version you can understand. Find out what God wants from you. Then see how that matches what the church wants from you. Talk to a priest. Get the facts and then go with what God is telling you to do.

ISSUES: Identity

Do you feel the pressure to always look your best at school, church, even just around friends? Who are you really? If asked to define yourself, what would you say? Is your honest answer "a child of Christ"? Because if you are a Christian, that is your primary identity—a daughter of the King of the universe. That's a pretty big deal and something to be proud of. He chose you to be his own child and will never, ever give you up. Find your comfort, peace, and identity in that today.

You know I never give up. [11]You know how I
have been hurt and have suffered, as in Antioch, Iconium, and Lystra. I have suffered, but
the Lord saved me from all those troubles.
[12]Everyone who wants to live as God desires,
in Christ Jesus, will be hurt. [13]But people who
are evil and cheat others will go from bad to
worse. They will fool others, but they will also
be fooling themselves.

[14]But you should continue following the
teachings you learned. You know they are true,
because you trust those who taught you.
[15]Since you were a child you have known the
Holy Scriptures which are able to make you
wise. And that wisdom leads to salvation
through faith in Christ Jesus. [16]All Scripture
is given by God and is useful for teaching, for
showing people what is wrong in their lives,
for correcting faults, and for teaching how to
live right. [17]Using the Scriptures, the person
who serves God will be capable, having all
that is needed to do every good work.

4 I give you a command in the presence of
God and Christ Jesus, the One who will
judge the living and the dead, and by his coming and his kingdom: [2]Preach the Good News.
Be ready at all times, and tell people what they
need to do. Tell them when they are wrong.
Encourage them with great patience and careful
teaching, [3]because the time will come when
people will not listen to the true teaching but
will find many more teachers who please them
by saying the things they want to hear. [4]They
will stop listening to the truth and will begin
to follow false stories. [5]But you should control yourself at all times, accept troubles, do
the work of telling the Good News, and complete all the duties of a servant of God.

[6]My life is being given as an offering to
God, and the time has come for me to leave
this life. [7]I have fought the good fight, I have
finished the race, I have kept the faith. [8]Now,
a crown is being held for me—a crown for being right with God. The Lord, the judge who
judges rightly, will give the crown to me on

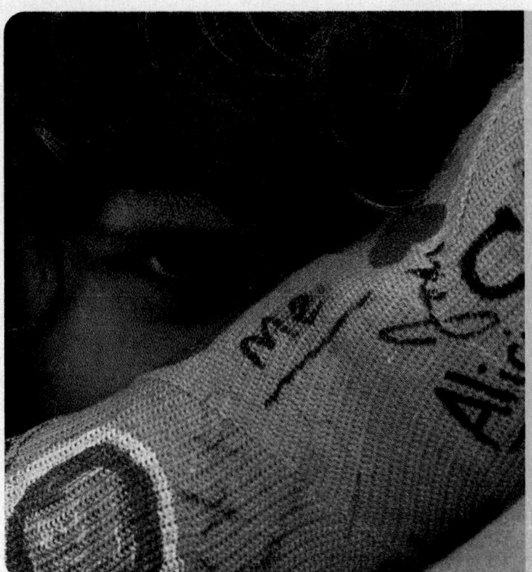

LEARN IT & LIVE IT

Philemon 7:
Learn It: We should show compassion to others.
Live It: Cook dinner for someone tonight and take it to them.

Hebrews 1:8-9:
Learn It: God favors Christ over the angels; and because of our unique relationship to Christ, we too are favored over them (see 1 Corinthians 6:1-3).
Live It: Treat yourself like a princess today. Go on a "date" with God.

Hebrews 2:1:
Learn It: We must be careful to follow the things we were taught.
Live It: Think for ten seconds before you make any decision today. Make sure your decisions are biblical and glorify God.

that day[n]—not only to me but to all those who have waited with love for him to come again.

PERSONAL WORDS

9Do your best to come to me as soon as you
can, 10because Demas, who loved this world,
left me and went to Thessalonica. Crescens
went to Galatia, and Titus went to Dalmatia.
11Luke is the only one still with me. Get Mark
and bring him with you when you come, because he can help me in my work here. 12I
sent Tychicus to Ephesus. 13When I was in
Troas, I left my coat there with Carpus. So when you come, bring it to me, along with my books, particularly the ones written on parchment.[n] 14Alexander the metalworker did many
harmful things against me. The Lord will punish him for what he did. 15You also should be
careful that he does not hurt you, because he fought strongly against our teaching.

16The first time I defended myself, no one

"THE LORD STAYED WITH ME AND GAVE ME STRENGTH SO I COULD FULLY TELL THE GOOD NEWS."

helped me; everyone left me. May they be forgiven. 17But the Lord stayed with me and gave
me strength so I could fully tell the Good News to all those who are not Jews. So I was saved from the lion's mouth. 18The Lord will save
me when anyone tries to hurt me, and he will bring me safely to his heavenly kingdom. Glory forever and ever be the Lord's. Amen.

FINAL GREETINGS

19Greet Priscilla and Aquila and the family of Onesiphorus. 20Erastus stayed in Corinth,
and I left Trophimus sick in Miletus. 21Try as
hard as you can to come to me before winter.

Eubulus sends greetings to you. Also Pudens, Linus, Claudia, and all the brothers and sisters in Christ greet you.

22The Lord be with your spirit. Grace be
with you.

Notes

4:8 day The day Christ will come to judge all people and take his people to live with him. **4:13 parchment** A writing paper made from the skins of sheep.

Titus

ONLY TRUTH MAKES PEOPLE CHRISTLIKE

Like Timothy, Titus was also a traveling companion of Paul. However, he finally settled down in Crete, the isle of pirates and thugs. He had a tough job! To help him out with a little advice, Paul wrote Titus a letter of general teachings for the church. In this letter, he talks about the roles of leaders in the church, the divisions of groups and their proper behavior, and finally an ethical program for the church to live in the world and act in accordance with Jesus' teachings of meekness, obedience, and gentleness. Paul describes in detail how Titus's church should be run in Crete. This was a real challenge for this renegade church, but Paul knew that Titus could handle these guys.

1 From Paul, a servant of God and an apostle of Jesus Christ. I was sent to help the
faith of God's chosen people and to help them
know the truth that shows people how to serve
God. [2]That faith and that knowledge come
from the hope for life forever, which God
promised to us before time began. And God
cannot lie. [3]At the right time God let the world
know about that life through preaching. He
trusted me with that work, and I preached by
the command of God our Savior.

[4]To Titus, my true child in the faith we
share:

Grace and peace from God the Father and
Christ Jesus our Savior.

TITUS' WORK IN CRETE

[5]I left you in Crete so you could finish
doing the things that still needed to be done
and so you could appoint elders in every
town, as I directed you. [6]An elder must not be
guilty of doing wrong, must have only one
wife, and must have believing children. They
must not be known as children who are wild
and do not cooperate. [7]As God's manager, an
elder must not be guilty of doing wrong, being
selfish, or becoming angry quickly. He must
not drink too much wine, like to fight, or try to
get rich by cheating others. [8]An elder must be
ready to welcome guests, love what is good, be
wise, live right, and be holy and self-controlled.
[9]By holding on to the trustworthy word just as
we teach it, an elder can help people by using
true teaching, and he can show those who are
against the true teaching that they are wrong.

[10]There are many people who refuse to
cooperate, who talk about worthless things
and lead others into the wrong way—mainly
those who say all who are not Jews must be
circumcised. [11]These people must be stopped,
because they are upsetting whole families by
teaching things they should not teach, which
they do to get rich by cheating people. [12]Even
one of their own prophets said, "Cretans are
always liars, evil animals, and lazy people
who do nothing but eat." [13]The words that
prophet said are true. So firmly tell those people they are wrong so they may become strong
in the faith, [14]not accepting Jewish false stories and the commands of people who reject
the truth. [15]To those who are pure, all things
are pure, but to those who are full of sin and do
not believe, nothing is pure. Both their minds
and their consciences have been ruined.
[16]They say they know God, but their actions
show they do not accept him. They are hateful
people, they refuse to obey, and they are useless
for doing anything good.

54% OF TEENS WANT TO HAVE CHILDREN WHEN THEY GROW UP.

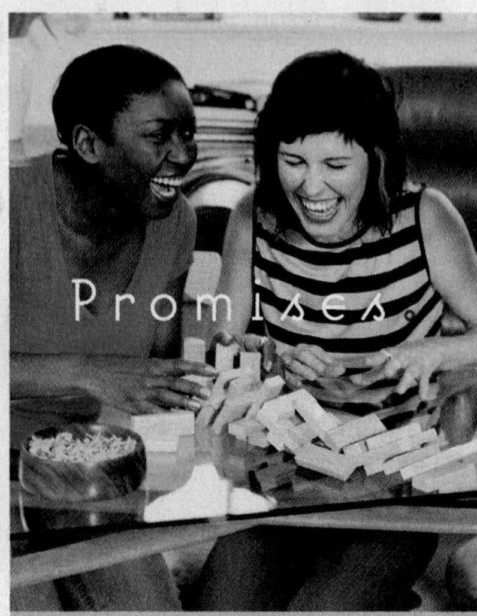

Titus 2:14

Sometimes people think that God's grace is nothing more than the forgiveness of sins. It would be enough if that's all there was to it—just the forgiveness of every sin in your whole life—even the ones you won't commit for another twenty or thirty years.

But God knows you need more than just a clean slate to become all he wants you to be. You also need a heart that's tender toward him, a mind that can be made to think like his, and a soul that yields its will to the wishes of his Spirit. This verse tells you that he "gave himself for us so he might pay the price to free us . . . and to make us pure people who belong only to him. . . ." You're included.

But gentle and patient to the end, he's also allowed your heart to be tested. He's also given you the power to stand up to temptation. Anything that doesn't agree with God or his Word is temptation. Know his Word so well that you are quick to recognize temptation. When you see it, run.

Your pure heart can feel impure sometimes. If it does, get clean. Ask God's forgiveness and receive it. His forgiveness purifies you.

He's changed your heart forever. Go and live like you believe it.

"HIS FORGIVENESS PURIFIES YOU."

FOLLOWING THE TRUE TEACHING

2 But you must tell everyone what to do to follow the true teaching. 2Teach older men to be self-controlled, serious, wise, strong in faith, in love, and in patience.

3In the same way, teach older women to be holy in their behavior, not speaking against others or enslaved to too much wine, but teaching what is good. 4Then they can teach the young women to love their husbands, to love their children, 5to be wise and pure, to be good workers at home, to be kind, and to yield to their husbands. Then no one will be able to criticize the teaching God gave us.

6In the same way, encourage young men to be wise. 7In every way be an example of doing good deeds. When you teach, do it with honesty and seriousness. 8Speak the truth so that you cannot be criticized. Then those who are against you will be ashamed because there is nothing bad to say about us.

Psalm 86:5
Lord, you are kind and forgiving and have great love for those who call to you.

DIDYA KNOW → 49% OF TEENS WANT TO LIVE CLOSE TO FAMILY.

9Slaves should yield to their own masters at all times, trying to please them and not arguing with them. 10They should not steal from them but should show their masters they can be fully trusted so that in everything they do they will make the teaching of God our Savior attractive.

11That is the way we should live, because God's grace that can save everyone has come. 12It teaches us not to live against God nor to do the evil things the world wants to do. Instead, that grace teaches us to live now in a wise and right way and in a way that shows we serve God. 13We should live like that while we wait for our great hope and the coming of the glory of our great God and Savior Jesus Christ. 14He gave himself for us so he might pay the price to free us from all evil and to make us pure people who belong only to him—people who are always wanting to do good deeds.

15Say these things and encourage the people and tell them what is wrong in their lives, with all authority. Do not let anyone treat you as if you were unimportant.

THE RIGHT WAY TO LIVE

3 Remind the believers to yield to the authority of rulers and government leaders, to obey them, to be ready to do good, 2to speak no evil about anyone, to live in peace, and to be gentle and polite to all people.

3In the past we also were foolish. We did not obey, we were wrong, and we were slaves to many things our bodies wanted and enjoyed. We spent our lives doing evil and being jealous. People hated us, and we hated each other. 4But when the kindness and love of God our Savior was shown, 5he saved us because of his mercy. It was not because of good deeds we did to be right with him. He saved us through the washing that made us new people through the Holy Spirit. 6God poured out richly upon us that Holy Spirit through Jesus Christ our Savior. 7Being made right with God by his grace, we could have the hope of receiving the life that never ends.

8This teaching is true, and I want you to be sure the people understand these things. Then those who believe in God will be careful to use their lives for doing good. These things are good and will help everyone.

9But stay away from those who have foolish arguments and talk about useless family

LEARN IT & LIVE IT

Hebrews 2:15:
Learn It: Jesus has freed us of our fear of death.
Live It: Next time you get scared of something, repeat this truth to yourself ten times. Read Hebrews 2 and learn all that God has provided and planned for us.

Hebrews 2:18:
Learn It: Jesus suffered and was tempted.
Live It: Don't give in to your temptation today. Remember that Jesus was able to stand strong against the devil. Use Scripture to fight off any temptations that you face.

Hebrews 3:13:
Learn It: We are supposed to encourage others.
Live It: Write a note to three of your friends today. Tell them how much you love them.

histories and argue and quarrel about the law.
Those things are worth nothing and will not
help anyone. 10After a first and second warning, avoid someone who causes arguments.
11You can know that such people are evil and
sinful; their own sins prove them wrong.

SOME THINGS TO REMEMBER

12When I send Artemas or Tychicus to you,
make every effort to come to me at Nicopolis,
because I have decided to stay there this winter. 13Do all you can to help Zenas the lawyer
and Apollos on their journey so that they have
everything they need. 14Our people must
learn to use their lives for doing good deeds to
provide what is necessary so that their lives
will not be useless.

15All who are with me greet you. Greet
those who love us in the faith.

Grace be with you all.

bible basics

The Ten Commandments can be found in Exodus 20 of the Old Testament. They are the rules God laid out for the nation of Israel and are considered moral law. We are still supposed to live that way today. Among the commandments are these: do not murder, do not lie, honor your father and mother, do not have any gods except God, and do not steal.

Philemon

HOW CHRIST MAKES A DIFFERENCE IN RELATIONSHIPS

Paul had met Onesimus, a runaway slave, and Onesimus had become a Christian while staying with him. After a while, though, Paul knew Onesimus needed to return to his master, Philemon, and make things right. So Paul wrote this reference letter for Onesimus, asking for Philemon's forgiveness and acceptance back into his home and church. Paul never really talks about slavery being good or bad, just how all people should treat each other. Instead of trying to start a revolution to fight the system, he works on changing the people inside the system through brotherly love. Because Onesimus and Philemon were both a part of the church, Paul wanted to demonstrate the love that should be or could be shown among those people.

1From Paul, a prisoner of Christ Jesus, and
from Timothy, our brother.
To Philemon, our dear friend and worker
with us; 2to Apphia, our sister; to Archippus, a
worker with us; and to the church that meets
in your home:
3Grace and peace to you from God our Father
and the Lord Jesus Christ.

PHILEMON'S LOVE AND FAITH

4I always thank my God when I mention you
in my prayers, 5because I hear about the love
you have for all God's holy people and the faith
you have in the Lord Jesus. 6I pray that the faith
you share may make you understand every
blessing we have in Christ. 7I have great joy and
comfort, my brother, because the love you have
shown to God's people has refreshed them.

ACCEPT ONESIMUS AS A BROTHER

8So, in Christ, I could be bold and order you
to do what is right. 9But because I love you, I
am pleading with you instead. I, Paul, an old
man now and also a prisoner for
Christ Jesus, 10am pleading with
you for my child Onesimus,
who became my child while I
was in prison. 11In the past
he was useless to you, but
now he has become useful for both
you and me.
12I am sending him back to you, and with
him I am sending my own heart. 13I wanted to
keep him with me so that in your place he might
help me while I am in prison for the Good News.
14But I did not want to do anything without asking you first so that any good you do for me will
be because you want to do it, not because I
forced you. 15Maybe Onesimus was
separated from you for a short
time so you could have him
back forever— 16no longer as
a slave, but better than a
slave, as a loved brother. I
love him very much, but you will love
him even more, both as a person and as a
believer in the Lord.

Psalm 145:8
The LORD is kind and shows mercy. He does not become angry quickly but is full of love.

Blab

Q. I was just wondering is MTV or rap music bad to watch and listen to?

A. God is present everywhere, even on MTV. But, don't feed your mind that stuff 24/7. Whatever you constantly feed your mind, that is what you will believe. So spend more time talking to God and reading the Word. Dig into that and then you will see him everywhere.

Q. Everyone at school hates me. What should I do?

A. Everyone does not hate you. You can't possibly know what every person is thinking. Stop being so emotional about it and start trying to be fun to be with. Maybe you are just quiet, or shy, or boring. They just might not know you. Try to come out of your shell. Try art, try music. Read the paper. Make conversation. They will start to see who you are and start acting more like friends.

Q. What do you think, as teenagers, that the age gap between people dating could be?

A. Adolescence is one of the times that bodies and emotions develop the fastest, so a nineteen- and fourteen-year-old dating is a lot different from a twenty-five-year-old and thirty-year-old dating. Stick with relationships close to your own age. The younger you are, the closer your ages should be. But also know that, at fourteen years old, that relationship will most likely not last forever. So don't get all wrapped up in it. Take it easy.

17So if you consider me your partner, welcome Onesimus as you would welcome me. 18If
he has done anything wrong to you or if he
owes you anything, charge that to me. 19I,
Paul, am writing this with my own hand. I will
pay it back, and I will say nothing about what
you owe me for your own life. 20So, my
brother, I ask that you do this for me in the
Lord: Refresh my heart in Christ. 21I write this
letter, knowing that you will do what I ask you
and even more.

22One more thing—prepare a room for me in
which to stay, because I hope God will answer
your prayers and I will be able to come to you.

FINAL GREETINGS

23Epaphras, a prisoner with me for Christ
Jesus, sends greetings to you. 24And also Mark,
Aristarchus, Demas, and Luke, workers together
with me, send greetings.

25The grace of our Lord Jesus Christ be with
your spirit.

TOPten

RANDOM WAYS TO BE A COOL SISTER

01	Next time your sibs get on your nerves, don't get mad at them.
02	Take them out for ice cream or coffee.
03	Give your sister some clothes you haven't worn in a long time.
04	Let them take you to one of their favorite places.
05	Plan something fun for your parents together.
06	Have a movie night with candy, popcorn, and sodas.
07	Pray for your siblings.
08	Invite them to hang out with you and your friends for a while.
09	Compliment them every now and then.
10	Let your sibs borrow your CDs when they have their friends over.

Hebrews

Every group of people has tags and labels they use to identify themselves as part of their group. For the Jews, their biggest tags were the rituals and rules God had given them through Moses. The Law, as these rules were called, represented God's agreement with the Jews. The writer of Hebrews (some scholars think it was Paul and others, Priscilla!) walked back through the whole history of the Jews starting with their earliest and most famous ancestors, Abraham and Moses. But the whole point of doing this was to show that Jesus was greater than any of their ancestors: he was the new prophet, priest, and king! The writer was trying to convince his Hebrew readers that Jesus was, indeed, the Messiah that all their ancestors had pointed them toward. Maybe the most famous chapter of Hebrews is chapter 11. The writer spells out that "you gotta have faith," and tells what it is and how to live it.

JESUS IS THE NEW AND GREATEST PROPHET, PRIEST, AND KING

GOD SPOKE THROUGH HIS SON

1 In the past God spoke to our ancestors through the prophets many times and in many different ways. 2But now in these last days God has spoken to us through his Son. God has chosen his Son to own all things, and through him he made the world. 3The Son reflects the glory of God and shows exactly what God is like. He holds everything together with his powerful word. When the Son made people clean from their sins, he sat down at the right side of God, the Great One in heaven. 4The Son became much greater than the angels, and God gave him a name that is much greater than theirs.

5This is because God never said to any of the angels,

"You are my Son.
Today I have become your Father." *Psalm 2:7*

Nor did God say of any angel,

"I will be his Father,
and he will be my Son." *2 Samuel 7:14*

6And when God brings his firstborn Son into the world, he says,

"Let all God's angels worship him."[n] *Psalm 97:7*

"GOD HAS CHOSEN HIS SON TO OWN ALL THINGS, AND THROUGH HIM HE MADE THE WORLD."

7This is what God said about the angels:

"God makes his angels become like winds.
He makes his servants become like flames of fire." *Psalm 104:4*

8But God said this about his Son:

"God, your throne will last forever and ever.
You will rule your kingdom with fairness.
9You love right and hate evil,
so God has chosen you from among your friends;
he has set you apart with much joy." *Psalm 45:6-7*

10God also says,

"Lord, in the beginning you made the earth,
and your hands made the skies.
11They will be destroyed, but you will remain.
They will all wear out like clothes.
12You will fold them like a coat.
And, like clothes, you will change them.
But you never change,
and your life will never end." *Psalm 102:25-27*

notes

1:6 "Let . . . him." These words are found in Deuteronomy 32:43 in the Septuagint, the Greek version of the Old Testament, and in a Hebrew copy among the Dead Sea Scrolls.

13 And God never said this to an angel:

"Sit by me at my right side
until I put your enemies under your
control."[n] *Psalm 110:1*

14 All the angels are spirits who serve God
and are sent to help those who will receive salvation.

OUR SALVATION IS GREAT

2 So we must be more careful to follow
what we were taught. Then we will not
stray away from the truth. 2 The teaching God
spoke through angels was shown to be true,
and anyone who did not follow it or obey it
received the punishment that was earned. 3 So
surely we also will be punished if we ignore
this great salvation. The Lord himself first told
about this salvation, and it was proven true to
us by those who heard him. 4 God also proved
it by using wonders, great signs, many kinds of
miracles, and by giving people gifts through
the Holy Spirit, just as he wanted.

CHRIST BECAME LIKE HUMANS

5 God did not choose angels to be the rulers
of the new world that was coming, which is
what we have been talking about. 6 It is written
in the Scriptures,

"Why are people important to you?
Why do you take care of human beings?
7 You made them a little lower than the
angels
and crowned them with glory and honor.
8 You put all things under their control."
Psalm 8:4-6

When God put everything under their control,
there was nothing left that they did not rule.
Still, we do not yet see them ruling over everything. 9 But we see Jesus, who for a short time
was made lower than the angels. And now he
is wearing a crown of glory and honor because
he suffered and died. And by God's grace, he
died for everyone.

10 God is the One who made all things, and
all things are for his glory. He wanted to have
many children share his glory, so he made the
One who leads people to salvation perfect
through suffering.

11 Jesus, who makes people holy, and those
who are made holy are from the same family.
So he is not ashamed to call them his brothers
and sisters.[n] 12 He says,

"Then, I will tell my fellow Israelites about
you;

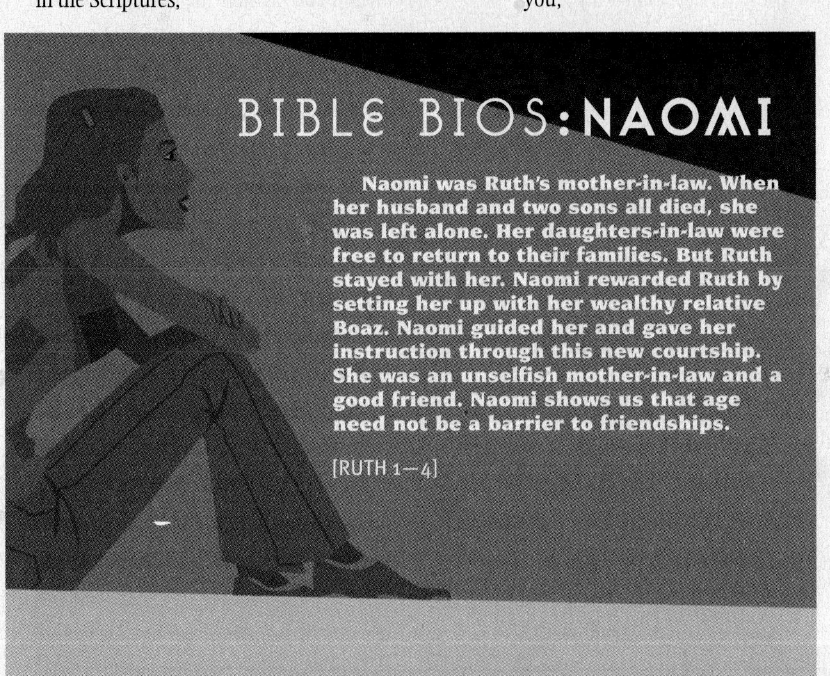

BIBLE BIOS: NAOMI
Naomi was Ruth's mother-in-law. When her husband and two sons all died, she was left alone. Her daughters-in-law were free to return to their families. But Ruth stayed with her. Naomi rewarded Ruth by setting her up with her wealthy relative Boaz. Naomi guided her and gave her instruction through this new courtship. She was an unselfish mother-in-law and a good friend. Naomi shows us that age need not be a barrier to friendships.
[RUTH 1—4]

Hebrews 2:18

It's not unusual to hear somebody excuse personal faults by saying, "Well, that's just the way I am"—as if it would be unfair to expect anything better out of him or her. It's true that everybody has flaws and everyone is susceptible to some temptations. Some people have a hard time being nice when things aren't going well for them; some people are tempted to cheat because they're so driven to make a good grade; some people are sucked in by the buzz they get from drinking or drugs. That's the way they are.

But Jesus never said that it was okay to do wrong because you have a weakness. He told people to do the right thing anyway. He wasn't being heartless. He wasn't looking down from some ivory tower, shouting, "You must resist temptation!" He was flesh and blood, just like you. He knew what it was like to be tempted. He isn't leaving you to overcome your weaknesses all by yourself. He's right there with you, giving you the strength to make the right choice. He's saying, "You can do it!" He's God. He's given you the strength to overcome and he knows you can!

"HE'S RIGHT THERE WITH YOU, GIVING YOU THE STRENGTH TO MAKE THE RIGHT CHOICE."

1:13 until . . . control Literally, "until I make your enemies a footstool for your feet." **2:11 brothers and sisters** Although the Greek text says "brothers" here and throughout this book, the writer's words were meant for the entire church, including men and women.

BEAUTY SECRET

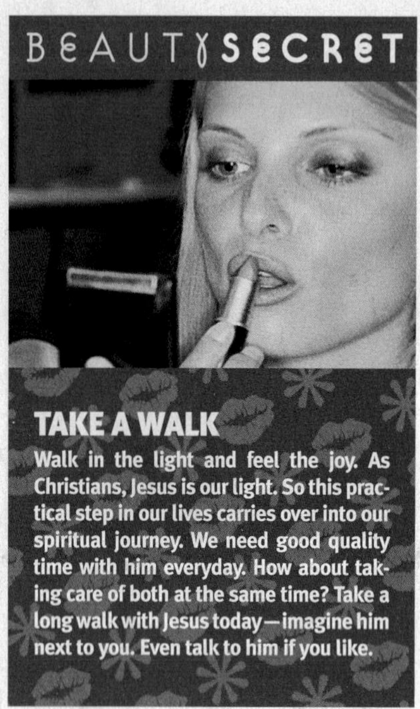

TAKE A WALK

Walk in the light and feel the joy. As Christians, Jesus is our light. So this practical step in our lives carries over into our spiritual journey. We need good quality time with him everyday. How about taking care of both at the same time? Take a long walk with Jesus today—imagine him next to you. Even talk to him if you like.

I will praise you in the public meeting."

Psalm 22:22

13 He also says,

"I will trust in God." *Isaiah 8:17*

And he also says,

"I am here, and with me are the children
God has given me." *Isaiah 8:18*

14 Since these children are people with physical bodies, Jesus himself became like them. He did this so that, by dying, he could destroy the one who has the power of death—the devil— 15 and free those who were like slaves all their lives because of their fear of death. 16 Clearly, it is not angels that Jesus helps, but the people who are from Abraham.[n] 17 For this reason Jesus had to be made like his brothers in every way so he could be their merciful and faithful high priest in service to God. Then Jesus could bring forgiveness for their sins. 18 And now he can help those who are tempted, because he himself suffered and was tempted.

JESUS IS GREATER THAN MOSES

3 So all of you holy brothers and sisters, who were called by God, think about Jesus, who was sent to us and is the high priest of our faith. 2 Jesus was faithful to God as Moses was in God's family. 3 Jesus has more honor than Moses, just as the builder of a house has more honor than the house itself. 4 Every house is built by someone, but the builder of everything is God himself. 5 Moses was faithful in God's family as a servant, and he told what God would say in the future. 6 But Christ is faithful as a Son over God's house. And we are God's house if we keep on being very sure about our great hope.

WE MUST CONTINUE TO FOLLOW GOD

7 So it is as the Holy Spirit says:

"Today listen to what he says.
8 Do not be stubborn as in the past
when you turned against God,
when you tested God in the desert.
9 There your ancestors tried me and
tested me
and saw the things I did for forty years.
10 I was angry with them.
I said, 'They are not loyal to me
and have not understood my ways.'
11 I was angry and made a promise,
'They will never enter my rest.' "[n]

Psalm 95:7-11

12 So brothers and sisters, be careful that none of you has an evil, unbelieving heart that will turn you away from the living God. 13 But encourage each other every day while it is "today."[n] Help each other so none of you will become hardened because sin has tricked you. 14 We all share in Christ if we keep till the end the sure faith we had in the beginning. 15 This is what the Scripture says:

"Today listen to what he says.
Do not be stubborn as in the past
when you turned against God."

Psalm 95:7-8

16 Who heard God's voice and was against him? It was all those people Moses led out of Egypt. 17 And with whom was God angry for forty years? He was angry with those who sinned, who died in the desert. 18 And to whom was God talking when he promised that they would never enter his rest? He was talking to those who did not obey him. 19 So we see they were not allowed to enter and have God's rest, because they did not believe.

4 Now, since God has left us the promise that we may enter his rest, let us be very careful so none of you will fail to enter. 2 The Good News was preached to us just as it was to them. But the teaching they heard did not help them, because they heard it but did not accept it with faith. 3 We who have believed are able to enter and have God's rest. As God has said,

"I was angry and made a promise,
'They will never enter my rest.' " *Psalm 95:11*

But God's work was finished from the time he made the world. 4 In the Scriptures he talked about the seventh day of the week: "And on the seventh day God rested from all his works."[n] 5 And again in the Scripture God said, "They will never enter my rest."

Q. What do you think about the way girls dress?
A. There's way too much showing most of the time. I think that's really gross.
GUYS SPEAK OUT

6 It is still true that some people will enter God's rest, but those who first heard the way to be saved did not enter, because they did not obey. 7 So God planned another day, called "today." He spoke about that day through David a long time later in the same Scripture used before:

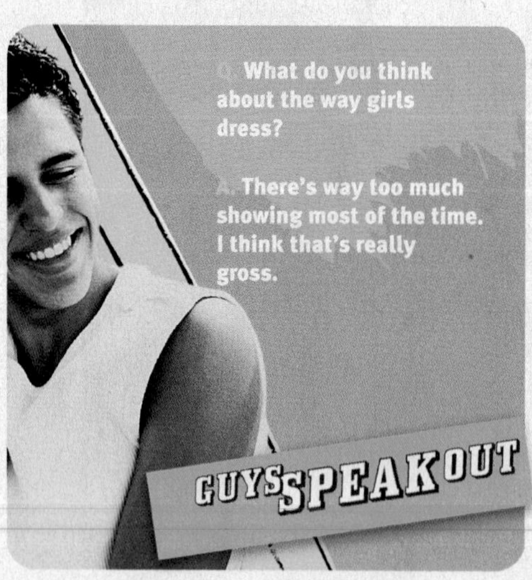

notes

2:16 Abraham Most respected ancestor of the Jews. Every Jew hoped to see Abraham. **3:11 rest** A place of rest God promised to give his people. **3:13 "today"** This word is taken from verse 7. It means that it is important to do these things now. **4:4 "And . . . works."** Quotation from Genesis 2:2.

ARE YOU AT PEACE?

QUIZ

1. IT'S MONDAY MORNING. 8:00 A.M. YOUR BIOLOGY TEACHER GIVES YOU A POP QUIZ. AS YOU GET OUT A PIECE OF PAPER, YOU FEEL:

A. EXTREME ANXIETY; YOU WORRY THAT YOU WILL NOT BE READY!
B. RELAXED; YOU STUDIED, AND YOU ARE SURE OF YOURSELF.
C. INDIFFERENT; WHAT DO GRADES MATTER ANYWAY?
D. NERVOUS; YOU WANT TO DO WELL, BUT YOU ARE STILL A LITTLE WORRIED.

2. YOU WALK INTO A GIRLFRIEND'S BIRTHDAY PARTY AT A RESTAURANT. YOU IMMEDIATELY REALIZE YOU ARE INCREDIBLY UNDERDRESSED FOR THIS SPECIAL OCCASION. UNSURE HOW TO HANDLE THE AWKWARD SITUATION, YOU:

A. MAKE A JOKE ABOUT YOUR MISTAKE AND SIT DOWN TO EAT LUNCH.
B. QUICKLY MAKE A DASH OUT THE DOOR, HOPING NO ONE SAW YOU.
C. SIT DOWN QUIETLY AND NERVOUSLY HOPE NO ONE WILL REALLY NOTICE OR CARE.
D. REALIZE THAT IT ISN'T THE OUTSIDE THAT MATTERS BUT YOUR TRUE SELF.

3. AFTER COMING HOME FROM SCHOOL, YOU RECEIVE A CALL FROM YOUR MOM TELLING YOU THAT YOUR GRANDMOTHER HAS JUST HAD A STROKE AND IS IN THE HOSPITAL. WHILE YOU ARE VERY UPSET ABOUT THIS TRAGIC NEWS, YOU:

A. FIRST PAUSE A MOMENT TO GATHER YOURSELF AND YOUR THOUGHTS TO PRAY.
B. FALL INTO HYSTERICS AND BEGIN PANICKING.
C. JUMP INTO A CAR AND GET TO THE HOSPITAL AS QUICKLY AS POSSIBLE.
D. CALL YOUR FRIENDS TO ASK FOR SUPPORT.

4. IT'S YOUR SENIOR YEAR, AND YOU ARE PREPARING FOR COLLEGE. YOU HAVE VISITED PROSPECTIVE SCHOOLS, AND NOW YOU ARE READY TO APPLY. YOU MAIL OFF AN APPLICATION TO YOUR TOP FIVE CHOICES, AND YOU ARE AWAITING THEIR ACCEPTANCE OR REJECTION LETTERS. YOUR BEST FRIEND CALLS TO TELL YOU SHE GOT HER FIRST ACCEPTANCE LETTER. YOU:

A. ARE EXCITED FOR HER AND ASK IF YOU GUYS CAN GO CELEBRATE.
B. BEGIN TO WONDER WHY YOURS ARE LATE AND IF YOU DIDN'T GET IN.
C. FANTASIZE THAT YOU WILL RECEIVE A REJECTION LETTER.
D. CALL AND ASK OTHER FRIENDS IF THEY HAVE RECEIVED LETTERS.

5. LATE FOR SCHOOL, YOU HOP IN YOUR CAR AND SPEED DOWN THE ROAD. A COP CLOCKS YOU SPEEDING 10 MPH OVER THE SPEED LIMIT, AND HE STOPS YOU. YOU GET A TICKET. WHEN YOU GET HOME THAT DAY, YOU:

A. TELL YOUR PARENTS IMMEDIATELY AND ASK FOR FORGIVENESS.
B. FORGET ABOUT IT. IT HAPPENED THAT MORNING AND IT SLIPS YOUR MIND.
C. DECIDE THAT YOU WANT TO KEEP THIS A LITTLE SECRET FOR A WHILE.
D. GO CRYING TO YOUR MOTHER, WORRIED ABOUT YOUR RECORD AND WHAT YOUR DAD MIGHT SAY.

KEY:

1. a = 4; b = 1; c = 2; d = 3
2. a = 1; b = 4; c = 3; d = 2
3. a = 1; b = 4; c = 3; d = 2
4. a = 1; b = 2; c = 4; d = 3
5. a = 1; b = 2; c = 3; d = 4

IF YOU SCORED BETWEEN 17 AND 20, YOU ARE A WORRYWART.

Chill out. You need to take a deep breath, lie down, and relax. Jesus tells us to consider the lilies. He tells us to consider the sparrows. Take a walk in nature and admire God's creation and see how he cares for it. You need to learn to cast your worries upon him.

IF YOU SCORED BETWEEN 13 AND 16, YOU ARE A PRINCESS OF STRESS!

You're not exactly having daily panic attacks, but you do have some issues with anxiety and stress. To combat these daily stressers, begin to notice what does and doesn't make you worry. Prioritize your obstacles. Your priorities will reveal that some things in life simply don't matter in the whole scheme of life, love, and history. Yet God knows even the hairs on your head. Rest in him.

IF YOU SCORED BETWEEN 9 AND 12, YOU ARE A HURDLE JUMPER!

Stress and worry are no strangers, but you have a pretty good grasp on how to handle these things. You have a sense of peace in life, and you know how to manage situations and problems as they arise. While you aren't exactly living life on a beach, you have good common sense and embrace life in its fullness.

IF YOU SCORED BETWEEN 5 AND 8, YOU ARE A PEACE SISTER!

No worries here. In fact, there is a fine line between being at peace and being numb or indifferent to life. You probably struggle with apathy at times, but mostly you have your priorities straight, a sense of inner strength, a belief in yourself and God, and an assurance that God is in control. Peace is a fruit of the Spirit that you seem to have in abundance. Share your gift, and plant a seed so that others can enjoy this wonderful fruit.

Hebrews 3:13

Most of us feel insecure when we are in a new place, doing new things, or meeting new people. Somehow we forget everything that is good and strong about ourselves. We can only see our weaknesses and think about our failures. You may have a friend who needs some encouragement in this area.

Verse 13 says she may need it every day. That's what being in the body of Christ is all about. Christians are supposed to encourage one another and remind each other that they are children of a loving God—empowered by his strength and covered by his grace. It's your official job as a Christian to encourage your friend. Be there when she needs you and cheer her on. Give her a big hug and tell her how wonderful she is. There will come a day when you'll be the one who needs those things. Your friend will be happy to return the favor.

"Today listen to what he says.
Do not be stubborn." *Psalm 95:7-8*

8 We know that Joshua[n] did not lead the people
into that rest, because God spoke later about
another day. 9 This shows that the rest[n] for
God's people is still coming. 10 Anyone who
enters God's rest will rest from his work as
God did. 11 Let us try as hard as we can to enter
God's rest so that no one will fail by following
the example of those who refused to obey.
12 God's word is alive and working and is
sharper than a double-edged sword. It cuts all
the way into us, where the soul and the spirit
are joined, to the center of our joints and
bones. And it judges the thoughts and feelings
in our hearts. 13 Nothing in all the world can be
hidden from God. Everything is clear and lies
open before him, and to him we must explain
the way we have lived.

JESUS IS OUR HIGH PRIEST

14 Since we have a great high priest, Jesus
the Son of God, who has gone into heaven, let
us hold on to the faith we have. 15 For our high
priest is able to understand our weaknesses.
When he lived on earth, he was tempted in
every way that we are, but he did not sin. 16 Let
us, then, feel very sure that we can come
before God's throne where there is grace.
There we can receive mercy and grace to help
us when we need it.

5 Every high priest is chosen from among
other people. He is given the work of
going before God for them to offer gifts and
sacrifices for sins. 2 Since he himself is weak,

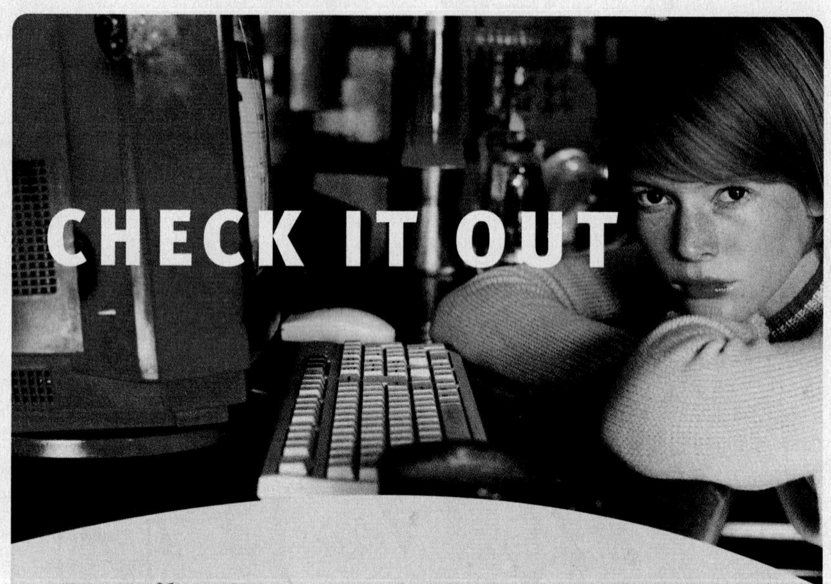

FreeVibe.Com—Anti-Drug Campaign

Wanna be the one? Here's what it takes: Are you between the ages of nine and eighteen? Do you have an opinion? Help people like you stay healthy and make informed decisions. Become an "I Count Advisor" and you will have the opportunity to say what you think about websites, advertisements, newsletters, logos, and other materials produced for the National Youth Anti-Drug Media Campaign. This program will operate completely via the Internet, so you must have an email address and access to the Net.

Go to www.freevibe.com/shoutout/vsignup_index.shtml.

notes

4:8 Joshua After Moses died, Joshua became leader of the Jewish people and led them into the land that God promised to give them. **4:9 rest** Literally, "sabbath rest," meaning a sharing in the rest that God began after he created the world.

LEARN IT & LIVE IT

Hebrews 4:14:
Learn It: Jesus is the great high priest.
Live It: Go to him freely today. Spend half an hour in prayer with Jesus. Just talk to him; tell him how much you love him.

Hebrews 6:10:
Learn It: God is fair.
Live It: Is something not going your way? Does it seem like the world is against you? God is fair. Don't complain.

Hebrews 6:18:
Learn It: God cannot lie.
Live It: Really believe that what he says is true. Dare to live your life that radically.

DIDYA KNOW

34% OF ALL TEENS SAY THEY ARE BORN AGAIN.

he is able to be gentle with those who do not understand and who are doing wrong things. 3Because he is weak, the high priest must offer sacrifices for his own sins and also for the sins of the people.

4To be a high priest is an honor, but no one chooses himself for this work. He must be called by God as Aaron[n] was. 5So also Christ did not choose himself to have the honor of being a high priest, but God chose him. God said to him,

"You are my Son.
Today I have become your Father."
Psalm 2:7

6And in another Scripture God says,
"You are a priest forever,
a priest like Melchizedek."[n] *Psalm 110:4*

7While Jesus lived on earth, he prayed to God and asked God for help. He prayed with loud cries and tears to the One who could save him from death, and his prayer was heard because he trusted God. 8Even though Jesus was the Son of God, he learned obedience by what he suffered. 9And because his obedience was perfect, he was able to give eternal salvation to all who obey him. 10In this way God made Jesus a high priest, a priest like Melchizedek.

WARNING AGAINST FALLING AWAY

11We have much to say about this, but it is hard to explain because you are so slow to understand. 12By now you should be teachers, but you need someone to teach you again the first lessons of God's message. You still need the teaching that is like milk. You are not ready for solid food. 13Anyone who lives on milk is still a baby and knows nothing about right teaching. 14But solid food is for those who are grown up. They have practiced in order to know the difference between good and evil.

6 So let us go on to grown-up teaching. Let us not go back over the beginning lessons we learned about Christ. We should not again start teaching about faith in God and about turning away from those acts that lead to death. 2We should not return to the teaching about baptisms,[n] about laying on of hands,[n] about the raising of the dead and eternal judgment. 3And we will go on to grown-up teaching if God allows.

4Some people cannot be brought back again to a changed life. They were once in God's light, and enjoyed heaven's gift, and shared in the Holy Spirit. 5They found out how good God's word is, and they received the powers of his new world. 6But they fell away from Christ. It is impossible to bring them back to a changed life again, because they are nailing the Son of God to a cross again and are shaming him in front of others.

7Some people are like land that gets plenty of rain. The land produces a good crop for

Psalm 145:9
The LORD is good to everyone;
he is merciful to all he has made.

RELATIONSHIPS

Your brother is trying to pick a fight with you again. You two have a history of nonsense arguments turning into knock-down-drag-out fights. He knows just what to say to get under your skin. Your blood is beginning to boil, beads of sweat are forming on your forehead. It's so tempting to lash back at him, but then you remember Proverbs 15:1: "A gentle answer will calm a person's anger, but an unkind answer will cause more anger." Why not knock the socks off your brother by doing what he least expects? Respond in love. Say something kind in return. You'll not only set a good example, but you'll avoid a fight at the same time.

notes

5:4 Aaron Aaron was Moses' brother and the first Jewish high priest. **5:6 Melchizedek** A priest and king who lived in the time of Abraham. (Read Genesis 14:17–24.) **6:2 baptisms** The word here may refer to Christian baptism, or it may refer to the Jewish ceremonial washings. **6:2 laying on of hands** The laying on of hands had many purposes, including the giving of a blessing, power, or authority.

Hebrews 5:8-9

Take the time to turn to and read Hebrews 2:18. You'll see that Jesus experienced suffering and temptation. But how did that make him perfect? He made the right choices in the midst of his suffering and temptation. Now he is the perfect One to save and strengthen you.

Jesus is perfect, but that does not distance him from you. He became a man, remained perfect, and died for your sin, so that he could get to know you. He wants a relationship with you. He wants to be there for you in your suffering. He can carry you through it. His strength is perfect when all your strength is gone. His perfection enables him to minister to you. He can anticipate your needs. And because he is perfect, he knows all the answers. He knows when you're empty. He knows when to send in the troops. You benefit from the perfection of Christ. He is a perfect Savior for the lost, a perfect intercessor for the needy, a perfect friend for everybody.

those who work it, and it receives God's blessings. [8]Other people are like land that grows
thorns and weeds and is worthless. It is in
danger of being cursed by God and will be
destroyed by fire.

[9]Dear friends, we are saying this to you, but
we really expect better things from you that
will lead to your salvation. [10]God is fair; he
will not forget the work you did and the love
you showed for him by helping his people.
And he will remember that you are still helping them. [11]We want each of you to go on with
the same hard work all your lives so you will
surely get what you hope for. [12]We do not
want you to become lazy. Be like those who
through faith and patience will receive what
God has promised.

[13]God made a promise to Abraham. And as
there is no one greater than God, he used himself when he swore to Abraham, [14]saying, "I will
surely bless you and give you many descendants."[n] [15]Abraham waited patiently for this to
happen, and he received what God promised.

[16]People always use the name of someone
greater than themselves when they swear. The
oath proves that what they say is true, and this
ends all arguing. [17]God wanted to prove that
his promise was true to those who would get
what he promised. And he wanted them to
understand clearly that his purposes never
change, so he made an oath. [18]These two things
cannot change: God cannot lie when he makes
a promise, and he cannot lie when he makes an
oath. These things encourage us who came to
God for safety. They give us strength to hold on
to the hope we have been given. [19]We have this
hope as an anchor for the soul, sure and strong.
It enters behind the curtain in the Most Holy
Place in heaven, [20]where Jesus has gone ahead
of us and for us. He has become the high priest
forever, a priest like Melchizedek.[n]

THE PRIEST MELCHIZEDEK

7 Melchizedek[n] was the king of Salem and
a priest for God Most High. He met

Q. How far is too far to go?

A. The question is not so simple. What you are wanting is someone to give you permission to do things. Would you be embarrassed to tell your mom, your little sister, your grandma, or even your pastor what you did? If you would be, don't do it.

Q. When I'm hanging out with some of my friends, I find myself acting differently, in ways that I know don't please God. What do you think?

A. Doing what is right, just because it is right and not because it's cool or popular, is called having values. If you value honoring God over people, then you can feel confident when you do what is right even if it makes people mad. Be faithful and he will be faithful. Don't let your friends bully you into behaving badly. Stand strong! He has given you the strength.

Q. I have been wondering lately what a girl should dress like. What I mean is, how baggy do the clothes have to be?

A. When you wear clothes with the intention of showing off certain parts of your body—really tight or short clothes—then guys are usually trying to see what you're trying to show off. It makes them think sexual thoughts about you. It's not good for you or them, so don't do it.

notes: **6:14 "I . . . descendants."** Quotation from Genesis 22:17. **6:20; 7:1 Melchizedek** A priest and king who lived in the time of Abraham. (Read Genesis 14:17–24.)

Elections are held on the Tuesday after the first Monday in November!
Rock the Vote!

November

1 How's school? Give your favorite and least favorite teachers a note of appreciation today.

2

3

4

5 Pray for a Person of Influence: Jeff Deyo's birthday!

6 Visit your grandparents or some elderly folks in a nursing home this weekend.

7

8 Take your dad out for a date tonight–just the two of you.

9

10

11 Veterans Day. Honor those vets who protect our country. Watch a great classic war movie.

12 Grace Kelly's birthday. Be extra feminine today!

14

15 Read your favorite psalm, and sing some praises to Jesus this morning.

16

18 Get your friends and have an adventure!

19

20 Take your sister to the mall and buy her a gift, just 'cause.

21

22

23 Billy the Kid's birthday. Watch an old John Wayne movie in his memory!

24

25 Pray for a Person of Influence: Amy Grant's birthday is today.

26

27

28 Pray for a Person of Influence: Today is Anna Nicole Smith's birthday.

29

30 Pray for a Person of Influence: Ben Stiller turns another year older today.

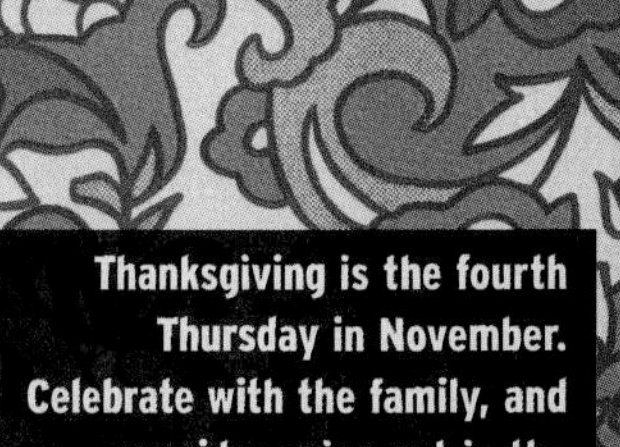

Thanksgiving is the fourth Thursday in November. Celebrate with the family, and consider going out in the community to help others less fortunate than you today.

Hebrews 6:17-18

Do you ever doubt God? Maybe you doubt the whole thing—God, the Bible, and all the Jesus stuff. Do you think that everyone who believes must be out to lunch? Maybe you do believe in God, but aren't sure that he's really going to come through for you. Hebrews says that the hope of Christ is right in front of you—"the hope we have been given." You are holding a record of the promises God has made to you. He has told the truth. He has kept his promises. His vows have never changed. Be encouraged to run to him because he never lies. You've got to make up your mind to believe that and you've got to decide that you are going to believe his Word. Until you've made that commitment, you'll constantly struggle with doubt.

The truth of his Word will replace your doubt. John 8:32 says "the truth will make you free." So immerse yourself in these pages. Commit to do more than just slide your eyes over the words. Really concentrate and study the Bible prayerfully. Read about how God has kept his promises. Read about the incredibly deep and powerful love he has for you. Read about his longing to know you and to be with you forever. Get these words into your heart and into your mind. Pretty soon, all your doubts will be replaced with the absolute certainty of God and of his truth.

"BE ENCOURAGED TO RUN TO HIM."

Abraham when Abraham was coming back
after defeating the kings. When they met,
Melchizedek blessed Abraham,
2and Abraham gave him a tenth
of everything he had brought
back from the battle. First,
Melchizedek's name means
"king of goodness," and he is king
of Salem, which means "king of
peace." 3No one knows who Melchizedek's
father or mother was,*n* where he came from,
when he was born, or when he died.
Melchizedek is like the Son of God; he continues being a priest forever.

4You can see how great Melchizedek was.
Abraham, the great father, gave him a tenth of
everything that he won in battle. 5Now the law
says that those in the tribe of Levi who
become priests must collect a tenth from the
people—their own people—even though the
priests and the people are from the family of
Abraham. 6Melchizedek was not from the
tribe of Levi, but he collected a tenth from
Abraham. And he blessed Abraham, the man
who had God's promises. 7Now everyone
knows that the more important person blesses
the less important person. 8Priests receive a
tenth, even though they are only men who live
and then die. But Melchizedek, who received a
tenth from Abraham, continues living, as the
Scripture says. 9We might even say that
Levi, who receives a tenth, also paid it
when Abraham paid Melchizedek a
tenth. 10Levi was not yet born, but he
was in the body of his ancestor when
Melchizedek met Abraham.

11The people were given the law*n*
based on a system of priests from the
tribe of Levi, but they could not be
made perfect through that system. So
there was a need for another priest to
come, a priest like Melchizedek, not
Aaron. 12And when a different kind of
priest comes, the law must be changed,
too. 13We are saying these things about Christ,
who belonged to a different tribe. No one from
that tribe ever served as a priest
at the altar. 14It is clear that our
Lord came from the tribe of
Judah, and Moses said nothing about priests belong-
ing to that tribe.

John 14:21
Those who know my commands and obey them are the ones who love me, and my Father will love those who love me. I will love them and will show myself to them.

JESUS IS LIKE MELCHIZEDEK

15And this becomes even more clear
when we see that another priest comes who is
like Melchizedek.*n* 16He was not made a priest
by human rules and laws but through the
power of his life, which continues forever. 17It
is said about him,

"You are a priest forever,
a priest like Melchizedek." *Psalm 110:4*

18The old rule is now set aside, because it
was weak and useless. 19The law of Moses
could not make anything perfect. But now a
better hope has been given to us, and with this
hope we can come near to God. 20It is important that God did this with an oath. Others
became priests without an oath, 21but Christ
became a priest with God's oath. God said:

"The Lord has made a promise
and will not change his mind.
'You are a priest forever.' " *Psalm 110:4*

22This means that Jesus is the guarantee of a
better agreement*n* from God to his people.

Q. Do you expect a girl to kiss you on a first date?
A. No way. You need to keep it simple in high school—no physical stuff for me yet.
GUYS SPEAK OUT

7:3 No . . . was Literally, "Melchizedek was without father, without mother, without genealogy." **7:11 The . . . law** This refers to the people of Israel who were given the Law of Moses. **7:15 Melchizedek** A priest and king who lived in the time of Abraham. (Read Genesis 14:17–24.) **7:22 agreement** God gives a contract or agreement to his people. For the Jews, this agreement was the Law of Moses. But now God has given a better agreement to his people through Christ.

23When one of the other priests died, he could not continue being a priest. So there were many priests. 24But because Jesus lives forever, he will never stop serving as priest.

DIDYA KNOW

THE LARGEST NUMBERS OF TEENS ARE CATHOLIC (22%) AND BAPTIST (16%).

25So he is able always to save those who come to God through him because he always lives, asking God to help them.

26Jesus is the kind of high priest we need. He is holy, sinless, pure, not influenced by sinners, and he is raised above the heavens. 27He is not like the other priests who had to offer sacrifices every day, first for their own sins, and then for the sins of the people. Christ offered his sacrifice only once and for all time when he offered himself. 28The law chooses high priests who are people with weaknesses, but the word of God's oath came later than the law. It made God's Son to be the high priest, and that Son has been made perfect forever.

"NOW A BETTER HOPE HAS BEEN GIVEN TO US, AND WITH THIS HOPE WE CAN COME NEAR TO GOD."

JESUS IS OUR HIGH PRIEST

8 Here is the point of what we are saying: We have a high priest who sits on the right side of God's throne in heaven. 2Our high priest serves in the Most Holy Place, the true place of worship that was made by God, not by humans.

3Every high priest has the work of offering gifts and sacrifices to God. So our high priest must also offer something to God. 4If our high priest were now living on earth, he would not be a priest, because there are already priests here who follow the law by offering gifts to God. 5The work they do as priests is only a copy and a shadow of what is in heaven. This is why God warned Moses when he was ready to build the Holy Tent: "Be very careful to make everything by the plan I showed you on the mountain."[n] 6But the priestly work that has been given to Jesus is much greater than the work that was given to the other priests. In the same way, the new agreement that Jesus brought from God to his people is much greater than the old one. And the new agreement is based on promises of better things.

7If there had been nothing wrong with the first agreement,[n] there would have been no need for a second agreement. 8But God found something wrong with his people. He says:

"Look, the time is coming, says the Lord,
when I will make a new agreement
with the people of Israel
and the people of Judah.
9It will not be like the agreement
I made with their ancestors
when I took them by the hand
to bring them out of Egypt.
But they broke that agreement,
and I turned away from them, says the Lord.
10This is the agreement I will make
with the people of Israel at that time,
says the Lord.
I will put my teachings in their minds
and write them on their hearts.
I will be their God,
and they will be my people.
11People will no longer have to teach their
neighbors and relatives
to know the Lord,
because all people will know me,
from the least to the most important.

Hebrews 8:6

Because of Jesus, things are much better for us than they were for our ancestors. We've got a new high priest, a new tent of worship, and a new agreement with God. The priests of our ancestors were sinful and wicked. Their sin kept them from representing the people well before God. Jesus is our new High Priest. His perfection has replaced the old priests, making him the only way to God the Father.

The old Meeting Tent of worship is now just a shadow of the real one in heaven. The new place of worship is where Jesus sits with the Father. Our worship isn't dictated by ritual, but by relationship. We worship out of our love for Jesus. The new agreement that God has made promises that, through Jesus Christ, we will belong to the Lord forever and he will belong to us as our God (see Jeremiah 31:31-34). The new agreement promises to forgive the sins of those who trust in Christ. Because of Christ, we can pray and fellowship directly with the Lord. We can personally ask for the forgiveness of our sins. We can sense his leading and compassion in our lives.

God has promised us better things. He's given us the best gift—a better relationship with him—through the work of Jesus and the Holy Spirit.

"WE WORSHIP OUT OF OUR LOVE FOR JESUS."

notes

8:5 "Be . . . mountain." Quotation from Exodus 25:40. **8:7 first agreement** The contract God gave the Jewish people when he gave them the Law of Moses.

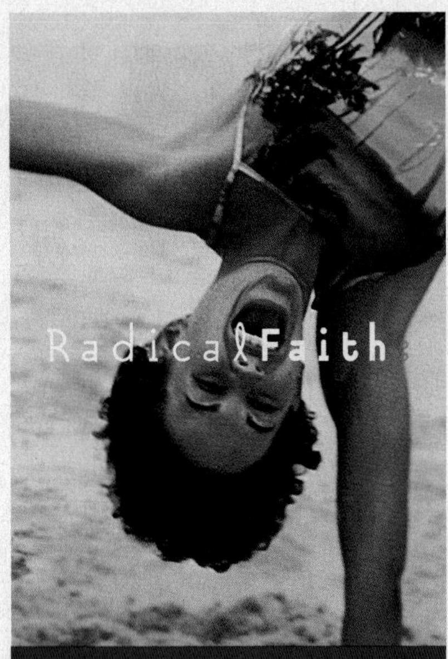

Hebrews 10:19-20

The Temple the Israelites built had a special room called the Most Holy Place (Hebrews 9:3-8). The door of this room was covered by a thick, heavy curtain because God's presence lived in the room. Because the presence of the Lord is so awesome, the people had to be separated from it. They were sinful and sin cannot stand in the presence of God's love and holiness. Only the high priest could go through the curtain, and he could do it only once a year. At that time, the high priest had to make one sacrifice for sins he and his family had committed and another sacrifice for the sins of the whole nation. The blood of the sacrifice took away the people's sins for the next year (see Leviticus 16).

At the moment Jesus died on the cross, the curtain in front of the Most Holy Place was torn from top to bottom (see Matthew 27:51). God's presence was made available to everyone! It's like God had been sitting behind a locked door for years and years; and only the high priest had the key. Then Jesus came along and unlocked that door for everyone. His blood takes away the sins of everyone who trusts in him. Now he's the High Priest.

Enter God's presence freely and as often as you want!

12I will forgive them for the wicked things
they did,
and I will not remember their sins
anymore." *Jeremiah 31:31-34*

13God called this a new agreement, so he has
made the first agreement old. And anything that
is old and worn out is ready to disappear.

THE OLD AGREEMENT

9 The first agreement[n] had rules for worship and a man-made place for worship.
2The Holy Tent was set up for this. The first
area in the Tent was called the Holy Place. In it
were the lamp and the table with the bread
that was made holy for God. 3Behind the second curtain was a room called the Most Holy
Place. 4In it was a golden altar for burning
incense and the Ark covered with gold that held
the old agreement. Inside this Ark was a golden
jar of manna, Aaron's rod that once grew leaves,
and the stone tablets of the old agreement.
5Above the Ark were the creatures that showed
God's glory, whose wings reached over the lid.
But we cannot tell everything about these
things now.

6When everything in the Tent was made
ready in this way, the priests went into the first
room every day to worship. 7But only the high
priest could go into the second room, and he
did that only once a year. He could never enter
the inner room without taking blood with him,
which he offered to God for himself and for sins
the people did without knowing they did them.
8The Holy Spirit uses this to show that the way
into the Most Holy Place was not open while
the system of the old Holy Tent was still being
used. 9This is an example for the present time.

bible basics

Holiness is absolute perfection. Only God is holy. He has never sinned, never made a mistake, never done anything wrong. God demands that people be holy also. This is a problem, because it's impossible. The only option is for us to ask Jesus to be our savior and claim his reputation as our own. That way, God looks at Jesus' perfect record and considers us to be holy instead of the sinful mess we are. Holiness is a lifestyle that says, "Anything that I do or say will honor Christ."

notes

9:1 first agreement The contract God gave the Jewish people when he gave them the Law of Moses.

LEARN IT & LIVE IT

1 Peter 2:13:
Learn It: We are to obey people in authority.
Live It: Do what your parents ask you to do today. Take out the garbage. Do your homework. Anything they ask, do it.

1 Peter 3:15:
Learn It: We are to respect Christ in our hearts.
Live It: Realize that even what you think in your heart about God—he hears. Are you respecting him?

1 Peter 4:8:
Learn It: Love will cause many sins to be forgiven.
Live It: Forgive someone you are holding a grudge against. Can you do it? Give it over to God today—promise him that you aren't going to worry yourself with that offense anymore.

God is love. Those who live in love live in God, and God lives in them. 17This is how love is made perfect in us: that we can be without fear on the day God judges us, because in this world we are like him. 18Where God's love is, there is no fear, because God's perfect love drives out fear. It is punishment that makes a person fear, so love is not made perfect in the person who fears.

19We love because God first loved us. 20If people say, "I love God," but hate their brothers or sisters, they are liars. Those who do not love their brothers and sisters, whom they have seen, cannot love God, whom they have never seen. 21And God gave us this command: Those who love God must also love their brothers and sisters.

FAITH IN THE SON OF GOD

5 Everyone who believes that Jesus is the Christ is God's child, and whoever loves the Father also loves the Father's children. 2This is how we know we love God's children: when we love God and obey his commands. 3Loving God means obeying his commands. And God's commands are not too hard for us, 4because everyone who is a child of God conquers the world. And this is the victory that conquers the world—our faith. 5So the one who wins against the world is the person who believes that Jesus is the Son of God.

6Jesus Christ is the One who came by water[n] and blood.[n] He did not come by water only, but by water and blood. And the Spirit says that this is true, because the Spirit is the truth. 7So there are three witnesses that tell us about Jesus: 8the Spirit, the water, and the blood; and these three witnesses agree. 9We believe people when they say something is true. But what God says is more important, and he has told us the truth about his own Son. 10Anyone who believes in the Son of God has the truth that God told us. Anyone who does not believe makes God a liar, because that person does not believe what God told us about his Son. 11This is what God told us: God has given us eternal life, and this life is in his Son. 12Whoever has the Son has life, but whoever does not have the Son of God does not have life.

WE HAVE ETERNAL LIFE NOW

13I write this letter to you who believe in the Son of God so you will know you have eternal life. 14And this is the boldness we have in God's presence: that if we ask God for anything that agrees with what he wants, he hears us. 15If we know he hears us every time we ask him, we know we have what we ask from him.

16If anyone sees a brother or sister sinning (sin that does not lead to eternal death), that person should pray, and God will give the sinner life. I am talking about people whose sin does not lead to eternal death. There is sin that leads to death. I do not mean that a person should pray about that sin. 17Doing wrong is always sin, but there is sin that does not lead to eternal death.

18We know that those who are God's children do not continue to sin. The Son of God keeps them safe, and the Evil One cannot touch them. 19We know that we belong to God, but the Evil One controls the whole world. 20We also know that the Son of God has come and has given us understanding so that we can know the True One. And our lives are in the True One and in his Son, Jesus Christ. He is the true God and the eternal life.

21So, dear children, keep yourselves away from gods.

notes

5:6 water This probably means the water of Jesus' baptism. **5:6 blood** This probably means the blood of Jesus' death.

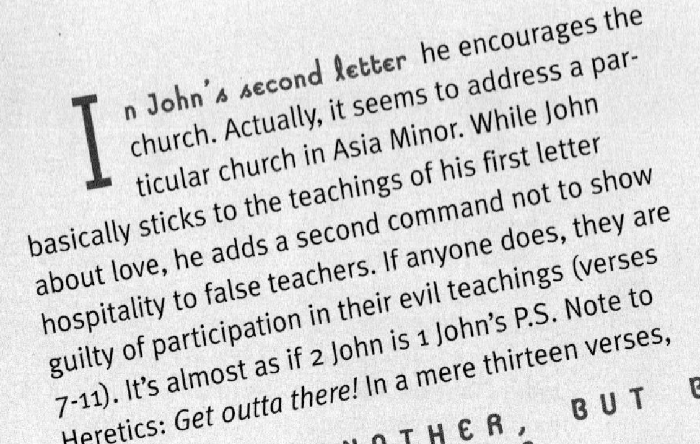

In John's second letter he encourages the church. Actually, it seems to address a particular church in Asia Minor. While John basically sticks to the teachings of his first letter about love, he adds a second command not to show hospitality to false teachers. If anyone does, they are guilty of participation in their evil teachings (verses 7-11). It's almost as if 2 John is 1 John's P.S. Note to Heretics: *Get outta there!* In a mere thirteen verses,

2 John

LOVE ONE ANOTHER, BUT BEWARE OF FALSE TEACHERS

John warns true Christians against the fake evangelists traveling around the land and preaching that spiritual things are good and physical things are evil. While this sounds pretty good, they actually went so far as to say that Jesus was only a spirit who looked human. Now that is heresy. The problem was that these guys weren't just in their churches; they were in their homes! John warns not to support these fakers. He says if people don't preach the genuine story of Jesus, don't let them in. Period.

GUYS SPEAKOUT
Q. Do you ever think about getting married?
A. Yeah, it's natural to think about your future spouse.

From the Elder.[n]
To the chosen lady[n] and her children:
1I love all of you in the truth,[n] and all those
who know the truth love you. 2We love you
because of the truth that lives in us and will be
with us forever.
3Grace, mercy, and peace from God the
Father and his Son, Jesus Christ, will be with
us in truth and love.
4I was very happy to learn that some of your
children are following the way of truth, as the
Father commanded us. 5And now, dear
lady, this is not a new command but is
the same command we have had from
the beginning. I ask you that we all love
each other. 6And love means living the
way God commanded us to live. As
you have heard from the beginning,
his command is this: Live a life of love.
7Many false teachers are in the
world now who do not confess that
Jesus Christ came to earth as a human.
Anyone who does not confess this is a
false teacher and an enemy of Christ.
8Be careful yourselves that you do not
lose everything you have worked for, but that
you receive your full reward.
9Anyone who goes beyond Christ's teaching and does not continue to follow only his
teaching does not have God. But whoever continues to follow the teaching of Christ has both
the Father and the Son. 10If someone comes to
you and does not bring this teaching, do not
welcome or accept that person into your
house. 11If you welcome such a person, you
share in the evil work.

RELATIONSHIPS

"And a servant of the Lord must not quarrel but must be kind to everyone, a good teacher, and patient" (2 Timothy 2:24). Put this verse into your memory. It's a good one to remember when you're not getting along with someone or when the tension at home is high and you're feeling frustrated. Pray to God for patience; ask him to give you a gentleness of heart and a peaceful spirit. Remember that when you are weak, he is strong.

12I have many things to write to you, but I
do not want to use paper and ink. Instead, I
hope to come to you and talk face to face so we
can be full of joy. 13The children of your chosen
sister[n] greet you.

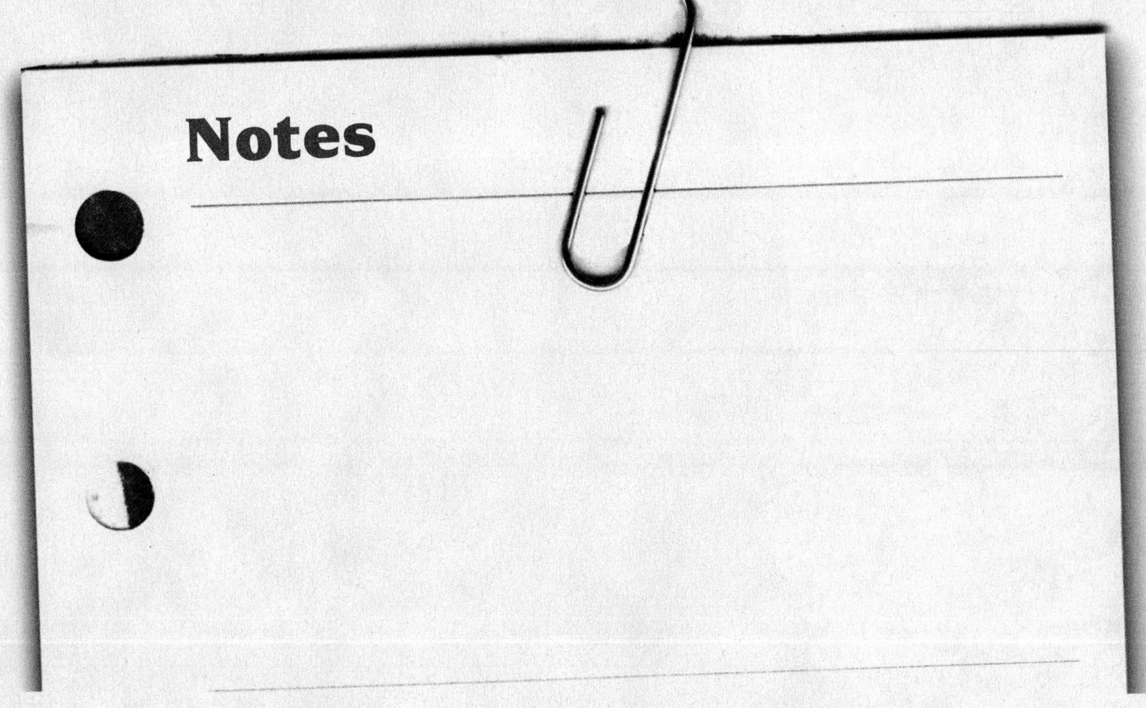
Notes

notes

1 Elder "Elder" means an older person. It can also mean a special leader in the church (as in Titus 1:5). **1 lady** This might mean a woman, or in this letter it might mean a church. If it is a church, then "her children" would be the people of the church. **1 truth** The truth or "Good News" about Jesus Christ that joins all believers together. **13 sister** Sister of the "lady" in verse 1. This might be another woman or another church.

3 John

GUIDELINES ABOUT CHRISTIAN HOSPITALITY

In this last but not least of John's letters, John encourages a friend, Gaius. You'd think that in the beginning years of Christianity believers were really super-nice to each other. But, guess what? It didn't quite happen that way. Evil people with false teachings and void of godly love had infiltrated the church. These evil people worshiped two things only: power and prestige. So, what does John do? He writes a letter filled with quick advice for beginners struggling with the issue. John's advice to believers is to keep doing what they know God wants them to do: Obey the truth, love others, and support those spreading the Good News, regardless of the risk. In this personal letter, he congratulates Gaius for obeying the true teachings about Jesus, and especially for showing hospitality to Christian missionaries.

From the Elder.[n]

To my dear friend Gaius, whom
I love in the truth:[n]

[2]My dear friend, I know
your soul is doing fine, and I
pray that you are doing
well in every way and that your
health is good. [3]I was very happy
when some brothers and sisters[n] came and
told me about the truth in your life and how
you are following the way of truth. [4]Nothing
gives me greater joy than to hear that my children are following the way of truth.

[5]My dear friend, it is good that you help the
brothers and sisters, even those you do not
know. [6]They told the church about your love.
Please help them to continue their trip in a way
worthy of God. [7]They started out in service to
Christ, and they have been accepting nothing
from nonbelievers. [8]So we should help such
people; when we do, we share in their work for
the truth.

[9]I wrote something to the church, but
Diotrephes, who loves to be their
leader, will not listen to us. [10]So
if I come, I will talk about what
Diotrephes is doing, about
how he lies and says evil
things about us. But
more than that, he refuses
to accept the other brothers and sisters; he even stops those who do want to
accept them and puts them out of the church.

[11]My dear friend, do not follow what is bad;
follow what is good. The one who does good
belongs to God. But the one who does evil has
never known God.

[12]Everyone says good things about
Demetrius, and the truth agrees with what
they say. We also speak well of him, and you
know what we say is true.

[13]I have many things I want to write you,
but I do not want to use pen and ink. [14]I hope
to see you soon and talk face to face. [15]Peace
to you. The friends here greet you. Please
greet each friend there by name.

Psalm 91:14
The LORD says,
"Whoever loves me,
I will save.
I will protect those
who know me."

DIDYA KNOW

28% OF TEENS FEEL THAT THEY SHOULD SHARE THEIR FAITH WITH OTHERS, BUT 56% OF BORN-AGAIN CHRISTIANS FEEL THIS WAY.

Blab

Q. What is the difference between the Holy Spirit and God?

A. The Holy Spirit *is* God. The Bible tells us about the Trinity. That is three persons of God that are one God, but also are distinct. Just like Jesus was down here while God the Father was in heaven, the Holy Spirit, God's Spirit, can be here while the Father and the Son are in heaven. The Holy Spirit is the part of God who comes to live inside you. He is the Counselor (Comforter, Helper) Jesus talked about sending.

Q. My best friend, who is a Christian, just came out to me on the phone last night! I guess he has kind of been confused about his sexuality for a while, but I honestly thought he was going to get over it. He didn't and last night he came out to me. I had no idea what to say or what to do.

A. Wow, that's really tough. The Bible clearly says that homosexuality is wrong (Romans 1:24-27), so you should share with him that you're concerned for him because he claims to know Christ yet is living in disobedience to God. Approach your friend with humility, because you are also a sinner. It hurts, but God has put you in this friend's life for a purpose. Love him, but don't back down from what you believe. Don't let him give you any details about any relationships or anything like that—tell him you really don't want to talk about that because you know it's against God. Be honest with him, but humble in your approach. And continue to pray that he'll come around.

Q. Is it wrong to wear a bra that fills out your shirt a little more?

A. 1. How old are you? 2. Why do you want to do it? If you're still young, just be patient. Your body is still in the process of filling out. In fact, it will continue to do this all the way through college. So don't give up hope and think that you will be forever flat-chested. If you're trying to get guys to like you more, it may work. But do you really want to date a guy who wouldn't go out with you if you were one cup-size smaller? I mean, seriously, what are his priorities? And check *your* priorities. Read Proverbs 31 to see what God says an attractive woman looks like.

notes

1 Elder "Elder" means an older person. It can also mean a special leader in the church (as in Titus 1:5). **1 truth** The truth or "Good News" about Jesus Christ that joins all believers together. **3 brothers and sisters** Although the Greek text says "brothers" here and throughout this book, the writer's words were meant for the entire church, including men and women.

Jude

BEWARE OF THOSE WHO PERVERT GOD'S GRACE

Jude was a man with a mission. Even though Christianity hadn't been around a long time, there were lots of people twisting and turning the truth of the Good News to mean something totally different. Christians often met with people who shortcut their beliefs. They encountered people who said they had found an easier, shorter, better way to heaven. What was it? Well, since Jesus had forgiven people of their sins, sin didn't matter anymore. In fact, they could sin all they wanted! But Jude had no patience for this kind of trickery and lying. He wrote his letter to the church to straighten out these kinds of deceptions and to remind them that what we do matters to God. He says there need to be knowledgeable Christians who can point to examples in Scripture. Jude encourages believers to put up their lives and defend their beliefs by the way they live.

1 From Jude, a servant of Jesus Christ and a brother of James.

To all who have been called by God. God the Father loves you, and you have been kept safe in Jesus Christ:

2 Mercy, peace, and love be yours richly.

GOD WILL PUNISH SINNERS

3 Dear friends, I wanted very much to write you about the salvation we all share. But I felt the need to write you about something else: I want to encourage you to fight hard for the faith that was given the holy people of God once and for all time. 4 Some people have secretly entered your group. Long ago the prophets wrote about these people who will be judged guilty. They are against God and have changed the grace of our God into a reason for sexual sin. They also refuse to accept Jesus Christ, our only Master and Lord.

5 I want to remind you of some things you already know: Remember that the Lord saved his people by bringing them out of the land of Egypt. But later he destroyed all those who did not believe. 6 And remember the angels who did not keep their place of power but left their proper home. The Lord has kept these angels in darkness, bound with everlasting chains, to be judged on the great day. 7 Also remember the cities of Sodom and Gomorrah[n] and the other towns around them. In the same way they were full of sexual sin and people who desired sexual relations that God does not allow. They suffer the punishment of eternal fire, as an example for all to see.

8 It is the same with these people who have entered your group. They are guided by dreams and make themselves filthy with sin. They reject God's authority and speak against the angels. 9 Not even the archangel[n] Michael, when he argued with the devil about who would have the body of Moses, dared to judge the devil guilty. Instead, he said, "The Lord punish you." 10 But these people speak against things they do not understand. And what they do know, by feeling, as dumb animals know things, are the very things that destroy them. 11 It will be terrible for them. They have followed the way of Cain, and for money they have given themselves to doing the wrong that Balaam did. They have fought against God as Korah did, and like Korah, they surely will be destroyed. 12 They are like dirty spots in your special Christian meals you share. They eat with you and have no fear, caring only for themselves. They are clouds without rain, which the wind blows around. They are autumn trees without fruit that are pulled out of the ground. So they are twice dead. 13 They are like wild waves of the sea, tossing up their own shameful actions like foam. They are like stars that wander in the sky. A place in the blackest darkness has been kept for them forever.

14 Enoch, the seventh descendant from Adam, said about these people: "Look, the Lord is coming with many thousands of his holy angels to 15 judge every person. He is coming to punish all who are against God for all the evil they have done against him. And he will punish the sinners who are against God for all the evil they have said against him."

notes

7 Sodom and Gomorrah Two cities God destroyed because they were so evil. **9 archangel** The leader among God's angels or messengers.

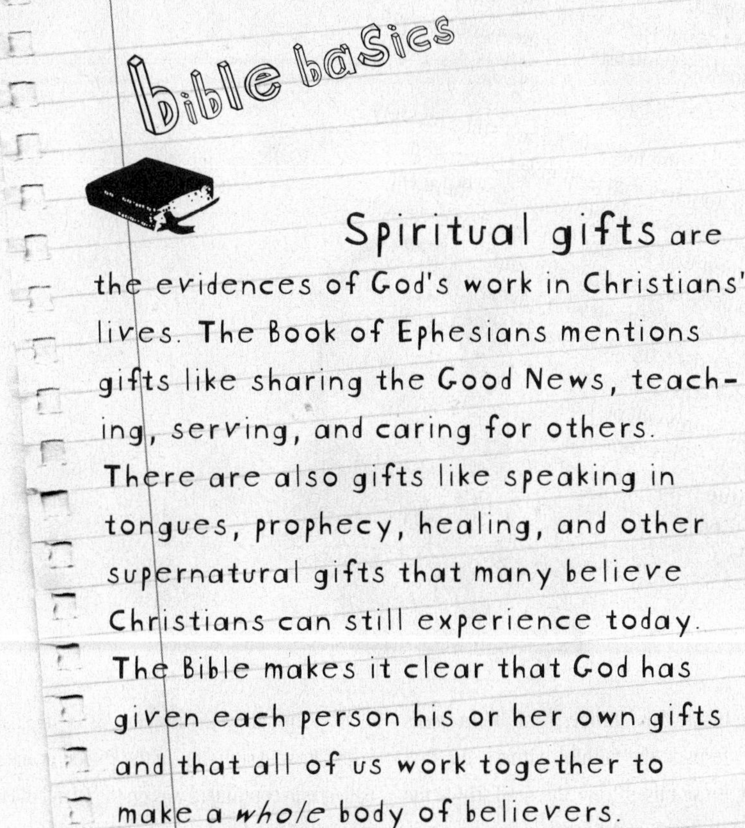

bible basics
Spiritual gifts are the evidences of God's work in Christians' lives. The Book of Ephesians mentions gifts like sharing the Good News, teaching, serving, and caring for others. There are also gifts like speaking in tongues, prophecy, healing, and other supernatural gifts that many believe Christians can still experience today. The Bible makes it clear that God has given each person his or her own gifts and that all of us work together to make a *whole* body of believers.

16These people complain and blame others,
doing the evil things they want to do. They
brag about themselves, and they flatter others
to get what they want.

A WARNING AND THINGS TO DO

17Dear friends, remember what the apostles
of our Lord Jesus Christ said before. 18They said
to you, "In the last times there will be people
who laugh about God, following their own evil
desires which are against God." 19These are
the people who divide you, people whose
thoughts are only of this world, who do not
have the Spirit.

20But dear friends, use your most holy faith
to build yourselves up, praying in the Holy
Spirit. 21Keep yourselves in God's love as you
wait for the Lord Jesus Christ with his mercy
to give you life forever.

22Show mercy to some people who have
doubts. 23Take others out of the fire, and save
them. Show mercy mixed with fear to others, hating even their clothes which are dirty from sin.

PRAISE GOD

24God is strong and can help you not to fall.
He can bring you before his glory without any
wrong in you and can give you great joy. 25He
is the only God, the One who saves us. To him be glory, greatness, power, and authority through Jesus Christ our Lord for all time past, now, and forever. Amen.

Jude 20

How's your prayer life? Stumbling, fumbling, falling asleep? Don't quite know where to start or how to end? Don't let your lack of practice keep you from spending time with Jesus. The Lord God promises to help you pray through the power of the Holy Spirit.

God is not impressed with big, long prayers or Bible-sounding words. He sees right through all that stuff, clear down to the bottom of your heart. He wants to know how you really feel. You can be totally honest with him. (He already knows the truth anyway.) He won't be distracted, won't spread rumors, won't act like your stuff is stupid. He loves to hear from you, so speak to him with reverence, in truth, and according to his will.

"HOW'S YOUR PRAYER LIFE?"

The final book in the Bible was written by John after he had a bizarre vision on the isle of Patmos. If there were a movie on this revelation, it would be like Stephen King meets Stephen Spielberg: the best horror movie with special effects galore. In this sci-fi book, John sees out-of-this-world creatures, the throne room of God, and the end times! Of course, scholars debate over what John really saw or whether these creatures and stories were symbols. And

Revelation

THE FINAL SHOWDOWN BETWEEN GOD AND SATAN

some of the images John talks about are still a mystery today. The book teaches that God gives Satan and human evil some leeway in this world, but there will come a day when God will say, "Enough," and we will all be judged according to our faith and our works. In the end, those who have their faith in Christ's righteousness will be invited into God's presence forever and Satan will be banished from the kingdom. It's a real and true happily-ever-after kind of story.

JOHN TELLS ABOUT THIS BOOK

1 This is the revelation[n] of Jesus Christ,
which God gave to him, to show his servants what must soon happen. And Jesus sent
his angel to show it to his servant John, [2]who
has told everything he has seen. It is the word
of God; it is the message from Jesus Christ.
[3]Happy is the one who reads the words of
God's message, and happy are the people who

DIDYA KNOW

65% OF TEENS SAY THAT THE DEVIL (OR SATAN) DOESN'T REALLY EXIST.

hear this message and do what is written in it.
The time is near when all of this will happen.

JESUS' MESSAGE TO THE CHURCHES

[4]From John.

To the seven churches in the country of
Asia:

Grace and peace to you from the One who
is and was and is coming, and from the seven
spirits before his throne, [5]and from Jesus
Christ. Jesus is the faithful witness, the first
among those raised from the dead. He is the
ruler of the kings of the earth.

He is the One who loves us, who made us
free from our sins with the blood of his death.
[6]He made us to be a kingdom of priests who
serve God his Father. To Jesus Christ be glory
and power forever and ever! Amen.

[7]Look, Jesus is coming with the clouds, and
everyone will see him, even those who
stabbed him. And all peoples of the earth will
cry loudly because of him. Yes, this will happen! Amen.

[8]The Lord God says, "I am the Alpha and
the Omega."[n] I am the One who is and was and
is coming. I am the Almighty."

[9]I, John, am your brother. All of us share
with Christ in suffering, in the kingdom, and in
patience to continue. I was on the island of Patmos,[n] because I had preached the word of God
and the message about Jesus. [10]On the Lord's
day I was in the Spirit, and I heard a loud voice
behind me that sounded like a trumpet. [11]The
voice said, "Write what you see in a book and
send it to the seven churches: to Ephesus,
Smyrna, Pergamum, Thyatira, Sardis, Philadelphia, and Laodicea."

[12]I turned to see who was talking to me.
When I turned, I saw seven golden lampstands
[13]and someone among the lampstands who
was "like a Son of Man."[n] He was dressed in a
long robe and had a gold band around his chest.
[14]His head and hair were white like wool, as
white as snow, and his eyes were like flames of
fire. [15]His feet were like bronze that glows hot
in a furnace, and his voice was like the noise of
flooding water. [16]He held seven stars in his
right hand, and a sharp double-edged sword

notes

1:1 revelation Making known truth that has been hidden. **1:8 Alpha and the Omega** The first and last letters of the Greek alphabet. This means "the beginning and the end." **1:9 Patmos** A small island in the Aegean Sea, near the coast of Asia Minor (modern Turkey). **1:13 "like . . . Man"** "Son of Man" is a name Jesus called himself.

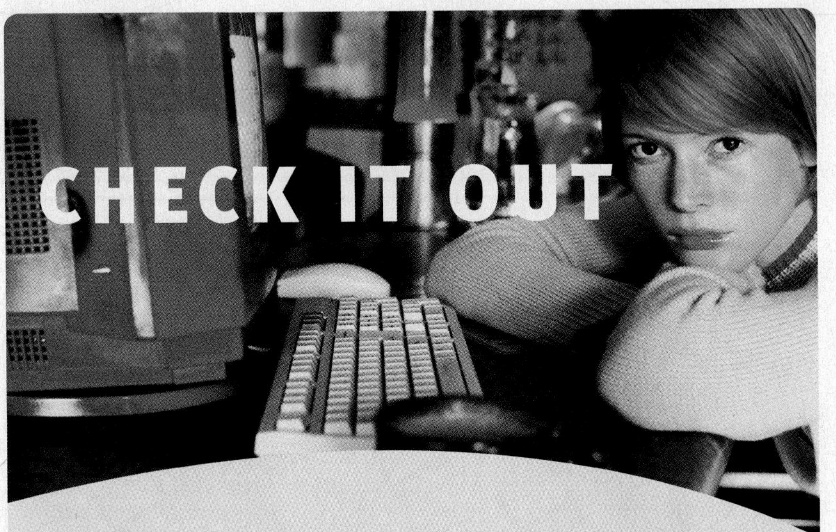

American Indian Education Foundation

The American Indian Education Foundation (AIEF) is the largest provider of scholarships to American Indian students in the United States. During the fall of 2001 AIEF provided 201 scholarships.

AIEF also has an unmatched record of success with student retention. In the previous three years 91.3% of our scholarship recipients have stayed in school or graduated. AIEF does not award scholarships based primarily on high school grade point averages. We look at a variety of factors, including the history of volunteerism and the student's commitment to returning to their Indian communities.

AIEF actively works to keep our scholarship recipients in school. This includes college packs to help the freshmen students with supplies that they will need to start college life, phone call and e-mail encouragement, and further financial support in times of crisis.

For more information, go to ***www.aiefprograms.org.***

came out of his mouth. He looked like the sun
shining at its brightest time.
17When I saw him, I fell down at his feet like
a dead man. He put his right hand on me and
said, "Do not be afraid. I am the First and the
Last. 18I am the One who lives; I was dead, but
look, I am alive forever and ever! And I hold the
keys to death and to the place of the dead. 19So
write the things you see, what is now and what
will happen later. 20Here is the secret of the
seven stars that you saw in my right hand and
the seven golden lampstands: The seven lampstands are the seven churches, and the seven
stars are the angels of the seven churches.

TO THE CHURCH IN EPHESUS

2 "Write this to the angel of the church in
Ephesus:
"The One who holds the seven stars in his
right hand and walks among the seven golden
lampstands says this: 2I know what you do, how
you work hard and never give up. I know you do
not put up with the false teachings of evil people. You have tested those who say they are
apostles but really are not, and you found they
are liars. 3You have patience and have suffered
troubles for my name and have not given up.
4"But I have this against you: You have left
the love you had in the beginning. 5So remember where you were before you fell. Change

LEARN IT & LIVE IT

1 Peter 5:7:
Learn It: Give your worries to God because he cares about you.
Live It: Whenever you start to stress today, banish that thought from your mind. Think about something else immediately; then remind yourself that God is taking care of your worries for you.

2 Peter 3:3:
Learn It: People will laugh at you for your faith.
Live It: Don't care. Can you do that? Put your rep on the line for Christ.

1 John 1:5:
Learn It: God is light, and there is no darkness in him.
Live It: Be that same light to the others around you today. Don't complain, grumble, gossip, or be pessimistic. Be light.

Blab

Q. One of my shirts shows a sliver of my belly when I lift up my arms. I'm only eleven, but my 'rents seem to think my bellybutton can lead to temptation . . . is that true?

A. I think the issue isn't so much whether or not your bellybutton is temptation, but whether or not you're going to obey your parents. If they don't want you to wear the shirt, then you need to honor and obey them in that. As far as it being a temptation is concerned, I think it is. I've certainly heard guys comment on girls that show off their midriffs. They think they're good looking, but all they can see is their outward appearance. They really have no interest in getting to know that girl. Don't make yourself out to be an object of some guy's lust.

Q. I'm thirteen and I've always dressed really sporty. I'm thinking I want to start dressing more like a typical girl; but when I went shopping with my friends, they all made fun of me for wanting to look at those clothes and said I would never wear those. How do I change my style?

A. You've got two options: 1. Gradual change or 2. Cold turkey. If you want to go with a gradual change, why don't you try getting some cute sporty skirts and dresses. Then you can gradually move to more feminine clothes. People may not even notice. Or, you can go cold turkey. This is what one of my friends did in high school. One day she had dyed black hair, very goth/hippie clothes. The next day she was back to her brunette-Ann Taylor look. Everyone was shocked, but they loved it. Maybe try shopping with your mom or one really close friend who will understand the dilemma. Tell them you want a makeover, and you want their help shopping. They'll be totally into it, and you won't feel the peer pressure from shopping with a whole bunch of friends.

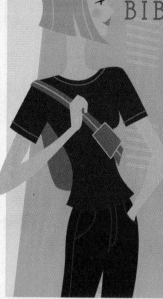

BIBLE BIOS: RUTH

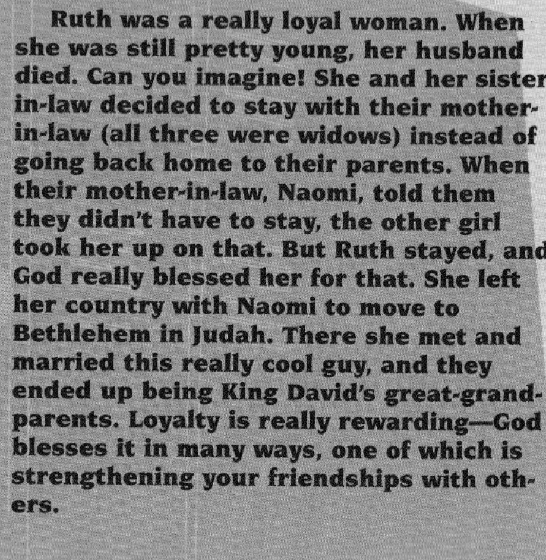

Ruth was a really loyal woman. When she was still pretty young, her husband died. Can you imagine! She and her sister-in-law decided to stay with their mother-in-law (all three were widows) instead of going back home to their parents. When their mother-in-law, Naomi, told them they didn't have to stay, the other girl took her up on that. But Ruth stayed, and God really blessed her for that. She left her country with Naomi to move to Bethlehem in Judah. There she met and married this really cool guy, and they ended up being King David's great-grand-parents. Loyalty is really rewarding—God blesses it in many ways, one of which is strengthening your friendships with others.

[RUTH 1–4]

your hearts and do what you did at first. If you
do not change, I will come to you and will take
away your lampstand from its place. 6But
there is something you do that is right: You
hate what the Nicolaitans[n] do, as much as I.

7"Every person who has ears should listen
to what the Spirit says to the churches. To
those who win the victory I will give the right
to eat the fruit from the tree of life, which is in
the garden of God.

TO THE CHURCH IN SMYRNA

8"Write this to the angel of the church in
Smyrna:

"The One who is the First and the Last,
who died and came to life again, says this: 9I
know your troubles and that you are poor, but
really you are rich! I know the bad things
some people say about you. They say they are
Jews, but they are not true Jews. They are a
synagogue that belongs to Satan. 10Do not be
afraid of what you are about to suffer. I tell
you, the devil will put some of you in prison
to test you, and you will suffer for ten days.
But be faithful, even if you have to die, and I
will give you the crown of life.

11"Everyone who has ears should listen to
what the Spirit says to the churches. Those
who win the victory will not be hurt by the
second death.

TO THE CHURCH IN PERGAMUM

12"Write this to the angel of the church in
Pergamum:

"The One who has the sharp, double-edged
sword says this: 13I know where you live. It is
where Satan has his throne. But you are true
to me. You did not refuse to tell about your
faith in me even during the time of Antipas,
my faithful witness who was killed in your
city, where Satan lives.

14"But I have a few things against you: You
have some there who follow the teaching of
Balaam. He taught Balak how to cause the
people of Israel to sin by eating food offered to
idols and by taking part in sexual sins. 15You
also have some who follow the teaching of the
Nicolaitans.[n] 16So change your hearts and
lives. If you do not, I will come to you quickly
and fight against them with the sword that
comes out of my mouth.

17"Everyone who has ears should listen to
what the Spirit says to the churches.

"I will give some of the hidden manna to

2:6, 15 Nicolaitans This is the name of a religious group that followed false beliefs and ideas.

TOPten

RANDOM VERSES
TO PRAY FOR YOUR LIFE

01	Matthew 6:31-34
02	2 Corinthians 1:3-4
03	John 3:16-18
04	Ephesians 6:11-17
05	James 1:19-20
06	Colossians 3:12-14
07	1 Peter 5:5
08	Matthew 6:14-15
09	Romans 15:30
10	Romans 12:3

everyone who wins the victory. I will also give to each one who wins the victory a white stone with a new name written on it. No one knows this new name except the one who receives it.

TO THE CHURCH IN THYATIRA

18"Write this to the angel of the church in Thyatira:

"The Son of God, who has eyes that blaze like fire and feet like shining bronze, says this:
19I know what you do. I know about your love, your faith, your service, and your patience. I know that you are doing more now than you did at first.

20"But I have this against you: You let that woman Jezebel spread false teachings. She says she is a prophetess, but by her teaching she leads my people to take part in sexual sins
and to eat food that is offered to idols. 21I have given her time to change her heart and turn away from her sin, but she does not want to
change. 22So I will throw her on a bed of suffering. And all those who take part in adultery with her will suffer greatly if they do not turn
away from the wrongs she does. 23I will also kill her followers. Then all the churches will know I am the One who searches hearts and minds, and I will repay each of you for what you have done.

24"But others of you in Thyatira have not followed her teaching and have not learned what some call Satan's deep secrets. I say to you that I will not put any other load on you.
25Only continue in your loyalty until I come.

26"I will give power over the nations to everyone who wins the victory and continues to be obedient to me until the end.

27'You will rule over them with an iron rod,
as when pottery is broken into pieces.'

Psalm 2:9

28This is the same power I received from my Father. I will also give him the morning star.
29Everyone who has ears should listen to what the Spirit says to the churches.

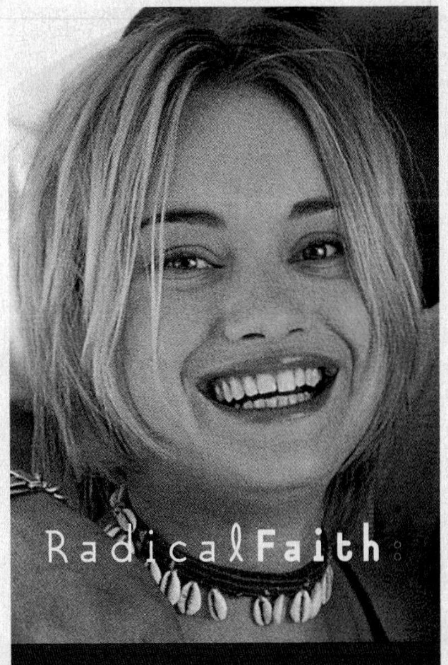

Revelation 2:3-4

Jesus was talking to some people who had done great things for him. They had worked hard and persevered; but in all of that, they somehow lost their first love for him. You probably know people like that. They go to church all the time, wear Christian t-shirts, and scream "Jesus" really loud at concerts. But they're missing a passion for him.

The Lord wants you to be known as a person who loves him. He'd rather have you be known as a gentle, humble lover of God than as the most eloquent preacher who just sounds good. All kinds of things will tempt you to love them more than you love Jesus, but don't give in. Hold on tight to your love for him. When other people walk away from an encounter with you, they should know one thing—that you have a passionate, fervent, fiery love for God that will not quit.

If you've gotten caught up in doing a bunch of stuff in the name of the Lord, slam on the brakes. Run into his presence. Pray and worship him. Start listening to him and hearing his voice. Let him melt your heart again. Ask him to rekindle your fire for him. Your service is made great because your love for him is great. Keep your passion burning for him!

ARE YOU VAIN?

1. YOU SPEND _____ MINUTES IN THE MORNING GETTING READY FOR SCHOOL.

A. 15
B. 30
C. 60
D. 90

2. WHEN PEOPLE GIVE YOU COMPLIMENTS, YOU USUALLY:

A. SAY, "THANK YOU VERY MUCH!"
B. SAY, "THANKS," AND RETURN A COMPLIMENT.
C. GET EMBARRASSED AND LOOK AT THE GROUND.
D. GET OFFENDED THAT THEY HADN'T NOTICED UNTIL NOW.

3. WHEN YOU OVERHEAR A GROUP OF BOYS WHISPERING AND LAUGHING AS YOU WALK BY, YOU IMMEDIATELY ASSUME THAT:

A. THEY ARE TALKING ABOUT THE GAME ON FRIDAY NIGHT.
B. THEY ARE TALKING ABOUT A GIRL OR GIRLS.
C. THEY ARE TALKING ABOUT YOU.
D. THEY ARE GOSSIPING ABOUT A STORY THAT INVOLVES YOU.

4. IF YOU HAVE A CRUSH ON A GUY, YOU ASSUME THAT:

A. HE WOULD DEFINITELY GO OUT WITH YOU IF HE KNEW YOU LIKED HIM.
B. HE WOULD DEFINITELY *NOT* GO OUT WITH YOU.
C. HE HAS A CRUSH ON YOU TOO.
D. HE HAS A SLIGHT INKLING THAT YOU LIKE HIM.

5. AS YOU WALK TO YOUR CLASS, YOU HEAR A WHISTLE BEHIND YOU. YOU:

A. TURN AROUND, ASSUMING IT WAS FOR YOU.
B. KEEP ON WALKING, THINKING IT WAS NOT FOR YOU.
C. QUICKLY GLANCE TO SEE WHO WHISTLED—CURIOUS.
D. KEEP ON WALKING WITH A LITTLE SWING OF THE HIPS.

Key:
1. a = 1; b = 2; c = 3; d = 4
2. a = 3; b = 2; c = 1; d = 4
3. a = 1; b = 2; c = 4; d = 3
4. a = 4; b = 1; c = 3; d = 2
5. a = 4; b = 1; c = 2; d = 3

IF YOU SCORED BETWEEN 16 AND 20, YOU'RE SO VAIN, I BET YOU THINK THIS QUIZ WAS ABOUT YOU.

Sister, you gotta lighten up. The world does not revolve about you. Here's what you need to do: Read James 4 every day this week. You need to pray that God will give you humility. No one likes to be around a prima donna. Be humble, and you'll find that you'll be more successful in life. Do something for someone less fortunate than you today.

IF YOU SCORED BETWEEN 12 AND 16, YOU ARE SAYING, "MIRROR, MIRROR ON THE WALL, WHO'S THE FAIREST OF THEM ALL?"

You're close to being annoyingly vain. Whenever you start to think that some whisper or rumor is all about you, step back. Count to ten. Then realize that you are not at the center of the universe. Look for ways to help other people this week, without being noticed for it.

IF YOU SCORED BETWEEN 9 AND 12, YOU ARE A TIARA WISHER.

You long to be beautiful, popular, and well respected, but you've got to balance yourself too. Check your priorities this week; whenever they start to get off track, refocus. Dive into the Scripture, and remind yourself that Christ is the reason you live and breathe and even exist. Pray a lot, and celebrate the fact that you're God's child.

IF YOU SCORED BETWEEN 5 AND 8, YOU ARE BASHFUL.

You are the essence of humility to those around you. You are a giving person who loves to serve others. Cherish what Jesus said about the humble—they will inherit the earth. Wow! Keep on serving others, and you will one day be served!

TO THE CHURCH IN SARDIS

3 "Write this to the angel of the church in Sardis:

"The One who has the seven spirits and the seven stars says this: I know what you do. People say that you are alive, but really you are dead. 2Wake up! Make yourselves stronger before what you have left dies completely. I have found that what you are doing is less than what my God wants. 3So do not forget what you have received and heard. Obey it, and change your hearts and lives. So you must wake up, or I will come like a thief, and you will not know when I will come to you. 4But you have a few there in Sardis who have kept their clothes unstained, so they will walk with me and will wear white clothes, because they are worthy. 5Those who win the victory will be dressed in white clothes like them. And I will not erase their names from the book of life, but I will say they belong to me before my Father and before his angels. 6Everyone who has ears should listen to what the Spirit says to the churches.

TO THE CHURCH IN PHILADELPHIA

7"Write this to the angel of the church in Philadelphia:

"This is what the One who is holy and true, who holds the key of David, says. When he opens a door, no one can close it. And when he closes it, no one can open it. 8I know what you do. I have put an open door before you, which no one can close. I know you have a little strength, but you have obeyed my teaching and were not afraid to speak my name. 9Those in the synagogue that belongs to Satan say they are Jews, but they are not true Jews; they are liars. I will make them come before you and bow at your feet, and they will know that I have loved you. 10You have obeyed my teaching about not giving up your faith. So I will keep you from the time of trouble that will come to the whole world to test those who live on earth.

11"I am coming soon. Continue strong in your faith so no one will take away your crown. 12I will make those who win the victory pillars in the temple of my God, and they will never have to leave it. I will write on them the name of my God and the name of the city of my God, the new Jerusalem,[n] that comes down out of heaven from my God. I will also write on them my new name. 13Everyone who has ears should listen to what the Spirit says to the churches.

TO THE CHURCH IN LAODICEA

14"Write this to the angel of the church in Laodicea:

"The Amen,[n] the faithful and true witness, the beginning of all God has made, says this: 15I know what you do, that you are not hot or cold. I wish that you were hot or cold! 16But because you are lukewarm—neither hot, nor cold—I am ready to spit you out of my mouth. 17You say, 'I am rich, and I have become wealthy and do not need anything.' But you do not know that you are really miserable, pitiful, poor, blind, and naked. 18I advise you to buy from me gold made pure in fire so you can be truly rich. Buy from me white clothes so you can be clothed and so you can cover your shameful nakedness. Buy from me medicine to put on your eyes so you can truly see.

19"I correct and punish those whom I love. So be eager to do right, and change your hearts and lives. 20Here I am! I stand at the door and knock. If you hear my voice and open the door, I will come in and eat with you, and you will eat with me.

21"Those who win the victory will sit with me on my throne in the same way that I won the victory and sat down with my Father on his throne. 22Everyone who has ears should listen to what the Spirit says to the churches."

JOHN SEES HEAVEN

4 After the vision of these things I looked, and there before me was an open door in heaven. And the same voice that spoke to me before, that sounded like a trumpet, said, "Come up here, and I will show you what must happen after this." 2Immediately I was in the Spirit, and before me was a throne in heaven, and someone was sitting on it. 3The One who sat on the throne looked like precious stones, like jasper and carnelian. All around the throne was a rainbow the color of an emerald. 4Around the throne there were twenty-four other thrones with twenty-four elders sitting on them. They were dressed in white and had

Psalm 91:4
He will cover you with his feathers, and under his wings you can hide. His truth will be your shield and protection.

DIDYA KNOW → **61% OF TEENS BELIEVE THAT IF A PERSON IS GENERALLY GOOD THEY'LL GO TO HEAVEN.**

Q. How serious should high school relationships be?
A. Not serious—you're still so young and can get into trouble easier than when you're older.
GUYS SPEAK OUT

3:12 Jerusalem This name is used to mean the spiritual city God built for his people. See Revelation 21–22. **3:14 Amen** Used here as a name for Jesus; it means to agree fully that something is true.

BEAUTY SECRET
THE NATURAL LOOK
Did you know you are most beautiful when you are most naturally . . . you? We may paint our faces, pierce our ears, wear cool clothes, and fix our hair, but in the end we are most attractive just as we are. Charm and beauty are sometimes helpful, but they certainly aren't everything. We need to remember that it's what's on the inside—not what's on the outside—that makes us truly beautiful.

golden crowns on their heads. [5]Lightning
flashes and noises and thundering came from
the throne. Before the throne seven lamps
were burning, which are the seven spirits of
God. [6]Also before the throne there was something that looked like a sea of glass, clear like
crystal.

53% OF TEENS BELIEVE THAT JESUS COMMITTED SINS WHILE ON EARTH.

In the center and around the throne were
four living creatures with eyes all over them,
in front and in back. [7]The first living creature
was like a lion. The second was like a calf. The
third had a face like a man. The fourth was
like a flying eagle. [8]Each of these four living
creatures had six wings and was covered all
over with eyes, inside and out. Day and night
they never stop saying:

"Holy, holy, holy is the Lord God Almighty.
He was, he is, and he is coming."

[9]These living creatures give glory, honor,
and thanks to the One who sits on the throne,
who lives forever and ever. [10]Then the
twenty-four elders bow down before the One
who sits on the throne, and they worship him
who lives forever and ever. They put their
crowns down before the throne and say:

[11]"You are worthy, our Lord and God,
to receive glory and honor and power,
because you made all things.
Everything existed and was made,
because you wanted it."

5 Then I saw a scroll in the right hand of
the One sitting on the throne. The scroll
had writing on both sides and was kept closed
with seven seals. [2]And I saw a powerful angel
calling in a loud voice, "Who is worthy to
break the seals and open the scroll?" [3]But
there was no one in heaven or on earth or under the earth who could open the scroll or
look inside it. [4]I cried hard because there was
no one who was worthy to open the scroll or
look inside. [5]But one of the elders said to me,
"Do not cry! The Lion[n] from the tribe of Judah, David's descendant, has won the victory
so that he is able to open the scroll and its
seven seals."

[6]Then I saw a Lamb standing in the center
of the throne and in the middle of the four living creatures and the elders. The Lamb looked
as if he had been killed. He had seven horns
and seven eyes, which are the seven spirits of
God that were sent into all the world. [7]The
Lamb came and took the scroll from the right
hand of the One sitting on the throne. [8]When
he took the scroll, the four living creatures
and the twenty-four elders bowed down before the Lamb. Each one of them had a harp
and golden bowls full of incense, which are
the prayers of God's holy people. [9]And they
all sang a new song to the Lamb:

"You are worthy to take the scroll
and to open its seals,
because you were killed,
and with the blood of your death you
bought people for God
from every tribe, language, people, and
nation.
[10]You made them to be a kingdom of priests
for our God,
and they will rule on the earth."

[11]Then I looked, and I heard the voices of
many angels around the throne, and the four
living creatures, and the elders. There were
thousands and thousands of angels, [12]saying
in a loud voice:

"The Lamb who was killed is worthy
to receive power, wealth, wisdom, and
strength,
honor, glory, and praise!"

[13]Then I heard all creatures in heaven and
on earth and under the earth and in the sea
saying:

"To the One who sits on the throne
and to the Lamb
be praise and honor and glory and power
forever and ever."

[14]The four living creatures said, "Amen,"
and the elders bowed down and worshiped.

6 Then I watched while the Lamb opened
the first of the seven seals. I heard one
of the four living creatures say with a voice like
thunder, "Come!" [2]I looked, and there before
me was a white horse. The rider on the horse
held a bow, and he was given a crown, and he
rode out, determined to win the victory.

[3]When the Lamb opened the second seal, I
heard the second living creature say, "Come!"
[4]Then another horse came out, a red one. Its
rider was given power to take away peace from
the earth and to make people kill each other,
and he was given a big sword.

[5]When the Lamb opened the third seal, I
heard the third living creature say, "Come!" I
looked, and there before me was a black horse,

notes

5:5 Lion Here refers to Christ.

and its rider held a pair of scales in his hand. 6Then I heard something that sounded like a voice coming from the middle of the four living creatures. The voice said, "A quart of wheat for a day's pay, and three quarts of barley for a day's pay, and do not damage the olive oil and wine!"

7When the Lamb opened the fourth seal, I heard the voice of the fourth living creature say, "Come!" 8I looked, and there before me was a pale horse. Its rider was named death, and Hades[n] was following close behind him. They were given power over a fourth of the earth to kill people by war, by starvation, by disease, and by the wild animals of the earth.

9When the Lamb opened the fifth seal, I saw under the altar the souls of those who had been killed because they were faithful to the word of God and to the message they had received. 10These souls shouted in a loud voice, "Holy and true Lord, how long until you judge the people of the earth and punish them for killing us?" 11Then each one of them was given a white robe and was told to wait a short time longer. There were still some of their fellow servants and brothers and sisters[n] in the service of Christ who must be killed as they were. They had to wait until all of this was finished.

12Then I watched while the Lamb opened the sixth seal, and there was a great earthquake. The sun became black like rough black cloth, and the whole moon became red like blood. 13And the stars in the sky fell to the earth like figs falling from a fig tree when the wind blows. 14The sky disappeared as a scroll when it is rolled up, and every mountain and island was moved from its place.

15Then the kings of the earth, the rulers, the generals, the rich people, the powerful people, the slaves, and the free people hid themselves in caves and in the rocks on the mountains. 16They called to the mountains and the rocks, "Fall on us. Hide us from the face of the One who sits on the throne and from the anger of the Lamb! 17The great day for their anger has come, and who can stand against it?"

Psalm 91:11
He has put his angels in charge of you to watch over you wherever you go.

THE 144,000 PEOPLE OF ISRAEL

7 After the vision of these things I saw four angels standing at the four corners of the earth. The angels were holding the four winds of the earth to keep them from blowing on the land or on the sea or on any tree. 2Then I saw another angel coming up from the east who had the seal of the living God. And he called out in a loud voice to the four angels to whom God had given power to harm the earth and the sea. 3He said to them, "Do not harm the land or the sea or the trees until we mark with a sign the foreheads of the people who serve our God." 4Then I heard how many people were marked with the sign. There were one hundred forty-four thousand from every tribe of the people of Israel.

5From the tribe of Judah twelve thousand
were marked with the sign,
from the tribe of Reuben twelve thousand,
from the tribe of Gad twelve thousand,
6from the tribe of Asher twelve thousand,
from the tribe of Naphtali twelve
thousand,
from the tribe of Manasseh twelve
thousand,
7from the tribe of Simeon twelve thousand,
from the tribe of Levi twelve thousand,
from the tribe of Issachar twelve thousand,
8from the tribe of Zebulun twelve thousand,
from the tribe of Joseph twelve thousand,
and from the tribe of Benjamin twelve
thousand were marked with the sign.

THE GREAT CROWD WORSHIPS GOD

9After the vision of these things I looked, and there was a great number of people, so many that no one could count them. They

Blab

Q. I have a guy friend and recently everyone has been saying, "You two make the perfect couple!" thinkin' we're going out. Hey, what can I say? I like the attention. Attention = the slight touches, hugs, winks, notes, walkin' in the hall together close, etc. But I don't like him like him. I'm just havin' fun. Do you have any comments or advice or even criticism for me?

A. It's perfectly normal for you to start wanting attention from guys as you get older. You just need to make sure that your priorities are in place. Remember what the Proverbs say about women who put too much emphasis on their physical relationships with guys. Study what it means to be a godly woman. One day you'll fall in love with and marry a guy that God has picked for you—and the physical relationship you will have with him will be totally awesome. Be patient, and learn a lot in these years you have while you're still single.

Q. There is a guy who I like and have known for about two years now. He is a Christian but not growing all that well, and he is a senior who will be going into the army after school, like for college, coming home on holidays and stuff. Do you think it would be too risky to keep getting to know him and maybe get up to actually dating even though he will be going away soon?

A. There is nothing wrong with getting to know someone, but there are a couple of red flags that you have to take note of and consider as potential danger signs. First of all, the big one, he is leaving. This will make it really hard on the relationship. But more important is that you two are not on the same spiritual level. It seems like you take your relationship with God much more seriously than he does. This will be a problem in the future of your relationship. It's better to stick with someone you are more in balance with.

notes

6:8 Hades The unseen world of the dead. **6:11 brothers and sisters** Although the Greek text says "brothers" here and throughout this book, both men and women would have been included.

were from every nation, tribe, people, and language of the earth. They were all standing before the throne and before the Lamb, wearing white robes and holding palm branches in their hands. [10]They were shouting in a loud voice, "Salvation belongs to our God, who sits on the throne, and to the Lamb." [11]All the angels were standing around the throne and the elders and the four living creatures. They all bowed down on their faces before the throne and worshiped God, [12]saying, "Amen! Praise, glory, wisdom, thanks, honor, power, and strength belong to our God forever and ever. Amen!"

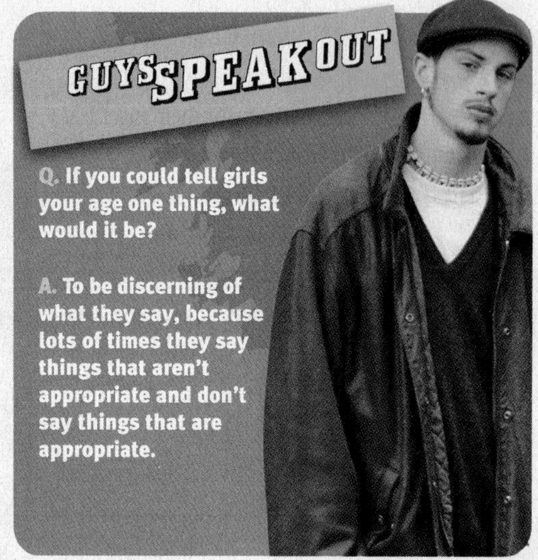

Q. If you could tell girls your age one thing, what would it be?

A. To be discerning of what they say, because lots of times they say things that aren't appropriate and don't say things that are appropriate.

[13]Then one of the elders asked me, "Who are these people dressed in white robes? Where did they come from?"

[14]I answered, "You know, sir."

And the elder said to me, "These are the people who have come out of the great distress. They have washed their robes[n] and made them white in the blood of the Lamb. [15]Because of this, they are before the throne of God. They worship him day and night in his temple. And the One who sits on the throne will be present with them. [16]Those people will never be hungry again, and they will never be thirsty again. The sun will not hurt them, and no heat will burn them, [17]because the Lamb at the center of the throne will be their shepherd. He will lead them to springs of water that give life. And God will wipe away every tear from their eyes."

THE SEVENTH SEAL

8 When the Lamb opened the seventh seal, there was silence in heaven for about half an hour. [2]And I saw the seven angels who stand before God and to whom were given seven trumpets.

[3]Another angel came and stood at the altar, holding a golden pan for incense. He was given much incense to offer with the prayers of all God's holy people. The angel put this offering on the golden altar before the throne. [4]The smoke from the incense went up from the angel's hand to God with the prayers of God's people. [5]Then the angel filled the incense pan with fire from the altar and threw it on the earth, and there were flashes of lightning, thunder and loud noises, and an earthquake.

THE SEVEN ANGELS AND TRUMPETS

[6]Then the seven angels who had the seven trumpets prepared to blow them.

[7]The first angel blew his trumpet, and hail and fire mixed with blood were poured down on the earth. And a third of the earth, and all the green grass, and a third of the trees were burned up.

[8]Then the second angel blew his trumpet, and something that looked like a big mountain, burning with fire, was thrown into the sea. And a third of the sea became blood, [9]a third of the living things in the sea died, and a third of the ships were destroyed.

[10]Then the third angel blew his trumpet, and a large star, burning like a torch, fell from the sky. It fell on a third of the rivers and on the springs of water. [11]The name of the star is Wormwood.[n] And a third of all the water became bitter, and many people died from drinking the water that was bitter.

[12]Then the fourth angel blew his trumpet, and a third of the sun, and a third of the moon, and a third of the stars were struck. So a third of them became dark, and a third of the day was without light, and also the night.

[13]While I watched, I heard an eagle that was flying high in the air cry out in a loud

LEARN IT & LIVE IT

1 John 3:11:
Learn It: We must love each other.
Live It: Write your dad a letter today telling him why you love him.

1 John 4:1:
Learn It: There are many false prophets in the world.
Live It: Study the Scriptures for forty-five minutes today. Do you know how to tell a false prophet from a true one?

1 John 5:14:
Learn It: Whatever we ask of God, he hears it.
Live It: Check your prayers—are you asking God for the things you should be? Realize that the Creator of the universe hears what you are saying to him and about him.

notes: **7:14 washed their robes** This means they believed in Jesus so that their sins could be forgiven by Christ's blood. **8:11 Wormwood** Name of a very bitter plant; used here to give the idea of bitter sorrow.

LEARN IT & LIVE IT

2 John 6:
Learn It: We are to live a life of love.
Live It: Pick flowers today and take them to your mom.

Jude 18:
Learn It: There will be people who laugh at God in the last days.
Live It: Defend your Savior. Don't allow people to scoff at him in your presence. Do what it takes to make sure he's respected.

Revelation 7:9:
Learn It: People from every tribe will worship God in heaven.
Live It: Love all people—even the ones who are different from you. This week make one new friend from a different race—through volunteer work, school clubs, etc.

voice, "Trouble! Trouble! Trouble for those who live on the earth because of the remaining sounds of the trumpets that the other three angels are about to blow!"

9 Then the fifth angel blew his trumpet, and I saw a star fall from the sky to the earth. The star was given the key to the deep hole that leads to the bottomless pit. 2Then it opened up the hole that leads to the bottomless pit, and smoke came up from the hole like smoke from a big furnace. Then the sun and sky became dark because of the smoke from the hole. 3Then locusts came down to the earth out of the smoke, and they were given the power to sting like scorpions.[n] 4They were told not to harm the grass on the earth or any plant or tree. They could harm only the people who did not have the sign of God on their foreheads. 5These locusts were not given the power to kill anyone, but to cause pain to the people for five months. And the pain they felt was like the pain a scorpion gives when it stings someone. 6During those days people will look for a way to die, but they will not find it. They will want to die, but death will run away from them.

7The locusts looked like horses prepared for battle. On their heads they wore what looked like crowns of gold, and their faces looked like human faces. 8Their hair was like women's hair, and their teeth were like lions' teeth. 9Their chests looked like iron breastplates, and the sound of their wings was like the noise of many horses and chariots hurrying into battle. 10The locusts had tails with stingers like scorpions, and in their tails was their power to hurt people for five months. 11The locusts had a king who was the angel of the bottomless pit. His name in the Hebrew language is Abaddon and in the Greek language is Apollyon.[n]

12The first trouble is past; there are still two other troubles that will come.

13Then the sixth angel blew his trumpet, and I heard a voice coming from the horns on the golden altar that is before God. 14The voice said to the sixth angel who had the trumpet, "Free the four angels who are tied at the great river Euphrates." 15And they let loose the four angels who had been kept ready for this hour and day and month and year so they could kill a third of all people on the earth. 16I heard how many troops on horses were in their army—two hundred million.

17The horses and their riders I saw in the vision looked like this: They had breastplates that were fiery red, dark blue, and yellow like sulfur. The heads of the horses looked like heads of lions, with fire, smoke, and sulfur coming out of their mouths. 18A third of all the people on earth were killed by these three terrible disasters coming out of the horses' mouths: the fire, the smoke, and the sulfur. 19The horses' power was in their mouths and in their tails; their tails were like snakes with heads, and with them they hurt people.

20The other people who were not killed by these terrible disasters still did not change their hearts and turn away from what they had made with their own hands. They did not stop worshiping demons and idols made of gold, silver, bronze, stone, and wood—things that cannot see or hear or walk. 21These people did not change their hearts and turn away from murder or evil magic, from their sexual sins or stealing.

THE ANGEL AND THE SMALL SCROLL

10 Then I saw another powerful angel coming down from heaven dressed in a cloud with a rainbow over his head. His face was like the sun, and his legs were like

83% OF TEENS BELIEVE THAT MORAL TRUTH DEPENDS ON THE SITUATION.

notes

9:3 scorpions A scorpion is an insect that stings with a bad poison. **9:11 Abaddon, Apollyon** Both names mean "Destroyer."

pillars of fire. 2The angel was holding a small scroll open in his hand. He put his right foot on the sea and his left foot on the land. 3Then he shouted loudly like the roaring of a lion. And when he shouted, the voices of seven thunders spoke. 4When the seven thunders spoke, I started to write. But I heard a voice from heaven say, "Keep hidden what the seven thunders said, and do not write them down."

5Then the angel I saw standing on the sea and on the land raised his right hand to heaven, 6and he made a promise by the power of the One who lives forever and ever. He is the One who made the skies and all that is in them, the earth and all that is in it, and the sea and all that is in it. The angel promised, "There will be no more waiting! 7In the days when the seventh angel is ready to blow his trumpet, God's secret will be finished. This secret is the Good News God told to his servants, the prophets."

8Then I heard the same voice from heaven again, saying to me: "Go and take the open scroll that is in the hand of the angel that is standing on the sea and on the land."

9So I went to the angel and told him to give me the small scroll. And he said to me, "Take the scroll and eat it. It will be sour in your stomach, but in your mouth it will be sweet as honey." 10So I took the small scroll from the angel's hand and ate it. In my mouth it tasted sweet as honey, but after I ate it, it was sour in my stomach. 11Then I was told, "You must prophesy again about many peoples, nations, languages, and kings."

THE TWO WITNESSES

11 I was given a measuring stick like a rod, and I was told, "Go and measure the temple of God and the altar, and count the people worshiping there. 2But do not measure the yard outside the temple. Leave it alone, because it has been given to those who are not God's people. And they will trample on the holy city for forty-two months. 3And I will give power to my two witnesses to prophesy for one thousand two hundred sixty days, and they will be dressed in rough cloth to show their sadness."

4These two witnesses are the two olive trees and the two lampstands that stand before the Lord of the earth. 5And if anyone tries to hurt them, fire comes from their mouths and kills their enemies. And if anyone tries to hurt them in whatever way, in that same way that person will die. 6These witnesses have the power to stop the sky from raining during the time they are prophesying. And they have power to make the waters become blood, and they have power to send every kind of trouble to the earth as many times as they want.

7When the two witnesses have finished telling their message, the beast that comes up from the bottomless pit will fight a war against them. He will defeat them and kill them. 8The bodies of the two witnesses will lie in the street of the great city where the Lord was

RELATIONSHIPS

"Where jealousy and selfishness are, there will be confusion and every kind of evil" (James 3:16). Do you have a younger brother or sister who gets all the attention from your parents? Or a sibling who's close to you in age, and excels more in sports than you do? It's tempting to let feelings of resentment build up toward that person. But resist that temptation. Those feelings, which seem harmless at first, will eat away at you until you are completely consumed by them. God does not intend for his children to live in such a way. Instead, ask that he enable you by his power to resist the temptation to give in to bitter jealousy. Ask him to pour his love for that person into you.

Crucifixion was a way that Romans executed people back during Bible times. Criminals were nailed to large planks of wood, which were stood upright; and victims were left hanging there to suffocate. This was a public death, and the criminals were often ridiculed or spat upon. Jesus was crucified because he claimed to be God's Son.

killed. This city is named Sodom[n] and Egypt,
which has a spiritual meaning. 9Those from
every race of people, tribe, language, and nation will look at the bodies of the two witnesses for three and one-half days, and they
will refuse to bury them. 10People who live
on the earth will rejoice and be happy because these two are dead. They will send each
other gifts, because these two prophets
brought much suffering to those who live on
the earth.

18The people of the world were angry,
but your anger has come.
The time has come to judge the dead,
and to reward your servants the
prophets
and your holy people,
all who respect you, great and small.
The time has come to destroy those who
destroy the earth!"
19Then God's temple in heaven was
opened. The Ark that holds the agreement

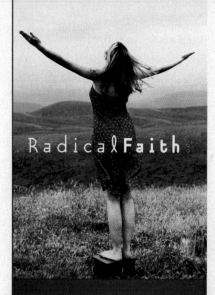

DIDYA KNOW → 30% OF TEENS BELIEVE THAT ALL RELIGIONS WORSHIP THE SAME GOD.

11But after three and one-half days, God put
the breath of life into the two prophets again.
They stood on their feet, and everyone who
saw them became very afraid. 12Then the two
prophets heard a loud voice from heaven saying, "Come up here!" And they went up into
heaven in a cloud as their enemies watched.
13In the same hour there was a great earthquake, and a tenth of the city was destroyed.
Seven thousand people were killed in the earthquake, and those who did not die were very
afraid and gave glory to the God of heaven.
14The second trouble is finished. Pay attention: The third trouble is coming soon.

THE SEVENTH TRUMPET

15Then the seventh angel blew his trumpet.
And there were loud voices in heaven, saying:
"The power to rule the world
now belongs to our Lord and his Christ,
and he will rule forever and ever."
16Then the twenty-four elders, who sit on
their thrones before God, bowed down on
their faces and worshiped God. 17They said:
"We give thanks to you, Lord God
Almighty,
who is and who was,
because you have used your great power
and have begun to rule!

God gave to his people could be seen in his
temple. Then there were flashes of lightning,
noises, thunder, an earthquake, and a great
hailstorm.

THE WOMAN AND THE DRAGON

12 And then a great wonder appeared
in heaven: A woman was clothed
with the sun, and the moon was under her
feet, and a crown of twelve stars was on her
head. 2She was pregnant and cried out with
pain, because she was about to give birth.
3Then another wonder appeared in heaven:
There was a giant red dragon with seven heads
and seven crowns on each head. He also had
ten horns. 4His tail swept a third of the stars
out of the sky and threw them down to the
earth. He stood in front of the woman who was
ready to give birth so he could eat her baby as
soon as it was born. 5Then the woman gave
birth to a son who will rule all the nations
with an iron rod. And her child was taken up to
God and to his throne. 6The woman ran away
into the desert to a place God prepared for her
where she would be taken care of for one thousand two hundred sixty days.
7Then there was a war in heaven. Michael[n]
and his angels fought against the dragon, and
the dragon and his angels fought back. 8But

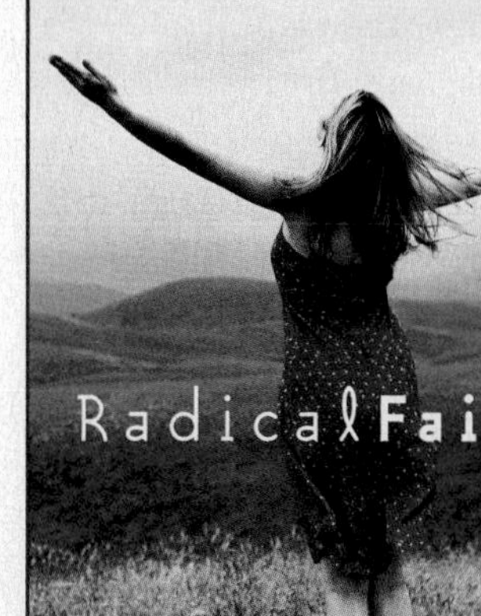

Revelation 19:16

What will you think when you see Jesus in his robe and read the words "KING OF KINGS AND LORD OF LORDS"?

There are kings and lords all over the earth—have been for hundreds of years. You've heard about them in history class—King David, King Saul, King Louis XIV, King Henry VIII. You've heard about them in literature class—Alfred, Lord Tennyson, and George Gordon, Lord Byron.

Kings and lords are known primarily for their power, their wealth, their military might, and their positions as rulers over groups of people. Jesus Christ puts it all to shame. You talk about power. His power can raise the dead. You talk about wealth. His Father owns the cattle on a thousand hills (see Psalm 50:10). You talk about military might. He's raising up an army that will someday defeat the raging forces of Satan. You talk about a ruler. He rules the whole world. Philippians 2:10 says that "every knee will bow to the name of Jesus—everyone in heaven, on earth, and under the earth."

He is the King of all the kings who have ever ruled and the Lord of every lord. Go ahead. Enthrone him in your heart. You'll never find a more loving, merciful, gracious King.

notes

11:8 Sodom City that God destroyed because the people were so evil. **12:7 Michael** The archangel—leader among God's angels or messengers (Jude 9).

the dragon was not strong enough, and he and his angels lost their place in heaven. [9]The giant dragon was thrown down out of heaven. (He is that old snake called the devil or Satan, who tricks the whole world.) The dragon with his angels was thrown down to the earth.

[10]Then I heard a loud voice in heaven saying:

"The salvation and the power and the
kingdom of our God
and the authority of his Christ have now
come.
The accuser of our brothers and sisters,
who accused them day and night before
our God,
has been thrown down.
[11]And our brothers and sisters defeated him
by the blood of the Lamb's death
and by the message they preached.
They did not love their lives so much
that they were afraid of death.
[12]So rejoice, you heavens
and all who live there!
But it will be terrible for the earth and
the sea,
because the devil has come down
to you!
He is filled with anger,
because he knows he does not have
much time."

[13]When the dragon saw he had been thrown down to the earth, he hunted for the woman who had given birth to the son. [14]But the woman was given the two wings of a great eagle so she could fly to the place prepared for her in the desert. There she would be taken care of for three and one-half years, away from the snake. [15]Then the snake poured water out of its mouth like a river toward the woman so the flood would carry her away. [16]But the earth helped the woman by opening its mouth and swallowing the river that came from the mouth of the dragon. [17]Then the dragon was very angry at the woman, and he went off to make war against all her other children—those who obey God's commands and who have the message Jesus taught.

[18]And the dragon stood on the seashore.

THE TWO BEASTS

13 Then I saw a beast coming up out of the sea. It had ten horns and seven heads, and there was a crown on each horn. A name against God was written on each head. [2]This beast looked like a leopard, with feet like a bear's feet and a mouth like a lion's mouth. And the dragon gave the beast all of his power and his throne and great authority. [3]One of the heads of the beast looked as if it had been killed by a wound, but this death wound was healed. Then the whole world was amazed and followed the beast.

"THIS MEANS THAT GOD'S HOLY PEOPLE MUST HAVE PATIENCE AND FAITH."

[4]People worshiped the dragon because he had given his power to the beast. And they also worshiped the beast, asking, "Who is like the beast? Who can make war against it?"

[5]The beast was allowed to say proud words and words against God, and it was allowed to use its power for forty-two months. [6]It used its mouth to speak against God, against God's name, against the place where God lives, and against all those who live in heaven. [7]It was given power to make war against God's holy people and to defeat them. It was given power over every tribe, people, language, and nation. [8]And all who live on earth will worship the beast—all the people since the beginning of the world whose names are not written in the Lamb's book of life. The Lamb is the One who was killed.

[9]Anyone who has ears should listen:
[10]If you are to be a prisoner,
then you will be a prisoner.
If you are to be killed with the sword,
then you will be killed with the sword.

This means that God's holy people must have patience and faith.

[11]Then I saw another beast coming up out of the earth. It had two horns like a lamb, but it spoke like a dragon. [12]This beast stands before the first beast and uses the same power the first beast has. By this power it makes everyone living on earth worship the first beast, who had the death wound that was healed. [13]And the second beast does great miracles so that it even makes fire come down from heaven to earth while people are watching. [14]It fools those who live on earth by the miracles it has been given the power to do. It does these miracles to serve the first beast. The second beast orders people to make an idol to honor the first beast, the one that was wounded by the deadly sword but sprang to life again. [15]The second beast was given power to give life to the idol of the first one so that the idol could speak. And the second beast was given power to command all who will not worship the image of the beast to be killed. [16]The second beast also forced all people, small and great, rich and poor, free and slave, to have a mark on their right hand or on their forehead. [17]No one could buy or sell without this mark, which is the name of the beast or the number of its name. [18]This takes wisdom. Let the one who has understanding find the meaning of the number, which is the number of a person. Its number is six hundred sixty-six.

THE SONG OF THE SAVED

14 Then I looked, and there before me was the Lamb standing on Mount Zion.[n] With him were one hundred forty-four thousand people who had his name and his Father's name written on their foreheads. [2]And I heard a sound from heaven like the noise of flooding water and like the sound of loud thunder. The sound I heard was like people playing harps. [3]And they sang a new song before the

14:1 Mount Zion Another name for Jerusalem; here meaning the spiritual city of God's people.

throne and before the four living creatures
and the elders. No one could learn the new song
except the one hundred forty-four thousand
who had been bought from the earth. 4These
are the ones who did not do sinful things with
women, because they kept themselves pure.
They follow the Lamb every place he goes.
These one hundred forty-four thousand were
bought from among the people of the earth as
people to be offered to God and the Lamb.
5They were not guilty of telling lies; they are
without fault.

THE THREE ANGELS

6Then I saw another angel flying high in the
air. He had the eternal Good News to preach to
those who live on earth—to every nation,
tribe, language, and people. 7He preached in a
loud voice, "Fear God and give him praise, because the time has come for God to judge all
people. So worship God who made the heavens, and the earth, and the sea, and the springs
of water."

8Then the second angel followed the first
angel and said, "Ruined, ruined is the great
city of Babylon! She made all the nations drink
the wine of the anger of her adultery."

9Then a third angel followed the first two
angels, saying in a loud voice: "If anyone worships the beast and his idol and gets the beast's
mark on the forehead or on the hand, 10that
one also will drink the wine of God's anger,
which is prepared with all its strength in the
cup of his anger. And that person will be put in
pain with burning sulfur before the holy angels and the Lamb. 11And the smoke from
their burning pain will rise forever and ever.
There will be no rest, day or night, for those
who worship the beast and his idol or who get
the mark of his name." 12This means God's
holy people must be patient. They must obey
God's commands and keep their faith in Jesus.

13Then I heard a voice from heaven saying,
"Write this: Happy are the dead who die from
now on in the Lord."

The Spirit says, "Yes, they will rest from
their hard work, and the reward of all they
have done stays with them."

THE EARTH IS HARVESTED

14Then I looked, and there before me was a
white cloud, and sitting on the white cloud
was One who looked like a Son of Man.[n] He
had a gold crown on his head and a sharp
sickle[n] in his hand. 15Then another angel came
out of the temple and called out in a loud voice
to the One who was sitting on the cloud,
"Take your sickle and harvest from the earth,
because the time to harvest has come, and the
fruit of the earth is ripe." 16So the One who
was sitting on the cloud swung his sickle over
the earth, and the earth was harvested.

17Then another angel came out of the temple in heaven, and he also had a sharp sickle.
18And then another angel, who has power
over the fire, came from the altar. This angel
called to the angel with the sharp sickle, saying, "Take your sharp sickle and gather the
bunches of grapes from the earth's vine, because its grapes are ripe." 19Then the angel
swung his sickle over the earth. He gathered
the earth's grapes and threw them into the
great winepress of God's anger. 20They were
trampled in the winepress outside the city,
and blood flowed out of the winepress as high
as horses' bridles for a distance of about one
hundred eighty miles.

THE LAST TROUBLES

15 Then I saw another wonder in
heaven that was great and amaz-
ing. There were seven angels bringing seven
disasters. These are the last disasters, because
after them, God's anger is finished.

2I saw what looked like a sea of glass mixed
with fire. All of those who had won the victory over the beast and his idol and over the
number of his name were standing by the sea
of glass. They had harps that God had given
them. 3They sang the song of Moses, the servant of God, and the song of the Lamb:

"You do great and wonderful things,
Psalm 111:2
Lord God Almighty. *Amos 3:13*
Everything the Lord does is right and true,
Psalm 145:17
King of the nations.
4Everyone will respect you, Lord, *Jeremiah 10:7*
and will honor you.
Only you are holy.
All the nations will come
and worship you, *Psalm 86:9-10*
because the right things you have done
are now made known." *Deuteronomy 32:4*

5After this I saw that the temple (the Tent of
the Agreement) in heaven was opened. 6And
the seven angels bringing the seven disasters
came out of the temple. They were dressed in
clean, shining linen and wore golden bands
tied around their chests. 7Then one of the four
living creatures gave to the seven angels seven
golden bowls filled with the anger of God, who
lives forever and ever. 8The temple was filled
with smoke from the glory and the power of
God, and no one could enter the temple until
the seven disasters of the seven angels were
finished.

THE BOWLS OF GOD'S ANGER

16 Then I heard a loud voice from the
temple saying to the seven angels,
"Go and pour out the seven bowls of God's
anger on the earth."

2The first angel left and poured out his bowl
on the land. Then ugly and painful sores came
upon all those who had the mark of the beast
and who worshiped his idol.

3The second angel poured out his bowl on
the sea, and it became blood like that of a dead
man, and every living thing in the sea died.

4The third angel poured out his bowl on
the rivers and the springs of water, and they
became blood. 5Then I heard the angel of the
waters saying:

"Holy One, you are the One who is and
who was.

notes

14:14 Son of Man "Son of Man" is a name Jesus called himself. **14:14 sickle** A farming tool with a curved blade. It was used to harvest grain.